The Coffee Exporter's Guide

THIRD EDITION

Geneva 2011

ABSTRACT FOR TRADE INFORMATION SERVICES

ID=42619   2011   SITC-071
                                            COF

International Trade Centre (ITC)
The Coffee Exporter's Guide. – [3rd ed.]
Geneva: ITC, 2011. xvi, 247 p.

Guide providing information on trade practices relating to exporting coffee – presents an overview of the world coffee trade and markets; deals with international coffee contracts (Europe and United States), logistics, insurance, dispute resolution, futures markets, risk management and hedging, trade financing, and related management issues; covers coffee quality with a special emphasis on quality control aspects; outlines new trends in the coffee trade such as electronic commerce, niche markets, organic certification, fair trade labelling, and other sustainability schemes; highlights climate change and environmental issues relevant to the coffee industry; includes a list of frequently asked questions from coffee producers and the respective answers.

Descriptors: **Coffee, Trade Practices, Contracts, Organic Products, Certification, Labelling, Climate Change, Electronic Commerce, Market Surveys, Manuals.**

English, French, Spanish (separate editions)

ITC, Palais des Nations, 1211 Geneva 10, Switzerland (*www.intracen.org*)

Cover design and illustration: © International Trade Centre, Kristina Golubic

P246.E/DMD/SC/11-XI

ISBN 978-92-9137-394-9
United Nations Sales No. E.12.III.T.1

FOREWORD

This third edition of *The Coffee Exporter's Guide* marks the 20th anniversary of this popular publication. First published as *Coffee - An exporter's guide* in 1992 and subsequently updated in 2002, this practical handbook has become the world's most extensive and authoritative publication on the international trade of coffee.

With neutral, hands-on information about the mechanics of trade in green coffee, the guide addresses value chain stakeholders in both coffee-producing and coffee-importing countries. A detailed overview of the world coffee trade is accompanied by advice on marketing, contracts, logistics, insurance, arbitration, futures markets, hedging, trade credits, risk management, quality control, e-commerce and more.

This new edition addresses trends which were barely apparent in the coffee industry ten years ago, such as climate change adaptation and mitigation, as well as the important role of women in the sector. It also features a more detailed comparison of the leading sustainability schemes – in addition to more established certification schemes for organic production and fair trade.

Over the years, this guide has been used by ITC and many others to train both newcomers and more experienced people in the coffee industry, who use the information regularly – both in daily routines and for major decisions.

We wish to thank the many industry experts, companies and institutions that have contributed in various ways to the guide. We are particularly grateful for the support from the International Coffee Organization, which has shared its knowledge for all three editions of the guide, and also has cooperated with ITC in other coffee projects over the years.

It is our hope that this guide, along with its companion website *www.thecoffeeguide.org*, will continue to serve as an essential training and knowledge-sharing tool to advance the interests of producers, exporters and those who support them in coffee-producing countries around the world.

Patricia Francis
Executive Director
International Trade Centre

ACKNOWLEDGEMENTS

Hein Jan van Hilten is the principal author of this guide as well as the previous editions from 1992 and 2002. He has spent some 50 years in the coffee industry, first as an exporter in East Africa and subsequently as an independent Coffee Development Consultant in numerous producing countries. Currently he serves on the Executive Board of the 4C Association, a mainstream sustainability initiative for the coffee industry, and moderates *www.thecoffeeguide.org*, ITC's electronic version of this guide.

The guide was made possible through the valuable contributions of expertise, experience and time by the people, companies and organizations below, whose assistance is acknowledged with thanks and appreciation.

Paul J. Fisher was also co-author of the 2002 edition of the guide. He has served many years in the coffee trading and roasting sectors. In recognition of his contribution to the industry, including his role in development of the widely used eCOPS™ (Electronic Commodity Operations Processing System), he was elected an Honorary Life Member of the Green Coffee Association (GCA) in 2011 and remains active in GCA affairs in an advisory capacity.

Michael A. Wheeler served many years as Executive Director of the Specialty Coffee Association of Europe, He contributed extensively to both this and the 2002 edition of this guide. At the International Coffee Organization he currently serves as Overseas Representative for the Papua New Guinea Coffee Industry Corporation and has chaired a number of committees at ICO.

Beatriz M. Wagner is a former Class A member of the Coffee, Sugar and Cocoa Exchange in New York and was a contributor also to the 2002 edition of the guide. Mrs. Wagner continues to lecture and consult on soft commodity trading issues. She is also co-author of ITC's guide on cocoa trade.

Gerd Uitbeijerse is a Master Mariner and former Senior Cargo Care Expert with leading shipping lines. He remains actively involved in cargo care matters through the Global Cargo Consultancy Management enterprise in the Netherlands.

Sunalini Menon is founder and CEO of Coffeelab Pvt. Ltd. in Bangalore, India. She is an internationally recognized coffee cupper and has contributed extensively to the chapters dealing with coffee quality, especially robusta.

Captain Reinhard Diegner has many years experience in commodity marine insurance, physical risk management and loss assessment, primarily from many years with a leading firm of underwriting agents in Germany.

Michael P. Flynn is a past Chairman of the European Coffee Federation's Contracts Committee. Currently he acts as an adviser to the Committee and has contributed extensively on issues related to contracts and arbitration.

Joost Pierrot has many years experience in the field of organics and contributed to the guide's sections on sustainability issues. He works as an Organic Development Consultant and has contributed to other publications in ITC.

Roel Vaessen is Secretary-General of the European Coffee Federation and serves on many industry bodies. He has contributed extensively on European Union issues as food safety and cargo security rules.

Morten Scholer, Senior Market Development Adviser in ITC, was responsible for overall management, coordination and strategic direction of the work in ITC.

ITC also wishes to thank the following industry personalities and organizations who over the years have contributed to the different editions of the Coffee Guide, especially so Abba Bayer who contributed extensively to the 1992 edition and who today is an Honorary Life Member of the Green Coffee Association in the United States. Special thanks are also due to the International Coffee Organization in London for its unstinting assistance with information on coffee statistics and related matters for all three editions.

Individual contributors

Peter Baker, Romeo S. Barbara, Maurice Blanc, Carlos H.J. Brando, Ivan Carvalho, Renaud Cuchet, Robin Dand, Frans Douqué, Norbert Douqué, Reinier Douqué, Pablo Dubois, Stephen Dunn, Dick Engelsma, Gerrit van Elst, John Eustace, Massimiliano (Max) Fabian, Judith Ganes Chase, M.P.H. Gathaara, Bernard Gaud, Gordon S. Gillett, Daniele Giovannucci, Michael C. Glenister, Gabriel Cadena Gomez, Jeremy Haggar, Jos Harmsen, Hidetaka Hayashi, Clive A. van Hilten, Patrick F. Installé, Birthe Thode Jacobsen, Phyllis Johnson, Rebecca L. Johnson, Sipke W. de Jong, Alexander Kasterine, Paul Katzeff, Soren Knudsen, Paula A. Koelemij, Karl Kofler, Surendra Kotecha, David Landais, Ted Lingle, Kerstin Linne, Sandy McAlpine, Jan Meijer, Kerry Muir, Robert F. Nelson, Henry Ngabirano, Kif Nguyen, Doan Trieu Nhan, Ronald J. Onzima, Luis Norberto Pascoal, Alain Pittet, R. Price Peterson, Gloria Inés Puerta Quintero, Paul Rice, Mike Ritchie, Elodie Robin, David Roche, Aimee Russillo, Josefa Sacko, Jasper P. van Schaik, John Schluter, Christian Schøler, Garth Smith, Susie Spindler, Dominic Stanculescu, Gerrit H.D. van der Stegen, Søren Sylvest, Joachim Taubensee, Panos Varangis, Rinantonio Viani, Martin Wattam, Joachim R. Wernicke, Birgit Wilhelm, Christian B. Wolthers, Eric C. Wood.

Organizations

The Coffee Quality Institute – United States of America, the Coffee Science Information Centre – United Kingdom, the European Coffee Federation – ECF, the International Women's Coffee Alliance – IWCA, the National Coffee Association of USA, Inc., NYSE Euronext Liffe – United Kingdom, the Specialty Coffee Association of America – SCAA, the Specialty Coffee Association of Europe – SCAE.

Dianna Rienstra copy edited the guide. Publication production and promotion was managed by Natalie Domeisen. Desktop publishing was done by Isabel Droste in ITC.

CONTENTS

CHAPTER 4   63

CONTRACTS 64

CHAPTER 5   83

LOGISTICS AND INSURANCE...................84

CHAPTER 10   163

RISK AND THE RELATION TO TRADE CREDIT

CHAPTER 11   187

COFFEE QUALITY

TABLES

FIGURES

BOXES

NOTE

Unless otherwise specified, all references to dollars ($) and cents (cts) are to Unites States dollars and cents.

All references to tons are to metric tons. The term 'billion' denotes 1 thousand million.

The following abbreviations are used:

AA	Against actuals
ACPC	Association of Coffee Producing Countries
ASP	Applications service provider
B/L	Bill of lading
BM&F	Brazilian Mercantile & Futures Exchange
CAD	Cash against documents
CDM	Clean Development Mechanism
CFR	Cost and freight
CFTC	U.S. Commodity Futures Trading Commission
CFC	Common Fund for Commodities
CFS	Container freight station
CHIPS	Clearing House Interbank Payment System
CIF	Cost, insurance, freight
CM	Collateral manager
COE	Cup of Excellence
COT	Commitment of traders
CSCE	Coffee, Sugar and Cocoa Exchange (New York)
CY	Container yard
DAF	Delivered at frontier
ECC	European Contract for Coffee
eCOPS	Electronic Commodity Operations Processing System (at ICE, New York)
ECF	European Coffee Federation
EDK	Ex dock
ETA	Estimated time of arrival
EU	European Union
EUREP	Euro-Retailer Produce Working Group
EUREPGAP	EUREP Good Agricultural Practice
EWR	Electronic warehouse receipt
FAO	Food and Agriculture Organization of the United Nations
FAQ	Fair average quality
FCA	Free carrier
FCL	Full container load
FCM	Futures commission merchant
FDA	U.S. Food and Drug Administration
FOB	Free on board
FOT	Free on truck/train
FLO	Fairtrade Labelling Organizations
GAP	Good Agricultural Practice
GBE	Green bean equivalent
GCA	Green Coffee Association (United States)

GHG	Greenhouse gas
GIS	Geographic information system
GP	General purpose (container)
GPS	Global positioning system
GSP	Generalized System of Preferences
GTC	Good till cancelled
HACCP	Hazard Analysis Critical Control Point
ICA	International Coffee Agreement
ICE	Intercontinental Exchange (New York)
ICO	International Coffee Organization
ICS	Internal Control System (organic)
IFOAM	International Federation of Organic Agriculture Movements
IPCC	Intergovernmental Panel on Climate Change
ISO	International Organization for Standardization
ITC	International Trade Centre
JIT	Just-in-time
LCH	London Clearing House
LCL	Less than container load
L/C	Letter of credit
LIFFE	London International Financial Futures and Options Exchange (NYSE Euronext Liffe)
MFN	Most favoured nation
NCA	National Coffee Association (United States)
NCAD	Net cash against documents
NCSE	New York Coffee, Sugar and Cocoa Exchange
NGO	Non-governmental organization
NY 'C'	Coffee 'C' Contract (at ICE, New York)
OTA	Ochratoxin A
PTBF	Price to be fixed
RTD	Ready-to-drink
SAS	Subject to approval of sample
SCAA	Specialty Coffee Association of America
SCAE	Specialty Coffee Association of Europe
STC	Said to contain
SURF	Settlement Utility for Managing Risk and Finance
SWIFT	Society for Worldwide Interbank Financial Telecommunication
TEU	Twenty-foot equivalent unit (container)
THC	Terminal handling charges
UCP	Uniform Customs and Practice for Documentary Credits
UNCTAD	United Nations Conference on Trade and Development
USDA	United States Department of Agriculture
VSA	Vessel sharing agreement
WTO	World Trade Organization
XML	Extensible mark-up language

CONVERSIONS TO GREEN BEAN EQUIVALENT

In accordance with internationally accepted practice, all quantity data in this guide represent bags of 60 kg net (132.276 lb) green coffee or the equivalent thereof, i.e. GBE: green coffee equivalent. Green coffee means all coffee in the naked bean form before roasting.

The International Coffee Organization has agreed the following conversion factors to convert different types of coffee to GBE:

- Dried cherry to green bean: multiply the net weight of the cherry by 0.5;
- Parchment to green bean: multiply the net weight of the parchment by 0.8;
- Decaffeinated green bean to green bean: multiply the net weight by 1.05;
- Regular roasted coffee to green bean: multiply the net weight of the regular roasted coffee by 1.19;
- Decaffeinated roasted coffee to green bean: multiply the net weight of the decaffeinated roasted coffee by 1.25;
- Regular soluble coffee to green bean: multiply the net weight of the regular soluble coffee by 2.6;
- Decaffeinated soluble coffee to green bean: multiply the net weight of the decaffeinated soluble coffee by 2.73;
- Regular liquid coffee to green bean: multiply the net weight of the dried coffee solids contained in the regular liquid coffee by 2.6;
- Decaffeinated liquid coffee to green bean: multiply the net weight of the dried coffee solids contained in the decaffeinated liquid coffee by 2.73.

Alternatively, for statistical purpose: 60 kg green coffee represents:

- 120 kg dried cherry;
- 75 kg parchment.

CHAPTER 1

WORLD COFFEE TRADE –
AN OVERVIEW

WORLD COFFEE TRADE – AN OVERVIEW

THE IMPORTANCE OF COFFEE IN WORLD TRADE

Coffee is an important commodity in the world economy, accounting for trade worth approximately US$ 16.5 billion in calendar year 2010, when some 97 million bags of 60 kg (5.8 million tons) were shipped. World production in coffee year 2010/11 is estimated at 131 million bags (7.8 million tons) while consumption in calendar year 2010 is estimated at 135 million bags (8.1 million tons).

Table 1.1   World coffee exports, by value and volume, 1990–2010

Calendar year	US$ billion	Million bags (60 kg net)	Cts/lb (EUV)*
1990	6.9	80.6	65
1995	11.6	67.6	130
2000	8.2	89.5	69
2005	9.2	87.6	79
2006	10.8	91.6	89
2007	12.8	96.3	100
2008	15.4	97.6	119
2009	13.3	96.2	105
2010	16.5	96.7	129

Source: ICO.

* Export unit value, rounded to nearest US cent.

Some 70 countries produce coffee. Three countries alone have in recent years produced around 55% of the world's coffee: Brazil (32%–34%), Viet Nam (12%–13%) and Colombia (8%–9%).

In 2010 the International Coffee Organization (ICO) estimated total coffee sector employment at about 26 million persons in 52 producing countries. See Doc. ICC 105-5 at *www.ico.org*.

For many countries, coffee exports not only are a vital contributor to foreign exchange earnings, but also account for a significant proportion of tax income and gross domestic product. For eight countries, the average share of coffee exports in total export earnings exceeded 10% in the period 2005–2010, although the importance of coffee in the economy of many countries is diminishing over time. This can be demonstrated by the fact that during the period 1995–2000, there were 15 countries which fell into this category, i.e. the average share of coffee exports in their total export earnings exceeded 10%.

Figure 1.1   Share of coffee in total exports by value, 2005–2010

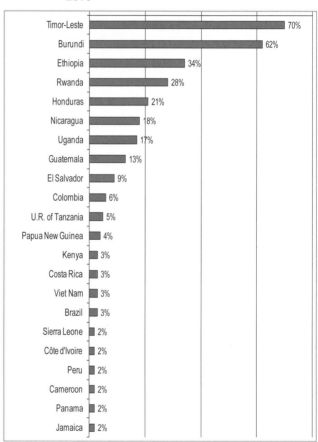

Source: ICO.

SUPPLY, PRODUCTION, STOCKS AND DOMESTIC CONSUMPTION

DEFINITIONS RELATED TO SUPPLY

Supply is generally defined as the sum of production in a given coffee year plus stocks carried over from the previous year.

Exportable supply, however, is defined as supply minus domestic consumption and an amount deemed to be required for working stocks.

Working stocks is not precisely defined. It relates to the volume of coffee required to maintain a steady and planned flow of exports to the market. It is generally perceived as the amount of coffee in the pipeline in an exporting country at any one time. Harvesting and export patterns vary from country to country. As a result, working stocks are not defined as a fixed percentage or proportion of a country's production or export capacity, but rather as an individual amount unique to every country. In many respects the calculation of working stocks is arbitrary, but it is generally based on historical data for each country.

Exportable production is total annual production less domestic consumption in producing countries. Availability for export is equivalent to the carry-over stocks from the previous year plus exportable production of the current year. Any difference between exportable production and actual exports (surplus or shortfall) results in an adjustment up or down of the carry-over stocks to the following year.

Crop year. Coffee is a seasonal crop. Seasons vary from country to country, starting and finishing at different times throughout the year. This makes statistics on worldwide annual production very difficult to collate: any single 12-month period may encompass a whole crop year in one country, but will also include the tail end of the previous year's crop and the beginning of the next year's crop in others. In order to compare supply aggregates as well supply with demand, where possible supply data has been converted from crop year to coffee year (which runs from October to September). It should be noted that this is not always possible.

READINESS FOR EXPORT

Of course there is a delay between the harvesting of coffee and its readiness for export due to processing, drying, conditioning and so forth. The following is the estimated timing of the approximate crop availability for export in selected countries:

Arabica
Brazil: 86% in July-December
Ethiopia: 75% in January – June
Honduras: 60% in January – June
Kenya: 70% in January – June
Peru: 68% in July – December
Colombia: availability is usually (but not always) spread fairly equally throughout the coffee year.

Robusta
Brazil: 75% January – June
Indonesia: 65% July – December
Uganda: 64% January – June
Viet Nam: 55% January – June

COFFEE PRODUCING COUNTRIES BY ICO QUALITY GROUP

For administrative reasons, mainly related to the organization of quotas in the past, the ICO divided coffee production into four groups on the basis of the predominant type of coffee produced by each member country.

Table 1.2   Crop years in producing countries

1 October-30 September	Benin Cameroon Central African Republic Colombia Costa Rica Côte d'Ivoire Democratic Republic of the Congo El Salvador Equatorial Guinea Ethiopia Gabon	Ghana Guatemala Guinea Honduras India Jamaica Kenya Liberia Mexico Nicaragua Nigeria	Panama Sierra Leone Sri Lanka Thailand Togo Trinidad and Tobago Uganda Venezuela (Bolivarian Republic of) Viet Nam
1 April-31 March	Angola Bolivia (Plurinational State of) Brazil Burundi Ecuador	Indonesia Madagascar Malawi Papua New Guinea Paraguay	Peru Rwanda Zimbabwe
1 July-30 June	Congo Cuba Dominican Republic	Haiti Philippines United Republic of Tanzania	Zambia

Source: ICO.

Table 1.3   ICO qualiy groups

Quality group	Producers
Colombian mild arabicas	Colombia, Kenya, United Republic of Tanzania
Other mild arabicas	Bolivia (Plurinational State of), Burundi, Costa Rica, Cuba, Dominican Republic, Ecuador, El Salvador, Guatemala, Haiti, Honduras, India, Jamaica, Malawi, Mexico, Nicaragua, Panama, Papua New Guinea, Peru, Rwanda, Venezuela (Bolivarian Republic of), Zambia, Zimbabwe
Brazilian and other natural arabicas	Brazil, Ethiopia, Paraguay, Timor-Leste, Yemen
Robustas	Angola, Benin, Cameroon, Central African Republic, Congo, Côte d'Ivoire, Democratic Republic of the Congo, Equatorial Guinea, Gabon, Ghana, Guinea, Indonesia, Liberia, Madagascar, Nigeria, Philippines, Sierra Leone, Sri Lanka, Thailand, Togo, Trinidad and Tobago, Uganda, Viet Nam

GEOGRAPHICAL DISTRIBUTION

Coffee is indigenous to Africa, with arabica coffee reportedly originating from Ethiopia and robusta from the Atlantic Coast (Kouilou region and in and around Angola) and the Great Lakes region. Today, it is widely grown throughout the tropics. The bulk of the world's coffee, however, is produced in Latin America and in particular in Brazil, which has dominated world production since 1840.

Brazil is the world's largest grower and seller of coffee. Viet Nam, which expanded its production rapidly throughout the 1990s, now holds the number two position, bringing Colombia into third place and Indonesia into fourth.

The figures below demonstrate the shift of regional shares of arabica and robusta production since 1981.

CONVERSIONS TO GREEN BEAN EQUIVALENT

In accordance with internationally accepted practice, all quantity data in this guide represent bags of 60 kg net (132.276 lb) green coffee or the equivalent thereof, i.e. GBE: green coffee equivalent. Green coffee means all coffee in the naked bean form before roasting.

The International Coffee Organization has agreed the following conversion factors to convert different types of coffee to GBE:

- Dried cherry to green bean: multiply the net weight of the cherry by 0.5;

- Parchment to green bean: multiply the net weight of the parchment by 0.8;

- Decaffeinated green bean to green bean: multiply the net weight by 1.05;

- Regular roasted coffee to green bean: multiply the net weight of the regular roasted coffee by 1.19;

- Decaffeinated roasted coffee to green bean: multiply the net weight of the decaffeinated roasted coffee by 1.25;

- Regular soluble coffee to green bean: multiply the net weight of the regular soluble coffee by 2.6;

- Decaffeinated soluble coffee to green bean: multiply the net weight of the decaffeinated soluble coffee by 2.73;

- Regular liquid coffee to green bean: multiply the net weight of the dried coffee solids contained in the regular liquid coffee by 2.6;

- Decaffeinated liquid coffee to green bean: multiply the net weight of the dried coffee solids contained in the decaffeinated liquid coffee by 2.73.

Alternatively, for statistical purpose: 60 kg green coffee represents:

- 120 kg dried cherry;
- 75 kg parchment.

Figure 1.2   Annual arabica production, 1981/86 and 2006/11

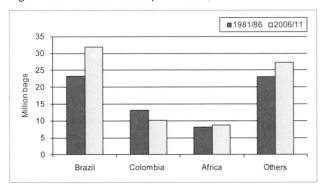

Source: ICO.

Figure 1.3   Annual robusta production, 1981/86 and 2006/11

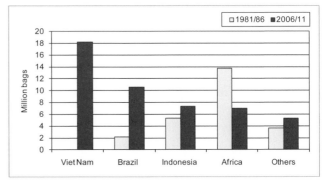

Source: ICO.

GRADING AND CLASSIFICATION

Green coffee is graded and classified for export with the ultimate aim of producing the best cup quality and thereby securing the highest price. However, there is no universal grading and classification system – each producing country has its own, which it may also use to set (minimum) standards for export.

Grading and classification is usually based on some of the following criteria:

- Altitude and/or region;
- Botanical variety;
- Preparation (wet or dry process = washed or natural);
- Bean size (screen size), sometimes also bean shape and colour;
- Number of defects (imperfections);
- Roast appearance and cup quality (flavour, characteristics, cleanliness, etc.);
- Density of the beans.

Most grading and classification systems include (often very detailed) criteria, e.g. regarding permissible defects, which are not listed here. The Origins Encyclopaedia at *www.supremo.be* is an example of a website which gives information on the export classification of coffees of most origins. Terminology on size and defects as used for classifications is also found at *www.coffeeresearch.org*.

The diversified classification terminology used in the trade is illustrated with a few examples below. It should be noted that descriptions such as 'European preparation' may differ from one country to another. The examples refer primarily to the trade in mainstream coffee and do not reflect the often more detailed descriptions used for niche markets.

Brazil/Santos NY 2/3

Screen 17/18, fine roast, strictly soft, fine cup.

Brazil/Santos NY 3/4

Screen 14/16, good roast, strictly soft, good cup (often seen quoted as 'Swedish preparation').

Colombia Supremo screen 17/18

High grade type of washed arabica, screen 17 with maximum 5% below. Often specified with further details.

Côte d'Ivoire (Ivory Coast) Robusta Grade 2

Grade 2; scale is from 0 (best) to 4 based on screen size and defects.

El Salvador SHG EP

Strictly High Grown (above 1,200 m; High Grown from 900–1,200 m and Central Standard from 500–900 m). Commonly used quality descriptions are European Preparation (maximum 6 defects per 300 g) and American Preparation (maximum 12 defects per 300 g).

Ethiopia Jimma 5

Sun-dried (i.e. natural) arabica from the Jimma region. Type 5 refers to a grading scale based on screen, defect count and cup quality.

Guatemala SHB EP Huehuetenango

Strictly Hard Bean is from above 1,400 m. Scale includes five altitude levels from below 900 m (Prime washed) to above 1,400 m. European preparation: above screen 15, allows maximum 8 defects per 300 g (American preparation: above screen 14, allows 23 defects).

India Arabica Plantation A

Washed arabica, screen 17. Classification is PB, A, B and C. Other classifications apply to unwashed (naturals) and robusta.

Indonesia Robusta Grade 4

The export grade scale goes from 0 (best) to 6. Grade 4 allows 45–80 defects. Region or other details are sometimes specified as quality, e.g. EK-1 and EK-Special. Processing depends on the region (island).

Kenya AB FAQ even roast clean cup

Kenya arabica grade AB, fair average quality. Internal grading system (E, AA, AB, PB, C, TT and T) is based on bean size and density, further detailed by liquor quality into 10 classifications. Top cupping coffees are mostly sold on actual sample basis.

Mexico Prime Washed Europrep

Prime Washed (prima lavado) from altitude between 600 m and 900 m, on a scale from 400 m to 1,400 m; Europrep is retained by screen 17 and allows maximum 15 defects per 300 g.

Papua New Guinea (PNG) Smallholder Y1-grade

Y1 is one of the grades on a scale covering bean size, defect count, colour, odour, roast aspects and cup quality; AA, A, AB, B, C, PB, X, E, PSC, Y1, Y2 and T.

Viet Nam Robusta Grade 2 maximum 5% blacks and broken

Grade 2 out of six grades: Special Grade and Grade 1 to 5, based on screen size and defects. (Descriptions are often supplemented with further details on moisture content, acceptable mix of bean types, bean size, etc.)

Table 1.4   Illustration of a defect count for sun-dried (natural) coffee

1 black bean	1
2 sour or rancid beans	1
2 beans in parchment	1
1 cherry	1
1 large husk	1
2–3 small husks	1
3 shells	1
1 large stone/earth clod	5
1 medium-sized stone/earth clod	2
1 small stone/earth clod	1
1 large stick	5
1 medium-sized stick	2
1 small stick	1
5 broken beans	1
5 green or immature beans	1
5 insect damaged beans	1

DOMESTIC CONSUMPTION

Domestic consumption in producing countries is estimated to have risen from about 26 million bags in 2000/01 to over 41 million bags in crop year 2010/11. The bulk of this increase is attributed to growth in the internal market in Brazil, which has increased from 13 million bags to more than 19 million bags over the same period – about half of all coffee consumed in producing countries. Industry sources point to the growth in real disposable incomes in Brazil and a policy of using better quality coffee for the internal markets as important factors behind this growth.

Elsewhere in Latin America, consumption is constrained by relatively low urban income levels although there has been some growth in Mexico and consumption remains reasonably substantial in Colombia.

By comparison consumption in Africa is negligible with the exception of Ethiopia, where there is a long and well-established tradition of coffee drinking.

In Asia, total consumption is reasonably high in India, Indonesia and the Philippines, although per capita consumption levels are relatively low. See table 1.6.

Table 1.5   Overview of world production by type, coffee years 2006/07–2010/11 (in millions of bags)

Coffee Year	2006/07	2007/08	2008/09	2009/10	2010/11*
World	**127.1**	**127.8**	**126.7**	**128.6**	**131.1**
Arabicas	**77.3**	**80.1**	**75.8**	**77.8**	**80.8**
Brazil	29.1	30.3	32.2	32.5	33.6
Colombia	12.6	12.5	8.7	9.0	9.2
Other Americas	23.1	24.2	22.8	21.8	23.2
Africa	8.3	8.7	7.6	9.6	10.3
Asia and the Pacific	4.2	4.4	4.4	4.9	4.4
Robustas	**49.7**	**47.7**	**50.9**	**50.8**	**50.4**
Brazil	10.2	10.7	10.6	10.9	12.7
Other Latin America	0.5	0.4	0.4	0.4	0.3
Viet Nam	19.3	16.5	18.5	18.0	18.5
Indonesia	6.4	6.9	8.1	8.6	6.8
Other Asia and Pacific	5.4	5.3	5.5	6.2	4.9
Côte d'Ivoire	2.8	2.6	2.4	1.9	2.2
Uganda	2.2	2.6	2.6	2.4	2.2
Other Africa	2.9	2.7	2.8	2.4	2.8
Shares (%)					
Arabicas	60.8	62.7	59.8	60.5	61.6
Robustas	39.2	37.3	40.2	39.5	38.4

Source: ICO and USDA.

* Preliminary.

Note: Totals may not add up owing to rounding. For more up-to-date statistics visit www.ico.org.

Table 1.6 Domestic consumption in coffee producing countries, crop year 2010/11 (estimated) ('000 bags)

Africa	5 181
of which:	
Côte d'Ivoire	317
Ethiopia	3 383
Asia and the Pacific	**8 328**
of which:	
India	1 800
Indonesia	3 333
Philippines	1 080
Viet Nam	1 583
Latin America	**27 501**
of which:	
Brazil	19 130
Colombia	1 400
Mexico	2 354
Venezuela (Bolivarian Republic of)	1 650
Total	**41 010**

Source: ICO and own estimates.

Note: Figures are rounded up to the nearest '000.

EXPORTS

Exports of coffee in all forms from producing countries have varied significantly from year to year, reflecting, by and large, the variations in world production. See tables 1.5 and 1.7.

STOCKS IN PRODUCING COUNTRIES

Extreme caution must be exercised when looking at producer-held stock figures, as the numbers involved do not necessarily reflect true availability. In some cases the official estimates will underestimate the amount held, as it is often impossible for the authorities to record the total volume held in private hands in a country, while in other cases the figures will exaggerate the amount available. This was certainly the case in the past when stocks played an important role in determining a producing country's quota at the ICO, as it was to a country's advantage to record the highest possible stock figure. Consequently poor-quality coffee, which was difficult to sell and indeed had very little value, was often included to inflate a country's stock figure, although this tends not to be the situation today.

Table 1.7 Overview of world exports by type, 2006/07–2010/11 ('000 bags)

Coffee years	2006/07	2007/08	2008/09	2009/10	2010/11*
Total exports	**98 388**	**96 032**	**97 433**	**92 521**	**105 000**
Arabicas	**59 908**	**57 854**	**58 630**	**56 202**	**64 025**
of which from:					
Brazil	24 067	22 303	27 318	26 540	29 603
Colombia	10 586	10 846	8 072	6 533	7 817
Other Latin America	17 063	17 248	16 397	15 317	17 803
Africa	5 633	5 131	4 777	4 953	6 231
Asia and the Pacific	2 559	2 326	2 066	2 859	2 571
Robustas	**31 111**	**30 541**	**32 263**	**29 191**	**33 277**
of which from:					
Brazil	1 571	2 025	1 377	1 082	2 127
Other Latin America	236	107	339	253	329
Viet Nam	18 066	15 751	17 381	14 578	17 105
Indonesia	2 934	4 696	5 905	5 320	4 880
Other Asia and the Pacific	2 243	1 991	2 067	2 576	4 059
Côte d'Ivoire	1 807	1 423	1 122	1 819	955
Uganda	2 144	2 711	2 407	1 960	2 116
Other Africa	2 110	1 837	1 665	1 603	1 706
Roasted coffee	**204**	**287**	**255**	**223**	**200**
Soluble	**7 165**	**7 350**	**6 285**	**6 905**	**7 498**
of which from:					
Brazil	3 313	3 508	2 849	3 162	3 142
Other Latin America	1 941	2 142	1 926	1 965	2 206
Africa	885	525	414	270	310
Asia	1 026	1 175	1 096	1 508	1 840
Shares (%)					
Arabicas	60.9	60.3	60.2	60.7	61.0
Robustas	31.6	31.8	33.1	31.5	31.7
Roasted	0.2	0.2	0.3	0.3	0.2
Soluble	7.3	7.7	6.4	7.5	7.1

Source: ICO.

*July/June.

Furthermore, stock verifications ceased in 1989 with the suspension of the quota system and although the figures produced from the verification exercise were questionable, they were the product of a reasonably rigorous procedure. Since then the figures have been based on national estimates and there has been no independent verification of the accuracy or otherwise of these figures. As a result, published statistics are subject to frequent revisions, some of which are substantial going back over a number of years. A degree of caution is therefore necessary when using these figures in any analysis. See table 1.7.

DEMAND, CONSUMPTION AND INVENTORIES

Most of the statistical material on trends in imports, re-exports and consumption of coffee worldwide is expressed in calendar years, which is largely how data on demand and consumption are reported and analysed by consuming countries and trade bodies. The summary data below are given in coffee years to facilitate comparisons with supply data provided elsewhere.

A straight comparison between the two sets of data is not possible as time lags produce differences between the basic and aggregate figures. To complicate the issue even further, statistics on coffee consumption tend to be misleading as no single set of statistics gives the whole picture. Import statistics, for example, are not a good indicator of

consumption as they do not take into account re-exports or changes in the level of stocks held in importing countries. To overcome this the ICO publishes figures on 'disappearance' that take these factors into account, but it is still impossible to allow for changes in the level of unreported stocks held by traders, roasters and retailers.

For countries, which are members of the ICO and for a few non-member countries where the relevant statistics exist, the figures relate to disappearance, whereas for the rest of the non-member countries they relate to net imports. Strictly speaking the two sets of figures are not the same, but are close enough to be incorporated in the table 1.9.

CONSUMPTION TRENDS

It is estimated that global consumption in coffee year 2010/11 will total 130.9 million bags. Of this total, 69.4 million bags were consumed in importing ICO member countries, 20.5 million bags were consumed in non-member countries, and the remaining 41.0 million bags were consumed in producing countries.

Consumption has grown by an average of around 1.2% a year since the early 1980s. Probably the most spectacular growth has been witnessed in Japan, where consumption has grown by around 3.5% a year over the same period, although it appears to have reached a plateau over the last 10 years. Japan is now the third largest importer of coffee in the world.

Table 1.8   Opening stocks by type, crop years 2006/07–2010/11 ('000 bags)

Coffee years	2006/07	2007/08	2008/09	2009/10	2010/11
World	**28 343**	**27 722**	**19 463**	**20 489**	**18 461**
Arabicas	**21 323**	**19 076**	**14 361**	**13 376**	**11 838**
of which from:					
Brazil	16 503	15 200	11 294	10 714	8 486
Colombia	855	819	366	25	27
Other Latin America	2 292	1 314	1 021	791	910
Africa	1 168	1 253	1 315	1 383	2 193
Asia and the Pacific	505	490	365	463	222
Robustas	**7 020**	**8 646**	**5 102**	**7 113**	**6 623**
of which from:					
Brazil	4 737	6 639	3 336	3 942	2 592
Other Latin America	8	4	3	4	6
Viet Nam	500	833	526	640	2 716
Indonesia	129	24	45	541	573
Other Asia and the Pacific	992	812	660	535	97
Côte d'Ivoire	282	124	458	970	418
Uganda	264	120	20	23	11
Other Africa	108	90	54	458	210
Shares (%)					
Arabicas	75.2	68.8	73.4	65.3	64.1
Robustas	24.8	31.2	26.6	34.7	35.9

Source: ICO.

There has been very little growth in coffee consumption in Europe over the last five years, with consumption showing signs of stagnation and possibly even decline. The situation is only slightly better in the United States, where overall consumption, despite the boom in the specialty sector, has remained virtually unaltered over the past five years.

The figures for consumption in non-ICO member countries suggest that there has been a surprisingly large upsurge in consumption in these countries since the turn of the century. On average, consumption has grown by over 6% per annum, although the recent economic turmoil has reduced coffee consumption in many of these countries – possibly only temporarily. However, these figures should be read with some caution, as the data for exports and hence consumption in these countries is not necessarily always collected from the same source.

Table 1.9 Consumption in importing countries/areas, 2006/07–2010/11 ('000 bags)

Importing countries/areas	2006/07	2007/08	2008/09	2009/10	2010/11*
World	**92 619**	**93 568**	**92 922**	**91 392**	**89 859**
North America of which:	**23 994**	**24 501**	**24 901**	**24 624**	**24 060**
United States	21 199	21 423	21 656	21 332	20 473
Western Europe of which:	**42 780**	**42 340**	**39 874**	**40 651**	**39 182**
France	5 581	5 331	5 329	5 562	5 632
Germany	9 082	9 912	8 409	9 554	8 584
Italy	5 840	5 918	5 752	5 743	5 760
Eastern Europe	**6 195**	**7 211**	**7 589**	**6 586**	**7 030**
Asia and the Pacific of which:	**12 908**	**13 780**	**14 280**	**13 564**	**13 745**
Japan	7 265	7 150	7 330	6 909	6 680
Others	**6 742**	**5 736**	**6 270**	**5 967**	**5 842**

Source: ICO.

* Preliminary estimate.

STOCKS OR INVENTORIES IN IMPORTING COUNTRIES

Stocks held in importing countries are usually referred to as inventories to distinguish them from stocks held in producer countries. Inventories tend to grow when prices are low and deplete when prices are higher, although the relationship is far from linear.

Consumer-held stocks were relatively stable throughout the 1980s, but increased dramatically with the suspension of quotas in 1989 and the collapse in prices. They fell in response to the price hike in 1994, but began to expand again with the collapse in prices during 2000 and 2001. By the end of 2010 they totalled just over 18 million bags, which is equivalent to about just over 10 weeks of consumer demand

Once again, some caution is required when looking at these figures as much of the data on consumer-held stock either is not published or is published only sporadically. Furthermore, as for producer-held stocks, a certain proportion of this should be seen as working stock, that is, the amount of coffee in the system or pipeline at any one time.

In the past, most analysts worked on the basis that around 8 million bags were required as consumer-held working stock. However, the adoption of the just-in-time stock management system by most of the world's major roasters, together with the improvement in logistics, has meant that the volume that probably should now be considered working stock has been reduced to maybe as low as 4 million bags.

The figure below shows the evolution of inventories since 1990 together with the composite indicator price.

Figure 1.4 Total inventories in importing countries and prices, 1990-2010

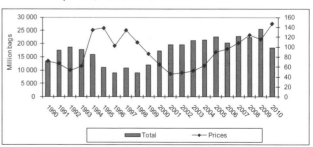

Source: ICO.

PRICES

There is no single price for 'coffee' because coffee, being a product of nature, is not a homogeneous product. However, broadly speaking the international coffee-pricing scene can be divided up as follows:

- Physicals – prices for green or physical coffee;
- Indicators – prices that track broad groups of comparable coffees;
- Futures – that project prices forward for standard qualities;
- Differentials – a system linking physical prices to futures prices.

Day-to-day physical coffee prices are determined by supply and demand. Price setting criteria are mostly quality (what is the quality of a given coffee or origin), and availability (how much or how little is being offered of a particular type of coffee). This confirms that not all coffee is the same. In fact each parcel of coffee is unique with regard to its characteristics, flavour and quality and hence attracts a different price. Of course other factors play a role as well, for example market expectations, speculative actions, changes in currency exchange rates and so on. However, by grouping more or less comparable types of coffee together, average prices can be calculated and even traded.

ICO indicator prices, published daily by the International Coffee Organization in London, represent and track the four main types of coffee available in the international market: (i) Colombian mild arabicas, (ii) Other mild arabicas, (iii) Brazilian and other natural arabicas, and (iv) Robustas. These indicator prices represent spot or cash prices, quoted in the market for coffee that is more or less immediately available (or within a reasonable time-span). The four categories enable the ICO to calculate market prices for these four broad groups and so monitor price developments for each. In addition, using an agreed formula, the ICO publishes a Daily Composite Indicator Price that combines these four into a single price representing 'all coffee'. This probably represents the best indication of a current 'international price for coffee'. This and other price information, also historical, is freely available at *www.ico.org*. For an overview of the ICO indicator pricing system itself see *www.ico.org/coffee_prices.asp*.

Futures prices reflect the estimated future availability and demand for coffee as a whole. Go to *www.theice.com* for arabica coffee futures prices in New York, and to *www.euronext.com* for robusta coffee futures prices in London. See chapter 8 for details of what average quality of coffee these futures markets represent. Price charts depict past price behaviour on these markets – a good source is found at *www.futures.tradingcharts.com*.

However, as mentioned, the ICO price indicators (which track prices) and the futures markets (which project prices) by necessity only do so for generally known, standard qualities of coffee. Futures markets are used to offset price risk in the green coffee market where different qualities of

coffee are traded. Traders therefore link individual prices with the futures price by establishing a price difference, the differential. Briefly, this differential takes into account (i) differences between an individual coffee and the standard quality on which the futures market is based, (ii) the physical availability of that coffee (plentiful or tight), and (iii) the terms and conditions on which it is offered for sale.

An example follows. By combining the New York or London futures price and the differential, one usually obtains the FOB (free on board) price for a particular type of green coffee. This enables the market to simply quote, for example, 'Quality X from Country Y for October shipment at New York December plus 5' (US cts/lb). Traders and importers know the cost of shipping coffee from each origin to Europe, the United States, Japan or wherever, and so can easily transform 'plus 5' into a price 'landed final destination'.

The study of physical coffee prices is complicated by the variability in the quality and appeal of individual coffees, making it extremely difficult to monitor the daily behaviour of differentials and physical prices. However, for general research purposes the price information available from the International Coffee Organization and the futures markets of New York and London often suffices. Nevertheless, it is important to appreciate that physical coffee price differentials can be extremely volatile and that at the moment there is no established mechanism or tool that allows exporters or indeed importers to hedge the risk inherent in physical coffee price differential volatility.

THE INTERNATIONAL COFFEE ORGANIZATION

IDENTIFICATION OF EXPORTS

In the early 1960s the International Coffee Organization (ICO) instituted an identification code for coffee exports to enable it to apply the export quota system that existed at the time. However, this coding system has become an important statistical tool in its own right and so remains valid in today's free coffee market.

Example: 002 – 1961 – 0978

- The first group (002, maximum three digits) identifies the country of origin, in this case Brazil. Other codes are 003 Colombia, 011 Guatemala, and so on.
- The second group (1961, maximum four digits) identifies the exporter. Exporters are registered with the local authority that issues ICO certificates of origin and receive a code number from such an authority.
- The third group (0978, maximum four digits) refers to the individual shipment to which the bags in question belong – in this example shipment number 978 made by exporter number 1961 during the coffee year in question.

To see the entire list of country codes and more on ICO Certificates of Origin go to *www.ico.org,* look under Documents – By meeting – Rules, where you can trace ICC 102-9. Coffee years run from 1 October to 30 September – individual shipment numbers recommence at 0001 every year.

The system allows easy identification of individual bags: the country of origin, the exporter, and the shipment number for that exporter. For shipment's in bulk (see chapter 5), the shipping marks, including the ICO numbers, are marked directly on the container liner, making them visible when the container doors are opened. The container number itself is marked on the ICO Certificate of Origin, thereby completing the link.

MAIN ELEMENTS OF THE INTERNATIONAL COFFEE AGREEMENT 2007

- It entered into force for 10 years on 2 February 2011, on expiry of the International Coffee Agreement (ICA) 2001. The Council will however review the Agreement five years after its entry into force and 'take decisions as appropriate'.

- Extension(s) of the Agreement for up to eight years can be decided upon by the Council.

- The Council remains the supreme decision-making authority within the organization, but it also operates through a number of other bodies namely:
  - The Finance and Administration Committee;
  - The Projects Committee;
  - The Promotion and Market development Committee;
  - The Statistics Committee;
  - The Private Sector Consultative Board, with the power to make recommendations on matters raised for its consideration by the Council;
  - The World Coffee Conference, which is called upon to discuss matters of interest to the industry at large and to be self-financing, unless the Council decides otherwise. World Coffee Conferences have been held in London 2001, Salvador, Brazil 2005 and Guatemala City 2010;
  - The Consultative Forum on Coffee Sector Finance, is a new institution created by the International Coffee Agreement 2007 and aims to facilitate consultations on topics related to finance and risk management in the coffee sector with a particular emphasis on the needs of small and medium scale producers and local communities in coffee producing area.

- The ICO's main objectives are to:
  - Promote international cooperation on coffee matters;
  - Provide a forum for consultations between governments and with the private sector;
  - Promote consumption and coffee quality;
  - Encourage the development of a sustainable coffee sector in economic, social and environmental terms;
  - Collect and publish economic, technical and scientific information, statistics and studies;
  - Provide a forum for the understanding of structural conditions in international markets and long term production and consumption trends that result in fair prices to both producers and consumers;
  - Promote training and the transfer of technology relevant to coffee to members;
  - Encourage members to develop appropriate food safety procedures in the coffee sector;
  - Develop and seek finance for projects that benefit members and the world coffee economy;
  - Facilitate the availability of information on financial tools and services that can assist coffee producers.

- The ICO's headquarters are to remain in London, unless the Council decides otherwise.

- The ICO will continue to maintain the system of indicator prices.

- Certificates of origin will continue to accompany all exports.

- The preamble acknowledges the exceptional importance of coffee to the economies of many countries and to the livelihoods of millions of people, as well as the contribution that a sustainable coffee sector can make to the achievement of the Millennium Development Goals. It also recognizes that collaboration between members can foster an economically diversified coffee sector and contribute to its development, as well as recognizing that increased access to coffee related information and market-based risk strategies can help avoid imbalances that give rise to market volatility, which is harmful to both producers and consumers.

Key events in the history of the International Coffee Agreement (ICA). (Based primarily on F.O. Licht. International Coffee Report, vol. 15. No. 21. See also *www.ico.org/ico/history.htm.*)

1963: First ICA comes into force at a time of low prices, regulating supplies through an export quota system.

1972: Export quotas suspended as prices soar.

1980: Export quotas restored and producers agree in return to abandon attempts to regulate the market unilaterally.

February 1986: Quotas suspended after a boom caused by drought losses to Brazil's crop sends prices soaring above the ceiling of the ICA's US$ 1.20–US$ 1.40 target range.

October 1987: Quotas reintroduced.

4 July 1989: Indefinite suspension of quotas after the system breaks down under the pressure of competing demands from exporters for market shares under the new ICA then being negotiated. Backed by the United States, Central American states and Mexico press for a much bigger slice of the market at the expense of Brazil (which resists this) and of African producers.

4 September 1989: Then-Colombian President Virgilio Barco writes to United States President George Bush appealing for help to bring back export quotas under a new ICA and receives an encouraging response on 19 September.

1 October 1989: ICA extension with its economic clauses suppressed takes effect.

February 1990: President Bush at a Latin American drugs summit in Colombia reaffirms commitment to a new ICA and a document is released setting out the Administration's thinking on its possible shape.

December 1991: During talks with Cesar Gaviria (Colombia's new President) Brazilian President Fernando Collor de Mello (elected in March 1990), agrees in principle to back efforts to restore quotas when the local industry – given the lead role in formulating policy – can agree a common position.

March 1992: Brazil finally gives the go-ahead to the negotiation of a new ICA with economic clauses.

June 1992: First round of the negotiations.

9 March 1993: Bill Clinton, victor in the November 1992 United States presidential elections, writes to President Gaviria supporting a new ICA, although with no sign of much enthusiasm.

31 March 1993: ICA negotiations collapse during the sixth round with little progress having been made and each side blaming the other for the impasse.

September 1993: In Brazil, 29 countries sign a treaty establishing the Association of Coffee Producing Countries (ACPC) with powers to regulate supplies and prices. Citing this as a reason, the United States pulls out of the ICO.

September 1994: New 'administrative' ICA without economic clauses (drafted in March) enters into force for five years.

March 1998: First talks open about the possibility of replacing the 1994 ICA.

July 1999: ICA talks break down.

September 1999: 1994 ICA extended for a further two years. During the first year, it is agreed a further attempt will be made to draw up a replacement treaty.

September 2000: Drafting of a new ICA completed.

October 2001: ICA 2001 enters into force for six years. It has no provisions for price regulation.

February 2005: The United States returns to full membership.

January 2006: Negotiations to replace the ICA 2001 begin

September 2007: A new 10-year International Coffee Agreement is approved and the 2001 ICA is extended, initially for one year, to enable ratification procedures to be completed.

September 2010: The 2007 ICA is extended for a fourth year to provide further time for participating countries to complete their ratification procedures.

September 2010: Japan officially withdraws from the Agreement.

2 February 2011: ICA 2007 finally comes into force.

Table 1.10 Membership of the ICO

Exporting members		Importing members	
Angola	Kenya	European Community	Malta
Brazil	Liberia	Austria	Netherlands
Burundi	Mexico	Belgium/Luxembourg	Poland
Central African Republic	Nicaragua	Bulgaria	Portugal
Colombia	Panama	Cyprus	Romania
Costa Rica	Papua New Guinea	Czech Republic	Slovakia
Côte d'Ivoire	Philippines	Denmark	Slovenia
Cuba	Sierre Leone	Estonia	Spain
Ecuador	Thailand	Finland	Sweden
El Salvador	Timor-Leste	France	United Kingdom
Ethiopia	Togo	Germany	Norway
Gabon	Uganda	Greece	Switzerland
Ghana	United Republic of Tanzania	Hungary	Tunisia
Guatemala	Viet Nam	Ireland	Turkey
Honduras	Yemen	Italy	United States of America
India	Zambia	Latvia	
Indonesia		Lithuania	
There are 11 countries (Benin, Bolivia (Plurinational State of), Cameroon, Democratic Republic of the Congo, Guinea, Madagascar, Malawi, Nigeria, Paraguay, Rwanda and Zimbabwe) which have all signed the new Agreement but had not completed the required procedures for full membership by November 2011.			

Table 1.11 World production by country, 1995/96–2010/11 ('000 bags)

	Average			Coffee years				
	1996/97 2000/01	2001/02 2005/06	2006/07 2010/11	2006/07	2007/08	2008/09	2009/10	2010/11*
TOTAL	**106 623**	**113 423**	**128 257**	**127 048**	**127 835**	**126 664**	**128 610**	**131 144**
Arabica group	*70 757*	*73 816*	*78 364*	*77 317*	*80 110*	*75 813*	*77 820*	*80 778*
North America	**20 034**	**16 717**	**17 542**	**17 089**	**18 504**	**17 777**	**16 674**	**18 148**
Costa Rica	2 347	1 882	1 544	1 580	1 791	1 320	1 462	1 589
Cuba	306	231	108	92	84	126	115	122
Dominican Republic	641	404	498	406	510	609	463	500
El Salvador	2 241	1 503	1 489	1 371	1 621	1 547	1 065	1 840
Guatemala	4 653	3 738	3 855	3 950	4 100	3 785	3 500	3 950
Haiti	433	374	347	361	359	357	350	307
Honduras	2 379	2 856	3 714	3 461	3 842	3 450	3 527	4 290
Jamaica	42	33	30	40	20	32	30	30
Mexico	5 472	4 076	4 240	4 200	4 150	4 651	4 200	4 000
Nicaragua	1 127	1 313	1 520	1 300	1 700	1 615	1 686	1 300
Panama	190	148	159	173	176	153	170	120
United States	203	160	129	154	151	133	106	100
South America	**40 117**	**45 608**	**47 320**	**47 725**	**48 459**	**45 907**	**46 564**	**47 946**
Bolivia (Plurinational State of)	170	146	141	148	137	139	141	139
Brazil	25 074	29 241	30 510	29 056	30 290	32 175	32 454	33 577
Colombia	11 102	11 705	10 382	12 541	12 504	8 664	9 000	9 200
Ecuador	539	540	492	695	515	384	437	427
Paraguay	30	33	24	24	25	21	25	23
Peru	2 203	2 929	3 658	3 691	3 468	3 594	3 657	3 880
Venezuela (Bolivarian Republic of)	999	1 014	1 114	1 571	1 520	930	850	700
Africa	**6 538**	**7 061**	**8 924**	**8 329**	**8 725**	**7 669**	**9 613**	**10 279**
Burundi	363	337	279	298	299	274	230	293
Cameroon	133	80	84	92	87	82	76	83
Democratic Republic of the Congo	88	91	63	60	67	64	68	56
Ethiopia	3 224	4 158	6 170	5 551	5 967	4 949	6 931	7 450
Kenya	1 297	903	727	826	652	572	750	833
Malawi	64	41	19	18	21	16	20	19
Madagascar	44	28	29	30	30	30	30	25
Rwanda	261	321	317	307	291	307	350	328
Uganda	340	412	598	540	650	640	600	560
United Republic of Tanzania	525	496	573	512	578	676	494	603
Zambia	52	98	37	57	55	33	26	15
Zimbabwe	147	97	29	38	28	26	38	14
Asia and the Pacific	**4 068**	**4 458**	**4 486**	**4 174**	**4 422**	**4 460**	**4 969**	**4 405**
India	1 855	1 934	1 563	1 754	1 561	1 311	1 593	1 595
Indonesia	790	839	1 677	1 263	1 628	1 899	2 139	1 457
Lao People's Democratic Republic	145	458	50	50	50	50	50	50
Papua New Guinea	1 138	883	959	863	988	1 005	992	945
Philippines	54	139	35	35	35	35	35	33
Sri Lanka	7	13	10	9	10	10	10	10
Timor-Leste	n.a.	n.a.	39	46	36	48	47	64
Yemen	79	193	193	200	150	150	150	315
Robusta group	*35 866*	*39 578*	*49 892*	*49 731*	*47 725*	*50 851*	*50 790*	*50 366*
America	**5 574**	**7 965**	**11 416**	**10 705**	**11 142**	**10 940**	**11 324**	**12 967**
Brazil	4 924	7 600	11 021	10 236	10 742	10 557	10 881	12 691
Ecuador	610	325	377	444	386	369	420	264
Guatemala	14	24	10	10	10	10	10	10
Guyana	9	3	3	3	3	3	3	2
Trinidad and Tobago	17	14	5	12	1	1	10	0

	Average			Coffee years				
	1996/97 2000/01	2001/02 2005/06	2006/07 2010/11	2006/07	2007/08	2008/09	2009/10	2010/11*
Africa	**10 340**	**7 390**	**7504**	**7 860**	**7 908**	**7 856**	**6 689**	**7 208**
Angola	59	32	30	35	37	26	24	29
Benin	0	0	0	0	0	0	0	0
Cameroon	1 174	710	680	744	708	667	614	668
Central African Rep.	191	62	82	87	70	79	75	100
Congo	5	3	3	3	3	3	3	2
Côte d'Ivoire	3 864	2 591	2 370	2 847	2 598	2 353	1 850	2 200
Democratic Republic of the Congo	666	315	330	317	349	335	357	294
Gabon	3	1	1	1	0	1	1	0
Ghana	39	17	26	29	31	27	25	20
Guinea	139	281	403	473	323	394	375	450
Liberia	5	19	29	53	40	30	10	10
Madagascar	644	461	584	587	614	726	467	523
Nigeria	52	49	45	51	42	51	40	40
Sierra Leone	45	26	54	31	42	87	30	80
Togo	286	129	157	134	125	138	140	250
Uganda	2 949	2 405	2 392	2 160	2 600	2 560	2 400	2 240
United Republic of Tanzania	219	285	319	307	326	380	278	302
Asia and the Pacific	**19 952**	**24 223**	**30 973**	**31 167**	**28 675**	**32 055**	**3 277**	**30 191**
India	2 756	2 724	3 100	3 404	2 899	3 060	3 234	3 389
Indonesia	6 286	5 665	7 346	6 367	6 937	8 093	8 553	6 778
Lao People's Democratic Republic	73	163	375	400	350	350	350	425
Malaysia	160	810	716	500	930	952	1 000	200
New Caledonia	9	1	1	1	1	1	1	1
Papua New Guinea	59	21	20	25	10	10	10	45
Philippines	746	498	417370	331	394	382	669	76
Sri Lanka	35	31	31	33	33	32	30	25
Thailand	1 252	789	755	766	653	675	930	752
Viet Nam	8 576	13 521	18 161	19 340	16 467	18 500	18 000	18 500

Source: ICO and USDA.

* Provisional.

n.a. = not available.

CHAPTER 2

THE MARKETS FOR COFFEE

THE MARKETS FOR COFFEE

THE STRUCTURE OF THE COFFEE TRADE

Broadly speaking, at the consumer level coffee can be divided into three commercial categories.

- **Exemplary quality**: limited availability – fine to unique taste experience.
- **Premium quality:** moderate availability – good to very good taste experience.
- **Mainstream quality**: very widely available – acceptable taste experience.

Precise figures are unavailable, nor is the situation static, but it is generally accepted that between 80% and 90% of all coffee consumed worldwide is of mainstream quality.

Figure 2.1 Leading coffee trading companies worldwide, 2010

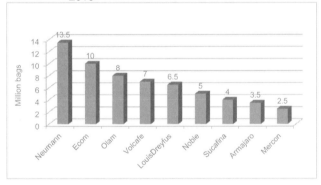

Source: Trade estimates – subject to constant change.

The structure of the coffee trade in North America, most of Western Europe and Japan is very similar. Coffee is generally purchased from the exporting countries by international trade houses, dealers and traders. The very largest roasters in Europe also maintain their own in-house buying companies, which deal directly with origin. In the main, however, roasters tend to buy their coffee from international trade houses or from specialized import agents who represent specific exporters in producing countries. The international trade plays a vital role in the worldwide marketing and distribution of coffee. Coffee is generally sold FOB (free on board), but many roasters, especially in the United States, prefer to buy on an ex-dock basis. Small roasters often prefer to buy in small lots on a delivered in-store or ex-store basis. This allows plenty of scope for the various middlemen involved in the trade to operate and perform useful functions, although the increasing concentration at the roasting end of the industry has led to a substantial reduction in their number.

Essentially, the coffee trade assists the flow of coffee from the exporting country to the roaster. Traders and dealers take responsibility for discharging the coffee from the incoming vessel and make all the necessary arrangements to have the coffee delivered to the roaster. Using the futures markets either for hedging or as a price guide, traders offer and provide roasters spreads of physical coffee for shipment one month to 18 months in the future. Many of these sales, especially for later shipment positions, are short sales: the seller will source the required green coffee at a later date.

Such positions are typically sold at a premium or a discount (the differential) against the price of the appropriate delivery month on the London or New York futures markets (selling price to be fixed – PTBF – see chapters 8 and 9 on futures markets and trading). This gives the roaster the right to fix the price for each individual shipping position at their option, usually up to the first delivery day of the relevant month. Some roasters might want a separate contract for each position, while others might have a single contract for six positions, for example July through December. Obviously selling so far ahead carries considerable risk. In some cases the coffee may not even have been harvested yet. To reduce their exposure, traders sometimes offer such forward positions as deliveries of a basket of acceptable coffees rather than committing to a single growth. This is becoming less common today than it was in the past, but it remains a significant feature of the trade in many parts of the world. Typical examples of such baskets are given below.

- Guatemala prime washed, and/or El Salvador central standard, and/or Costa Rica hard bean, versus the appropriate delivery months of the New York futures market.
- Uganda standard grade, and/or Côte d'Ivoire grade 2, and/or Indian robusta AB/PB/EPB grades, versus the appropriate delivery months of the London futures market.

These baskets represent coffees that are acceptable for the same purpose in many blends of roasted coffee; traders can fulfil their delivery obligations by providing one of the specified growths. Any shipment would, however, still be subject to the roaster's final approval of the quality.

Not all coffee is always immediately sold to a roaster. Before arrival an individual parcel of coffee may be traded several times before it is eventually sold to a roaster. This trading in physical coffee should not be confused with trading coffee contracts on the futures exchanges and terminal markets. Given the variability of supply, the coffee market is inherently unstable and is characterized by wide fluctuations in price. The futures market therefore plays an important role in the coffee trade, as it does with other commodities, by acting as the institution that transfers the risk of price movements to speculators and helps to establish price levels. These markets do not handle significant quantities of physical coffee, although dealers do occasionally deliver coffee or take delivery of coffee in respect of contracts that have not been closed out. Participants in the industry use the futures markets primarily for hedging.

The structure of the trade in other importing countries is broadly similar, although naturally there are variations. In some countries, such as the Nordic countries, there are no main traders or importers as such, but rather just roasters and brokers/agents. In others, such as in Eastern Europe, importers either import directly or increasingly via the international trade houses based in the main coffee centres of Hamburg, Antwerp, Le Havre and Trieste.

WHY IS COFFEE TRADED IN UNITED STATES DOLLARS?

This question is often asked, particularly at times when the United States dollar is weak. When local currencies in coffee producing countries strengthen against a falling dollar growers suffer, or do not benefit if global prices rise. What are the possibilities of selling in currencies other than United States dollars, for example the euro, considering the European Union is by far the world's largest consumer of coffee?

There are many sides to this issue, but the points below suggest that although change is always possible, for the time being it is unlikely.

- **Coffee is a global commodity that is traded worldwide on a daily basis.** It would be very difficult to maintain this global liquidity if some coffees were priced in different currencies. Point in case: in 1992 the London robusta market moved from using British pound sterling to United States dollars for that reason, thereby also facilitating arbitrage between the New York and London futures markets.
- **Price risk management would become very difficult if the market had to interpret both futures price movements, and currency movements for each and every hedging transaction.** 80% to 90% of the market is mainstream coffee that is priced and/or hedged against the New York and London futures markets, both priced in United States dollars. Also, New York is by far the world's leading futures exchange and would be most unlikely to move away from the United States dollar. Finally, using different currencies in a single transaction could mean that a correct decision on the coffee price might be totally offset by a wrong assumption on the currency front.
- **The currencies of many countries are loosely linked to the United States dollar in the sense that they often follow dollar movements,** particularly so in Latin America where the United States is the predominant trading partner. This is not the case in most of Africa where the European Union plays that role.

- **The United States market will of course continue to purchase in dollars and many, if not all, origins will oblige.** If elsewhere coffee were traded in a different currency, this might possibly distort prices and add currency-based arbitrage to an already quite speculative coffee trade.

One should also bear in mind that buyers will always protect themselves. If having to buy in a different currency means more risk or a disadvantage, then this will be priced into the transaction. Therefore, it is difficult for individual exporters or smaller producing countries to pursue this unless such a change was in the context of a general industry move, triggered by some external event or situation.

STRUCTURE OF THE RETAIL MARKET

Retail sales of coffee (both roasted and instant) in the main importing countries are channelled through a combination of retail shops owned by the roasters themselves, their own direct sales force supplying supermarkets and hypermarkets, and wholesalers and food brokers. Supermarkets today play a much larger role in the retailing of coffee than they ever did before and supermarket own brands now account for a sizeable proportion of retail coffee sales. Roasted coffee is sold in ground form or as whole bean and is packaged in various types and sizes of cans and packets. Soluble coffee is generally sold in jars, although sachets are becoming increasingly popular, especially in emerging markets and in particular, for the '3-in-1' products where instant coffee is pre-mixed with sugar and a creamer.

Single-serve instant portions are also gaining ground in established markets, as are coffee pads or pods and capsules for use in domestic filter coffee and espresso machines. What these have in common is convenience of preparation, consistency of quality and easy mess-free disposal of spent coffee grounds. More recently there has been a significant shift towards single-serve filter coffee brewing methods in the United States and Europe with the development of new single serve filter machines as well as the single-serve pour-over filter system, known generally as the 'chemex' system. There is also a strongly growing, although still small, market for ready-to-drink (RTD) liquid coffee beverages sold in cans or bottles.

Roasters have two distinct market segments:

- **The retail (grocery) market,** where coffee is purchased largely, but not exclusively for consumption in the home;
- **The institutional (catering) market,** where coffee is destined for the out-of-home market e.g. restaurants, coffee shops and bars, hospitals, offices, and vending machines.

The percentage share of each segment varies from country to country, but in most countries, retail sales for in-home consumption generally account for 70% to 80% of the overall market. There are exceptions, especially in countries where there is a well-established catering trade and eating out is part of the country's traditions, for example in Italy, Spain and Greece.

Each segment accepts a wide range of products, the quality and taste of which depend largely upon the coffee growths that make up the blends, the degree of roast, the type of grind, and so on. Most small roasters tend to specialize in one segment, while larger and in particular multinational roasters usually service both. The major part of the retail market is, however, controlled by a handful of huge multinational roasters and the degree of concentration is increasing. Although this trend was temporarily halted by the growth in the specialty trade, it is once again accelerating with the rapid acquisition of small specialty roasters by the multinationals.

Figure 2.2   Leading coffee roasting companies worldwide, 2010

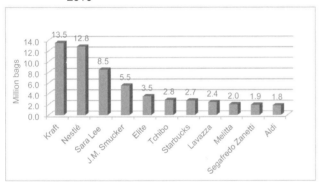

Source: Trade estimates – subject to constant change.

DEMAND

Coffee is one of the world's most popular beverages. Gross imports of all types of coffee have quadrupled from 33 million bags in 1949 to 132 million bags in 2010. However, statistics on gross imports are a poor indicator of demand as they ignore re-exports. In 2010 re-exports accounted for some 38.9 million bags, although in the past they were not as important as they are today. Data on re-exports is not available prior to 1964, but figure 2.3 shows the growth in gross exports since 1949 and in total net imports since 1963. Net imports reflect what is consumed in the country of importation plus any surplus that goes into inventories.

A more accurate indicator of consumption is provided by statistics on disappearance, which take into account re-exports and changes in the level of stocks held in importing countries. Table 2.1 shows world gross imports, net imports, disappearance and inventories by form of coffee over the period 2005–2010.

Figure 2.3   World coffee imports, 1949–2010

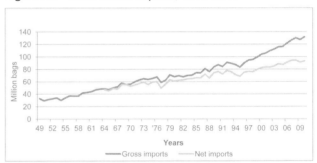

Source: ICO.

Table 2.1   World gross and net imports, disappearance and inventories by form of coffee, 2005–2010 (in millions of bags)

		2005	2006	2007	2008	2009	2010
A.	**Gross imports**	**116.3**	**121.7**	**126.5**	**130.1**	**127.4**	**131.6**
	Green	89.7	93.3	95.9	98.2	97.3	99.4
	Roasted	10.9	12.3	12.9	14.0	14.0	15.2
	Soluble	15.7	16.1	17.7	17.9	16.1	17.0
B.	**Gross re-exports**	**28.9**	**30.6**	**32.9**	**35.6**	**36.1**	**38.8**
	Green	8.3	8.9	9.4	11.7	11.2	12.2
	Roasted	10.4	11.6	12.4	13.6	14.0	15.1
	Soluble	10.2	10.1	11.1	10.4	10.9	11.5
C.	**Net imports**	**87.4**	**91.1**	**93.6**	**94.5**	**91.3**	**92.8**
	Green	81.4	84.4	86.5	86.5	86.1	87.2
	Roasted	0.5	0.7	0.5	0.4	0.0	0.1
	Soluble	5.5	6.0	6.5	7.5	5.2	5.5
D.	**Disappearance**	**88.2**	**90.2**	**93.1**	**94.8**	**92.3**	**93.6**
E.	**Inventories as at 31 December***	**20.2**	**19.1**	**21.1**	**21.4**	**22.4**	**18.4**

Source: ICO.

* Comprises all stocks in consuming countries including stocks in free ports.

ROAST AND GROUND COFFEE

Estimates suggest that some 100 million bags or 76% of all coffee consumed in the world (including that consumed in producing countries) is roast and ground. In importing countries, about 75% of consumption is roast and ground, and of this about 87% is roasted in-country. The remainder is imported from other consuming countries and also, but to a lesser extent, from producing countries.

In some regions the cross-border trade in coffee roasted by importing countries themselves is growing strongly. The European Union dominates this trade, and in 2010 had 77% of world exports of roasted coffee. Producing countries accounted for around 1.5% of this trade in roasted coffee. The United States, Canada and a small number of other countries made up the remaining 21.5%.

The market for roast and ground coffee is dominated by large multinationals (Kraft Foods, Nestlé and Sara Lee/DE), despite the fact that in many countries there has been a resurgence in small, locally-based roasters. The bulk of roast and ground coffee consumed in importing countries is blended (usually before roasting) to ensure a certain uniformity in the finished product. Blending increases the roasters' flexibility, making them less dependent on a single source of supply. It also allows them to compensate for seasonal changes in the taste of coffee beans and to switch to other coffees if there are any problems with availability or price.

Roasting develops the coffee's flavour and fragrance; the higher the roast the more the flavour is developed. Lightly roasted beans produce a thin, almost straw-coloured liquid with little flavour except perhaps acidity, although the weight loss is less. A darker roast will give a dark liquid, which may have lost acidity but has gained body and stronger flavour, although the weight loss will be higher. The darker the roast, the greater the cell destruction and fragmentation. This facilitates the extraction of solubles, but too dark a roast merely leaves a burnt flavour.

Roast and ground coffee has a shorter shelf life than soluble coffee. It loses quality the longer it is exposed to air, so it is frequently packed in vacuum or gas-flushed packs.

INSTANT OR SOLUBLE COFFEE

The term 'instant coffee' or 'soluble coffee' encompasses spray-dried powder, freeze-dried powder and liquefied forms of coffee such as liquid concentrates. All of these methods of processing involve dehydrating brewed roasted and ground coffee. The freeze-dried method produces a superior but more expensive product.

Figure 2.4 shows that world consumption of soluble coffee is rising relatively strongly after a number of years of stagnation, expanding from 22.8 million bags (green bean equivalent) in

2000 to 31.1 million bags in 2010, although as a percentage of overall consumption it has remained relatively flat.

Figure 2.4   Consumption of soluble coffee – 2000, 2005 and 2010

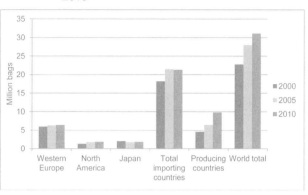

Source: NKG Statistics.

In Europe, growth in demand has been relatively modest at around 0.2% a year in recent years, which is considerably slower than the overall growth in consumption for all types of coffee. In the United Kingdom, where soluble coffee accounts for around 75% of total consumption, demand was beginning to show signs of actual decline, but has been revitalized in recent years by the growing interest in speciality instant coffees (such as instant cappuccino). Elsewhere in Europe, however, the introduction of new specialty instant coffee products also increased demand for soluble coffee, but the trend appears to have been short lived. The Deutscher Kaffeeverband estimate that the instant coffee share of demand in Germany rose from 6.2% to over 7.5% between 1998 and 2005 reflecting this surge in demand for these speciality instant products, only to fall back to 4.1% in 2010.

Much of the recent growth in soluble coffee consumption can be attributed to a rise in demand in Eastern Europe, and East and South-East Asia – both regions where soluble coffee enjoys a high market share. In East and South-East Asia there has been tremendous growth in the demand for the product known as '3-in-1', a beverage that combines the convenience of soluble coffee with a non-dairy creamer and sugar, usually in single-serve sachets purchased one at a time.

In 2010, just under 70% of the soluble coffee consumed in importing countries was processed into soluble coffee in those countries. The corresponding figure in 2000 was 83%, which suggests that producing countries may be seeing a significant increase in their share of the soluble coffee market in importing countries. Imports of soluble coffee are often referred to as offshore powder. Consumption of instant coffee in producing countries themselves varies considerably. In the Philippines and Thailand instant coffee accounts for around 95% of coffee consumption. In Brazil, the largest exporter of soluble coffee, domestic consumption of instant coffee only accounts for around 5% of overall coffee consumption. In India most soluble coffee is also exported, although it does account for around 35% of local consumption. In Mexico the figure is about 47%.

Globally, Nestlé and Kraft Foods account for just under 75% of the world market, with Nestlé alone supplying around half the world demand for instant coffee.

DECAFFEINATED COFFEE

Decaffeinated coffee was developed in Europe, but achieved its first broad market in the United States during the 1950s. World consumption of decaffeinated coffee is difficult to gauge owing to the lack of separate data on this type of coffee in many importing countries.

In the United States, consumption of decaffeinated coffee was relatively stable from 2000 to 2005, accounting for 8%–9% of mainstream sales and about 20% of sales of specialty coffee. Sales thereafter increased significantly, but fell back to 13% in 2011 (from 16% in 2009) according to the latest NCA Coffee Drinking Study. Consumption of decaffeinated coffee has been fairly static elsewhere since 2000, and in many countries low-caffeine coffee products are now an established part of the manufacturers' range. These products are not caffeine free, but are either a mixture of regular coffee and decaffeinated coffee or blends of coffees with a naturally low caffeine content. These products are sold as 'light' coffee.

Table 2.2   Consumption of decaffeinated coffee as a percentage of total consumption, 2010

Country	%	Country	%
Australia	7	Italy	7
Austria	4	Japan	Low
Belgium/Luxembourg	8	Netherlands	12
Brazil	Low	Norway	Low
Canada	8	Portugal	4
Denmark	6	Spain	16
Finland	1	Sweden	Low
France	7	Switzerland	4
Germany	7	United Kingdom	10
Greece	1	United States	13

DEMAND BY GEOGRAPHICAL AREA

NORTH AMERICA

United States of America

Green coffee makes up the bulk of imports into the United States. Rather surprisingly given the growth in specialty coffee consumption in the United States, the origin mix of its green coffee imports has shifted away from washed arabicas towards Natural arabicas and robustas. A significant proportion of this shifting supply pattern can be put down to changes in the availability and origin of supply and in particular to supply problems in Colombia and Central America but higher prices particularly in the last two to three years has accelerated the switch to these other coffees. In 2005, 48% of United States imports of green coffee from producing countries came from the Colombian Milds and Other Milds groups. By 2010 this was down to just 43%.

Imports from Brazil vary from year to year and in 2010 increased to over 28% of green bean imports from 21% in 2005, while imports of robusta coffee (including estimated imports of robusta from Brazil) have increased marginally from just over 25% in 2005 to 27% in 2010. There is no doubt that the initial increase in the use of robusta reflected the greater consumption of espresso blends containing robusta coffee, as well as its incorporation in many of the mainstream blends as a means of keeping prices lower. However, the somewhat constrained increase in robusta use is thought by some analysts to reflect consumer resistance to the altered taste profile that the greater use of robusta created.

Roast and ground (or regular) coffee: Over 85% of the coffee sold for home consumption is roast and ground coffee. By 2011, 85% of total consumption, based on cups consumed per person per day, takes place at home. According to the National Coffee Association of USA the drip coffee maker dominates American coffee preparation, although the single-cup brewing systems are growing.

Specialty coffee: This sector has transformed and improved the image of coffee in the eyes of the American consumer. In 1991 it was estimated that there were just 500 gourmet or specialty coffeehouses, yet by 2010 there were an estimated 10,000-plus. This number excludes other coffee venues such as coffee carts, kiosks, vending machines and cafes in bookstores, sporting arenas and transportation facilities, which have also seen an explosion in numbers.

Even so, brewed coffee remains the most popular type of coffee consumed in the United States in 2011, accounting for 92 out of every 100 cups of coffee consumed – up from 85 cups per 100 in 2010. This reflects the surge in the adoption of home-use single-cup filter brewing systems. Soluble coffee consumption on the other hand, which had witnessed something of a resurgence, now appears to be in decline and in 2011 accounted for around eight cups per 100 – down from 11 cups in 2010. Similarly gourmet or specialty coffee beverages (both roasted and instant) appears to be in decline, accounting for 36 cups per 100 cups consumed in 2011, which is down from the 40 cups per 100 recorded in 2010, possibly reflecting consumer reaction to the downturn in global economic activity. The coffee sector in the United States has undergone radical change in the last decade. Following the acquisition of Folgers and a sizable portion of Sara Lee/DE in the United States, J.M. Smucker is now the largest coffee roasted and manufacturer in America followed by Kraft Foods.

Table 2.3   Coffee consumption in North America, 2010

Country	Population (millions)	Net imports (million bags)			Main suppliers (green bean)	Per capita consumption (kg/year)	Additional information
		Green beans	Roasted	Soluble			
United States	318	20.68	-0.64	1.15	Brazil 28% Viet Nam 18% Colombia 13%	4.1	83% of America's re-exports of processed coffee goes to Canada
Canada	34	2.14	0.91	0.53	Colombia 27% Brazil 22% Guatemala 14%	6.3	98% of Canada's re-exports of processed coffee goes to the United State

Source: ICO and other trade sources.

Note: Green bean equivalents are used for roasted, soluble and per capita consumption figures.

Canada

The coffee market in Canada is estimated to have increased at a compound annual growth rate of 3.1% since 2004 with Kraft being the leading roaster. The market is fairly fragmented with a large number of smaller roasters, but is beginning to consolidate following a number of high-profile mergers and acquisitions. Roast and ground coffee accounts for 72% of the total market.

EUROPE

The European Union has 27 member states with a population of 500 million. According to the European Commission, the EU is the largest barrier-free market in the world, bigger than the United States, Canada and Mexico together.

In terms of green coffee imports, the 27 EU member states accounted for an estimated 51.3 million bags in 2010 (European Coffee Federation data), including intra-EU trade, and 45.9 million bags excluding intra-EU trade. The ICO's figures are 52.2 million bags and 46.9 million bags respectively.

One consequence of the EU's single market is that there is no intra-EU import or export, only movement of goods. This is more than just terminology. It means that the vast majority of imports are declared at the point of entry into the EU and not at the point of destination. This tends to increase gross import figures for those countries with the major points of importation (in essence, the major ports). At the same time, the single market means that the earlier documentary requirements for cross-border traffic no longer exist. Operators are required to report cross-border traffic to the statistical bodies, but only above a certain value and/or volume. Eurostat, the EU statistical office, has developed models to extrapolate total intra-EU movement of goods on the basis of the reported data, but these models have their limitations.

For these reasons, data on the movement of green as well as finished coffee within the EU have inevitably become less accurate. However, not only do many of the statistics for individual EU country coffee imports produced by both the EU authorities and the ICO not always present the total picture, but there are also differences between them. Most individual EU member country statistics must, therefore, be treated with some caution.

After deducting intra-EU trade, net total green bean imports into EU for 2010 work out at some 45.9 million bags. The five largest suppliers were Brazil (33%), Viet Nam (20%), Indonesia (6%), Honduras (6%) and Peru (5%).

Sustainability: Since 2003, the European industry has been working on a comprehensive concept to 'mainstream coffee on its way to sustainability', through an initiative known as the Common Code for the Coffee Community or 4C. This aims at establishing a scheme of continuous improvement of the social, ecological and economic principles in the production, processing and trading of mainstream coffee (which constitutes between 80%–90% of all coffee traded). The 4C Association was formally established in early 2007 with its secretariat in Bonn, Germany. The first 4C coffee became available in October 2007. See *www.4c-coffeeassociation. org.*

Speciality: Although many Western European countries have traditionally consumed high-quality coffees, in recent years the speciality concept has gained considerable acceptance amongst European consumers. See also chapter 3, Niche markets, and *www.scae.com*.

Summary data on the coffee imports of individual EU countries plus selected other European countries is shown in table 2.4.

In this context, green coffee means not-decaffeinated and from all sources – so also from other European countries. Green bean imports are identified by country of origin, but not all was necessarily imported directly from origin.

The source for most import/export data for the EU countries that were members as at 31 December 2010, as well as for Norway and Switzerland, is the European Coffee Federation's European Coffee Report 2010–2011, which itself draws on data provided by Eurostat and member associations. Other data are taken ex ICO and other trade statistics. Luxembourg's coffee statistics are combined with those for Belgium, although it is an EU member. The full ECF 2010 –2011 Coffee Report and earlier issues can be viewed and downloaded from *www.ecf-coffee.org.*

Table 2.4   Coffee consumption in Europe, 2010

Country	Population (millions)	Net imports (million bags)			Main suppliers (green bean)	Per capita consumption (kg/year)	Additional information
		Green beans	Roasted	Soluble			
European Union							
Austria	8.4	0.55	0.25	0.11	Brazil 24% Viet Nam 22% Honduras 7% Unidentified via Germany 22%	6.4	Germany is Austria's main trading partner in processed coffee taking 62% of its imports of processed coffee from Germany, but re-exporting 30% of its output back to Germany.
Belgium/ Luxembourg	11	1.60	-0.37	-0.12	Brazil 28% Viet Nam 16% Honduras 10% Peru 7%	5.9	One roaster, Sara Lee / DE, accounts for around half of the market. Belgium also has many small roasters, particularly in the specialty sector.
Bulgaria	7.5	0.38	-0.04	0.54	Viet Nam 25% Indonesia 22% Brazil 10% Honduras 9%	3.2	99% of roasted coffee imports were ex EU sources, as were 69% of soluble imports.
Cyprus	0.9	0.03	0.01	0.04	Brazil 92%	5.0	98% of soluble imports were ex EU sources, as were 87% of roasted coffee imports.
Czech Republic	10	0.32	0.08	0.07	Brazil 27% Viet Nam 16% Indonesia 14%	2.7	99% of roasted coffee imports were ex EU sources, as were 87% of soluble imports.
Denmark	5.5	0.66	0.11	0.09	Brazil 14% Viet Nam 6% Uganda 5% Unidentified via Germany 55%	9.5	Imports of roasted coffee were almost exclusively ex EU sources with 77% coming from Sweden. The EU accounted for 82% of soluble imports.
Estonia	1.3	0.01	0.08	0.02	Viet Nam 24% Brazil 20% Indonesia 12% Uganda 11%	4.7	92% of its green coffee imports are re-exported to the Russian Federation, similarly 40% of its re-exports of soluble coffee go to the Russian Federation.
Finland	5.4	1.10	-0.06	0.04	Brazil 45% Colombia 10% Nicaragua 7% Guatemala 6%	12.1	Four roasters account for around 97% of the market; 96% of its imports are arabica and 4% robusta.
France	63	4.28	1.62	-0.03	Brazil 21% Viet Nam 11% Ethiopia 5% Honduras 4%	5.7	Kraft Foods and Sara Lee/DE account for 60% or more of the roast coffee market by volume. Nestlé accounts for almost two-thirds of the soluble market.
Germany	82	12.69	-2.24	-1.39	Brazil 35% Viet Nam 19% Peru 7% Honduras 6%	6.8	Two roasters, Kraft Foods and Tchibo, account for about 55% of the market. The market share of single serve pods and espresso coffee now accounts for 21% of the overall market.
Greece	11	0.40	0.15	0.45	Brazil 69% Viet Nam 9% India 9%	5.3	Soluble coffee accounts for just over 45% of the market. 99% of roast coffee imports and 74% of soluble coffee imports come from EU countries.
Hungary	10	0.21	0.09	0.09	All imports of green coffee come via the EU with Germany accounting for 92% of these imports	2.3	India and Brazil apart, soluble imports were almost exclusively ex EU sources.

Country	Population (millions)	Net imports (million bags)			Main suppliers (green bean)	Per capita consumption (kg/year)	Additional information
		Green beans	Roasted	Soluble			
Ireland	4.6	0.04	0.02	0.09	Nicaragua 6% Colombia 5% Indonesia 5% unidentified via the United Kingdom 60%	2.0	Over two-thirds of total imports are processed coffee, 63% of which comes from the United Kingdom.
Italy	60	7.71	-2.06	0.15	Brazil 34% Viet Nam 19% India 13% Indonesia 6%	5.8	Five roasters, of which Lavazza is the largest, account for around 70% of the market. The single serve segment, which is growing by 20% per annum, is changing the dynamics of the market. Italy re-exports 28% of what its imports – reflecting its success in marketing Italian espresso brands overseas.
Latvia	2.2	0.05	0.02	0.03	Virtually all imports of green coffee come via the EU – with 80% from Germany	2.6	99% of its imports of roasted coffee and 62% of its imports of soluble coffee come from the EU.
Lithuania	3.3	0.01	0.20	0.02	Virtually all imports of green coffee come via the EU with Germany accounting for 64% of these imports	4.1	84% of re-exports of roasted coffee and 58% of re-exports of soluble coffee go to other EU countries, most notably Latvia.
Malta	0.4	0.00	0.01	0.01	Indonesia 40% Costa Rica 40%	1.8	Green bean imports are less than 1,000 bags and virtually no re-exports recorded.
Netherlands	17	0.99	0.22	0.12	Brazil 33% Viet Nam 15% Guatemala 6% Honduras 6%	4.8	ECF data puts imports of green coffee almost double that of the ICO at 1.91 million bags, reflecting the problems of collecting accurate import data for individual EU countries.
Poland	38	1.65	-0.17	0.61	Viet Nam 4% Lao People's Democratic Republic 3% Unidentified via Germany 83%	3.3	99% of its roasted coffee imports and 65% of its imports of soluble coffee originate in the EU.
Portugal	11	0.76	-0.08	0.08	Viet Nam 19% Brazil 15% Uganda 10% Cameroon 9%	4.1	Nestlé's market share is around 33%, with approximately 70 roasters covering the balance, many operating in small, local niche markets.
Romania	21	0.36	0.30	0.14	Viet Nam 29% Indonesia 14% Brazil 13% Uganda 8%	2.2	Over 99% of its imports of roasted coffee and 58% of its imports of soluble coffee are from the EU.
Slovakia	5.4	0.06	0.25	0.04	Brazil 27% Viet Nam 24% Ethiopia 17%	3.7	Over half of its imports of roasted coffee is re-exported mainly to EU destinations; similarly 59% of its imports of soluble coffee are also re-exported mainly to the Czech Republic.

Country	Population (millions)	Net imports (million bags)			Main suppliers (green bean)	Per capita consumption (kg/year)	Additional information
		Green beans	Roasted	Soluble			
Slovenia	2.0	0.14	0.04	0.03	Brazil 46% Viet Nam 22% India 6% Unidentified via Italy 11%	6.1	72% of its imports of soluble coffee come from Austria, while 50% of its roasted coffee imports come from Italy.
Spain	45	4.02	0.17	-0.95	Viet Nam 35% Brazil 21% Uganda 6% Colombia 5%	4.3	The top three roasters control about 60% of the market. Some 300 smaller roasters cover the remainder and dominate the out-of-home market, where espresso is in high demand.
Sweden	9.3	1.66	-0.46	0.01	Brazil 44% Peru 10% Colombia 8% Ethiopia 7% Kenya 7%	7.9	Dominating roasters are Kraft Foods with about 40% of the market, Zoegas 20%, Lofbergs Lila 15% and Arvid Nordquist 10%. A small number of roasters share the balance.
United Kingdom	62	2.21	0.55	0.34	Viet Nam 19% Brazil 16% Indonesia 15% Colombia 12%	3.0	Soluble coffee accounts for around 80% of the market, but tea still dominates the hot beverage market. Nestlé accounts for around 50% of the soluble coffee market; Kraft Foods just over 20%.
Other European countries							
Norway	4.8	0.59	0.08	0.07	Brazil 46% Colombia 17% Guatemala 12%	9.2	Almost 85% of the market is shared by six roasters, some of which are also importers.
Russian Federation	142	1.44	0.15	2.07	Viet Nam 37% Brazil 30% Indonesia 11%	1.6	Roasted coffee is expanding rapidly and accounted for 29% of the market in 2010, but soluble still dominates; 40% of the instant coffee consumed in the Russian Federation is produced locally.
Switzerland	7.7	1.99	-0.48	-0.50	Brazil 30% Viet Nam 15% Colombia 9% India 7%	8.0	The main roaster, Migros, accounts for around 45% of the market. The re-export of processed coffee continues to grow strongly with both roasted coffee and soluble coffee growing by around 20% over the year.

Source: ICO, ECF and other trade sources.

Note: Green bean equivalents are used for roasted, soluble and per capita consumption figures.

Data on Eastern European countries mostly originate from the ICO and F.O. Licht's International Coffee Report.

ASIA AND AUSTRALASIA

Coffee consumption is growing strongly throughout Asia and Australasia, primarily as a result of rising disposable income, but also as a result of the adoption of a more Western lifestyle throughout the region. In particular, consumption is showing exceptional growth in many of the producing countries of the region, most notably India, Indonesia, Viet Nam and Malaysia as well as China. In the more mature markets of the region, i.e. Japan, Australia and New Zealand, consumption is also expanding, but at a much lower rate.

China (including Hong Kong, China and Macao, China)

China (population 1.34 billion) is a producer as well as a consumer, consuming an estimated 700,000 bags in 2010, with internal production, primarily in the Yunnan Province, of around 500,000 bags in 2010. Chinese arabica is becoming fairly well known abroad and certainly in Europe, where the bulk of the green bean exports were destined.

Nestlé, which is the market leader and accounts for around 68% of the retail value of the coffee market in China, has been active in promoting internal production and obtains as much as it can of its raw material requirements from local sources. It has achieved very good market penetration and its Nescafé brand, including ready-to-serve coffee mixes, is widely available throughout the country.

However, over the last 10 years or so there has also been an explosion in the number of new American-style coffee bars opening up in all the major cities. Starbucks alone has opened more than 470 new shops in different cities throughout China since 1999, and other similar companies have also been expanding at the same rate. As a result, coffee is acquiring a more modern image and is becoming a very popular beverage with the young.

Japan

Demand for coffee continues to grow in Japan with average weekly consumption amounting to 10.9 cups in 2010 up from 10.0 cups in 2002. Instant coffee remains the most popular form of coffee accounting for 4.8 cups per week, while roasted coffee accounts for 3.3 cups, canned coffee 1.9 cups and liquid coffee 1.0 cups.

Republic of Korea

The Republic of Korea has had a thriving coffee market for a number of years based primarily on instant coffee, but the explosion of speciality coffee shops, both local and overseas owned, and a definite shift towards espresso-based coffee has helped to push consumption ahead very positively by around 7% annually over the past four years. Nevertheless, instant coffee still accounts for 85% of the total market, which a recent survey put at 22.8 billion cups of coffee or 452 cups for every Korean per year.

OTHER IMPORTING COUNTRIES

Other importing countries combined account for approximately 11 million bags. Data for selected countries from this group appear in table 2.6. This is a diverse group in which consumption levels per capita vary significantly. In some of these countries per capita consumption exceeds those recorded in a number of the more mature markets.

Table 2.5   Coffee consumption in selected countries in Asia and Australasia, 2010

Country	Population (millions)	Net imports (million bags)			Main suppliers (green bean)	Per capita consumption kg/year	Additional information
		Green beans	Roasted	Soluble			
Australia	22	1.08	0.06	0.23	Viet Nam 25% Papua New Guinea 17% Brazil 17% Indonesia 8%	3.5	Instant coffee accounts for +80% of all coffee sales. Nestlé, Cantarella and Sara Lee dominate the market.
China	1 338	0.08	0.09	0.13	Production = 500 000 bags; gross imports of green bean = 540 000 bags from Viet Nam 75%, Indonesia 10%	0.03	Almost all production is exported, mainly to Germany and Japan. The United States is largest supplier of roasted coffee, 30%; Malaysia largest in soluble coffee, 32%. Consumption: 700 000 bags (est.).
Japan	127	6.84	0.11	0.31	Brazil 30% Colombia 19% Indonesia 14% Viet Nam 13%	3.4	Instant coffee sector is dominated by Nestlé, 60%, and Ajinomoto, 30%. Largest suppliers of roasted coffee are UCC and Key Coffee.
Malaysia	28	0.99	0.01	-1.49	Production = 1.1 million bags; gross imports of green bean = 1.0 million bags from Viet Nam 48%, Indonesia 45%	1.3	Malaysia exports 1.8 million bags of instant coffee a year to the Philippines 34%, Singapore 21% and Indonesia 10%.
New Zealand	4.4	0.16	0.08	0.09	Viet Nam 26% Brazil16% Papua New Guinea 10% Colombia 10%	3.5	Instant coffee dominates the market. Nestlé accounts for +40% of all coffee sales.
Republic of Korea	49	1.73	0.08	-0.14	Viet Nam 31% Brazil 19% Colombia 13% Honduras 11%	2.0	Exports of instant coffee exceed 278,000 bags to China 29%, Israel 14%, Russian Federation 13% and Australia 10%.

Source: ICO and other trade data.

Note: Green bean equivalents are used for roasted, soluble and per capita consumption figures.

Table 2.6   Coffee consumption in selected countries, 2010

Country	Population (millions)	Net imports (million bags)			Main suppliers (green bean)	Per capita consumption (kg/year)	Additional information
		Green beans	Roasted	Soluble			
Algeria	35	2.01	<0.01	<0.01	Côte d'Ivoire 50% Viet Nam 25% Indonesia 11%	3.4	Algeria has potential to significantly increase consumption in light of its installed roasting capacity of around 4 million bags of green coffee. However, consumption is only growing at around 0.5% annually.
Argentina	40	0.50	0.01	0.10	Brazil 98%	0.9	Roasted coffee accounts for around 60% of the market in Argentina with Grupo La Virginia the largest roaster in the market. The instant coffee market is dominated by Nestlé Argentina SA.
Israel	7.6	0.45	0.03	0.08	Viet Nam 38% Brazil 8% Uganda 7% India 5%	4.4	Israel enjoys a thriving café culture based largely on espresso-based drinks, although the more traditional Turkish style coffees still account for a significant part of the consumption. Coffee consumption in Israel is growing at just over 6% annually.
Morocco	32	0.55	0.01	-0.09	Indonesia 25% Viet Nam 25% Guinea 17% Uganda 10%	0.9	Nestlé was the leader in value terms in coffee in 2010, accounting for 29% value share, but roasted coffee still accounts for the bulk of consumption.
Serbia	7.3	0.51	0.01	0.03	Brazil 64% Viet Nam 18% India 10%	4.0	Two companies dominate the market, Grand Prom with a 48% share of the market by value and Straus Adriatic with 30%. One survey suggests that 90% of coffee consumers in Serbia drink black or Turkish coffee.
South Africa	50	0.40	0.02	0.14	Viet Nam 58% Indonesia 16% Brazil 5%	0.7	Instant coffee dominates the coffee market in South Africa, with a share of 92%. The leading player is Nestlé. The roasted coffee market is characterized by a large number of medium and smaller roasters.
Tunisia	11	0.25	<0.01	0.05	Brazil 40% Cameroon 31% Viet Nam 11% Indonesia 10%	1.7	Reports suggest that coffee consumption is increasing among young people, but tea remains the most popular beverage.
Turkey	73	0.30	0.02	0.28	Brazil 98%	0.5	Although Turkish coffee is important in the out-of-home market, instant coffee dominates the in-home market accounting for over 90%. The leading player is Nestlé.
Ukraine	46	0.10	0.29	1.10	Viet Nam 22% India 16% Cameroon 8%	1.9	Soluble coffee and coffee-based mixes, imported mainly from Brazil and the European Union, account for more than 70% of Ukraine's coffee consumption. Green coffee represents only a small share of imports.

Source: ICO and other trade data.

Note: Green bean equivalents are used for roasted, soluble and per capita consumption figures.

PRODUCING COUNTRIES

Domestic consumption in producing countries is estimated to have totalled 41 million bags in 2010 – up from just over 26 million bags in 2001. The bulk of this increase is attributed to growth in the internal market in Brazil, which is not only the world's largest coffee producer, but also the world's second-largest consumer, accounting for 19 million bags in 2010.

The structure of Brazil's domestic industry is relatively diverse, characterized by a large number of small to medium-sized roasters, possibly as many as 1,400. Nevertheless, concentration is a continuing process. The top five roasters are, in order of importance: Sara Lee, Santa Clara, Marata, Melitta and Damasco. Roast and ground coffee dominates the market with over 90% of all sales and although the country is a large exporter of soluble coffee, instant coffee accounts for only approximately 5.5% of the overall domestic market in Brazil.

Consumption in Brazil

The industry association (ABIC) puts domestic consumption in Brazil at approximately 6.0 kg per person in 2010, whereas the ICO puts it at 5.8 kg. This is now considerably higher than that of the United States and more than double the low that Brazilian per capita consumption fell to in 1985 (2.3 kg). Consumption stagnated around this level until steps were taken in 1989 to improve the quality of coffee available on the domestic market. In particular, the industry introduced what became known as the *Selo de Pureza* or purity seal. This, together with an active marketing policy aimed at encouraging consumption by providing more information on the product, formed the basis of a successful push to increase consumption. Coffee products are only eligible for the Purity Seal if they comply with certain basic conditions. In addition, ABIC continues its Coffee Quality Program, aimed at educating consumers about aroma, body, flavour, degree of roasting and grinding. Participating roasters display the Quality Seal on their retail packaging. ABIC also runs an internal accreditation programme for coffee shops, hotels and restaurants that use quality beans and in so doing helps promote the coffee culture in Brazil. Finally, the promotion of sustainability in the coffee chain is also actively pursued.

Brazil's success in raising domestic consumption is of interest to many other coffee producing nations hoping to raise their domestic use. In response the ICO commissioned *A Step-by-step Guide to Promote Coffee Consumption in Producing Countries,* which uses the Brazilian experience and that of a few other countries to create a methodology to promote consumption. See *www.ico.org/promoting_consumption.asp.*

Table 2.7   Coffee consumption in selected origins, 2010

Country	Population in millions	Production (million bags)	Imports (million bags)			Per capita consumption kg/year	Additional information
			Green beans	Roasted	Soluble		
Brazil	195	48.10	0	0.01	0.01	5.8	Domestic consumption 19 million bags. Total imports only amount to 21,000 bags – mainly of roasted coffee from Europe.
Ethiopia	83	7.45	0	0	0	2.3	Domestic consumption 3.4 million bags, which is around 40% of overall production.
India	1 171	4.98	0.38	<0.01	0.01	0.1	Domestic consumption 1.8 million bags, growing at 6% annually. The rapid growth is attributed to (i) rising disposable income, (ii) shifting urbanization, and (iii) growth in population with 54% aged under 25.
Indonesia	240	8.86	0.20	0.01	0.31	0.9	Domestic consumption 3.3 million bags. Out-of-home consumption accounts for 22% of the total market. Roasted coffee dominates the market, but 3-in-1 preparations are rapidly gaining market share with 30% of the market.
Mexico	113	4.00	0.50	<0.01	0.10	1.2	Domestic consumption 2.4 million bags. Almost 60% of consumers consume soluble coffee, 23% consume roasted coffee and 15% a combination of both. Nestlé is the market leader.
Viet Nam	87	18.50	0.05	<0.01	0.05	1.1	Domestic consumption 1.6 million bags. Instant coffee accounts for the bulk of consumption with Nestlé as the market leader.

Source: ICO and other trade data.

Note: Green bean equivalents are used for roasted, soluble and per capita consumption figures.

Elsewhere in Latin America, consumption is constrained by relatively low urban income levels although there has been some growth in Mexico and consumption remains reasonably substantial in Colombia. By comparison, consumption in Africa is negligible with the exception of Ethiopia, where there is a long and well-established tradition of coffee drinking.

In Asia, total consumption is high in India, Indonesia and Viet Nam, although per capita consumption levels are still relatively low.

FACTORS INFLUENCING DEMAND

Income is an important factor affecting the demand for coffee. In many ways this is not surprising, especially as coffee is still perceived by many to be a luxury item, especially in low-income countries. There is clear evidence that consumption is highly dependent not only on absolute income levels, but also, and probably more importantly, on changes in real-income levels.

In countries that have a history of drinking coffee, there seems to be a direct correlation between the level of income and the level of consumption. The highest consumption per capita is found in the Nordic countries: Denmark, Finland, Iceland, Norway and Sweden – all of them at around 10 kg per person per year. Other European countries such as Germany, Switzerland, the Netherlands and Austria also have a history of drinking coffee and also enjoy relatively high personal incomes. It is noticeable that countries with a tradition of drinking coffee and lower personal incomes, such as Spain, Portugal and Greece, have a considerably lower rate of consumption. Given that coffee is still considered to be a luxury item in many consuming countries, it is not surprising that as a general rule, changes in real incomes have a greater effect on consumption in low-income countries than in high-income countries.

LIFESTYLE, DIET AND COMPETING DRINKS

While price and incomes obviously play a major role in determining the demand for coffee, it is difficult to ignore the effect other factors may have on overall consumption – for example competition from alternative beverages, adverse publicity as a result of various health studies, advertising, or lifestyle. Coffee is traditionally recognized as an everyday beverage that is frequently seen as a stimulant and an aid to alertness, but also seen as a social lubricant fulfilling a very necessary function enabling people to socialize. 'Let's have a coffee' is a phrase often used to cover a general request for an informal get-together, regardless of whether coffee is to be drunk or not. It is interesting to note that coffee is more likely to be consumed at breakfast, lunch or dinner if these are taken as family meals rather than eaten alone. However, as meals are becoming less formal and structured in many countries, more coffee is being consumed out of home, although the home remains the most popular place to consume coffee.

The type of food consumers prefer may also have an effect on the amount of coffee they drink. Either through habit or taste, coffee seems to complement some foods more than others. This might explain why coffee is generally less popular in restaurants serving Asian foods than in those serving traditional Western European cuisine.

Competition from other beverages has also been an important factor affecting the demand for coffee. Over the last 30 years or so, soft drinks have become more popular, invariably at the expense of coffee, especially among young people. However, the situation is far from static and the new American-style coffee bars appear to reversing this trend, although the situation varies from country to country. Consumption of soft drinks in the United States has shown rapid growth since the mid-1960s: the percentage of the population drinking soft drinks grew from 47% in 1975 to 58% in 2011. It does, however, appear to have reached a plateau as very little growth has been achieved over the last four years. However, In Germany coffee remains the most popular beverage and although the consumption of herbal teas, fruit juices and mineral water is rising, it does not appear to be doing so at the expense of coffee. In Japan coffee is gaining ground at the expense of other beverages, but more slowly than in the early 1980s.

Price may be a major factor in the change to alternative beverages, but health worries and advertising also provide strong motives to switch to other beverages. Over the years a number of studies have suggested that coffee – in fact invariably caffeine, but the stigma attaches to coffee rather than to all beverages containing caffeine – is linked in some way to some cancers and other diseases.

The publicity given to the findings of these studies has contributed significantly to the decline in the consumption of coffee in some developed markets. A number of the cola drinks on the market contain high levels of caffeine – but not as high as most coffees. Studies have found that coffee may have some beneficial health effects, e.g. helping to relieve stress and inhibiting the viruses that cause cold sores, measles and polio, as well as preventing some types of cancer and possibly delaying the onset of Parkinson's disease. Unfortunately, this positive information does not gain wide publicity and does not yet appear to counteract the effects of the adverse publicity. The Institute for Scientific Information on Coffee (ISIC) is highlighting some of these benefits of coffee through its Positive Communication on Coffee Programme. Visit *www.coffeeandhealth.org* and see also ICO's *www.positivelycoffee.org*.

ADDING VALUE – AN OVERVIEW

Downstream processing is often seen as a way of adding value to a raw product at origin. Unfortunately, this is not as straightforward as it at first appears if it were, there would be a far greater trade in processed coffee products from origin than there is today.

In 2010 (calendar year) just 7.6% of all coffee exports from producing countries were processed coffee. This is almost 40% higher than 10 years ago, but given the low starting point this is still fairly slow progress. The bulk (97%) of this export is instant coffee, as roasted coffee exports have never exceeded 0.3% of total coffee exports from producing countries.

The consuming market for coffee is dominated by a few very large companies, mainly multinationals, which sell their product by promoting their brand name and image through large-scale advertising. Normally advertising expenditure is equivalent to between 3% and 6% of sales revenue.

Most coffee is sold through supermarket chains, which generally, stock a relatively limited range of brands that meet their criteria for sales per unit of shelf space. In that environment it is difficult and costly for new brands and new suppliers to penetrate the market, but it is not impossible as there are always some openings for new suppliers.

Smaller packers and roasters, however, have managed to secure a place in practically every consuming country to a greater or lesser degree, often selling coffee under either their own brand names or providing supermarket chains with own label (also known as private label) coffee to be sold under the brand name of the supermarket. Own label or secondary brands generally sell at a substantial discount and are not usually advertised in the media. Instead they are promoted in store.

In the past such brands were usually considered to be inferior in quality, but that is no longer the case and as a result, own label coffees have been able to capture a significant share of the market. The own label area offers the best opportunity for coffees processed at origin because such coffees cannot afford large advertising expenditure. But with increasing concentration at the retail level the scope for new entrants is becoming more limited. Furthermore, the own label market is fiercely price competitive.

Soluble coffee packed for supermarkets retails at a discount of typically 10%–30% on the price of the leading comparable brands. For spray-dried soluble coffee the retail market is not only oversupplied, but is also shrinking as consumers switch to better quality freeze-dried and agglomerated soluble coffees.

SOLUBLE COFFEE

The soluble coffee market is dominated by two multinational firms: Nestlé and Kraft Foods. One or the other or both have a presence in every main consumer market and probably in many producing country markets as well. In addition there is often a third large supplier in each main market. For example in the United States Procter & Gamble enjoys a reasonably large share of the market, while the Ueshima Coffee Company (UCC) is of some significance in Japan. The larger companies manufacture soluble coffee in their own plants and rarely obtain soluble coffee from outside suppliers.

Nestlé also operates a small number of soluble processing plants in producing countries, primarily aimed at supplying the domestic market, but also nearby regional markets.

The scope for outside manufacturers lies in supplying product for:

- Secondary (own label) brands that have no manufacturing facilities (although this market tends to be rather sluggish);
- Specialist packers of own label coffee in consuming countries.

Most supermarket chains prefer to buy from a specialist packer rather than direct from origin, and usually insist that bulk supplies are repacked in retail jars. For all practical purposes, an origin supplier seeking to enter the own label market would be best advised to trade through a specialist packer in a consuming country, especially as in most cases the finished retail product is a blend of coffee from several sources.

There are several specialist packers of soluble coffee for own label product in consuming countries. Some operate their own processing plants, but also often purchase soluble coffee for blending from other sources to fulfil contracts that are beyond their capacity, or when imported soluble is cheaper than their own product. Other specialist packers have no processing capacity of their own and merely blend and repack products from other sources.

The retail market for soluble coffee has three general segments:

- **Premium brands of freeze-dried soluble.** Nestlé and Kraft Foods dominate in this segment, but there is some significant participation by other brands, particularly supermarkets' own labels. Both Brazil and Colombia supply freeze-dried soluble coffee to this market, which is still growing. Although not the most popular form of soluble coffee, in general freeze-dried is gaining market share in every consuming country at the expense of other types of soluble coffee. It has obtained 40% to 45% of the soluble coffee market in Japan, the United States and the United Kingdom and a little over 30% in Spain and Australia. Extra premium blends of freeze-dried coffee composed solely or mainly of arabica and sometimes from a single origin are also marketed in this sector.

- **Standard brands of spray-dried soluble.** These generally consist of coffee that has been agglomerated. Agglomeration is a process that not only improves solubility, but also transforms the coffee powder into more attractive granules. Agglomerated coffee is the most popular form of soluble coffee. It accounts for more than half the sales in the majority of consuming markets, although it is losing market share to freeze-dried coffee.

- **Cheap blends of spray-dried powder.** This is often soluble coffee that has been imported from origin and repacked. Considerable excess manufacturing capacity has resulted in extreme price competition and although this is by far the cheapest type of soluble coffee available in many markets, it is losing market share to all other types of instant coffee. It does, however, constitute the larger share of the market in the Russian Federation and many other Eastern European and Asian markets as well as in producing country markets.

The total market for soluble coffee is showing signs of strong growth after being relatively flat in the 1990s. Estimated consumption in countries that do not produce coffee was 21 million bags GBE in 2010, of which 30% was manufactured in producing countries.

SOLUBLE COFFEE – OUTLOOK

The bulk of the soluble coffee exported from producing countries is spray-dried powder. Brazil accounts for just under half of all soluble coffee exports. Intense price competition coupled with diminishing demand has led to a marked reduction in the spray-dried powder manufacturing capacity in many consuming countries, although a significant proportion of that reduced capacity has been transferred to other, usually emerging, markets. It does not appear, therefore, that there is a very secure future for new entrants planning to supply spray-dried powder.

Freeze-dried soluble continues to make significant progress, although processing is comparatively expensive and the product quality demands a high proportion of the more expensive arabica. The process is therefore unsuitable for countries that produce only robusta. The market has primarily been developed by Nestlé and Kraft Foods, although a number of other companies are actively involved in the sector, particularly those producing own labels. Brazil and Colombia are important suppliers and while the market for freeze-dried coffees is growing there are concerns that there is already tremendous manufacturing over-capacity in both Brazil and a number of consuming countries such as Germany. Freeze-dried coffee accounts for around 30% of all sales of soluble coffee. Trade opinion suggests that the market for soluble coffee as a whole is likely to grow only slowly over the next 10 years; by contrast, the market for freeze-dried coffee is expected to continue growing at a much faster rate.

The opportunity for new suppliers must be weighed against current excess manufacturing capacity, which is probably sufficient to cover most, if not all, the anticipated increase in demand for a number of years. Although most exports of soluble coffee are as finished product (in primary or bulk so not retail packaging) some sales are made as frozen concentrate for finishing in the country of destination.

Exports of soluble coffee by coffee producing countries for the period 2005–2010 are shown in table 2.8. Most of the coffee exported was produced in the country of shipment.

Soluble coffee is also produced in Malaysia for use in regional markets and in the Philippines for domestic consumption.

SOLUBLE COFFEE – MANUFACTURING METHODS

Extraction. Optimum extraction of soluble coffee solids depends on the temperature of the extraction water and its rate of flow through roasted, ground coffee. In practice incoming water can be approaching 200° C under high pressure. Extraction requires a row of interconnecting percolators or cells, using a continuous reverse flow principle. Each cell is filled in turn with fresh coffee. Incoming hot water is introduced into the cell containing the least fresh, most extracted coffee, where it collects those soluble solids that are vulnerable to the high temperature and carries these to the next cell in the cycle, and so on. In each cell the coffee liquor collects more soluble solids.

By the time the sixth cell in a cycle has been reached the liquor's temperature has been reduced and so inflicts minimum damage on the delicate flavour constituents of the freshest roast coffee that are essential to the final quality. The liquor is then drawn off and cooled. It now consists of approximately 85% water and 15% soluble coffee. Meanwhile, the first cell in the cycle (that underwent extraction with the hottest water), is emptied of the spent grounds and is recharged with fresh coffee to start the cycle again. Thus, there is always one cell outside the process, which requires seven cells altogether.

Evaporation is necessary to reduce the liquor's water content to 50%. But first the liquor is centrifuged to remove non-soluble particles. To evaporate liquor at normal pressure would require very high temperatures that would cause the liquor to acquire off flavours and lose valuable coffee aromas as well. Consequently, evaporation takes place under low vacuum and low temperature conditions.

Spray-drying requires a large cylindrical tower with a conical base. The concentrated liquor is introduced into the top under pressure, with a jet of hot air. The falling droplets dry into a fine powder that cools as it descends. These particles may then be agglomerated into granules by wetting them in low-pressure steam, allowing them to stick together. The wet granules are then dried as they descend through a second tower and are sifted to provide a uniform final granule size.

Freeze-drying consists of freezing the coffee liquor into a ¼ inch (about 6 mm) thick cake on a moving conveyor at a temperature of -45° C. The frozen cake is then broken into small particles and the ice crystals are removed under very high vacuums, being converted directly to water vapour by a process known as sublimation. Freeze-drying is more energy expensive but is gentler on the product as less heat is applied to evaporate the water content. Consequently, freeze-drying is used for the finer and more expensive blends of instant coffee.

Table 2.8   Exports of soluble coffee by exporting countries, 2005–2010 (in bags, green bean equivalent)

	2005	2006	2007	2008	2009	2010
Total	**6 121 305**	**5 547 293**	**6 845 865**	**7 217 775**	**6 244 132**	**7 124 876**
Colombian Milds	**632 648**	**627 111**	**585 465**	**697 653**	**585 451**	**613 004**
Colombia	626 690	622 731	583 173	696 494	584 461	603 390
United Republic of Tanzania	5 958	4 380	2 292	1 159	990	9 614
Other Milds	**1 451 597**	**1 528 089**	**2 286 563**	**2 192 170**	**2 256 260**	**2 750 631**
Ecuador	597 189	599 174	749 271	746 025	659 875	806 744
El Salvador	458	54	241	51	108	404
Guatemala	23	478	1 605	2 679	2 535	2 337
Guyana	394	1 665	1 851	1 510	0	600
Haiti	0	0	0	0	52	702
India	338 377	409 397	829 496	770 263	937 587	1 205 765
Jamaica	586	760	1 823	2 091	1 840	2 484
Mexico	444 319	430 176	624 842	601 930	610 151	687 671
Nicaragua	57 481	60 795	53 523	42 593	39 511	43 583
Peru	14	0	0	0	0	0
Panama	8	222	61	1 653	237	302
Venezuela (Bolivarian Republic of)	12 714	25 368	23 848	23 375	4 416	39
Zimbabwe	34	0	2	0	0	0
Brazilian Naturals	**3 547 915**	**2 957 191**	**3 384 918**	**3 366 521**	**2 881 018**	**3 226 267**
Brazil	3 525 169	2 948 212	3 372 692	3 364 816	2 881 018	3 226 267
Nepal	43	43	43	43	0	0
Paraguay	22 703	8 933	12 183	1 650	0	0
Yemen	0	3	0	12	0	0
Robustas	**489 145**	**434 900**	**588 918**	**961 522**	**519 838**	**534 973**
Côte d'Ivoire	192 755	165 113	381 343	340 017	350 922	276 775
Guinea	0	0	236	0	0	0
Ghana	139	89	78	225	48	22
Indonesia	223 384	192 029	149 283	602 804	154 005	234 201
Lao People's Democratic Republic	0	31	21	86	0	58
Madagascar	182	0	0	0	0	0
Nigeria	160	0	2	140	0	0
Philippines	33 636	35 314	32 105	4 435	6 656	6 338
Sierra Leone	31	16	0	23	15	2
Sri Lanka	300	1 657	703	58	53	468
Trinidad and Tobago	692	408	313	576	607	660
Viet Nam	37 866	40 243	24 834	13 158	7 532	16 449

Source: ICO. For more up-to-date statistics go to *www.ico.org*.

DECAFFEINATED COFFEE

Caffeine is a natural substance found in the leaves, seeds or fruits of more than 60 plant species worldwide. The level of its presence in non-decaffeinated coffee depends on a number of factors: different types of coffee contain varying levels of caffeine. Factors determining this include the variety of the coffee tree itself and where grown, soil, altitude, climate etc.

The decaffeination process is applicable to both soluble coffee (spray-dried and freeze-dried) and roasted coffee. Decaffeinated coffee enjoyed a considerable rise in popularity during the 1980s, especially in the United States, but its performance in the market during the 1990s has not been very strong.

Decaffeinated coffee is seen as having to compete with other specialty coffees and although consumers of decaffeinated coffee tend to be very loyal to the product, caffeine no longer appears to be an issue that most consumers are particularly concerned about.

Despite technological improvements in the decaffeination process over the last 15 years, and in particular the development of what many see as better processes which use water and carbon dioxide rather than methyl chloride, the product is losing market share. It is estimated that decaffeinated coffee currently accounts for around 10% of all coffee sales. Usually, it commands only a small premium over non-decaffeinated coffee and frequently is sold for the same price. Consequently the economics of the decaffeination are tight.

In 2010, trade sources estimated that the cost of the process ranged from US\$ 0.50/kg–US\$ 0.65/kg of green bean, for the cheapest process using methyl chloride, to about double that for the more expensive methods. Incidentally, there is a substantial market for extracted, crude caffeine in industries such as pharmaceuticals and soft drinks.

THE DECAFFEINATION PROCESS

Arabica coffee beans contain 1%–1.5% caffeine, whereas robusta contains more than 2%. Caffeine is an alkaloid with stimulant properties that are pleasing to the majority of coffee drinkers, but not to all. Decaffeination caters for those who do not want the stimulant effect of caffeine.

The caffeine in the green coffee beans has to be extracted. Different processes are used. The solvents are water, organic extraction agents or carbonic acid. The processing steps are vaporization, decaffeination and drying. All these steps are carried out using the green coffee bean.

First, the green coffee is treated with vapour and water to open up the bean surface and the cell structure to access the crystalline caffeine taken up on the cell walls. The second step is extracting the caffeine by an extraction agent that extracts only the caffeine. The caffeine extraction is not a chemical process, but a physical one. No chemical changes take place. Instead differences in the characteristics of the extraction agent, which has to absorb the caffeine, and the beans containing the caffeine, are used. The extraction agent absorbs the caffeine selectively. Once the extraction agent is saturated with caffeine the next processing step removes the caffeine and the extraction agent can be used again. This cycle is repeated until practically all the caffeine is removed from the coffee bean. Then the wet coffee, from which the caffeine has been removed, is dried until once again it reaches its normal moisture content. It can then be roasted as usual.

The following decaffeination agents are allowed in the European Union: methylene chloride, ethyl acetate, carbon dioxide and watery coffee extract from which the caffeine is removed by active carbon. All conventional decaffeination methods have undergone intensive scientific examination and are considered safe. In the European Union the absolute caffeine content in roasted, decaffeinated coffee may not exceed 0.1%, or 0.3% in soluble coffee. In the United States, 'decaffeinated' is generally taken to mean that the caffeine content has been reduced by 97%, or to less than 3% of the original content.

ROASTED COFFEE

The market for roasted coffee is somewhat less concentrated than that for soluble coffee. Although market concentration in the roast and ground sector increased significantly, particularly during the 1980s and in the late 1990s, the development of the specialty sector has slowed the trend and the number of small roasters operating worldwide did increase significantly again for a while. Small roasters rarely buy direct from origin, but make their purchases through importers who are able to offer some security of supply and cost savings for small lots. In many cases importing direct from origin involves buying a full container load of around 300 bags (18 tons), which is simply too large an order for most small roasters.

As a result of the development of the specialty and gourmet sectors in many countries, single origin roasted coffee is now widely available. However, blends of roasted coffee from different origins remain the most predominant roasted coffee product in the overall market today and this makes it difficult for producers to enter the retail market on their own. The trade in roasted coffee from origin is limited: in 2010 only 222,500 bags were exported from origin in roasted form compared to 7.1 million bags GBE of soluble and 89.3 million bags of green coffee. In total, roasted coffee accounted for just 0.23% of all coffee exports, but the published statistics on this trade are notoriously inaccurate with reported imports from producing countries greatly exceeding reported exports from those origins. Even so, and perhaps hardly surprisingly, Brazil was recorded as the largest exporter of roasted coffee in 2010, a position it has held undisputed for the past five years, although prior to that the Dominican Republic and occasionally Colombia vied with Brazil for the top place.

There are several obstacles to exporting roasted coffee from origin. None of them are insurmountable, but together they form a significant barrier to this trade. Roasted coffee rapidly loses its flavour unless it is vacuum packed or gas flushed. A supplier wishing to export must therefore install an appropriate packing facility.

Furthermore, consumers are becoming increasingly sophisticated and demand high quality packaging that requires a significant level of investment. Additionally, legislation in importing countries frequently insists that packs are marked with a 'sell by' or 'use by' date.

Transporting the product to market from origin can take a considerable amount of time and this puts the exporter at a disadvantage compared to a local roaster that is able to offer the retailer a product with a longer shelf life. Exporters of roasted coffee therefore need to develop speedy distribution systems in order to minimize this disadvantage. This usually requires the active collaboration of agents or specialized importers or roasters in the target market(s).

READY-TO-DRINK AND EXTRACTS OR CONCENTRATES

Canned, ready-to-drink (RTD) coffee was originally developed by the Ueshima Coffee Company. In 2010, it accounted for close to 20% of total consumption in Japan, where it is sold mainly through vending machines. RTD liquid coffee in plastic bottles and in PET packs is also very popular and is generally sold in supermarkets. It currently accounts for just under 10% of all coffee consumption in Japan.

Canned coffee products are also finding a good market in many emerging markets in Asia, particularly in China, although the success of the product depends very much on its availability in vending machines. RTD coffee products are particularly suitable for iced coffee drinks, and as such are beginning to make inroads in the North American and Western European markets.

Originally the obvious requirement for success was access to vending machines and vending sites. As a result, soft drink manufacturers currently dominate this sector of the market. But the major roasters are now pushing hard as well, not least because market sources consider the prospects for RTD coffee excellent because of its convenience.

Sales of shelf-stable (i.e. not refrigerated or frozen) coffee products for use as iced coffee etc. are the most likely area of growth because such products can be sold off supermarket shelves like any other dry goods. Another potential winner could be concentrated liquid coffee. The frozen concentrate is designed for commercial and out-of-home consumers such as hotels, restaurants and offices for which, it is reported, it will produce a 'fresh' cup of coffee in a few seconds.

How much these developments do for coffee consumption or indeed coffee quality is debatable – the coffee content is usually not very high and the coffee taste is often masked by flavouring. Nevertheless, it is a new and growing niche market. Brazil and Colombia are the main manufacturers of concentrate at origin. Unfortunately, it is difficult to see how smaller producers without a substantial home market to support a manufacturing capability can participate.

TRADE PRICES, INVESTMENT COSTS AND TARIFFS

IMPORTS AND PRICES OF ROASTED AND SOLUBLE COFFEE

Average imports of roasted and soluble coffee of the seven leading importing countries and the origin of those imports are shown in figure 2.5 and figure 2.6.

Figure 2.5 Imports of roasted coffee by origin, average 2005–2010

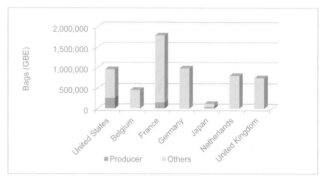

Source: ICO.

These seven countries account for the bulk of the imports of both roasted and soluble coffee. And as can be seen, with the exception of the United States and France, imports of roasted coffee from producing countries barely register on the chart. Imports of roasted coffee into the United States have been increasing significantly from 2005 to 2010, with a noticeable increase in imports of roasted coffee from Mexico, Colombia and more recently Viet Nam. Imports of soluble coffee from producing countries are clearly more significant and form a larger share of the trade in the United States, Germany, Japan and the United Kingdom.

Figure 2.6 Imports of soluble coffee by origin, average 2005–2010

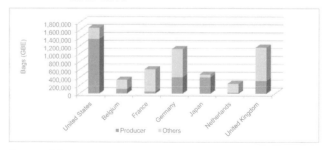

Source: ICO.

The average export unit-value of soluble coffee is compared with the ICO composite indicator in figure 2.7. Generally the export unit value tracks the indicator, usually at a lower level, but occasionally at a premium. However, because of intense competition, the value added, on an FOB basis, is less than popularly supposed.

Figure 2.7 Export value of soluble coffee from ICA producing countries compared with the ICA Composite Indicator Price, 1990–2010

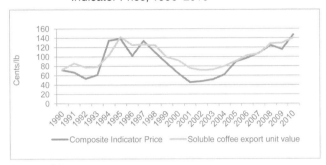

Source: ICO.

Export unit-value statistics show that the prices of Brazilian soluble are generally lower than both the New York market prices for Brazilian green coffee and, at times, the London market prices for robustas. On the other hand, Colombian prices correspond more closely with New York prices, although the unit-value of exports of Colombian soluble (an aggregate of spray-dried and freeze-dried) remains for the most part just slightly above the quoted green coffee price. One of the reasons for producing countries to continue with this is that coffee transformed in the country of origin does not have to possess all quality characteristics of coffee which can be exported in green form. The transformation into soluble may therefore allow the use of lower grades. Nevertheless, the value added by the manufacture of soluble at origin is likely to be, at best, marginal and a run of low prices may not allow the speedy recovery of costs of new installations.

As is seen in figure 2.8, roasted coffee sells at a premium over both the ICO composite indicator and the New York market for Other milds, but this trade is more specialized and export prices may include the provision of retail packs. Nevertheless, the trade remains negligible.

Figure 2.8 Export value of roasted coffee from ICA members compared with the ICA Composite Indicator Price, 1990–2010

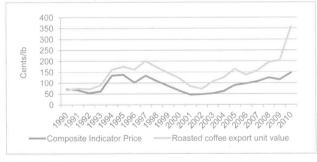

Source: ICO.

TARIFFS AND TAXES

It has long been recognized that tariffs and taxes influence coffee consumption. The coffee community considers tariffs and taxes to be part of a broader group of legal, political and administrative barriers to coffee consumption (as mentioned

for example in Article 24 of the 2007 International Coffee Agreement).

Significant progress in reducing tariffs and taxes on coffee imports into consuming countries has been made through the various rounds of the General Agreement on Tariffs and Trade (GATT) and more recently through negotiations under the auspices of the World Trade Organization. However, while most tariff barriers have been removed for green coffee, there remain a number of tariffs imposed on processed coffee that continue to act as a barrier to importation of processed coffee into consuming countries. In addition, there are also a number of non-tariff barriers still in place, such as quantitative restrictions and internal taxes that continue to inhibit consumption.

CLASSIFICATION OF COFFEE PRODUCTS TRADED INTERNATIONALLY

Among the trade-related product nomenclatures, the following three are of particular interest to coffee:

- **HS – Harmonized System:** The Harmonized Commodity Description and Coding System (Harmonized System) is the system for classification of goods in international trade and for customs tariffs. It has been developed under the auspices of the World Customs Organization. HS assigns a six-digit code to general categories. In most countries, these codes are broken down to a more detailed level referred to as the tariff line. Details at *www.wcoomd.org*.

- **CN – Combined Nomenclature:** This is the European Union's eight-digit coding system. It is based on the HS. Details at *www.europa.eu.int*.

- **SITC – Standard Industrial Trade Classification:** SITC was developed by the United Nations. It is commonly used for trade statistics and by trade analysts. The current version is Revision 4.

TARIFFS IMPOSED ON COFFEE AND COFFEE PRODUCTS

The world's leading coffee importing countries and regions (United States, Canada, European Union and Japan) do not levy any import duties on green coffee imports. The United States and Canada also do not levy import duties on processed coffee (roasted, soluble). The Russian Federation no longer levies any general import tariff on green coffee imports, but roasted coffee imports are rated at 10% with a minimum of EUR 0.20 per kg. The European Union applies different import tariff regimes for processed coffee, depending on an individual producing country's status in terms of the Generalized System of Preferences (GSP), Economic Partnership Agreements (EPA) or Bilateral Trade Agreements. For information on selected individual import country regimes visit *www.ecf-coffee.org* and look for their 2010/11 Annual Report under Publications. Alternatively visit *www.exporthelp.europa.eu/index_en.html*.

Value added tax (VAT) is levied on both roasted and soluble coffee sales by most European countries with the percentage ranging from 3% in Luxembourg to 25% in Denmark and Hungary. Of course these are internal taxes and do not directly concern exporters, but it is nevertheless useful to know. Excise duties are also levied by Belgium, Denmark, Germany, Latvia and Romania. For a full list see the ECF 2010/11 Annual Report as well as *www.exporthelp. europa.eu.*

PROMOTING COFFEE CONSUMPTION

The promotion of coffee consumption worldwide is vital for the entire coffee industry. Competition from other beverages is intense and the total amount of money spent on advertising soft drinks, for example, far exceeds the amount spent on coffee. Well-coordinated national and international generic (general) campaigns are necessary not only to encourage people, particularly in emerging markets, to take up coffee drinking, but also to retain the loyalty of existing consumers.

This is not to ignore the fact that roasters worldwide invest tens of millions of dollars in brand promotion, the costs of which are estimated to be between 3% and 6% of total sales. Although such promotion is not generic, it does encourage consumption of coffee in general. Nevertheless, there is a distinct need for the entire industry to engage in generic promotion of the type as undertaken by the ICO in the Russian Federation and China in the 1990s as the

campaigns had very positive effects on consumption in both countries. By 2011 the ICO no longer had the funds to finance such campaigns.

The ICO does offer *A Step-by-step Guide to Promote Coffee Consumption in Producing Countries,* which uses primarily the Brazilian experience and methodology on how to promote consumption in producing countries and any emerging coffee market. This comprehensive guide can be downloaded from *www.ico.org.*

The annual United States Winter Coffee Drinking Study is a good example of a survey on coffee consumption. See *www.ncausa.org* for details.

Table 2.9   Classification of coffee products traded internationally

	HS code	CN code	SITC Rev.4
Coffee in green form (not roasted)	0901.10	0901 10 00	07110
Not decaffeinated	0901.10	0901 11 00	07111
Not decaffeinated, arabica		0901 11 10	
Not decaffeinated, robusta		0901 11 20	
Not decaffeinated, other		0901 11 90	
Decaffeinated	0901.12	0901 12 00	07112
Decaffeinated, arabica		0901 12 10	
Decaffeinated, robusta		0901 12 20	
Decaffeinated, other		0901 12 90	
Roasted coffee	0901.20	0901 20 00	07120
Not decaffeinated	0901.21	0901 21 00	
Decaffeinated	0901.22	0901 22 00	
Coffee husks and skins	0901.90	0901 90 00	07113
Coffee substitutes containing coffee	0901.90	0901 90 00	07132
Extracts, essences and concentrates of coffee (Various CN codes for a range of sub-products)	2101.11	2101 11 xx	07131
Preparations with a basis of these extracts, essences or concentrates or with a basis of coffee (Various CN codes for a range of sub-products)	2101.12	2101 12 xx	07131

Table 2.10   Tariffs for import of coffee in selected countries (in percentage unless otherwise indicated)

Product code	Description	Category	EU	Norway	Switzerland	Japan	United States
0901.11.00	Green coffee not decaffeinated	MFN	0	0	0	0	0
		GSP	0	0	0	0	0
		LDC	0	0	0	0	0
		General	0	0	0		
0901.12.00	Green coffee decaffeinated	MFN	8.3	0	0	0	0
		GSP	4.8	0	0	0	0
		LDC	0	0	0	0	0
		General	0	0	0	0	
0901.21.00	Roasted coffee not decaffeinated	MFN	7.5	0	SwF 63/100 kg	12	0
		GSP	2.6	0	0	10	0
		LDC	0	0	0	0	0
		General	0	0	0	20	
0901.22.00	Roasted coffee decaffeinated	MFN	9	0	SwF 63/100 kg	12	0
		GSP	3.1	0	0	10	0
		LDC	0	0	0	0	0
		General	0	0	0	20	0
0901.90.10	Coffee husks and skins	MFN	0	0	0	0	0
		GSP	0	0	0	0	0
		LDC	0	0	0	0	0
		General	0	0	0	0	10
0901.90.90	Coffee substitutes containing coffee	MFN	11.5	0	SwF 70/100 kg	12	US cts 1.5/ kg
		GSP	8	0	0	0	US cts 1.5/ kg
		LDC	0	0	0	0	0
		General	0	0	0	20	US cts 6.6/ kg
2101.11.00	Extracts, essences and concentrates of coffee	MFN	9	0	SwF 182/100 kg	8.8 – 24	0
		GSP	3.1	0	0	0	0
		LDC	0	0	0	0	0
		General	0	0	0	12.3 – 16	0
2101.12.00	Preparations with a basis of extracts, essences or concentrates or with a basis of coffee	MFN	11.5	0	SwF 80.8 – SwF 123.45/100 kg	15 – 29.8 + ¥1 159/kg	8.5 – 10
		GSP	8	0	SwF 0 – SwF 79.45/100 kg	0	0 – 10
		LDC	0	0	0	0	0 – 10
		General	0	0	0	12.3 – 35 + ¥1 363/kg	0 – 10

Note: The tariff headings contain several sub-categories – hence the range of tariffs is given. The Generalized System of Preferences (GSP) is a specific additional measure aimed at the lowering of tariffs for imports from developing countries. It formally exempts WTO member countries from so-called most favoured nation (MFN) for the purpose of lowering tariffs for developing countries, without also doing so for developed countries. The preferential GSP tariff rates are beneficial but still present a barrier in the majority of coffee importing countries. LDC refers to least developed country.

CHAPTER 3

NICHE MARKETS, ENVIRONMENT AND SOCIAL ASPECTS

NICHE MARKETS, ENVIRONMENT AND SOCIAL ASPECTS

THE SPECIALTY MARKET

It is often neither viable nor possible to add value to green coffee by processing at origin. Many coffees are suitable only for blending or processing into neutral or anonymous end products, including soluble. For such coffees it is not possible to add monetary value as prices are determined solely by market conditions. However, reliable and consistent grading procedures, strict compliance with contractual obligations and regular delivery will add value in the sense that the product will be preferred by primary buyers over those from less consistent origins. Certain growths of coffee, on the other hand, may be highly prized for their flavour characteristics and attract a suitable premium. Examples include Jamaican Blue Mountain, Hawaii Kona, Top Kenya AA and Guatemalan Antiguas.

Some of these growths regularly attract extremely high premiums. For example, in the early 2000s Jamaican Blue Mountain attracted such a large premium that the unit value of coffee exported from Jamaica was over 13 times higher than the average of all 'Other milds' producers and more than 16 times higher than the average achieved by all origins. The top Kenyan grades regularly achieve prices more than double that achieved by other growths with some small parcels selling in early 2011 for as high as US$ 20/lb.

Coffees, especially the winning coffees, sold through the Cup of Excellence programme, www.cupofexcellence.org, attract exceptionally high premiums, but the lot size is generally very small. The programme involves much more than just promoting the winning lots. The Cup of Excellence programme offers the origin the chance to highlight its coffee quality and focus marketing attention on the country concerned. Colombia has managed to consistently command sizeable price premiums for its coffee because it has always adopted an active marketing and publicity policy, which over time resulted in many brands throughout the world being labelled as 100% Colombian. Over time, other producers could also try to ensure that the label of the blend containing their coffee at least carries a reference to the composition of the blend. Unfortunately, very few roasters are actually willing to do this. In any case, a roaster who markets such a blend will need to be assured of consistent quality and regular delivery.

Consumer awareness of the origins they drink does lead to product loyalty and the development of a brand image. This results in some, albeit limited, protection from the vagaries of the market. But if roasters are unable to obtain regular supplies from one exporter, they will of course be encouraged to seek alternative sources.

THE MEANING OF SPECIALTY

The term 'specialty coffee' originated in the United States. It was initially used to describe the range of coffee products sold in dedicated coffee shops, in order to differentiate these coffees from coffee generally available through supermarkets and other retail outlets. The term 'gourmet' is also used, but is now applied to so many products that it has lost all relevance.

Specialty today refers both to whole bean sales and to coffee beverages sold in coffee bars and cafés, as opposed to restaurants and other catering establishments. The range includes higher quality coffees, both single origin and blends, unconventional coffees such as flavoured coffees and coffees with an unusual background or story behind them. However, with the rapid growth in the number of specialty coffee retail outlets and more particularly the expansion of the specialty coffee product range into more mainstream outlets such as supermarkets, the term has become much looser. It is fair to say that 'specialty coffee' has become a generic label covering a range of different coffees, which either command a premium price over other coffees or are perceived by consumers as being different from the widely available mainstream brands of coffee. The term has become so broad that there is no universally accepted definition of what constitutes 'specialty coffee', and it frequently means different things to different people.

Given this lack of precision in definition it is extremely difficult to describe the market in a global way. The best approach appears to be to look at the specialty market from different country or regional viewpoints. However, the very notion 'gourmet' or 'specialty' suggests some degree of exclusivity. It is unlikely that one could market thousands of tons of a particular coffee and still call it 'exclusive'.

The first lesson: one should not 'overdo it'. It is, and always has been, a mistake to consider specialty coffee a different industry from the rest of the coffee business. Supply and demand will not only determine the general level of coffee prices, but will also determine the premium paid for 'quality'.

The second lesson: producers need to target any special coffee very carefully because the term 'specialty' covers a large and growing number of different products, each of which has its own niche.

NICHE MARKETS – DEFINITION

A niche combines a set of conditions that enable a single species or a single product to thrive within the greater ecological or commercial environment. Much of global coffee production consists of mainstream-type coffees. However, there are many other coffees, often of limited availability, with greatly varying taste characteristics that appeal to different groups of consumers, and which sell at a premium over mainstream coffees. Simply put, where the producers or exporters of such a coffee and such a group of consumers get together, a niche market is created.

Two main factors determine whether a coffee can find a niche market: quality and availability. 'Availability' is easily understood, but 'quality' is a subjective term which means different things to different people. See chapter 11, Coffee quality.

QUALITY SEGMENTATION OF COFFEES

Broadly speaking, coffees can be divided into three commercial categories.

- **Exemplary quality** coffees have a high intrinsic value with a fine or unique cup. Usually of quite limited availability. Mostly retailed under straight estate or origin names. Usually very well presented washed coffees, including some superior washed robustas, but also includes some naturals (Ethiopian Harar, Yemeni Mochas, some Indonesian arabicas) and top organic coffees, which are usually, but not always, roasted by comparatively small firms and marketed through fairly exclusive outlets, e.g. retail coffee shops or bars and upmarket delicatessens.
- **High quality or premium brands**, good cupping coffees, well presented, but not necessarily visually perfect. Retailed both as straight origins and as blends. Includes good quality, well prepared organic coffees, and washed as well as superior quality natural robustas. The market for this quality band is much broader and includes a good percentage of today's specialty coffee. Also produced by leading multinational coffee companies and marketed through normal retail outlets such as supermarkets.
- **Mainstream quality**, average quality, reasonably well presented, but certainly not visually perfect. Will offer a decent, clean but not necessarily impressive cup.

In today's specialty market all three types of coffee are represented: exemplary and high quality coffees either as stand-alone or as a named blend component, and mainstream quality in many of the ready-to-drink and flavoured drinks that are sold alongside filter coffee and espresso.

Obviously, for smaller exporters of top quality coffee, the exemplary segment initially offers more promise. However, producers or exporters of good quality coffee have three basic options open to them.

- Sell to the leading roasters (through the usual trade channels) if volume sales are required and the coffee sold lacks the flavour characteristics necessary to be marketed on its own.
- Sell to specialty roasters either direct or through importers or agents. The latter in most cases is the more realistic option as these importers or agents have a wide coverage of the small roasters and other retail outlets, which are too small to import direct.
- Focus on specialty coffee retailers either by selling direct (for roasting in store) through specialty wholesalers or by selling through specialty roasters. However, the number of specialty coffee retailers importing direct is extremely small.

Premiums for specialty coffee can be considerable at the retail level, but the premiums available for producers are inevitably much lower, although they can still be significant. It is sobering to realize that mainstream qualities, including robusta, account for an estimated 85%–90% of world coffee consumption, while the share of exemplary and high quality coffee is no more than 10% or perhaps 15% of the world market. This suggests that for many producers it would be inadvisable to ignore the mainstream market altogether. Instead, they should concentrate on both: specialty for their top quality and mainstream for the remainder of their production.

A further point to note is that sales to small roasters are mostly on extended credit terms, something only an importer can easily afford. Inventory costs, late payment costs and even the risk of payment defaults are therefore part of the cost equation. Also, most roasters purchase subject to approval of the quality on delivery. This means the importer will be left with any coffee that does not meet the roaster's expectations. In other words, the premium for specialty coffee at the wholesale level includes many more factors than just the quality.

EXCLUSIVE MARKETING ARRANGEMENTS

There are times, especially with a new and limited coffee, that a producer may agree to sell this coffee only to a particular company, or to only a few companies that do not compete in the same geographic region. Importers and roasters at times like to have such an arrangement because it prevents their competitors from marketing the identical name at a different price in the same marketplace. They can then create a marketing strategy that sets, them and the coffee – sometimes called 'partnership coffee' or 'relationship coffee' – apart from the competition.

Potential benefits for the producer

- The agreements are usually long term and as such can help create price stability. This expectation of premiums allows producers to focus on the coffee instead of the marketplace, and to be able to pay for the extra effort it takes to maintain the quality.

- An exclusive arrangement generally means roasters will be spending marketing dollars in introducing the coffee to their clients, i.e. a roaster will promote this particular coffee rather than just blend it. Promotional dollars behind the coffee mean increased consumer awareness, which can lead to longer term loyalty.

- Exclusivity creates a certain sense of loyalty and communication between the producer and the importer/roaster that may otherwise not be possible. It is also in the best interest of the receiving company that the quality is optimal – as such it may provide technical help and other assistance that would otherwise not have been available to the producer.

Potential disadvantages for the producer

- An exclusive arrangement may limit the coffee's exposure. If it is with a smaller company or companies with limited market share, then the chance to create a broader consumer base is lost. This could imply that when the agreement comes to an end the producer is left with a coffee that enjoys only limited awareness and requires further effort to build market share.

- An exclusive arrangement usually contains price constraints. Sometimes beneficial for the producer, but depending on market movements and the demand for this particular coffee, this could also have negative effects. One can find oneself locked in with one buyer when in reality a better price might be available elsewhere.

- The producer is relying on one or a few companies to promote his coffee, but generally has no guarantee this will in fact happen, or that it will be enough to be effective. Even though it is also in the buyer's best interest to ensure this, he or she may in fact not do so.

In conclusion, producers entering into such arrangements must make every effort to know their business partner. There certainly are companies that are less than serious, that make promises they cannot keep, and that sometimes may even forego the agreed payment structure when this suits them. It is imperative therefore that all contractual arrangements are reviewed by a legal adviser, both in the producer's own country and in the buyer's country.

To be effective these agreements must be true partnerships. The producer must do his or she share to deliver the quantity and quality the buyer requires. The buyer must do his or her share to pay a timely, fair price and to promote the coffee to his or her consumer base in a way that ensures ongoing demand. In other words, create relationships that can be formalized in a marketing agreement.

THE SCOPE FOR SPECIALTY COFFEE

On the consumption side the potential for specialty coffee appears to be almost limitless, mostly because of constant product innovation. But not all of today's specialty products

necessarily use very good coffee, and some contain very little coffee indeed. Also, there is no universal agreement on what constitutes specialty coffee, and it frequently means different things to different people. But without a clear understanding of what is really specialty coffee, an accurate market assessment becomes extremely difficult.

In the United States the Specialty Coffee Association of America (SCAA – www.scaa.org) describes true specialty grade coffee as having maximum five defects in a standard sample with all cups free of all taints and showing distinctive positive characteristics. Go to www.scaa.org and/or www.coffeeinstitute.org/scaa.html for more on the SCAA's definition of what constitutes specialty grade coffee, defect counts, etc.

On the above basis we would estimate that no more than 5% of green coffees could make specialty grade. If we were to include what the SCAA calls high-end premium coffee (eight defects, clean cup) then maybe the specialty market is 10% of all of the green coffee business in the United States, a percentage that many trade sources consider realistic. On the other hand, Daviron and Ponte in their book The Coffee Paradox (ISBN 1 84277 456 5 hb – ISBN 1 84277 457 3 pb, published by www.zedbooks.co.uk) estimated the total size of the specialty market in the United States in calendar year 2000 at 17%. The National Coffee Association's National Coffee Drinking Survey 2011 puts Gourmet coffee beverages at 36% of the market, including both roasted coffee and specialty instant coffee products. But the difficulty with specialty or gourmet coffee is to properly define it. For example, is average Starbucks quality specialty coffee or is it high-quality mainstream coffee?

In Western Europe many countries have traditionally consumed high quality coffees, at least equal to the good premium types that are produced by mainstream roasters. This is perhaps why the Speciality Coffee Association of Europe (SCAE – www.scae.com) describes specialty (or speciality) coffee as an end product, rather than as a green bean product, by saying that 'speciality coffee is defined as a crafted coffee-based beverage, which is judged by the consumer (in a limited marketplace at a given time) to have a unique quality, a distinct taste and personality different from, and superior to, the common coffee beverages offered. The beverage is based on beans that have been grown in an accurately defined area, and which meet the highest standards for green coffee, and for its roasting, storage and brewing.'

This interpretation then places the emphasis more on the fact that specialty coffee is not only expected to be different, but also a more luxurious and superior product with a certain element of exclusivity. It also suggests that the term 'specialty coffee' is really a generic label covering a range of different coffees, which either command a premium price over other coffees, or that are perceived by consumers as being different. In Europe, the term often tends to be associated with coffee for the American market, and the name also conjures up images of flavoured coffees.

Therefore, until such time as there is general agreement on what constitutes specialty coffee it is not possible to accurately quantify how much is produced, or how much is consumed. The general consensus appears to be that specialty coffee in all its different forms may account for around 10% of world consumption. It certainly is gaining market share fairly rapidly, but of course world consumption as a whole is rising as well, which makes it likely that the 10% will probably remain the upper limit for some time to come.

The specialty market in the United States

The United States specialty market has seen strong development over the past 20 years or so, which has helped not only arrest the fall in United States consumption, but also grow the overall market. Much of this has been driven by the Specialty Coffee Association of America, which has promoted the whole concept of quality. In the last three to four years there has been tremendous growth in single serve brewing systems, which allow consumers to experiment with different coffees. They are frequently single origin, but also flavoured and other manipulated products, so much so that according to the latest survey from the National Coffee Association of USA, (NCA – www.ncausa.org), single-cup brewing systems are now the second most frequently cited brewing method, with 7% past day penetration. This number is significantly higher than in 2010, when it was 4%, which indicates that single-cup brewing systems are actively growing and at the same time expanding the market for specialty coffees. The only downside is the fact that these systems significantly reduce product waste (i.e. reduce excess brewing) and thus do not necessarily immediately expand the market volume wise.

Increasing sales of espresso-type drinks also mean growing demand for low-acid coffees, such as Brazils and robustas, at the expense of traditional specialty mild arabicas. Note also that espresso drinks generate higher profit margins than do traditional cups of coffee. Furthermore, on the roaster/retailer side – coffee bars and shops ranging in size from international chains at one extreme, to firms with just a few stores at the other – the trend has been to follow the example of the Starbucks operation. Not only to get bigger, mostly through merger or acquisition, but also to 'commoditize' and simplify business. This can mean eliminating or reducing the number of 'straight' origin coffees that are carried, resulting in increasing dependence on blends because higher sales mean larger and more centralized buying requirements. This makes it increasingly cumbersome to deal with many small suppliers.

So-called 'signature blends' are often used in the branding strategy of larger companies. At the same time, mainstream roasters have been upgrading their image by offering 'quality' coffees, but many have very different perceptions of what this means. Some of the large United States mega-discount stores have installed 30-pound capacity computerized coffee roasters and are selling freshly roasted 'specialty' coffee at much lower prices than the traditional specialty stores. The

quality may not always be there, but the coffee is fresh. Some such chains have also started importing roasted beans direct from some producing countries in partnership with roasters at origin. Major restaurant chains such as McDonald's and Dunkin' Donuts are now offering specialty coffees and this line appears to be enjoying good sales growth. Given this strong industry growth and the accompanying proliferation of specialty coffee products, the SCAA together with the Coffee Quality Institute (CQI – www.coffeeinstitute.org) has created the Q Grading System, which effectively establishes a standard for certified specialty coffee. See details in chapter 12, Quality control. The aim is to provide producers, exporters, importers, roasters and retailers of specialty coffee with the means to have the quality and authenticity of their product independently certified. The programme builds on the existing SCAA Green Coffee Classification System and Grading Chart; see www.scaa.org and www.coffeeinstitute. org.

The specialty market in Japan

The specialty market in Japan is not dissimilar to the market in the United States, and it too has distinctive segments:

- Almost mythical name coffee: Blue Mountain, Hawaiian Kona etc.;
- Good quality, straight origin estate or area coffees;
- Decent standard qualities;
- Branded blends.

There are no dedicated specialty importers, but most importers handle at least some specialty coffees and increasingly service smaller downstream buyers directly; although there is also a network of coffee dealers and wholesalers. Interestingly, larger roasters maintain their own coffee outlets within large department stores – in so doing, they of course achieve widespread exposure.

The Japanese market basically offers producers the same sales prospects as does the United States with the exception that it is very difficult to gain recognition for new individual coffees. This is because creating a stand-alone brand image for an individual coffee would be enormously expensive and without guarantee of success. Disclosure of origin at retail level is provided for in consumer legislation, but as the composition of blends is flexible and they are sold under the roasters' own brand names, usually only the main components are identified by country of origin (and never by individual grower or producer). As a result, price resistance in Japan, other than for a few stand-alone top coffees, is probably greater than in the United States specialty market. For more information visit the website of the Specialty Coffee Association of Japan (SCAJ – www.scaj.org).

Other emerging specialty markets would appear to be strongly influenced by trends in the United States. Operators in the United States have opened or franchised specialty stores in Australia, China, Republic of Korea, Singapore and elsewhere.

The specialty market in Northern Europe

The Northern European specialty market is part of the world's largest market for coffee. Europe's total imports are double those of the United States. But the great concentration of buying power in the hands of very few roasters has not made it easy for small producers to add value through improved quality, or through promotion in Europe. This is mainly because their production is deemed insufficient to be considered for sale as straight origin coffee, but also because specialty coffee in Europe is a true niche market in a continent where much good quality coffee is already readily available.

The true specialty target segment consists mostly of real enthusiasts searching for something different, rather than large numbers of people who are disappointed in their daily cup of coffee, as was the case in the United States.

The entry of Europe's mega-roasters into this field demonstrates that they appreciate its potential. Competition between them and smaller specialty roasters will probably limit the latter's potential market more than has been the case in the United States, where until fairly recently the large roasters did not have any real 'quality' to offer.

In many European countries the opposite applies and both sides are therefore targeting more or less the same niche market, with large operators benefiting from economies of scale the smaller ones cannot match. The establishment in 1999 of the Specialty Coffee Association of Europe was an important innovation in this somewhat uneven playing field. By the middle of 2011, the SCAE had almost 1,600 members in 77 countries, so not only in Europe, and had established 35 national chapters. It now organizes regular trade shows, training events and competitions, and offers a growing range of member services. It is also interesting to note the recent massive increase in the number of micro-roasters operating in Europe. They usually either serve a very local area or, as is becoming more frequent, a select clientele via the Internet, or occasionally both.

Exporters should note that the area to be covered is vast, with hugely varying quality preferences. Smaller producers in particular will almost certainly have to depend on specialty importers or agents to access the European market efficiently.

The specialty market in Southern Europe

The Southern European specialty market, mainly Italy, is entirely different from that of most other European countries.

Italy is a gateway into a number of Eastern European markets. Many Italian importers and roasters traditionally supply ready-made specialty blends (green or roasted, for roast and ground or for espresso) to nearby countries in Eastern Europe as well as the many small roasters that operate in Italy itself.

The Italian market counts over 1,500 individual roasters. There is a substantial mainstream segment, but many small specialty roasters exist and flourish. Many of these buy ready-made, ready-to-roast green coffee blends from the specialty importers, especially for the strong espresso segment. But many of these smaller roasters are facing strong competition from the larger and medium sized roasters through the introduction of the singleserve pod systems that have been growing at an annual rate of around 20% over the last four years.

Larger specialty roasters, such as Lavazza and Illy, export substantial quantities of Italian espresso blends all over Europe and the United States, so the sales opportunities for specialty type coffee that meets the quality requirements for the espresso trade are quite substantial.

For a review of those requirements and how they differ from traditional specialty coffee see the section on coffee tasting in chapter 12, Quality control.

THE DIFFERENCE BETWEEN MAINSTREAM AND SPECIALTY ROASTERS

Many people and articles, as well as this guide, attempt to differentiate between what they call the mainstream and the specialty coffee industry. But it is not entirely clear where the one stops and the other begins. For example, if the Swiss multi-national roaster Nestlé is considered to be mainstream, what then is its single-serve R&G capsule-making subsidiary Nespresso? Alternatively, if size or turnover are the criteria, where then to place Starbucks?

Large or mainstream roasters are moving into the specialty market, for example, by offering organic and single-origin coffees or by establishing their own specialty operation, sometimes under a different name. Such moves reflect the growing importance of the specialty segment, but somewhat blurs the distinction between the two. It is therefore better perhaps to ask what causes different retail products to be classified as mainstream or specialty.

'Mainstream' simply reflects the fact that an estimated 85% to 90% of all coffee roasted is of fair average quality, mass-produced and marketed. Such coffees are available in quantity and are usually presented as blends, often through supermarkets, etc. Roasters who are predominantly active in this market segment are therefore known as 'mainstream roasters'. Their buying capacity is huge and there is strong concentration in this market with Kraft and Nestlé currently the world's leading roasters.

'Specialty' usually refers to individually presented coffees, often but not always of somewhat limited availability. With the exception of the Starbucks Company in the United States, the turnover of most specialty roasters is relatively limited but, in recent years the number of small roasters worldwide has shown strong growth. However, the term specialty increasingly also refers to coffees that are different, for example, in the way they are presented. This is part of the specialty attraction, although it is fair to say that for the average latte one does not require top-grade coffee. A simple blend will do.

To complicate matters further there is also no denying that the output of some of the larger European roasters has always included top-quality coffees, often far superior to the average specialty coffee. Yet such roasters are usually classified as mainstream because of their size and the conventional marketing methods most employ. Their products are not perceived as being 'different'. At the same time, other retail products elsewhere may be classified as specialty even though they may be based on average-quality or mainstream-type coffee.

The specialty market itself is divisible in three sub-segments: Exemplary coffees, usually presented as single origin or single source, High quality coffees that may include blends, and Average quality coffee that is presented 'differently', for example lattes. Therefore, one should probably classify individual roasters by the products they market, rather than by the type of coffee they may be buying.

The Nespresso Company combines technical innovation (special home brewing equipment) with high-quality coffees. It stands alone from the Nestlé Group, and both the company and its products should definitely be classified as being part of the specialty segment.

In a way, the Starbucks Company does the same because it relies on innovative retail and presentation methods that have set it apart from other roasters/retailers. This includes the constant promotion of high-quality origin coffee, but it is increasingly selling blends as well as its new instant coffee brand 'Via'. However, the company firmly belongs to the specialty segment because it is marketing specialty type coffees.

The Swedish roaster Gevalia is a different example. The company ranks amongst the major specialty sellers (mostly by mail order) in the United States, yet is owned by the multi-national mainstream roaster Kraft Foods.

ORGANIC COFFEE

Organic products have come a long way since small groups of consumers started buying organic food directly from farms or from small health food shops, where quality was secondary as long as the products were organic. But then in the early 1990s supermarket chains started paying systematic attention to organic food. Year after year they have taken over market share from the specialized shops, to the point where they drive most of the growth in the market share of organic food today.

It is estimated that almost 10 million hectares of land in Europe is cultivated organically. Austria is leading with as much as 20% of the total farm area under organic cultivation. The market share for organic products in Western countries ranges between 0.5% and 8% for food

generally, but varies widely for different product groups. The United States remains the largest single market for organic products, followed by Germany. Consumption growth rates have been slowing since 2008 in some countries, especially in the organic sector in the United Kingdom. However, the United States is continuing to grow (almost 10% to US$ 27 billion in 2010, which is about 4% of all food and beverage sales in that market).

WHAT ARE ORGANIC PRODUCTS?

Organic agriculture means holistic production management systems that promote and enhance agro-ecosystem health, including biodiversity, biological cycles and soil fertility. Organic production systems are based on specific and precise production, processing and handling standards. They aim to achieve optimal agro-ecosystems that are socially, ecologically and economically sustainable. Terms such as 'biological' and 'ecological' are also used in an effort to describe the organic production system more clearly.

Requirements for organically produced foods differ from those for other agricultural products. The production procedures, and not just the product by itself, are an intrinsic part of the identification and labelling of, and status claims for, such products. See the FAO/WHO Codex Alimentarius Commission Guidelines for the Production, Processing, Labelling and Marketing of Organically Produced Foods (1999) at *www.codexalimentarius.net*.

Advocates of organic agriculture believe that conventional agriculture, with its use of chemical inputs, will not be sustainable in the long run as it leads to soil degradation and pollution of the environment, and poses health risks for both consumers and producers. Therefore, organic agriculture replaces manufactured inputs (fertilizers, pesticides, herbicides, etc.) by natural compost and vermiculture, biological pest controls and the growing of legumes and shade trees. (Vermiculture is the raising of earthworms to aerate soil and/or produce vermicast: the nutrient-rich by-product of earthworms, used as a soil conditioner.)

The International Federation of Organic Agriculture Movements (IFOAM; founded 1972) has formulated basic standards for organic products. See *www.ifoam.org* for the full text. These standards are at the base of the legislation that has been introduced in the European Union (1992), the United States (2000), Japan (2001), and a number of other countries (including Argentina, Bolivia (Plurinational State of), India and Mexico) that have created national legislation to regulate the market for organic products.

Western countries have developed extensive legislation for organic products. The conditions that must be met before coffee may be marketed as organic are both comprehensive and well defined. No coffee may be brought to the marketplace and labelled organic unless it is proved to conform to the regulations. In other words, coffee can be marketed as organic only when it is certified as such by a recognized organization or certifier, based on regular inspection of all stages of production, processing, transporting and roasting of the coffee.

The first organic coffee cultivation was recorded at the Finca Irlanda in Chiapas, Mexico (1967). The first organic coffee to be imported into Europe from a small farmers' cooperative came from the UCIRI cooperative in Oaxaca, Mexico (1985).

WHY BUY OR GROW ORGANIC COFFEE?

Why do consumers choose organic coffee?

- **Health considerations.** Many consumers perceive organic foods as healthier. However, this motive is less important for coffee than it is for some other crops in that roasted coffee hardly ever contains harmful residues. But there is also a growing number of consumers whose health worries extend to the workers who have to work with the chemicals that are used in the traditional production system.
- **Demand for specialty coffee.** Although the quality of organic coffee is not necessarily better than that of conventional coffees, the market for organic coffee is increasingly demanding higher quality, which is why organic coffees are often positioned in the specialty segment. The first organic coffees to appear on the market in the 1980s were good quality arabicas from Mexico, but nowadays organic robusta, as well as lower grades of organic arabica are also available. Some quality estates or exporters have their coffees certified as organic to underline their quality, hoping it will be perceived as truly special.
- **Environmental concerns.** Other consumers are concerned about the negative impact of agro-chemicals on the environment. They are not necessarily concerned only about health issues, but primarily want to be sure that the products they buy are produced in an environmentally friendly way in order to prevent pollution, erosion and soil degradation.

Why produce organic coffee?

In principle producers are motivated by the same concerns as consumers, but in addition they want to secure their social and cultural future by realizing the premium that certified organic coffee obtains. This benefit depends on the demand for organic coffee, which in turn determines the amount of the premium that can be obtained and the extra costs involved in organic production.

Growing organic coffee

Growing any organic product, including organic coffee, is more than just leaving out fertilizers and other agro-chemicals. Coffee produced in this way should instead be called 'natural' coffee and, to the surprise of many, the industry looks upon this as non-sustainable production. This is because in the long run the soil will be depleted by natural production, which is often referred to also as 'passive cultivation' or 'organic by default'.

To achieve sustainable production it is necessary to make active use of various organic agriculture techniques, including the composting of organic material, mulching of the soil under the trees with organic material, use of biological pest control, and investing in shade regulation. The principle of sustainable agriculture is that a value corresponding to that harvested should be returned to the soil. All possible methods have to be used to enhance the fertility of the soil. This is why passive production of coffee, even when no chemicals are used, is viewed as non-sustainable and not as organic.

Usually, a producer may simultaneously grow both conventional and organic coffee, although this is not recommended. There must be a clear separation between the two types and adequate barriers to prevent contamination with agro-chemicals from neighbouring fields.

Coffee may normally be sold as organic only once organic cultivation has been practised for at least three years before the first marketable harvest. This also means three years of inspection. These years are called the conversion period.

In specific cases, depending on previous agricultural practices, this conversion period may be reduced, but only after approval of the certifying organization, which in turn has to report such a decision to the authority granting the required import permit. For a producer who can prove that no agro-chemicals have been used in the past, it is important to try to reduce the conversion period. If a producer can document that no agro-chemicals have recently been used, it is certainly worthwhile discussing the possibility with the certifier.

PROCESSING AND MARKETING ORGANIC COFFEE – THE AUDIT TRAIL

Not only coffee cultivation, but also all subsequent steps in the production chain, have to be certified. On-farm processing, storage, transport, export processing, shipping, export, import, roasting, packaging, distribution and retailing all have to be certified organic. Contact with conventionally produced coffee must be excluded and so there has to be a separation in space and/or time. Spraying or fumigation with toxic agents is never permitted and special measures must be taken to prevent contact with areas where fumigation has taken place. Adequate records are to be kept of incoming and outgoing coffee so that the entire product flow can be documented and accounted for, often referred to as traceability. All the steps in the chain should therefore be documented and administered in a way that makes it possible to trace back the origin of the product from one step to the next (track and trace), ensuring that no contamination with conventional coffee has occurred. This traceability minimizes the risk of fraud at all stages and is a very important part of the inspection process by certifying organizations.

The flavouring of roasted coffee is permitted when natural flavouring substances or preparations are used. For packaging roasted coffee, flushing with nitrogen or carbon dioxide is permitted. For the decaffeination of coffee, chemical solvents (e.g. methylene chloride) are not permitted, but the water method or the supercritical carbon dioxide method (the CO_2 method) may be used.

ORGANIC CERTIFICATION AND IMPORT

As already indicated, the importation and sale as organic of both green and processed coffee must comply with the legal regulations of the consuming countries. This compliance needs to be verified by a third party; the procedure is called certification. It is important to realize that different rules apply in different countries.

The certification procedure includes a number of steps. Note that there is a clear distinction between the certification of an operator to produce organic coffee and the certification of an export shipment to be imported as organic coffee.

- **Registration.** The producer selects a certification organization (certifier for short) and signs a contract. The producer provides information on their farm/processing facilities and is registered.
- **Inspection.** At least once a year the certifier inspects the production and processing facilities.
- **Certification.** The inspection report is the basis for deciding whether a master certificate can be granted.
- **Control certificate (formerly called transaction certificate).** This must be issued for every export shipment to the European Union, the United States and Japan, indicating the exact quantity and organic origin, after which the goods may be exported/imported as organic.

The certification process includes an assessment of the grower's production and export capacity against which the authenticity of future export transactions will be tested. This is to ensure that sellers of organic products do not exceed their registered capacity. Also, in the European Union, organic products can be labelled as such only once the entire production and handling chain, from the grower through to the importer, has been inspected and certified.

Organic regulations

In the initial development stages there was no legal definition of organic food and so farmers' organizations and others formulated their own standards and issued certificates and seals to offer consumer guarantees. The next phase was when IFOAM united these different standards into its 'Basic standards for organic production and processing'. These standards provide a framework for certification bodies and standard-setting organizations worldwide to develop their own certification standards. In an effort to harmonize standards and certification, and to provide a universal quality seal for organic products, IFOAM also has an accreditation programme for certification organizations. See *www.ifoam.*

org for more information on this accreditation programme and for links to other publications, e.g. the differences between European Union and United States regulations for organic agriculture. In the third development phase, different countries or states (e.g. Germany, California) developed laws on organic agriculture and processing, which were eventually incorporated in formal EU or United States regulations.

Today (late 2011), the bulk of organic coffee is certified against one of the following standards:

- Council Regulation (EC) No. 834/2007 of 28 June 2007 on organic production and labelling of organic products and repealing Regulation (EEC) No. 2092/91 that came into force 1 January 2009 for the European Union;
- National Organic Program for the United States (NOP);
- Japan Agricultural Standard (JAS).

Importing organic coffee into Europe

In the European Union, the market for certified organic food is regulated by Council Regulation (EC) No. 834/2007 and subsequent amendments thereto. (Visit *www.eur-lex.europa. eu* and type 2007 (year) and 834 (document number) into the search function to see Regulation 834/2007 and subsequent additions.) All major European certifying organizations are subject to this regulation, although in some respects some, such as Naturland in Germany or Soil Association in the United Kingdom, apply stricter standards. For more information see also *www.ifoam.org.*

Equal values. The international trade in organic products and regulations for their certification are based on equivalence or 'equal values'. That is to say, organic products imported into the EU must have been produced in accordance with standards that are equivalent to those applicable within the EU itself. This is clearly stated in Article 33 of EC 834/2007. But equivalence is not always interpreted in the same way, for example, when an individual competent body insists on the foreign standard being identical, rather than equivalent, to the corresponding EU regulation. In some instances such differences could be considered as non-tariff or technical trade barriers.

The same article provides that a non-EU country can be approved by the European Commission if its production system complies with principles and inspection measures, equivalent to those laid down in EC 834/2007. Such a country is then added to a list of approved countries.

Accreditation of certification organizations. The European standard known as EN 45011 and the corresponding ISO 65 guide both stipulate that certification organizations should be accredited by a recognized accreditation body. Aspiring exporters of organic coffee to the European Union should therefore verify that:

- The proposed certifying organization has an EN 45011/ISO 65 accreditation, which they should be able to submit on request. It is important to note that the European Union does not recognize certifiers that certify clients against organic standards that do not conform to EU specifications. For example, the use of sodium nitrate is permitted by some non-EU certifiers, but is prohibited under EU regulations.

- The proposed certifier can certify directly against EU regulations because a certifier may certify against a number of different standards.

Importation and inspection. Aspiring exporters should satisfy themselves that the proposed importer is fully aware of and follows the required EU customs documentation, i.e. that importer is certified against EU regulations. But exporters must also be aware of the fact that for each shipment EU customs will demand to see an original inspection or control certificate (formerly called transaction certificate) for verification and endorsement. Therefore, exporters must apply for these on time because without such documentation EU customs will only clear a shipment as conventional coffee.

Inspection certificates are issued by the certifying body and this is where the earlier inspection of production capacity comes in, i.e. the master certificate that was issued by the certifier to confirm the seller's authenticity and capacity. At the end of a year it can then be seen whether the total exports for which inspection or control certificates were issued correspond with the production capacity stated in the master certificate.

Once cleared through EU customs the organic product enjoys free movement to other member states. But when all or part of a consignment is to be re-exported as organic to a destination outside the EU then, depending on the country of destination, the original EU importer may have to obtain a new inspection certificate from a competent EU certifying organization. This is by law, but because the market requires it.

EU organic production logo. Most certifying bodies have their own quality labels. As a result, many different labels exist in the European Union for the designation of organic products. Increasing trade in roasted coffee within the European Union therefore forces roasters to display several labels on their retail packets, an arrangement that does not provide the clarity one would expect.

Regulation EC 834/2007 now stipulates that the EU organic production logo shall be obligatory for all organic pre-packaged food produced within the European Community. However, the simultaneous use of national or private logos shall not be prevented.

For more information on organic certification and regulations in the EU, in addition to *www.ifoam.org*, also visit to *www. intracen.org/exporters/sectors*. Click on Organic Products and then Certification. The site also provides a useful glossary of organic certification concepts.

Importing organic coffee into the United States

Prior to 2002, private and state agencies certified organic practices and national certification requirements did not exist.

As a result, there were no guarantees that 'organic' meant the same thing from state to state, or even locally from certifier to certifier. Consumers and producers of organic products therefore jointly sought to establish national standards to clear up confusion in the marketplace, and to protect the trade against mislabelling or fraud.

As required by the Organic Foods Production Act (OFPA), the National Organic Standards (part of the National Organic Program, NOP) became effective on 21 October 2002. OFPA itself was adopted in 1990 to establish national standards for the production and handling of foods labelled as 'organic'.

Today organizations that are fully NOP-compliant (certified) may label their products or ingredients as organic, and may use the 'USDA Organic Seal' on organic products in the United States, irrespective of whether they are produced domestically or are imported. As a result of NOP, there is a single national label in the United States to designate organic products, thereby avoiding the label confusion that exists in Europe. A list of accredited certifying agents can be found on the websites of the United States Department of Agriculture, *www.ams.usda.gov/nop* and the Independent Organic Inspectors Association, *www.ioia.net*.

Like the European Union, the United States also requires a control or transaction/export certificate for each shipment, showing date, weight/quantity, and origin. However, unlike to European Union, NOP does not require the 'master certificate' for the processing unit.

Information on trade in organic products can also be found at *www.ota.com*, the website of the Organic Trade Association – look for *about/sectorcouncils/coffee/index.html*.

Importing organic coffee into Japan

The Japan Agricultural Standard (JAS) for Organic Agricultural Products entered into force in April 2002. Enacted by the Ministry of Agriculture, Forestry and Fisheries, JAS regulates the production and labelling of organic food items produced in Japan. Although coffee is not grown in Japan, JAS nevertheless also covers organic coffee (and tea) under 'organic agricultural products'. The JAS standard has been further revised in 2005. For more information visit *www.maff. go.jp/e/jas/index.html*.

Only ministry-accredited certifying bodies may issue JAS organic certification for coffee to be imported into Japan. Interested certifying bodies in producing countries may also apply for accreditation under JAS. Subject to meeting the JAS standard for their products, set by the Agriculture Ministry, suppliers of organic coffee and tea may display the JAS mark, which also gives Japan a single organic label for the entire Japanese market.

WORLD MARKET FOR ORGANIC COFFEE

Different trade sources have varying views on the size of the market for certified organic coffee. This is not helped by the fact that few consuming countries register organic coffee imports separately. To note also that the 27 EU member countries increasingly report coffee imports as a single market, making provision of individual country data even more difficult. Nevertheless, indications are that consumption of certified organic coffee in North America and Europe has been growing fairly strongly since 2005, with growth figures averaging 5% to 10% annually, although this has slowed in the last couple of years.

A 2010 study by ITC (Trends in the Trade of Certified Coffees by J. Pierrot, D. Giovannucci and A. Kasterine; March, 2011 – See *www.intracen.org/exporters/organic-products* – Information and Technical Papers) puts 2009 imports at around 1.7 million bags or almost 1.4% of the 126 million bags of 2009 world gross imports (excluding re-exports). Of this, 45% went to Europe, 41% to North America and 14% to Asia and elsewhere. Estimates for 2010 suggest that the market might have grown by around 3% to 1.75 million bags.

Peru remains by far the leading exporter, with exports of 406,000 bags in 2009 and 423,000 bags in 2010. Other leading producers include Colombia, El Salvador, Ethiopia, Guatemala, Honduras, Indonesia and Mexico, with Ethiopia, Honduras and Mexico currently each exporting over 100,000 bags annually. However, it should be noted that official or recorded export figures are not always complete as not all exporting countries provide the necessary data, making it difficult to be precise.

Growth in Japan is very much linked to quality: organic coffee of excellent quality generates increasing consumer interest, something that augurs well for further growth in this segment. Growth potential for average quality organic coffee on the other hand is limited.

North American growth is also linked to quality. The fact that profit margins on certified products as organic usually are higher plays a role as well, so mainstream roasters and retail chains are showing increasing interest. Almost half of all Fairtrade certified coffee is certified organic as well, whereas certification by both the Rainforest Alliance and Utz Certified is not only growing strongly, but also includes a substantial amount of certified organic.

On the production side there remains the mistaken belief amongst some that organic coffee does not need to show quality. As a result, some organic production simply cannot find premium buyers and ends up being exported uncertified, i.e. as conventional coffee.

Nevertheless, premia for decent quality organic coffee have probably stabilized somewhat and, under normal market conditions, may range from about 10% upward, however always depending on quality. Therefore, moving into organic coffee continues to remain out of bounds for producers who are unable to provide the required quality, or who underestimate the cost (fees, learning costs, workload and sometimes lower yields, at least in the first few years) that go with making the move.

ORGANIC COFFEE AND SMALL PRODUCERS

Numerous grower organizations and smallholders are aware of the market for organic coffee. Because many of them do not use, or use a minimum of agro-chemicals, conversion seems a logical option especially when coffee prices are low. As well as the problem of possible oversupply, potential producers should also carefully consider the costs of certification. They have to assure themselves not only that their future output will be in accordance with the rules of organic production, but also that the proposed inspection system is in accordance with the regulations in the import markets that are to be targeted.

To assist in this regard the organic sector has developed an internal control system (ICS) that provides a practical and cost-effective inspection option. Generally, if a grower group has more than 30 members it qualifies for an ICS. Although an ICS can be quite burdensome, it is a means to reduce the costs of inspection. Otherwise each individual member must be inspected every year, which is extremely expensive, especially for larger groups with a geographically far-flung membership. With a proper ICS, only a random sample of the total number of producers has to be inspected by an independent certifying organization. Major ICS elements include:

- Internal standards, including sanctions;
- Personnel;
- Infrastructure;
- Training and information;
- A 100% internal farm control at least once a year;
- Monitoring of product flow.

The magnitude of the random sample to be taken by the external inspection body under an ICS system is a major item of debate within the European Union, but as a rule of thumb most competent authorities seem to accept the square root method for external inspections, i.e. 100 members = 10 inspections, 400 members = 20 inspections and so forth. Note also that some roasters submit random green coffee samples for chemical analysis to verify the accuracy of the inspection and certification process.

CERTIFICATION COSTS AND VIABILITY

Production and export

It is impossible to give a precise indication of the cost of certification. It depends on the time needed for preparation, travel, inspection, reporting and certification, and the fees the certification organization charges. Not only the agricultural production of the coffee, but also the wet and dry processing as well as the storage and export process have to be inspected and certified. Fee structures vary considerably and it is therefore advisable to review in detail which inspection and certification organization offers the best service at the lowest price. Some charge a fee per hectare, others a percentage of the export value. As a norm, the cost of inspection and certification should not exceed 3%–4% of the sales value of the green coffee, although it should be noted that some grower organizations pay more than this.

Local certifiers (i.e. those established in the same producing country or region) are usually, but not always, cheaper than the international agencies. However, local certificates are not necessarily or easily recognized by importing countries, so their validity has to be carefully checked. A number of international certifiers have branch offices in producing countries and locally employed staff carry out inspections at lower expense than external personnel. Another option for international certifiers is to use a recognized local inspection body with which they have a cooperation agreement.

Also to be taken into account are increased production costs and sometimes a fall in the yield per hectare. So, not only does the producer have to bear the inspection and certification costs, but production might also fall, at least for a couple of years. Some sources suggest yields may fall by some 20%.

Inspection costs tend to be higher in the initial phase as the certifiers need time to get to know the producer and to register fields and facilities. To overcome the start-up problems during the conversion period, coffee growers in a number of countries can have access to funds to finance the costs of certification. Nevertheless, if the average annual inspection and certification cost for example comes to US$ 5,000 or more there is little financial point in converting to certified organic if the annual exportable production amounts to only two or three containers. These costs are extremely difficult to assess because they depend entirely on the nature and intensity of the conventional cultivation practices before the conversion to organic agriculture.

A further cost and a real problem for the producer is the conversion period from conventional to full organic production. During this time the coffee cannot be sold as organic and so does not realize any premium. Meanwhile, premiums for organic coffee are difficult to indicate because they depend on the quality of the coffee and on the market situation at a given moment. In recent years premium quotations have ranged from 10 cts/lb to as high as 75 cts/lb, depending on quality and availability. As a rule of thumb, however, the potential producer premium (FOB) for the organic version of a particular coffee compared to the equivalent non-organic quality can probably be put at 10% to 20%. This compares with consumers generally accepting to pay retail prices of around 20% more for organic coffee than they do for conventional coffee. Some exceptional coffees realize higher premiums ,but there is a strong feeling in trade circles that, realistically, this is the maximum that should be expected. Consumer interest tails off rapidly if premiums go beyond this unless the coffee's quality is absolutely outstanding.

The high of 20% is an indication only. Actual producer premiums fluctuate alongside coffee prices as a whole: high coffee prices probably reducing the premium percentage and, conversely, low coffee prices probably encouraging somewhat higher premium percentages. It remains to be seen therefore whether or how the much higher coffee prices ruling in early 2011 may alter this picture (Fairtrade offers a fixed premium for organic coffee over its minimum guaranteed price for conventional coffee that meets Fairtrade criteria). See table 3.2 for details.

Contrary to popular belief the liquor of organic coffee is not necessarily better than that of its conventional equivalent. Where it is not, the premium over conventional coffee has to be justified purely by the organic aspect and is therefore strictly limited by supply and demand unless and until the quality is such that the organic coffee in question can achieve a true stand-alone position in the market – its own niche. Then the premium potential becomes entirely demand driven, just as is the case for some well-known conventional specialty or gourmet coffees, and such organic brands achieve premiums of 25% or even higher over conventional coffee.

But as the supply of organic coffee grows, so growers should be more cautious when venturing into this field. Just as producers of conventional specialty coffee have experienced, it is equally difficult to launch new stand-alone brands of organic coffee. Organic coffees that do not offer quality as such, or that are available in large quantities, will sell at much lower premiums over their conventional equivalent, perhaps as low as 5% because, just like any other standard type coffee, they end up as bulk blenders. Chapter 11, Coffee quality, makes it clear that to produce good quality coffee of any kind takes much work and strict management. Organic certification will always complement such efforts, but cannot replace hard work and integrity.

Remember:

- Check which certifier is the most acceptable and the most appropriate for the target export market. If possible, determine which certifier the prospective buyer(s) may prefer. Make sure the preferred certifier is accredited and approved in the target market.

- Obtain quotations from various certifiers and ask for clear conditions (especially how many days will be charged) and timelines. Conditions are usually negotiable. Remember certifiers are offering a service, not favours, and should serve their clients, not the other way around.

- Ensure your potential export production warrants the conversion cost, i.e. calculate the opportunity cost of converting to organic production.

Information on costs and current sales prices for comparable coffees is available on many websites and can relatively easily be compared.

Importing, roasting and retailing

The green coffee importer and the coffee roaster also have to be inspected and certified. Inspection costs in the European Union vary from US$ 500 to US$ 900 per year per import/production location. In addition, the importer (who does not process the coffee, but only trades it) pays a licence fee of 0.1% to 0.7% of the sales value or US$ 0.20/kg to US$ 0.50/kg, depending on turnover. Roasters pay a licence fee of 0.1% to 1.5% of the sales value of the roasted coffee, depending on turnover. As already mentioned, every EU importer of organic coffee must apply for an individual import permit for each of their suppliers and for each consignment.

See ITC's website at *www.intracen.org/exporters/organic-products* for more general information on organic products and organic certification.

MAPPING TECHNOLOGY IN COFFEE MARKETING: GPS AND GIS

USING GPS AND GIS – THE PRINCIPLE

Modern agricultural mapping technology is one of the key elements in the implementation of efforts to reduce poverty and to monitor agricultural activities in developing countries. Remote sensing technology in the form of multi-spectral satellite imagery, geographical positioning systems (GPS) and digital aerial photography has improved dramatically in recent years and forms the foundation of geographical information systems (GIS).

GIS and remote sensing, in combination with geographical positioning systems, are the instruments that are being used to measure and audit agricultural activities. The importance of mapping agricultural activities in developing countries is firstly to assist in monitoring and calculating agricultural activities on an ongoing basis. Secondly, land use and land management forms an integral part of agricultural development but this process can only really be successfully managed using GIS and updated remote sensing technology.

If you cannot measure it, you cannot manage it

Using GIS as part of the mapping process assists in the creation of spatial models that indicate the most viable agricultural activities in particular areas. This in turn enables authorities to improve infrastructure around viable agricultural activities, whereas GIS web map capabilities can be used as a marketing tool to encourage investment and create agricultural concession areas. Finally, GIS platforms to monitor agricultural activities, land use and land management enable both governments and the donor community to plan ahead in the fight against poverty.

A number of governments, most notably in the coffee sector in Brazil and Colombia, combine satellite imagery information with data collected regularly from a large number of ground stations in order to reduce the margin of error in their coffee crop estimates. Apart from coffee, satellite imagery also assists in the collection of information on soya, maize, rice, sugar cane, citrus, wheat and cotton crops.

MAPPING TECHNOLOGY IN COFFEE MARKETING

Not only can authoritative information about where or how a coffee is grown contribute to making it a successful specialty or organic coffee, but it can also help prevent misrepresentation. Modern technology enables one to show on a map not only where a coffee is grown, but also the special characteristics of that area such as altitude, soils, vegetation type, slope, rainfall and special environmental attributes. By demonstrating this information in maps or graphics, producers can show why their coffee is unique, or at least different from the majority of other coffees in their country or region. If, in addition, producers seek an authorized, enforceable 'appellation' for their coffee then they also need the spatial information necessary to legally or formally define the extent of the appellation zone and thus lead to the authentication of the appellation and the coffee in question. A growing number of consumers also demands more assurance that the coffee was produced in an environmentally friendly way, that it was properly harvested and processed, and that it actually comes from a specific region or farm. Technologies are now available and are being applied in the field to help producers' and farmers' organizations address these issues and many more.

Actual projects

The United States Agency for International Development (USAID) is funding projects in Peru, Guatemala, Costa Rica, the Dominican Republic and some African countries that use the following approach to address these issues.

- The physical location of each farm (longitude, latitude and altitude) is mapped and recorded by project extension agents using a global positioning system (GPS) unit.
- Data are collected on how producers grow their coffee including varieties, altitude, application of pesticides, and other details that may be important for marketing or certifying. Extension agents also collect data on practices and quality and whatever else defines the 'uniqueness' of the coffee at the farm, farmers group, or 'appellation zone' levels. Socio-economic data are collected as well.
- This information (production and location) is entered into a spatial database or geographic information system (GIS). This works like a more traditional database, but includes location information for each record.

- Maps are created showing not only where the farms are located, but also whatever characteristics are of interest about each farm and the coffee produced on that farm.

These projects are implemented by the US Geological Survey's National Center for Earth Resources and Science (EROS), national coffee agencies and agricultural research institutions, and the Tropical Agricultural Centre for Training and Research (CATIE) for Costa Rica. The initiative is called GeoCafe due to its combination of geographic and coffee information. The GeoCafe systems being developed lead to better overall production management; promote the establishment of mechanisms that facilitate coffee monitoring and trace-back; and facilitate access to information over the Internet on coffee production, processing and marketing. At the same time, they provide information about the coffee to potential buyers, thereby assisting the marketing effort. For example: Where is a particular type of coffee produced and by whom? Which farms are located at a certain altitude? What are the climatic and soil conditions on these farms? What forest cover is there?

Although for individual small farmers the need for such systems is limited, it is a very useful information and management tool for farmers' organizations, cooperatives and estates, particularly those promoting their coffee under specific logos or appellations.

The results of the GeoCafe projects can be viewed on the Internet. Any user can look at the maps, zoom in and out to see details, or even ask to see all of the farms meeting some criteria (e.g. 'show me all farms in this zone growing arabica at an altitude over 1,000 m').

Visit the sites below to view actual maps and other information: *www.dominicancoffee.com, www.guatemalancoffees.com, www.edcintl.cr.usgs.gov/ip/geocafe.*

The technology behind GeoCafe is well known and mature. GeoCafe is fully customizable and no complex programming is needed to operate and maintain a basic application. The costs of implementation are not high, since the technological platform has been already developed, and most of the data acquisition is done by partner agencies using internal resources (when available). With minor adaptations, the GeoCafe system can be adapted to other crops or other uses (e.g., watershed management and conservation, and environmental monitoring).

The website of the US Government Geological Survey, *www.usgs.gov,* provides information on a large number of different applications that are of interest to those working with GPS and GIS.

FUTURE USES OF GPS AND GIS – THE WAY FORWARD

New technologies are being developed to aid in data collection. Handheld devices already exist that combine spatial data (GPS locations) and traditional data collection

(specific non-spatial information). These data are entered into the device and downloaded into the database at the end of each day or week.

Ongoing initiatives open the way for online querying, information access, and mapping projects in other agricultural areas and sectors, not only in Latin America but also elsewhere, for example in Africa. And also for products as cocoa, cashew nuts, or bananas to name a few.

In the area of authentication – proving that a coffee or a product actually comes from a specific area or source – technologies such as smart tags are also being developed. Such tiny computerized tags, attached to each bag or container, can contain any set of information required to meet the market's authentication requirements, and could even be tracked by satellite if such control was necessary.

Remote sensing and spatial mapping today provide information on natural vegetation, watersheds, land-cover, land-use, forestry and other crop areas, etc. But of course, the benefits are not limited to agriculture. The same technologies assist with urban development and town planning, infrastructure verification, protection of wetlands, and mapping of informal settlements. The list is almost endless and covers matters of interest to developed and developing countries alike.

As an example see *www.geospace.co.za.* For more information, a search on Google using the words Geographic Information Forum produces a lengthy list of relevant websites like, for example, *www.ppgis.net* – the Open Forum on Participatory Geographic Information Systems and Technologies. Advanced users of mapping technology and related subjects will find *www.registry.gsdi.org/index.php* of interest.

Potential sources of geographical positioning equipment

This guide does not recommend any particular equipment or supplier. But a quick search on the Internet, using the key words: GPS equipment manufacturers or suppliers, produces a huge amount of information.

The amount of available information is overwhelming and the best approach would probably be to make contact with the projects mentioned earlier to determine their preferred choice of equipment. Sources close to these suggest that Garmin International, *www.garmin.com/us* supplies many sets to coffee producing areas. Another leading supplier is Magellan System Corporation, *www.magellangps.com.* Both of them supply simple but robust models – some of them at a few hundred dollars or less. Other sites offering a selection of equipment include *www.tvnav.com* and *www.thegpsstore.com,* but the list of potential supply sources is almost endless. For use in the coffee sector one should always select a model with altimeter. Some mobile phones (cell phones) have a GPS facility built in.

In most countries, institutions such as the National Mapping or Geographical Survey Service and others, including some government departments, already use GPS equipment and should be able to offer advice on local experience and preferences. Especially for use in remote areas, simplicity and durability of the equipment are of paramount importance. In other words, do not invest in unnecessarily sophisticated features that are unlikely to be used.

GIS software – for creating a spatial database and mapping – is primarily used by groups of cooperatives and large estates. See ESRI at *www.esri.com* as an example.

Latitude, longitude and altitude

For an introduction to latitude/longitude visit, for example, *www.istp.gsfc.nasa.gov/stargaze/Slatlong.htm.* For detailed educational and technical information on GPS/GIS use any Internet search engine combining the words Geographical Positioning Systems or visit *www.trimble.com/gps/index.shtml.*

Here is a GPS reading example from Ethiopia:

N 07 01 44.0;
E 038 50 16.1;
1,720 m.

- The latitude North of Equator. 07 are degrees (from 0 to 90), 01 refers to minutes (from 0 to 59) and 44.0 are seconds (from 0 to 59);
- The longitude East of the Greenwich line (which goes North-South through Greenwich in London, United Kingdom), also in degrees (from 0 to 180), minutes and seconds; and
- The altitude above sea level.

TRADEMARKING AND GEOGRAPHICAL INDICATIONS IN COFFEE

TRADEMARKS AND LOGOS

A registered trademark or logo can help protect a successful product from being fraudulently duplicated. The Colombian Juan Valdez trademark needs no explanation or description. It is virtually known worldwide and is protected against fraudulent use because it is registered in all the main import markets. But the cost of developing and registering a trademark can be high and prospective applicants may even find that their favourite choice is already in use, or is too close to an existing registration to be accepted.

It is advisable therefore to begin by conducting a search of existing registrations to see if anyone else has already claimed your proposed mark or name. Searches can be made over the Internet on the sites below that also provide information on procedures and regulations pertaining to trademarking and related matters generally in the EU, the United States and Japan:

- European Union: *www.oami.europa.eu*
- United States: *www.uspto.gov*
- Japan: *www.jpo.go.jp*

The EU and US sites also provide information on the Madrid Agreement that deals with the International Registration of Marks. Information on trade related aspects of intellectual property rights (TRIPS) generally is found at *www.wto.org* – look for TRIPS under trade topics, then Intellectual property. For the registration of both trademarks and geographic indications (or appellations of origin, which is possibly more appropriate for coffee) an application will have to be filed first of all with your national authorities. These authorities will also be able to advise whether anyone else has already registered what you wish to protect because you cannot register the same (or even a similar) mark or name that someone else may have registered before you. This principle of prior verification applies to foreign countries as well.

Eventually one will have to employ a legal firm to conduct a search of existing registrations. Note also that the degree of protection offered by trademark legislation varies from country to country. These considerations suggest that trademarking should be considered only where the product warrants it, and where the degree of protection is such as to make the effort and cost worthwhile. But certainly, where a producer goes to the trouble and cost to create an appellation for their coffee and backs it up with registration in a GIS database, then trademarking of the name will complete the safeguarding process.

TRADEMARKS VERSUS GEOGRAPHICAL INDICATIONS

A trademark provides protection to the owner of the mark by ensuring the exclusive right to use it to identify goods or services, or to authorize another to use it in return for payment. The period of protection varies, but a trademark can be renewed indefinitely beyond the initial time limit on payment of additional fees. Trademark protection must be enforced by the registered owners of the mark at their own expense, utilizing appropriate legal redress where necessary. In most legal systems courts have the authority to enforce trademark ownership rights against infringement.

In a larger sense, trademarks promote initiative and enterprise worldwide by rewarding the owners of trademarks with recognition and financial profit. Trademarks also hinder the efforts of unfair competition. For further details visit *www.wipo.org,* the website of the World Intellectual Property Organization (WIPO) Geneva, Switzerland.

Almost all countries in the world register and protect trademarks by maintaining a register of trademarks. Trademarks may be one or a combination of words, letters and numerals. They may consist of drawings or logos, symbols, three-dimensional signs such as the shape and packaging of goods, etc.

A **geographical indication (GI)** provides an indication of where something comes from. It can be used on goods or services that have a specific geographic origin and that possess qualities or a reputation that are intrinsically due to that place of origin. As we know, all agricultural products typically have qualities that derive from their place of production and are influenced by specific local factors, such as climate and soil but some have acquired a certain distinctiveness and recognition. As such, GIs may be used for a wide variety of agricultural products, such as for example 'Tuscany' for olive oil produced in a specific area in Italy; or 'Champagne' for sparkling wines from a well-defined region in France, or Jamaica Blue Mountain for its coffee.

A geographic name itself is not necessarily a GI. In order for a geographic name to function as a GI, it must indicate more than just origin; it must communicate that the product from this region has a particular quality or has a particular reputation that is specifically connected to the noted region.

Appellation of origin is a special kind of geographical indication. It is used for products that have a specific quality that is exclusively or essentially due to the geographic environment in which the products are produced. The concept of geographical indications encompasses appellations of origin. Wines from France are maybe the products most frequently associated with appellations, e.g. AOC Alsace means Appellation d'Origine Controlée Alsace. This certifies that the wine is from the Alsace region.

Logos used for trademarks and geographical indications

A trademark is a sign (logo) used by an enterprise to distinguish its goods and services from those of other enterprises. It gives its owner the right to exclude others from using that trademark.

A geographical indication tells consumers that a product is produced in a certain place and has certain characteristics that are due to that place of production. All producers who make their products in the place designated by a geographic indication, and whose products share typical qualities, may use it. Producers outside the geographic indication may not use the name or logo, even if the quality of their product is the same or better. Usually it is more difficult (but not impossible) to register trademarks that lay claim to a geographic name. This because of the realization that it is not always obvious that an applicant for such a mark can claim to represent all potential interested parties from the region, area or district in question. One way around this could be

to obtain officially sanctioned approval for the application from a relevant governmental or semi-governmental body from the target geographic region, area or district. Another approach could be to use a graphic (i.e. decorative) logo that refers to the area, and which would be used by many in that area subject to specified requirements. Rather than a geographic 'word mark', the graphic trademark is then filed as a collective mark for goods produced from that area, by members of the area.

For a complete overview on the subject of geographical indications, including several coffee case studies, look for ITC's Guide to Geographical Indications on the ITC website *www.intracen.org/publications* where the book can be downloaded free of charge in pdf format.

Presentations made during a seminar on Geographical Indications for Coffee held at the International Coffee Organization in May 2008 can be viewed at *www.dev.ico.org/event_pdfs/gi/gi.htm.*

SUSTAINABILITY AND SOCIAL ISSUES IN THE COFFEE INDUSTRY

Coffee has always been connected with emotions and opinions; therefore the debate about socio-economic aspects of coffee production is decades old already. One regular topic, especially in times when coffee prices are low or when there is political turmoil in coffee producing areas, is the working and living conditions of coffee farmers and workers on coffee plantations.

Advocacy groups and NGOs lobby for improved livelihoods and fair treatment of coffee growers and plantation workers. Some consumer activists wanted to change the system from within and started constructing alternatives to the dominant free market coffee economy. They began to import coffee, tea and other commodities from small producer organizations, which they sold through so-called 'Third World' shops.

These early steps blossomed, boosted by an initiative in the Netherlands in 1988 when an NGO, Solidaridad, took the initiative to start the Max Havelaar certification system for Fairtrade coffee (and subsequently also for other products) with the goal of bringing these coffees into conventional supermarket channels. This in turn spurred the creation of other certification labels orientated towards sustainability, which retailers and manufacturers embraced, seeing such cause-related marketing as a means of product differentiation, but at the same time promoting sustainability as well as fulfilling their corporate social responsibility objectives. Producers in turn generally receive better prices for their coffee, although not all schemes necessarily guarantee a better return.

A more recent general development is that the mainstream coffee industry is increasingly accepting responsibility for the conditions under which the coffee is produced. Coupled with growing interest in and support for environmental causes in importing countries generally, this has led to the introduction of terms such as responsibly produced or environment-friendly or environmentally sustainable coffee. For a good introduction to the subject go to *www.conservation.org*, the website of Conservation International, and look for the Conservation Principles for Coffee Production, which are listed as sustainable livelihoods for coffee producers; ecosystem and wildlife conservation; soil conservation; water conservation and protection; energy conservation; waste management; and pest and disease management.

All these and related aspects gained considerable public interest during the years 2001-2005 when the ICO Composite Indicator Price fell below 50 cts/lb. This period of shockingly low producer prices became known as the Coffee Crisis and motivated the appearance of new initiatives as, for example, the 4C Coffee Association that promotes a mainstream verification standard

As a result differentiation of coffee products through sustainable certification labels now comes in many forms, but the main agencies are as follows:

- Fair Trade; *www.fairtrade.net*
- Rainforest Alliance; *www.rainforest-alliance.org*
- Utz Certified; *www.utzcertified.org*
- The Common Code for the Coffee Community (4C Association) *www.4c-coffeeassociation.org*

These various initiatives are rapidly gaining market share and by 2010 it was estimated that they represented around 5% of the total world trade in coffee.

SUSTAINABILITY, CERTIFICATION, VERIFICATION, CORPORATE GUIDELINES

Sustainability has been defined by some as 'meeting the needs of the present generation without compromising the ability of future generations to meet their needs'. It can then be further defined in environmental, economic and social dimensions with biodiversity perhaps as the key measure of environmental sustainability in the natural world. This concept appeals to coffee growers and consumers who are not necessarily interested in, or who see no rationale to the production of organic coffee as such, perhaps because they believe that low yields coupled with increasing availability of organic coffee will always prevent small growers from generating the high incomes that some proponents of organic coffee production believe can be achieved. Others do not see the market potential as sufficiently large, and still others simply believe that it is possible to achieve more or less the same objectives without going the organic way, which for mainstream producers would be very difficult if not entirely impossible to do.

This is not the place to pronounce for or against any of these arguments, but if a production process maintains

biodiversity presumably one may consider that it sustains rather than harms the environment. If so, and when linked with consideration for social and ethical issues, this concept presents a broad alternative for the more directly focused objectives of some individual labels.

Sustainability in itself, of course, does not need the guarantee of a certification or verification. Often, producers are already improving performance and efficiency significantly through the use of good agricultural practices (GAP) and/or good management practices (GMP). Certainly, this does not imply the need for an audit procedure. Nevertheless, consumers generally wish to be able to place a certain trust in claims such as 'this is an environmentally friendly' or 'socially responsible' product. Hence, the existence of different ways and means to provide such guarantees to roasters and retailers alike that allow them to offer what is sometimes also called 'no-worry coffee'.

Certification guarantees (through a certificate) that specific rules and regulations of voluntary standards are met in a certain environment (e.g. individual producer, producer group, cooperative or even region). These producers have to meet certain requirements – social, economical, environmental – and certification calls for independent third-party confirmation of this status, conducted by an accredited auditor. Mostly, certifications have to be renewed on an annual basis.

Roasters buying certified coffee benefit from the guarantee provided by the certificate and by using the logo and related information on their retail packaging. Certification protects both buyer and supplier, often also resulting in better marketing opportunities because there is a specific demand for certified products.

Verification also ensures that certain agreed criteria and practices are met, but does not use a certificate to market the claim to the final consumer. Instead, company standards or internal supply chain standards rely on verification processes that are not as rigid and costly as a certification process that has to be conducted by appointed auditors. Instead, local third-party actors such as NGOs – or even second-party actors – may be asked to verify adherence to specific criteria. In addition, the timing between repeat verifications may be significantly less onerous than an annual re-certification process. In the coffee sector the most prominent example of a verification scheme is the 4C Association – the Common Code for the Coffee Community. 4C offers guidelines for better coffee farming that link up with GAP and GMP, while aiming at continuous improvement. The claims 4C makes are therefore not as specific as those of certification schemes and it refrains from using an on-pack (retail) logo.

Corporate guidelines or buying standards broadly pursue the same objectives and also set standards that aim at improving sustainability. Different from open certification and verification schemes, corporate guidelines or standards are company-specific. That is, retail credit can only be claimed by the buyer that initiated the standard. By far the best-known examples of such standards are the Starbucks C.A.F.E. Practices Program and the Nespresso AAA Sustainable Quality™ both of which, in addition to the usual sustainability issues, also deal with coffee quality.

For more on this see: *www.scscertified.com/retail/rss_starbucks.php* and *www.nespresso.com*.

The quest for sustainability does not end with coffee production. The end objective for the coffee industry is to extend sustainability throughout the entire supply chain. In this respect it is noteworthy that in March 2011 the well-known roaster Illycaffé (*www.illy.com*) in Trieste, Italy, was formally awarded the certification of Responsible Supply Chain Process by the certifiers DNV Business Assurance, a unit of Det Norske Veritas (*www.dnv.com*). The event marked the 20th anniversary of the introduction of the Ernesto Illy Brazil Award for Coffee Quality. The certification marks the organization's ability to provide a sustainable approach to processes and stakeholder relations all along the production chain, and specifically in the supply chain.

INTEGRATED FARMING SYSTEMS

Integrated farming systems, which are one such linked approach and might in the end perhaps be the most promising, focus on minimizing the use and negative effects of agro-chemicals. Basically this means that in all phases of production and processing one tries to minimize the impact on the environment. This approach does not exclude the use of agro-chemicals, but rather attempts to reduce their use to a minimum. Moreover, more attention is given to the reduction of energy consumption, packaging materials, and so on. Documentation and certification can be achieved within the framework of the ISO 14001 system, with the producer or processor documenting where and how in each step of the production and processing system they are reducing the environmental impact (see *www.iso.org*). See also chapter 12, Quality control, which covers the ISO 9001 standard used by some coffee estates and commercial coffee growers.

THE EUROPEAN RETAIL PROTOCOL FOR GOOD AGRICULTURAL PRACTICE

The European Retail Protocol for Good Agricultural Practice (Eurepgap: see *www.eurep.org*) was originally introduced by European retail chains for sourcing their fresh produce purchases.

Eurepgap forms the basis of this code. The protocol was established by over 30 leading European retailers working together in the European Retailers Produce Working Group (EUREP) to harmonize their agricultural standards for fruits and vegetables. The protocol is now an established part of their sourcing strategy and enjoys wide acceptance. It is consumer-driven and provides an assurance of basic good agricultural practices and social conditions.

Work was completed in 2004 to allow green coffee supplies to be brought under the same principles, more appropriately called a code of conduct or a code of practice. See *www.eurep.org/newdesign/index_html*.

CODES OF CONDUCT

Codes of conduct or codes of practice such as Eurepgap are a good example of how purchasing power translates into change at the producing end. The retailer demands certain assurances of the roaster, who in turn requires their suppliers to conform. This is not to say that all this has come about entirely spontaneously. The 1990s saw a number of food scares that have undoubtedly focused consumer attention on the how and what of the food and drink they consume. But even so, as in some other industries, one can probably mark the 1990s as a turning point for the policies of the larger roasters with respect to social responsibility. Pressure through lobbying and campaigns may have contributed to this attitude change.

An increasing number of individual companies and associations such as the Specialty Coffee Associations of America and of Europe are engaged in a variety of activities related to what may broadly be called codes of conduct or initiatives which address social accountability, i.e. the Starbucks Coffee Company C.A.F.E. Practices, the Nespresso AAA Sustainable Quality™ Program, and some of the initiatives undertaken by Coffee Kids Organization.

For further information on social accountability issues (SA8000 framework) see *www.sa-intl.org,* the website of Social Accountability International. See also *www.saiplatform.org*.

THE MAIN SUSTAINABILITY SCHEMES IN THE COFFEE SECTOR

FAIRTRADE LABEL ORGANIZATION

The Fairtrade initiative aims to enable organizations of smallholder producers of coffee (and cocoa, tea, honey, bananas, orange juice and sugar) to improve their conditions of trade, e.g. more equitable and more stable prices. Currently, Fairtrade efforts in coffee and other products like cocoa, honey and rice are concentrated on smallholder producers only. Conversely, in products like tea, sugar, bananas and other fruits the emphasis is also on estates (improving conditions for the labour force).

The Max Havelaar Foundation was established in the Netherlands in 1988, and since then another 25 countries have followed suit. In 1997 the different national institutions established an umbrella organization known as the Fairtrade Labelling Organizations International (FLO) with offices in Bonn, Germany.

Their objective is to provide the necessary instruments to assist and enable small growers to take their development into their own hands. This is achieved by incorporating in the producer price not only the cost of production, but also the cost of providing basic necessities such as running water, healthcare and education, and the cost of environmentally-friendly farming systems. Consumer support for this more equitable trading is then linked to participating growers through the Fairtrade labels on retail packaging in consuming countries. Simply put, the higher prices consumers pay for Fairtrade products reach the growers' organization through a combination of guaranteed minimum prices and premiums.

The FLO's role is to:

- Promote Fairtrade coffee in consumer markets (this is done by the national labelling initiatives);
- Identify and assist eligible groups of small growers to become inscribed in the FLO coffee producers' register, i.e. to obtain FLO certification;
- Verify adherence by all concerned to the Fairtrade principles, thus guaranteeing the label's integrity;
- Fairtrade is a certification programme that all smallholders' organizations and roasters who satisfy the criteria can join. But in the end success in the retail market depends on consumer support.

The Fairtrade labels aim to make the initiative and the growers behind it visible and therefore marketable on a sustained basis. The labels enable FLO and others to provide sustained publicity and support where it counts most – in the consuming countries – for example, by building a public image of quality, reliability and respect for socio-economic and environmental concerns that consumers recognize and appreciate.

Fairtrade does not aim to replace anyone in the traditional marketing cycle and works on the basis that there is a place for each, provided all accept the Fairtrade goal of selling the largest possible volume of smallholder coffee at a fair price: fair for growers and consumers alike. The labels provide a guarantee to the consumer of adherence to this principle while leaving production, purchasing, processing, marketing and distribution where it belongs, in the coffee industry.

Using Fairtrade labels

Coffee to be sold under a Fairtrade label must be purchased directly from groups certified by FLO. The purchase price must be set in accordance with Fairtrade conditions of which the following are the most significant:

- The purchase price should be the reference market price or the Fairtrade minimum price (whichever is higher), plus the Fairtrade premium, plus the organic differential where applicable.
- Reference market prices are those of the New York (arabica) and London (robusta) futures markets, as described below:
  - **Arabicas:** the New York 'C' market at NYSE: ICE shall be the basis plus or minus the prevailing differential for the relevant quality, FOB origin, net shipped weight. The price shall be established in United States dollars per pound.
  - **Robustas:** the London terminal market at NYSE Liffe shall be the basis plus or minus the prevailing differential for the relevant quality, basis FOB origin, net shipped weight. The price shall be established in United States dollars per metric ton.
- Fairtrade minimum prices are guaranteed minimum prices. They have been set as per the table below,

Table 3.1   Total worldwide sales of FLO-certified coffee, 2004–2010 (60 kg bags)

	Not comparable to new (green bean) data				New and comparable		Estimated
	2004	2005	2006	2007	2008	2009	2010
Europe	279 400	352 065	429 915	521 065	767 300	855 717	950,000
North America	123 385	210 685	430 600	504 565	578 567	636 917	700,000
Australia/New Zealand	n.a.	1 650	4 765	7 500	18 500	26 567	35,000
Japan	915	2 165	2 450	3 685	5 833	6 533	7,300
Others						483	600
Total	403 700	566 565	867 730	1 036 815	1 370 200	1 526 216	1 692 900

Source: FLO/Bonn and TransFair USA.

NB: Due to reporting differences, the data for 2008 and 2009 are green bean equivalent and comparable with other certifications. However, 2004-2007 are not. 2010 figures are estimates based on extrapolated growth rates. Calculations are based on FLO consumer country sales rather than coffee exported from origin with average distribution being roasted (97%) and soluble coffees (3%) – converted to GBE.

differentiated according to the type of the coffee. If the reference price is below the Fairtrade minimum price level, then the Fairtrade minimum price applies.

- These prices (either reference price or minimum price) shall then be increased by a fixed premium of 20 cts/lb (of which at least 5 cts for productivity and/or quality improvements).
- For certified organic coffee with officially recognized certification, that will be sold as such, a further organic differential of at least 30 cts/lb per pound of green coffee will be due.
- This calculation took effect on 1 April 2011.

Table 3.2   Fairtrade premiums

Type of coffee	Fairtrade minimum price regular or conventional cts/lb	Fairtrade premium cts/lb	Organic premium cts/lb
Washed arabica	1.40	20	30
Natural arabica	1.35	20	30
Washed robusta	1.05	20	30
Natural robusta	1.01	20	30

The Fairtrade price formula can effectively be summarized as (a) the Fairtrade minimum price or, if market prices are higher, the relevant futures market price (plus or minus the normal differential that would apply to that coffee) plus (b) the Fairtrade premium (listed in the above table) plus (c) any differential that might be applicable for organic coffee.

Minimum tonnage

Mention has already been made of the difficulty of shipping small lots that do not fill an entire container. FLO itself does not impose minimum volumes on grower organizations, but for practical reasons shipments must be in container size lots, meaning a minimum exportable production of about 18 tons.

In practice, small producer groups in some countries do manage to combine shipments so as to fill a container, for example by establishing an umbrella organization to coordinate this and other activities to achieve the necessary economies of scale. FLO's start-up requirements also serve a developmental objective. Taking into account membership and other characteristics, producer groups should at least have the potential to reach a volume of business that will achieve sustainable development impact.

Applying for FLO certification

FLO certification provides access to all FLO member organizations. See *www.fairtrade.net*. Participating organizations of small coffee growers must meet criteria consisting of requirements against which the producers

will actually be monitored. (Look for Generic Fairtrade Standards for Small Farmers' Organizations on the same website.) Criteria include:

- Minimum entry requirements, which all must meet when joining Fairtrade, or within a specified period;
- Progress requirements, i.e. show improvement over the longer term.

Application procedure

The applying organization directs its request to FLO International. The certification unit of FLO sends an application pack to the applicant containing general information on FLO and the Fairtrade market, FLO standards, detailed information on the initial certification process and the application form. If the first evaluation, based on the application form, is positive, the applying organization will be visited by an FLO inspector who will examine the organization on the basis of the minimum requirements of FLO. All relevant information is then presented to the FLO Certification Committee charged with the certification of new producer groups. Once approved the certification will be formalized by means of a signed producer agreement with FLO and a certificate indicating the duration of validity of the certification (to be renewed every two years).

UTZ CERTIFIED

UTZ CERTIFIED – Good inside (UTZ) was until early 2007 known as Utz Kapeh = 'good coffee' in a Maya language from Guatemala. UTZ is one of the largest sustainability programmes for responsible coffee production and sourcing in the world. Founded as a producer-industry initiative, UTZ is an independent organization. By setting a 'decency standard' for coffee production and helping growers to achieve it, UTZ recognizes and supports responsible producers.

The UTZ sustainability programme is centred on the UTZ CERTIFIED Code of Conduct. This Code is based on international production standards and contains a set of strict product specific criteria for socially and environmentally appropriate coffee growing practices and economically efficient farm management. Independent third-party auditors are engaged by UTZ CERTIFIED to check whether the producers meet the code requirements.

UTZ CERTIFIED believes that increasing sustainability should also reinforce the independent position of farmers, which is why farmers are trained in the professionalization of their agricultural practice and operational management to improve the quality, volume and value of their crops.

UTZ certification is available to any interested parties, roasters and growers alike. Interested growers (individuals or groups) receive technical assistance to help them implement the changes necessary to achieve certification.

A web-based system, the traceability system, monitors the UTZ CERTIFIED coffee throughout the coffee chain, allowing roasters and brands to always trace back where and how their coffee was produced. The UTZ certification provides roasters with the assurance that coffee they have purchased was grown and harvested in a responsible way. In 2011 UTZ CERTIFIED joined the 4C Association with the aim of increasing cooperation and aligning the two organizations' codes of conduct in order to create a mechanism or means of support to enable producers to step up from the 4C baseline standard to the UTZ CERTIFIED level.

Different from some other certification schemes, UTZ CERTIFIED offers a way forward towards a type of market-driven recognition that is open to all who can qualify, that is available to both mainstream and specialty coffee, and that precludes no one from participating. As a result, the agency is increasing its penetration and in 2010 over 121,000 metric tons of UTZ CERTIFIED coffee was sold by registered UTZ CERTIFIED companies in 42 countries. This represents an increase of almost 50% in the volume sold the previous year. By the end of 2010, a total of 162 individual producers (in groups – mostly smallholders) and 476 others (estates and others) had been certified by the agency in 23 origin countries.

Visit *www.utzcertified.org* for more information.

RAINFOREST ALLIANCE

In terms of environmental and sustainability requirements the Rainforest Alliance (RA) certification scheme is certainly amongst the more ambitious. Based on multi-crop farm management guidelines continuously developed since 1992 by the Sustainable Agriculture Network, or SAN, a coalition of independent NGOs, its work has attracted considerable support, including substantial grant funding from the United Nations Development Program.

Rainforest Alliance coffee production standards incorporate the ten Social and Environmental Principles of the Sustainable Agricultural Network:

- Social and Environmental Management System. Agriculture activities should be planned, monitored and evaluated, considering economic, social and environmental aspects and demonstrate compliance with the law and the certification standards. Planning and monitoring are essential to efficacious farm management, profitable production, crop quality and continual improvement.

- Ecosystem Conservation. Farmers promote the conservation and recuperation of ecosystems on and near the farm.

- Wildlife Conservation. Concrete and constant measures are taken to protect biodiversity, especially threatened and endangered species and their habitats.

- Water Conservation. All pollution and contamination must be controlled, and waterways must be protected with vegetative barriers.

- Fair Treatment and Good Conditions for Workers. Agriculture should improve the well being and standards of living for farmers, workers and their families.

- Occupational Health and Safety. Working conditions must be safe, and workers must be trained and provided with the appropriate equipment to carry out their activities.

- Community Relations. Farms must be "good neighbours" to nearby communities, and positive forces for economic and social development.

- Integrated Crop Management. Farmers must employ Integrated Pest Management techniques and strictly control the use of any agrochemicals to protect the health and safety of workers, communities and the environment.

- Soil Conservation. Erosion must be controlled, and soil health and fertility should be maintained and enriched where possible.

- Integrated Waste Management. Farmers must have a waste management programme to reduce, reuse and recycle whenever possible and properly manage all wastes.

SAN standards are based on an internationally recognized IPM model, which allows for some limited, strictly controlled use of agrochemicals. Farmers certified by the Rainforest Alliance do not use agrochemicals prohibited by the US Environmental Protection Agency and the European Union, nor do they use chemicals listed on the Pesticide Action Network's 'Dirty Dozen' list.

RA considers that by following the standards, farmers can reduce costs, conserve natural resources, control pollution, conserve wildlife habitat, ensure rights and benefits for workers, improve the quality of their harvest, and earn the Rainforest Alliance Certified seal of approval. The seal allows producers to distinguish their coffee. This is helpful in establishing long-term marketing relationships because the certification guarantees that the farm is managed according to the highest social and environmental standards. The certification process includes: (i) preliminary site visit by SAN technicians to determine the changes necessary to achieve certification (diagnostic); (ii) a comprehensive audit of farm operations (certification audit); (iii) based on an evaluation report, the certification committee determines whether the farm merits certification; and (iv) a contract that governs and monitors the use of the Rainforest Alliance Certified seal of approval, the handling of certified products and marketplace promotion.

In 2010, sales of RA-certified coffee were 114,884 metric tons green bean and are the culmination of phenomenal annual growth for the past eight years. RA-certified coffee is now produced on 44,648 coffee farms around the world

For more information on RA and SAN visit *www.rainforest-alliance.org*.

THE 4C ASSOCIATION – MAINSTREAMING SUSTAINABILITY IN COFFEE

Like other major food sectors, the mainstream coffee sector witnesses growing general concern over issues as food safety, import security, producer well-being, environmental and climate change related problems, and transparency, and how final consumers react to some of these topics. Even though mainstream consumers are not necessarily looking for labelled products, they are increasingly interested in social and environmental conditions generally. These consumers believe and expect that their suppliers are taking care to provide them with 'no worry products' that are both safe and of good quality. They certainly would not want to hear one day that they have been 'buying' child labour, forced evictions or the application of prohibited chemicals.

Inspired by these facts and developments such as the UN Millennium Goals, the 4C Association (*www.4C-coffeeassociation.org*) emerged as an initiative of important stakeholders across the entire coffee sector in 2003 and was officially established in December 2006. The 4C Association is an inclusive, membership driven organization of coffee farmers, trade and industry, and civil society. Members work jointly towards improving economic, social and environmental conditions in the coffee chain through the promotion of more sustainable and transparent practices for all who make a living in the coffee sector.

The main pillars of the 4C Association are a Code of Conduct, Rules of Participation for trade and industry, Support Services for coffee farmers, a Verification System and the participatory Governance Structure.

4C has three membership chambers: Producers, Trade and industry, and Civil society. Chamber members elect their representatives to the 4C Council, the Association's managing body. The council in its turn appoints a small Executive Board. This democratic arrangement ensures that the Association's decision-making organs are under the control of its members with guaranteed equal representation for all three categories. The Association is funded through membership fees and public contributions, including co-funding from government agencies. Membership fees are weighted according to financial means, thus differentiating significantly between small-scale producers and industry members such as coffee traders, roasters, soluble manufacturers or retailers with private label coffee.

4C's Common Code for the Coffee Community introduces baseline criteria for the sustainable production, processing and trading of green coffee and eliminates unacceptable practices. Through its global network, the 4C Association provides support services to coffee farmers, including training, access to tools and information. Many tools and support services are free of charge for coffee producers as they are funded in large parts from the membership fees from the trade and industry members and complemented by public contributions. In addition, 30% of the membership fees of industry and 50% to 70% of those of the intermediary buyers go directly to the 4C Support Services budget.

Through the continuous improvement concept of its Code Matrix and the Support Services, 4C helps farmers of all sizes, particularly also smallholders, and their business partners to access a baseline level of economic, environmental and social sustainability.

The 4C Standard is a pure business-to-business concept for the coffee supply chain, offering an entry level sustainability baseline for producers from which they might step up towards more demanding sustainability standards. Conceptualized as a business-to-business standard and not as a consumer label, the 4C Association is pre-competitive and does not provide a label to market 4C Compliant Coffee towards the final consumer on the coffee pack.

Instead, 4C industry members may communicate their commitment and membership using a membership statement on coffee packs. The membership statement does not refer to the quality or quantity of roasted coffee, but is a means for 4C industry members to emphasize their support of the 4C Sustainability Approach. Except on coffee packs, the logo of the 4C Association may be used widely in publications, websites, brochures etc.

4C Units are the suppliers of 4C Compliant Coffee. The 4C Association believes that sustainability is not in the hands of coffee farmers alone – all actors along the chain need to join forces to make sustainability happen. Therefore, 4C verification is performed at the 4C Unit level and a 4C Unit may be established at any stage of the coffee chain, from producer/producers' groups to roaster level. 4C Units have to be located in producing countries. The managing entity of the 4C Unit assumes responsibility and coordinates the implementation of 4C with its individual suppliers. This mechanism actually allows the 4C Association to also address and include the manifold unorganized smallholders who would otherwise not have access to the market for sustainable coffee. Everyone in the coffee market chain from producers to transporters, collectors and warehouses, millers and processors, traders and exporters, roasters, and retailers can register as a 4C Unit.

4C Verification is the backbone of credibility for the 4C system. In the 4C system, 4C Verification checks compliance against the baseline standard of 4C, consisting of 28 parameters that represent a mix of environmental, social and economic considerations. All defined 10 Unacceptable Practices must be excluded and at least a minimum level of compliance (called 'average yellow') is required within each dimension of sustainability to successfully pass verification. All 4C verification is conducted by independent third party verification or certification organizations that have successfully participated in 4C verifier training and are accredited to ISO/Guide 65.

4C and other standards are benchmarking that benefits the coffee industry. Being designed as a baseline standard for the mainstream sector, and therefore complementary to more demanding standards, the 4C Association aims at benchmarking with other standards in order to reduce the burden of multiple certification/verification for producers, while also directing its support services to those producers that are not certified. The first benchmarking was achieved with the Rainforest Alliance in mid-2008. The 4C Code of Conduct being a baseline standard, benchmarking with the Rainforest Alliance's Sustainable Agriculture Network (SAN) standard is non-reciprocal. This means that holders of the Rainforest Alliance Certificate may apply for a 4C License without additional costs or verification procedures, whereas 4C License holders need to step up to SAN standards in order to become Rainforest Alliance certified. Being 4C Compliant of course makes it easier for such growers to make the move upwards. As a result of the 2008 benchmarking exercise, 4C members holding Rainforest Alliance certification are now being offered an additional marketing window because they can sell any surplus production as 4C Compliant Coffee. As mentioned earlier, UTZ Certified began the process of benchmarking in 2011.

OTHER SUSTAINABILITY LABELS

Biodynamic coffee usually is high-quality arabica at high premiums with a low market share. A well-known example is coffee from the Finca Irlanda (Chiapas, Mexico) where organic cultivation began in the 1960s. Biodynamic products are organic and can be marketed as such, but they meet even higher production standards and represent a true niche market. For more see *www.demeter-usa.org*.

Especially in the United States and Canada, there is a market for so-called bird-friendly or shade grown coffee. Limited use of agro-chemicals is permitted and the emphasis is put on the conservation of shade trees on plantations in order to preserve bird life and biodiversity. Shade grown coffee is not the same as organic coffee, but there are specific standards and a certification system has been developed by the Smithsonian Migratory Bird Center, *www.nationalzoo.si.edu/ scbi/migratorybirds/coffee,* and other institutions and NGOs in Canada, the United States and Mexico. Shade grown represents a step along the way towards environmentally sustainable coffee. So far the market for such coffees is small and mostly limited to North America.

CERTIFICATION AND VERIFICATION

CERTIFICATION AND MARKETABILITY IN COFFEE

Over time certification has become an almost indispensable marketing tool for many agricultural products, particularly perishables such as fruit and vegetables. The flower label required on principle by many Western retail chains for imported fruit and vegetables is a good example.

However, these are products that are sold directly to the end-consumer, i.e. they are not transformed, and, as such,

the certification is used to ensure market access. This is because the label proves to the end-user that producers subscribe to good agricultural and management practices; protect the environment; practice safe pesticide use; and engage in resource protection generally. Thus, the product is accepted as both safe and environmentally friendly. For coffee the situation is rather different because coffee growers in the main provide green coffee to overseas roasters who in turn produce and retail the finished product. Therefore, in most instances the identity of the producing countries, let alone the individual producer, is not known to the end-user. Consequently there is much less consumer awareness of the production process and whether certification (or verification) by itself enhances a coffee's marketability, is therefore a pertinent question.

In the coffee industry, certification schemes also guarantee that specific rules and regulations of voluntary standards are met. On-pack labels then make this known to the end-user on the producer's behalf and, often, the end-user is expected to pay a premium to recompense the grower for this specific effort.

Verification similarly ensures that certain agreed criteria and practices are met, but does not use certificates or on-pack claims to market this to the end-user. Typically a mainstream market tool that offers market access rather than premia, verification is meant to improve efficiency, sustainability and profitability for growers on the one hand, whilst enabling buyers to make more informed decisions on the produce they purchase and process. Currently, the mainstream market accounts for between 85% and 90% of all green coffee exported from producing countries.

Over time, it may be expected that buyers of mainstream coffee will increasingly insist on certain guarantees as regards the manner in which the coffee they buy is produced, perhaps to the gradual exclusion of those producers unable or unwilling to provide them. Verification would appear to be the most likely tool for this, in many cases enhanced by certification for a particular type of niche market.

It should also be noted that the scope for premium priced coffee, purely based on quality, is in theory unlimited because it has direct and universal appeal to many more end-users. The market for quality or specialty (gourmet) coffee is increasing constantly, i.e. this market segment is demand driven and is showing strong growth.

However, the scope for premium prices based on certification rather than on quality is limited because of demand reasons. This is so because for many if not a majority of end-users the intrinsic quality of a product is of more importance than is certified compliance with a code of conduct or standard. Therefore, the potential for certified coffees that require to be sold at a premium mostly lies in niche markets. However, the supply of such coffees is not necessarily always demand driven and over time some may be subject to oversupply. While certification definitely adds to a coffee's image and may enhance its value, in the longer term certification by itself (so without the 'quality') is no guarantee for premium prices. But it can add to a coffee's marketability.

Table 3.3   Comparative overview of sustainability schemes for coffee

Aspect	Organic	Fairtrade	Rainforest Alliance*	UTZ CERTIFIED	Common Code 4C
Premium	No assured premium paid – it varies considerably from market to market (but 15 to 20 cts was paid in some countries in 2011, if double certified with Fairtrade then it gets an automatic 20 cts premium).	Fixed premium always assured (but overall level of demand not always in tandem with production).	No assured premium (but 5 to 8 cts range was common in 2011).	No assured premium paid (but 2 to 5 cts was common in 2011).	No assured premium (but may be paid in certain circumstances if seller/buyer so agree)
Yield and quality	Short-term impact on yields may be negative; possibly positive impact on quality.	Only indirect (and possibly positive) impact on yields and quality (through higher income, thus increased possibility of purchasing inputs and hiring labour).	Potentially negative yield impact; positive impact on quality.	Possibly positive but limited.	Possibly positive through improved farming and processing methods.
Labour inputs	Higher labour inputs.	Higher labour inputs linked to collective processes such as coordination, meetings etc.	Higher labour inputs.	Moderately higher labour inputs.	Moderately higher labour inputs.
Other income impacts	Possibility of selling other organic products from the farm; income diversification.	Possible indirect impact through wider trade networking offering possibility of selling other Fairtrade products.	Possibility of selling forest by-products and fruit.	Increasing visibility of UTZ may improve conditions of trade.	Over time improved conditions of trade may be possible.
Market access, networking	Access to well-established and reliable market.	Access to well-established, reliable market; technical assistance from Fairtrade importers.	Buyers and markets increasing steadily.	Number of buyers and markets increasing steadily.	Potentially easier access to large segment of the mainstream market.
Extension, credit	Possibly more effective extension from field staff supported by NGOs and some buyers, but limited support from public system.	Access to trade financing and traditional credit sources due to Fairtrade membership and improved financial position of cooperatives.	More effective agro-forestry extension from supportive NGOs, but limited support from public system.	Potentially better extension services from supportive NGOs and some buyers, but limited support from public extension services.	Potential support from 4C-support platform and participating buyers; limited support from public extension services.
Organizational capacity; community impact	Potential increase in mutual support among farmers to solve farming management problems.	Increased organizational capacity of participating farmers; access to training; better organizational ability to serve members; community projects.	Mutual support amongst farmers for forest management.	Strengthening organizational capabilities (if registration is done via farmer groups rather than as individuals).	Strengthening of organizational capabilities through potential assistance from 4C-support platform; access to training.
Environment	Potential adoption of new farming techniques to improve soil fertility as well as drought and erosion resilience.	Limited environmental benefits.	Improved bio-diversity and agro-ecological conditions; enhancement of soil fertility.	Limited environmental benefits through the gradual elimination of inappropriate farming and processing methods.	Limited environmental benefits through the gradual elimination of inappropriate farming and processing methods.
Risk, planning capabilities	Risk reduction through reduced external inputs; no mono-cropping; improved soil resilience; planning may improve.	Better planning for coffee production, personal and household needs; guaranteed price reduces risk.	Reduced pest management and social risk; planning may improve.	Potential for some reduced pest management and social risk; planning may improve.	Better planning and reduced risk through improved market access may be possible.

Source: Based on original work and further input from Daniele Giovannucci and Stefano Ponte; 4C table by Jan van Hilten.

* Also applies to most shade grown coffee.

For more information on these and other standards visit ITC's *www.standardsmap.org*.

SUSTAINABILITY AND GENDER

WOMEN'S EMPLOYMENT AND OWNERSHIP IN THE COFFEE SECTOR

Most if not all sustainability initiatives pay considerable attention to social and labour issues, but the status of women in the coffee sector is generally not singled out. The 2010 Stanford Social Innovation Review, *www.ssireview.org* found that only 1 out of the 10 initiatives it assessed listed gender governance as a requirement, four listed women's labour rights and three listed women's health and safety. The assumption may well be that general attention to labour rights and other social aspects in the coffee sector also takes care of this. But even so, this does not really do justice to the important role so many women actually play.

In 2008, ITC conducted a survey on the role of women in the coffee sector. Twenty-five persons, mainly women, in 15 coffee producing countries in Africa, Asia and Latin America, provided information. The survey showed considerable differences between individual countries with, for example, women doing little of the field and harvest work in Brazil (highly mechanized and often alternative jobs for women), but as much as 90% in some African countries (nearly all manual). Women play only a small role in in-country trading in most countries, whereas in Viet Nam this is around 50%. The data gathering was limited to 15 very different countries only, but at least made it possible to indicate a kind of 'typical' role of women in the sector.

Female ownership in the value chain in coffee producing countries is also variable, but generally modest at all levels. Ownership is difficult to describe for several reasons, for example, the distinction between ownership and user-rights is sometimes unclear as is co-ownership for married couples. The findings showed significant variations, but simplified one could say that women typically own around 15% of land, of traded products (coffee) and of companies related to coffee in coffee producing countries.

Table 3.4   Women's employment in the coffee sector

Women in the workforce in % of total	Variations low – high	'Typical'
Field work	10 – 90	70
Harvest	20 – 80	70
Trading in-country	5 – 50	10
Sorting	20 – 95	75
Export	0 – 40	10
Other (certifications, laboratories, etc.)	5 – 35	20

Table 3.5   Women's ownership in the coffee sector

Women's ownership in % of total (including co-ownership)	Variations low – high	'Typical'
Land used for coffee production – including user rights	5 – 70	20
Coffee – when harvested	2 – 70	15
Coffee – when traded domestically	1 – 70	10
Companies in the coffee sector (exporters, laboratories, certifiers, transportation, etc.)	1 – 30	10

WOMEN'S ASSOCIATIONS IN THE COFFEE SECTOR

Possibly the most opportune way to advance women and promote women's rights in the coffee sector is through women's associations where there is joint agreement on objectives, where issues and matters of particular interest to women can be discussed freely, and where there is an absence of peer pressure. Topics at the top of the agenda in the associations are typically (i) lack of access to land (linked to heritage legislation), (ii) lack of education and skills, (iii) lack of access to capital and options for savings, and (iv) the inability to locate good markets for coffee.

The potential of such associations is receiving increasing attention from donor organizations with an interest in gender issues and it is becoming more common to find specific gender components in coffee sector projects. In addition, the need to economically empower women in coffee is seen as a major opportunity by women who participate in associations.

Women's coffee associations were first initiated in the United States in 2002. The most prominent are today the following:

- International Women's Coffee Alliance, IWCA, *www. womenincoffee.org* coordinates information sharing and training of women. It has establishes so-called chapters in primarily Central America (Costa Rica, El Salvador, Guatemala and Nicaragua), the Caribbean (Dominican Republic) and South America (Colombia and Brazil (in formation)). New chapters were established in 2011 in Africa (Burundi, Kenya and Rwanda) where more are in preparation, including Ethiopia, Uganda and United Republic of Tanzania. Chapter members include women and men representing various segments of the coffee supply chain. They are legalized entities that have a voice in their countries and seek the support of national trade support institutions, corporations and not-for-profit organizations.

- Café Femenino Foundation, *www.coffeecan.org* and *www.cafefemeninofoundation.org,* commenced by assisting poor communities in Peru. It currently works in around 10 countries in Latin America and is now turning to Africa.

- The Coffee Quality Institute, CQI, *www.coffeeinstitute.org* offers a leadership programme with mentors (from the Unites States) and fellows primarily in Central America and South America. Availability depends on funding which, currently, is restricted.

A few countries have small national or in-country regional associations or women's groups in the coffee sector, for example in Mexico, Colombia, Peru, Kenya and India.

Worth mentioning here is also the valuable work done by Grounds for Health (GFH), *www.groundsforhealth.org*. GFH is a not-for-profit organization founded to provide healthcare services to women in coffee-growing communities. GFH offers cervical cancer screening and treatment in several Latin American countries and more recently in East Africa.

CHAPTER 4

CONTRACTS

CONTRACTS

INTRODUCTION TO CONTRACTS

International trade in coffee would not be possible without general agreement on the basic conditions of sale. Otherwise it would endlessly be necessary to repeat each and every contract stipulation for a proposed transaction, essentially very time consuming and open to mistakes. To avoid this the coffee trade has developed standard forms of contract of which the most frequently used are those issued by the European Coffee Federation (ECF – *www. ecf-coffee.org*) in the Netherlands and the Green Coffee Association (GCA – *www.greencoffeeassociation.org*) in the United States. Although many individual transaction details must be still agreed before a contract is concluded, the basic conditions of sale, unchanging conditions that apply time and time again, can be covered simply and easily by stipulating the applicable standard form of contract. Even so, an offer to sell (or a bid to buy) must stipulate the quality, quantity and price, the shipment period, the conditions of sale, the period during which the offer or bid is firm (valid), and so on.

WHEN THINGS GO WRONG

There will always be problems and mistakes, delays and even disasters, both avoidable and unavoidable. The most important rule is: Keep the buyer informed! If a problem is advised in time the buyer may be able to re-position the contract and resolve the problem. If buyers are not promptly informed it becomes impossible for them to protect themselves and, indirectly, often the exporter as well. If it is clear the quality is not quite what it ought to be, do not hope to get away with it – tell your buyer. If a shipment will be delayed, do not wait to announce this but tell the buyer immediately. Article 11(v) of the European Contract for Coffee (ECC) specifically requires that the buyer be kept informed without delay. If a claim is reasonable, settle it, promptly and efficiently. The buyer is not an enemy but a partner, and should be treated as such.

Arbitration (chapter 7) always dents reputations and usually spells the end of a business relationship. Correctly settled claims can help to cement relationships. Bear in mind that many buyers will not bother to lodge smaller claims or pursue them through to arbitration – their time is too expensive. Instead they will simply strike the name of the offending party off their list of acceptable counterparts, often without saying so.

MITIGATION OF LOSS

When loss is likely, both the seller and the buyer are required to mitigate the loss as much as possible: that is, they must keep the loss to a minimum. Regardless of who is liable to pay, both parties are responsible to keep the loss to a minimum. A good example is when documents are lost. Yes, it is the responsibility of the seller to trace and present them as soon as possible. Yet, the buyer cannot just let the coffee sit on the dock incurring late penalties (demurrage, container charges, etc.). The buyer is required to take all reasonable action necessary to keep the late charges to a minimum and when claiming damages has to prove both the reasonableness of the claim and that all possible action was taken to keep the loss to the unavoidable minimum.

VARIATIONS TO STANDARD FORMS OF CONTRACT

Commercial contracts can be and often are concluded with conditions other than those of the standard forms of contract, as long as these are well understood and are clearly set out in unambiguous language (leaving no room for differing interpretations). For example, one might agree to change the shipment quantity tolerance in Article 2 of the ECC from 3% to 5%. In this case the contract should then include a paragraph to the effect that 'Article 2 of ECC is amended for this contract by mutual agreement to read a tolerance of 5%'.

If a modification to an existing contract is agreed it should be confirmed in writing, preferably countersigned by both parties. Adding the words 'without prejudice to the original terms and conditions of the contract' ensures that the modification does not result in unintended or unforeseen change to the original contract. If a modification is not confirmed in writing then one of the parties could subsequently repudiate or dispute it. Human memory is fallible and there is nothing offensive in ensuring that all matters of record are on record.

The same applies to business under GCA contracts. Some North American roasters have small booklets containing their proprietary terms and conditions, which all suppliers must sign on to before they can be approved vendors. In the GCA XML (electronic) contract there is a huge field (350 characters) of entitled exceptions.

COMMERCIAL OR 'FRONT OFFICE' ASPECTS

SPECIFYING 'QUALITY': ON DESCRIPTION

Quality can be specified in any one of a number of ways.

On description: The quality will usually correspond to a known set of parameters relating to country of origin, green appearance and liquor quality. Most of the descriptive parameters are open to varying interpretations. For example, in the description 'Country XYZ arabica grade one, fair average quality, crop 2012, even roast, clean cup', the only real specifics are that the coffee must be of the 2012 crop in country XYZ and that the bean size and defect count should correspond to what country XYZ stipulates for grade one arabica.

Fair average quality (FAQ): This essentially means the coffee will be representative of the average quality of the crop, but there is no defined standard for this.

Even roast: This implies that the roasted coffee will not contain too many pales (yellow beans) and will be of reasonably even appearance.

Clean cup: This indicates that the liquor should not present any unclean taste or off-flavour, but otherwise says nothing about the cup quality. Nevertheless, buyers know roughly what the cup quality ought to be and, for example, if the cup were to be completely flat or lifeless, they would argue that this is not consistent with fair average quality for country XYZ.

The trade in robusta is largely based on descriptions. These convey the quality being sold fairly well because the liquor quality of robusta does not normally fluctuate as widely as that of arabica. Descriptions greatly facilitate the trade in coffee, but it should never be forgotten that the roaster (the end-user) will always consider the liquor quality when assessing the overall quality of a coffee. The quality represented by FAQ will vary from season to season. 'FAQ of the season' means the quality must be comparable to the average quality shipped during that crop year; arbitrators will judge any claims on that basis. If quality tends to vary widely within a country and a season, the seller may go further and stipulate FAQ of the season at the time and place of shipment.

SPECIFYING 'QUALITY': ON SAMPLE BASIS

Because descriptions provide a minimum of detail concerning quality they are seldom if ever used for the trade in high quality coffee. In addition, buyers know that different sellers have their own interpretation of FAQ and so prefer to deal with shippers whose interpretation is acceptable to them. However, traders wishing to short-sell XYZ arabica grade one FAQ forward does not necessarily know in advance which shipper or exporter they will later buy from.

In this case the term 'first class shipper' can be added to the description, thereby implying that a reputable exporter will ship the coffee. But the term first class is open to interpretation as well and so the contract may instead stipulate the names of exporters of whom the buyer approves, one of whom must eventually ship the coffee. Large roasters are quite flexible about the origin of standard or commercial grade coffee, and to widen their purchasing options often leave the seller, often a trade house, free to deliver an agreed quality from one of a number of specified origins and shippers.

Subject to approval of sample (SAS): This is one way to eliminate most of the quality risk inherent in buying unseen coffee from unknown shippers, as buyers are not obliged to accept any shipment that they have not first approved. SAS obliges the exporter to provide an approval sample before shipment. There are three generally recognized possibilities:

- SAS, no approval no sale. If the sample is not approved the contract is automatically cancelled.

- SAS, repeat basis. If the first sample is rejected, a second or even a third sample may be sent. Sometimes the contract will mention how many subsequent samples can be submitted. This option provides maximum quality security without immediately jeopardizing the contract, and works well in long-standing relationships.

- SAS, two or three samples for buyer's choice. When the buyer's quality requirements are very specific, and in order to save time, multiple samples may be submitted at the same time. To avoid confusion such contracts should stipulate whether repeat samples may be sent or whether no approval means no sale.

Theoretically, an exporter who feels aggrieved by what seems to be an unreasonable (intentional) rejection and cancellation could declare a dispute and proceed to arbitration (chapter 7). However, the chance of success would be extremely slim if not non-existent, not least because an arbitration panel might rule it has no jurisdiction over what was in essence a purely conditional contract that never became binding (because the buyer did not approve a sample). Exporters should therefore be fairly selective when agreeing to sell subject to approval of sample.

Stock-lot sample: Selling on stock-lot sample avoids potential approval problems. The sample represents a parcel that is already in stock so there should be no discrepancy between the sample and the shipment, including the screen size (even if the screen size was not stipulated). Day-to-day business would become too cumbersome if one insisted on stock-lot samples for all deals, but for newly established exporters or for those wishing to break into a niche market or to trade top quality coffees, stock-lots usually are the best route.

Once a satisfactory delivery has been made, an exporter may wish to sell a similar quality again. Rather than send new samples, the exporter may offer 'quality equal to stock-lot X'; this guarantees that the coffee is of comparable quality, suitable for the same end-use as the original purchase. The words 'equal to' must be used because the sample was not drawn from the new lot of coffee. If the exporter feels that the quality is very similar, but that a little latitude is needed as to the coffees bean size or green appearance, they may say 'quality about equal to stock-lot X'. Usually, such business is only between parties in a long-standing relationship who know each other well.

Type: Once a few transactions have been satisfactorily concluded, buyer and seller may decide to make the quality in question into a type. Both parties are now confident that the quality will be respected and business can proceed without samples (although some roasters will still insist on pre-shipment samples). Usually the quality of a type (like a recipe) is kept confidential between shipper and buyer. Top or exemplary coffees are mostly sold on sample or type basis, whereas medium and standard qualities are more often traded on description.

THE SHIPPING PERIOD

The most often-encountered trade terminology includes:

- **Date of shipment:** the 'on board' or 'shipped' date of the bill of lading. Contracts should always stipulate from which port(s) shipment is to be made. For FCA contracts the date of delivery is the date of the carrier's receipt.
- **Spot goods:** have already arrived overseas, e.g. available ex warehouse Hamburg.
- **Afloat:** coffee that is en route, i.e. on board a vessel that has sailed but has not yet arrived.
- **Named vessel (or substitute):** shipment must be made on a specified vessel. Adding 'or substitute' ensures that shipment can also be made if the shipping line cancels the named vessel or replaces it with another. Many contracts simply stipulate the shipping line that shall carry the goods.
- **Immediate shipment:** shipment within 15 calendar days counted from the date of contract.
- **Prompt shipment:** shipment within 30 calendar days counted from the date of contract.
- **Shipment February (or any other month):** shipment is to be made on any day of that month (single month); 'February/March seller's option' means shipment will be made on any day within those two months (double month).

The shorter the shipping period, the shorter the roaster's exposure to market fluctuations and the more precise physical and financial planning can be. Buyers generally look for less exposure, and double months are not popular. For example, shipment March/April means that shipment can be made at any time during a 61-day period, which does not go well with the increasingly prevalent just-in-time (JIT) philosophy (see chapter 5). Sellers in landlocked countries or those with inefficient shipping connections are often forced to sell on double months. By contrast, countries as Brazil and Colombia can guarantee coffee to be available in Europe within 21 days from the date of sale (10 days or so for the United States). Inability to offer precise shipping options

(named vessel, immediate or prompt shipment, first half of a month) is a marketing handicap.

DELIVERY COMMITMENT

Offers and contracts must stipulate the point at which the exporter will have fulfilled its commitment to deliver, that is, the point at which risk and responsibility are transferred to the buyer.

Free on board (FOB): the goods will be loaded at the seller's expense onto a vessel at the location stipulated in the contract, e.g. FOB Santos. The seller's responsibilities and risk end when the goods cross the ships rail, and from then on the buyer bears all charges and risk. Under the ECC contract the price to seller is expressed as FOB, but the buyer is currently responsible for insuring the goods from the last place of storage ahead of loading on board, e.g. the port warehouse, which is not the case under the GCA FOB contract. Most coffee contracts stipulate the price to the sellers in terms as FOB, but the ECC can be described as an ill-defined cost and freight contract. The use of FCA contracts seems to be on the increase.

Free carrier (FCA): in landlocked countries the sale is often FCA, with buyers themselves arranging transport to the nearest ocean port and onward carriage by sea. International transporters, usually linked with shipping lines, often offer one-stop services, taking the goods in hand in Kampala, Uganda, and delivering them to Hamburg, Germany, for instance, using a single document known as a combined bill of lading covering both inland and maritime transportation. Risk of loss is transferred when the coffee is delivered to the freight carrier at the place of embarkation. All freight charges, including loading onto an ocean vessel, railcar, trailer or truck (combined bill of lading), are payable by the buyer. The exporter provides the customs clearance documentation. Unless special arrangements have been made with the carrier, such shipments must be re-stuffed at the port of shipment if an LCL (less than container load) bill of lading is required.

Cost and freight (CFR, previously called C&F): the seller is responsible for paying costs and freight (but not insurance) to the agreed destination.

Cost, insurance, freight (CIF): the seller is also responsible for taking out and paying the marine insurance up to the agreed point of discharge. Very rarely used nowadays.

In all cases it is the seller's responsibility to deliver the shipping documents to the buyer. When a parcel is loaded on board ship, a mate's receipt is issued to the ship's agent. This is the legal basis for the bill of lading, which should be prepared and issued immediately. Shippers are entitled to the bill of lading as soon as the goods have been loaded. Some agents release them only once a vessel has sailed, but this is incorrect and causes unnecessary cost.

The International Chamber of Commerce's *Guide to Incoterms® 2010* contains a more detailed description of these and other shipping terms. However, the standard contracts used in the coffee trade all state or imply that also under an FOB sale the seller is responsible for booking freight space, arranging shipment and producing a full set of shipping documents. These stipulations in standard coffee contracts differ from, and supersede, the Incoterms®' definition of FOB.

OCEAN FREIGHT

Most coffee contracts are effectively FOB – in that the receivers pay the freight. Receivers prefer this because they can negotiate rates of freight that individual exporters or producing countries may be unable to obtain. For this reason, bills of lading do not always indicate the freight charge, or simply state 'freight as per agreement'.

As they are liable to pay the freight, receivers consider that they should also negotiate the rates (and argue, indirectly, that they are in fact better placed to do so). This may be so, but whenever the freight from a particular port increases buyers adjust their cost calculation for the origin in question as they calculate the cost of all coffee on the basis landed port or roasting plant of destination. If the freight rate from a particular country increases, the prices bid for coffee from that origin will eventually compensate for this – if freights from comparable origins have not also risen. This is because the market compares like with like, that is, the landed cost. Ultimately therefore it is the producers who pay the freight charges. However, without the current arrangements some freight rates would likely be higher. See also chapter 5, Logistics.

Terminal handling charges (THC): are an important part of container transport costs and can vary considerably between shipping lines, sometimes to the point where an apparently attractive rate of freight is in fact not attractive at all. Shippers should keep themselves informed of the THC raised directly or indirectly by individual shipping lines at the ports they load from as they can face unexpected costs if buyers specify a line whose freight is low (buyers' advantage) but whose THC are high (shippers' disadvantage).

WEIGHTS

Most standard forms of contract stipulate that natural loss in weight exceeding a certain percentage is to be refunded by the sellers. This is known as the weight franchise. Coffee is hygroscopic, which means that it attracts or loses moisture depending on climatic conditions. It may therefore lose a little weight during storage and transport. To counter this weight loss, a number of exporters have traditionally packed a little more per bag than they invoice. This helps to ensure that arrival weights are as close to the agreed shipping weight as possible. Buyers know from experience what losses in weight to expect from most origins and take this into account when calculating the cost landed destination or roasting

plant. However, shipping in bulk has greatly reduced weight loss and as a result such a franchise has been reduced to a minimum (0.5% under both the ECC and the GCA contracts).

Net shipped weights: the weights established at the time of shipment are final, subject to the stipulations of the underlying standard form of contract. Under an FCA contract the parties can also agree that the net delivered weight be final together with the procedures and conditions that shall apply.

Net delivered weights or net landed weights: the goods will be reweighed upon arrival and final payment will be made on the basis of the weights then established.

If buyers are suspicious about the accuracy of the shipping weights they may require an independent weigher to supervise the weighing. Sellers may stipulate the same when selling basis net delivered weights or when weights are disputed and reweighing is ordered.

PAYMENT: CONDITIONS

Usually, and advisedly so, the conditions of payment will have been agreed in advance and will therefore already be known to both parties, especially if the business relationship has existed for some time. But when offering to a new buyer the payment conditions must be specified.

Letters of credit – Uniform Customs and Practice. In the context of this guide a letter of credit is a contract between a bank and a seller whereby the bank undertakes to pay the seller an agreed sum against delivery of an agreed set of shipping documents.

Terms and conditions governing letters of credit are laid down in what is known as the Uniform Custom and Practice for Documentary Credits, issued by the International Chamber of Commerce. The most recent version, the UCP 600 became effective from 1 July 2007. Because of its importance, UCP is discussed at the end of this chapter.

Payment against letter of credit (L/C) requires the buyer to establish an L/C before shipment is effected. A letter of credit is an undertaking from the buyer's bank to the exporter's bank that payment will be made against certain documents such as the invoice, certificate of origin, weight note, certificate of quality and bill of lading (for sea transport) or waybill (for road or rail transport). The exporter should check that the documents specified in the letter of credit are obtainable. Sometimes buyers require verification of documents by an embassy or consulate not located in the exporter's country, or they may include documents the exporter is not contractually required to provide.

The timing of letters of credit is very important. The L/C must be available for the exporter's use from day one of the agreed shipping period, and it must remain valid for negotiation for 21 calendar days after the last date that shipment is permitted to be made. Watch the timing very carefully: once the expiry date has passed, the letter of credit is only as good as the buyer's willingness to extend it.

If the terms and conditions of an L/C are not met, the exporter's bank will not pay the exporter until the buyer has confirmed that all is in order. This may involve sending the documents abroad without payment. If at that stage the buyer refuses to make payment, the exporter may be left with an unpaid shipment in some foreign port. The importance of conforming to all the conditions in a letter of credit cannot be stressed enough. Exporters should always consult their bankers before they assume that a letter of credit is acceptable.

An ordinary (i.e. revocable) or unconfirmed letter of credit is nothing more than an uncertain promise to pay if certain documentation is submitted. However, the UCP 600 have moved away from revocable credits, i.e. with effect from 1 July 2007 all credits became by default irrevocable.

An **irrevocable letter of credit** cannot be cancelled once established. The exporter can be certain that funds will be available if valid documents are presented. Even so, the exporter's bank may pay the exporter only when it has received the funds from the bank that established the letter of credit. This can create problems if, for example, the buyer argues that the documents are not correct or the buyer's bank is slow in making payment.

Under a **confirmed and irrevocable letter of credit** the exporter's bank confirms that payment will be effected upon the timely presentation of valid documents without reference to the establishing bank. By adding its confirmation, the exporter's bank therefore guarantees payment. If the negotiating bank discovers a minor discrepancy in the documents, such as a spelling error, it may still negotiate them providing the exporter signs a guarantee that in case of refusal by the buyer, the exporter will refund the payment received until the matter is settled.

Whenever exporters feel that letters of credit are required, they should insist that they are confirmed and irrevocable. Even then, extreme care must always be taken to ensure that all details are respected, even to the spelling of words and shipping marks.

ALTERNATIVE PAYMENT METHODS

Payment net cash against documents (NCAD or CAD) on first presentation. The buyer is expected to make payment when the documents are first presented. Exporters will agree to this method of payment if they know their buyers well and have confidence in their financial strength and integrity. An exporter can submit the documents through the intermediary of its own bank, which then asks a correspondent bank abroad to present them to the buyer, collect the payment and remit the funds, less all collection costs, to the instructing bank for the account of the exporter. (This includes the [reasonable] charges raised by the buyer's bank because that bank is now acting on the instructions of the seller's bank and, therefore, the seller.) See ECC Article

19(d), European Free Carrier Contract for Coffee (EFCACC) 18(c) and the relevant section in the GCA contract.

In this way, the documents remain within the banking system until payment has been received, thus ensuring that the exporter does not lose control of the goods. If the exporter is in need of prompt payment it can ask their own bank to advance them all or part of the invoice value. This is known as negotiation of documents. The exporter remains responsible for the transaction – if the buyer does not pay, the exporter's bank will demand its money back.

Documents in trust. Assuming the exporter's bank does not object, documents may also be sent direct to the buyer with the request to make payment upon receipt of the documents. This is known as sending documents in trust. As the term implies, the decision to do this depends entirely on the trust the two parties place in each other.

Payment net cash against documents upon arrival: payment is due when the goods arrive at the port of destination. When selling on this basis an exporter should always stipulate that payment must be made after expiry of a certain period, whether the goods have arrived or not. Otherwise there will clearly be problems if for some reason the goods arrive six months late or do not arrive at all because the vessel has been lost. Contracts should therefore *always* stipulate 'payment net cash against shipping documents upon arrival of the goods at [destination] but not later than 30 [or 60] days after date of bill of lading'.

PAYMENT: CREDIT POLICY

Exporters must decide for themselves which payment conditions to accept. They must assess the financial status of their buyers and act accordingly. Some information can be obtained from bank references that indicate a client's creditworthiness. Although such reports are useful, they cannot provide all the desired information nor do they place any responsibility on the bank that issues them. Exporters using borrowed working capital are usually subject to stringent conditions concerning the buyers they can sell to, and on what payment conditions.

When entering into contracts and deciding on payment terms, sellers should investigate the identity of their buyers. International trading groups often work through foreign and local subsidiaries whose commitments are not necessarily guaranteed by the parent firm, even though they may trade under the same or similar names. When in doubt a seller can demand a guarantee from the parent firm that it accepts responsibility for the contracts with, or documents handed to, a given subsidiary.

In some countries the monetary authorities dictate payment policy for exports, for instance by insisting that all exports must be covered by letters of credit to avoid possible loss of foreign exchange. This kind of blanket regulation results in some of the world's largest corporations with impeccable credentials being asked to establish L/Cs. Many buyers simply refuse to establish letters of credit, and those that do establish them calculate the cost and inconvenience involved. Ultimately it is the grower who pays for such bureaucratic attitudes.

SCOPE AND VALIDITY OF AN OFFER

The scope and validity of an offer (or bid) must be specified – when does acceptance constitute a firm commitment for both parties?

An exporter wishing only to publicize a potential availability at an approximate price uses terminology such as price idea or we offer/quote subject to availability or subject unsold. To the buyer this suggests there is a good chance of obtaining the coffee in question if the indicated price is agreed to. Although the exporter is not bound to sell, the buyer has some reason to be annoyed if the exporter refuses to do so for no obvious reason (e.g. was simply fishing for price information).

A firm offer, however, does commit the seller if the buyer accepts the offer within a reasonable time. 'Reasonable' is open to interpretation, so sellers must stipulate a time after which the offer lapses. The same applies to bids from buyers: these too must be specific. 'Subject to immediate reply' says that the reply should be immediate, but even 'immediate' is not precise. It is always better to say, for example, 'subject to reply here by 3 p.m. our time'. The choice of time limit depends on the situation of the exporter and the type of buyer to whom the offer is addressed. An exporter who is keen to sell may wish to try various markets at the same time. If they have only limited stocks of the coffee in question they cannot make multiple firm offers and will instead offer subject to availability or subject unsold. Alternatively, they can make firm offers for short periods to individual buyers by telephone or, increasingly, by e-mail. Conversely, they can give a buyer or, more probably, an agent an entire day to work an offer, but the exact time at which the offer expires should always be stated.

Modern communications offer almost instantaneous exchanges, especially through e-mail and other electronic means, enabling exporters to contact many potential buyers within short periods of time. It is not only the face of trade that is changing, but also the methodology and terminology. (See chapter 6, E-commerce and supply chain management.) But what will not change is that acceptance, verbal or otherwise, within the time limit of a firm offer or bid constitutes a firm and binding contract. Disputes can be submitted to arbitration, but the best approach is to ensure that the wording of offers or bids is clear and precise.

Example: 'We offer firm for reply here today by 5 p.m. our time 1,000 bags XYZ arabica grade one as per sample 101 at 170 cts/lb, FOB [port], NSW (net shipping weight), shipment November/December 2012 our option, payment NCAD first presentation'. This assumes that the applicable standard form of contract has previously been agreed by the parties; for a new buyer the applicable standard contract should therefore be mentioned as well.

Counter offers: if a buyer counter bids a lower price against a firm offer this automatically releases the seller. The offer is no longer binding, because the buyer has rejected it by counter offering. If the seller rejects the counter offer the buyer cannot subsequently revert to the original offer: when they countered, that firm offer lapsed unless of course the seller agrees to reinstate it.

USING INTERMEDIARIES – WHO IS WHO

Agents. Modern communications, especially e-mail, permit regular contact with many more clients than was the case just 10 years ago and the traditional agency function is increasingly making way for direct trade. Even so, it is not always feasible to deal directly with individual buyers in more than just a few markets, especially when time differences come into play, and many exporters still use agents.

A local agent is on the spot, speaks the language, knows the buyers and usually can discuss more than just the one origin most exporters represent. This makes an agent an interesting conversation partner who is more likely to get a buyer's attention. And for exporters, agents provide a two-way information flow because they know local conditions and often gain insight into the activities of competitors.

Agency agreements must make it clear what each party is permitted and expected to do. If an agent is given exclusivity in a given market (sole agency) then the exporter can demand that the agent does not market also for any of the exporter's direct competitors. Larger agency firms sometimes represent a stable of exporters, including some from the same origin, and smaller exporters may have to accept this because they cannot generate sufficient business to make a sole agency worthwhile for the agent. Such firms that do not work under an actual agency contract really function more as preferred sales channels than as true agents.

Brokers work within a given geographical area, bringing local buyers and sellers together. Like agents they declare the name of both the buyer and the seller, and receive a commission but do not represent a party. **Traders** buy or sell in their own name and for their own account. Agents or brokers who do not declare the buyer's name operate as traders because they 'take the coffee over their own name'.

Importers and **traders.** Growing interest in niche products and markets, accompanied by the reappearance of small roasters (e.g. in the United States), has revitalized many importers that are once again increasingly fulfilling the traditional function of sourcing specific types of coffee (specialty, organic, but also mainstream qualities) in producing countries and bringing these to market. Today, many importers represent single estates and individual exporters under agreements where, in exchange for exclusivity of supply, they undertake to stock and promote particular types of coffee. This potentially attractive alternative to the commission agency option mentioned above is discussed further in chapter 3. Their ability to carry stocks is of great importance, as it also enables less widely traded coffees to be immediately available in the main import markets. Larger, more vertically integrated trade houses usually handle more easily traded coffees, standard qualities that are relatively widely bought and sold. Some of the very large houses at times almost operate as market makers in that their pricing becomes a reference point, even for origin, as shown below.

First and second hand. Coffee sold direct from origin is 'first hand' (there were no intermediate holders). If the foreign buyer then re-offers that same coffee for sale, the market will know it as 'second hand'. But international traders also offer certain coffees for sale independent of origin: in so doing they are going short in the expectation of buying in later at a profit. To achieve such sales they may actually compete with origin by quoting lower prices than the producers themselves. Market reports then refer to 'second hand offers' or simply the 'second hand'. Traders can buy and sell matching contracts many times, causing a single shipment to pass through a number of hands before reaching the end-user, a roaster. Such interlinked contracts are known as 'string contracts'.

DOCUMENTATION OR 'BACK OFFICE' ASPECTS

INTRODUCTION TO DOCUMENTATION

International coffee transactions are executed by transfer of title rather than by the physical handing over of coffee. Title to goods shipped under contract by sea from one country to another is represented by the bill of lading, accompanied by a set of additional documents, together known as the shipping documents. The document of title for goods already stored in the port or place of delivery under a spot contract can be a warehouse receipt or storage warrant issued by a recognized public warehouseman. The only difference between the traditional chain of paper documents and electronic documentation is that the paper is largely eliminated. This is why electronic documentation is sometimes also called paperless trading. Using electronic documentation does not change the contractual responsibility of the seller or the buyer. The only differences are in how and when documents are issued, and how and when they are made available to the buyer. However, as yet electronic bills of lading are not widely used in the coffee trade.

Shipping documents must always comply in all respects with the conditions of the contract between the parties. If they do not, a seller may not be paid on time, or, in extreme circumstances, may lose the money altogether. The shipping documents must therefore show or state that (i) they represent the contracted and shipped coffee, (ii) a known series of shipping rules has been complied with, and (iii) they conform in all respects to the sales contract between the parties and to the standard form of contract on which that sales contract is based. Shipping documents must also be presented on time. Nothing is more annoying than late documents.

LETTERS OF CREDIT

Where payment against a letter of credit is stipulated the seller should obtain full details of the buyer's letter of credit as soon as possible. This is to ensure that the required documentation is in fact obtainable, that there will be sufficient time to obtain such documentation, and that there are suitable shipping opportunities to the named port of destination within the stipulated period of shipment. The European Contracts for Coffee only require a full and complete letter of credit to be available for use from the first day of the contractual period for shipment, even though the letter of credit may well contain stipulations on what must be done before loading. Therefore, it may be wise to provide specifically in the contract for earlier receipt of the full and complete letter of credit. Sellers should also ensure that the letter of credit remains valid for the negotiation of documents for at least 21 days after the date of shipment. See also chapter 10.

Both ECF and GCA stipulate this. If the length of validity is not carefully checked one could fulfil all the L/C conditions only to find it has lapsed.

Buyers calculate all costs (from FOB through to delivery at final destination) to arrive at the final cost 'price landed roasting plant', taking into account any extra costs. For example, an origin that habitually delivers documents late (i.e. after the vessel has arrived) is penalized as the buyer will provide for this eventuality in the calculation to 'landed plant'. In fact the importer actually saves money by not having to finance the goods for the expected period of time, but should the goods arrive before the documents then serious trouble will arise. If a letter of credit is demanded, the bid price will be lowered correspondingly to cover the costs. Such a bid would also be lower than that for similar coffees from other origins that do not require a letter of credit.

DESTINATIONS, SHIPMENT AND SHIPPING ADVICE

If the port of destination is not known it is not easy for the seller to organize shipment. For forward shipment or FCA contracts the ECC currently stipulates that the port of shipment must be declared by the 14th calendar day prior to the first day of the contractual shipping period (GCA stipulates 15 days' notice). Otherwise it might not be possible to complete the processes required for shipment within the agreed period. See also 'Port of destination' for more on how the GCA approaches this particular aspect. For immediate and prompt shipment or FCA contracts the destination must be declared at the latest on the first calendar day following the date of sale (and at the time of contract by GCA).

Shipment must be made during a vessel's last call at the agreed port of loading during that particular voyage. This rule is intended to exclude vessels that trade up and down the coast of a country with several ocean ports until enough cargo has been accumulated to make the main journey more profitable.

The coffee must be shipped on a port to port or a combined transport bill of lading issued by a shipping line which, using one or more vessels, will carry the goods throughout the voyage without further intervention by seller or buyer. The line issues a bill of lading at the port of origin to cover the entire voyage, enabling the buyer to see the details of shipment on the first vessel and to claim the coffee at final destination from a subsequent vessel. See also chapter 5, Logistics.

Transshipment: the first vessel discharges at an intermediate port and the goods are reloaded onto another vessel to the final destination. This is increasingly frequent as shipping companies rationalize operations and container vessels become larger. In particular, the use of containers has encouraged the development of shipping hubs: larger or more central ports that are fed containers from outlying ports by smaller or feeder vessels for loading onto large container vessels.

Shipping advice: as soon as the required information is available, the seller must advise certain specific details of the shipment. However, note that under the ECF's FCA contract sellers have just two calendar days to transmit advice of delivery.

For a shipment on terms other than CIF (which the seller insures), the shipping advice enables the buyer to insure the shipment and either to make the necessary arrangements to receive it at the port of destination or (where the bill of lading allows such a choice) to declare an optional port of destination in time for the shipping company to arrange discharge there. A series of time limits in ECC are designed to ensure that these objectives are met, and to give the buyer the freedom to procure a replacement parcel elsewhere if no shipment is forthcoming.

The details to be included in the advice of shipment or delivery are listed in the ECF contracts. The buyer is entitled to receive such advice, or an advice of delayed shipment/ delivery, or an advice of *force majeure*. Failure to receive an advice theoretically entitles the buyer to take the drastic step of cancelling the contract and claiming recompense for any loss suffered.

More stringent security measures at ports of entry in both the United States and the European Union require shippers to provide more detailed shipping advices. For example, GCA states that for FCA, FOB, CIF, CFR or EDK shipment contracts the shipping advice must include all U.S. Food and Drug Administration (FDA) required information.

DELAYED SHIPMENTS

The seller must advise the buyer of delayed shipment as soon as, for example, they become aware that a vessel may not load within the contracted period due to problems connected with the operations of the vessel itself such as a delay on the inbound voyage. Sellers must also show, using independent documentary proof, that a late shipment is not their fault.

If a problem of a much wider scope and of a more serious nature arises that prevents the seller, as well as other shippers, from shipping within the contracted period then, in addition to sending the notification of delayed shipment immediately this becomes evident, under certain circumstances the seller may be able to claim *force majeure*. Under ECF contracts the effect of both an advice of delayed shipment (or delivery) and an advice of *force majeure* is initially to extend the period allowed for shipment. Cancellation of the contract follows if the problem continues after that period (although cancellation would be rather unusual). However, GCA does not specify any extension and explicitly excludes events taking place before arrival of the goods at port of shipment.

Experienced exporters know that quick and frank admission of shipping problems usually helps them to reach an amicable settlement with their buyers. Failure to ship is bad enough, but failure to keep buyers informed is even worse as it prevents them from making alternative arrangements in time.

THE BILL OF LADING

The bill of lading usually contains:

- The name of the seller at origin (the shipper); the name of the buyer (the consignee); and, specified by the buyer, the name of the party to whom delivery is to be made and who is to be notified of the arrival of the shipment (the notify address);

- The bill of lading's unique number, the name of the vessel, the port of loading, the destination, and the number of originals that have been issued;

- Details of the cargo and whether shipped LCL/LCL or FCL/FCL, together with the container and seal numbers, where shipment is in containers;

- A statement that the coffee is on board or shipped, i.e. not simply received by the shipping company for shipment, and that there is no record of damage to the coffee (a clean bill of lading), and the date of onboard shipment.

A 'received for shipment' LCL bill of lading may be acceptable if this has previously been agreed by the buyer.

Bills of lading are issued in sets of identical originals, normally two or three, with a variable number of non-negotiable copies for record purposes only. Each original can be used independently to claim the coffee shipped, although not everyone holding an original bill of lading will automatically be handed the goods by the shipping company at destination. Who is allowed to claim the goods depends on how the bills are made out.

TITLE TO AND ENDORSEMENT OF A BILL OF LADING

When bills of lading are made out or endorsed to a named consignee, then only that consignee can take delivery of the shipment. A bill of lading made out to a named consignee can be endorsed only by that consignee, not the shipper. Once a consignee has been named the original shipper no longer has any power to alter the bill of lading in connection with title to the shipment.

If the consignee is not known at the time the shipper instructs shipment on a particular vessel then the bills of lading may also be made out to order. In this case, only the party to whom they are endorsed with the words 'deliver to …' or 'deliver to the order of …' can take delivery. This endorsement is made by the shipper who is named on the bill of lading. Occasionally buyers stipulate in their shipping instructions that the goods be consigned to order.

A bill of lading is a negotiable instrument and can be passed from a shipper through any number of parties, each party endorsing it to assign title to the next party. The only condition is that title can be assigned only by the party shown on the bill as having title at the time. Any failure to respect this condition breaks what is known as the chain of title; all purported assignments of title after such a break are invalid. Before paying for documents a buyer will therefore carefully examine the bill of lading to see that they are named on it as consignee, either on the face or on the reverse in an endorsement. In the latter case, the buyer will also make sure that the endorsements show an unbroken chain of title through to them.

There is one exception to the general rule that a consignee must be named on a bill of lading to take delivery of a shipment. This is when the bill is a bearer bill. In this case, anyone holding (or bearing) the bills (or one bill of the set) can take delivery. Bills are considered bearer bills when the word bearer is entered in the space marked consignee when the bills are first made out. Alternatively a title-holder endorses the bills with the words deliver to bearer, or a named title-holder endorses the bills in blank, i.e. by stamping and signing them without naming any other party in his endorsement. Although this may be simple and convenient, it means that anyone who obtains all or any of the originals (including a thief or a buyer who has not yet made payment) can take delivery of the shipment. Bills of lading are therefore usually made out to or endorsed to a named consignee.

The greatest security of all is afforded by issuing or endorsing a bill to a buyer nominated bank with an instruction to the bank to endorse and hand the bill over to the buyer when, and only when, payment has been made.

DISPATCHING BILLS OF LADING

Because in theory each original bill of lading in a set can be used to claim the goods at destination, a buyer will want to be in possession of all the originals in a set before making payment. Documents are often sent in two dispatches with the bills of lading split between them, simply to minimize the risks of all of them being lost or delayed. Only when the buyer has received both dispatches will payment be made, unless the first contains a bank guarantee for any missing bill

of lading. Many exporters use courier services and send all documents at once.

CERTIFICATES

ICO certificates of origin are issued for every international shipment of coffee from producers to consumers (whether the importing country is an ICO member or not), and are used to monitor the movement of coffee worldwide. The forms contain details of identity, size, origin, destination and time of shipment of the parcels in question. ICO certificates were particularly important when ICO export quotas were in force as they were also used to enforce the quota limits for individual exporting countries. The certificates are now less important and some consumer countries no longer insist on them. But it is in the interest of exporting countries to comply with ICO regulations on certificates of origin as they enable the ICO to monitor coffee movements and produce accurate statistics on each country's exports.

Moreover, all ICO exporting members are required to ensure that all coffee issued with certificates of origin complies with the minimum quality standards indicated by ICO resolution 407. See also chapter 11, Coffee quality.

Preferential entry certificates: Countries that levy duties or taxes on coffee imports sometimes grant duty exemptions to certain exporting countries. Entitlement to remission of duty or tax is obtained by submitting an official certificate of exemption (EUR1, GSP and others). Individual sales contracts often state that an exemption certificate must be provided where appropriate. This certificate must accompany the shipping documents, failing which the buyer is entitled to deduct the duty difference from the invoice and pay only the balance. The seller will be able to obtain refund of the shortfall by submitting the required certificate retroactively, but only if the buyer in turn is able to obtain this within the applicable time limit from the authorities in the country of importation. Sellers who are in doubt about whether such a certificate is required should ask their local chamber of commerce or trade authority. Note also that under ECC a buyer may stipulate a country of importation other than that of the port of destination.

Insurance certificates: Under a CIF contract the seller must provide an insurance certificate, issued by a first-class insurance company, showing that insurance has been taken out in accordance with the terms of the sales contract. The certificate must enable the buyer to claim any losses directly from the insurance company. The certificate entitles the holder to the rights and privileges of a known and stipulated master marine insurance policy that may cover a number of shipments. The certificate represents the policy and is transferable with all its benefits by endorsement in the same manner as bills of lading.

Other certificates: There are an increasing number of other certificates available for special contractual requirements. Some, such as weight and quality certificates, are supplied by recognized public or private organizations in the country of origin, and have various formats. Others, such as health, phytosanitary and non-radiation certificates, are often supplied on application by government bodies, in a set format prescribed by local law and regulations. The variety of formats available for special purpose certificates is so great that it is not practical or useful to discuss them here.

Shippers should be familiar with the format of local certificates and should investigate their availability and cost before entering into any contractual obligation. Otherwise they may be unable to supply a document at all or may require a price increase to cover costs.

MISSING AND INCORRECT DOCUMENTS

ECC states that, provided the missing document does not prevent the importation of the coffee into the country of destination, a European bank guarantee shall be accepted for the missing document(s). Sellers under the GCA contract must provide a guarantee issued by a bank in the United States. Exporters who have not arranged with a bank in Europe or the United States to issue such guarantees should consider specifying in all their contracts that guarantees issued by a first-class international bank will be accepted.

In principle, a set of shipping documents made up of some documents and some guarantees can be acceptable, and it is possible for payment to be made and delivery to a buyer to take place even though no original documents and only guarantees have passed between seller and buyer. But when the absence of documents prevents the importation of a shipment, buyers will not make payment on the basis of a guarantee as they will be unable to gain access to the shipment. While bank guarantees from seller to buyer are generally acceptable for missing contractual documents, guarantees for missing bills of lading must be made out to the shipping company and forwarded to the buyer for use. Shipping companies provide their own pre-printed guarantee forms for this purpose.

A buyer may also accept the seller's personal guarantee for missing documents without a bank's involvement. The seller may take steps to rectify errors in documents, especially when the documents relate to prompt landing and importation of a shipment (e.g. bills of lading) and when the time saved by amending them on the spot either benefits the buyer or prevents charges to the seller. The buyer can give the bills of lading to the shipping company's agent at destination who will amend them on receipt of authority from the seller via the shipping company's agent at the port of shipment.

Occasionally an entire set of documents is lost or destroyed in transit. The shipping company can then be requested to issue duplicate bills in return for an unlimited bank guarantee as indemnity against possible future liability to a holder of the supposedly lost documents.

As far as incorrect documents are concerned, obvious clerical errors that do not materially affect a document do not entitle a buyer to delay or refuse payment under ECC. If mistakes

invalidate a document or affect its reliability, the document is regarded as a missing document and a guarantee can be submitted in its place. The seller then returns the document itself for re-issue or amendment.

STANDARD FORMS OF CONTRACT

Changes to standard forms of contract are rare but do occur. For ECF contracts (under review by the end of 2011) see the latest version at *www.ecf-coffee.org* – look for Contracts under Publications. For GCA contracts go to *www.greencoffeeassociation.org* and look for Contracts under Resources.

OVERRIDING PRINCIPLE

The standard forms of contract set out generally accepted rules, practices and conditions in the international trade in coffee for which the terminology and precise meaning have been standardized under the aegis of leading coffee trade bodies (for Europe the ECF, and for the United States the GCA). The GCA contracts are also available in an electronic or XML (extensible mark-up language) version, together with a price fixing letter, a price fix rolling letter and a destination declaration letter. The data files are available, free of charge, from the GCA at *www.greencoffeeassociation.org.* For more information on using the XML versions exporters should contact their American buyers or agents.

Both ECF and GCA publish a number of contracts dealing with different types of transactions. Most coffee is traded using these standard contracts. Others exist but are rarely used.

All ECF and GCA contracts state expressly that no contract shall be contingent on any other and that each contract is to be settled between buyers and sellers without reference to any other contracts covering the same parcel.

Although intended to cover 'string contracts' this also means exporters cannot claim inability to ship because someone else, say an interior supplier, let them down. (Traders sometimes buy and sell matching contracts many times, causing a single shipment to pass through a number of hands before reaching an end-user. Such contracts are called string contracts.)

EUROPEAN COFFEE FEDERATION CONTRACTS

There are four ECF contracts in all, of which the ECC and the EFCACC are relevant for exporters as they cover coffee to be dispatched from origin. The other two contracts mostly deal with the trade in coffee within import markets: the European

Contract for Spot Coffee (ECSC) and the European Delivery Contract for Coffee (EDCC). While important for importers and traders they are of little direct interest to exporters. Go to *www.ecf-coffee.org* for the full contracts.

ECC and EFCACC cover both coffee shipped in bags and coffee shipped in bulk using lined containers. Note that although hardly any bagged coffee is still shipped without the use of containers, ECC does not stipulate that containers must be used. It allows it, provided the bill of lading states that the shipping company is responsible for the number of bags. Parties wishing to conclude individual transactions on a different basis must therefore ensure that the sales contract stipulates on what basis containerization shall be permitted. EFCACC on the other hand stipulates that delivery of coffee in bags shall be made in containers, under LCL/FCL conditions, whereby the carrier is responsible for the number of bags and the condition and suitability of the containers.

Incoterms®. Both ECF and GCA contracts make no reference to these, not because of any disqualification or disagreement, but because Incoterms® are a general (i.e. not coffee-specific) set of international trade definitions. The exclusion is purely to safeguard the stand-alone status and clarity of the ECF and GCA contracts that have been written by and for the trade in coffee.

See Exclusions in this chapter and go to *www.iccwbo.org/incoterms/understanding.asp* for more on Incoterms®.

The main implication of this exclusion is that, as for CFR or CIF contracts, under an FOB contract the seller is acquitted of responsibility only once the goods pass the ship's rail. This is the same for GCA contracts. Under ECC the stipulation means that any buyer wishing to impose the use of a particular shipping line or vessel must make this known at the time of concluding the contract. But under GCA this has already been formalized in that the standard GCA conditions state that for FCA and FOB sales the buyer reserves the right to nominate the carrier. EFCACC also stipulates that buyers shall nominate the carrier.

GREEN COFFEE ASSOCIATION CONTRACTS

Many North American roasters purchase coffee 'ex dock': the importer/trade house deals with all the formalities of shipment and landing, including customs clearance and passing the obligatory sanitation check of the FDA. This latter check is particular to the United States and all contracts for importation into the United States carry the stamp-over clause 'No pass – no sale'. This means that if any or all of the coffee is not admitted at port of destination in its original condition by reason of failure to meet the requirements of governmental laws or acts, the contract shall be deemed null and void as to that portion of the coffee which is not admitted in its original condition at point of discharge. Further, that any payment made for any coffee denied entry shall be refunded within 10 calendar days of denial of entry. For more on this go to *www.cfsan.fda.gov* or apply for the information booklet

Health and Safety in the Importation of Green Coffee into the United States from the National Coffee Association of USA. If coffee is refused entry under a contract that does not bear this over-stamp, in addition to having to refund payment as above the seller may also be required to make a replacement delivery within 30 days.

Effective 1 January 2006, contracts should stipulate whether they cover Commercial Grade or Specialty Grade coffee. This will determine the type of arbitration that would be held – if nothing is specified, then the contract is automatically assumed to cover Commercial Grade coffee.

There are nine GCA contracts. Four of them deal with coffee that is sold outside of the country of destination, four deal with coffee sold inside the country of destination, and one deals with coffee delivered at the border or frontier. The main distinction between the contract types is based on how cost and risk are allocated between the parties. Go to *www.greencoffeeassociation.org* for the full contracts.

Free carrier (FCA). Risk of loss is transferred when the coffee is delivered to the freight carrier at place of embarkation. All freight charges, including loading onto an ocean vessel, railcar or trailer, are payable by the buyer.

Free on board (FOB). Risk of loss is transferred when the coffee crosses over the ships rail. Terminal handling costs at the place of loading are for account of the shipper. Free on railcar (FOR) and free on truck or trailer (FOT) are variations of FOB, the only difference being the type of conveyance. The buyer pays the freight charges.

Cost and freight (CFR). As for FOB except that freight is included in the price and paid by the seller.

Cost, insurance and freight (CIF). As for CFR, but the seller also pays marine insurance and provides a certificate of insurance.

Delivered at frontier (DAF). Under DAF contracts, risk of loss is transferred when the coffee is delivered to a named point at the frontier. Delivery takes place on arriving means of transport (trailer, truck, rail car), and is cleared for export, but not cleared for import.

Ex dock (EDK or xDK). When coffee is sold ex dock, risk of loss transfer takes place on the dock at port of destination, after all ocean freight and terminal handling charges are paid, and customs entry and all government regulations have been satisfied.

Ex warehouse (EWH or xWH), delivered (DLD) and spot (SPT) contracts are outside the scope of normal export business and not discussed here.

Price to be fixed (PTBF). This does not feature in ECC but GCA stipulates that such contracts shall specify the differential (value) that is added to or subtracted from an agreed price basis. When applicable the number of lots of coffee futures should also be mentioned, as well as whether buyer or seller has the right to execute the fixation. If there is margin payable between time of fixation and time of shipment/delivery, it must be determined at time of contract. Finally, the earliest and the latest fixation date shall be specified at time of contract. Any changes are to be by mutual agreement and in writing.

ECF AND GCA CONTRACTS

THE MOST IMPORTANT ARTICLES AND CONDITIONS

Quantity

Tolerance to ship 3% more or less than the contracted weight. Applicable to both ECF and GCA. The intention is not to frustrate shipment if on arrival in port five bags are missing out of 500. But the tolerance applies only if the cause is beyond the sellers control. If buyers suspect deliberate manipulation they may lodge a claim.

Weights at shipment

Weight franchise of 0.5% on coffee sold 'net shipped weight' in ECC and EFCACC. Any weight loss on arrival in excess of 0.5% is to be refunded by the seller. Until the end of 1997 the tolerance was 1%. The present figure is a direct consequence of the growth in bulk shipments, in the sense that there should hardly be any weight variation if coffee is correctly shipped in lined and sealed containers. Shippers of bagged coffee often include a small tolerance (excess weight) per bag to avoid claims. GCA standard contracts state that for coffee sold on a shipped weight basis, and unless otherwise specified on the contract, the franchise is 0.5%.

Independent evidence of weight. The shipping weight shall be established at the time and place of shipment, or at the time and place of stuffing if the coffee is stuffed into the shipment containers at an inland location. In either case, sellers shall provide independent evidence of weight. This stipulation in both ECC and EFCACC provides buyers with some independent evidence that a container for which the bill of lading or waybill states 'said to contain' in fact does hold a certain amount of coffee. This does not alter the shipper's responsibility in any way unless the parties agree that shipping weights shall be final (together with the procedure and conditions that shall apply). GCA does not make this stipulation. The requirement to provide independent evidence of shipping weights applies equally to coffee sold 'delivered weights'.

Supervision by buyer's representatives (independent weighers). Buyers can demand this under both ECC and GCA provided they give due notice and pay the costs. The seller is obliged to provide the certificate together with the shipping documents but the buyer cannot withhold payment if the seller does not provide it. It is possible that the supervising weigher failed to hand the certificate to the

exporter, or omitted to attend the weighing when asked to do so.

Weights on arrival (landed weights)

Establishment of arrival weights. ECC and EFCACC require that weighing (and sampling) take place no later than 14 calendar days (15 for GCA) after discharge at the final port of destination or, in case of unforeseen complications, from the date the goods become available for weighing. Under both ECC/EFCACC and GCA shippers have the right to appoint supervisors at their expense.

ECC and EFCACC stipulate that on arrival containers (bagged and bulk) may be on-carried to an inland destination and weighed there provided they are on-carried not later than 14 calendar days from the date of final discharge at the port of destination, and provided weighing (and sampling) take place under independent supervision, at buyer's expense, not later than seven calendar days after arrival at the inland destination. The point of containerization is to minimize handling and the object of this clause is to permit receivers to bring the coffee without unnecessary handling as near to its final destination as possible, for example a roasting plant. (If coffee is weighed at a roasting plant then such weights may also be called 'factory weights'.) GCA provides that coffee in bags is to be weighed either within 15 days of availability at port of destination (landed weights), or within 15 days of date of tender at buyer's plant (plant weights). Coffee in bulk is to be weighed during unloading within 21 days of availability at final destination, or 21 days after all United States government clearances have been received (silo weights).

But the GCA approach is quite different from that of the ECF contracts in that it requires that the actual transaction contract state when, where, how and by whom, coffee is to be weighed for settlement purposes, that is, weighing responsibilities including liability for costs must be specified at the time of contract. If coffee is removed from the stipulated place of weighing or the time limits expire before the weighing takes place, then the net shipped weight will stand.

Packing

ECC and EFCACC state that the coffee shall be packed in sound uniform natural fibre bags suitable for export and in conformity with the legal requirements for food packaging materials and waste management within the European Union valid at the time of conclusion of the contract. This is important and exporters must know what types and quality of bags are acceptable, not only in the European Union but also in other countries. Be careful not to confuse 'port of destination' with 'country of destination' as the two may not always be the same. To read the EU Packaging and Packaging Waste Disposal Directive go to *www.europa.eu* (official publications, use EUR-Lex).

See also the Draft Code of Hygienic Practice for the Transport of Foodstuffs in Bulk and Semi-Packed Foodstuffs of the Codex Alimentarius Commission at *www.codexalimentarius. net* and chapter 12, Quality control.

GCA stipulates that coffee bags shall be made of sisal, henequen, jute, burlap or similar woven material, without any inner lining or outer covering. Bulk coffee shall be in a bulk container liner. Depending on the contract so-called super sacks (jumbo bags) made of synthetic fibre may also be used. Soluble coffee is commonly shipped in cardboard cartons with a plastic liner. All forms of packaging must conform to food grade packaging standards at the country of destination.

Quality

The quality of the coffee must be strictly as per contract. If there is a difference and the resultant claim cannot be settled amicably then it will go to arbitration. A buyer cannot lodge any formal claim before paying for the shipping documents. Effective 1 January 2006, GCA contracts should stipulate whether they cover Commercial Grade or Specialty Grade coffee. This will determine the type of arbitration that would be held – if nothing is specified, then the contract is automatically assumed to cover Commercial Grade coffee.

Claims are usually settled by granting an allowance that the seller must pay, together with the buyer's costs and expenses. But if the coffee is unsound or the quality is radically different from that specified then the buyer may seek to have the contract discharged by invoicing back the coffee. In awarding invoicing back the arbitrators shall establish the price bearing in mind all the circumstances concerned. Basically this means they may order the contract cancelled and instruct the sellers to refund the entire cost of the coffee plus any relevant damages.

Note that an excessive moisture level is one factor towards declaring a coffee unsound. See also chapters 5 and 12.

Under GCA all quality issues FCA, FOB, CFR, CIF and DAF are settled by allowance, except gross negligence and fraud. In the latter case the arbitration will be a technical arbitration that might convene a quality panel to verify negligence or fraud.

Freight

Where coffee is sold CFR/CIF the costs of bringing the goods to the port of destination are for the account of the seller. If the rate of freight increases between the time of sale, and the time of shipment then the increase is for the sellers account. Only increases that enter, into force after the shipment took place shall be for the buyers account. This is indicative of the trade's wish to control freights and shipping through the use of FOB contracts. Exporters who have to use national flag carriers therefore also have to accept they are potentially liable to pay for such freight increases.

Place of embarkation. ECC does not speak of this, but GCA states that for FOB, CFR and CIF contracts this shall be defined as the named seaport of the country of origin; for both the GCA and ECF FCA contracts it is defined as the place where custody of the coffee is turned over to the carrier for transport. The place of embarkation or point of delivery must always be clearly noted on the bill of lading or carrier's receipt.

Port of destination. If this is not advised when the contract is concluded, the buyer must declare it at the latest by the deadline stipulated by either ECC or GCA. Otherwise a buyer could simply refuse to declare a port of destination and so frustrate the execution of a contract (for example, if the price had become unfavourable due to change in the market). Note that the ECC text states that the deadline is met when the declaration is made at the buyer's place of business, i.e. all the buyer has to do is send the declaration by cable, fax, e-mail, telex or other means of written electronic communication. The shipper cannot declare the buyer in default simply because no declaration has been received; if a declaration is overdue, the shipper should make inquiries rather than just let events unfold. GCA does not say this but clearly the same principle of due diligence applies. However, whereas ECC sets a clear deadline for lodging a technical claim, GCA sets a limit of one year from the date the issue arises. Note also that ECC Article 27 states that communication by fax, e-mail or other means of written electronic communication is at the parties' own risk (basically because proof of dispatch and receipt is not automatic).

Sometimes by the time the declaration (of destination) falls due the coffee has not yet been sold on and the buyer may not be in any position to declare a final destination. In the past the buyer would then declare a range of ports (e.g. Rotterdam, option Bremen/Hamburg), called options or optional ports. Then the goods would be stowed on board in such a way as to make discharge possible at any of the named ports, with the cost or option fees for buyer's account.

But on modern container vessels such stowage is difficult if not impossible. Exporters should satisfy themselves therefore that the shipping line will in fact accept such cargo before they agree to ship to optional ports. Transshipment is a much more frequently used option but current transshipment practices often make it difficult to confirm the final vessel. Shipping advices against FOB contracts, and indeed bills of lading, can only mention the vessel that first loads the goods, leaving tracking of the goods to the buyer. Note also that bills of lading may stipulate the place of delivery as CFS (a container freight station) at or associated with the port of destination, regardless of the port of discharge.

NB: To note that GCA also states that, in the case of a contract for forward shipment, if the buyer fails to declare the destination then the seller may ship to New York. ECC does not include any such provision.

What this means in fact is that where a buyer fails to declare the destination in time, this GCA clause offers the seller the choice whether to make shipment or not, always provided that such shipment is made within the contracted period. The underlying philosophy is to give a shipper an alternative if the buyer totally refuses to cooperate. The shipper will then ship to New York and, if the buyer refuses to honour the documents, the goods are sold in the open New York market. The shipper then sends an invoice to the original buyer for any loss. If the buyer refuses to settle the shipper then goes to arbitration and wins a judgment that will be relatively easy to enforce in the Unites States, based on New York law. When a buyer refuses to give a destination, contract performance becomes secondary to legal action. New York is a coffee market with major liquidity and the assumption is that just about any coffee can be sold there. However, with the exception of Japan and Canada, little coffee is traded on the GCA contract to non-American destinations. The entire procedure is a last resort, but it gives possible finality to an argument that otherwise could go on forever.

Shipment

Shipment must be made at the vessel's last scheduled call at the port of shipment before commencing the final voyage. This is reminiscent of when traditional break bulk vessels used to discharge and load cargo at a range of ports in the same region and in so doing might call at the same port on the way in and on the way out. Modern container vessels rarely if ever do so but the stipulation is nevertheless a valid one and applies to both ECC and GCA.

Shipment must be made by conference line or other acceptable vessel (ECF), or metal-hulled, self-propelled vessels which are not over 20 years of age and not less than 1,000 net registered tons, classed A1 American Record or equivalent, operating in their regular trade (GCA). This prevents shippers from using any old tramp vessel that happens to be available. (Tramp vessels make irregular port calls to discharge and look for new cargo, i.e. the exact opposite of liner vessels.) Note also that at some future stage European Union authorities may introduce legislation covering the type, class, condition and age of ships that may enter European Union ports. Information on vessel registration and vessels themselves is available at *www.lloydslistintelligence.com,* by subscription only.

Shippers will pass on to the shipping line all relevant instructions received from buyers. These apply equally to shipment in bags in containers, and to shipments in bulk. This is important – in case of subsequent problems shippers may be asked to furnish proof they did so.

Shipment in bags

Shipment in containers, suitable for the transport of coffee, shall be permitted under LCL/FCL conditions, whereby the shipping company is responsible for the number of bags and the condition and suitability of the containers.

However, shipping lines increasingly discourage LCL/FCL (or LCL/LCL) and in future shippers may not always be able to satisfy buyer's wishes in this regard. In this case their only option will be to effect weighing and stuffing under independent supervision at their expense as all other shipments in containers shall require agreement of the

parties. Again, GCA leaves the matter of the shipment basis to the parties to the contract.

LCL, or less than container load: the shipping line accepts responsibility for the number of bags. FCL, or full container load: the line accepts responsibility only for the container, not for the contents, by stating for example, 'STC (said to contain) 300 bags of coffee' on the bill of lading. See also chapter 5, Logistics and insurance.

Shipment in bulk

Unless otherwise agreed, shipment shall be made under FCL/FCL conditions. This reflects the move from break bulk to almost universal containerization. Unless otherwise stated, FCL/FCL is now the norm. This means that bulk is increasingly, if not always, loaded and weighed under independent supervision, but shippers still have to pass on to the shipping line all relevant instructions received from buyers, and in case of damage may be asked to provide proof of having done so. GCA leaves the matter entirely to the parties, who must stipulate the agreed shipping basis in the contract.

Delay in shipment

Sellers shall not be held responsible if they are able to prove their case. The most important point this article makes is that the buyer must be kept informed at all times without undue delay. This is absolutely essential. Delays in shipment usually affect buyers adversely and they must be enabled to take measures to protect themselves. Failing to respect this clause not only is entirely unprofessional but can also result in unforeseen consequences, possibly even cancellation of the contract.

On-carriage of containers

Buyers may discharge containers at inland destinations. The point of containerization is to minimize handling and the only object of this clause is to permit receivers to bring the coffee without unnecessary handling as near to its final destination as possible, for example a roasting plant. In case of weight claims buyers have to prove weighing took place under independent supervision. GCA permits the same. In addition it defines the port of entry as all dock and warehouse facilities within a 50-mile radius of ships berth that are used for the discharge of ships cargo (or all freight facilities within a 50-mile radius of a border crossing).

Advice of shipment

Both ECC and GCA require that advice of shipment must be transmitted as soon as known. In practice only gross negligence could explain why one would not advise buyers as soon as possible, which only leaves the question of whether or not the advice actually reaches them promptly. But ECC and GCA approach this question very differently. ECC considers it may not be within the seller's control and so, in theory, it suffices if buyers receive the notice before the vessel arrives at the port of destination. Only someone with no interest in good business relationships would consider this normal practice, however.

EFCACC on the other hand stipulates that advice of delivery must be transmitted within two calendar days of the date of delivery.

There is an important provision in the ECC articles dealing with advice of shipment and/or delivery. If a shipping or delivery advice is not received by noon on the fourteenth calendar day after the expiry of the contractual shipping or delivery period, and if there has been no notification of a delay and no *force majeure* has been pleaded, then damages may be claimed or the buyer may cancel the contract altogether. This could leave a forgetful exporter with an unsold and most likely uninsured shipment. See Article 13(d) of the ECC and Article 12(d) of the EFCACC for full details.

GCA on the other hand states that for FCA, FOB, CFR, CIF and EDK contracts, written advice with all details must be transmitted not just as soon as known, but not later than on the day of arrival of the vessel at destination and/or five business days from bill of lading date, whichever is later. The advice may be given verbally with e-mail or fax confirmation to be sent the same day. This is included because of the close proximity of many Latin American producing countries to the United States, but it applies to all contracts.

Shipping documents

Sellers must provide shipping documents in good time (including a full set of 'clean on board' bills of lading, i.e. bills stating that the goods were received on board ship in apparent good order), enabling the buyer to clear the goods upon arrival. Failure to provide documents in time will incur demurrage and other costs, and could even lead to cancellation of the contract under both ECC and GCA. Delivery documents under EFCACC are to be made available promptly but latest within 14 days of the carrier's receipt, otherwise penalties or in extreme cases cancellation may apply.

ECC Article 18 and EFCACC Article 17 stipulate the documents buyers are entitled to receive and those they are entitled to request.

Insurance

The vast majority of the trade in coffee today is on FOB terms. In this regard ECC Article 15 contains three extremely important stipulations.

In the case of CFR and FOB contracts the buyers have to cover the insurance ahead of the contractual shipment period. Without this stipulation the coffee might be loaded without any insurance cover in place, leaving the exporter at risk. In case of doubt an exporter should insist on proof of insurance.

The current (late 2011) version of the ECC stipulates that the insurance shall commence from the time the coffee leaves the ultimate warehouse or other place of storage at the port of shipment. This is because it can be extremely difficult to determine at what point the marine insurer became liable for any damage or loss incurred once the goods have left the ultimate place of storage. If after leaving the ultimate place of storage but before crossing the ship's rail the goods were destroyed by fire, or fell into the water, then the seller might receive no bill of lading at all and would be unable to submit shipping documents for the buyer to pay. This is why ECC also states that the sellers have the right to the benefit of the policy until the documents are paid for.

In the above example the buyer would have to claim the loss or damage under their insurance cover on the seller's behalf. But even if a vessel sinks immediately after loading the seller will receive a bill of lading and the buyer will have to pay for it. Until payment is made, the benefit of the insurance cover remains contractually vested in the sellers.

GCA on the other hand relies instead on the transfer of risk stipulation that applies for each contract: shippers and buyers must cover insurance accordingly.

EFCACC stipulates that insurance shall be covered prior to the contractual delivery period, that sellers shall have the right to the policy until the documents are paid for, and that insurance shall extend from the time the coffee is delivered to the carrier for an amount 5% above the contract price. (Prior to delivery insurance is of course seller's responsibility). See also chapter 5.

Export licences

Under both ECF and GCA contracts the exporter is not only responsible for obtaining export licences but also for the consequences if such a licence is later cancelled or revoked. Similarly, buyers are responsible for obtaining any import licences required.

Duties, fees and taxes

Both ECF and GCA contracts stipulate that all and any such costs in the country of export are always for the account of the exporter, irrespective of whether they already existed at the time of concluding the contract or were imposed afterwards. At the import end such costs, if any, are for account of the buyer unless the seller is in breach by not supplying required documentation (see below).

Certification of preferential entry

Certificates entitling the coffee to completely or partially duty-free entry into the stated country of destination (which may be different from that of the port of destination) must accompany the shipping documents. If they are not available the buyers are entitled to deduct the duty difference from the payment to the seller. They will only be obliged to refund this (less any expenses) if the subsequent submission of the certificate is accepted by the customs authorities in the country of import.

(The United States and Canada do not levy import duties or taxes on green coffee.)

Payment

The coffee remains the property of the sellers until it has been paid for in full. No third party can lay claim to any coffee that has not been paid for. This is important when documents are sent in trust. If a buyer is declared insolvent after the documents are received but before they have been paid, then the judicial authorities (or liquidators) have no claim to the goods, although in some countries national insolvency law takes precedence over individual contract stipulations. How far sellers can enforce this clause in European Union and other importing countries therefore depends on local law.

In the United States there are no doubts in this respect. When invoked, bankruptcy law (11 USC § 365 (e)(1) overrides all GCA terms and conditions. Most coffee is sold on payment terms in the United States and Canada and the risks are great. Selling 'net 30 days from delivery' means the seller is granting the buyer possession 30 days before payment. If the buyer goes bankrupt, the seller may lose the value of the coffee.

There can even be problems with payments that are made within the 90 days prior to a bankruptcy. This is called the preference period and if the liquidator or trustee can show that the payments were not normal (i.e. extraordinarily late or extraordinarily early), then a supplier might be forced to return the payments to the bankruptcy pool.

ECF and GCA contracts both state that letters of credit must conform exactly to the contract, must be available for use from day one of the agreed shipping period, and must remain valid for negotiation for 21 calendar days after the last date shipment can be made. This allows time for the seller to obtain all the required documents and possible consular visas.

Force majeure

Partial performance, non-performance or delayed performance of a contract can be justified only as a result of unforeseeable and insurmountable occurrences, but only if these arise after the conclusion of the contract and before the expiry of the performance period allowed by the contract. And furthermore only if the seller informs the buyer as soon as the impediment arises, provides evidence and keeps the buyer fully informed of developments. In other words, make sure your buyer knows what you know yourself. Under ECF contracts a successful plea of *force majeure* can extend the performance time limit by up to a maximum of 45 calendar days, after which the contract lapses. Disputes have to be settled by arbitration.

GCA follows the same principle but does not specify any extension. It also states that in no case shall the seller be excused by any such causes intervening before arrival of the affected portion of the coffee at the point of embarkation of the original shipment. Thus, delays within producing countries do not constitute *force majeure*. Disputes dealing with *force majeure* will by nature be technical and as such are subject to a one-year filing time limit (see also chapter 7).

Submission of claims – ECF contracts

Quality claims. Not later than 21 calendar days from the final date of discharge at the port of destination.

All other claims (technical claims). Not later than 45 calendar days from:

- The final date of discharge at the port of destination, provided all the documents are available to the buyer (i.e. the coffee has been shipped); or
- The last day of the contractual shipping period if the coffee has not been shipped.

These limits may be extended if the arbitral body at the place of arbitration (mentioned in the contract) considers that one or other of the parties will suffer undue hardship.

Submission of claims – GCA contracts

Under GCA rules time limits are based instead on the filing of a demand for arbitration, not on when the defending party is notified.

Quality claims. A demand for arbitration must be filed with the GCA within 15 calendar days from date of discharge or after all government clearances have been received, whichever is later.

Other claims (technical claims): The only time limit is that a demand for arbitration must be filed with the GCA not later than one year from the date the dispute first arose. Usually one would expect to see a number of exchanges between the parties to the contract before this but there is no contractual obligation on either of the parties to do anything but file a demand for arbitration within the year. (Depending on the type of contract dispute, the United States legal system allows three-to-seven years for the filing of judgement. Quality claims are subject to a 15-day limit because quality deteriorates over time.)

Default

Default occurs if one of the parties does not execute its part of the contract. After declaring the offending party to be in default the injured party can claim discharge of the contract with or without damages (but excluding any consequential, i.e. indirect, damages). If the offender fails to pay these or disputes them then the matter shall be decided by arbitration.

The default clause is stipulated separately in the ECF contracts, mainly because the notion of a claim assumes an incorrectly executed contract. Default on the other hand deals with the cost and damage to the injured party of the total and possibly wilful non-execution of a contract.

As in the case of invoicing goods back for a radical difference in quality, there are no fixed rules for determining default damages. In the European Union the process depends on the arbitral body under whose jurisdiction the arbitration is held. The GCA contracts provide for arbitration in different American locations provided a location other than New York has been specified in the contract. If no location is specified then arbitration will automatically be held in New York with the arbitrators setting the damages if any are awarded.

Arbitration

Any dispute that cannot be resolved amicably shall be resolved through arbitration at the place stated in the contract. Unless a different American location has been specified in the contract, the GCA contracts automatically place arbitration in New York, to be held in accordance with the law of New York State. However, the ECF is the umbrella body for a number of national coffee associations in sovereign countries, quite a few of which have their own arbitral bodies, rules and legal systems (see chapter 7, Arbitration).

In this context the most important are the United Kingdom (London), Germany (Hamburg) and France (Le Havre), followed by Italy (Trieste), Belgium (Antwerp) and the Netherlands (Amsterdam). All ECF contracts provide that disputes shall be resolved by arbitration but the actual commercial contract must state where this shall take place. If not then arbitration will be delayed while the ECF Contracts Committee determines where it will be held and the defending party may find itself having to deal with arbitration proceedings in a location it is not familiar with.

Communications

Article 27 of ECC (26 in EFCACC) lists the Notices that are required to be given under different Articles – and how they can be given (fax, e-mail etc.) and should be recorded. GCA allows fax and e-mail or equivalent electronic message.

Exclusions

The following laws and conventions do not apply to ECF standard forms of contract:

- The Uniform Law on Sales and the Uniform Law on Formation to which effect is given by the Uniform Laws on International Sales Act 1967;

- The United Nations Convention on Contracts for the International Sale of Goods of 1980; and

- The United Nations Convention on Prescription (Limitation) in the International Sale of Goods Act 1974 and the amending protocol of 1980.

GCA's Legal Framework and Contract Rulings simply state that 'The UN Convention on Contracts for the International Sale of Goods shall not apply to this contract'.

UCP 600 IN SALES CONTRACTS

The Uniform Customs and Practice for Documentary Credits or UCP 600 is a set of internationally recognized rules and standards published by the International Chamber of Commerce (ICC – *www.iccwbo.org*).

Where the rules are incorporated the seller has the advantage that he will know in advance the criteria against which the banks will examine the shipping documents in deciding whether or not to pay under a letter of credit. For the buyer the major advantage of incorporation is that he will know in advance the criteria against which the price for the goods will be paid against tender of documents. However, for the buyer to be under an obligation to open a letter of credit governed by the UCP 600, the sale contract needs to include an express condition imposing such an obligation on the buyer. Only with such a condition in place can the seller object if the buyer were to open a letter of credit that is not governed by the UCP, e.g. 'Payment by irrevocable letter of credit, incorporating UCP 600'.

However, buyers may still stipulate in the credit that certain aspects of the UCP rules are excluded, provided of course this was laid down in the sales contract.

IRREVOCABLE AND CONFIRMED CREDITS

The UCP 600 have moved firmly away from revocable credits and Article 2 defines a credit as 'any arrangement, however named or described, that is irrevocable and thereby constitutes a definite undertaking of the issuing bank to honour a complying presentation'. Moreover, Article 3, headed 'Interpretations', states that a credit is irrevocable even if there is no indication to that effect. Finally, Article 10 makes it clear that a credit cannot be cancelled without the agreement of the beneficiary.

However, it is not impossible for revocable credits to be opened since Article 1 of the UCP 600 allows any part of the rules to be modified or excluded. It is consequently still possible for a buyer to establish a revocable credit. It remains prudent, therefore, for sellers to continue to stipulate in their sale contracts that the buyer will open an irrevocable, confirmed letter of credit. Sellers should, of course, also make sure when the credit arrives that it incorporates UCP 600 or expressly describes itself as irrevocable.

A 'confirmed credit' brings the advantages of 'a definite undertaking of the confirming bank, in addition to that of the issuing bank'. However, UCP 600 does not assume a credit to be confirmed where the text does not say otherwise. Consequently, as before, if a seller wants to impose upon his buyer an obligation of a confirmed letter of credit, he must impose such an obligation in the sale contract (e.g. 'Payment by irrevocable letter of credit to be confirmed by first class New York bank acceptable to the Sellers…') and – when the letter of credit is received – to make sure that it has been confirmed by an acceptable confirming bank.

NON-DOCUMENTARY REQUIREMENTS

It is a common occurrence for documentary credits to contain instructions that are not expressly attached to a document that needs to be tendered. However, if for example the credit stipulates shipment on a vessel of a particular class, but does not require the tender of a classification certificate, then under UCP 600 the bank is under no obligation to inquire as to the age of the vessel named in the bill of lading. This means that if a buyer is particularly anxious to ensure that payment is only made if the bank is satisfied, say, that the vessel carries a particular classification, the buyer should:

- Stipulate in the sale contract for the tender of a copy of the classification certificate under the letter of credit; and
- Stipulate for the tender of the same document in the letter of credit.

In this way, the buyer ensures, first, that the seller cannot complain that the letter of credit requires more documents than does the sale contract and, second, that the seller will only be paid on tender of a conforming classification certificate. The seller needs to consider, when agreeing the terms of the contract, whether he or she will be in a position to satisfy the obligation the buyer is seeking to impose upon him. For example, how easy will it be to get hold of a copy of such a classification certificate?

TIME ALLOWED TO BANKS TO EXAMINE THE DOCUMENTS

Time to examine documents is vitally important. UCP 500 gave each bank involved in the credit a 'reasonable time, not to exceed seven banking days following the day of receipt of the documents' to examine the documents. Acceptance or rejection of the documents was therefore required within this period.

Under UCP 600 this has been changed to five banking days following the day of presentation. However, if a bank decides on the second day that the documents are in order, must payment then be made immediately or can the bank wait till the full five days are up? Whereas Article 14(b) gives each bank five banking days to decide whether to pay, Article 15 says that a bank must honour the credit (pay) or give notice of refusal immediately it comes to that decision. See also Articles 14(b) and 16(d) – and note that a 'banking day' is defined in Article 2. It is not simply a day the bank is open, but 'regularly open at the place at which an act subject to these rules is to be performed'.

To avoid becoming ensnared in disputes of this kind, sellers could stipulate in the sales contract that a condition be included in the letter of credit stating, for example:

'Payment by confirmed irrevocable letter of credit, incorporating UCP 600, providing for payment within three banking days of presentation of the following documents …'

FORCE MAJEURE

This Article (36) is largely unchanged although express reference is now made to terrorism. The stipulation that under UCP the expiry date of a credit is not extended as a result of *force majeure* remains unchanged, i.e. a credit will simply expire even though *force majeure* may prevent the seller from utilising it.

But something sellers may not always be aware of is that documents under letters of credit may also be presented for payment at the issuing bank (as well as any nominated bank) – see Article 6a. This can be important if the nominated bank is affected by force majeure and, for example, may be closed.

INCOTERMS®

Incoterms® are standard international trade definitions used every day in countless numbers of contracts for the sale of good – both domestic and international. ICC model contracts facilitate trade especially for smaller companies that may lack access to adequate legal advice on issues relating to the writing of contracts. However, they do not apply to the stand-alone standard forms of contract for green coffee shipments of the ECF and the GCA of New York.

Nevertheless, there are exporters who prefer to apply at least some of the definitions used by Incoterms® to their green coffee shipments (for which they of course require the buyer's agreement) whereas the ECF/GCA standard forms of contracts do not cater for the export of manufactured goods such as roasted and packaged coffee. It is therefore appropriate to provide at least an introduction to Incoterms®.

The Paris-based International Chamber of Commerce was established in 1919. Since then, it has expanded to become a world business organization with thousands of member companies and associations in around 120 countries representing every major industrial and service sector. Today's ICC is also the main business partner to the United Nations and its affiliated agencies in matters of international trade.

ICC publishes various sets of internationally recognized rules and standards since 1936. The most well known to the coffee trade are probably Incoterms® themselves, and UCP 600 or the Uniform Customs and Practice for Documentary Credits.

The Incoterms® rules have been developed and maintained by experts and practitioners brought together by ICC and have become the standard in international business rules setting. They help traders avoid costly misunderstandings by clarifying the tasks, costs and risks involved in the delivery of goods from sellers to buyers. Incoterms® rules are recognized by the United Nations Commission on International Trade Law (UNCITRAL) as the global standard for the interpretation of the most common terms in foreign trade. UNCITRAL (*www.uncitral.org*) is the Commission that formulates and regulates international trade in cooperation with the World Trade Organization (WTO).

The terms are updated from time to time – the latest version (Incoterms® 2010) came into effect on 1 January 2011. However, parties to a contract could agree to continue using an earlier version. In this case they should specify which one the contract is based on, for example Incoterms® 2000. The full set of Incoterms® 2010 rules can be obtained from the ICC website: *www.iccwbo.org/incoterms*. Guidance Notes explain the fundamentals of each Incoterms® rule, such as when it should be used, when risk passes, and how costs are allocated between seller and buyer. The Guidance Notes are not part of the actual Incoterms® 2010 rules, but are intended to help the user accurately and efficiently steer towards the appropriate Incoterms® rule for a particular transaction. The ICC also offers a helpful wall chart that illustrates the obligations of each party under different delivery conditions.

TWO DISTINCT CLASSES OF RULES

1. Rules for any mode or modes of transport:

   EXW: Ex Works

   FCA: Free Carrier

   CPT: Carriage Paid To

   CIP: Carriage and Insurance Paid to

   DAT: Delivered At Terminal

   DAP: Delivered At Place

   DDP: Delivered Duty Paid

This class includes the seven Incoterms® 2010 rules that can be used irrespective of the mode of transport selected and irrespective of whether one or more than one mode of transport is employed. They can be used even when there is no maritime transport at all. It is important to remember, however, that these rules can be used in cases where a ship is used for part of the carriage.

2. Rules for sea and inland waterway transport:

   FAS: Free Alongside Ship

   FOB: Free On Board

   CFR: Cost and Freight

   CIF: Cost, Insurance and Freight

In this class of Incoterms® 2010 rules, the point of delivery and the place to which the goods are carried to the buyer are both ports, hence the label 'sea and inland waterway rules'. Under the last three Incoterms® rules, all mention of the ship's rail as the point of delivery has been omitted in preference for the goods being delivered when they are 'on board' the vessel. This more closely reflects modern commercial reality and avoids the rather dated image of the risk swinging to and fro across an imaginary perpendicular line.

TERMINAL HANDLING CHARGES

Under Incoterms® rules CPT, CIP, CFR, CIF, DAT, DAP, and DDP, the seller must make arrangements for the carriage of the goods to the agreed destination. While the freight is paid by the seller, it is actually paid for by the buyer as freight costs are normally included by the seller in the total selling price. The carriage costs will sometimes include the costs of handling and moving the goods within port or container terminal facilities and the carrier or terminal operator may well charge these costs to the buyer who receives the goods. In these circumstances, the buyer will want to avoid paying for the same service twice: once to the seller as part of the total selling price and once independently to the carrier or the terminal operator. The Incoterms® 2010 rules seek to avoid this happening by clearly allocating such costs in articles A6/B6 of the relevant Incoterms® rules.

RULES FOR DOMESTIC AND INTERNATIONAL TRADE

Incoterms® rules have traditionally been used in international sale contracts where goods pass across international borders. In various areas of the world, however, trade blocs, like the European Union, have made border formalities between different countries less significant. There is also greater willingness in the United States to use Incoterms® rules in domestic trade. Consequently, the subtitle of the Incoterms® 2010 rules formally recognizes that they are available for application to both international and domestic sale contracts. As a result, the Incoterms® 2010 rules clearly state in a number of places that the obligation to comply with export/import formalities exists only where applicable.

CHAPTER 5

LOGISTICS AND INSURANCE

LOGISTICS AND INSURANCE

BASIC SHIPPING TERMS

Break bulk: means coffee is stowed in the ship's hold in bags – the cargo is loose. Sometimes the bags are left in the loading slings to speed up discharge at destination, at the expense though of less freight capacity per cubic metre. The disadvantages of break bulk shipping are numerous: the goods can be exposed to the weather during loading and discharge; the bags can be torn; there is a risk of contamination from other cargo during the voyage; and bags may be lost or mixed with other shipments. Marine insurance is usually higher for break bulk cargo.

Containerized cargo: (both in bags and in bulk) remains in the container throughout the journey, often to the final inland destination. Most, if not nearly all, coffee now travels in containers and break bulk services are no longer on regular offer. As a result, shipping small (less than container load) parcels has become a problem (discussed later in this chapter).

Container transit in general is faster, more efficient and more secure than break bulk. Modern container vessels spend only short periods in port as all cargo is assembled before arrival, and container handling can proceed irrespective of weather conditions. Strict schedules can be maintained, and turnaround times are shorter. Ro-ro (roll-on roll-off) vessels carry containers on trailers that are simply driven on and off the ships. This does away with the need for gantry cranes. Ro-ro vessels are mostly used between smaller ports, for example in Europe, although some bagged coffee is also exported from West Africa on so-called flatbed trailers.

Nowadays, most if not all, coffee is shipped internationally in containers with break bulk only occurring on some coastal stretches, for example from ports that lack the required lifting equipment or that use lighters to transfer cargo to coasters waiting offshore. But such cargo (coffee in bags) would then be containerized at the port where transfer to the deep ocean going vessel takes place.

NB: For an extensive glossary of shipping and shipping-related terminology visit *www.safmarine.com* and look for 'Glossary of Terms' under Support – Useful information. Other shipping lines offer similar information.

SHIPPING SERVICES

Liner services: are regular, scheduled shipping services between fixed groups of ports that operate regardless of cargo availability. Tramping vessels, however, make irregular, opportunistic calls at ports when cargo is available. In theory importers can also charter vessels for larger tonnages, but chartering is a complex business and conditions for each charter must be negotiated individually. However, major shipping lines themselves often include chartered vessels in their scheduled liner services, using standard charter contracts.

Unless specifically stated to the contrary, all coffee contracts automatically stipulate that shipment will be by liner vessel, operated under a regular, scheduled service.

Conferences: are groups of ship owners who jointly offer regular sailings by guaranteeing the number of vessels to be available during the year between different ports and their schedules. Most scheduled ocean liners used to operate under liner Conferences (known simply as Conferences) through which they scheduled and guaranteed sailings to and from an agreed range of ports, thereby eliminating duplication among their members. The system was thought to benefit both sellers and buyers because freight rates were fairly stable, schedules were published well in advance, and regular and dependable services were provided. However, in October 2008 the European Union discontinued its block exemption from anti-trust rules for shipping line Conferences. This means that shipping lines may no longer deal with freight rate negotiations en block and instead must now negotiate freight rates and schedules separately with their individual shippers and/or receivers. Similar moves appear to be afoot in the United States and elsewhere.

Vessel sharing agreement (VSA): or alliances are a variation on the traditional Conference system. In VSA, several carriers may offer a joint service by agreeing a frequency and capacity from and to certain ports. The lines share the vessels each contributes but each carrier markets and sells freight space on an individual basis. Individual freight contracts can still be negotiated with each line and depending on the space available receivers can also nominate a choice of carriers for the goods. (For most shipments, the receiver rather than the shipper is the freight payer and negotiator.) The advantage for the shipping lines is better cost-control and increased efficiency; for receivers there is more flexibility in that they can negotiate rates and in a sense 'play the market'. But the number of sailings is not necessarily guaranteed and may be varied, for example to stabilize freight rates.

SHIPPING HUBS

Shipping hubs and container feeder vessels are becoming increasingly important as the shipping industry evolves to meet the demands of globalization and the proportion of bigger vessels in world fleets is growing. Already some vessels can carry as many as 11,000 to 15,000 TEU (20-foot equivalent units) and some major shipping lines announced in 2011 having placed orders for a new class of container vessel that will carry 18,000 TEU. These ships will be longer and wider than anything ever built before but it is stated that their revolutionary design and propulsion systems would considerably reduce costs and cut CO_2 emissions per container carried. This latter aspect fits well with the increasing interest in 'green supply chain management' and forecasts are that still larger vessels may become operational in the foreseeable future. However, such mega-vessels will call only at ports with the required deep water and offering both the cargo and the mechanized capability to handle it quickly and efficiently. As a result, smaller ports increasingly feed cargo to the nearest regional hub, in rather the same way as airlines have been doing for years. In some origins this practice is already well established, but elsewhere it is creating some problems for the industry, also because the supply of smaller feeder vessels is not necessarily keeping up with the growing number of very large container ships (VLCS).

It is not uncommon for receivers of coffee to have proper advice of shipment, within contract terms, but still not know the name of the vessel that will deliver at the final port of discharge. This is because the name of the transshipment or mother vessel is not always known at the time of loading.

Internet-based track and trace services offer solutions provided the shipping advice includes the container numbers (which shippers are obliged to provide in the shipment advice). Larger receivers working on the just-in-time supply system require carriers to inform them direct by e-mail, within a given time limit, of all transshipment arrangements, including the name of the mainline vessel and its estimated time of arrival (ETA) at destination. Not immediately obvious perhaps, but other issues can arise when authorities in a transshipment port impose certain conditions on cargo that is to be transshipped there.

For example, in late 2006 Panama directed that any vents on containers carrying green coffee for transshipment in Panamanian ports (Balboa and Manzanillo) must be secured with insect-proof netting and must be accompanied by a phytosanitary certificate. A green placard with the words GREEN COFFEE in capital letters also has to be affixed to all four container walls. This is to safeguard against Broca (borer) infestation being transmitted from other coffee producing countries. Non-compliance means a container will not be allowed to be discharged for onward shipment, a potential cause of considerable logistical and financial problems.

OCEAN FREIGHT AND SURCHARGES

Ocean freight: is mostly quoted as a lump sum per container, regardless of the payload. Coffee in bulk containers is usually shipped under FCL/FCL conditions (loading and discharge costs are not included in the freight rate), whereas bagged coffee in containers is shipped LCL/FCL (loading supervised by the shipping line and cost included in the freight rate) or FCL/FCL. The cost of loading and discharging containers varies between container terminals and between shipping lines, sometimes considerably, and can be an important cost item.

Ocean freight includes variable elements beyond the control of shipping companies. The most important are the cost of fuel and exchange rate fluctuations. If a European shipping line agrees a freight rate expressed in United States dollars, movement in the rate of exchange of the dollar against the euro will be reflected in its income. To avoid having to speculate on potential fluctuations in fuel prices or currencies, freight contracts instead allow for price adjustments whenever notable changes occur.

Surcharges: due to adjustment of fuel costs are called bunker surcharge (BS) or bunker adjustment factor (BAF). They are usually applied as a sum per container. A surcharge due to currency fluctuations is called currency adjustment factor (CAF), expressed as a percentage of the freight sum. BS or BAF is applied to the basic rate of freight and CAF to the resulting sum. Contracts may also provide for surcharges when other costs change, such as port usage charges or tolls on seaways and canals. Shipping lines may also levy special increases on freight from or to ports where congestion causes excessive delays to vessels. 'All in' rates of freight are also available, particularly to large shippers and receivers. These remain fixed for specific periods during which no BAF or CAF surcharges can be applied.

War risk: is another potential cause for surcharging freights as ship owners pass on higher insurance premiums for vessels operating on difficult or dangerous trade routes. Such unforeseen costs are a result of *force majeure* and may be passed on to shippers or receivers, usually at a flat rate per container. More about insurance later in this chapter.

Other surcharges may be levied as well, depending on the carrier and the voyage. These may include cargo documentation/customs fees, piracy surcharge, stacking charges, transshipment fee etc.

Freight charges are of great importance to producing countries, because for the roaster the real cost of coffee is the price 'landed roasting plant'. If coffees bought from country A and from country B are used for the same purpose, the two qualities are substitutional and should therefore be priced the same.

If for example the freight from country A is notably higher than freight from B, then A's asking price has to be lower to match the landed cost of B. And if freight rates from country B were to fall then the FOB price or differential for that coffee will eventually rise accordingly if freight rates elsewhere do not follow suit.

Freight rates fluctuate all the time and are also negotiable. It is very likely that different companies will apply different rates during the same time period, making it pointless to list actual rates in this guide. It is much more important to have a good grasp of the general principles governing freights.

Freight rates are often governed by factors more numerous and complex than, for example, the distances involved. Currently, the dominant practice is for shippers and receivers to negotiate individual freight agreements with shipping lines, sometimes on a worldwide basis. As a result, actual freight rates for many receivers are not general knowledge with many bills of lading simply stating 'freight as per agreement' or 'freight payable at destination'.

It remains advisable, however, for industry bodies, both in exporting as well as importing countries, to meet on a regular basis with individual shipping lines that are important in the transport of coffee to review issues of mutual interest. These include shifts in coffee production and demand, port developments in origin and at destination, technical and physical issues (such as hygiene and food safety), and other topics relating to coffee logistics and levels of service.

Freight portals on the Internet: can match available cargo with available space, and vice versa. Trucking and freight rates can be sought and offered so large shippers and receivers can relatively easily ask transporters and shipping lines to tender for certain land and sea cargoes. These are fast moving developments that enable large users of sea and land transportation to strike competitive deals.

Increasing security concerns place more and more emphasis on the creation of an audit trail by the tracing and tracking of all containerized cargo, including coffee. As a result, the importance and range of functions of freight portals is growing, also as part of the general move towards seamless electronic documentation and information sharing in transport and the bulk commodity trade in general. For an example go to *www.inttra.com* or to any major shipping line website.

TERMINAL HANDLING CHARGES

Terminal handling charges (THC) and post-terminal charges are important components of the cost of transporting containerized coffee. (THC cover the cost of the loading and discharge of containers, not charges for inland transportation etc.) A freight quotation by itself may be attractive, but the cost of bringing a container on board or getting it to the roasting plant after discharge may well be higher than the norm and so offset any perceived advantage. Receivers keep a close watch on terminal charges; these charges are an important part of their evaluation of the competitiveness of individual carriers.

Remember that unless stated otherwise in the contract, under an FOB contract the shipper is liable for THC at origin and the receiver is liable at destination. If a receiver negotiates a lower rate of freight but at the same time the terminal handling costs at origin increase, the outcome is that freight costs are being moved around the supply chain – in this case to the detriment of the exporter. (Under an FCA contract the receiver is liable for both sets of THC so this is not an issue.)

BILLS OF LADING AND WAYBILLS

A bill of lading is firstly a receipt: the carrier acknowledges that the goods have been received for carriage. But it is also evidence of the contract of carriage and a promise to deliver that cargo. The contract commences at the time the freight space is booked. The subsequent issue of the bill of lading confirms this and provides evidence of the contract, even though it is signed by only one party: the carrier or its agents.

A bill of lading is also a transferable document of title. Goods can be delivered by handing over a bill of lading provided the shipment was consigned 'to order' and all the subsequent endorsements are in order. See also chapter 4, Contracts.

If a bill of lading is lost, or does not arrive in time for the receiver to take delivery, for example when transit times are short, then the carrier will usually be able to assist by delivering the goods against receipt of a guarantee. The guarantee safeguards the carrier in case the claimant is not the rightful owner of the goods. Wrongful delivery would constitute a breach of contract and the carrier will therefore insist on a letter of indemnity (LOI) from the receiver backed by a bank guarantee whose wording meets the carrier's specifications, usually for an amount of 150% to 200% of the actual CIF value of the goods, valid for one to two years. Although there is no express time limit beyond which the holder of a bill of lading can no longer claim the goods, a guarantee good for one or possibly two years should adequately cover the carrier's obligations. Nevertheless, a letter of indemnity can never invalidate the actual contract of carriage which is the bill of lading.

However, carriers are not obliged to deliver goods against guarantees. That decision is entirely at their discretion and the receiver may have to negotiate the terms with the carrier, who may wish to consult the original shipper. Note that ECF contracts clearly state that buyers are under no obligation to take delivery under their guarantee and if 28 calendar days after arrival the bill of lading is not available then the buyer may declare the seller to be in default. The remedy here would be for the exporter to provide the guarantee instead. GCA does not specifically refer to missing documents and leaves settlement of any unresolved claim or dispute in this regard entirely to arbitration.

DIFFERENT TYPES OF BILLS OF LADING

The carrier's responsibility commences on the physical acceptance of the goods for carriage. If this occurs at an inland point a combined transport bill of lading will be issued. If the handover is in a port then a port-to-port bill of lading will be issued.

The term 'through bill of lading' should not be used, as it means that the issuing carrier acts as principal only during the carriage on its own vessel(s) and acts as an agent at all other times. This implies that the responsibilities and liabilities may be spread over more than one carrier under different (possibly unknown) conditions at different stages of the transport chain.

Under a combined transport bill of lading the carrier accepts responsibility, subject to the normal stipulations in the bill of lading, for the whole carriage, inland and marine: from door to door, or from door to container yard or container station. The carrier arranges both the marine and the inland transport, but it should be noted that marine and overland transport are governed by different international conventions. This can have an effect on the settlement of claims – the financial liability of the carrier for inland carriage is not necessarily the same as it is for the marine voyage (on board ship, i.e. 'from tackle to tackle'). Usually the carrier will assist in any claims procedure initiated by the receiver and/or insurance company, but will not necessarily accept responsibility for settlement if the damage occurred during the overland stage. For example, a truck is stopped at gunpoint and the driver is asked to 'disappear': no liability. Or an accident occurs because of driver negligence: liability may exist depending on local jurisprudence.

Obviously, large receivers will find it easier to solve such matters than will smaller companies. Note that for FCA contracts (also known as 'free on truck' in some origins) it is the buyer's responsibility to lodge the necessary claims under their insurance policy, and insurance cover should therefore commence at the inland point of loading.

Whether a bill of lading is of port-to-port or combined transport depends on whether the box 'place of receipt' (or 'place of delivery') has been filled in.

SEA WAY BILLS

Like a bill of lading, a sea way bill is a receipt and evidence of a contract of carriage, often used for through cargo. But such a bill is not a document of title. Unlike bills of lading, sea way bills cannot be issued 'to order', they cannot be negotiated, i.e. they cannot be endorsed. The advantage is that there is no need to transmit paper documentation to the point of destination to secure delivery because delivery is made, automatically and only, to the named consignee. They can be used when payment does not depend on the submission of documents, for example because the shipment is between associated companies or because payment has been made in advance. Thus, sea way bills can facilitate paperless transactions. See also chapter 6, E-commerce and supply chain management.

CONTRACT OF CARRIAGE: FOB, FCA AND CIF/CFR

The coffee trade uses three basic contract conditions: FOB, FCA and CIF (or CFR), of which the first two are most common.

FOB – free on board. The seller's obligations are fulfilled when the goods have passed over the ship's rail at the port of shipment. For contracts stipulating FOT (free on truck) and FOR (free on rail) this occurs when the goods have passed over the truck's tailgate or the railcar's loading gate.

Under present-day FOB contracts it is nearly always the buyer who arranges the contract of carriage and who is liable for all costs and risk from that point onwards. Nevertheless, ECC clearly states that it should in fact be considered as an ill-defined cost and freight contract even though the price may be defined in FOB terms, i.e. the freight being for account of the buyers. The exporter's contractual responsibility effectively still ends only when the coffee crosses the ship's rail. ECC also states that the buyer is responsible for insuring the goods from the time the goods leave the ultimate warehouse or other place of storage at the port of shipment. This is important because it is increasingly difficult to establish the precise time a container leaves the stack on the quayside and is transferred across the ship's rail. Under GCA contracts the risk of loss transfers upon crossing of the ship's rail and exporters must insure accordingly.

FCA – free carrier. The seller's obligations are fulfilled when the goods, cleared for export, are handed to the carrier or the carrier's official agent(s) at the named place or point of handing over. (Sometimes also called free in container or free in warehouse.) The buyer's responsibility starts here and they are liable to pay all and any inland transportation costs as well as the cost of loading at the port of shipment.

The total freight cost takes all this into account. Not everyone is willing to purchase on the basis of FCA though, especially if the goods are not handed over at the carrier's own premises or at a recognized container filling station. Remember that inland and marine transports are covered by different international conventions and even though a shipping line may arrange for the inland transport it will not necessarily accept liability for events occurring before the goods reach the port of shipment or cross the ship's rail.

CIF – cost, insurance and freight (or CFR – cost and freight). The shipper arranges and pays the contract of carriage but otherwise the transfer of risk is as under FOB.

Table 5.1 Cost distribution between sellers (S) and buyers (B)

	FOB	CIF/CFR	FCA
Loading at sellers' premises	S	S	S
Inland transport (from the named place)	S	S	B
Trade documentation at origin	S	S	S
Customs clearance at origin	S	S	S
Export charges	S	S	S
Loading terminal handling charges (THC)	S	S	B
Ocean freight	B	S	B
Unloading terminal handling charges (THC)	B	B	B

In the United States, a considerable amount of business is transacted FCA (or perhaps also FOT) because of the coffee imported from Mexico through the land border between the two countries (around 2 million bags a year). Seller and buyer should be clear on the difference between the two terms.

Basically, in the case of FCA risk of loss transfers to the buyer the moment the goods are received by the carrier, whether for overland or maritime transport, whilst in the case of FOT (or FOR) that risk transfers to the buyer when the goods are placed on the truck or railcar.

Customs documentation charges or **Cargo declaration fees.** These are a new type of charge, introduced by shipping lines to cover the cost of complying with maritime cargo security regulations now in force for both the United States and the European Union. Cargo that does not comply with these regulations may not be loaded and the lines have to ensure only correctly documented cargo is loaded. Whilst there is no denying that there is an administrative and IT cost to this, many exporters consider these charges to be linked to importation and therefore should be paid by the receiver. However, so far the general consensus on the receiving side is that these charges are part of the cost of bringing cargo to FOB, i.e. they form part of the export charges and as such are to be paid by shippers.

CARRIER'S LIABILITY – BURDEN OF PROOF

FCL – full container load. This simply means the seller/shipper was responsible for stuffing the container and the cost thereof. But the contents of a sealed container cannot be verified from the outside.

The FCL bill of lading simply states 'received on board one container STC [said to contain] X number of bags [or for bulk: kg] of coffee, shipper stow and count'. In other words, in an FCL bill of lading the shipping line acknowledges receipt of the container, undertakes to transport it from A to B without losing or damaging it, and to deliver it. But the shipping line does not commit itself as regards the contents. See also chapter 10, Risk and the relation to trade credit.

There is no clear connection between FCL or LCL and Incoterms®. The terms FCL and LCL are common in most coffee producing countries but do not always have exactly the same meaning. Combining FCL with the term CY (container yard: container is received), and LCL with CFS (container freight station: goods are received), removes any room for confusion. However, CY and CFS are not freight terms, but represent delivery locations.

LCL – less than container load. This means the carrier is responsible for the suitability and condition of the container, and the stuffing thereof. The carrier pays for this and then charges an LCL service charge. The bill of lading will state 'received in apparent good order and condition X number of bags said to weigh Y kg'. Now the carrier accepts responsibility for the number of bags but still not for the contents of the bags, nor for the weight.

In the interests of service to clients, although not in all coffee producing countries, shipping lines will agree to carry coffee as LCL provided the containers are filled or stuffed on the carrier's premises, ideally at a container freight station (CFS). It has become accepted practice in some countries for containers to be stuffed at the seller's premises at their expense, under the supervision of the carrier or the carrier's appointed agent. A higher rate of freight will still apply than for an FCL shipment, but this arrangement is nevertheless of great value to smaller shippers or to those who are still relatively unknown. Importers and their bankers increasingly check on the credibility of exporters, including the documentation they supply, and do not accept unknown FCL bills of lading.

For some exporters and origins, the stuffing and weighing of containers 'under independent supervision' is now the order of the day, not only for LCL shipments, but also for FCL in order to satisfy the legitimate security concerns of all involved in the coffee trade. Such services are often provided by collateral managers who verify correct procedure in an exporter's operations on behalf of the bank that finances the business, sometimes right through to delivery at the receiving end. See also chapter 10.

Claims on shipping lines have dropped as a result of these services, suggesting that past discrepancies in containerized cargo were at least partly the result of inadequate supervision during stuffing. The main cause of claims on containerized coffee in bags has, however, always been condensation damage, which is much less likely to occur when coffee is shipped in bulk.

The term LCL is something of a misnomer in that containers are nearly always full and freight is charged per container, not by weight. The reason the term is often used is that it permits marine insurers and/or receivers to lodge insurance claims directly on shipping lines.

But just as roasters argue that roasting and distribution is their core business, not the transporting, storing and financing of green coffee stocks, so shipping companies consider their business is to carry sealed containers safely and efficiently from A to B, and not to be concerned with the contents. Shipping lines have to eliminate the LCL bill of lading entirely, in time. This in turn will see increased use of independent weighers and supervisors, although the reliability of such services will still vary from port to port, and from country to country. If after such inspections weight or quality claims still arise there will be serious differences of opinion between shipper and receiver. This is mainly because it is not always understood that providing a certificate of weight or quality does not absolve the shipper from contractual obligations.

CARRIER'S OBLIGATIONS – THREE CONVENTIONS

Each case of damage to goods needs to be examined on its own circumstances and merits, but it is useful to understand the background. International conventions governing maritime contract of carriage issues include the The Hague-Visby Rules, the Hamburg Rules and now the Rotterdam Rules adopted by the UN General Assembly in 2009. The first two define a Contract of Carriage as referring only to the carriage of goods by sea, whereas the newly adopted

Rotterdam Rules define a Contract for Carriage as one that may combine carriage by sea and other modes of transport.

These conventions define a carrier's obligations, for example such as having to exercise due diligence to make the vessel seaworthy and to care for the cargo. In general the Rotterdam Rules strengthen the rights of shippers and owners of cargo but of course this type of convention covers many aspects and some of the texts may even be open to different interpretations. However, in terms of who has to prove what, it still remains for the claimant to prove any loss or damage is due to the carrier's failure to adequately perform its duties. Shippers and receivers alike should be familiar with the numerous clauses and conditions contained in the fine print on bills of lading, but this is not always the case.

This means a shipping company will accept responsibility only if it can be conclusively proven that damage to the goods occurred during transit, i.e. en route while the goods were under its control. However, unless the cause of such damage is obvious it may be very difficult to prove the point and exporters can fully expect that receivers of damaged goods will hold them responsible. But at the same time receivers are duty bound to preserve and exercise all rights against third parties. They must also always lodge claims with the shipping company, with their underwriters and any other involved party. There is more information on marine insurance and claims later in this chapter.

Nevertheless, the burden of proof rests with the exporter/shipper, unless there is concrete evidence that the loss or damage was due to an external event, an event that took place after the container was handed over for shipment. Of course, if an FCL shipment is lost or destroyed in its entirety then in most instances everyone will have little option but to accept the exporter's declaration as to the original contents and their condition.

However, if upon discharge containerized goods are found to be damaged without any obvious link to an external event then the burden of proof can become very heavy.

On a separate but related issue: If really serious damage occurs en route, due to unforeseen events beyond anyone's control – *force majeure* or Acts of God – then under the contract of carriage (bill of lading) a shipping company may decide to declare what is known as General Average. Such a declaration will result in proportional claims being lodged against all the owners/receivers of all the goods that were on board at the time the event took place. This kind of situation can become extremely complicated and may at times result in lengthy litigation.

TRANSSHIPMENT ISSUES

The growing size and capacity of container vessels to already up to 15,000 TEU, and in future rising to as many as 18,000, is resulting in increased incidences of transshipment whereas transshipment routings may also become more diverse. Increased transshipment also means that ever more strict instructions must be given, in writing, as to the type of 'cargo care' that is required whereas details of the shipment's routing must be known and agreed in advance. From some origins it is now not at all unusual for shipments to be transshipped three times, in some instances even four times. For example, from the local port by feeder vessel via a larger national port to a regional shipping hub where the large 'mother vessels' call. Or, from the national port to the regional hub and then transshipment again abroad, for example discharge at Antwerp and onward shipment to Helsinki. This means increased transit times, particularly if a feeder vessel is late and misses the mother vessel's slot at the hub port.

Modern container vessels spend the vast majority of time at sea – days in port are kept to a minimum and 'late cargo' simply gets left behind. Such events make it difficult for importers to guarantee 'on time delivery' to their roaster clients and causes additional costs (particularly financing), which they will wish to recoup.

However, because most, if not nearly all, green coffee shipped from origin is sold basis FOB (free on board) or FCA (free carrier) the exporter's responsibility usually ends when the goods cross the ship's rail or are handed to the stipulated carrier. Naturally this presupposes that shipment is made in accordance with the terms and conditions of the contract, i.e. those of the under-lying standard form of contract as well as those that may have been stipulated by the buyer, including any 'cargo care' notes. But, of course, quality and other claims always remain a possibility. See also chapter 4, Contracts.

Even though selection of the carrying vessels is sometimes left up to the exporter, especially FOB buyers should also engage with the process by being well informed about shipping opportunities from a particular port and by insisting that the most suitable options and routings are chosen. Once the goods are on board ship they have become the buyer's responsibility in the sense that he or she has to ensure the goods are insured, will have to settle the freight and, of course, will have to take delivery. If any claims arise after loading due to delays and/or damage then it is for the buyer to lodge these with the shipping company if he or she thinks there is a case for doing so.

However, the exporter is duty-bound to make sure that he keeps the buyer informed of all and any changes to the shipping process, also when information reaches him about changes in transshipment dates, vessels or schedules after the goods were shipped. All parties to a transaction must always exercise due diligence: that is, they must be able to prove that at all times they acted correctly. The shipping agents at origin should monitor transshipment cargo and keep their principals fully informed – this is not always the case though. Nevertheless, in the vast majority of cases it is the buyer who, at least initially, is liable to cover any extra costs although, where appropriate, an exporter might perhaps be asked to assist with the lodging of claims etc. It would make good sense to assist where possible.

NB: Once a buyer realizes that shipping delays are becoming a regular occurrence for goods shipped from a particular port then the buyer will adjust his cost calculation from FOB origin port of shipment to Ex Dock at destination accordingly. On a case-by-case basis, usually it is the buyer who suffers the consequences but, in the longer run, it is always exporters who bear the cost because they will receive lower bid prices. Which of course are passed on to the grower.

Unfortunately, there are no magic solutions to the transshipment issue. A port can drop off the international schedules of the major shipping companies, i.e. main or 'mother' vessels no longer call there, for example due to insufficient deep water; insufficient cargo on offer; or inefficient cargo handling. If so, then that port and everyone utilizing it will have to adjust and make the best of it through improved efficiency and other cost saving measures. For example:

- Keep up to date and make sure your buyer knows not only what you know, but also as soon as you come to know it.
- Ensure you choose the right shipping agent. One who will not simply book on 'friendly' vessels, but who will offer the most efficient routing and transshipment connections.
- Make sure all appropriate 'cargo care' details are stated in the cargo booking. Do not rely on the shipping agent to take care of this.
- Demand the origin shipping agent monitors the cargo all the way, keeping you informed. Liaise closely with the shipping companies, both coastal/regional and international. Usually, this is best achieved through the forum of an exporters' association, a coffee authority, a chamber of commerce or other such body that brings together a number of parties with individual but similar interests.
- Conduct regular reviews of recent shipping experiences, highlight buyers' concerns and claims/comments, etc.
- Stress the fact that, in the final analysis, all extra costs come off the producer price, meaning this is an industry issue – not just one concerning exporters.

SMALL LOT LOGISTICS

Exporters and buyers of small lots that are **less than a container load** face both logistical and cost constraints. Indeed, many importers will not consider anything less than a container load: 19 to about 21 tons in a 20-foot container depending on the type of coffee.

This effectively bars many potential small producers of specialty or organic coffee from direct participation in the overseas market. As a result, many small pockets of quality or exemplary coffee in producing countries go unrecognized, simply because they vanish in the mainstream of a country's total exports. Yet, improved and simplified processing

technology today allows even very small grower groups to produce quality coffee. But if this cannot be marketed successfully, then what is the point?

The Cup of Excellence programme, *www.cupofexcellence. org* (see chapter 6), and the specialty industry as a whole have identified many pockets of excellent quality in different countries but the logistics of getting small lots from A to B are daunting. Few if any carriers today will even quote freight rates per ton, let alone accept mini-lots. Simply put: on container vessels there is no room for break bulk or loose cargo, only for containers.

Within modern shipping there are few alternative options and it is true to say that transport now represents the one great limitation on smaller producers wishing to access the specialty market.

OPTIONS FOR SMALL LOTS

Combine or consolidate cargo. Finding compatible cargo to fill a standard container at least close to capacity can be difficult, and still means having to wait until a full load is assembled. Organic coffee may not be shipped in the same container with other coffee because of the risk of contamination.

Mini-containers within a single, large container could be a solution but these would probably have to be disposable because of the difficulty of attracting suitable return cargo. This is where flexible intermediate bulk containers (FIBCs or bulk bags, super bags, jumbo bags – go to *www.fibca.com*) can possibly play a role. However, most roasters, especially smaller ones, are not equipped to handle bulk bags. But, when hermetically sealed such bags also help to preserve quality, which is especially important for the more expensive specialty coffees. See for example *www.grainpro.com*.

In many countries freight consolidators (specialized freight forwarders) do arrange for the consolidation of compatible cargo to utilize containers more effectively, but this may not be so easily done from smaller ports in producing countries. Also, one would have to be absolutely certain that the other goods in such a consolidated container load will not impact on the coffee and that the buyer is in agreement.

Another and probably less complicated variant, depending on the buyer, is to combine a small parcel of top coffee with a parcel of easily sold, cheaper quality, for example 50 bags exemplary and 250 bags of a generally traded, run-of-the-mill coffee, together in one container shipped as FCL.

In some countries (Nicaragua for example) producer associations help growers of certified exemplary coffee to create container loads by combining different shipments for specific markets. There are also instances where specialty buyers join together in combining shipments. But this requires much organization and great support from exporters and importers alike.

Pay for dead freight. Some buyers or shippers sometimes simply absorb the cost of dead freight (the cost of any empty space in a container) especially when the coffee in question is of high value. How much dead freight can be absorbed will vary from transaction to transaction but there is little doubt that producers of very small quantities stand little chance of becoming regular exporters if they cannot consolidate with others. It does not really make sense to ship a container FOR 25 or 50 bags.

Air freight. Alternatively, if a small lot of expensive 'exemplary' coffee can bear the cost of paying freight for a full container then it may sometimes be just as cost effective to use airfreight instead. However, Customs and security issues play a role here – coffee is not normally exported/imported in this way and so airlines and airfreight companies do not always know how to handle the attendant administrative procedures.

Finally, yet another problem facing shippers of small lots of top quality coffee is that quality can be lost if transit times are too long, for example due to multiple transshipments.

SHIPPING IN CONTAINERS

Bagged coffee in 20-foot 'dry containers' (and today even in 40-foot containers) is a major improvement over the old break bulk method, but still involves extensive handling and does not fully exploit a container's carrying capacity. This is important as transport and freight costs are charged per container rather than by weight. The cost of handling bagged cargo is also escalating continuously, especially in importing countries.

When correctly lined with cardboard or sufficiently strong Kraft paper, and if properly stuffed, standard 20-foot dry containers are suitable for transporting bagged coffee. This is not to suggest they are suitable for prolonged storage of coffee, because they are not. Some receivers do specify ventilated containers for shipments from certain areas. These provide ventilation over their entire length, usually top and bottom, but not all shipping lines offer them. They are expensive, and at the same time more and more coffee is shipped in bulk instead.

Bulk shipments were first experimented with in the early 1980s. After a period of exhaustive trials, mostly on coffees from Brazil and Colombia, the conclusion was that standard containers are perfectly suitable for the transportation of coffee in bulk. But they must be fitted with appropriate liners (usually made of polypropylene) and the coffee's moisture content must not exceed the accepted standard for the coffee in question.

Some container facts:

- **TEU** stands for twenty foot equivalent unit: maximum total weight 30.48 tons, maximum gross payload 28.28 tons (i.e. including the weight of packaging, liners, etc.).

- **FTE** stands for forty foot equivalent unit: maximum total weight 30.4 tons, maximum payload 26.4 tons. Newer and somewhat taller FTE's have a slightly higher payload at maximum 27.5 tons. FTE's are becoming more common in the carriage of bagged coffee as they are easier to stow on board ship. However, shippers should bear in mind that as yet not all end-receivers are equipped to handle FTE's.

- **GP** in the United States stands for general purpose container – the European Union equivalent is **DC** or dry container, i.e. both are the same. The net load of a standard, general-purpose, steel TEU container is on average about 21,000 kg green coffee. However this varies, depending on the type of coffee being shipped. Large beans can be as low as 19,000 kg – small beans perhaps as much as 24,000 kg. It is impossible to use the entire theoretical payload capacity of a TEU because coffee is relatively bulky and so space is the limiting factor here. For a FTE the limitation is not space but the maximum permissible weight.

- Ocean freight for coffee shipments is always charged per container. As such it is entirely up to the shipper to decide how much of the available space to use and respectively how much space to leave empty (dead space).

- Wooden container floors (where fitted) must have been treated against infestation – details of the treatment method is found on the CSC (Container Safety Convention) plate on the container door. This is important because of rules on Wood Packaging Material (WPM) that is used in international shipments. See for example *www.aphis.usda.gov* – Importation of Wood Packaging Material. Note also that materials other than wood for use as container flooring are under development.

- When making a booking with a shipping line always give the instruction 'stow away from heat, cool stow and sun/weather protected' or 'stow in protected places only/away from heat and radiation', i.e. no outer or top position. 'Stow under deck' or 'under waterline' is not appropriate with modern container vessels, since the fuel tanks are often situated in the hull and can radiate heat. Abbreviations also used are **AFH** = Away From Heat and **KFF** = Keep From Freezing.

See also *www.containerhandbuch.de* (version in English).

BAGGED COFFEE IN CONTAINERS: RISK OF CONDENSATION

Condensation occurs because moisture is always present in the air and hygroscopic (water-attracting) materials such as coffee normally contain a certain amount of moisture as well. Coffee with moisture content in excess of 12.5% (ISO 6673) should never be shipped, whether in containers or bagged, as beyond this point the risk of condensation and therefore fungi growth occurring becomes unacceptably high. The only exceptions could be specialty coffees that traditionally have high moisture content, such as Indian monsooned coffees.

This is not to suggest that a moisture content of 12.5% is commercially acceptable for all coffee – for certain coffees, certain origins and certain buyers it is definitely not. The figure of 12.5% simply represents a known technical point at which the risk of damage from condensation and growth of mould during storage and transport becomes unacceptably high. Shippers who normally ship their coffee at moisture percentages below 12.5% should definitely continue to do so.

NB: In certain areas there are shippers who habitually ship at higher moisture contents. but this guide is not in a position to express an opinion on this.

An increasing number of buyers now include maximum permissible arrival moisture content in purchasing contracts. Increasing preoccupations with food health and hygiene in consuming countries suggest strongly that exporters will be well advised therefore to acquaint themselves with their buyers' requirements in this regard.

Coffee is often loaded in tropical or otherwise warm areas for discharge at places where the temperatures are very much lower. Warm air holds more water vapour than cold air; when warm, moist air cools down to dew point, then condensation occurs. Dew point is the temperature at which a sample of saturated air will condense.

Put differently: coffee travelling from producing countries during the Northern Hemisphere summer experiences much less temperature change than when travelling during the Northern Hemisphere winter. Vessels may then arrive when snow and ice conditions are prevalent, particularly in Northern Europe. Of course such conditions are entirely beyond anyone's control, including the shipping company. On other routes cargo may experience multiple climate zones during transit. For example from the Pacific Ocean ports of Guayaquil (Ecuador) and Buenaventura (on Colombia's West Coast) to the East Coast (Atlantic Ocean) of the United States. When passing Cape Hatteras in the State of North Carolina on the East Coast vessels may in winter sometimes experience a drop in outside temperature of up to 20° C (36°F) in just four hours.

During transit the temperature outside the container gradually cools down and the steel container allows the chill to conduct from the outside of the panels through to the inside. On arrival the container has cool roof and side panels, and moist warm air in the space above the cargo and within the stow. Most of the moisture will have been given up by the coffee beans themselves.

When the temperature of the panels falls below the dew point of the air inside the container, condensation starts and will continue until the dew point of the interior air falls to that of the air outside.

Apart from making sure that the coffee's own moisture content is acceptable, condensation cannot really be avoided and all one can do is try to prevent the condensation falling onto the coffee as droplets. If temperature changes are gradual and enough time passes then the coffee beans will absorb the excess moisture from the air within the container and the container will again be 'dry'. But temperature differences of 8° C to 10° C over short periods of time almost inevitably will

result in condensation taking place. In severe cases water droplets, mostly consisting of dislocated moisture from the coffee itself, form on the interior roof and side panels, and then drip on to the cargo causing water damage and mould. Correct stowage does mitigate against the air above the cargo reaching dew point. This can be supported by adding a drying agent or desiccant always provided these are approved for use with foodstuffs and are accepted by the final receiver. For more on this see for example *www. stopak.com, www.dessicantsonline.com,* or *www.dry-bag. nl.*

In summary, differences in temperature plus the time factor and the speed of events combine to release moisture from the coffee. Given enough time the coffee surface will reabsorb the moisture. If events unfold too fast or there is too much moisture, then the coffee cannot reabsorb what it gave up and condensation will continue as long as the temperature difference between the steel of the container and the air inside it is greater than 8° C. A simple demonstration: a glass of cold liquid 'sweats' because its temperature is below the dew point of the surrounding air. The moisture on the outside of the glass comes from the surrounding air, not from the liquid or the glass itself. When the glass warms up, its temperature eventually reaches that dew point, which causes the moisture on the outside to dry again: it evaporates back into the surrounding air.

In producing countries condensation occurs when containers are stuffed at high altitude locations with high temperatures during the day that fall rapidly at night, leading to the same scenario. The risk is increased if full containers are left outside in the radiant heat of the sun, so containers should not be stuffed too far ahead of the actual time of shipment.

The only answer to all such weather-related events is to exercise the utmost care when lining and stuffing containers, and to ensure correct stowage on board ship. See also *www.tis-gdv.de* of the Transport Information Service of the German Insurance Association. Alternatively, contact your local shipping company representative for information on container stuffing and related issues.

Container vessel in Finland during winter, covered in snow.
Photograph courtesy Maersk Line Cargo Care.

Container approval form

Type	□ 20'	□ Steelbox	□ Normal ventilated
	□ 40'	□ Plywood	□ Mini-vents

Condition	□ New		**Rust**
	□ Used		□ None
		□ Normal wear and tear	□ A little
		□ Severe wear and tear	□ Some
		□ Unacceptable	□ Unacceptable

Watertightness	Checked from inside/doors closed □ Yes
	□ No (why) _____

Doors

Closing devices		Left side		Right side	
	Top	□ OK	□ Defect	□ OK	□ Defect
	Middle	□ OK	□ Defect	□ OK	□ Defect
	Bottom	□ OK	□ Defect	□ OK	□ Defect
Door sealing		Left side		Right side	
	Top	□ OK	□ Defect	□ OK	□ Defect
	Middle	□ OK	□ Defect	□ OK	□ Defect
	Bottom	□ OK	□ Defect	□ OK	□ Defect
Ventilation		□ Open	□ Taped	□ Other _____	

Cleanliness	□ Front wall panel	□ Right side wall panel	□ Roof panel
	□ Doors	□ Left side wall panel	□ Floor
Humidity of floor checked	□ No	□ Yes _____ %	
Odour	□ Odour free	□ Foreign smell like	

Container number: _____

Container approved by: _____

Date and venue	Name in capital letters	Signature

NB: Before entering a container check that there are no labels attached indicating it may previously have carried dangerous goods or, in the case of fumigation, what kind of substance was used. Before entering such a container also check that it has been properly de-gassed.

When ordering a container from the carrier, specify in writing that the container must be suitable for the carriage of coffee beans, i.e. foodstuffs, that you reserve the right to reject any container you detect to be unfit, and that you will claim compensation for losses resulting from unsuitable containers. This is no guaranteed protection, but it will alert the carrier. Even so, you remain fully liable for the selection of a suitable container, so firmly reject any suspect container – irrespective of who supplies it. Note that where the shipping line delivers the empty container to the shipper's premises (carrier haulage) and it is validly rejected, then the line will have to pay for replacing it. But if the shipper's transporter collects it from the shipping line (merchant haulage) and it is subsequently rejected, then the shipper will be liable for the cost thereof.

Use a **container approval form** like the example on the previous page. This will serve as a guideline for the personnel in charge of loading and will also remind them to pay the necessary attention. A copy could be left inside the container to demonstrate that you did pay the necessary attention.

The basic premise is that condensation cannot always be avoided but it is possible to avoid the condensed water vapour coming back into the coffee. It is important to consider the following:

- **Containers must be technically impeccable**: dry, clean, odourless and watertight; free of corrosion on the roof and sides; intact door locks, rubber packing and sealing devices.

- If possible **check the moisture content of the floor**. At least insist on a dry container that has not been washed recently. Note that it takes a long time for the floor to dry out and that without an instrument (Penetro meter) you have no reliable means of checking the floor's moisture content which, ideally, should not exceed 12% for bagged cargo. Up to 14% place extra protection (cardboard/Kraft paper) – if over 14% to 16% use plastic with cardboard/paper on it for this. Above this use dry pallets, but note that containers with a floor moisture content above 18% are basically not suitable for bagged coffee.

- When stuffing takes place at the shipper's or at CFS premises (in LCL status) **the shipping line must inspect the containers**. An inspector, acting on behalf of the shipping line, should go inside the container and close the doors. If any daylight is visible the container must be rejected immediately.

- When stuffing takes place at the shipper's premises (in FCL status) **the shipper or its representative should inspect the containers** as above and of course conduct the goods tally.

- The inspector should also particularly check for **obnoxious smells** by remaining inside the closed container for at least two to three minutes. There are occasional incidents of coffees arriving with a strong phenolic smell which renders them unfit for use. A phenolic smell or taste is reminiscent of disinfectant or an industrial cleaning agent such as carbolic acid. Inspectors should reject containers that show evidence of a prior load of chemical cargo or that have an IMCO/

IMO dangerous cargo sticker or label affixed. For more information on the **International Maritime Dangerous Goods Code (IMDG)** and **dangerous cargo labels** go to *www.imo.org,* the website of the International Maritime Organization. Note that coffees tainted by **chemical contamination or smell** will attract claims on arrival ranging from 50% to 100%, to which must be added the costs of destruction.

- **Wooden container floors** (where fitted) must have been treated against infestation – details of the treatment method is found on the Container Safety Convention (CSC) plate on the container door. This is important because of the already-mentioned rules on Wood Packaging Material (WPM) that are used in international shipments.

- The actual **stuffing of the container should take place under cover**, just in case there is a rain shower. **Bags should be sound**: no leaking, slack or torn bags; no wet bags; and no stained bags. The number of bags loaded is to be tallied and signed for by both warehouse staff and loading supervisor (in case of LCL shipments representing the shipping line).

- **The container should never be filled to absolute capacity** in that there should always be some room above the stow. (Applies equally to bulk cargo.)

- Best practice for bagged cargo is to **line the container with cardboard or two layers of Kraft paper**, preferably corrugated with the corrugation facing the steel structure, so that no bag comes in contact with the metal of the container. When stuffing is complete a double layer of Kraft paper should be fitted on top of the bags all the way to the floor in the doorway. This will ensure that the paper will at least partly absorb any possible condensation from the roof. In a fully lined container there will be cardboard or Kraft paper also between the bags and the corner posts, in the junction between the upright walls and the floor, at the back of the container and at the doors, and covering the top of the stow as well. Cardboard is stronger and preferable to Kraft paper

- **Desiccants** or **dry bags** are sometimes used. They are meant to avoid the air in the container reaching dew point (100% relative humidity) during the voyage. The need depends on local circumstances but desiccants should only be used with the express prior permission of the receiver. Many receivers do not permit their use under any circumstances and it is up to the exporter to determine their acceptability. Other materials that can help manage conditions inside a closed container also exist, but fall outside the scope of this guide.

- **Liners for bulk coffee should be 100% sound,** which means no pinholes etc. If condensation forms and drips from the roof it may collect in puddles on the liner and soak through if pinholes exist, which means a claim can be made.

- Under International Maritime Dangerous Goods Code (IMDG) rules coffee still being under **fumigation** or not yet properly 'aired' should be booked, documented, labelled and handled for shipment as IMO Classified (Class 9 UN no. 3359 'fumigated unit').

BAGGED COFFEE IN CONTAINERS: STUFFING AND SHIPPING

Coffee is hygroscopic and contains water. When out in the open the container roof heats up during the day and cools down at night. If there is relatively free air circulation then the warm, humid air released from the coffee rises to the cooler steel plates, where condensation can be severe. The effect of this thermal flow is serious when coffee is stowed in bags because there are air channels within the stow, simply because of the shape of the bags. Those air channels are even larger when stowing is across as illustrated in the chart below. Using the saddle stow blocks these air channels between bags to quite an extent as also shown in the pictures below.

Individual receivers may and do stipulate their own stowage patterns and there is no standard method. However, the golden rule is to try and minimize the air within the stow (i.e. between the bags) as much as possible because cooling of that air during transit contributes to condensation.

Another way.

Stowage complete.

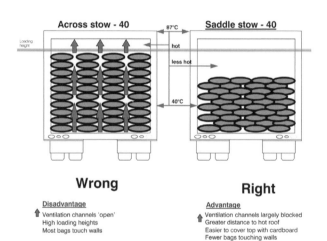

Wrong

Disadvantage
⬆ Ventilation channels 'open'
High loading heights
Most bags touch walls

Right

Advantage
⬆ Ventilation channels largely blocked
Greater distance to hot roof
Easier to cover top with cardboard
Fewer bags touching walls

One way.

Transit time: Experience shows that most of the condensation problems encountered during maritime transport are caused at origin (containers are stuffed too early ahead of actual shipment or not properly lined), or immediately after offloading (particularly for containers arriving in winter). It is therefore of the utmost importance to limit transit times (by using dedicated sailing/routings) and the dwell periods and land legs of the transit as much as possible.

Note that without knowing the exact stowage position of a container it is very difficult to prove that the cause of damage was wrong positioning of the container on board the ship. The damage might already have happened on shore, before loading. In any event, improper stuffing of a container (bags touching the roof or bulk coffee not levelled) can never be compensated for by demanding special care from the carrier.

BULK COFFEE IN CONTAINERS: SEVERAL ADVANTAGES

Recent years have seen a substantial increase in the movement of coffee in bulk, using normal dry containers fitted with a liner. Exact data are not readily available, but informed shipping sources suggest that for a number of large producing countries most shipments, other than to the United States, are now 'in bulk'.

Shippers save on the cost of bags (and there is no need to dispose of them at the receiving end), minus the cost of the liner. Also, a container can hold between 21-24 tons of coffee in bulk which, depending on the type of coffee, can represent a potential payload increase of almost 17% over bagged coffee. At the receiving end the inland transport of say 50,000 tons green coffee in bulk a year for a large roaster is reduced from 2,777 movements of 18 tons to 2,380 movements of 21 tons. In Brazil, for instance, 2 million bags shipped in bulk means close to 1,000 fewer individual containers.

Other obvious advantages are time and labour savings because bulk containers are emptied mechanically, using a tilt chassis. (Jumbo bags or super sacks are much larger than conventional bags, holding as much as 500 kg or more. They are mostly used for intermediate transport cum storage and must not be confused with liners that make use of the container's entire load capacity which jumbo/super sacks cannot.) But there are also other advantages, which are not always immediately apparent:

- **Coffee in bulk arrives in a better condition than coffee in bags when shipped under similar conditions.** Air in between the beans and in between the bags is called interstitial air. Interstitial air in a bulk load hardly moves because the individual beans are obstructing the free flow of air so the hot air cannot easily move to the top of the container. As a result, the temperature of the inside air at the top of the container is lower for bulk coffee than for coffee in bags and the risk of condensation is reduced.

- **There are far fewer claims on coffee shipped in bulk.** Shipping in bulk avoids most of the problems associated with bagged cargo: no baggy smells any more, no weight losses due to handling, generally better preservation of quality. When correct liners and procedures are used, and the coffee is shipped at the correct moisture content, there are far fewer claims on coffee shipped in bulk than there are on coffee shipped in bags – according to some sources claims are reduced by up to two-thirds. Good quality liners also help to preserve coffee quality.

In recent years, a few of the originators of the bulk coffee shipping process have patented in the United States some of the more ingenious parts of the bulk liner. The patents are on the strapping and bulkhead systems that hold the liner in place when the container doors are opened. All major importers and roasters in the United States have been cautioned to use only licensed liners for coffee shipments. As no one has contested the patent claims, the United States coffee industry has more or less agreed to use only licensed liners for coffee shipments. Shippers should check with their United States buyers what brands of liners are licensed under present patents.

Most shipping companies and freight forwarders will be able to provide information on the availability and cost of liners, but it may be advisable to obtain your buyer's agreement before choosing any particular type or make. Note also that coffee should only be shipped in bulk with the buyer's prior consent.

BULK CONTAINERS: LINING AND FILLING

The same inspection procedure must be carried out as for bagged coffee: a container is either suitable or it is not.

The liner itself is best described as an oblong sack or envelope whose size is equivalent to the inner space of a 20 foot container (TEU). It is attached to hooks in the upper corners after which loose coffee is blown in, gradually filling the entire container with coffee. Container liners are used in the containerized bulk shipment of dry free-flowing cargo such as coffee. They are quick and simple to install and enable bulk cargo to be shipped door to door with a minimum of handling, thereby minimizing cargo spillage and waste.

Liners are usually made from virgin polyethylene (film or woven polyolefins), allowing coffee to be transported safely in an enclosed chamber, thus avoiding contamination from pollutants and salt sea air. The liner protects the coffee from external influences such as moisture and, in case of condensation occurring on the container's inside walls, it ensures that this does not affect the coffee.

Once full the liner is sealed and not opened again until discharge at destination, either into the reception system of a roasting plant, or into a silo storage system, for example in a port. Bulk shipping means no export bags are required anymore and more coffee fits into the container (variable but generally about three tons more), thus saving on transport costs. Bulk coffee is discharged mechanically at the receiving end, thus avoiding the use of expensive manual labour. In Western Europe the disposal of empty coffee bags costs money as well. Today, large roasters may receive as much as 90% in bulk but, medium-sized and especially smaller roasters are more likely to still use bagged coffee for ease of blending. Nevertheless, being able to supply coffee in bulk is a definite advantage with cost savings for both shipper and receiver. To note that containers carrying bulk coffee should display a warning sign 'bulk cargo' or such-like statement.

FIXING THE LINER

The inner polypropylene liner must fit snugly against the walls, roof and floor when full – improper placing of the inlet could cause tearing – and the load must be as evenly levelled as possible. The liner's roof must not sag, but must be tight so at no time will the inlet or roof rest on the coffee after loading. Ideally, built-in reinforced straps in the liner's front panel (bulkhead) will prevent bulging when the container is full, thus allowing for easy closing of the doors. (Strapping ropes can also be used.) There should not be any pressure on the doors when closed after loading. The liner must be properly fastened to the container's interior, also at the far end: at the point of discharge the container is tilted to enable the coffee to slide out of the liner, rather than the filled liner sliding out of the container.

Containers can be filled in two ways. One method is to take the coffee from the silo with the aid of a blower or to empty individual bags into the blower's reception hopper. Blowing air into the liner makes it align itself with the walls, roof and floor of the container. Once the liner fits correctly inside the container, the blower then spews the coffee into the now fully-lined container. During this process the displaced air must be able to escape. Some types of piping may cause static electricity build-up and should preferably be earthed.

Do not blow a heap into the centre, leaving space at the rear and the doors, but fill the liner evenly. To ensure the coffee stays away from the hot container roof, avoid as much as possible contact between the stow and the liner's roof panel, preferably by a margin of about 70 cm. Some receivers stipulate that there must be space between the liner's roof panel and the top of the coffee load.

Another way is to fill the container using a telescopic conveyor belt that extends into the lined box. This eliminates the need for air pressure and therefore the risk of damage to the beans.

Bulk coffee in liners – an example. Photograph courtesy Maersk Line Cargo Care.

CONTAINERS AT THE RECEIVING END

INLAND CONTAINER STATIONS

Unlike bagged coffee in containers, bulk coffee in lined containers can be transported and stored outside for limited periods fairly safely under ECC rules. Containers may be weighed and sampled at inland stations provided they were on-carried within 14 calendar days of arrival at the seaport and were weighed and sampled within seven calendar days of arriving at the inland station. (Whether or not carriers raise any extra charges for such extra time is between them and the receiver.) This permits large receivers to take delivery at inland terminals. They then call the containers forward just in time for direct discharge at the roasting plant.

The objective of the just-in-time (JIT) supply line principle is to carry only the immediately necessary physical stocks, with planned arrivals to make up for drawdown. Large trade houses have the capacity to supply JIT direct from their own stocks but cannot supply all a roaster's requirements, also because roasters do not want JIT to limit their purchasing options. The alternative is to buy from smaller exporters and origins 'basis named vessel' where the buyer dictates the shipping line and the vessel to be used.

Receivers are also expected to take all reasonable measures to avoid condensation occurring, especially in winter. If the goods are not required for some time then they will be discharged in a port silo complex for call-up when required. Many ports now offer dedicated silo storage facilities or 'silo parks', which receive and store bulk. Services include blending and cleaning/sorting on demand. Deliveries to roasting plants are then made in bulk trucks that discharge by tilting, or in bulk bags. Some bulk trucks are compartmentalized and can hold different qualities, which are discharged separately by a conveyor belt that runs below the compartments.

Coffee in bags for larger end-users now increasingly goes to a silo installation for transformation into bulk, obviously at a cost.

DISCHARGE

Technology and mechanization are constantly improving supply chain management and an increasing number of bulk containers go directly from the quay or container station to the roasting plant. Here they are discharged, automatically and by a single person (sometimes the driver of the vehicle).

At the roasting plant or silo storage facility the container truck is backed onto a reception pit where the seals are checked and cut. The doors are opened, the liner is cut and the container is then gradually angled upwards by the lorry's tilt-chassis, causing the coffee to pour out. The tilting mechanism is plugged into the computerized reception mechanism, which then controls the rate of tilt and hence the rate of pour. Once the discharge is complete the liner is removed and put away for dispatch to a recycling plant. This is much more efficient than when bags had to be unloaded, cut open and tipped out manually

QUALITY AND SAMPLING

To receive the wrong quality of coffee creates huge problems for any roaster. If anything this has been reinforced by modern just-in-time supply chain practices.

Large roasting plants slot incoming containers into the production line on the basis of the quality, i.e. to be used in blend or production run number X. The quality is known in the sense that the purchasing department has previously approved a sample of the coffee and it has been allocated a purchase or quality code. The plant has received the shipping sample and has verified its conformity with the purchase code.

It is extremely important to the roaster that the shipping sample is fully representative of the actual shipment because at the roasting plant the container is discharged directly into a receiving silo. This leaves little room for manoeuvre – reversing the operation is both awkward and time-consuming. Of course, someone watches the actual discharge to ensure no excessive foreign matter or clumps of coffee are present. Clumps suggest water or condensation damage and a potential risk of mould.

After dumping the coffee passes through a transfer duct into the electronic weighing silo. During this passage a time switch opens a valve at regular intervals, permitting a small amount of beans to fall into a sample receptacle. In this way the entire load is automatically sampled, from beginning to end. The resulting sample is then thoroughly mixed and checked to ensure it matches the purchase or quality code. This system is much more accurate than the old way of using a sampling iron on perhaps 10% of the bags. After approval and weighing the coffee is then transferred to the final storage silo pending supply to the roasting process. During this transfer any foreign matter, dust and chips are removed, again automatically.

WEIGHTS AND SUPERVISION

Weighing technology in importing countries has progressed from the random check weighing of a certain percentage of the bags to the accurate computerized weighing of each complete parcel, increasingly by using weighing silos.

The ECC states that the sellers shall refund any loss in weight in excess of 0.5% of the shipping weight. Unless weighing at origin is extremely accurate some argue that this implies 'delivered weights' irrespective of what the contract states

because many containers travel long distances to the coast from inland filling stations. But the underlying reasoning is that coffee in bulk does not dry out to any noticeable extent and so should not incur any noticeable loss in weight either.

Experience suggests that 90% to 95% of bulk containers discharge within the laid down weight tolerance of 0.5% and that any loss exceeding 0.2% is likely to be due to incorrect filling. There is therefore no particular reason for shippers to add a little extra weight to avoid weight claims (as is sometimes done for bagged coffee). Note though that large receivers seldom bother to claim for small weight differences, preferring to simply strike a recurrent offender off their list of approved suppliers.

Some receivers use the weighing mechanism in the container gantry crane to establish whether the gross weight of a container appears to be within acceptable limits. Should an individual container present cause for concern it will be discharged and weighed under independent supervision. This is not feasible in arrival ports but is possible by special arrangement at inland container yards.

But, the container can only be discharged into the electronic weighing system of the roasting plant or silo park operation. This makes the term 'supervision' somewhat theoretical, because all that will be produced is a computer print-out and verification of the container and seal numbers. Of course, the supervisor could certify that the weighing system had been correctly and formally calibrated in accordance with the laws of the country where it is situated. The operators of such weighing installations should be able to produce a valid calibration certificate on demand.

CONTAINER WEIGHTS AT SHIPMENT

There have been instances where coffee containers have arrived at destination severely underweight or even totally empty, with all seals etc. intact. Strange as this may seem it is nevertheless fact and seeing that theft while on board ship seems rather unlikely, this raises the obvious question: who, if anyone, checks container weights at the time of loading on board vessel? What happens currently?

- Containers arrive at ship's side for loading already locked and sealed. Therefore, all that is visible during loading are locked and sealed steel boxes.
- Port container or gantry cranes do have a weight indicator, but the operator, who is a third party, will not necessarily always observe this nor is he/she in a position to know what the weight of a particular container should be. Container weights vary according to the contents whereas sometimes even empty containers are carried for repositioning.
- In theory it is possible to ask the port for a weighing slip, but this means extra costs. It is also not really feasible to interrupt loading in case variances were to be observed. Modern container vessels carry large numbers of

containers and spend little time in port. Schedules are very strict and interruptions are unacceptable.

- In some ports containers are loaded using the ship's own gear (lifting equipment), for example if port equipment is in short supply. Such on-board equipment is not necessarily fitted with weight indicators.

So far the conclusion has been that checking container weights during loading is not a viable proposition unless someone is prepared to incur, possibly substantial, costs.

However, in recent years evidence has come to light of shippers overloading and under-declaring container weights (probably not coffee containers) to the point where vessel security becomes compromised as evidenced by a number of incidents at sea and in port. In December 2010, the World Shipping Council – www.worldshipping.org – therefore asked the International Maritime Organization – www.imo. org – to establish an international legal requirement that all export containers must be weighed before they are loaded.

Weighing containers is by itself not difficult – the issue is how to avoid interrupting the regular flow so as not to interfere with yard, port and ship operations. This may mean changes in the way containers are brought into the port or container yard, or how they are handled there. One potential way is to fit mobile container positioning equipment with weight indicators and to record the results with 'exceptions' being directed away from the regular flow. Another would be for accredited third party verifiers to provide accurate container weights before entry into port or yard.

Whatever the case may be, as and when it materializes, the weighing of loaded containers immediately ahead of shipment should be an added security advantage to coffee shippers and receivers alike.

OUTLOOK

Today (late 2011), the carriage of coffee in containers, whether in bags or in bulk, has become universal and it is unlikely that much if any coffee is still shipped internationally as break bulk or loose cargo. Furthermore, estimates are that as much as 70% of all mainstream coffee is now shipped in bulk. Because mainstream coffee makes up over 90% of all coffee traded, this makes it likely that not less than 65% of all coffee traded internationally is shipped in bulk. But the real figure could be (much) higher. Exact data on the amount of coffee carried in bulk versus that in bags are not available and this information is based on feedback from coffee shipping and trading sources. Large mainstream roasters are the major receivers of bulk coffee and a number of them today accept nothing else into their plants. But for importers and medium to small roasters, especially specialty roasters, the proportion of bulk is much less because medium to small roasters are more likely to blend by bag count instead of container count.

As mentioned, most large modern roasting plants no longer accept bagged coffee and producing countries or exporters that persist in using bags will see much of their cargo transiting through silo parks at destination. Here the bagged coffee is de-bagged and transferred into silos for subsequent delivery in bulk, sometimes after blending. This is both costly and time consuming and will increasingly render uncompetitive those mainstream suppliers who cannot or will not 'do bulk'.

COST AND CONVENIENCE

Bulk shipments require less handling, cost less in terms of packaging, and incur lower port and freight charges than bagged cargo. At the receiving end they eliminate manual labour and reduce transport costs, with the product basically presented 'ready for use' at the roasting plant. With exact and reliable just-in-time scheduling, coffee increasingly travels directly from origin to the roasting plants.

European Union countries hold importers directly responsible for the disposal of waste materials such as jute and sisal bags, a task that roasters can do without. The European Union is also increasingly pressuring road transport to travel outside peak traffic hours: coffee in bulk fits this development because at the terminals it can be handled mechanically, outside normal working hours.

Containerization and cargo safety issues are under constant research in areas as vacuum packing for green coffee; improved desiccants and use of moisture absorbing materials (MAMs); different fumigation and container cleaning methods; electronic seals including door opening registration alarms; satellite tracking; and securing inland transportation; etc.

CONTAINER SECURITY AT CUSTOMS

Previous sections have referred to security issues such as quality, performance and finance. But there are also physical risks that may occur once the container leaves the loading station. It may be tampered with for reasons of theft or smuggling, both occurrences that are on the rise worldwide. Favourite locations for this type of crime are ports and container terminals, or during road or rail transport.

RECEIVING CONTAINERS – UNITED STATES

The aftermath of the terrible events of 11 September 2001 in New York brought much stricter inspection controls on containers, and even coffee samples entering the United States and probably also other countries. There are many millions of containers in use worldwide, carrying much of the world's cargo, and relatively few of them are ever physically inspected because to do so would cause bottlenecks that would not sit well with just-in-time logistics. To deal with such concerns, the U.S. Food and Drug Administration (FDA) has introduced a Food Bioterrorism Regulation that requires all those handling food products, including green coffee, to be registered with it. See *www.cfsan.fda.gov* and *www.ncausa. org*. See also the information on HACCP and the United States in chapter 12.

In addition, US Customs have initiated C-TPAT (Customs-Trade Partnership against Terrorism), a government-business programme to strengthen overall supply chain and border security. For more on this search for C-TPAT on *www.cbp. gov*. C-TPAT is more extensive where US Customs review company security and control systems. It is voluntary, but once an importer has been registered costs will be lower as there will be fewer customs inspections. Foreign companies shipping to the United States that may not have links with a C-TPAT registered importer can make use of an Agency Service offered by the National Coffee Association of USA.

The NCA C-TPAT programme is to help the industry partner with the United States Government to enhance homeland security while easing potential burdens on commerce. The NCA has partnered with the Global Security Verification (GSV) cross sector industry initiative (*www.importsecurity. com*) and Intertek (*www.intertek.com*) to develop the industry's shared information platform designed to facilitate importers' and exporters' participation and compliance with C-TPAT requirements. The platform will be a registry of foreign suppliers and their C-TPAT related security practices. Industry importers that are current members and/or seeking C-TPAT membership can utilize the NCA C-TPAT shared information platform for efficient and cost-effective means of collecting and maintaining necessary documentation. In addition to the supplier registry, the platform is designed to provide valuable information and tools to users to facilitate application to the C-TPAT program. Visit *www.ctpat.ncausa. org* which also describes the registration process itself.

Under the Container Security Initiative (CSI) all high-risk cargo is to be inspected before loading at origin and to this end US Customs have established a presence in a number of foreign ports. For food shipments US Customs now require advance notice, no more than five days before arrival and no later than noon the day prior to arrival for discharge. In addition, the '24 Hour Advance Manifest Rule' obliges shipping companies to transmit cargo manifest details to US Customs 24 hours prior to a vessel's ETA at the port of loading. Cargo for which the required details have not been transmitted as per this rule will not be loaded. Should a certain shipment be considered suspect then US Customs will issue a DNL message: Do Not Load. See more on *www.cbp.gov*.

RECEIVING CONTAINERS – EUROPEAN UNION

In early 2004, the United States and the European Union also signed a shipping security deal that will extend the Container Security Initiative screening programme to all EU states. Since then, the European Commission has adopted Commission Regulation (EC) No. 1875/2006 of 18 December 2006 aimed at increased security for shipments entering or leaving the EU and providing greater facilitation for compliant operators. The Regulation has implemented four measures as follows:

- A risk management framework ensuring customs control of goods crossing the EU.
- An Authorized Economic Operator (AEO) Certificate will be granted to reliable economic operators.
- Traders will have to supply customs authorities with advance information on goods brought into, or out of, the EU.
- Customs authorities will be required to exchange information electronically on exports between the Customs offices involved in the procedure (export control system).

A copy of the Regulation can be downloaded from the following link: *www.eur-lex.europa.eu/LexUriServ/site/en/ oj/2006/l_360/l_36020061219en00640125.pdf*. The following offers a brief explanation of what this means:

Authorized Economic Operator. Reliable and compliant traders will benefit from simplifications in the customs procedures and/or from facilitation with regard to customs controls relating to safety and security under the Authorized Economic Operator (AEO) certification scheme. The AEO concept should ensure a safer and more secure end-to-end supply chain. Being recognized as an AEO will constitute an added value for the operator as it demonstrates compliance with solid security criteria and controls. This will provide a competitive advantage to participating companies.

Information on goods prior leaving or entering the EU territory. Traders will have to supply customs authorities with advance information on goods brought into, or out of, the EU (entry and exit summary declarations). This will enable customs authorities to carry out better risk analysis, e.g. before goods arrive in the customs territory, and to focus on high risk cargo due to the availability of risk information at an early stage. It will also allow quicker processing and release upon arrival, resulting in a benefit for traders.

NB: This is of particular importance to coffee exporters in that the advance information on shipments must be sent to the EU Customs at the first point of arrival 24 hours before the loading of a container on the vessel. See Annex 30A of the Regulation for further details. Different time limits apply to various modes of transport but the 24-hour requirement covers virtually all coffee shipments.

What is now known as the European Union (EU) Advance Cargo Declaration Regime entered into force on 1 January 2011.

For further information visit *www.ecsa.eu/publications/101.pdf* or *www.ecsa.eu* (look under Publications). See also the FAQ section at *wwwec.europa.eu/ecip/help/faq/index_en.htm*

Export control system. Customs authorities will be required to exchange information electronically on exports between the Customs offices involved in the procedure. This constitutes the first step in the full computerization of the EU Customs; the so-called electronic Customs project (IP/05/1501). Once all Member States are connected to the export control system then EU exporters will receive the proof of export immediately after the exit of goods, enabling all related processes (VAT refunds, etc.) to be speeded up.

Further information on the security aspects of the Customs Code can be found at: *www.ec.europa.eu/taxation_customs/ customs/policy_issues/customs_security/index_en.htm*

Most shipping lines are well aware of, and well versed in, the application of the different directives in the United States and the European Union and are mostly dealing with them by electronic means. They are more or less forced to do so on shippers' behalf because potentially they are liable for substantial fines where no or incorrect advance information is provided. Because of this additional administrative workload some shipping lines have introduced a new category of fees to cover the cost – as explained at the beginning of this chapter.

CONTAINER SEALS

Apart from locks, the first defence against tampering are the numbered seals the shipping company provides to seal a container's doors. If a seal is broken or damaged then it may well be that the container has been tampered with. But instances have been recorded where traditional seals have been broken and replaced without any visible sign of this having occurred. Because of this some exporters add locks of their own to physically secure container doors.

Containers and their seals must also be physically checked each time a container changes hands, for example from origin terminal to ship, from ship to arrival terminal, from arrival terminal to truck, and from truck to roasting plant. Ideally, each time a Container Interchange Receipt should be established that records the seal's condition, the seal number, and the exterior condition of the container itself. Should there be something wrong with any of these then the receipt trail could show under whose responsibility this happened, in turn enabling a claim to be lodged if necessary. The last check takes place just before the container will be opened. Shipping lines also use these receipts to claim redress for any physical damage to the actual container itself.

Security of containers is not just to protect the coffee. In recent years, illegal drugs have also been found in coffee containers (as a result of port to port conspiracies, unconnected with the coffee trade). The international coffee trade and the shipping community are actively working with customs authorities worldwide to help stop the use of coffee shipments as a vehicle for illegal drugs. Obviously, container seals are the first line of defense in this battle.

Modern seals incorporate increasingly sophisticated technology that makes undetected tampering much more difficult. But physical verification is still required. Seals by themselves cannot prevent containers being opened – they are not a deterrent but rather a means of verification. Even so, seals are no better than the person who places them. If that person cannot be trusted then one cannot be sure the seal was really placed at all, i.e. that it was not faked. It is not for this publication to explain different ways in which the placing of seals has previously been faked. Instead, one solution is to use clear seals that show the mechanism, with the number printed on the inside under a clear elevation that works as a magnifying glass.

However, even intact seals prove only that the cargo seems not to have been interfered with after the seals were affixed. Bulk containers have been known to be attacked by forcing a pipe through the rubber door seals and into the liner, after which coffee is simply siphoned out. This is easily prevented by placing a plank upright on the floor inside and in front of the doors before shutting them. However, there have also been instances where containerized cargo has disappeared during inland transit to port, yet doors and seals were perceived as intact. Where this occurs with any regularity shippers really only have one option: invest in security measures such as having trucks travel in escorted convoys, only allowing night stops in authorized locations, etc.

If a container's seal and seal number are sound and correct on arrival of an FCL shipment, but the condition or weight of the coffee is not, then the receiver will claim from the shipper/ exporter, also if stuffing took place under supervision. When goods are shipped FCL, the responsibility lies with the person supplying them unless the bill of lading shows the container was accepted as sound but at destination it is delivered damaged. To repeat, the burden of proof always lies with the shipper.

For goods shipped on an LCL basis, shipping lines can be held responsible only for the number and the apparent good order and condition of the bags, Therefore, if on arrival the seal and seal number of a container shipped on an LCL basis are sound and correct, but the condition or number of the bags is not, then the receiver will claim from the shipping line.

CONTAINER TRACKING AND SMART CONTAINERS

Most reputable shipping lines provide container tracking tools, track and trace, through their own websites. Containers are not yet tracked electronically (implanting microchip transmitters is still too expensive) but every move is notified and recorded in the tracking system, making up-to-date information available. As individual carriers traditionally work with proprietary computer systems and programmes for such services, receivers have to contact each carrier individually, which is cumbersome. However, shipping portals are increasingly standardizing the way shippers, receivers and clearing agents interact with carriers by providing access through a single platform.

Other service tools will include sailing schedules, container bookings, bill of lading information and event notifications. Large shippers/receivers can have direct (authorized) access to such portals and may for example operate entirely with electronic information, including bills of lading. Eventually, such portals will also interact with both e-commerce and paperless trading systems. For more on this go to *www.inttra.com* Smaller or occasional shippers and receivers mostly still rely on hard copy (printed) bills of lading, but the portal can arrange to print the document at the most appropriate location. This saves time and minimizes the risk of mail being lost. However, as mentioned in chapter 6, more widespread use by the coffee trade of electronic documentation probably depends on major shipping lines generally moving to electronic bills of lading.

Depending on their sophistication, modern container seals can record and transmit all actions that might occur during a voyage, particularly also the opening/closing of container doors. Using technologies such as Radio Frequency Identification (RFID) passive devices are read by scanning whereas active devices (battery powered) can themselves transmit information. These are useful tools for keeping track of cargo and facilitating cross-border trade, for example by reducing customs formalities in Europe. But security concerns are also placing electronic seals in the forefront of anti-terrorism activities. Until fairly recently, a container load of simple food items like bottled water, flour or sugar did not pose any major security risk, as theft was unlikely. But today there is a real risk of terrorist action (contamination, poisoning, etc.) and also low-value food cargo requires high levels of security.

The Smart Container pilot project by US Customs represents another potential approach, but whichever direction is taken, electronic seals or smart containers, one or both will become an integral part of coffee logistics. Although the cost of active (able to report) electronic seals is coming down and re-usable ones are increasingly available, cost still remains an obstacle, not least because of the massive number of container shipments that take place daily.

INSURANCE

UTMOST GOOD FAITH

All insurance contracts are subject to the principle of utmost good faith. The insured must truthfully inform the underwriter of every material fact that may influence the insurer in accepting, rating or declining a risk. This duty of disclosure continues throughout the life of the policy. Insurance is in effect a partnership between the owner of the commodity who wishes to avoid or minimize the risk of loss or damage and the insurance company that will take on that risk against payment of a fee. The owner of the commodity must practice risk avoidance, just as the insurance company must make good legitimate losses.

Insurance is the most obvious and the oldest form of risk management, and has been practiced since long before futures markets and other risk management instruments came into being. It is beyond the scope of this guide to go into the precise detail of what constitutes a good insurance policy. There are almost endless variations on a very basic theme: if the loss was unavoidable then the cover should stand.

But insurance cover is only as good as what is stated in the policy document. One view is that only what is expressly included is covered. Another and more attractive view is that anything that is not specifically excluded is covered.

THE RISK TRAIL TO FOB

To judge the need for insurance cover, one first needs to analyse the type of risk that exists, how prevalent it is and what potential loss it represents. Only then consider whether or not cover should be purchased. Always look at the monetary value of coffee when considering risk. As coffee prices fluctuate, so does the value of a truck or container load. It is not always recognized that a container load of coffee can be more valuable than a load of television sets or other electronic goods.

THE RISK TRAIL TO FOB: FARM GATE TO PROCESSING

Money in transit. An obvious risk – buying agents carry cash. An insurance company may offer cash in transit cover as part of a general policy, but the extent of such a cover is always limited so be sure to find out exactly what is covered and what is not. When coffee values change the amount of necessary cash will change as well.

Ownership at inland buying stations. At this stage coffee is often packed in unmarked bags and is very difficult to identify. Keep stocks at such stations to a minimum and transfer them to a central location as soon as possible. Unless there is a good, formal record system at the buying station it may be difficult to insure risk at this stage. Be certain to advise the insurance company of all circumstances, including negative aspects, to prevent difficulties arising after a loss occurs.

Inland transit. Often inland transit is by small trucks under variable conditions of transport quality. Arrivals must therefore be checked for quality, weight and moisture content. To make fraudulent manipulation more difficult samples should be taken by a member of the quality control department rather than by warehouse staff.

THE RISK TRAIL TO FOB: WAREHOUSING AND PROCESSING

Warehousing. The better organized this function is, the easier it is to obtain cover and negotiate the best terms and conditions. Like banks, insurance companies wish to know and understand how a business operates. Ensure coffee is stored in an easily identifiable manner, using a numbered bay system in the warehouse with the bay numbers and boundaries painted on the floor. Coffee must always be stored on dry, clean wooden baulks or pallets, off the floor, away from walls.

Keep back-up warehouse records in a secure and separate location. Otherwise the loss of both stocks and records can become very convenient for some, while creating a nightmare for the owner. Make weekly stock checks, preferably using people who do not know what is expected and therefore can only report what they find. All stacks should bear a clearly visible stack card, showing the detail and history of the coffee stored. There should never be unidentified coffee in any warehouse. Unidentified can become unknown and may progress to non-existent – mystery disappearance or 'going over the wall'.

Make regular random weight checks to verify that bags are of the correct weight and that scales have not been tampered with. Occasionally tear down a stack, again at random, to verify there is no hole or empty drum in the middle.

Other obvious general risk factors include flooding, fire, lightning, explosion, plane crash, theft, burglary and embezzlement. Others are deterioration due to excessive moisture content, prolonged storage or infestation (but not all of these latter types of risk are insurable).

The buildings themselves can pose risk if roofs are not tight, drainage pipes are blocked, ventilation is inadequate or the walls and floor are of poor quality. The area in which the warehouse is located may pose risks if neighbouring buildings are used to store or produce hazardous or smelly goods.

Processing. Usually the risk of faulty or improper processing cannot be insured. Processors must depend on the qualifications of their staff and good quality control at the purchasing end to achieve the expected results. Nevertheless, accurate storage and processing records with daily out-turn reports will go a long way to alerting one to any unexpected and unwelcome variations.

Processing is always a weak point in that out-turns cannot be forecast exactly. Ensure scales are correctly set, bags are weighed to the proper weight and, above all, do not allow any unmarked coffee to lie around. Unmarked bags or bags without tags could be the first stage of an unscheduled voyage out of the warehouse.

THE RISK TRAIL TO FOB: TRANSPORT TO PORT

There are no uniform patterns for inland transportation to the port. Each producing country has different arrangements, but all have some risk principles in common.

- The truck that collects the coffee at your facility must have been properly cleaned, as you do not know what it carried before. Closely inspect all trucks for smells and other contamination. Look for holes in the roof or flooring through which water could penetrate or through which coffee might be stolen by the use of probes.

- The same applies when containers are used for inland transportation. In addition, take a very close look at the locking devices of the doors and at the door hinges.

- It is also recommended to check the moisture of any wooden flooring of any such truck or container with a moisture-measuring instrument. Even a moisture content of well in excess of 20%, a situation in which coffee would definitely become damaged, cannot be verified by simply touching or feeling the floor.

- If the inland container is also to be used to ship the coffee, then be sure that the container is properly lined, with the coffee fully enveloped by strong Kraft paper or cardboard (depending on the season and your type of trade) or an adequate container liner in the case of a bulk shipment.

- Depending on climatic conditions, heat radiation may be a potential hazard. Even if that is not the case, coffee in a container should never be stored in the open for any prolonged period.

- Ensure that only known and trusted parties or persons handle the coffee. It is advisable to operate with as few truckers or trucking companies as possible in order to build a mutual relationship. It may also be wise to clearly define which trucks and which drivers may be used.

- Keep in contact with the driver(s) by mobile phone and/ or use a Global Positioning System (GPS) to monitor a truck's progress.

- Do not permit overnight trucking or prolonged stops at unknown places. If the distance to the port is too far to make it in a single day trip, then make sure the driver reports with the truck at places that can be trusted, and stays overnight only in a safe and secured compound. Under certain circumstances convoy systems can also be of help.

- In some countries it is advisable to consider using security services. Before adopting such safety measures and so incurring cost, always ask how quickly you will be notified of something being wrong, and who will do what within what period of time after such information is received. Have an established accident or crisis management procedure.

- Ensure the coffee is delivered to a safe and suitable location, and that the operator is familiar with the handling of coffee. On arrival the goods should be properly checked and a certificate of receipt issued. This is to ensure there is a credible paper trail that the insurer can verify.

- Remember, the climate in most shipping ports is far from ideal for coffee. In high temperatures and high humidity coffee absorbs moisture, possibly to a level where permissible limits for safe transportation are exceeded and where severe condensation and mould may become unavoidable.

Exporters should bear in mind that at all times the coffee travels and is stored at their risk. There is also the obligation to deliver a particular quality and quantity at a given time and place. Poor management of the risks to FOB may ruin any chance of claiming a mishap on *force majeure* (i.e. as unforeseeable events beyond anyone's control – see chapter 4, Contracts).

DELIVERY TO FOB: FCL (OR CY) TERMS

Up to this point there is no difference between shipping FCL (full container load) (CY) or LCL (less than container load) (CFS), because it is always the shipper's responsibility and risk that the coffee arrives at the point and time contracted for, usually FOB a particular vessel. (For a more detailed explanation of the terms LCL and FCL, see the beginning of this chapter) The following are the additional responsibilities and risks an exporter assumes when shipping FCL.

- The shipper is responsible for selecting a suitable container. This is not limited to deciding whether a type of container is suitable in principle; each individual container must be suitable for the carriage of foodstuffs. As per the bill of lading only the shipper is responsible for selecting a suitable container, for controlling its condition and for preparing it in every respect for the voyage.

- The shipper is responsible for proper lining of the container, or for enveloping the coffee in a suitable form.

- The shipper is responsible for loading the correct quantity. Only evidence that the container has been tampered with will absolve the exporter from having to make good any short weights. The shipper is responsible for what is loaded into the container, right until the doors are closed.

- It is solely the task of the shipper to prepare the container for the carriage of goods. Any damage that cannot be proved to have occurred from external causes is for the account of the shipper. In this context, changes in weather or temperature are not an external cause.

- The shipper is responsible for proper stowage and must request the carrier to 'stow away from heat, cool stow and sun/weather protected' or 'stow in protected places only/away from heat and radiation' (i.e. no outer or top position). The ECC also stipulates that shippers shall pass on all relevant shipping instructions received from buyers to the carrier.

Remember, the burden of proof is always on the shipper, that has to show that everything was in good order when the container left their premises or was loaded. If there is any doubt, the shipper will be held responsible, regardless of any supervision certificates issued by any party at origin.

Such weight or supervision certificates do not provide an ultimate safeguard because only the verifiable facts at destination count. This does not prevent shippers from employing trustworthy persons with good knowledge to control and verify what is being done – their simple presence may already be enough to avoid manipulations. But, unless expressly agreed, such inspectors or inspection companies seldom assume any financial liability arising from their work.

DELIVERY TO FOB: FCL (OR CY) TERMS IN BULK

Bulk shipments are made almost exclusively on FCL (full container load) terms. In only very few ports do shipping companies offer the service of bulk loading coffee that is delivered to them in bags. For bulk shipments, be aware of all risks already mentioned above for FCL shipments, and also of the following additional factors.

- While the need to select a suitable container for bagged coffee is essential and obvious, this is even more so for coffee in bulk because separating out any damaged beans is far more difficult and expensive. In particular, the container must be clean, free of taint, watertight, and with locking and sealing devices intact. Only responsible, experienced and reliable persons should be entrusted with the checking of containers before stuffing.

- Using the appropriate liner is essential. These are made from woven polypropylene or similar material that allows the coffee to breathe. The liner must be fixed to the container in such a way that:
  - It does not slide out during tilting and emptying of the container;
  - The liner's roof does not lie on the coffee; and
  - The bulge does not touch the doors, but is well away from them (this because the bulging effect increases during transit).

- The liner must be filled properly with the correct quantity and quality of coffee. The surface of the coffee must be as level as possible to provide maximum distance to the container roof, and to prevent the liner from resting on top of the coffee.

- Sealing the container is a good option to secure evidence of what has been done. The carrier will probably also affix a seal. If so, check carefully that the seal is correctly applied, and the seal number is noted and mentioned in the shipping documents. (The ECC requires shippers to provide seal and container numbers in their shipping advices.)

DELIVERY TO FOB: LCL (OR CFS)

LCL (less than container load) means the carrier is responsible for the suitability and condition of the container, and the stuffing thereof for which they charge an LCL service charge. The bill of lading will then state 'received in apparent good order and condition X number of bags said to weigh Y kg'. The carrier accepts responsibility for the number of bags but not the contents or the weight. The exporter's liability is reduced, but not eliminated, because again, the carrier can only be blamed if the cause of any arrival discrepancies can be proved to be external.

TERMINATION OF RISK

Depending on the terms of the contract of sale contract, risk may terminate at different stages of the shipping process.

FCA (can be either **CY** or **CFS**). The buyer or their agent takes delivery at an inland place, probably at the seller's mill or warehouse, the receiving station or on the carrier's truck. No risk of physical damage or destruction attaches to the exporter after this point, but the exporter remains responsible for errors or omissions that occurred while the goods were under their care and responsibility.

In other words, if you deliver an FCL container that is unsuitable (e.g. tainted) then you remain responsible for all the consequences. The same goes for short weights beyond the permitted tolerance. But if the container is stolen after it leaves the premises, then the loss is not the responsibility of the exporter.

FOB (and **CFR**). As discussed in chapter 4, Contracts, there are differences between FOB according to Incoterms® and FOB as per the ECC and GCA contracts for coffee. In insurance terms, the following applies:

- **Incoterms®.** FOB means that you must bring the goods safely and in sound condition on board ship at your risk and expense. See *www.iccwbo.org/incoterms*.
- **ECC.** FOB means that the risk, or rather the obligation to keep the goods insured, passes to the buyer when the coffee leaves 'the ultimate warehouse or place of storage at the port of shipment'. This certainly does not mean that the entire inland haulage or storage is at the buyer's risk – all it means is the very short time span from the last place of storage immediately before shipment. (This stipulation removes any uncertainty regarding insurance cover being in place for FOB shipments. The seller's contractual responsibility ends 'when the goods cross the ship's rail', but for insurance purposes it is difficult to establish when exactly this happens.) In the case of container shipments it means the removal of the container from the stack in the port of shipment for direct placing under ship's tackle – not the removal of the coffee from the warehouse for stowing it into containers. ECC then goes on to state that 'the sellers shall have the right to the benefit of the policy until the documents are paid for'. This ensures that the exporter has recourse to the buyers' insurance policy in case the goods or the container itself are damaged, destroyed or stolen between the time the container is placed in the export stack in the port and its receipt on board.

- **GCA:** Under GCA contracts, however, title to the goods is transferred when they cross the ship's rail and the shipper is therefore obliged to insure up to this point. The structure of the American coffee trade is different from that in Europe. The vast majority of American roasters buy coffee 'ex dock' so it is the trade house or importer that deals with marine insurance matters whereas in Europe many roasters buy basis FOB.

CIF. In addition to paying the ocean freight the shipper must also arrange and pay for an insurance that must be in conformity with the stipulation of the ECC: warehouse to warehouse, all risks including SRCC (strikes, riots, civil commotions commodity trade) risk, and war risks at a value of CIF + 5%. Very few CIF sales take place nowadays – as is seen earlier in this chapter.

STANDARD FORMS OF CONTRACT

Changes to standard forms of contract used in the coffee trade are relatively rare but do occur and by the end of 2011 the ECC was under review. To see the latest version visit *www.ecf-coffee.org* and look for Contracts under Publications. For GCA contracts visit *www.greencoffeeassociation.org* and look for Contracts under Resources.

INSURANCE: THE COVER

INSURING RISK

The preceding texts are intended to assist in assessing the risks and obligations, other than purely commercial ones, that accompany particular types of contracts. The need for insurance will be obvious to everyone – the scope of cover that is needed depends on the total exposure to risk and is best assessed by seeking professional guidance from an insurance broker, an underwriter or one's bankers. This guide cannot provide a comprehensive overview of all potential options and solutions.

Just as it is essential to fully appreciate and quantify one's exposure to certain risks, so one must understand the obligation to inform the underwriters fully of all the factors of the risk to be insured against. If this is not done it may be considered that the risk was misrepresented, rendering the insurance null and void. The relationship between client and underwriters is in many ways very similar to that between borrower and banker – full disclosure is the best approach.

Insurance is a business with firm rules and regulations. The costs of insurance coverage are not based on firm tariffs, however, but are the result of the underwriters' experience with the particular type of risk. Underwriters keep check of the amount of premium collected and the losses paid out. This loss experience will determine whether premiums are reduced, remain the same or are increased.

Alternatively the scope of cover may be reduced or even cancelled entirely. It is therefore in the exporter's own interest to avoid losses and claims, that is, to practice loss avoidance.

Finally, parties taking out insurance should always determine whether or not the cover they purchase includes loss as a result of terrorist action. If this is not specifically mentioned in a policy document then it may not be covered.

TYPES OF COVER

Open cover

If you have regular needs for insurance, it is advisable to enter into a contract that is valid for a period of time – usually one year. Within the principal contract all necessary stipulations are discussed and agreed once, and they apply for the entire period. This means that within its period of validity the cover is always available when needed. Compared to insuring on a case-by-case basis this provides additional safety, better rates and a better relationship with underwriters.

Maximum exposure or limit of liability

With an open cover the insurance contract will stipulate the limit of the underwriters' liability to compensate the insured for a single occurrence. The amount of liability may vary depending on each stage of transport or storage. On a case-by-case basis (insurance per certificate) the amount stated in the insurance certificate is the limit of liability. The considerable increase in green coffee prices, especially arabica, in 2010/11 once again highlights the need to regularly review all insured limits to make certain the value covered remains adequate.

Extent of insurance – all risks

In reality the phrase 'all risks' certainly does not mean that all possible risks are covered. Normal storage and transport insurance principally covers only losses due to physical damage to goods that occurs suddenly and originates from external sources or events. For example, underwriters will never cover the risk of goods becoming unfit for use as a consequence of excessive moisture content or improper preparation. They will firmly reject all such claims.

'All risks' normally covers all the physical risks mentioned earlier. The contract may however also include a list of perils, particularly for storage insurance. Be very careful with such lists. Only the items (perils) they mention are covered by the insurance – nothing else. If the list states only fire, lightning and flooding, then risks such as contamination, infestation, wetting or theft are not covered.

Risk avoidance

It is the duty of the insured and whoever is acting on their behalf (i) to take all reasonable measures to avoid or minimize losses recoverable under the insurance, and (ii) to ensure that all rights against third parties (warehousemen, transporters, port authorities, etc.) are properly preserved and exercised.

Loss in weight

One matter clearly not covered under 'all risks' is loss in weight that does not result from obvious theft or torn bags. Exporters wishing to cover potential weight losses, for example when shipping coffee in bulk, must expressly apply for such cover. Carefully check first whether it would not be better instead to ensure that the correct quantity is always shipped, possibly even with a small excess or 'tolerance'.

Duration of cover

There will be a clear stipulation from which moment until which moment cover is granted. Read that part of the policy or certificate very carefully; if you experience a loss outside that given timeframe, you are not covered. Note too that 'warehouse to warehouse' does not mean any warehouse that may be suitable – it is always a warehouse at the stated place of destination. This may well be different from the final destination the goods may travel to.

Exclusions

The policy or certificate may contain exclusion of particular risks, for example the nuclear energy exclusion clause. Another likely exclusion is for war on land, not to be confused with coverage against SRCC risks (strikes, riots, and civil commotion). There will also be other exclusions, sometimes based on the location of a particular risk.

Deductibles or franchises

It may well be that the underwriter does not cover all of the risk and only agrees to insure 80%. Alternatively, the first thousands of dollars of any claim will not be paid. Indirectly, this is the same thing. The objective of such stipulations is to ensure that the client, the insured, makes every effort to avoid claims occurring, that is, they practice risk avoidance.

Agreeing to deductibles – also called franchises – will also save some premium, but avoid a situation where in case of a major disaster the total amount of such deductibles could put the company's financial health at risk.

Premiums

The policy will stipulate the amount of premium to be paid, how the monthly declarations shall be made to the underwriters, and the way and time limit within which invoices need to be paid. Remember that unpaid premiums can result in cover lapsing. Underwriters usually view single risks as more speculative and more expensive to administer than declarations under an open cover or declaration policy.

Rates under open covers are generally much lower than those for single risks.

CLAIMS FROM RECEIVERS AT DESTINATION

It is known that the vast majority of shipments are contracted FOB, and that receivers cover the marine insurance. As a result, their relationship and arrangements with the providers of that cover are not of direct interest, but exporters need to understand why the receiver claims from them, rather than from the carrier or the carrier's insurance company.

The burden of proof rests on the shipper unless and until there is concrete evidence that the loss or damage was due to an external event that took place after the container was closed and sealed. At the same time, it must be appreciated that serious partners of good standing are not interested in claiming loss or damage where it does not exist. Some receivers take the trouble to immediately inform shippers when they believe there could be a claim on an arrival, perhaps adding a digital photograph showing the problem (e.g. wetness, mould or clotting of the beans).

Depending on the type of problem the shipper is then given a time limit within which to respond, for example by arranging for an appointed representative to witness the discharging. Because the shipper has only insured till FOB it is unlikely that their own insurance company will become involved, unless of course the evidence suggests that the damage or loss could have occurred before loading. As a precaution, shippers are always advised to transmit such claims to their underwriters.

Even so, damage due to the improper selection of a container, improper lining or stowing etc., is never part of the insurance cover to FOB unless it has been expressly agreed (liability insurance for faulty workmanship). Unexplained differences in weight or number of bags will also not be covered unless the cover was against loss in weight 'irrespective of cause', something few underwriters will consider.

Appointment of surveyors

'Appointment of surveyors' is an often-heard term. 'Lloyd's agents' is another. But the trade in coffee is increasingly specialized, and the burden of proof is increasingly placed on the exporter, including for health-related issues. It is unlikely that the average insurance surveyor will have the required expertise in condensation issues, for example. In some countries this kind of specialized expertise is more easily obtained than in others; if shippers consider they might be at risk they could be well advised to determine in advance whom they could call on to represent them in case of claims. Compiling information for different importing countries on qualified, professional surveyors and other available coffee experts (surveyors may not understand quality issues for example and a coffee quality expert may not be expert in transport matters) would be a useful exercise in collaboration between coffee trade associations in producing and consuming countries.

In any case, when a notification of a potential claim is received, it is best to react with all due haste and in particular the following:

- Inform your own insurance company, and the carrier, as a matter of course.
- Obtain the fullest information about the extent of the loss or damage.
- If necessary request someone (your agent for example) to visit the site.
- If things appear to be serious, appoint a qualified surveyor to attend on your behalf, always keeping your own underwriters informed.

WAR RISK INSURANCE IN SHIPPING

There are instances where underwriters declare certain areas to be 'war risk zones'. Not because of actual war, but because of piracy attacks. For example, the Malacca Straits in June 2005 and much more recently the Arabian Gulf area, as well as large stretches of the Indian Ocean, due to a spiralling number of attacks emanating from the Somali coast. Piracy problems are also encountered along the coast of West Africa. When a 'war risk zone' declaration is made shipping companies may decide to recoup any additional insurance premium they may have to pay by charging 'war risk' as a separate, additional freight cost to shippers. This is of interest to coffee producers because inevitably in today's coffee economy, such costs will be passed back to the producer in the form of lower prices.

The decision on the Malacca Straits Declaration was taken by the Joint War Committee or JWC, part of the Lloyd's Insurance Market Association, following a report on shipping security it had commissioned because of piracy attacks; the appalling situation along the Somali coast is general public knowledge. Strictly speaking, 'war' means a dispute between nations, conducted by military and/or naval attack. But this was not the case in the Malacca Straits, nor is it so along the Somali coast.

The insurance industry uses a number of acknowledged definitions of what covers certain types of risk. Among them are the **Institute War Clauses (Commodity Trades)** that speak of 'loss or damage to the coffee caused by war, civil war, revolution, rebellion, insurrection or resulting civil strife or any hostile act by or against a belligerent power'. War clauses also deal with capture, seizure, damage due to derelict mines, etc. as well as general average or salvage charges. But 'war' does not equal piracy. Yet, where such acts occur frequently, underwriters have to consider this additional risk and do so by declaring the area in question to be a 'war risk zone'. Individual insurance companies then determine what level of additional premium to apply – this calculation will depend on their assessment of the situation as well as the reinsurance arrangements they have in place.

The implementation of such a move, i.e. the levying of higher insurance premiums for 'war risk', was previously arranged jointly by the underwriters concerned that then advised the relevant shipping conferences. Usually, this resulted in a standard, across-the-board charge applicable to all shipping lines. Today, this is no longer the case, mostly as a result of the introduction of strict anti-cartel legislation that forbids 'joint price setting' by underwriters and shipping companies alike.

See the beginning of this chapter for an explanation of 'shipping Conferences'.

Other clauses relevant to the trade in coffee are (i) the **Institute Commodity Trades Clauses (A)**, dealing with loss/damage to goods, general average and salvage charges, and liability under the 'both to blame collision' clause which appears in some bills of lading; and (ii) the **Institute Strikes Clauses (Commodity Trades)** dealing with loss/damage caused by strikers, locked-out workers or people taking part in labour disturbances, riots or civil commotions, and any terrorist or person acting from a political motive in addition to general average or salvage charges connected with the foregoing.

Individual shipping companies, faced with demands for additional premium on vessels sailing through or passing the declared danger zone, basically have three options:

- Purchase the additional insurance cover;
- Cover it themselves through their in-house insurance pool; or
- Do nothing and take the risk.

Within all three options a commercial decision then has to be made on whether or not to charge 'war risk' as a separate, additional freight cost to shippers or receivers. This is done with bunker (fuel) surcharges, for example. By quoting freight and surcharge together the 'war risk' issue in question automatically becomes part of the contract of carriage, the bill of lading.

However, insuring cargo against 'war risk' is not the responsibility of the shipping company: the conditions of the contract of carriage firmly place the onus on the owners of the goods. Thus, the additional premium mentioned here is that payable for the insurance of the vessel. A premium paid by the shipping company that may result in a surcharge on the ocean freight it in turn charges to shippers.

Of course the owners (receivers) of the cargo most likely also have to pay additional 'war risk' insurance to cover the goods they ship. If all these additional costs become substantial it is inevitable that prices will suffer: new costs or cost increases that are introduced between 'production'

and 'landing of the goods abroad' in the end usually fall on producers in the form of lower prices.

Finally, the foregoing only provides a brief overview of what usually takes place between declaring that 'war risk' exists, and shippers or receivers being asked to pay a surcharge for this. The legal definitions and interpretations of what constitutes 'war risk' are extremely complicated and cannot be explained here, nor can the level of surcharges individual companies might apply be easily estimated.

The unprecedented increase in piracy attacks emanating from the Somali coast affects East and Central African coffee producers in that war risk surcharges on their main export routes have been driven to very high levels indeed, with as much as US$ 200 per TEU reportedly being charged by some shipping lines in 2011. Fortunately, coffee prices had risen substantially by then, but over the longer term there can be little doubt that such surcharge levels, together with the increased premiums receivers have to pay for insuring their goods, in the end directly impact on the economies of the countries concerned. These additional charges of course apply to all their maritime import and export cargo, not just coffee.

For more information on piracy threats and counter measures visit *www.imo.org* and go to their Knowledge Centre.

CHAPTER 6

E-COMMERCE AND SUPPLY CHAIN MANAGEMENT

E-COMMERCE AND SUPPLY CHAIN MANAGEMENT

E-COMMERCE AND COFFEE

Modern communication technology, Internet, e-mail, mobile phones, etc. has enabled many to access information on coffee markets and pricing almost effortlessly, often almost irrespective of where one might be located. Use of the Internet is widespread also in the dissemination of statistics, shipping information and other useful information, while networking services as Facebook and Twitter enable the instantaneous exchange of news and views on coffee matters and issues globally. It is surprising that despite initial enthusiasm and an almost global acceptance of electronic operations in many spheres of economic activity, green coffee trading via electronic market places has not taken off.

Price information is widely available on the Internet and coffee futures are all traded electronically on both LIFFE (www.euronext.com) and ICE (www.theice.com). However, no electronic marketplaces actively trading in green coffee have emerged as yet. A number of serious attempts have been made, but failed to attract the required interest and we were not aware of any electronic market place that was actively trading physical or green coffee (as opposed to coffee futures) by end 2011.

When it comes to actual trading then traditional methods continue to be the order of the day, i.e. direct contact between seller and buyer using e-mail, telephone, telex and fax. Why is this? Apart from the fact that the international coffee trade remains very fragmented with numerous actors, there are probably two major reasons:

1. Buyers need to know what quality they may be purchasing because coffee is not homogeneous. The reason futures markets work is that they trade a fully standardized product; anyone wishing to deliver (tender) coffee to a futures market first has to have that coffee stored, graded and certified. This ensures that anyone taking delivery from a futures market knows in advance what kind of coffee can be expected. Of course most operators on the futures markets never tender or receive physical coffee, but the basis to do so is there which is what makes trading possible.

Coffee quality varies enormously and development of internationally accepted green coffee standards that roasters could trust enough to receive coffee 'unseen' has to date proved impossible. Roasters need advance samples of the physical coffee they receive and they need to be able to reject substandard deliveries. But at the same time, they also need to safeguard their supply line. This is

why direct dealings with trade houses and exporters remain the preferred option. There are mainstream roasters that use electronic documentation throughout but unless and until a number of them give solid backing to the idea of an open electronic marketplace for green coffee, there is little chance of one emerging any time soon.

In fact it is questionable whether the mainstream coffee industry (85%-90% of all coffee roasted) presently has any interest in advancing beyond the electronic trading and execution of futures and options. This enables the industry to purchase physical green coffee at a differential to the futures markets. Final prices are then established using electronically traded futures. Put differently, today's futures markets all operate electronically and are used as a tool for the pricing of most physical or green coffee, leaving only the sourcing and implementation of the actual purchases to be carried out through direct contacts.

This is not the same as an 'electronic market place for green coffee', but seems to be all the market requires at this stage. This is why otherwise great ideas as Eximware, www.eximware.com, and Intercontinental Exchange's (ICE) eCOPS system, www.theice.com have failed to advance into green coffee trading. Futures markets operate combined electronic trading and documentation systems successfully, but this is a very different environment from the trade in physical, in green coffee.

Many specialty coffee sellers would like to see an electronic marketplace where green coffee can be offered and bought at prices that are not based on the futures markets, but on actual quality. But this ideal always comes up against the fact that no serious importer or roaster will purchase specialty coffee unseen, i.e. without being able to assess the quality and knowing the supplier before committing to a purchase.

Therefore, until such issues are resolved, instead of this business-to-business (B2B) model, the most obvious e-commerce activity in the coffee world will likely remain that of business-to-consumers (B2C), in which roasters, importers and some specialized producers with the requisite logistical capability sell small amounts, often in retail packs, directly to individual consumers or wholesale to small retailers. See chapters 8 and 9 for more on futures and differentials. See also chapter 3 on the difference between mainstream and specialty roasters.

Undoubtedly, the technology exists to make Internet-based, e-commerce coffee trading feasible. It will not take off, however, until enough market participants are comfortable with using it to provide the critical mass necessary to make it viable. Electronic market platforms, we suggest, allow buyers and sellers of a particular product to make contact and exchange information, after which some might proceed to initiate actual transactions directly, i.e. not via the platform. See for example *www.leatherline.org,* also operated by the International Trade Centre (ITC). Electronic market places on the other hand would allow them to also enter into and execute legally binding transactions, requiring much more complex and demanding systems to deal with electronic B2B trades. Examples of platforms offering coffee linkages include *www.eFresh.com* and *www.koffeelink.com.*

2. Efficient commerce comes first. Supply chain management is not e-commerce – instead of 'electronic marketplaces', what is required first of all is standardization of the way in which industry or a group of companies operate. Before we can have successful e-commerce in coffee, we need efficient commerce, and this is where the Internet offers huge potential that is increasingly being exploited. Prime examples already operating in the coffee industry include the London LIFFE CONNECT™ futures trading system, the GCA's XML contract, the eCOPS system, shipping portals and logistics tracking systems. These are widely used by many participants in the coffee trade.

However, one of the original expectations of electronic documentation was that such systems could eventually link all or at least most actors along the entire coffee chain. And that the logical outcome of such a process would, over time, facilitate the emergence of electronic market places where buyers and sellers of green coffee would meet.

Electronic documentation has developed into something quite different from the original vision. In today's coffee trade most such systems with automatic database updates generate internal documents only. They then e-mail or send confirmations to third parties. These third party documents must then be entered manually into the database of the party receiving them.

The problem for fully automated documentation systems is twofold. Experience has shown that (i) few in the coffee trade are (yet?) willing to pay a third party for document generation, and (ii) individual companies want to maintain their own database. Documents that update a communal database might save duplicating data entry, but in the coffee trade the communal database concept is still perceived as less than secure. Many large coffee companies today employ electronic databases and documentation systems but these are used internally. They are seldom linked to other parties in the coffee trade and certainly play no role when it comes to trading green coffee. This then relegates the concept of electronic market places for green coffee still further into the future.

However, electronic documentation systems are here and they are being used extensively although not as fully as one would have expected. To date one of the main stumbling blocks also appears to be a reluctance to move to negotiable electronic bills of lading, resulting in the continued physical transfer of shipping documents against payment. As mentioned in chapter 5, some receivers use sea way bills, whereby cargo is deliverable only to the party specified at the time of loading. Such bills are not negotiable and eliminate the need to transmit paper documentation to obtain delivery at destination. But this can only work between closely linked parties and other documents might still be in paper form. However, should major shipping lines decide to make a general move to electronic bills of lading then it is logical the coffee trade would adapt and fully fledged electronic documentation systems for physical coffee transactions would come into their own.

It is important to understand how such systems can or should work.

EFFICIENT COMMERCE – THE ICE eCOPS SYSTEM

eCOPS, the ICE's Electronic Commodity Operations Processing System, in 2004 replaced the ever-growing stream of paper documentation necessary for the delivery of coffee to the New York futures market. This became possible when negotiable electronic warehouse receipts (EWRs) replaced the old paper ones. EWRs had already been used in the United States cotton trade since the early 1990s.

Other electronic documents are the warehouse bill of lading (local shipping advice), contract summary, shipping advice, FDA and Customs entry, sampling order, delivery order, commercial invoice, notice of assignment, trust receipt, weighing request, exchange invoice, notice of transfer, bank release, weight note, sampling confirmation, quality certificate and grade certificate. Most of these are not of direct interest to exporters as such, but this range of previously paper documents demonstrates a seamless exchange of data, title and, therefore, goods and money.

eCOPS does include an electronic maritime bill of lading option that in theory enables exporters to link into this entire system once electronic bills of lading become accepted in the coffee trade.

The integrity of the eCOPS EWRs and other documentation is ensured by restricting issuance authority to licensed operators only, and eCOPS generated EWRs are accepted as collateral by the commercial banking system. All companies that deal with Exchange coffee are connected to eCOPS, but as yet the system is not widely used for non-Exchange goods. However, since 2003 every change of ownership of Exchange Certified Coffee has been successfully tracked by eCOPS, not only in the United States but also in the European ports of Antwerp, Hamburg/Bremen and Barcelona. Some United States coffee warehouses have moved to issuing eCOPS EWRs for all coffee they handle, Exchange certified or otherwise.

However, as mentioned previously, the eCOPS system too has not been able to transform itself into a true B2B electronic market place. For more on eCOPS and updates on further developments go to *www.theice.com* and look for eCOPS.

EFFICIENT COMMERCE – SUPPLY CHAIN SECURITY AND EFFICIENCY

Supply chain security has become extremely important as evidenced by the Importer Security Filing (ISF) requirements for the United States and the Import Control System (ICS) now in force for the European Union (see also chapter 5). Globally import and export cargo security measures now require the sharing of information around the world, thus allowing government systems to screen against what may be considered risky cargo.

These security systems are electronically managed and involve large amounts of information to be collected, processed and shared speedily to ensure no undocumented or risky shipments are allowed to travel. Failure to comply fully may result in serious fines being levied against carriers and importers alike. And, as security concerns grow so will the complexity of the legislation to address these, all of which will add to the responsibilities of operators along the modern supply chain.

Shipping lines have so far been at the vanguard of developing the necessary infrastructure because cargo that is inadequately documented in terms of these regulations may not be loaded at origin. This increasing reliance on electronic documentation and the consequent streamlining of data collection processes is now exposing smaller exporters and importers to the advantages that electronic documentation brings. This includes reduced risk of errors and possibly fraud, as well as faster and more accurate information flows.

Alos, electronic linkages within the coffee trade will continue to grow, because more and more of the required software can now be leased on a pay-as-you-go basis, which avoids the previous problem of having to invest in software that becomes outdated within a relatively short time. The end result is likely to be a more efficient and more secure supply chain, even if the actual electronic trading of green coffee remains excluded.

INTERNET AUCTIONS

There is growing interest in Internet auctions for selling specialty coffee. The concept and many of the legal, technical and practical aspects were developed under the auspices of the ICO/ITC/CFC Gourmet Coffee Project and involved the Brazilian Specialty Coffee Association (BSCA) working in association with the Specialty Coffee Association of America (SCAA). The first auction was held in Brazil in 1999. The idea has subsequently been developed into the Cup of Excellence programme, owned by the non-profit Alliance for Coffee Excellence. Since 1999, more than 60 COE auctions have taken place in Bolivia (Plurinational State of), Brazil, Colombia, Costa Rica, El Salvador, Guatemala, Honduras, Nicaragua and Rwanda. Similar Internet auctions have also been held in other countries, outside the COE programme.

Although the individual lots sold may mostly be very small, the auctions generate enormous publicity and interest. The coffees and their stories do put a country and an area 'on the quality map', and there is an increasing number of success stories where individual coffee growers have subsequently been able to create sustained follow-up business at very good prices with some of the auction buyers.

The logistics of hosting an Internet auction are complex and involve developing a suitable portal that can handle real time defined bids from different sources. The process of signing up international buyers and importers is also a difficult and time-consuming task, as is establishing a tasting panel of recognized cuppers who select the best coffees in a competition among hundreds of candidates. Origins interested in hosting a Cup of Excellence Internet auction may contact the organizers at *www.cupofexcellence. org*. Note that such auctions focus on the small exemplary segment of the specialty market and do not lend themselves to broader-based selling of coffee.

PAPERLESS TRADE

TAKING THE PAPER OUT OF THE COFFEE TRADE: AN EXAMPLE

Today, larger companies in particular have automated back office systems that link in with shipping portals and, sometimes, selected suppliers and/or buyers. Nevertheless, as also explained in chapter 5, nearly the entire coffee trade still uses paper documentation in its dealings. Actual negotiations are conducted by phone, fax, and e-mail, but final agreements such as contracts, delivery orders, bills of lading, letters of credit and other vital documents require an original signature and mostly continue to be presented physically to the respective parties.

Furthermore, the quality and type of shipping documentation that circulates can be quite variable and delays may be considerable when faulty documents have to be returned and resubmitted, or cargo release is delayed because the documents are not available, causing significant and unnecessary cost.

Banks and others in the trade chain are very interested both in electronic security and the standardization of trade documentation. Taken together, if clear and enforceable standards apply, these would provide the certainty that the shipping documentation submitted is valid and negotiable, which is not always the case today.

For many exporters the time lapse between actual shipment and receipt of payment, executed through physical transmission of paper documents, can take as much as 15 to 25 days. In a truly paperless electronic system, the transfer of documents, transfer of title and financial settlement can be reduced to four days or even less, depending on the complexity of the business process.

Typical traditional document flow

Day 1   Coffee loads
Day 2   Carrier prepares bill of lading
Day 3   Shipper receives bill of lading (can be much later in some coffee producing countries)
Day 4   Shipper processes bill of lading to bank
Day 5   Bank receives bill of lading
Day 6   Non-working day
Day 7   Non-working day
Day 8   Bank processes documents
Day 9   Documents in transit to selected European bank
Day 10   Documents in transit to selected European bank
Day 11   The European bank receives documents
Day 12   The European bank sends documents to buyers
Day 13   Non-working day
Day 14   Non-working day
Day 15   Buyer receives and processes documents
Day 16   Payment effected
Day 17   Shipper receives payment

Typical electronic documentation flow

Day 1   Coffee loads, bill of lading raised by carrier
         Bill of lading instantly transmitted to shipper
         Shipper uses bill of lading to generate other documents
         Shipper transmits to selected European bank
Day 2   Documents received and processed by bank
         Bank transmits to buyer
Day 3   Buyer processes documents and effects payment
Day 4   Shipper is credited with the payment

Clearly the benefits will vary from country to country, but that they are potentially substantial is obvious, especially when credit is tight and expensive, and when exporters depend on fast turn-around of their capital. However, as explained, the coffee trade has as yet not fully accepted to use truly paperless systems and appears to be satisfied with partial solutions. Nevertheless, it is good to understand how truly paperless systems really function – also because the increasing demand for rapid and accurate advance security information on coffee shipments is bringing ever more coffee trade players into the field of electronic information sharing. This is not to say that the electronic documentation process described in the sections that follow will be rapidly

adopted by the international green coffee trade, but it is and remains an option which is why this overview is provided.

BIRD'S EYE VIEW

Imagine the electronic progress of a coffee shipment from sale to delivery as a highway along which there are a number of stops where different actions take place: the coffee is contracted, bagged, weighed, transported, stuffed into containers, cleared, shipped, invoiced, paid, discharged, cleared, trucked inland and delivered to the roaster. At each stop documents and advices are initiated and are slotted into the electronic master envelope that represents the physical shipment. When the envelope reaches the buyer it contains all the required documentation and the buyer pays for the goods.

This is no different from the traditional way of physically collecting all the paper and signatures at every stage and couriering them to the buyer or their bank. Except the electronic method is entirely secure, it is neutral and it takes much less time. It also provides a precise and instantaneous record of each step or action that is taken along the way, and of who takes it. At all times each party will know who said what to who, thus avoiding misunderstandings and mistakes.

THE ELECTRONIC ENVIRONMENT

Major international companies have seen that the electronic sharing of non-confidential data and information can shorten delivery, marketing and financing cycles, while maintaining acceptable inventory levels, thereby reducing cost and liberating working capital throughout the trade chains. Optimizing the supply chain results in efficiency gains for all parties, and minimizes the complications and risks involved in international trade and shipping.

Electronic information flows also make it much easier to act proactively when a potential control issue looms; the situation at each stage of the execution of an international shipment is visible, instantly and constantly. Finally, increases in efficiency and security may also add to cash market liquidity.

Such major change does not happen overnight. We have seen the telex and fax gradually being replaced by e-mail. But what to do with electronic data which is not standardized? How to make optimal use of Internet technology? How to bring the community of coffee exporters, traders, importers, roasters, carriers, warehousemen, government authorities, financial institutions and other service suppliers closer together in sharing data, thereby avoiding duplication and errors? How to create efficiencies for each member of the community in their function within the supply chain and for the coffee community as a whole? What about the security of the data transmission? Will such comprehensive data be used effectively and without compromising the competitive advantage individual companies may have developed over the years?

Various global shippers have focused their efforts on providing browser-based information services on contracts, delivery orders, shipments and quality. These initiatives have played a meaningful role in the process of automation and creation of supply chain visibility. But in the long run they are probably not a sustainable solution because they do not allow for efficient, industry-wide data integration.

Two mainstream solutions have now evolved: e-marketplaces for commodity trading and secure messaging platforms to allow for data integration within the supply chain.

FROM B2B-EXCHANGE TO E-MARKETPLACES

When e-commerce over the Internet was introduced, the operations were rightfully considered as B2B exchanges. Bringing buyers and sellers together, price discovery, and matching supply and demand were the main criteria bringing coffee traders and roasters to the Internet. Through specialization these B2B exchanges then developed into private exchanges or evolved into e-marketplaces, enlarging their scope to cover several commodities.

These e-marketplaces facilitate the electronic execution of coffee contracts, but this covers only the 'front office' segment of trading coffee. The 'back office' component (execution of contracts, shipments, payments) continues to be largely paper based. Logically, e-marketplaces need to be able to link the members of the coffee industry and service suppliers, so as to offer the best levels of service and data distribution to the back offices and planning systems of exporters, traders, importers, roasters, warehouses and other service providers.

CENTRALLY AVAILABLE DATA VERSUS STRAIGHT THROUGH PROCESSING

While e-marketplaces provide electronic functions and may replace back-office functions within each of the individual trading partners, the data remain on the servers at the e-marketplace. For certain functions it is ideal if the various parties in the supply chain have access to these centralized data. However, certain types of data need to be held in the databases of the participants themselves, for reasons of corporate security or enterprise resource planning (ERP): production scheduling, accounting, contract and position management systems and so on that are outside the scope of an e-marketplace. Such data need to be transferred among the different players.

In paperless trade this is done not through physical transfers of documents or rekeying the data, but through electronic messaging of the data, between participants or via the e-marketplace.

If the electronic data are in a standard format, which can be recognized by participating systems, information can be transferred directly from computer to computer. This is also known as **straight through processing**. This means the data do not have to be intercepted by users for verification and subsequent re-entry in the system – often the origin of errors. They can be integrated directly into the individual user's application or database.

When combined with the central functions provided by the e-marketplaces, straight through processing allows for efficiencies and cost savings at all functional levels of the supply chain. Administrative tasks are reduced and supply chain visibility and efficiency between trade chain partners is increased.

LEGAL FRAMEWORK REQUIRED

Managing and limiting risk is essential in the international coffee trade and shipping environment. Knowing and trusting one's counterparts is not always easy. Managing the risks inherent in negotiable documents requires security, non-repudiation and certainty of delivery.

Some companies have been using e-commerce for some time despite the lack of specific international or national legislation, however, the lack of legal clarity has slowed acceptance. The electronic exchange of data does not in itself pose a problem, but when the data represent contracts, negotiable instruments or payments, a clear legal and neutral framework is required. In the absence of uniform national legislation, this framework can take the form of a multilateral contract that binds all participants to rules of conduct that are necessary for these transactions to work.

CONTRACT AND TITLE REGISTRY

The contract will clearly define which electronic messages replicate the provisions of the classic paper documents, such as contracts and bills of lading. It also provides data security and integrity, and establishes that these messages cannot be repudiated. These are all essential elements in electronic messaging. It would also establish a central registry of titles, so that legitimate transfer of title can be made, basically for any type of negotiable documents, whether bills of lading, contracts, warehouse warrants or letters of credit. Of course, the legality of such a system would have to be tested in a number of jurisdictions, between them covering many countries.

COMPLIANCE, VERIFICATION AND SETTLEMENT

Any system will have to be able to handle and verify the compliance of all types of international trade documentation. From commercial documents to government-issued certificates and financial settlement tools such as document compliance checking and exchange of business documents against payment, so eliminating expensive and time-consuming manual activities. Also, in a properly established system electronic documents of title should provide a basis for trade goods to be used as collateral for financing. Finally, the overall aim should be to connect the entire trade community: exporters, importers, carriers, banks and other intermediaries, thereby making the movement of goods and financial settlement cycles entirely paperless.

Different options include web-based browser solutions that focus on particular functions, industries or geographic sectors. Other solutions such as TradeCard, PayPal and IdenTrust focus more on financial settlement. Some existing service providers restrict themselves to specific markets, some overlap with others, and in some cases they are complementary.

SECURE TRANSFER OF DATA AND DOCUMENTS

Neutrality is an important aspect when choosing a service provider. Exporters, traders and roasters will generally feel more comfortable with a visibly neutral platform. They also prefer a legal framework in which supply chain participants can communicate data and documents within a closed community, yet within an open technology environment providing more effective business processes throughout the supply chain.

Individual participants will continue needing to keep data on their own servers and will strive to establish 'straight through processes' to their particular customers. But over time communities served by different providers will require cross-provider links between those networks. Service suppliers to the trade who are active across multiple industries, such as carriers, warehouses and banks, require access and transferability.

Both the open technology used and the transparency of cross-provider transfer of data will eventually allow companies to interact across borders and industries. Already several systems collaborate and promote collaboration between supply chain members, so they will seek similar connections between different networks. Three examples:

- **Bolero**, developers of an electronic trade facilitation system originally known as Bill of Lading Europe. See *www.bolero.net*.

- **IdenTrust.** This is a certification authority and scheme that enables digital signatures to be deployed by applications. SWIFT provides network and interface services to IdenTrust. See *www.identrust.com*.
- **GS1 US.** Previously Transora, GS1 US is a supply chain standard development and information sharing platform, linking multiple sectors and businesses. See *www.gs1us.org*.

Transactions must be handled through a provider or trustee that furnishes depository services. That is to say, all those wishing to use electronic transfer of original documents will have to be linked to a provider of depository services, at least until individual providers can themselves be linked to each other and carry out each other's deliveries, adhering to the strictest standards of integrity and verification of the documentation.

The international banking community has been using protocols and systems for many years: SWIFT (Society for Worldwide Interbank Financial Telecommunication) and CHIPS standards (Clearing House Interbank Payments System). Today these systems handle approximately 95% of all international United States dollar payments. Bolero and IdenTrust are based on similar principles and are logical extensions of the original considerations that led to SWIFT's formation.

SWIFT is one of the founders of Bolero and IdenTrust and manages the technical operations of the Bolero system under contract, thus linking Bolero directly into the international banking system. According to its 2010 report there are 9,700 live users in 209 countries transmitting over 4 billion messages a year with peak traffic at over 18 million in a single day. Details at *www.swift.com*.

SPECIFIC ASPECTS

SECURITY, COMMON GROUND AND DISPUTE RESOLUTION

The trade in coffee would not be possible without security, some form of common ground and the effective, neutral resolution of disputes. The existing trade execution system has been developed and fine-tuned over many decades. Electronic systems will have to satisfy the same concerns and meet if not surpass the same standards to address the new issues arising from the use of electronic documents.

In the paperless chain, security will be provided primarily by the legal framework, exactly as is the case with SWIFT, CHIPS, IdenTrust and others.

Common ground will be provided by the multilateral contract with the main operator acting as trustee for the entire operation. As in the traditional coffee trade, rules and regulations will have to be clearly defined and would preferably be overseen by the system users themselves, coming together rather as the coffee trade comes together in the GCA and the ECF.

GUARANTEED ORIGINALS AND NO MISTAKES

An electronic chain has its own in-built security insofar as it guarantees that what is transmitted is the original. Changes, additions, deletions and any mismatches, including the identity of who submitted them and when, are noted, recorded and advised. This removes a major cause for loss and argument in the coffee trade: incorrect documentation and who is to blame for it. An electronic system guarantees that the documents are correct as received, but cannot by itself say anything about the coffee these cover, so the importance of collateral management remains unchanged.

The system would record exactly what was done, by whom and when, for each individual contract by means of a unique identifier which also tracks the progress of each individual document. An identifier is generated whenever a new transaction is initiated. This can be done by the buyer or the seller, depending on what was agreed between them.

In its simplest form all this means, for example, that a buyer who erred in the description of the goods in a letter of credit, or that instructed the wrong shipping marks, cannot later claim it was the shipper's fault and withhold payment.

WHAT ARE THE BENEFITS OF E-COMMERCE?

- Banks and their collateral managers can exercise better control over the execution of the transactions they fund, an important factor when financing trade in commodities. Depending on industry demand, electronic warehouse receipts could also be linked into the system, for example to start the funding chain of the coffee that is to be procured, processed for export and shipped. Or coffee could be tendered to commodity exchanges such as New York and London, linking into systems as eCOPS.
- All concerned, including the bankers, can see the progress of the goods and, therefore, the progress of the transaction.
- Shipping documents are prepared, issued and transmitted more quickly, resulting in earlier payment.
- Turnover is faster, meaning more business within the same amount of working capital, or a reduction of the working capital required.
- Costs are lower: less interest, no errors, no lost or late documents, no arguments and no waiting for shipping documents.

- Sellers have better control. So do importers and roasters, who can trace both coffee and documents.
- In some consuming countries special arrangements permit coffee to be cleared through customs ahead of arrival, resulting in direct dispatch from ship to final destination. This could bring many exporters closer to participation in the just-in-time supply systems of larger roasters.

ELECTRONIC TRADE EXECUTION IN PRACTICE

Contract. Once a deal is established the contract details are automatically transmitted to the principal parties to the trade, using the secure messaging platform and the contract XML standard. (XML means extensible mark-up language.)

Back office link. This is automatic, as both parties have received the contract confirmation and the information has been integrated into their back-office systems through their user interface. The contract data are now ready for further execution.

Price fixing. The price is fixed either by using an e-marketplace or directly between the parties by trading futures via their futures broker, using the network to confirm the transactions.

Letter of credit. If called for, the network is used to establish the letter of credit through a message from the opening bank to the exporter's bank.

Shipping instructions. For a FOB contract the importer will provide shipping and document instructions to the exporter and the opening bank via the network. The opening bank in turn sends an undertaking to the exporter's bank, detailing the commercial documents to be presented under the letter of credit.

Pre-shipment finance. On the basis of the letter of credit (or other undertaking) the exporter can apply for pre-shipment finance, using the protocols provided by the system (and their relationship to the banking system). Upon approval the bank's collateral manager will be automatically linked into the transaction.

Freight. The importer can negotiate freight through a carrier's electronic service provider (e.g. INTTRA or GTNexus), confirmed through the network's electronic messaging system.

Shipment. The exporter advises the coffee's availability and makes a container booking using electronic messaging. (This incidentally also facilitates the establishment of the ship's stowage plan.) The importer books for voyage and space with the carrier as per this advice. These messages are simultaneously copied to other involved parties, for example, the handlers of the cargo to the export terminal, the warehouse and the agency supervising weighing and stuffing. The foregoing presupposes that all of those involved, including customs, have updated their electronic back-office systems using data obtained from a web interface or using their own document management software.

Bill of lading. Using details from the booking and document instructions received earlier, the carrier issues an electronic bill of lading and registers it under the network title registry for release to the exporter. The exporter is notified through the system and will endorse the bill of lading to the appropriate party, usually the bank that financed the goods, which is then registered as pledgee on the bill of lading. Alternatively, the bill of lading can also be issued directly in a bank's favour.

Shipment advice. This is sent via the network using the XML standard for electronic shipping advices.

Dispatch. The exporter combines the commercial invoice with the other export documents received from the different service providers and authorities and packages these into a network message that the network forwards to either the buyer or the bank.

Verification. The documents are verified electronically with the instructions registered under the L/C undertaking. If there is any discrepancy the system notifies all parties and asks for refusal or acceptance of the documents.

Presentation of documents. If the documents are correct they are transmitted for inspection and/or approval (as per the L/C protocol) to the importer's bank or, in the case of CAD (payment cash against documents on first presentation) directly in trust to the importer. When the importer's bank makes payment, the electronic documents are released automatically to the importer. Alternatively, the L/C opening bank, which was acting as pledgee on the bill of lading, will endorse the bill of lading to the importer once the electronic funds transfer has been confirmed through the SWIFT clearing system.

At the receiving end. Before or upon arrival of the vessel, the carrier notifies all concerned (importer, clearing agent, Customs, inland roasting plant, etc.) of the vessel's ETA, followed by a notice of arrival, using XML. The importer settles the freight, releases the bill of lading to the carrier or shipping agency at the port of destination, and copies the bill of lading together with the commercial invoice to the clearing agent, all through the electronic network system and all at the same time. Again, each party knows instantaneously who said what to whom.

Final delivery. If the coffee is going to an inland roasting plant, notifications of cargo arrival, sample orders and delivery orders will pass electronically between the importer and the roaster. If the roaster operates on a vendor managed inventory basis then the importer will place the coffee either at the roasting plant, or at an intermediate container station, or in a warehouse or silo park pending final delivery. All this is done through network instructions to the clearing agents, trucking company and warehousemen. Again, everyone knows what is happening, and the roaster can see where the coffee is.

Finally, the importer issues an XML invoice and delivery order to the roaster, copied to the clearing agents, truckers and warehousemen. Upon payment this delivery order acts as transfer of title as per the conditions determined in the ECF or GCA standard form contract.

END RESULT AND OUTLOOK FOR 'PAPERLESS TRADE'

The foregoing is a realistic scenario of the execution of a coffee contract from origin to delivery at the destination market to a roaster. The example makes optimal use of electronic means of transferring data without the need for rekeying, as is also the case for example with ICE's eCOPS.

All electronically issued data are reused through back-office integration, or through making the data available through online service providers or e-marketplaces, facilitating the trade or the services performed by different service suppliers.

It appears to be a complicated process, but thanks to electronic messaging, use of XML standards and secure electronic transfer of title and financial settlement, the administrative handling is far less cumbersome than in the paper environment. The efficiencies realized will translate into direct cost reductions and savings across the supply chain. Equally important are the reduction in finance cycles and the possible reduction in inventory cycles, easier management, and improved cash flow.

For many exporters the business process described above can take 15 to 25 days from shipment to receipt of payment when executed through physical transmission of paper documents. Using an electronic system, the transfer of documents, transfer of title and financial settlement can be reduced to four days or less, depending on the complexity of the business process and the state of preparedness in the exporting country.

The use of back-office systems, often linking multiple locations within large companies, is increasingly widespread and can be expected to continue growing as these make the trade in coffee more efficient, more secure and less costly. However, electronic supply chain management is not yet widely used in the coffee trade although it is expected to grow. So far though, other than linkage with the futures markets of New York and London, most systems are not used for actual green coffee trading activities. More at, *inter alia, www.bolero.net, www.theice.com, www.coffeenetwork. com, www.eximware.com, www.commoditiesOne.com, www.iRely.com, www.ekaplus.com* and *www.essdocs.com.*

TECHNICAL QUESTIONS

WHO COULD USE AN ELECTRONIC SYSTEM?

A local IT infrastructure and legal framework must be in place first. If they are, anyone with Internet access, or whose bank, coffee authority or IT provider is linked into the system, can access it, either as a full member or by buying the service on a retail basis.

In practice only those countries whose customs and possibly coffee industry authorities have accepted the system and have installed the necessary capability will benefit. It seems likely that larger producing countries will be more interested because for them the potential economies of scale are tremendous. The roasting sector will also participate more and more because of the control and information the network provides, which will permit some to move from just-in-time systems to vendor managed inventory systems.

Even if a roaster is not linked into the system, the importer can surrender the electronic documents and have them replicated as paper originals by the original issuing authority, for instance the carrier or warehouse.

For the buyer it is essential, however, that the exporter is linked into the system. Given the cost savings and reduced working capital requirements the system provides, this linkage can become an important issue when considering the viability of any particular transaction or business relationship with an origin country or an individual exporter.

STANDARDS

Easy communication of data and documents within the coffee supply chain requires certain standards for contracts and contract amendments, pricing, optional conditions, declarations and so on. Standards are also needed for the electronic documents for contract execution, such as sample and delivery orders, bills of lading, warehouse receipts and warrants.

Electronic standards have been developed for the United States coffee industry in collaboration with the membership of the GCA, the National Coffee Association of USA and ICE. These use XML (extensible mark-up language) format so both humans and computers can read them and they allow electronic transfer and integration into back-office systems (straight through processing). The GCA electronic contract includes additional options: price fix letter, price fix rolling letter and a destination declaration letter.

The technology provides both simplification and an optimal number of choices when creating a contract, transmitting a delivery order or shipment advice, or presenting a commercial set of documents.

ACCESS

The system as described is not an actual IT application or browser, but rather provides an 'electronic highway' between the different parties in the electronic community. In short, it is open platform technology. Like CHIPS or SWIFT, such a system can keep track of all documents transmitted on its system (platform). It can provide proof of who said what to whom and when, and it can confirm that messages, contracts, shipping instructions, sampling orders, documents, delivery orders and so on were received in a timely manner and in good order.

To access such an electronic highway participants would probably use accredited application providers and possibly middleware companies, using software that can be implemented as stand-alone document packages, or integrated with back-office systems or enterprise resource planning systems.

Different parties have different needs, so different applications will have to be available for banks, carriers, traders, processors and others in the trade chain. Different solutions also apply to different sizes of companies. Bigger operations will need packages to be integrated with their existing software, while smaller companies may not have the need, the knowledge or the means to acquire sophisticated software.

In future, even the smallest exporter will probably be able to link into the electronic highway, either through an e-commerce site or by simply buying into an appropriate service through a bank or other service provider. This will certainly be the case in countries with well-developed and easy Internet access, provided Customs and other government authorities are in agreement and the necessary legal steps have been completed. Banks in coffee producing countries are likely candidates to take a direct interest as they then could retail the service to individual clients on a user fee basis.

Note that any electronic document handling system will have to be able to link up with the electronic bill of lading solutions that major shipping companies may eventually come up with.

CHAPTER 7

ARBITRATION

ARBITRATION

THE PRINCIPLE OF ARBITRATION

A contract becomes final and binding when buyer and seller agree on a transaction: verbally, by e-mail, by fax or otherwise. For this to be possible all standard terms and conditions must have been agreed to previously, including how possible disputes will be resolved. Arbitration provides a neutral, specialized platform to resolve a dispute when amicable settlement proves impossible.

The international trade in coffee is complex by nature and so dispute resolution can be quite complicated as well: it requires experience and insights not easily found outside the coffee trade itself. Disputes also need to be resolved quickly and fairly, preferably amicably, with buyer and seller agreeing to a mutually acceptable solution. But if this proves impossible then arbitration provides the means to resolve the matter in an impartial manner without involving a court of law where proceedings could be subject to delays (possibly holding up disposal of the goods) and where expert knowledge may not be easily accessible. Also, the exercise could be very costly. This is the main reason why the European Coffee Federation (ECF) and the Green Coffee Association (GCA) standard contracts expressly exclude recourse to the law for the settlement of disputes, stating instead that this shall always be through arbitration. Go to *www.ecf-coffee.org* and *www. greencoffeeassociation.org* for the full contract texts.

Arbitration rules have been set by the professional coffee associations in importing countries. The most important arbitration centres in Europe are London, Hamburg and Le Havre. Other arbitration centres are Amsterdam, Antwerp, Genoa, Rome and Trieste. In the United States arbitrations have always been held in New York but since 2006 they can also be held in other locations as approved by the GCA. Interested parties should contact their US connection or the GCA for an up to date list of GCA-approved locations.

ARBITRATION CENTRES

Under GCA rules arbitrations are held in New York unless a different GCA-approved location has been specified in the contract. Appeals are always heard in New York.

Under ECF contracts arbitrations can be held in different countries, something that could make a difference.

Even though there is one single European Contract for Coffee (ECC), there will always be subtle differences in interpretation, custom and national law governing arbitration in different localities, for example between London and Trieste. It is therefore important that the place where any arbitration will be held is agreed ahead of concluding a transaction, and is so stipulated in the contract. This will also avoid having to be a party to proceedings in an unfamiliar environment and, possibly, language.

United Kingdom
The British Coffee Association, London
Website: *www.britishcoffeeassociation.org*

Germany
Deutscher Kaffeeverband e.V., Hamburg
Website: *www.kaffeeverband.de*

France
Chambre arbitrale des cafés et poivres du Havre
115, rue Desramé, 76600 Le Havre
Telephone: +33 2 35216161
Fax: +33 2 35218060

United States of America
Green Coffee Association, New York
Website: *www.greencoffeeassociation.org*

Netherlands
Royal Netherlands Coffee and Tea Association, Rijswijk
Website: *www.knvkt.nl*

Belgium
Union professionelle du commerce anversois d'importation de café (UPCAIC), Antwerp
E-mail: bvdaki-upcaic@skynet.be

Italy
Associazione Caffè Trieste, Trieste
Website: *www.assocaffe.it*

TYPES OF DISPUTE AND CLAIMS

There are two types of disputes:

- **Quality disputes** – resolved through quality arbitration;
- **Technical disputes** – (any other dispute) resolved through technical arbitration.

Because quality disputes affect the fate of a parcel of coffee (delays are costly and at the same time the quality deteriorates) the rules and time limits for lodging a claim are different from those for technical disputes:

- **ECF contracts.** Quality claims must be lodged within 21 calendar days from date of final discharge at port of destination. All other claims (technical): not later than 45 calendar days from discharge provided the documents were available to the buyer, or from the last date of the contractual shipping period if the coffee has not been shipped.

- **GCA contracts.** Quality claims must be lodged within 15 calendar days after discharge or within 15 calendar days after all government clearances have been received. All other claims (technical): no time limit for lodging the claim, but a demand for technical arbitration must be lodged within one year from the date the issue first arose.

Either party to a contract can lodge a claim, preferably in writing, by notifying the other party within the stipulated time limits that a dispute has arisen. Should amicable settlement prove impossible then the claimant can proceed to arbitration. Suppliers must carefully consider their handling of claims. It is almost inevitable that forcing a claim to be settled through arbitration will signal the end of the relationship with the buyer in question.

Buyers are most likely to claim on matters of quality, weight, delayed or non-shipment, incorrect or missing documentation, etc. Suppliers' claims are more likely to center on late, incomplete or even non-payment or, for example, frustration of a contract by a buyer that fails to provide shipping instructions.

Fewer and fewer quality claims make it to arbitration because the supplier/shipper does not want to risk the relationship, whereas especially larger buyers do not bother to pursue relatively minor claims, preferring to simply strike the offending supplier off their register, sometimes even without notification.

COMMON ERRORS

The buyer is not the enemy. Keeping buyers informed usually means that most if not all of a problem can be resolved amicably. Hiding 'bad news' on the other hand guarantees trouble. Knowingly shipping sub-standard quality demonstrates disregard for contract integrity, or a lack of quality knowledge, or both. Not reporting that a shipment may be delayed can cause much greater damage than may immediately be obvious.

Buyer and seller are partners in a transaction. Both are obliged to play their role to ensure the successful completion and to minimize the impact of potentially harmful situations. Keeping the buyer informed of any problems enables timely corrective action to be taken, thereby saving costs and damages. Arbitrators will take this into account when it comes to making an award. And if a claim is received, deal with it. Promptly and efficiently. Do not ignore a claim in the belief that it will 'go away'. And if a claim does result in arbitration proceedings being initiated, cooperate fully because otherwise the exercise will proceed without your input.

Remember also that those who see the coffee trade from only one side, such as exporters, do not always appreciate why and how certain actions or lack of action can cause their counterpart to suffer loss or damage, and it is not uncommon for some to feel subsequently that they have been treated unfairly in the arbitration proceedings. Look for local assistance because local representatives usually have more experience with the arbitration system and can guide an exporter through some of the details. A local representative might not know exactly how an arbitration award was decided, but he or she should clearly understand the proceedings and be able to explain more or less how the outcome was determined. This is very helpful for an exporter in deciding whether or not to appeal against an award.

APPOINTING ARBITRATORS

Appointing an arbitrator does not mean acquiring a defender who will advance one side of a dispute no matter what. Arbitration means that the arbitrators impartially consider and pronounce on the merits of a case, irrespective of by whom they were appointed.

Only well known, experienced and respected members of the coffee trade can become arbitrators. They are selected by their peers to serve on their association's panel of arbitrators. As per his or her particular sphere of expertise, an arbitrator may serve on the quality panel, the technical panel or both. Depending on the rules of the association concerned arbitrators can be appointed by the parties to the dispute, or by the association itself. Where the parties to a dispute appoint their own arbitrators, usual practice is that these arbitrators themselves then select a third, the umpire.

AWARDS

An award is the verdict of the arbitrators, arrived at in accordance with the arbitration rules of their local arbitral body and national law. Under GCA contracts arbitrations always take place in the United States. However, under ECF contracts they can be held in different countries, something that could make a difference.

Most awards are subject to appeal, within the time limits set by the arbitral body at the place where the arbitration was held. The limits and procedures are different for each arbitral body whose rules should therefore be consulted.

FAILURE TO COMPLY WITH AN AWARD

Under ECF rules, if one of the parties fails to comply with an arbitration award which has become final, the other party may request the coffee association under whose rules the arbitration was held to post (publicise) the name of the defaulting party and/or bring it to the notice of the members and, through the ECF, to any person or organization with or having an interest in coffee. Each of the recipients of such notification may in turn bring it to the notice of its own members or otherwise publicise it. In addition, in order to enforce an arbitration award, a party may also have direct recourse to the courts of the place where the defaulting party is established. GCA rules allow 30 days for an award to be satisfied, after which a comparable procedure kicks in if the party in whose favour the award was given so requests.

VARIATIONS TO STANDARDS CONTRACTS

Of course contracts can be, and very many are, concluded with conditions differing from those of the standard forms of contract (GCA and ECC – see chapter 4, Contracts), as long as these are well understood and are clearly set out in unambiguous language, leaving no room for differing interpretations. For example, one might agree to change the weight tolerance in Article 2 of the ECC from 3% to 5%, in which case the contract should include a paragraph to the effect that 'Article 2 of ECC is amended for this contract by mutual agreement to read a tolerance of 5%'.

If a modification to an existing contract is agreed it should be confirmed in writing, preferably countersigned by both parties. Adding the words 'without prejudice to the original terms and conditions of the contract' ensures that the modification does not result in unintended or unforeseen change to the original contract. A modification that is not confirmed in writing could subsequently be repudiated or disputed by one of the parties, for example during arbitration proceedings. Human memory is fallible and there is nothing offensive in ensuring that all matters of record are on record.

ARBITRATION IN THE UNITED KINGDOM

THE BRITISH COFFEE ASSOCIATION

The British Coffee Association (BCA) provides a two-tier arbitration service: arbitration at the first stage by a tribunal of three arbitrators and, where required, an appeal procedure through a board of appeal of five arbitrators. Arbitrators are appointed by the BCA from members of the BCA Panel of Arbitrators. All disputes referred to the BCA on or after 1 February 2012 are determined subject to the provisions of the Arbitration Act 1996 and of any statutory re-enactment, modification or amendment for the time being in force ('The Act'), and the British Coffee Association Arbitration Rules 2012.

THE ARBITRAL PROCEEDINGS

Proceedings before a tribunal are referred to as 'first-tier proceedings' and proceedings before a board of appeal as 'appeal proceedings'. The seat of all arbitral proceedings is London, England.

Parties to proceedings have the right to apply to the courts to determine questions as to the substantive jurisdiction of the arbitral tribunal or board of appeal but in the latter case only if the original objection had already been made in the first-tier proceedings. Tribunals and boards of appeal may seek legal advice from or allow an independent legal adviser to attend at the hearing of any oral evidence or oral submissions. Tribunals and boards of appeal may also seek expert opinion from and/or allow an independent expert or assessor to attend at the hearing of any oral evidence or oral submissions for the purpose of providing expert opinion.

All written statements must be in English and supporting evidence in other languages must be accompanied by an independent translation. All written correspondence, submissions and notices are communicated in legible form by a prompt method of communication, including e-mail or fax unless otherwise directed by either tribunal or board of appeal.

Each party to proceedings (both tribunal and board of appeal) have the right upon application in writing to the BCA to require the BCA to remove one arbitrator only in which event a substitute arbitrator shall be appointed by the BCA. A party seeking to exercise this right is not required to give reasons for doing so. This right must be exercised within three London working days of the date of the appointment of the arbitrator which that party seeks to have removed.

In accordance with its general duty a tribunal or board of appeal has the power to order on its own initiative or on the application of a party: that the arbitral proceedings shall be consolidated with other arbitral proceedings; or that concurrent hearings shall be held;

A party may be represented in the arbitral proceedings by a representative (which expression shall include legal practitioners) except that: (i) at a hearing of oral evidence and/or oral submissions a party may not be represented by one or more legal practitioners unless permitted by the tribunal or board of appeal; and (ii) at a hearing of oral evidence a natural person ordered or permitted to give oral evidence may not give that oral evidence by way of a representative and must give that oral evidence in person.

It is the general duty of a tribunal or board of appeal to: (a) act fairly and impartially as between the parties, giving each party a reasonable opportunity of putting its case and dealing with that of its opponent; and (b) adopt procedures suitable to the circumstances of the particular case, avoiding unnecessary delay or expense, so as to provide a fair means for the resolution of the matters falling to be determined.

NB. If without showing sufficient cause a party after due notice fails to attend or be represented at hearings or fails to submit written evidence or make written submissions, then a tribunal or board of appeal may continue the proceedings in the absence of that party or, as the case may be, without any written evidence or submissions on that party's behalf, and may make an award on the basis of the evidence before it.

TIME LIMITS FOR INTRODUCING ARBITRATION CLAIMS

It is essential that claimants adhere to the rules of the standard form of contract on which the sale was based. ECC rules require quality claims to be submitted not later than 21 calendar days from the final date of discharge at the port of destination. All other claims must be submitted not later than 45 calendar days from:

- The final date of discharge at the port of destination, provided all documents are available to the buyers;
- The last day of the contractual shipping period if the coffee has not been shipped.

If amicable settlement (always the preferred solution) proves impossible then the formal decision to initiate arbitration proceedings must be notified within the following time limits:

- Quality disputes: not later than 28 calendar days from the date the claim was formulated;
- Other disputes: not later than 90 calendar days from the date one party formally notifies the other that the dispute apparently cannot be resolved amicably and arbitration proceedings will be initiated.

These time limits must be respected, or the outcome of the arbitration can be jeopardized. If unavoidable delays do arise then, in the interests of justice or avoiding undue hardship, ECC rules authorize the arbitral body at the place of arbitration to extend the time as it may think appropriate.

CLARITY IS ESSENTIAL

Claimants should provide a clear statement of the problem, how it arose and the remedy sought. It is not sufficient for example to simply state 'We claim an allowance'. If an allowance is sought then it must be quantified, e.g. 'US$ 4 per 50 kg is claimed on quality grounds'. The statement must be in writing and must be supported by copies of all relevant documentation, including copies of exchanges between the parties. All should be catalogued, numbered and presented in chronological order. If the dispute concerns quality the arbitrators will give directions on the production of the necessary samples. Respondents should provide all relevant documentation to all concerned and should specifically address the points raised by the claimant.

STANDARD TIMETABLE FOR FIRST-TIER PROCEEDINGS

Claimants and respondents ensure receipt by the BCA of five copies of their submissions, which include supporting evidence, within the following deadlines: (a) the claimant's claim submissions: within 21 days from the date the first-tier proceedings were commenced; (b) the respondent's defence submissions and counterclaim submissions (if any): within 21 days from the date the respondent received the claimant's claim submissions from the BCA; (c) the claimant's reply submissions and defence to counterclaim submissions (if any): within 21 days from the date the claimant received the respondent's defence submissions and counterclaim submissions (if any) from the BCA; (d) the respondent's reply to defence to counterclaim submissions: within 21 days from the date the respondent received the claimant's reply submissions and defence to counterclaim submissions from the BCA.

PROVISION OF SAMPLES

If a claimant wishes a tribunal to examine any sample, the claimant ensures receipt by the BCA of the sample, together with a concise statement of the purpose for which the sample is being provided, at the same time as receipt by the BCA of the claimant's application for arbitration. If a respondent wishes a tribunal to examine a sample the respondent ensures receipt by the BCA of the sample, together with a concise statement of the purpose for which the sample is being provided, no later than at the same time as receipt by the BCA of the respondent's defence submissions. If a party wishes to submit a sample at a later stage in first-tier proceedings for examination by a tribunal that party does so only with the permission of the tribunal.

AWARDS MADE BY A TRIBUNAL

A tribunal may make one final award on all matters to be determined. Alternatively a tribunal may make more than one final award on different aspects of the matters to be determined, pursuant to Section 47 of the Act, including but not limited to separate awards on interest, costs and jurisdiction. In addition, a tribunal has power to order on a provisional basis any relief which it would have power to grant in a final award.

COMMENCING APPEAL PROCEEDINGS

A party wishing to commence appeal proceedings (the 'appellant') ensures receipt by the BCA within 28 days from the date of the tribunal's award against which the appellant wishes to appeal of: (a) a non-returnable fee payable to the BCA in the amount published by the BCA from time to time; and (b) a written application for appeal proceedings to be commenced (the 'application for appeal'); (c) failing which the right to commence appeal proceedings shall be time barred unless the party wishing to commence appeal proceedings applies for an extension of time, in which case the BCA shall appoint a board of appeal to pronounce on the application.

The application for appeal should: (a) name the other party or parties (each a 'respondent') to the intended appeal proceedings; and (b) identify the tribunal's award against which the appellant wishes to appeal; and (c) request the BCA to appoint a board of appeal. It shall be accompanied by: evidence that the appellant has transmitted a copy of the application for appeal to each respondent; and a copy of the tribunal's award against which the appellant wishes to appeal.

Upon receipt by the BCA of both the non-returnable fee and the application for appeal, the appeal proceedings are deemed to have been commenced and the BCA shall: (a) forward a copy of the application for appeal to each respondent; and (b) appoint five arbitrators to form a board of appeal (unless already appointed as per above); and (c) forward to the board of appeal: a copy of the application for appeal; and a copy of the tribunal's award against which the appellant wishes to appeal.

STANDARD TIMETABLE FOR APPEAL PROCEEDINGS

Appellants and respondents ensure receipt by the BCA of seven copies of their submissions, which include supporting evidence, within the following deadlines: (a) the appellant's claim submissions: within 21 days from the date the appeal proceedings were commenced; (b) the respondent's defence submissions and counterclaim submissions (if any): within 21 days from the date the respondent received the appellant's claim submissions from the BCA; (c) the appellant's reply submissions and defence to counterclaim submissions (if any): within 21 days from the date the appellant received the respondent's defence submissions and counterclaim submissions (if any) from the BCA; (d) the respondent's reply to defence to counterclaim submissions: within 21 days from the date the respondent received the appellant's reply submissions and defence to counterclaim submissions from the BCA. A board of appeal may vary the above timetable in accordance with its general duty to act fairly and impartially.

Note that under BCA rules appeal proceedings are new proceedings in which the parties may submit new submissions and new supporting evidence to the board of appeal. But a board of appeal may consider submissions or supporting evidence submitted to the tribunal in the first-tier proceedings and/or correspondence or documents generated during the first-tier proceedings only if copies of the same are provided to it by a party in the appeal proceedings in accordance with the above timetable.

PROVISION OF SAMPLES

If a party wishes the board of appeal to examine a sample not submitted for examination during the first-tier proceedings that party can do so only with the permission of the board of appeal.

AWARDS OF INTEREST

A tribunal or board of appeal may award simple or compound interest from such dates, at such rates and with such rests as it considers meets the justice of the case.

COSTS OF THE ARBITRATION

A tribunal or board of appeal may make an award allocating the costs of the arbitration as between the parties, subject to any agreement of the parties. The expression 'costs of the arbitration' means: (a) the fees and expenses of tribunals and boards of appeal; (b) the fees and expenses of the BCA; and (c) the legal or other costs of the parties. Unless the parties otherwise agree, a tribunal or board of appeal shall award costs on the general principle that costs should follow the event except where it appears that in the circumstances this is not appropriate in relation to the whole or part of the costs.

The fees and expenses of the tribunal or board of appeal and the fees and expenses of the BCA shall be calculated: (a) at the time any final award is made; or (b) upon the tribunal or board of appeal becoming aware that the arbitral proceedings are subject to settlement between any of the parties or have been abandoned by one or more parties; (c) and the sum calculated shall be notified to the parties.

For detailed information on costs contact the BCA at *www.britishcoffeeassociation.org*.

ARBITRATION IN GERMANY

THE DEUTSCHER KAFFEEVERBAND E.V.

The Deutscher Kaffeeverband e.V. (DKV) in Hamburg is the umbrella organization for the German coffee trade and industry. The court of arbitration of the Deutsche Kaffeeverband e.V. at the Hamburg Chamber of Commerce (HCC) deals with principal arbitration cases on technical disputes. Proceedings are administrated by the HCC. Quality disputes are dealt with by the Association of Hamburg Coffee Import Agents.

TECHNICAL ARBITRATION BY THE DKV

Arbitration panel. The panel usually consists of three members. Each party to the dispute appoints an arbitrator, who has to be owner, member of the board of directors, managing director, personally liable partner, fully authorized signatory or duly authorized employee of a firm which is registered in the German Commercial Register or Cooperative Societies Register. Both arbitrators appoint an umpire. If they cannot agree on the umpire, then the umpire will be appointed by the Hamburg Chamber of Commerce. The Chamber will also appoint an arbitrator for the defendant, if the defendant fails to do so himself. The panel can be enlarged by two additional arbitrators on the demand of any party. Remember that arbitrators in a dispute are not partial to any side – they are neutral members of the official arbitration board.

Requests for arbitration must be made in writing to the arbitration board of the DKV at the Hamburg Chamber of Coffee and shall state the grounds for the dispute, a precise claim and proof of agreement regarding the competence of the arbitration board. The plaintiff also has to provide the name and address of the plaintiff's arbitrator and his declaration of assent.

HCC informs the other party of the claim, requesting a written response that must include the name of the arbitrator who will act for the defendant and his declaration of assent. Unlike some other markets, there is no fixed time limit within which the defendant must respond. Instead it is left to the discretion of HCC to set the limit for the first response, but once the arbitration panel is constituted then it sets all subsequent time limits. All submissions must be in writing in five copies.

Hearing and award. The date and the organization of the hearing are arranged by the umpire and HCC notifies the parties in writing. Arbitrators examine the written submissions and may invite further voluntary evidence from outside witnesses and experts. Both parties to the dispute are also summoned for oral pleading of their case. A legal adviser from the HCC has to attend all meetings and participates in the deliberations but has no vote. Decisions are reached by simple majority vote and the award, setting out the grounds for the verdict, is delivered in writing through the HCC.

Appeal. There is no appeal as such against a DKV award. An award can be submitted to the Hamburg Hanseatic High Court which is competent for all judicial rulings and functions required in accordance with German civil process law (ZPO). If the court disaffirms the award on formal legal grounds then the arbitration must be repeated, with the same arbitrators and umpire officiating unless the court specifically ruled otherwise.

Costs and fees are linked to the value of the dispute: up to EUR 10,000 the fee is EUR 1,000. Then an additional 10% for the next EUR 5,000; 9% for the next EUR 10,000; 8% for the next EUR 15,000; 7% for the next EUR 25,000; 6% for the next EUR 35,000; 5% for the next EUR 200,000; 4% for the next EUR 700,000; and 2% for the next EUR 1,000,000. For disputed sums over EUR 2,000,000 the additional fee is 0.5% of the amount in excess of EUR 2,000,000.

In addition to the above the HCC shall charge a flat-rate sum in the amount of 15% of these fees with a maximum of EUR 20,000.

Value added tax (VAT), where applicable, comes on top of all said fees, as well as necessary expenses of the arbitrators and the HCC. On submitting the statement of claim, the plaintiff has to make a security payment amounting to the anticipated costs of the proceedings.

QUALITY ARBITRATION IN HAMBURG

The contract must clearly state where arbitration will be held and under which rules.

Arbitration panel. Hamburg Private Arbitration in the Coffee Import Trade. Each party appoints their own arbitrator; together the arbitrators appoint the umpire. If a contract was concluded through an agent that agent is assumed to be the seller's arbitrator unless the agent appoints someone else to act for them. If the arbitrators fail to appoint an umpire then the chairperson of the Association of Hamburg Coffee Import Agents and Brokers will do so.

Requests for arbitration must be made in writing to the association. If asked to do so the association will also appoint arbitrators or umpires. No time limits are laid down for these appointments, but they must be made without undue delay.

Hearing and award. The hearing is based on the original contract submitted by the claimant. Unless otherwise agreed, for bagged coffee arbitration samples must be drawn from 10% of the lot and must be sealed, either by both parties jointly or by an independent sworn sampler. For coffee shipped in bulk a 2 kg sealed sample is required, usually of each individual container. If the arbitrators fail to reach agreement then the decision of the umpire will be final. In the interest of neutrality the parties' identities are withheld from the umpire until after a verdict has been reached. Should the umpire inadvertently become aware of the buyer's identity then the umpire must withdraw, thereby necessitating a new hearing. Awards are issued on the official Association certificate and signed by both arbitrators and the umpire.

Appeals. The Hamburg rules do not allow for appeals against awards in quality arbitrations. The awards are final and the arbitrators and umpire need not provide the grounds for their verdict.

Unsound coffee or radical quality differences, including excessive moisture content. ECC Article 7 states that where arbitrators establish that the coffee is unsound or of radically different quality, and award invoicing back, then they shall also establish the price having in mind all the circumstances. As an example, the quality difference might be so enormous that it is obvious the shipper made no serious attempt to supply what was sold. The more seldom Bremen arbitrations deal with this somewhat differently, but both sets of rules make special provision for such cases, and describe them as 'fraud and negligence'.

The question of fraud or negligence can be pursued only if the claimant requests this. In this type of case the arbitrators and three umpires are limited to pronouncing a 'suspicion of fraud and gross negligence' and to fixing an adequate allowance. The claimant may contest this and demand a technical arbitration to order annulment of the contract rather than payment of an allowance. The panel's reasoning must therefore be provided in writing by the umpires for possible use in such an arbitration.

Costs and fees. 1–1,000 bags: EUR 100 per arbitrator/umpire. For each additional 1,000 bags or portion thereof: an additional 100 EUR per arbitrator/umpire.

ARBITRATION IN FRANCE

THE CHAMBRE ARBITRALE DES CAFÉS ET POIVRES DU HAVRE

The Chambre arbitrale des cafés et poivres du Havre (CACPH) is the main arbitral body for coffee and brings together arbitrators from both the French and the Swiss coffee trade. CACPH conducts both quality *(arbitrage de qualité et expertise)* and technical arbitrations *(arbitrage de principe)*. Linked quality and technical issues within the same dispute can be dealt with simultaneously in a 'joint arbitration' *(arbitrage mixte)*. Requests for arbitration must be made in French or in English on the official form provided.

If legal counsel is to be involved this must be indicated on the request form. The rules provide for a two-tier system of adjudication: arbitration at the first instance and an appeals procedure. All time limits are calendar days and run from the date material is forwarded, including 72 hours deemed necessary for transmission. Late delivery automatically extends the time limit according to the delay involved.

DOCUMENTS TO BE SUBMITTED AND TIME LIMITS

Quality disputes

- Contract or sales confirmation;
- Invoice;
- Out-turn sample, sealed under independent supervision or by the parties jointly;
- Where relevant, a jointly sealed original sample of the coffee that was sold.

The request to CACPH must be submitted no later than 30 days from the formal notification by one of the parties that they are to proceed to arbitration. The defendant has 15 days from the date CACPH dispatches the notification to countersign and return it. Failure to respond will result in the arbitration proceeding without any input from the defendant.

Technical disputes

- Statement of the matters in disputes and claims made;
- All relevant documents (contracts, invoices, bills of lading, certificates, etc.).

The request for arbitration must be lodged within 30 days as above, to be followed by the complete dispute file in five copies, including statements of facts and claims, within a further 10 days. The other party must lodge their defence within 30 days from the date CACPH transmits the dispute file to them.

The plaintiff then has 15 days to respond after which the defendant has a further 15 days to make a final response. Failure to respond will result in the arbitration proceeding without any input from the defendant.

ARBITRATION PANELS

All arbitrators are designated by CACPH and their names are made known to the parties. Arbitrators may not have any connection with the matter in dispute. If they find that they do then they must withdraw unless the parties agree that they can continue.

For quality arbitrations and appeals: three arbitrators, appointed by the board of directors.

For technical arbitrations: in the first instance three arbitrators and on appeal five, again appointed by the CACPH board.

Parties to a dispute may challenge arbitrators only on grounds which arose, or became apparent, after they were appointed and must do so within three days of the event, failing which the panel shall stand as nominated. All arbitration hearings are private but in technical arbitrations the parties may be present or may be represented by legal counsel. They can also be represented by a member of the coffee trade but only with the prior approval of the panel.

Awards and appeals

Quality awards are issued within eight weeks from registration of the original request. Any appeal must be lodged within 15 days from the date the award was dispatched, copied to the other party. Appeal procedures and time limits are the same as for arbitration in the first instance.

Technical awards are made within three months from the date of hearing although this can be extended with the agreement of the CACPH board. Any appeal must be lodged within 20 days from the date the award was dispatched, copied to the other party, with the complete dispute file in seven copies being lodged with CACPH not more than 10 days later. Procedures and time limits are the same as for arbitration in the first instance.

NB: Awards are pronounced in French to enable the parties to obtain execution by the 'Tribunal de Grande Instance du Havre'. Awards can however be translated by sworn translators.

Costs and fees are set by the arbitrators, who also stipulate who shall be liable for them. No arbitration procedure will be initiated unless the required deposit for costs and fees (determined by CACPH for each individual case) has first been made.

ARBITRATION IN THE UNITED STATES

THE GREEN COFFEE ASSOCIATION

The rules of the Green Coffee Association (GCA) set out comprehensive arbitration and appeal procedures. Over 95% of the coffee imported into the United States and Canada is sold under GCA contracts so these rules apply to a large part of world imports and are of some considerable importance.

The rules differ in some important aspects from those in Europe. For example, for technical disputes GCA sets no time limit for lodging the claim and instead sets a limit of one year from the date the issue first arose for the filing of the demand for technical arbitration hearings. ECF on the other hand sets a time limit for lodging the claim of 45 days from the date of discharge at port of destination (provided all documents were available to the buyers), or from the last day of the shipping period in the case of non-shipment. This is followed by a further 90 days for the filing of the demand for arbitration, counted from the date one party formally notifies the other that arbitration will be initiated.

GCA permits the use of legal counsel whereas ECF requires prior approval for this. The GCA freely permits the use of witnesses and legal counsel, but it does not allow new evidence to be presented at an appeal, whereas the British Coffee Association's rules allow new evidence at any time. In the United Kingdom arbitrators are appointed by the BCA whereas in Germany claimant and defendant each appoint one arbitrator who together select a third, the umpire. For GCA arbitrations held outside of New York buyer and seller shall each nominate an arbitrator who jointly appoint a third. The same procedure applies for GCA arbitrations held in New York, but the parties may also agree to have all three selected by the GCA secretary, by lot, from the appropriate GCA arbitration panel. In addition to the technical panel the GCA has separate quality panels for washed arabica, natural arabica, robusta, specialty coffee and decaffeinated coffee.

GCA members annually submit names of coffee professionals who they feel are qualified to settle quality and/or technical disputes. The arbitration committee reviews the experience of each individual, and determines for which list he or she is qualified. These lists form the pool of names from which the GCA secretary then chooses arbitrators by lot. The secretary must also be vigilant not to select arbitrators who may have a conflict of interest because of relationships with either party to a dispute.

Once the arbitrators are selected, the arbitration is entirely under their control as stated in the GCA Rules of Arbitration:

> The Association does administer and interpret the arbitration procedure and these Rules and it designates the arbitrators. It is, however, the arbitrators who conduct the hearings, determine and decide the issue, and they alone have the power and authority to make an award. Arbitrators shall be in complete charge of the arbitration. They shall conduct the same with the purpose of establishing equity and fair dealings in matters of trade and commerce.

All GCA arbitrations are monitored by the legal staff of the IntercontinentalExchange (ICE) to ensure they are run efficiently and that the results are both impartial and in full compliance with the laws of the land. Since 1999 the administration of the GCA has fallen under the auspices of the Exchange (now ICE but previously known as the New York Board of Trade or NYBOT).

QUALITY ARBITRATIONS

The GCA contract stipulates that:

Coffee shall be considered accepted as to quality unless within 15 calendar days after discharge of the coffee, or within 15 calendar days after all government clearances have been received, whichever is later, either:

- Claims are settled by the parties to the contract; or
- Arbitration procedures have been filed by one of the parties in accordance with the provisions of the contract.

If neither of the above has been done within the stated period, or if any portion of the coffee has been removed from the point of discharge before representative sealed samples have been drawn by the GCA, in accordance with its rules, seller's responsibility for quality claims ceases for that portion so removed.

To initiate a quality arbitration, the claimant must submit a signed and notarized demand for arbitration in triplicate explicitly setting forth the precise complaint(s) in detail on GCA form A-2. This must be accompanied by the original contract, a sampling order to the order of the GCA, and the requisite arbitration fee. When GCA receives the defendant's answer it copies it to the claimant, who may either file a reply with GCA or allow the arbitration to proceed in accordance with the original submission. All arbitration forms are available from *www.greencoffeeassociation.org*.

On receipt of the arbitration demand, the defendant responds by filing their signed and notarized answer in triplicate on GCA form B-2, together with the requisite fee. This answer must be filed with GCA within five business days from receipt of the arbitration demand if the defendant's office is located in New York City. If the defendant's office is not in New York City, the GCA secretary can, at his or her discretion, extend any time requirement beyond that prescribed to give the defendant an equivalent period to that allowed to a resident.

If the claimant files an answer to the defendant's reply, the defendant can file an additional response or they can allow the arbitration to proceed on the basis of their original answer.

Procedure

When the final answer or reply has been filed, or the time when the same is due has expired, the GCA secretary determines the panel of arbitrators to be used. Any arbitrator known to be connected with either party shall be removed from the list.

If the arbitration is outside of New York, the secretary shall then supply the list of potential arbitrators to the petitioner and the respondent and ask them each to select one arbitrator. The secretary shall then ask the two arbitrators selected, to choose a third arbitrator from the same list. This is referred to as the Alternate Panel Selection method.

If the arbitration location is in New York, and the Alternate Panel Selection method is not specified at time of contract, the GCA secretary will select the panel by lot. If the arbitration location is not specified at time of contract, the arbitration will be in New York with the GCA secretary selecting the panel by lot.

Arbitrations involving grade or quality must be held at one physical location acceptable to the arbitrators and the association. GCA prepares an extract of the arbitration papers that have been filed, deleting all names and references to the parties, including all marks on the samples to be tested and ensures that all pertinent data and samples are submitted to the arbitrators. This secrecy applies to arbitrations where the GCA chooses the arbitrators. If the alternative selection of arbitrators is invoked, the parties waive their right to anonymity with the arbitrators. The arbitrators shall then make an award within five business days.

The arbitrators independently cup and grade six cups for each chop submitted for arbitration, according to the claimant's demand, and make their own conclusions. The arbitrators review their findings and issue either a unanimous decision, or a majority and a minority decision. GCA notifies the parties to the dispute as quickly as possible, but not later than five business days after the decision on the award is reached.

The arbitrators are also required to assess the costs of the arbitration against the unsuccessful party; they can also instruct the parties to share the costs.

Award and appeal

An award must be made and the parties notified by GCA within five business days after a quality arbitration is held. If the award is to be contested, an appeal must be filed with GCA within two business days after receipt of the award, on GCA form D in triplicate, duly signed and notarized and accompanied by the requisite fee. No new claims or counterclaims may be submitted on appeal.

All appeals are held in New York and the appeal arbitration panel consisting of five new arbitrators, so excluding the original three, is selected by GCA. The arbitrators grade and cup the original sample in the same way as the first panel to reach a decision. Their decision to uphold or change the original award is final.

The appeal award must be made within five business days of the sitting and the unsuccessful party must settle the award within seven calendar days of the date of receipt of the notice of the award.

GROSS NEGLIGENCE AND FRAUD

Under GCA rules all quality issues under FCA, FOB, CFR, CIF and DAF contracts are settled by allowance. GCA considers that it is a technical issue whether or not quality is inferior to such an extent that the normal remedy of an allowance is insufficient. Therefore the claimant must file a demand for a technical arbitration. The technical arbitration panel might in its turn convene a quality panel to verify whether negligence or fraud took place but this would not be made known to the claimant who would only receive the decision of the technical panel.

TECHNICAL ARBITRATIONS

Actions the claimant and the defendant must take. These are the same as for quality arbitrations, but the demand and response must be submitted on GCA forms A-1 and B-1. All relevant papers (shipping documents, correspondence, certificates, statements, etc.) must accompany these forms, which are available from *www.greencoffeeassociation.org*.

Technical arbitration hearings can be held in person at any facility deemed acceptable by the GCA and the arbitrators, or by conference phone call, or Internet meeting site. It is not necessary that arbitrators, parties and their legal representatives, and the GCA secretary be physically present at the same location. The secretary will arrange for a stenographic record of testimony if this is requested by either party.

Each party has the right to request an oral hearing. If they exercise this right, they may appear with an attorney and witnesses provided the arbitrators and the other party were been given prior notice of this and the arbitrators have not objected. The other party may then also appear with an attorney. The arbitrators always have the option of asking GCA legal counsel to be present.

All oral testimony must be made under oath; the entire procedure is recorded. All communications must be addressed to the chairperson of the arbitration panel; no one is permitted to communicate directly with the arbitrators or witnesses, except with the chairperson's approval.

Procedure

After the final replies have been received from all parties, the GCA secretary selects a panel of three arbitrators from the association's register of technical arbitrators and ensures that they have no connection with any of the disputants. A mutually satisfactory time and a date are set. The arbitrators may approve a delay of five days if acceptable reasons are submitted in writing.

The arbitrators receive copies of all the documents that have been filed and review them independently before the date of the arbitration. They elect their own chairperson to conduct the arbitration and hearings. The arbitrators may request the GCA counsel to attend and act as a legal adviser, but GCA counsel has no voice or vote in any decisions. The arbitrators assess costs on either or both of the parties.

Award and appeal

The award must be made within five business days of the arbitrators receiving copies of the transcript of the proceedings.

If the award is to be contested, an appeal must be filed within two business days of receipt of the award on form D in triplicate, duly signed, notarized and accompanied by the requisite fee. Five new arbitrators are selected to hear the appeal. They can review only the original documents and transcripts; no new evidence may be submitted. Their decision is final. The appeal award must be made within five business days of the arbitrators receiving the transcript of the hearings.

Settlement of the award must be within seven calendar days of the date of receipt of the notice of the award by the unsuccessful party.

PRACTICAL CONSIDERATIONS

Although the GCA arbitration system is designed so that exporters can use the system directly from source countries, it is advisable to have local representation at the arbitration. The GCA administration will provide all reasonable assistance to assure a fair hearing regardless of how far away a respondent may be, but there are certain facts and procedures of which the system assumes all participants have a good understanding.

To protect oneself from oversight, it is a simple matter for an exporter to nominate a local importer to appear on their behalf in arbitration. Most importers will perform this service free of charge and the practice is quite common. Local representation helps in a number of ways. First of all, documents and sampling usually move along more efficiently. When a piece of paper or a sampling order is misplaced, local people can trace the problem more quickly. Second, local representatives usually have more experience with the arbitration system and can guide the exporter through some of the details.

For example, it is clearly stated that blanket contentions are not admissible in quality arbitrations. That is to say, one cannot simply ask for a quality allowance because 'the coffee is bad'. An experienced person would point out that a quality complaint should not only be detailed, but also be all encompassing. There have been quality arbitrations where a claimant has complained only about the grade of the coffee. When reviewing the samples the arbitrators also found cup deficiencies, but felt unable to include the cupping problem in their award because the claimant did not claim on the cup. An experienced claimant would make a claim for certain grade defects (e.g. black beans, sour beans or husks) 'that sometimes reflect in the cup quality'.

The need for local representation in technical arbitrations is more obvious. The details of why and how contractual obligations are determined can be complex. An exporter's experience is usually mostly sales oriented, whereas importers (and most technical arbitrators for that matter) have the broader experience of being both buyer and seller in the international coffee market.

The final advantage to having local representation is gaining a better understanding of the award. Most awards are very simple statements like: 'Based upon the evidence submitted, we award X to the seller [or buyer], and the cost of the arbitration to the buyer [or seller].' It is rare that an award includes any explanation as to why the arbitrators decided the way they did.

Because most arbitrators are experienced coffee people, with equal experience as international buyers and sellers of coffee, they understand both sides of the transaction. Those who see the coffee trade from only one side, such as exporters, do not always appreciate why and how certain actions or lack of actions can cause their counterpart to suffer loss or damage, and it is not uncommon for some to feel they have been treated unfairly in the arbitration proceedings. Someone who has not experienced the business from both sides cannot always see how the other party was legitimately hurt by their actions and may sometimes think that the other party won the award because of a bias in the arbitration system.

In quality arbitrations the arbitrators do not know who the parties are. They see only the complaint and the defendant's reply, without names. After this the coffee does the talking. Therefore, bias in quality arbitrations is virtually impossible. In technical arbitrations, the arbitrators do see the names of the parties, but they are both buyers and sellers of coffee and so understand both sides of the business. Before being appointed they are pre-screened about any personal contacts they may have with the parties to the dispute, and GCA legal counsel monitors the proceedings. A local representative might not know exactly how the arbitration award was decided, but they should have a clear view of the proceedings and be able to explain more or less how an outcome was determined. This is very helpful for an exporter in deciding whether or not to appeal.

COSTS AND FEES

The arbitration fee for GCA-members shall be as follows:

- US$ 450 minimum up to 250 bags on any question solely of grade or quality of coffee. For each additional bag over 250 bags there shall be a fee of 50 cts per bag.

- US$ 650 minimum up to 250 bags from appellants only on an appeal from the award rendered on any question solely of grade or quality of coffee. For each additional bag over 250 bags there shall be a fee of 75 cts per bag.

- US$ 650 minimum up to 250 bags on any question other than one solely involving grade or quality of coffee. For each additional bag over 250 bags there shall be a fee of 50 cts per bag.

- US$ 850 minimum up to 250 bags from appellants only on an appeal from the award rendered on any question other than one solely involving grade or quality of coffee. For each additional bag over 250 bags there shall be a fee of 75 cts per bag.

From the fees received the association shall pay a fee to the arbitrators as follows:

- Arbitrations on any question solely of grade or quality of coffee, US$ 100 per arbitrator;

- Arbitrations on any question other than solely of grade or quality of coffee, US$ 100 per arbitrator.

In the event that arbitration is withdrawn or cancelled before an answer is filed, the sum of US$ 200 shall be retained by the Association as a filing fee out of the arbitration fee deposited providing a hearing has not yet begun. The balance of the arbitration fee shall be returned to the depositor except as provided below. When a hearing has been scheduled and held on a technical arbitration or appeal and any settlement is reached between the parties or they mutually agree to withdraw the arbitration or appeal, such settlement or agreement shall provide for forfeiture of the arbitration fee to the association by the depositor as the panel sees fit.

When a decision has been rendered by the panel, the arbitrators shall assess the arbitration fee on one or both of the parties as they see fit. All other expenses incurred, shall be borne in such manner as fixed in the award. Other deposits received are refunded to the parties entitled to them, except for non-member fees or any cancellation fees.

All non-members party to an arbitration shall be charged an additional fee for each arbitration or appeal, over and above the scheduled fees charged to members as provided above:

- US$ 300 on any question solely of grade or quality of coffee;

- US$ 300 on any other question.

The non-member fee when arbitrating against another non-member is:

- US$ 500 on any question solely of grade or quality of coffee;

- US$ 2,000 on any other question.

This additional fee is retained by the association regardless of the result. It must be paid, together with the regular arbitration fee charged to members, to the GCA at the time the submission to arbitration, and/or answer thereto is filed with the GCA secretary.

CHAPTER 8

FUTURES MARKETS

FUTURES MARKETS

ABOUT FUTURES MARKETS

The extreme volatility of the price of coffee brings drastic price changes over months, weeks or days, or even within the same trading day. Crop prospects vary widely due to unforeseen events, for example drought, frost or disease. High coffee prices encourage production growth, while low prices result in falling output. The balance of supply and demand is subject to many uncertainties that affect price trends and therefore represent price risk. All levels of the coffee industry are exposed to risk from sudden price changes.

Coffee futures represent coffee that will become available at some point in the future, based on standard contracts to deliver or accept a pre-determined quantity and quality of coffee at one of a known range of delivery ports. The only points to be agreed when concluding a futures contract are the delivery period and the price. The delivery period is chosen from a pre-set range of calendar months, called the trading positions. Market forces determine the price at the time of dealing.

There are two main futures market centres, New York and London, serving the global coffee industry:

- In New York, the Intercontinental Exchange (NYSE: ICE), for arabica (the New York C Contract – market symbol KC) – see *www.theice.com*.
- In London, the London International Financial Futures and Options Exchange (NYSE Liffe), for robusta (market symbol RC) – see *www.euronext.com*.

For ease of reference these markets will from now on mostly be referred to in this guide as New York arabica or New York C Contract and as London robusta, Liffe or LIFFE.

Other futures markets trading in coffee are found in Brazil and Singapore, whereas Viet Nam inaugurated two domestic exchanges in 2011.

INTERNET ACCESS

The growth of the Internet has made access to price information on the main markets easier than ever before. The exchanges have their own websites, and all the major commodity news services (Reuters, CRB, etc.) supply price quotes for the major coffee futures markets. There are also Internet sites relating specifically to the coffee business that provide market quotes. Most sites are easy to navigate and usually include a page with the latest futures price quotations.

To locate market information on the Internet, it is helpful to understand the market coding systems. Using the symbols mentioned above, LKDX12 would refer to a quote on the London robusta market for the November 2012 delivery period. In the same way, KCZ12 would symbolize a quote on the New York arabica contract for the December 2012 delivery period. Some Internet sites are easier to navigate and read using these official market symbols; other sites spell everything out in plain English.

Free access price quotations are subject to a 20 to 30 minute delay. Anyone requiring up-to-the-minute quotations must register with a subscription service, which means paying monthly fees for real-time quotes. There are numerous such subscription services with fees ranging anywhere from US$ 200 to US$ 1,000 per month, depending on what other news and trading services the subscription package includes.

THE FUNCTION OF FUTURES MARKETS

Coffee futures exchanges were originally created to bring order to the process of pricing and trading coffee and to diminish the risk associated with chaotic cash market conditions. The futures prices that serve as benchmarks for the coffee industry are openly negotiated in the markets of the coffee futures exchanges (primarily New York and London).

To support a futures market, a cash market must have certain characteristics: sufficient price volatility and continuous price risk exposure to affect all levels of the marketing chain; enough market participants with competing price goals; and, a quantifiable underlying basic commodity with grade or common characteristics that can be standardized. The futures exchange is an organized marketplace that:

- Provides and operates the facilities for trading;
- Establishes, monitors and enforces the rules for trading;
- Keeps and disseminates trading data.

The exchange does not set the price. It does not even participate in coffee price determination. The exchange market supports five basic pricing functions:

- Price discovery;
- Price risk transfer;
- Price dissemination;
- Price quality;
- Arbitration.

The exchange establishes a visible, free market setting for the trading of futures and options which helps the underlying industry find a market price (price discovery) for the product and allows the transfer of risk associated with cash price volatility. As price discovery takes place, the exchange provides price dissemination worldwide.

Continuous availability of pricing information contributes to wider market participation and to the quality of price. (More buyers and sellers in the marketplace mean better liquidity and therefore, better pricing opportunities.). To ensure the accuracy and efficiency of the trading process, the exchange also resolves trading disputes through arbitration.

THE TWO MARKETS – CASH AND FUTURES

To clearly understand the coffee futures market, a distinction must be drawn between physical (cash) coffee and coffee futures.

In the coffee cash market, participants buy and sell physical, green coffee of different qualities that will be delivered either immediately or promptly. The cash transaction therefore involves the transfer of the ownership of a specific lot of a particular quality of physical coffee. The cash price for the physical coffee is the current local price for the specific product to be transferred. (Note that sales of physical, green coffee for later (forward) delivery, called forward contracts, are not to be confused with futures contracts.)

In the coffee futures market, participants buy and sell a price for a standard quality of coffee. The futures transaction centres around trading a futures contract *based* on physical coffee (or its cash equivalent) at a price determined in an open auction – the futures market. The futures price is the price one expects to pay, or receive, for coffee at some future date.

- **Cash price.** The price now for coffee (by trading the physical product for immediate or prompt delivery).
- **Futures price.** The expected price for coffee (by trading the different positions of the futures contract).

The futures contract is a standardized legal commitment to deliver or receive a specific quantity and grade of a commodity or its cash equivalent on a specified date and at a specified delivery point. Its standardization allows the market participants to focus on the price and the choice of contract month.

Traders in the futures markets are primarily interested in risk management (hedging), investment opportunities, or speculation, rather than the physical exchange of actual coffee. Although delivery of physical coffee can take place under the terms of the futures contract, few contracts actually lead to delivery. Instead, purchases are usually matched by offsetting sales and vice versa, and no physical delivery takes place.

In addition to its pricing functions, the coffee futures market also serves to establish standards of quality and grade that can be applied throughout the industry.

PRICE RISK AND DIFFERENTIAL

Because the futures contract is standardized in terms of the quantity and quality of the commodity, the futures price represents an average range of qualities and is therefore an average price. The price for each individual origin and even quality of physical coffee is not necessarily the same: it may be higher or it may be lower. Historically the futures price and the cash price tend to move closer together as the futures delivery date draws near. While such convergence does occur in an efficient market, prices for physical coffee often fluctuate quite independently from the futures market. The physical premium or discount, the differential, represents the value (plus or minus) the market attaches to such a coffee compared to the futures market. This price differential can reflect local physical market conditions, as well as coffee quality and grade.

Price risk therefore has two components:

- **The underlying price risk.** The prices for arabica or robusta futures as a whole rise or fall;
- **The differential risk or basis risk.** The difference between the price on the physical coffee market for a particular quality or origin, and the price on the future market (known as the basis or differential) increases or decreases.

Futures markets can be used to moderate exposure to the price risk because they represent the state of supply and demand for an average grade of widely available deliverable coffee. They cannot be used to moderate the differential or basis risk, which attaches entirely to a particular origin, type or quality of coffee.

Price risk is almost always greater than differential risk, so the risk reduction capability of the futures market is an important management tool. Differential or basis risk can, admittedly, be very high at times and should never be ignored. It is helpful to examine historical differential pricing to identify periods of increased differential risk. There might be seasonal patterns, for example.

LIQUIDITY AND TURNOVER

Liquidity is a crucial factor in determining the success of a futures market. A futures market must have enough participants with competing price goals (buyers and sellers) to ensure a turnover high enough to permit the buying and selling of contracts at a moment's notice without direct price distortion. Large transaction volumes provide flexibility (liquidity) and enable traders to pick the most appropriate contract month, corresponding to their physical delivery commitments, to hedge the price risks inherent in those physical transactions. More bids to buy and offers to sell in the market at any given time create greater pricing efficiency for the participants seeking a price for the commodity. Currently only the New York and London markets provide this flexibility on an international scale, while the Brazilian market, although extremely active, is mostly relevant to local interests.

Speculators and hedgers competing for price generally means that futures and cash prices move in the same direction over time and as a futures contract approaches delivery, the futures price and the cash price will often converge. Futures prices do not always reflect cash market reality though, especially over the very short term when large volumes may be traded for purely speculative reasons. The volume of futures trading and the underlying quantity of physical coffee it represents easily exceed total production of green coffee, or indeed the volume of the physical trade as a whole.

The large volumes on the futures markets not only influence futures prices, but inevitably have an influence on the price of physical coffee as well. It is important for those involved in the physical coffee business to be aware of the activity of speculators and derivative traders. For that reason, the futures industry regularly examines and publishes the ratio of speculative and hedging activity in the market.

Speculators are absolutely necessary to the efficient functioning of a futures market. Speculative activity directly improves liquidity and therefore serves the hedgers' long-term interests. During the last 10 years or so, the activity of hedge funds and the development of options on futures markets have both led to an increase in short-term speculative activity.

While options on futures provide another speculative opportunity in the futures market, options also represent an important risk management tool that has become very useful in recent years. See also chapter 9, Hedging and other operations.

Not all options result in actual futures contracts. However, they do represent potential quantities to be traded on the strike dates should the holders decide to exercise their options rather than simply letting them expire. In any event, the large turnover in actual futures demonstrates the impact of the futures markets on the daily trade in physical coffee. In recent years, physical prices have largely been determined by applying a differential to prices in the futures market; that is, the combination of the differential (plus or minus) and the price of the selected futures position gives the price for the physical coffee.

The tables 8.1 and 8.2 demonstrate the huge growth in volume of the trade in options and futures.

Table 8.1 Annual turnover in futures compared with gross world imports, 1980–2010 (millions of tons)

Year	New York	London	Total futures	World imports*
1980	15.2	5.5	20.7	4.1
1985	11.1	5.1	16.2	4.5
1985–1989	17.7	5.4	23.1	4.7
1990–1994	37.3	5.5	42.8	5.3
1995–1999	37.6	6.6	44.2	5.6
2000	33.7	7.4	41.1	6.1
2001	37.4	7.7	45.1	6.2
2002	46.2	9.5	55.7	6.3
2003	54.6	11.6	66.2	6.5
2004	71.3	15.3	86.6	7.0
2005	67.8	16.3	84.1	7.0
2006	75.0	17.8	92.8	7.3
2007	84.6	22.2	106.8	7.6
2008	92.6	21.9	114.5	7.8
2009	72.4	25.2	97.6	7.6
2010	93.9	27.9	121.8	7.9

* Gross imports from all sources.

Table 8.2 Annual turnover in options and futures, 1990–2010 (millions of tons)

Year	New York	London	Total options	Options + futures
1990	4.8	0.2	5.0	41.0
1990–1994	12.9	0.7	13.6	56.3
1995–1998	16.9	0.8	17.7	42.1
1999	23.3	0.9	24.2	76.9
2000	15.5	0.6	16.1	57.2
2001	13.6	0.4	14.0	59.1
2002	18.1	0.7	18.8	74.5
2003	22.6	0.7	23.3	89.5
2004	33.5	1.2	34.7	121.3
2005	40.3	0.8	41.1	125.2
2006	47.2	2.3	49.5	142.3
2007	49.5	3.3	52.8	159.6
2008	48.0	2.8	50.8	165.3
2009	24.4	1.9	26.3	123.9
2010	39.2	4.8	44.0	165.8

VOLATILITY

The extreme volatility of coffee prices can be seen historically in both the size and suddenness of price moves. In April 1994, for example, New York arabica 'C' futures were around 85 cts/lb – after frost damage in Brazil they reached 248 cts/lb: a rise of close to 300% in less than three months. Eventually values fell back to around 90 cts/lb, but by May 1997 prices had reached over 300 cts/lb. And by mid 2001 the nearest position on the New York arabica 'C' contract had fallen to below 50 cts/lb: a 30-year low just four years after the 1997 highs. By end 2005 the near position once again stood above 100 cts/lb, reaching the 300 cts/lb level again in the first half of 2011. *www.futures.tradingcharts. com/chart/CF/M* offers charts showing the price movements over the last eight to nine years.

Modern communications can move markets quickly, ensuring that all events affecting price become known to all market players more or less simultaneously. And when as a result everyone wants to buy or sell, but there are no sellers or buyers, then without any trading the price may jump or fall by as much as 10 cts/lb or more, depending on the starting price level. In times of extreme volatility this gap means a trader can be left with a position they cannot liquidate when they wish to because there is no trade.

LEVERAGE

Leverage is a significant characteristic of the futures market. In light of coffee price volatility, it is important to be aware that futures contracts are leveraged instruments, meaning that a trader does not pay the full market price for each contract.

Instead, futures traders pay a small portion of the contract's total value (usually less than 10%) in the form of margin, a good faith deposit to ensure contract performance. A New York arabica 'C' contract trading at 200 cts/lb would be worth US$ 75,000 (each contract is for 37,500 lb of coffee). If the margin requirement is about US$ 5,400 per contract, buying 10 contracts at 200 cts/lb means posting a margin of US$ 54,000, representing a long (unsold) position worth US$ 750,000. Leverage offers advantages, but it carries an equal amount of risk. If the market moves down 10 cts before a selling trade can be achieved then the loss of US$ 37,500 in this case represents about 70% of the original investment of US$ 54,000 and will require payment of a variation margin (see later in this chapter). Of course, the hedger would be realizing a comparable gain in the cash market of the value of the planned physical transaction.

Large margin calls (additional payments necessary to maintain the original margin level) sometimes further increase volatility when inability or unwillingness to raise the additional deposits causes traders or speculators to liquidate their positions, thus fuelling the price movement up or down still further.

ORGANIZATION OF A FUTURES MARKET

CLEARING HOUSE

The clearing house conducts all futures business, including the tendering (delivery) of physicals under the terms of the futures contract. Usually set up as a corporation, separate and independent from the exchange, the clearing house guarantees and settles all exchange trades. Through its system of financial safeguards and transaction guarantees, the clearing house protects the interests of the trading public, members of the exchanges and the clearing members of the clearing corporation.

ICE Clear U.S. or 'Clearing Corporation' is the designated clearing house for ICE Futures U.S. – i.e. for the New York arabica contract. Although an ICE Futures U.S. subsidiary, ICE Clear U.S. has its own separate membership, board of directors, elected officers and operating staff.

In London the clearing house is owned by leading banks.

TRADING OF FUTURES

Traditionally the trading of futures contracts on the exchange floor was permitted only between exchange members. However, with the advent of electronic trading, anyone with the appropriate trading rights agreement with a clearing firm, direct or through brokers, can now trade futures electronically but will have to offer substantial guarantees before a trading account can be opened. In origin countries licensed commercial banks may offer such facilities.

Purchases and sales positions for the same contract month offset each other and are built up on a daily basis. Rather than carry such trades until maturity, the clearing house matches offsetting positions and clears them from the records of the brokers who handled them. The clearing house takes the place of the buyer or seller; it performs the role of seller to all buyers, and that of buyer to all sellers. In this way a maximum number of direct settlements is automatically possible at the close of each trading day.

FINANCIAL SECURITY AND CLEARING HOUSES

Financial security for the market is assured by the clearing house, which establishes and enforces rules and guidelines on the financial aspects of all exchange transactions. The clearing house checks, settles and reports each day's business and guarantees the fulfilment of each contract. This is assured through the payment of margins and the collection of all outstanding obligations from members within 24 hours. In addition, members pay into a permanent guarantee fund, enabling the clearing house to assume financial responsibility if a member defaults.

The clearing house also assigns tenders and re-tenders of deliverable coffee after ensuring each lot meets certain set standards of quality, storage, packing, and so on.

THE PRINCIPAL FUTURES MARKETS FOR COFFEE

Establishing a futures market requires extensive research and preparation, whereas success will depend largely on the financial backing that can be attracted. A further prerequisite is that the new futures operation can attain the liquidity necessary to create a true market place that attracts not only local interest, but also foreign operators. The United States and the United Kingdom markets are world market makers, whereas the Brazilian market is of special interest because it operates in a producing country.

THE NEW YORK ARABICA CONTRACT

The original Coffee Exchange of the City of New York was founded in 1882 to deal in futures contracts for Brazilian arabica. The New York Board of Trade or NYBOT was established in 1998 as the parent company of the Coffee, Sugar and Cocoa Exchange (CSCE) and the New York Cotton Exchange (NYCE).

Today's 'C' contract or NYKC covers mild arabica coffee and currently allows delivery of coffee from 19 producing countries. Some of these coffees are traded at basis price, while others are traded at differentials above or below the basis price.

In January 2007 the New York Board of Trade merged with ICE – *www.theice.com,* resulting in the introduction on 2 February 2007 of the electronic trading of six NYBOT soft commodity futures contracts, including arabica coffee, alongside the existing open outcry trading.

Open outcry trading was halted early 2008. Since then all Futures and Against Actuals or AA transactions are carried out electronically. Options, however, trade side by side, i.e. both electronically and through open outcry. The electronic trading hours for options are the same as for futures but open outcry trading of options only operates from 0800 hours to 1330 hours New York time. See later in this chapter for an explanation of AA transactions.

TRADING HOURS, QUOTATIONS, PRICE FLUCTUATION LIMITS

Electronic trading hours. Hours are as follows (London equivalent time in brackets): Open 3.30 a.m. (8.30 a.m.), Settlement window 1.28–1.30 p.m. (6.28–6.30 p.m.), Close 2 p.m. (7 p.m.). However, the ICE platform also offers a pre-open facility where traders can enter bids and offers on outright positions. Pre-open orders will not be available for execution until the electronic market session opens. They are shown in the electronic order book and are executed on a first-in-first-out (FIFO) basis when the electronic market opens. Pre-open sessions operate from 8 p.m. to 1.30 a.m. New York time on working days, and on Sunday evenings prior to a Monday trading session. Readers are advised to check on *www.theice.com* for any changes.

Quotations. For all bids and offers quotations are in United States cents and decimal fractions of a cent. No transactions, except against actuals (AA) transactions, are permitted at a price that is not a multiple of five one-hundredths of one cent per pound, or five points per pound.

Price fluctuation limits. There are no general limits for daily price fluctuations on the 'C' contract. The Board of Managers, however, may prescribe, modify, or suspend maximum permissible price fluctuations, without prior notice. In times of maximum volatility it is common to have limits imposed; historically, these limits have been between 4 and 8 cts per pound maximum daily fluctuation. Based on the New York 'C' contract size of 37,500 lb, a 4-cent variation is equivalent to US\$ 1,500 per contract. Jobbers and floor brokers calculate this by taking US\$ 3.75 for every point of movement, so each 1 cent move equals 100 points times 3.75, or US\$ 375.

The daily settlement price. For all open positions this is based on the trades occurring between 12.28 and 12.30 p.m. New York time.

DELIVERIES, DELIVERY MONTHS, TENDERABLE GROWTHS AND DIFFERENTIALS

Deliveries: can be made at the ports of New York (at par) as well as Houston, New Orleans and Miami; deliveries to the last three ports incur a discount or penalty of 125 points, or US\$ 468.75 per 37,500 lb contract (100 points = US\$ 0.01, i.e. 1 point = 1/100 cent). In Europe deliveries can be made at Antwerp, Bremen/Hamburg and Barcelona, subject again to a 125 point discount from the New York delivery price.

Delivery months: (or trading positions) are March, May, July, September and December. Ten trading positions are always quoted, giving a two-year period. For example: July 2012 (N12), September 2012 (U12), December 2012 (Z12), March 2013 (H13), May 2013 (K13), July 2013 (N13),

September 2013 (U13), December 2013 (Z13), March 2014 (H14) and May 2014 (K14). The first or nearest month is known as the current or spot month. When months repeat, the further out positions are sometimes referred to as red: in this example the March 2014 and May 2014 positions would be known as red March and red May.

Table 8.3   Tenderable growths and differentials at ICE

Tenderable growths	Deliverable at
Costa Rica, El Salvador, Guatemala, Honduras, Kenya, Mexico, Nicaragua, Panama, Papua New Guinea, Peru, Uganda, United Republic of Tanzania	Basis or contract price
Colombia	Plus 200 points per pound
Burundi, India, Venezuela (Bolivarian Republic of)	Minus 100 points per pound
Rwanda*	Minus 300 points per pound
Dominican Republic, Ecuador	Minus 400 points per pound
Brazil**	Minus 900 points per pound

* Effective with the March 2013 expiration, the differential for Rwanda will be minus 100 points.

** Deliverable effective with the March 2013 delivery expiration.

CERTIFICATION OF DELIVERIES

No coffee can be submitted for tendering without having first obtained a certificate of grade and quality from the exchange. All coffee submitted for certification is examined by a panel of three licensed graders. The examination is blind, or neutral, as the graders know the country of origin but not who submitted the sample. The quality is determined on the basis of six evaluations and measurements:

- Green coffee odour (no foreign odours);
- Screen size (50% over screen 15, no more than 5% below screen 14);
- Colour (greenish);
- Grade (defect count);
- Roast uniformity;
- Cup (six cups per sample).

Brazilian arabica will be deliverable effective with the March 2013 expiration. This means that in future both washed and semi-washed Brazilian arabicas may be tendered, but the exchange has not addressed this directly. Instead it has added a new standard to the rules as follows:

'Coffee "C" shall consist of one (1) growth, in sound condition, free from all unwashed and aged flavours in the cup, of good roasting quality and of bean size and colour in accordance with criteria established by the Exchange.'

The reference to 'aged flavours' is not linked to Brazilian arabica, but refers to all growths and is accompanied by simultaneous changes in the age penalties that exchange graded tenderable lots incur after a certain period of storage, also effective with the March 2013 expiration.

If a lot is passed, the exchange will issue the certificate, which includes a complete rating on any grade imperfections. One appeal against rejection is possible on each lot with the whole process repeated by five graders instead of the original three. The appellant has the option to submit a new sample or to run the appeal on the original sample. It is quite normal for coffee that grades well, but has failed on cup to be appealed automatically in the hope that the unsound cup in the first test was an anomaly.

The certificate establishes the basis, or standard, deliverable for these growths. Each growth is allowed a maximum of 23 imperfections (out of 350 grams), with a deduction of 10 points for each full imperfection by which it exceeds the number permitted in the basis. Sample size is 5 lb for parcels up to 300 bags, 8 lb for 301–500 bags and 10 lb for more than 500 bags.

Exchanges continuously monitor cash market conditions and adjust contracts or create new ones to reflect those changes. This reflects the fundamental relationship between cash and futures. If the futures market does not accurately represent the cash market, then it cannot perform its primary pricing functions.

As an example, in recent years the 'C' contract added Panamanian coffee to its tenderable growths, reduced the discount for a number of other growths and added European delivery points. In addition, new grading procedures as well as changes in bagging standards have been implemented.

INTEGRATING FUTURES AND CASH MARKETS: THE eCOPS SYSTEM

ICE's direct involvement with the grading, certification and warehousing of physical coffee is an indication of how interconnected the futures and cash markets have become. The New York Exchange is also directly involved in the establishment of electronic transfer of ownership of lots of coffee through standardized electronic contracts and other paperwork that must accompany the movement of coffee through the marketing chain.

In 1992, the then NYBOT introduced COPS or Commodity Operations and Processing System, a computerized commodity delivery system that addressed sampling, quality, weighing, and title transfer as well as confirming title status of deliveries. This transformed the entire delivery process for the coffee industry by reducing the complex, time consuming, costly and inefficient paper trail for each delivery against a futures contract.

eCOPS has now replaced the paper delivery trail with electronic versions of warehouse receipts, delivery orders, sampling orders, weight notes, invoices, insurance declarations and a number of other accompanying documents. Other areas such as bills of lading and customs entry documentation will be added as the system grows. For more on eCOPS see also chapter 6 or go to *www.theice.com* and look for eCOPS.

SUPERVISION BY CFTC

The U.S. Commodity Futures Trading Commission (CFTC) is charged with the supervision of trading in commodity futures. The CFTC reports directly to the United States Congress and its aim is to protect the trading public from possible abuses by the futures industry, such as manipulation of the market and other deceptive practices that might prevent the market from correctly reflecting supply and demand factors. It also seeks to ensure that the members of the exchange are financially viable.

Exchange bylaws, rules and regulations are statutory and therefore have the force of law. The provisions of the CFTC Act require every intermediary that deals with members of the public investing in futures to be registered with the National Futures Association, a self-regulatory body created by the Act. The ICE Exchanges, through the use of electronic surveillance and professional personnel, actively monitor trading activity and enforce trading rules and regulations.

COMMITMENT OF TRADERS REPORT

The CFTC actively promotes market transparency and to this end publishes the Commitment of Traders (COT) reports, which clearly show the position of large commercial and non-commercial traders. Positions of 50 contracts or more must be reported to the CFTC. This is of great value to small players in that it allows them to see information that otherwise would be available only to very large operators.

In the coffee market it is not uncommon for large speculative hedge funds to hold 20%–25% of the open (uncovered) interest, long or short, and it is important for producers and exporters to know in which delivery months these funds hold their positions. Because of the speculative nature of such fund positions, it is equally important to know their size because if the tonnage of either their long or short position moves to extremes, very fast action could become imminent (liquidation of the longs or buying against the shorts as the case might be).

The CFTC produces a weekly COT on futures, and a fortnightly COT on futures and options combined – available on the CFTC's home page at *www.cftc.gov*. The reports provide information on four categories of market players: Commercial, SWAP Dealers, Managed Money and Other Reportables.

THE LONDON ROBUSTA CONTRACT

Following the removal in 1982 of exchange controls in the United Kingdom, the London International Financial Futures and Options Exchange (LIFFE) was set up to offer market participants better means to manage exposure to both foreign exchange and interest rate volatility. In 1992 it merged with the London Traded Options Market, and in 1996 it merged with the London Commodity Exchange (LCE). This is when soft and agricultural commodity contracts were added to the financial portfolio.

Contracts currently traded are cocoa, robusta coffee, white sugar, wheat, barley and potatoes. There is also a weather contract. Following the purchase of LIFFE by NYSE the exchange was renamed NYSE Liffe – although in the trade it is still referred to as LIFFE. Commodity futures have been traded in London for many years – robusta coffee futures first started trading in 1958. Quotations then were in pound sterling but from 1992 onwards both futures and options have been trading in United States dollars.

Market symbol RC – website *www.euronext.com*

ELECTRONIC TRADING AT LIFFE

Trading takes place electronically by submitting an order, via a trading application (front-end software) into the LIFFE CONNECT™ central order book. Having received the orders the system's Trading Host stores all orders in the central order book. It also performs order matching with corresponding orders (this is an electronic representation of the marketplace), where the criteria for determining trade priority depend on the contract being traded. Traders can submit orders; revise price, volume or a 'good till cancelled' order's date; pull orders; and make wholesale trades. After a trade has been executed, trade details are sent into the Trade Registration System in real-time throughout the day for post-trade processing.

Traders do not know who their trading counterpart is, either before or after the trade. Dramatic as this move seemed at the time, the end-result has been increased liquidity and considerably easier access through linkages with global communications networks that provide electronic access on an equal footing, virtually regardless of location. LIFFE has broken new ground in that rather than obliging market participants to use LIFFE access software, a series of independent software vendors were contracted to design 'tailor-made' front-end solutions.

Participants may change or withdraw unfulfilled orders at any time and are able to 'see' all available offer and bid prices, including the number of lots on offer or bid for at those prices, and many other market details at any one time. To find out how to link into the LIFFE CONNECT™ trading system go to *www.euronext.com,* or ask for their brochure 'How the market works'. Price information is also available free of charge at *www.euronext.com/trader/priceslistsderivatives/ derivativespriceslists-46171-EN.html,* but with a 15 minute time delay.

ROBUSTA CONTRACT FEATURES AT LIFFE

Market symbol: RC

Trading hours are from 9 a.m. to 5.30 p.m. United Kingdom time. The exchange is open Monday through Friday except for listed public holidays.

The price basis is US$/ton ex warehouse.

The contract unit is 10 tons with a minimum price fluctuation of US$ 1/ton.

Delivery months are January (F), March (H), May (K), July (N), September (U), and November (X). As in New York, ten trading positions are always quoted.

The last trading day is the last business day of the delivery month (till 12.30 p.m.); tenders may be made any day during the delivery month.

Delivery points. Exchange-nominated warehouses in London and the United Kingdom home counties, or in a nominated warehouse in, or in the Board's opinion sufficiently close to Amsterdam, Antwerp, Barcelona, Bremen, Felixstowe, Genoa-Savona, Hamburg, Le Havre, Marseilles-Fos, New Orleans, New York, Rotterdam and Trieste.

TENDERABLE GROWTHS, PACKING, DIFFERENTIALS AND CERTIFICATION

Tenderable growths and packing

Robusta coffee from any country of origin that meets the minimum quality requirements is tenderable, provided it is freely available for exportation.

Coffee may be delivered in sound normal bags of maximum 80 kg gross each (bulk shipments must be bagged into tenderable lots), or in sound food grade flexible intermediate bulk containers (FIBC or big bags) weighing not less than 900 kg gross and not more than 1,100 kg gross.

Differentials

Premium Class: up to a maximum of 0.5% defects by weight and up to a maximum of 0.2% foreign matter by weight and a minimum of 90% over screen 15 round and a minimum of 96% over screen 13 round per 300 g; at an allowance of US$ 30 premium per ton.

Class 1: up to a maximum of 3.0% defects by weight and up to a maximum of 0.5% foreign matter by weight and a minimum of 90% over screen 14 round and a minimum of 96% over screen 12 round per 300 g at contract price.

Class 2: up to a maximum of 5.0% defects by weight and up to a maximum of 1.0% foreign matter by weight and a minimum of 90% over screen 13 round and a minimum of 96% over screen 12 round per 300 g; at an allowance of US$ 30 discount per ton.

Class 3: up to a maximum of 7.5% defects by weight and up to a maximum of 1.0% foreign matter by weight and a minimum of 90% over screen 13 round and a minimum of 96% over screen 12 round per 300 g; at an allowance of US$ 60 discount per ton.

Class 4: up to a maximum of 8.0 % defects by weight and up to a maximum of 1.0% foreign matter by weight and a minimum of 90% over screen 12 round per 300 g; at an allowance of US$ 90 discount per ton.

Coffee shall not be tenderable if in the opinion of the graders one or more of the following applies:

- The lot is not robusta coffee;
- The lot is unsound for any reason other than having the defects listed above;
- The lot contains more than 8.0% defects by weight per 300 g;
- The lot contains less than 90% over screen 12 round;
- The lot contains more than 1.0% by weight of foreign matter per 300 g;
- The lot has a detectable foreign odour including, but not limited to, mould, fermentation or smoke.

Age allowance

- US$ 5 discount per ton per calendar month for the period of 13 to 48 months following the date of grading.
- US$ 10 discount per ton per calendar month for the period of 49 calendar months and onwards following the date of grading.

Certification

Grading samples are examined by three members of the Exchange grading panel, who award a grading certificate based on the screen test, the measuring of both defects and foreign matter by weight, and an olfactory (smell) test – the coffee is not liquored (tasted).

SUPERVISION BY LCH

The London Clearing House (LCH) acts as the central counter party for all trades executed on the LIFFE exchange, and is contractually obliged to ensure the performance of all trades registered by its members.

Apart from LIFFE's internal regulations on members' financial resources, staff competency and systems suitability, a considerable body of United Kingdom legislation governs the general trade on futures markets. The Financial Services Act 1986 requires, among other things, every person dealing with the futures-trading public to register with the Securities and Futures Association. This is a self-regulatory body created by the Act (enhanced by the Financial Services and Markets Act 2000) that seeks to assure the financial viability of all Exchange members. LIFFE now also issues a weekly Commitments of Traders Report.

OUTLOOK FOR AN ELECTRONIC EXCHANGE

LIFFE is the largest electronic exchange in the world in terms of value, and has the potential to cope with substantially higher trading volumes. Depending on market demand it could also be expanded to incorporate acceptance of electronic warehouse warrants for tendering purposes. Clearing of physical coffee against futures (against actuals) is already available.

Through electronic documentation systems (see chapter 6, E-commerce and supply chain management) it is theoretically also possible to link coffee purchases in origin countries and the subsequent export shipments with the relevant hedging positions on the exchange. Such additions are of interest especially to the banking system that finances such operations, but would require considerable further development. See chapter 10, Risk and the relation to trade credit.

BOLSA DE MERCADORIAS & FUTUROS – BRAZIL

The first commodity exchange in Brazil was founded in São Paulo in 1917. The present Bolsa de Mercadorias & Futuros (BM&F) was established in 1985; in 1991 it and the original exchange merged and in 1997 a further merger with the Brazilian Futures Exchange of Rio de Janeiro consolidated BM&F's position as the leading derivatives trading centre in the MERCOSUR free trade area. The exchange conducts business in many fields of which coffee is just one. Details at *www.bmfbovespa.com.br.*

Through the GLOBEX system BM&F is linked to exchanges in the United States and elsewhere and its coffee contracts are accessible to non-residents of Brazil. This enables foreign traders and roasters to hedge purchases of Brazilian physicals against Brazilian futures, thus avoiding the differential risk that comes with hedging on other exchanges.

SEPARATE CONTRACTS FOR SPOT AND FUTURES

The contract size (100 bags of 60 kg each, meaning it is accessible also to smaller growers), clearly demonstrates that BM&F operates in a producing country.

The spot contract trades physical coffee. Type 6 or better, hard cup or better, is graded by BM&F and stored in licensed warehouses in the city of São Paulo. Prices are quoted in Brazilian reals per 60 kg bag and all contracts must be closed out at the end of each trading day. This contract is aimed at operators in the local market. Brazil is not just the world's largest producer – it is also the world's second largest consumer of coffee.

The arabica futures contract trades seven positions. These are March, May, July, September and December plus the next two positions of the following year. Basis: type 4–25 (4/5) or better, good cup or better, classified by BM&F, with prices quoted in US$ per 60 kg bag. Delivery may be made in BM&F licensed warehouses in 29 locations in the states of São Paulo, Paraná, Minais Gerais and Bahia (deliveries outside the city of São Paulo incur a deduction for freight costs). Using United States dollars facilitates linkage with the export market.

OPTIONS

Put and call option contracts. These contracts are also traded, based on the BM&F arabica futures contract expiring in the month after the delivery month of the option, also priced in United States dollars. There are seven trading positions: February, April, June, August and November, plus the next two positions in the following year. Buyers may decide to exercise options from the first business day following the day a position has been initiated up to the last trading day before expiry as follows:

Put option. The buyer (holder) of the option may decide to sell, and the seller (issuer) of the option must buy the corresponding position on the arabica futures contract.

Call option. The buyer (holder) of the option may decide to buy, and the seller (issuer) must sell the corresponding position on the arabica futures contract.

All transactions are at the strike price for which the option was taken and settlement is effected according to all the usual exchange regulations. Options are exercised only if they show a profit – otherwise they are simply allowed to expire.

CLEARING SERVICES, TURNOVER AND LIQUIDITY

Clearing services are provided by the exchange's clearing members, who are liable for the settlement of all transactions. Clearing members must maintain the minimum net working capital set by the exchange's clearing division and must post collateral to finance the clearing fund. They are also subject to limits in respect of the trading positions for which they accept liability.

Commodity brokers and local traders are in turn bonded to the clearing members for all transactions they execute, from registration to final settlement. There is no clearing house to take the role of counterpart in all transactions as is the case in New York and London.

TURNOVER – FUTURES AND OPTIONS

Over the years turnover has grown steadily:

- 2008: trading reached 838,090 arabica futures contracts or almost 84 million bags. But the open interest at year-end was just 15,066 contracts, whereas trade in options was just 54,853 contracts with the year-end open interest standing at 5,831 contracts.
- 2009: 596,435 futures contracts were traded, but again the year-end open interest was low at 18,538 contracts. Trade in options was just 5,155 contracts.
- 2010: 640,754 futures contracts were traded and the year-end open interest was 14,108 contracts. Trade in options was 17,453 contracts.

SINGAPORE EXCHANGE LTD – THE SGX ROBUSTA COFFEE CONTRACT

Launched in April 2010, the SGX Robusta Coffee Contract moved to the Singapore Exchange Ltd in January 2011.

The interesting aspect is the option to effect delivery in different locations, but to date activity has been modest.

SGX Coffee is a physical delivery futures contract, traded in five metric tons per lot of robusta coffee with specific quality standards defined by the exchange. There are two trading windows for the contract capturing both Asian and European trading hours: T session: 1000 hours to 1900 hours and the T+1 session: 2000 hours to 0200 hours (next day).

Delivery will be made via Warehouse Receipts representing coffee stored in bonded warehouses in Ho Chi Minh City, Viet Nam or Singapore. This is an interesting aspect, but nevertheless it remains to be seen whether this venture will be more successful than others that have ceased trading, like for example the arabica and robusta contracts that were traded in the past at Indian exchanges and the failed attempts in New York to establish a viable robusta contract.

For contract details visit *www.sgx.com* and go to products then commodities then robusta coffee futures.

VIET NAM – TWO EXCHANGES FOR ROBUSTA

In early 2011, both the Vietnam Commodity Exchange (VNX) in Ho Chi Minh City and the Buon Ma Thuot Coffee Exchange Center (BCEC) in Dak Lak commenced offering robusta coffee futures trading. See *www.vnx.com.vn* and *http://bcec.vn* respectively.

Located in Ho Chi Minh City, VNX was established as Viet Nam's first fully fledged commodities exchange in September 2010. The VNX Robusta Contract (five metric tons) is linked to both the London NYSE Liffe and Singapore SICOM exchanges and offers the choice of either quality specification at the time of initiating a trade. In terms of liquidity this link will assist in that VNX can offset contracts on either exchange should local liquidity not be sufficient. Exchange licensed warehouses will store coffee to be tendered and the intention is to try and arrange that in future samples may be sent to London for grading at the NYSE Liffe exchange. If this becomes reality then over time such an arrangement could lead to NYSE Liffe certified coffee being available ex warehouse Ho Chi Minh City. Potentially this could assist the holders to raise finance against such stocks and increase liquidity on VNX.

BCEC on the other hand commenced operations in 2005 as a spot market for physical coffee that before sale would be warehoused and inspected by the exchange. The intention was to provide an open market system that allowed farmers to access all available information and so negotiate better prices, whereas buyers would be assured of both contract integrity and quality. However, by early 2011 only small amounts of green coffee had been transacted in this way with farmers seemingly objecting to having to deliver coffee to the BCEC complex in the city of Buon Ma Thuot, preferring to sell to more easily accessible collectors instead. Nevertheless, the new futures contract is intended to offer individual farmers, traders, collectors and exporters the possibility of selling and buying coffee forward. To enable individual farmers to take part, the contract is for just two metric tons.

These are potentially interesting initiatives, but it should be noted that to date no serious alternatives to the London and New York exchanges have evolved. Turnover at SICOM in Singapore remains very small and coffee futures trading in India stopped some years ago because of a lack of liquidity.

THE MECHANICS OF TRADING IN FUTURES

The following paragraphs describe the actual workings of a futures market, based on the procedures and customs applicable to the New York and London Exchanges.

It is necessary to gain a good understanding of the mechanics of the market before attempting to grasp the commercial principles that govern traders' actions. These are discussed in chapter 9.

FLOOR PROCEDURE

In traditional open outcry or floor-based trading, the initiation of a transaction takes place on the floor of the exchange. Exact floor procedures vary from market to market. Exchanges as LIFFE for London robusta (screen only) and ICE for New York arabica (screen only except for options) have moved trading to a screen-based environment and automated the entire process.

In both floor and screen-based trading, there is usually some form of open auction during which buyers and sellers make their trades in public. Unlike the physical market, no privately arranged deals are allowed.

The transaction is negotiated across the floor, providing all participants an opportunity to respond to the current bids and offers. The negotiation is concluded the moment a buyer and a seller agree with each other and the seller registers the contract as a sale to the clearing house. Thereafter, the two traders are responsible only to the clearing house. In this way, the clearing house is a party to every transaction made by both buyers and sellers.

Automated or electronic trading is different, but maintains the transparency of open outcry trading in that all bids and offers can be viewed by all participants. The computer system matches equivalent bids and offers without human intervention. Once the orders are matched, the clearing procedure is exactly the same as the old open outcry system.

Futures contracts are standardized in that all terms are given, except the exact date of delivery, the names of the seller and buyer, and the price. The market rules are legally enforceable contract terms and therefore cannot be substantially altered during the period of the contract. Every futures contract specifies the quantity, quality, and condition of the commodity upon delivery; the steps to be taken in the event of default in delivery; and the terms of final payment.

DELIVERY

Most futures transactions do not result in physical delivery of the commodity. Depending on their strategy, futures traders usually make conscious decisions either to avoid delivery or to accomplish it. That is, they either make an offsetting transaction ahead of the delivery, thereby avoiding physical coffee being tendered to them; or they consciously force the exchange to deliver (tender) physical coffee by allowing the contract to fall due. Delivery must be completed between the first and the last trading days of the delivery month, although the exact terms vary from one market to the other.

While the futures contract can be used for delivery, its terms are not convenient for all parties. For example, the terms of delivery of futures contract provide the seller with the exclusive right to select the point of delivery. This situation can obviously create difficulties for the buyer. In addition, the actual coffee delivered, while acceptable under the futures contract, may not match the buyer's specific quality needs.

OFFSETTING TRANSACTIONS

A trader who buys a futures contract and has no other position on the exchange is long. If this purchase is not eventually offset by an equivalent sale of futures then the buyer will have to take delivery of the actual commodity. Alternatively, a trader who sells a futures contract without an offsetting purchase of futures is said to be short.

Traders who have taken either position in the market have two ways of liquidating it. The first involves the actual delivery or receipt of goods. Most traders choose the second option, which is to cancel an obligation to buy or sell by carrying out a reverse operation, called an offsetting transaction. By buying a matching contract a futures trader in a short position will be released from the obligation to deliver. Similarly, a trader who is long can offset outstanding purchases by selling.

Against actuals (AA). It is possible to liquidate futures positions in the spot market privately under a pre-arranged trade. This type of transaction, called an against actuals trade, avoids the complexities of making a physical delivery under a futures contract. However, such AA transactions must take place under the rules of the exchange that supervises the futures contract.

Open interest. The total of the clearing house's long or short positions (which are always equal) outstanding at a given moment is called the open interest. At the end of each trading day, the clearing house assumes one side of all open contracts. If a trader has taken a long position, the clearing house takes the short position, and vice versa.

The clearing house guarantees the performance of both sides of all open contracts to its members and each trader deals only with the clearing house after initiating a position. In effect, therefore, all obligations to receive or deliver commodities are undertaken with the clearing house and not with other traders.

FUTURES PRICES

Futures prices and spot prices. Futures markets provide a public forum to enable producers, consumers, dealers and speculators to exchange offers and bids until a price is reached which balances the day's supply and demand. Remember that only a negligible proportion of the physical coffee trade actually moves through exchange markets.

The futures price is intended to reflect current and prospective supply and demand conditions whereas the spot price in the physical market refers to the price of a coffee for immediate delivery. In the futures market the spot price normally reflects the nearest futures trading position.

Carries and inversions. When the quotation for the forward positions stands at a premium to the spot price, the market is said to display a carry (also called forwardation or contango). The price of each successive forward position rises the further away it is from the spot position. In order to provide adequate incentives for traders to carry stocks, the premiums for forward positions must cover at least part of the carrying costs of those who accept ownership. Therefore, when stocks become excessive, the futures market enables operators to enter the market to buy the commodity on a cash basis and to sell futures, thereby carrying it. The carry will eventually rise to a level where the premium covers the full cost of financing, warehousing and insuring unused coffee stocks. This level of the forward premium is known as the full carry. The holders of surplus coffee are now covered for the full costs of holding these stocks.

The size of the forward premium or discount between the various forward trading months quoted at any time reflects the fundamentals of the coffee market. When coffee is in short supply, the market nearly always displays an inversion (backwardation), with the forward quotation standing at a discount to the cash price.

This inversion encourages the holder of surplus stocks to supply them to the spot market and to earn the inversion by simultaneously purchasing comparable tonnages of forward futures at a discount to the spot price.

Differences between forward and futures market prices

Forward markets are used to contract for the physical delivery of a commodity. By contrast, futures markets are 'paper' markets used for hedging price risks or for speculation rather than for negotiating the actual delivery of goods. On the whole, prices in the physical and the futures markets move parallel to each other. However, whereas the futures price represents world supply and demand conditions, the physical price for any particular coffee in the forward market reflects the supply and demand for that specific type and grade of coffee, and the nearest comparable growths.

Prices in both physical and futures markets tend to move together because traders in futures contracts are entitled to demand or make delivery of physical coffee against their futures contracts. The important point is not that delivery actually takes place, but that delivery is possible, whether this course of action is chosen or not. Any marked discrepancy between the prices for physicals and futures would attract simultaneous offsetting transactions in the two markets, thus bringing prices together again.

However, buying futures in the hope of using the coffee against physical delivery obligations is extremely risky because the buyer of futures contracts does not know the exact storage location or the origin or quality of the coffee until delivery is made. The coffee that is finally delivered may be unsuitable for the buyer's physical contractual obligations, leaving them with more rather than less risk exposure. On the other hand, physical coffee on a forward shipment or delivery contract that is of an acceptable quality can usually be delivered against a short position on the futures market as the buyer can choose the origin and where to make the physical delivery (or tender). This feature makes futures contracts particularly suitable as a hedge against physicals.

TYPES OF ORDERS

Fixed price order for the same day. This means that an Exchange member is asked to buy or sell a given number of lots (contracts) for a particular month at a set price, for instance, two lots of coffee for December at US$ 1.70/lb. The contract must be completed during the day on which the order is given. If possible, the broker will buy (sell) at a lower (higher) price but never at a higher (lower) price. This ensures that the client will get the desired price if a contract is made, but they run the risk of not having a contract made at all if the floor trader cannot execute the order on that day.

Fixed price, open order is a similar order, except that the instructions stand for an indefinite period of time until the order is satisfied or cancelled by the client. This type of order is popularly known as good till cancelled.

Market order. This is an order that gives the broker more flexibility, and allows him to make a contract for the best possible price available at the time.

Different orders are often made, subject to certain conditions. For example, a broker may be instructed to make a contract if the price reaches a certain level. Orders that are conditional on specific terms set by the client can also be made. Examples of such orders are those to be carried out only at the opening or closing of the market or those to be carried out within a certain period of time. (Orders have to queue at the opening and closing of the market and are therefore not all filled at the same price, particularly when trading volume is high in an active market. If one stipulates a price then an order may not be executed if that price is not touched, or is exceeded.)

Market orders and fixed price orders for the same day are the most common, but orders are also made to suit the requirements of clients. Clients who follow exchange movements closely frequently revise their orders in response to changing market conditions. Those less involved in hourly market movements usually place open orders, or orders subject to certain conditions. For example, a stop-loss order – which is triggered into action as soon as a predetermined price level is reached – limits the client's losses relative to the level at which the order is executed. Placing more general conditions on the order gives the broker greater flexibility to react to changes in the market and leaves the final decision to them.

Positions

Open position. This is the number of contracts registered by the clearing house which are not offset by other contracts or tenders when the contracts become spot (the nearby contract month). For example, a coffee trader may have a position with the clearing house of 30 purchase contracts and 40 sales contracts. Some of the purchases and sales may be for the same delivery month, but the trader may have labelled them as 'wait for instructions' if those contracts represent separate hedging transactions for that trader. This means the trader will enter into additional futures deals to offset them once they unwind the physicals against which the original hedge was taken. In other words, the open position of that particular operator remains 70 lots until some of the contracts are offset or 'washed out'.

The clearing house reports only the total of all operator positions, rather than that of any one member, which is left to the broker to report. The CFTC's commitment of traders (COT) report breaks down the total open interest on the New York 'C' contract by category of traders. Large traders are called reportable, while small traders are non-reportable. The COT report then further breaks down the open interest by commercial and non-commercial reportable traders. It is a very handy tool for exporters to get an idea of the long or short positions of the large speculative hedge funds.

Margins

Trading deposits (margins). These are required upon initiation of a futures trade. Further deposits may be required daily to reflect the changes in the price of the contracts, when the market moves against a trader's position. If additional funds are required to restore the original margin (ranging from 5%-10% of the contract's nominal value) then variation margins must be paid in unless adequate security, for example treasury bills, had already been deposited when the account was established. Conversely, if the futures price move is favourable to the trader, the gains transferred into the account above the margin requirement level become immediately available to the trader.

Clearing house members must maintain specific margins depending upon their net open position with the clearing house. Margins are also needed for members of the trading public who lodge their contracts with members of the exchange. Original margins are normally set at approximately 10% of the market value of a contract and variation margins must be paid in full upon demand. Margin money collected by the exchange member from the public must be deposited in segregated customers' accounts. Note that the original margin requirements in this category are minimum figures and that exchange members may require additional security from their clients if they feel the minimum margin is not enough.

Original and variation margins are adjusted from time to time for the following reasons: to reflect increased or decreased market levels; to add security to volatile positions, particularly in months carrying no limit; and to discourage excessive concentration of trading positions in any one month. Investors should note that margin requirements can be changed without prior notice.

Financing margins

Financing margin calls on open contracts can make the use of futures markets very expensive for producers and exporters, partly because variation margins are always paid in cash. This does not apply to trading deposits, which can be covered by securities such as bank guarantees and treasury bills.

Any user of futures markets should be aware that unanticipated calls for variation margins can be costly in terms of demands on their cash flow and the interest forgone on cash deposited with the clearing house. Therefore, a user should carefully consider how margin calls will be financed before entering into any commitments. See also chapter10.

An (extreme) example: on 24 June 1994 the 'C' contract closed at 125.50 cts/lb. Just two weeks later the market closed at 245.25 cts/lb owing to frost damage in Brazil. This translated into a variation margin of US$ 45,000 per lot so an exporter with a short of 10 lots against physical stocks would have had to pay US$ 450,000 to meet the margin call – and within 24 hours at that. As a result of margin financing problems the open interest at that time was halved within weeks. Of course, exporters would benefit from the increased value of their physical stocks in a situation like this, but might not always find it easy to convince any but the most experienced commodity finance banks of the validity of this argument.

Merchants and brokers are often willing to help producers and exporters to overcome the problems that margin calls can create. In some cases, the broker will finance all the margin costs but in return the broker will expect a higher rate of commission or a discount on physical contracts. Brokers can be particularly useful in solving the additional problems connected with distant futures transactions. Often a high premium can be picked up for forward physicals, but there is no liquidity for such far dates in the futures markets.

However, most if not all of today's forward business in physicals is conducted on a price to be fixed basis, which has reduced the need to enter into far forward futures deals. For information on price to be fixed, or PTBF, see chapter 9.

Traders and others who pay their own margins are entitled to receive cash payments of all credit variation margins. Additionally, if they pay the trading deposit in cash, they are entitled to receive interest on that money.

Trade houses play an important role in aiding producers, exporters and industry to overcome margin requirements. When a trade house enters into a transaction for physical coffee, either on a price to be fixed basis or on an outright price basis, it is usually also the trade house that takes up the obligation and risk of margin financing. This is of significant benefit to the coffee trade and plays an integral part in establishing long-term delivery contracts. Of course, the trade house itself must have strict financial and third-party (counter-party) risk controls in place in order to avoid any excess margin calls in times of increased market volatility.

CHAPTER 9

HEDGING AND OTHER OPERATIONS

HEDGING AND OTHER OPERATIONS

HEDGING – THE CONTEXT

Coffee prices are inherently unstable. Irrespective of whether one is a producer, exporter, importer or roaster one must have a strategy to manage price volatility. For operators using borrowed funds most banks will insist upon a solid risk management strategy. Most of these strategies are designed using coffee futures and options to offset the price risk inherent with holding coffee inventories, or commitments to deliver coffee. Hedging can sometimes also be done by offsetting a sale of one type of physical coffee with the purchase of another type of coffee. This type of hedging is very difficult as the physical coffee market is not as liquid as coffee futures and it may be difficult to find a buyer at short notice for that particular coffee.

The text in this chapter presupposes that the reader has read chapter 8, Futures markets. Similarly, before proceeding to chapter 10, Risk and the relation to credit, readers should first acquaint themselves with the information provided on hedging and related operations.

PRINCIPLE, RISKS, PROTECTION

Hedging is a trading operation that enables management of the risks posed by unforeseen price movements. There are many strategies for hedging. Most of these strategies call for the use of coffee futures or options to offset normal price risk incurred with either (i) holding unsold stocks or inventories of coffee = being long or through (ii) forward sales of coffee not yet bought = being short.

Hedging does not eliminate risk, it is only a way to manage risk. Professional risk managers, sometimes referred to as 'traders', know many different hedging strategies and what kind of price protection each strategy will generate.

Hedging allows one to offset price risk through opposing but matching transactions in both physicals and futures. But only the price risk, not the basis or differential risk, can be hedged. Over the years hedging activity has risen strongly, mainly because few banks will finance transactions where price risk is not managed. But hedging in severely volatile markets requires increasingly large capital outlays, at times rising to unaffordable levels for all but the strongest hands. Successful hedging strategies therefore require backing

from experienced banks, well-versed in the financing of the commodity trade.

RISKS

Coffee producers are a natural 'long' in the coffee market. They always have coffee that is subject to price changes. The coffee producers' own might be stocks of already harvested coffee, or coffee still on their trees. They also have future coffee production that will be subject to price swings in the market. They might not know the exact quantities of their production in the next or the following year, but experienced coffee producers have a good idea how much a farm will produce in any given crop year. Hence, the next or the following year's production must be seen as part of the producer's long position.

Coffee roasters are a natural 'short' in the market. As long as a roaster stays in business, he or she needs to buy coffee, hence they are short. Inventory and forward purchases might reduce the need to buy coffee nearby, but as business continues, they will roast what they have and will need to buy more at the market price. Price swings can greatly affect their business and while they have a good idea of their futures sales volume, they have no idea of the price they will pay for coffee, unless they hedge.

Exporters and importers are true middlemen. They must buy coffee when the producer wants to sell and they must sell coffee when the roaster wants to buy. Exporters and importers can be naturally long or short, depending on whether they have more purchases or sales in their physical (green coffee) position.

TYPES OF PRICE RISK

Before active futures markets came into being coffee was bought and sold at fixed prices, meaning purchase and sale contracts would show a simple amount per pound or per ton. This type of pricing is also called 'outright' pricing. If one bought coffee at US$ 1.60/lb that had not already been sold (bought long), one could only hope and pray that the price would stay the same or go higher. If one sold coffee at US$ 1.60/lb that had not already been bought (sold short), the hope would be that the price would stay the same or go down in value. Anytime you closed such a contract, you were totally exposed to any price movements in the coffee market.

Another type of pricing is coffee bought or sold on a differential basis. When buying or selling coffee on a differential basis, one is committing to deliver or take delivery of coffee, not at a fixed price but at a difference to the futures market. Theoretically one can buy or sell at a difference to any published price in the coffee business (i.e. ICO Indicators), but almost all differential business is done against futures markets. More specifically, it is normal that robusta coffee is bought or sold against the London LIFFE Contract and arabica coffee is bought or sold against the New York ICE 'C' Contract. The reason differential contracts are mostly priced against future markets is that the future markets are liquid and prices can be fixed anytime these markets are open for trading.

Differentials link prices for widely differing types and qualities of green coffee with prices on the futures markets where standard qualities and quantities of coffee are traded. In recent years, increasing activity on the futures markets has translated into more and more severe price volatility, not always linked to changing fundamentals in the coffee market such as supply and demand. As a result, differentials for many individual origins now fluctuate not only in response to domestic changes in, for example, quality or availability, but increasingly also because of (sometimes unexpected) movements on the futures markets that are caused by speculative influences.

Historically, it has been quite normal to buy Brazil mid grade arabica at ICE 'C' with a differential of around minus 15 cts per pound FOB whereas Colombian UGQ (usual good quality) might for example trade at ICE 'C' plus 15 cts per pound FOB. While some of the other Milds coffees from Central America and East Africa have tended to trade near equal to or 'basis' with ICE 'C'. It is also normal that the trading or delivery month used for the differential would be the month immediately following the shipment period. For example, June shipment arabicas would be sold as a differential to July ICE 'C'.

It is important to note that buying or selling on a differential basis does not eliminate price volatility risk. For example, in 2010 some Colombian coffees which had been trading at around ICE 'C' plus 15 cts/lb, went up to ICE 'C' plus 80 cts/lb. If one had sold Colombian coffee at ICE 'C' plus 15 and were forced to cover the coffee at ICE 'C' plus 80, there would have been a loss of 65 cts/lb on the differential, before the contract itself was even fixed. This example is extreme, but it did happen and it will happen again with some quality of coffee.

Despite the extreme example just shown, it is safe to say that price differentials are generally less volatile than futures prices. With differential or Price To Be Fixed (PTBF) Contracts, one can reduce the price risk by taking positions, either long or short and avail those positions to all the risk management tools available in the futures and options

markets. But remember, it is impossible to entirely eliminate all of the risk. Nevertheless, most large end-users tend to purchase on PTBF basis and anyone wishing to partake of their business will have to be conversant with trading in this way. More will be discussed about PTBF contracts later in this chapter.

THE SELLING HEDGE

A party holding unsold stocks of a commodity, e.g. a producer, exporter, processor or importer/dealer, etc. is interested in safeguarding against the risk that the price may fall. This risk is offset by a forward sale of a corresponding tonnage on the futures market: the short or selling hedge. If prices decline, long holders would lose on the physical coffee they own. However, they would be compensated by profits made at the exchange because the futures contract would have been bought back at a lower price as well. This relies on the assumption, usually accurate, that futures prices also decline when physical prices fall.

A straightforward example (see below) would be that of an exporter in Guatemala who on 15 September buys 1,000 bags of prime washed arabica coffee ready for shipment in October. As there may be no buyers on that day willing to pay their asking price (FOB), the exporter sells four lots of the New York 'C' December position instead. They do this because the price obtainable will be very close to their asking price, plus or minus the differential, for the physical coffee. If the market for the physical coffee goes down, they will protect themselves from the lower price they may eventually have to sell at, by simultaneously buying in their short sale of New York 'C' December. Should the market go up, they will make up their loss on the December futures by the higher price they will receive when they sell the 1,000 bags of physical coffee – assuming that the prices for futures and the physical coffee move in tandem.

Differentials usually (but not always) tend to be lower when futures prices are high, and higher when futures are low. It is important however to be aware that at times differentials can be extremely volatile and although these variations can sometimes work in favour of an exporter, they can also at times leave all operators with a nasty surprise. Differentials vary as a result of a number of factors including production or supply problems at origin or outside influences on futures markets. Of course, not all hedging operations are necessarily profitable.

THE BUYING HEDGE

Roasters may have customers who want to purchase a certain percentage of their requirements at a fixed price for monthly deliveries up to a year ahead. But it would be both economically and physically impractical to purchase spot green coffee and finance and warehouse it for that period of time, so the roaster's alternative is to buy futures positions

Box 9.1   The selling hedge – an example

- **The market goes down**

Physical transaction:

15 September:	Exporter buys 1,000 bags of 152 lb each from grower	@ US$ 1.62/lb
30 October:	Exporter sells 1,000 bags	@ US$ 1.61/lb
	Loss of $0.01/lb on 152,000 lb	*= (US$ 1,520)*

Futures transaction:

15 September:	Exporter sells 4 lots December 'C' (150,000 lb)	@ US$ 1.72/lb
30 October:	Exporter buys 4 lots December 'C' (150,000 lb)	@ US$ 1.70/lb
	Profit of 200 points x 4 lots or $0.02/lb	*= US$ 3,000*
	Gross profit before commissions	= US$ 1,480

- **The market goes up**

Physical transaction:

15 September:	Exporter buys 1,000 bags of 152 lb each from grower	@ US$ 1.62/lb
30 October:	Exporter sells 1,000 bags	@ US$ 1.65/lb
	Profit of $0.03/lb on 152,000 lb	*= US$ 4,560*

Futures transaction:

15 September:	Exporter sells 4 lots December 'C' (150,000 lb)	@ US$ 1.72/lb
30 October:	Exporter buys 4 lots December 'C' (150,000 lb)	@ US$ 1.74/lb
	Loss of 200 points x 4 lots or $0.02/lb	*= (US$ 3,000)*
	Gross profit before commissions	= US$ 1,560

Note for the example above: Most countries in Latin America use bags of 69 kg (152 lb) although bags of 46 kg and 75 kg are also seen. Brazil and most countries in Asia and Africa use 60 kg bags. All ICO statistics are expressed in 60 kg bags equivalent though.

for as far forward as necessary to cover the sale of the roasted coffee.

Thus, in covering their needs for green coffee in a general way by purchasing the various forward months on the exchange, the roaster is in a position to buy a specific growth and quantity of physical coffee as and when needed for roasting, to fulfil their spread sale of roasted coffee. Upon purchasing the actual coffee they require, they then either sell out their position on the exchange or tender it as an 'AA' (against actuals) through the exchange with the agreement of the dealer from whom they are purchasing the physicals.

The dealer or importer who has entered into a forward sale of up to 12 monthly deliveries to a roaster can purchase the various trading months of the futures contract to protect their sale until they are able to buy the physical coffee to be delivered against the forward sale. Once physical coffee

is purchased, they sell back that part of their long position in futures on the exchange. As in the selling hedge, both parties have protected their price risk, regardless of market fluctuations up or down.

THE BUYING HEDGE – AN EXAMPLE

Example

On 2 January, a roaster sells roasted coffee equivalent to 500 bags arabica coffee per month, February through to January the next year at the (fixed) price of US$ 1.73/lb (GBE – green bean equivalent, net GBE sales price, i.e. roasting costs and margins have been deducted). They now protect that price by simultaneously buying the monthly positions of the 'C' contract as follows:

5 lots (1,250 bags) of March	@ US$ 1.68/lb
5 lots (1,250 bags) of May	@ US$ 1.70/lb
5 lots (1,250 bags) of July	@ US$ 1.72/lb
5 lots (1,250 bags) of September	@ US$ 1.74/lb
4 lots (1,000 bags) of December	@ US$ 1.76/lb

i.e. 24 lots (6,000 bags) at an average of 171.83 cts/lb or 1.17 cts/lb below the GBE selling price.

With this activity the roaster has immediately hedged most of the price risk involved. They can now deal with the purchase of the physical coffee at their convenience by periodically buying physicals to roast and ship to their customer, while simultaneously selling the corresponding amount of futures.

For example, on 1 February, they buy 1,250 bags of spot milds at US$ 1.70/lb, and simultaneously sell the five lots of March 'C' at US$ 1.70/lb. They apply their profit of 2 cts from the sale of the 'C' to lower the cost of their physical purchase to US$ 1.68/lb. On 1 April, they buy 1,250 bags of spot milds at US$ 1.69/lb and sell the five lots of May 'C' at US$ 1.69/lb. They apply the 1-cent loss from the 'C' sale to the cost of their physical purchase, resulting in a price of US$ 1.70/lb. And so on.

The roaster continues to buy in the approved physicals of their choice as needed, whether 250 bags at a time or 1,250 bags at once, and sells out the equivalent futures. Their hedging objective is to maintain their average differential of 1.17 cts/lb or better on the purchase of their physical coffee compared to their position on the futures market. The example above also shows that large roasters often price green coffee down to two decimal prices which demonstrates the competitiveness of the mainstream coffee business.

TRADING AT PRICE TO BE FIXED

THE PRINCIPLE OF TRADING PTBF

The trading described above assumed that buyers and sellers worked with fixed or outright prices. It also focused on the primary market or price risk, not on the basis risk or differential risk that cannot be offset by hedging. In recent years more and more physicals have been traded at prices that are to be fixed against the futures markets: the PTBF contract.

The PTBF contract is a great tool for price risk management as it combines the act of hedging with the act of buying or selling physical coffee. Immediately after a PTBF contract is signed, price risk changes from outright price to differential price. As mentioned earlier, differential price risk is inherently lower in volatility than outright price risk. Secondly, once a PTBF contract is signed, the buyer and seller can fix their respective prices anytime a futures market is open without having to wait for a bid or offer in a physical market which may lack liquidity. Yes, the buyer's price can be different than the seller's price for the same contract and the text that follows will show how this can happen.

It is necessary to caution that the PTBF contract is a risk management tool. Like any tool, if it is used improperly, it can cause more damage than good. There are numerous examples of how parties enter into PTBF contracts without proper knowledge of how they work. Instead of managing risk, the parties can unknowingly increase their risk beyond their means. There are known examples of exporters fixing PTBF contracts without actually having bought the physical green coffee – pure speculation. Or, delaying fixing until long after the physical green coffee was bought is just more of the same.

Yet the fact remains, a well executed PTBF contract will limit price risk to changes in the price differential and does give the ability to fix purchase or sale prices whenever future markets are open. However, to take advantage of this last attribute, buyers and sellers of PTBF contracts must have access to trading of coffee futures.

Initiating a PTBF contract. A relevant delivery month of the futures market is chosen. Because the quality of the physicals (the green coffee) is worth more or less than the quality on which the futures contract is based, the price stipulation will read (for example) 'New York 'C' December plus (or minus) 3 cts/lb', or 'London Robusta November plus (or minus) US$ 30/ton': the plus 3 or plus 30 is the differential.

Differentials for Colombians are normally a premium to the 'C' contract while natural Brazil arabica is normally a discount. Viet Nam grade 2 robustas are usually a discount to LIFFE while a good Uganda robusta is normally at a premium. The relevant month of the future market is usually the month traded nearest to the delivery month of the physical coffee. December delivery Colombians would normally trade against December 'C' contract. The number of futures contracts used to fix the price of the physical delivery is determined by taking the total quantity of the physical contract and dividing it by the size of each futures contract. If there is fraction of a futures contract involved, the total number of contracts will be rounded up or down.

It is important that all these contract terms – differential, futures month(s), number of futures contracts – are specified at the time of the contract initiation.

The contract constitutes a firm agreement to deliver and accept a quantity of physical coffee of a known quality and under established conditions. These conditions are based on the quotation for the specified delivery month of the futures market at the time of fixing, plus or minus the agreed differential. The advantage to the buyer and seller is that each has secured a contract for physical coffee, but the price remains open.

In other words, the buyer has now separated the operational decision to secure physical coffee (thereby avoiding problems of shortages) from the financial decision to fix the cost of that coffee, which they prefer to postpone. This arrangement provides flexibility for both buyer and seller. The obligation to deliver and accept physicals now exists, but as the price remains open.

FIXING PTBF CONTRACTS

Beside the differential that is determined at the initiation of the contract, there are three other prices: (i) the price that the seller fixed at, (ii) the price that the buyer fixed at, and (iii) the invoice price.

As mentioned earlier, it is preferable if not imperative that sellers and buyers of PTBF contracts have access, directly or via an intermediary, to futures trading accounts so they can fix at their command. The seller can fix the price he sells in a PTBF contract simply by selling the number of futures specified in the contract, in his, i.e. the seller's, futures account. The buyer can also fix his buying price by doing the opposite, i.e. buying the number of futures specified in his own futures account. The invoice price for the PTBF contract is set when either buyer or seller transfers these lots to the counterparty. In the case of 'PTBF buyer's call' it is the buyer who transfers futures to the seller. In the case of 'PTBF seller's call' it is the seller who transfers shorts from his or her futures account to offset the longs in the buyer's account, fixing the invoice price. In all PTBF contracts, the selling price for the coffee is the invoice price plus the profit or loss in the seller's futures account. The buying price for the coffee is the invoice price plus the profit or loss in the buyer's futures account.

USING PTBF – AN EXAMPLE

- On 20 August the exporter sells short 2,000 bags of Prime Mexican October shipment of the same year PTBF against NYKC December, again of the same year, less 6 cts/lb, FOB Laredo.

- On 20 September the exporter is able to buy the physicals at 160 cts/lb FOB equivalent and decides to buy or lock in at this price. NYKC December is trading at 169 cts/lb. The exporter calls their FCM (Futures Commission Merchant) and asks him to sell eight contracts December 'C' contract at 169 cts/lb.

- There is a market uptick and the FCM is able to sell at 169.50. Thus the sale price for the physicals is fixed at 169.50 less 6 = 163.50 cts/lb FOB Laredo. The seller has locked in a profit of 3.5 cts/lb. His PTBF price is locked at 163.50 cts/lb but this is not the invoice price.

- On 20 October, the buyer wants to lock in his price. NYKC is now trading at 189.50 and the buyer asks his FCM to execute at this level. The FCM buys 8 lots at 189.50 for account of the buyer. Thus the buy price for the physical coffee is fixed at 189.50 less 6 = 183.50cts/lb. Still this is not the invoice price.

- The next step in the PTBF contract is the establishment of the invoice price. This is commonly called Contract Price Fixation but as we have shown it is a misnomer as it merely establishes the invoice price for delivery of the physical goods. If the contract is 'seller's call', it is the seller's right to transfer the lots to the buyer, thereby fixing the invoice price. If it is 'buyer's call', it is the buyer's right to transfer the futures to the seller to establish the invoice price. For purposes of this example, the PTBF contract is 'seller's call'.

- On 18 November, which happens to be First Notice Day for NYKC December, the seller decides to fix the invoice price. December futures are trading that day between 180.00 and 182.00. He asks his FCM to post an AA (Against Actuals) transfer of eight lots short December 'C' to the buyer's account at 181.50. By posting an AA within the range of the day, he is assured he will get that price and this is common practice for all Exchanges. Once the transfer is complete the lots move out of the seller's account at 181.50 and move into buyer's account at 181.50, fixing the invoice price of the PTBF contract at 181.50 less 6.00 cts/lb= 175.50 cts per pound.

- The seller will receive 175.50 cts/lb when he delivers the coffee but he must subtract the loss in his futures account of 181.50 less 169.50 = 12 cts/lbs. So his sale price is 175.50 less 12.00 = 163.50 cts/lb, the same as his fixation of 20 September.

- The buyer must pay 175.50 cts/ lb when the coffee is delivered but he also lost in his future account. He bought at 189.50 and sold at 181.50 for a loss of 8.00 cts/lb. So he pays 175.50 cts/lb invoice price plus his futures loss of 8.00 cts/lb for total price of 183.50 cts/lb, the same as his fixation of 20 October.

The example above shows how the PTBF contract should work. The net sales price and the net buying price are different from the invoice price. There are variations to this. If, for example, the seller fixes his sales price and makes the futures transfer to the buyer on the same day, the net sales price and the invoice price are the same. This also works for buyer's call. If the buyer does his fixation at the same time and same price he transfers lots to the seller, his net buying price is the same as the invoice price.

However, the example demonstrates the ideal situation, that is to say it assumes that both parties (i) are well-versed in these kinds of transactions, and (ii) have unfettered and easy access to futures trading accounts, either directly or through intermediaries as banks, brokers and others. But this is not necessarily the case in all origin countries or for all exporters.

WHY SELL PTBF

Why then sell PTBF in the first place? The fact is that many exporters (who often double up as processors as well) have to be constantly present in the market, i.e. they must buy when 'their' growers or collectors want to sell. But buying coffee without a home for it can be dangerous and many exporters (and their bankers) therefore like to see that such purchases have a potential home. After all, trading coffee requires substantial funds of which most exporters need to borrow at least the major part which requires bank approval of the trading operation (as discussed in chapter 10). But selling forward at a fixed price, i.e. without already having the coffee, is equally dangerous. PTBF contracts on the other hand allow one to 'fix' the price at a later date, while at the same time providing an assured home for the coffee that will be bought. As explained earlier, the differential risk remains and it is up to each individual operator to determine how much of that risk is acceptable.

In its most basic form, PTBF sales contracts should be fixed when the physical coffee is purchased, possibly each time a container load has been reached. In this case larger contracts must allow for multiple fixations. How much coffee to accumulate before 'fixing' is an individual decision, but selling PTBF is a risk management tool and not intended for speculation. Having both the coffee and a 'fixed' sales contract means all market risk (price and basis) is eliminated.

How to fix? The seller has to rely on the buyer to do so on his behalf. When the seller calls for the fixation the buyer sells the appropriate amount of futures in the manner that should have been agreed earlier in the contract. For example, at the market opening, midpoint or close. Again, an individual arrangement. The seller has to believe that the buyer will not take advantage of what is after all a conflict of interest situation, meaning the parties must know each other and trust each other. This role is played by most trade houses and leading importers who do such trades 'within the differential'. Their objective is, for example, to buy PTBF at 'plus 5' and sell PTBF at 'plus 15' and it is they, as intermediaries, who now undertake the entire process outlined in the previous section.

Trading PTBF is also risky for the intermediary buyer. What if the exporter/shipper asks for fixation without actually owning the coffee? By so doing that exporter becomes fully exposed to market volatility. Should things go badly wrong and the exporter defaults then the importer who arranged the fixation will be in serious difficulty. He or she would have to cover the entire loss on the futures he or she sold and would still have to fulfil his or her own sales contract for the underlying physical coffee. Some buyers today therefore only allow fixing from a certain date, particularly for extended forward contracts.

SELLERS NEED DISCIPLINE!

A PTBF sale does not mean the seller has made their price decision – that will only be the case once they fix. But many a seller has been unable to bring themselves to fix at an unattractive level, and in falling markets a good number even of sellers roll open fixations from one futures position to the next, preferring to pay the cost of the switch. Usually this is the difference in price between the two positions plus the buyer's costs of arranging the operation. In other words, a PTBF sale is like being a passenger in an elevator without knowing whether it is going up or down, with 'fixing' being the floor buttons. If you do not push the button you may end up somewhere unexpected.

To avoid falling into the 'fixation trap' (an inability to decide), set internal stops to ensure that fixing takes place automatically when a certain time has elapsed or a price, up or down, is reached. Fixing orders can be given basis GTC (good till cancelled). But, as explained previously, in a very volatile and fast moving market situation the 'gap trading' phenomenon may make the timely execution of such GTC orders difficult if not impossible.

The producer or exporter who has both the coffee and a PTBF sale (i.e. they have the differential but no base price), must appreciate that although they have eliminated the differential risk, a decision not to fix leaves them totally exposed to the market or price risk. As already said, this is not very different from straightforward speculation. It is a well known fact that some shipment contracts allow fixation to be delayed, at exporter's request, sometimes even until after the goods have already been shipped. As has been stressed repeatedly already, PTBF is a trading mechanism that of course can also be used speculatively and it is up to each individual operator to determine what level of risk is acceptable.

NB: When fixed price sales are not feasible, one simple alternative is to sell PTBF and to fix immediately, thereby fixing both the futures price and the differential that, together, make up the final sales price. Concerns such as 'are we fixing too early?' or 'what if the market goes up?' can be dealt with by also buying a call option, accepting that the cost of this comes out of the sales price for the physicals.

MARGINS

For sellers to lock in their sale price on a PTBF contract they need to sell futures for their account. For the buyer to lock in his buy price they need to buy futures for his account. The futures account for both parties stays open until the transfer of lots is made offsetting the futures transaction (longs less shorts = 0).

While the futures accounts stay open, there are daily margin calls that must be paid. If the market goes up the shorts pay margin. If the market goes down, the longs pay margin. On a PTBF contract, the margins will be recovered when the futures transactions are squared, i.e. when the actual coffee is delivered and invoiced. Remember, however, there can be a long time between fixation of price and the actual delivery of the coffee. The parties must have enough cash to finance these margin calls until coffee delivery. Most commodity bankers will follow a margin call and grant additional financing but only if they are confident that the PTBF contract is properly executed and backed up with real coffee and a real commitment to sell.

OPTIONS

PUT AND CALL OPTIONS

Another approach to risk management has also demonstrated a growing usefulness: the purchase or sale of options on futures as price insurance. Obviously this 'insurance' is purchased at some cost, but the strategy enables one to limit potential losses in the futures market without having to pay margin calls whilst still being able to benefit from upside price potential. The purchase of options is particularly attractive to small producers who may wish to establish a price floor (above the cost of production) without committing capital to a margin account.

Options alone or in combination with futures offer greater flexibility for risk managers in the design of their hedging strategies. There are two options around which all option strategies are based: the call and the put. There are also two actions: you can buy or sell options.

Buying a call option confers the right, but not the obligation, to buy a futures contract at an agreed price between the date of concluding the contract and the time the option contract expires. If the buyer decides to exercise the option then the seller of the option is obliged to deliver the futures.

Buying a put option confers the right, but not the obligation, to sell a futures contract at an agreed price: the seller of the option is obliged to accept the futures if the option is exercised.

Of course the option holder will only exercise the option if it makes financial sense, that is, if the option shows a profit.

When one buys an option, the risk is limited to the price premium one pays for the option. If one sells or writes an option, i.e. one that was not previously bought, the risk is potentially unlimited.

The main thing to remember about options is that when you purchase an option, you pay a premium and your potential for loss is limited to the amount of that premium. The option can be exercised at any time, no matter how far the market moves, so there is potential for unlimited return less the amount of the premium. Also, you are not required to deposit any margin when purchasing options. Options work rather like insurance; the payment of a premium provides a level of protection against loss.

When you sell (or write) options, the reverse is true. The option writer is paid a premium (limited return) and must perform no matter how far the market moves (unlimited risk). Option writers must maintain margin accounts. Because of the potentially unlimited risk, only experienced hedgers and traders should consider selling or writing options.

PRICING OPTIONS

There are two prices quoted for options, the strike price and the premium. The strike price is the price quoted in an option; the price at which the option can be exercised. The premium, or cost of the option, is determined by the option Greeks – these are letters from the Greek alphabet used to identify different risks:

- **Option Greek Delta.** The amount by which the price of an option changes if the price of the underlying coffee future changes by one.
- **Option Greek Gamma.** The sensitivity of an option's delta to a change in the price of the underlying entity. In other words, gamma measures the rate of change of delta in relation to the change in the price of the underlying entity.
- **Option Greek Theta.** The amount by which the price of an option changes when the time remaining for the expiry date of the option falls by one day. As the time remaining for the expiry date of the option reduces, the price of the option falls. Thus option Greek Theta is always negative.
- **Option Greek Vega.** The implied volatility of an underlying stock is one of the most influential factors in determining the price of an option. Option Greek Vega measures the amount by which the price of the option changes when the implied volatility of the underlying future changes by one.

Basically the price for an option is based on three factors: the intrinsic value, the time to expiration (or time value), and the implied volatility. The cost of an option is related to how close the strike price is to the market price ruling at the time the option contract is concluded. As with futures there is an active trade in option contracts. To summarize:

- The strike price is the price quoted in an option; the price at which the option can be exercised.
- The intrinsic value of an option is the strike price as a differential to where the market is trading. If this intrinsic value is negative then it is considered to be zero.
- The time value of the option is also a factor in determining the premium. A longer time until expiration of the option increases the likelihood that the option will be exercised.

INTRINSIC VALUE – AN EXAMPLE

If December futures are trading at 154 cts/lb then a December call with a 150 cts/lb strike price might be quoted at a 6.50 cts/lb premium. The intrinsic value then is 4 cts/lb because the option is in the money. But a December call with a strike price of 160 cts/lb might trade at a 3 cts/lb premium, meaning the intrinsic value is nil because the option is 'out of the money'. Of course the buyer of an option has the choice of paying a higher premium to establish a greater level of price protection.

'Out of the money' options will not usually be exercised.
Out of the money 'puts' are often sold by roasters, as they
are always short. Out of the money 'calls' can be sold by
producers as they are always long but it should be done
cautiously risking a small percentage of an annual crop.

Some large producers, for example in Brazil, are comfortable
selling call options in spite of the infinite risk. This is because
producers are always long coffee. They have coffee stocks
and future production on the trees. If a future market is
above their cost of production, they often sell a small
percentage of their production by selling call options. If the
call options are struck, they can put their coffee against the
struck options pocketing the strike price and the premium.
It is the same as selling forward futures but at a premium to
the futures market. The downside for the producer is that he
must leave the call option percentage of his crop unsold,
unhedged and not fixed in price until the call options expire.
If a producer were to sell everything and the call options
outstanding were struck, the producer would be net short,
at least until the next crop arrives.

Implied volatility, which is based on a mathematical formula,
evaluates the premium on the expected price volatility of the
underlying futures contract. It is important to realize that the
price of an option can change because of time and volatility
factors even when the underlying futures price does not
move.

Option strategies are extremely diverse, and almost any
strategy can be developed using options (obviously at a
cost and a risk). A variety of names have been attributed
to various strategies – strangles, condor, calendar spread,
butterfly, and many others.

The scope of option trading is vast and an explanation of all
the strategies would take a book in itself. Call options are
of little direct interest to producers and exporters. Selling
or writing options is only for experienced hedgers and
involves potentially unlimited risk. Both therefore fall outside
the scope of this publication but more information can be
obtained from both IntercontinentalExchange (ICE) in New
York and NYSE Liffe in London.

BUYING PUT OPTIONS – AN EXAMPLE

Instead of selling futures, producers and exporters can
establish a minimum price, or price floor, by buying a put
option. With a put option in a falling market one can still
have a short hedge at a reasonable level. For calculating
value, the price floor will be the strike price less the premium
paid for the option. The advantage of the option is that if the
market goes up the option can simply be allowed to expire,
while the physicals can be sold at the higher level (from
which the premium paid for the option should be deducted
to arrive at the net sales realization).

If December futures are trading at 154 cts/lb an exporter or
producer might perhaps be able to buy a December 150

cts/lb put for a premium of 2.5 cts/lb. A put is an option to
be short, so there is no intrinsic value in being short at 150
cts/lb in a 154 cts/lb market. Furthermore, the right to be
short at 150 cts/lb costs 2.5 cts/lb, so the value of the option
is really 147.50 cts/lb. In this scenario, the option holder is
guaranteed a price floor at 147.50 cts/lb if the market goes
down, but they will still be able to take advantage of any
upswing in prices if the market rises.

HEDGING

HEDGING – THE ADVANTAGES

Hedging offers definite advantages to commodity producers
and costs comparatively little. Hedging with futures allows
a producer to lock in a price that reflects the producer's
business goals (a profit). The producer should therefore
determine the actual price available in the futures market
that will support the cost of production plus a profit. If prices
fall, the producer still achieves something near the originally
intended pricing goals. If prices rise, the producer foregoes
a larger profit margin.

The loss of this potential (speculative) extra profit is balanced
by the protection afforded against dramatic and damaging
declines in the market. There are also other advantages in
addition to this price-insurance aspect of hedging.

First, hedging offers a flexible pricing mechanism. Anyone
who feels they have made the wrong decision on the
exchange can have an alternative order executed easily
and immediately. Second, hedging operations involve only
small initial outlays of money. If the price of futures goes
up, the producer who has sold futures may be asked to
pay additional margins; but the price of their physicals will
also have risen. Third, because a futures contract provides
considerable price protection, banks and other financial
institutions are more likely to finance producers, exporters
and traders who hedge their crops and positions than those
who do not.

Finally, commodity trade banks and risk solution providers
put together different risk mitigation instruments that are
tailored to a client's requirements. For example, a put option
can be graduated to extend over the usual marketing season
by spreading equal portions over two or three futures trading
positions, at different strike prices if so wished. Each individual
portion can then be exercised individually. Alternatively, a
solution provider may simply guarantee a minimum price.
For payment of a premium, they undertake to make good
any shortfall between the insured price (the minimum price
the producer wishes to secure) and the price ruling for the
stated futures trading positions (New York or London), either
at a given date or based on the average price over a number
of trading days. In doing this the producer buys a 'floor', a
guaranteed price minus the cost of the premium.

SWAP AGREEMENTS

The straight meaning of the term 'swap' is to barter or exchange and this is very much to the point. For example, producers can 'swap' price risk by giving up the benefits from future price rises in exchange for a guaranteed minimum price. Such a swap agreement could even cover more than one crop year, with tonnages and settlement dates set for each quarter. In other words, they are written or tailored to address different, individual requirements. Swaps are often mentioned in commodity market reports but, generally speaking, are of limited interest to exporters.

In the case of coffee swaps, the price fixing necessary to finalize them would rely on the relevant futures market without actually having to trade futures. This avoids the problems that using futures can cause like having to raise margin calls, particularly when distant positions are to be dealt with. In addition, futures trading or hedging does not always address individual price insurance requirements.

Swap agreements are negotiated directly between those wishing to acquire them and solution providers who are prepared to offer or write them. Because such agreements are concluded separately from formal futures trading they are usually known as over-the-counter (OTC) products. Swap agreements are extensively used in financial and energy markets, but less so in agricultural commodity markets. Yet, demand for them could be on the increase, also because financial institutions are increasingly risk averse.

This is pertinent because one difficulty faced by both parties to a swap agreement is performance risk, especially for longer-dated agreements. Different from futures, there is no central clearing mechanism for agricultural swap agreements and, as a result, default is possible. This then limits their attraction as a price insurance vehicle.

To address this, in February 2009 ICE in New York introduced a clearing facility for agricultural swap agreements – initially for sugar, coffee and cocoa. To quote ICE literature in this respect:

1. Cleared swaps are OTC agreements that are eligible to be cleared by ICE Clear U.S. (the Clearing House), but which are not executed on ICE Futures U.S. (the Exchange), either electronically or on the trading floor. A cleared swap contract is created when the parties to an off-Exchange, OTC transaction agree to extinguish their OTC contracts and replace it with a cleared swap contract. This will provide the same efficiencies and benefits that centralized clearing offers traders of contracts listed for trading on the Exchange – including credit risk intermediation and the ability to offset different positions initiated with different counter parties.

2. This process is accomplished by the submission of each side of an OTC transaction to the Exchange and the acceptance of each side by the Clearing Members of each party to the swap. Cleared swap contracts will offer eligible OTC market participants in these products the ability to clear transactions through ICE Clear U.S. In addition, Clearing Members will be able to hold the cleared swaps and the margin deposited with respect to them in the same account as they hold position and margin deposited with respect to futures traded on the Exchange.

In brief therefore, execution of an OTC product that is turned into a 'cleared swap contract' becomes guaranteed by ICE Clear U.S., just as is the case with Exchange traded futures contracts. It seems logical this should enhance their suitability to be considered as price and credit risk limitation mechanisms.

In 2009, NYSE Liffe in London introduced cash-settled futures and options on its Bclear service for cocoa, robusta coffee and white sugar.

HOW TRADE HOUSES USE FUTURES

ARBITRAGE

The most common form of arbitrage for coffee is the robusta/arabica quality spread because the two major futures markets clearly show the arbitrage value, New York being arabica based and London robusta. If the price difference between two comparable arabica and robusta delivery positions is considered overstated or understated then the arbitrageur will buy the one and sell the other according to their convictions, speculating that the difference will move in their favour.

Trade houses for the most part go far beyond simple robusta/arabica arbitraging. Remember, there are over 60 countries that produce hundreds of different qualities and types of coffee. A good trader will look to all the quality options. Perhaps they will buy Brazil coffee trading at 8 cts/lb under New York 'C', while selling short Colombians at plus 12 cts/lb New York 'C', arguing that, comparatively speaking, Brazil is cheap and Colombians expensive. This sounds good, but in recent years it has been entirely possible to lose on both sides of such an arbitrage.

There are other forms of arbitrage. One that is very common in an oversupplied market is the 'cash and carry'. When the spot position is at a discount, high enough to cover the costs of carrying inventory to the next delivery period, this is called a 'cash and carry'. A 'cash and carry' in itself is not an arbitrage, but when the costs to carry are different for different markets, one can arbitrage the variation in carry costs.

ARBITRAGE – AN EXAMPLE

The carry cost for the NYKC September to December is based upon the following costs:

- Financing (cost of money);
- Insurance;
- Storage;
- Weight discounts (0.5% after the first two months of storage, 0.125% for each month stored after that);
- Age discounts (0.5 cts or 50 points for the first 150 days, after that 25 points per month for the first year, 50 points per month for the second year, 75 points per month for the third year, and 100 points per month for coffee over three years).

The costs for a simple August shipment of cash market coffee on 'cash and carry' basis, September through December, are all of the above, except for any quality discounts. Depending upon the type of coffee and its actual arrival date, there might be no weight discount. One can take delivery of fresh coffee in September and deliver it on in December without a discount. It is thus possible to arbitrage the cash market 'cash and carry', which is approximately 2.5 cts/lb, with the futures market 'cash and carry' of approximately 4 cts/lb based upon the average age of the certificates. In this example, a trader can pick up 1.5 cts for every pound of coffee carried from September to December.

- In August buy fresh coffee at September less 1 ct/lb;
- Simultaneously sell the same coffee at December less 1 ct/lb;
- September/December is trading at 4 cts: the 'cash and carry' for the futures market;
- Effectively the trader bought fresh coffee September delivery at a 4 cts discount to the price they sold December;
- It costs 2.5 cts/lb to carry the coffee from September to December in the cash market (storage, interest, and insurance only) leaving the remaining 1.5 cts/lb as profit.

TRADER SPECULATION

When traders say they are 'fully hedged', it is usually a sign that they have a bad position. In order to cover costs as an importer or trader, one simply must speculate. This speculation is not always outright long or short, but most of the time it is. Traders do, however, play quality and time differentials, and these are a different type of speculation.

A good trader is disciplined. Operations are always accounted for as what they are. A good trader will never use a hedge lot to offset a bad speculative trade. Nor will a good trader mix quality arbitrage with spread trading.

Keeping 'the book' well defined sounds easy but it is the downfall of many traders that they try to dress up their positions, that is, make them look better than they really are. Another sign of a good trader is the ability to take a loss. Traders cannot be right all the time. They only need to be right 60% of the time to be profitable.

The ability to take losses and move on is an essential element in trading, applicable to exporters as well.

COMMODITY SPECULATION

Commodity speculation is the purchase and sale of a commodity in the expectation that the reversal of the purchase or sale will yield a profit as a result of a change in the market value of the commodity. There is a certain amount of pure speculation in commodity futures, although its magnitude is difficult to gauge.

Throughout the 1970s, high levels of inflation and exchange rate uncertainty were associated with a greater degree of nominal price volatility for primary commodities. This in turn gave a tremendous boost to futures speculation, sometimes referred to as the other side of the exchange. The participation of speculators in the futures market contributes to that market's liquidity, essential for avoiding undue price distortions that can be caused by laying on or lifting hedges.

However, excessive speculation can lead to wider price fluctuations – markets become 'overdone on the upside and on the downside' (prices move to greater extremes than expected) – until the excess of either the long or short positions is finally unwound. By virtue of an individual or firm's expectations and willingness to take risks, speculators aim to make an uncertain profit from their operations in the market. Speculators may form their price expectations on the basis of the futures prices, the spot price, both spot and futures prices, or perhaps on the basis of the price spread alone, and take positions reflecting their expectations in the markets.

Certain features of futures exchanges attract speculation. These include the standardization of the futures contract, the relatively low costs of transactions and the comparatively low initial funding required (leverage).

DIFFERENCES BETWEEN HEDGING AND SPECULATION

Hedging is often confused with speculation. In both cases operators are concerned with unforeseen price changes. They make buying and selling decisions based on their expectations of how the market will move in the future. However, where hedging is essentially a means to avoid or reduce price risk, speculation relies on the risk element. For instance, it would be irrational to carry out a selling hedge if the market were absolutely certain to rise. In the absence of absolute certainty about future market movements, hedging offers an element of protection against price risk, whereas speculation involves deliberately taking a risk on price movements, up or down, in the hope of obtaining a profit.

One of the principles of speculation involves the opportunity for gain that the investor achieves by agreeing to accept some of the risk passed off by the hedger. In other words, the hedger gives up some opportunity in exchange for reduced risk. The speculator acquires opportunity in exchange for taking on risk.

Buyers and sellers of coffee who aim to minimize their price risks in the physical market assume opposite positions, or risks, in the futures market. At any moment there will be a number of buying and a number of selling hedge operations. However, it is unlikely that demand for hedges against buying risks will exactly balance demand for hedges against selling risks. The resulting surplus of buying and selling risks that has not been covered by the usual hedgers is taken up by speculators.

To absorb the vast amounts of futures entering the coffee exchanges, numerous speculators willing to buy one or two lots are required. Likewise, considerable purchasing pressure occurs when traders or roasters hedge to cover their future needs. Prices would increase unless speculators were willing to step in as sellers.

If producers who wish to hedge could always find counterparts who also wished to do so, there would be no need for speculators. However, this situation is unlikely to occur regularly, partly because the periods in which producers carry out hedging operations normally do not coincide with the periods in which consumers try to hedge. The speculator provides the link between these two different periods and interests. Nevertheless, large speculative positions can 'push' the market either way and producers/exporters should monitor developments closely since their objective is to lock in profitable prices rather than partake of speculative activities.

TYPES OF SPECULATORS

In any futures market the extent of speculative involvement can be high. The coffee markets are no exception. The New York market attracts the most attention, and longer-term speculative involvement can reach as much as 30% of the open interest. Day traders can account for an extremely large percentage of the daily volume.

Day traders are so-called because they always square their position at the end of each trading day – they never carry any long or short position overnight. The day traders in coffee are referred to as 'locals' as many operate for themselves. They take short-term positions (for minutes or hours) based on the order flow they see in the market and are well positioned to take advantage of price aberrations caused by other market participants. They will be prepared, for example, to deal at a few points under the market level if they judge that the distortion will be short-lived and that

prices will return to their previous levels. Thus, locals can liquidate their contracts at a profit, although the profit may be quite small. Because the locals receive a beneficial commission rate they can repeat this operation several times a day.

Commodity and hedge funds provide the greatest source of speculative activity and their financial power can greatly influence price movements. Funds operate on a variety of mathematical trigger mechanisms such as moving averages, trends and momentum indicators.

Over the years they have become more sophisticated in the complexity of the systems they use and some now incorporate an element of in-depth market research within their strategies. The fund managers generally have a large portfolio of markets to trade and will therefore view coffee as only one facet in their total risk management. A hedge fund could lose in coffee and make profit in other non-related markets (such as bonds or currencies) to return an overall profit.

Professional coffee traders do not have the luxury of this diversification or the financial backing that the funds control, and thus must be aware of the fund positions in the market in order to manage their own coffee books accordingly. Hedge funds normally take longer-term market positions.

Speculative funds that trade in coffee have been around for years but in recent years, their volume has grown. Also in the last few years there has been the entry of index funds into the coffee and other markets. These funds are large and have affected the dynamics of the market. While speculative funds move in and out of the market and can create short term changes in supply and demand, index funds enter a market as part of a long-term investment strategy for coffee within a basket of other commodities. They never liquidate their positions and usually only rebalance their positions once a year. This means that once a year, the fund's managers may decide to add or subtract a certain quantity of coffee futures in order to balance the fund and adjust the percentage of coffee contracts relative to the other commodities in the index fund. Hence, these funds maintain certain long positions by rolling forward futures contracts. In essence these funds create an additional demand for coffee and this investment demand does influence prices.

In the United States the Commitments of Traders Report documents activities of both speculative funds and index funds. Exporters as well as all industry hedgers should monitor the activity of these funds and accept that real supply and demand for coffee can be affected in both the short and long term. When these funds buy or sell in unison, they create much larger volumes in future trading than the coffee industry can offset and in so doing can move prices.

Websites of interest include *www.cftc.gov* of the U.S. Commodity Futures Trading Commission, *www.commitmentoftraders.com*, and *www.newedge*, which offer charts and spreadsheets showing the weekly commitments of traders of index funds.

High velocity traders have been around for a while in the equity markets but are relatively new to the commodity industry. It has been suggested that 60 % of volume today (end 2011) on the New York Stock Exchange is created by high velocity traders. These funds use proprietary algorithms to electronically buy and sell large quantities of futures, in microseconds, sometimes nanoseconds, in order to make a return on investment.

The problem for the coffee industry is that these high velocity traders can also move prices but, unlike speculative funds and index funds, they do not maintain large positions for any length of time. This makes it virtually impossible to see what they are doing to the market. Normally high volume is good for liquidity, but these funds trade so fast and aggressively that the only feature they add to the market is higher volatility. Industry hedgers need to be aware of this....

Professional coffee traders do not have the luxury of this diversification or the financial backing that the funds control, and thus must be aware of the fund positions in the market in order to manage their own coffee books accordingly. Hedge funds normally take longer-term market positions.

Coffee trade houses as well as large non-coffee related speculators take strategic positions in the futures market. Such positions could be to anticipate a directional move or to take advantage of price differences between different market positions – for instance a discounted switch structure in the same market or an arbitrage between the New York arabica and London robusta markets.

Non-professional speculators operate in commodity markets that are likely to experience sudden changes in price and hence offer a greater profit potential. They tend to be guided by information and comments from second-hand sources such as bulletins published by brokers, daily newspapers and, more recently, information on the Internet. This category of speculators normally involves small investors, many of who rely on the advice of commission houses.

SPECULATIVE STRATEGIES

Stop-loss order. Just as margin calls protect the clearing house from overexposure to the risk of financial losses, stop-loss orders offer protection to the speculator. Although they are willing to bear some losses from an adverse movement of prices, speculators cannot risk seeing a large proportion of the value of their assets wiped out. Speculators give a stop-loss order in order to moderate their losses. This order is triggered once the price of the 'stop' is reached, at which time the broker seeks to trade at the price given in the order or as close as possible if the market permits the order to be executed. Because the objective of the stop-loss order is to get out of a position, such orders have to be carried out ruthlessly. Stop-loss instructions are given the moment a trading position is taken, or sometimes even before, so the taking of any position automatically puts them in place. It is also quite customary to employ a 'trailing stop'. For example, if the initial position taken is good and the market trend continues as expected, the stop can be moved accordingly and so 'trail' the trend, thereby locking in increasing amounts of profit.

There are several aspects worth considering: first, the position to be adopted (long or short) as suggested by the market analysis, and the size of the transaction; second, the financial resources available for the operation; third, the target profit expressed in points; fourth, the loss, also expressed in points, that the speculator is prepared to absorb if the market moves in an unexpected direction; and finally, the changes in the level of the stop-loss orders that will ensure a paper profit.

It is important for speculators to decide the maximum loss they are willing to bear before taking a position. Once a position begins to lose points, there is a strong temptation to justify the losses and continue to invest, rather than to accept that the original decision was a mistake.

Likewise, speculators should define the expected profit (in points) and only liquidate their position when the target has been reached. It is just as common to attempt to take the profits before the positions have reached the maximum level as it is to continue to sustain losses even after prices have sunk below reasonable levels.

Straddling. This is another method of trading on the commodity markets. It involves simultaneously purchasing one delivery period and selling another delivery period. This can be undertaken in a variety of ways:

- The transactions can be carried out with two futures positions on the same exchange. This is sometimes referred to as a spread or switch.
- The two futures positions can be taken on two different exchanges.
- Positions can be taken on two separate exchanges of related merchandises, for example, arabica in New York and robusta in London. This is also generally called *arbitrage*.

Straddle operations have the advantage of offering lower risks to operators although, not surprisingly, at lower profits. In a sense, a straddle is a form of hedge. Exchanges usually encourage straddling by requiring less deposit than for a single purchase or sale. When operators undertake straddles they are long and short of futures contracts for different months or maturities, usually in the same commodity market. Operators buy one month's contract in a product and sell another month's contract in the same product or, in some cases, a related product.

The purpose of taking two futures positions is to take advantage of a change in price relationships, also called the 'spread'. The intention is to earn a profit from expected fluctuations in the differential between the prices of the two months. If during the interval prices rise, the profit made from the long position will be compensated by the loss on the short position, and vice versa if prices decline. What really matters in a straddle operation, therefore, is the price spread between periods. It is of no consequence in which direction the market moves. If, for example, the price spread between the July and December position seems greater than usual, with the forward position at a premium, it makes sense to buy the near position and sell the forward position. This assumes that the differential will be reduced at a later date, in which case the trader will gain.

The spread will narrow if one of the following situations arises:

- The near position rises while the forward position remains unchanged;
- The near position rises higher than the forward position;
- The near position remains unchanged while the forward position falls;
- The near position falls less than the forward position.

STRADDLING – AN EXAMPLE

A speculator sells New York 'C' December 2012 (KCZ12) and buys March 2013 (KCH13) at 360 points premium March. In abbreviated fashion, they are buying March/December at 360. As December gets closer to the first notice day and the level of certified stocks is rather high, the market will move out to a full 'carry' estimated by the trade to be 425 points. Our speculator now buys December/March (buys KCZ12 and sells KCH13) at 425, locking in a 65-point profit per lot. At US$ 3.75 per point, the profit is US$ 243.75 per lot. See chapter 8 for more on 'carries and inversions'.

TECHNICAL ANALYSIS OF FUTURES MARKETS

Technical analysis is the study of the market itself rather than an evaluation of the factors affecting the supply of, and demand for, a commodity (which is called fundamental analysis). The important components of technical analysis are prices, market volume and open interest. As this technical approach only considers the market, it must take into account fluctuations that reflect traders' actions and that are not necessarily associated with supply-and-demand cycles. The basic assumption of all technical analyses is that the market in the future can be forecast merely by analyzing the past behaviour of the market (although many in the coffee trade find this hard to accept).

Detailed technical analysis is not possible for all or even most traders. The most important elements for accurate decision-making are close contacts with the markets and with knowledgeable individuals in the trade. However, if charting specialists supply the analysis within a usable period of time, technical analysis can provide useful additional information, particularly for medium-term forecasts.

The main tools of technical analysis are past price patterns that are shown in various forms of charts or graphs. The changes in the volume of open positions (i.e. the number of futures or option contracts outstanding on a given commodity) and the total volume of operations in the market are also examined. Charts often use a moving average to record and interpret price trends. In most charts, an average moves with time as the newest price information is incorporated into the average and the oldest price is discarded. For example, a simple three-day moving average of the daily closing price of a commodity changes as follows: on Wednesday, the sum of closing prices on Monday, Tuesday and Wednesday is divided by three; on Thursday, the sum of closing prices for Tuesday, Wednesday and Thursday is divided by three; and so on. Analysts can average prices over a period of hours, days, months or even years, depending on their needs.

The value of the moving average always lags behind the current market price. When prices are rising in bull markets, the moving average will fall below the current price.

However, the moving average in a bear market will be higher than the current price. When the trend in prices is reversed, the moving average and the current price cross each other.

While advocates of charting accept that fundamental factors are the prime determinants of commodity prices, they point out that these factors cannot predict prices. They argue that the graphs incorporate all the fundamental factors that shape prices and also reflect the subjective market reaction to these factors. The alternative argument holds that although the price curve and other elements of the graph are real and objective, the interpretation is necessarily subjective. Thus, the same graph can give contradictory signals to different readers.

In reality there is likely to be substantial overlap between the fundamental approach and the charting approach. It is common for operators to determine the market trend by studying fundamental factors and to then select the right time to enter the market by referring to the charts. Similarly, chart advocates also study other factors beyond the limit of technical analysis. They may consider the number of marketing days left before a position expires, the amounts notified for delivery on the exchange, the situation of the longs, and the possibility of accepting deliveries on the exchange without adverse results.

Many companies specialize in producing charts for various commodities and most have their own websites where it is possible to access charting information such as price history, volumes, open interest and technical studies. In addition, all of the Internet coffee information sites, such as *www.theice.com*, *www.euronext.com*, *www.coffeenetwork.com*, *www.tradingcharts.com* and *www.futures.tradingcharts.com* have charting ability and analysis. Most of these websites carry not only price, but also volume and open interest, all of which are discussed in other parts of this chapter.

OPEN INTEREST

The total of a clearing house's outstanding long or short positions is called the open interest. If a broker who is long in a futures contract sells their position to another trader who wants to be long on futures, the open interest does not change. However, if they sell their position to a trader who is short and is therefore closing out their position, the open interest is reduced. The total size of the open interest indicates the degree of current liquidity on a given market.

When considering the open interest, it is important to distinguish between the types of operators entering the exchange. The term 'strong hands' describes those who are able to make margin payments over an extended period of time whereas 'weak hands' are operators who cannot easily meet the substantial variation margins demanded whenever prices move significantly.

In general, strong hands are comparatively resilient to price changes. One type of strong hand is an operator who uses the exchange for hedging purposes. They may want to liquidate a position, not as a result of price movements but because of an opportunity to carry out an operation in physicals. Once the hedging operation has begun they will not be affected by price changes. Another type of strong hand is the speculator who holds large amounts of capital. Such operators can withstand a setback on the market without being forced to sell their positions because they have the financial resources to cover the margins. Small non-professional speculators who generally operate through a broker are considered weak hands because they are more vulnerable to changes in price.

Looking at prices in isolation can give some indication of whether buyers or sellers are dominating the market, but it will not distinguish new purchases from hedging operations. If new purchases are the predominant activity, it is possible to forecast the continuance of the market's upward trend as these purchases signify that new operators are entering the market in the hope that the market will rise. However, if these purchases are largely for hedging purposes to cover short positions, the market is considered weak because once these short positions are covered the buying pressure will subside.

VOLUME OF OPERATIONS

The volume of operations, or turnover, is equivalent to the number of trades in all futures contracts for a particular commodity on a given day. Technical analysts regard volume and open interest as indicators of the number of people or weight of interest in the market and thus of the likelihood of a price rise. A gradual increase in volume during a price upturn could suggest a continuation of the trend.

The rise in volume could also result from an anticipation of higher prices in the future, but in fact it may indicate that long or short positions are leaving the market because of a fall in prices. In general, the volume of trade is a good guide to the breadth of the outside support given to a price movement on the market.

RELATIONSHIP BETWEEN OPEN INTEREST, VOLUME AND PRICE

The elements of charting must be interpreted together as they are meaningless on their own. When changes in open interest and volume are analysed in conjunction with the price charts, they may indicate several trends, described in the paragraphs that follow.

When both volume and open interest are expanding against a background of rising prices, a so-called bullish trend on the market is indicated. A rise in open positions is a consequence of the ongoing entry of new long positions and new short positions into the market. However, with every subsequent upward movement in prices, the shorts that previously entered the market will incur worsening losses that will be increasingly difficult to sustain. Eventually, traders with short positions will be forced to buy, which will add more buying pressure to the market.

A persistent rise in both volume and open interest with prices rising is a good indicator of a bull market. In this scenario more new participants are willing to enter the market on the long side, looking for higher levels. When the volume and open interest start to decline this could be a signal of a trend reversal. As mentioned earlier, for the New York market, the commitment of traders (COT) report, published by the U.S. Commodity Futures Trading Commission, *www.cftc.gov*, yields a great analysis of the opened interest, not only by trader category, but also by weekly change.

If daily volume and open interest are falling and prices are declining, a so-called bearish trend is confirmed. When there are more sellers than buyers in the market, long positions suffer increasing losses until they are forced into a selling position. Declining volumes together with declining prices in turn mean that it will be some time before the lowest price of this bearish trend is reached.

An explosion of volume can also signal a turning point in the market if a day's trading at very high price levels is recorded against a very large volume and if subsequent price movements, either up or down, are accompanied by lower levels of volume. This is a good sign that a reversal is imminent. Similarly, a collapse in prices after a severe downtrend, recorded against a high volume, can signal an end to the bearish trend.

CHARTING

The two most commonly used charts in technical analysis are the bar chart, and the point and figure chart. There are many technical studies that can be added to these charts such as trend lines, moving averages and stochastics (probabilities).

Bar charts use a vertical bar to record the high and low range of a price for each market day. The length of the bar indicates the range between the highest and lowest quotations. The vertical line is crossed by a small horizontal line at the closing price level. Therefore, in just one line per day it is possible to show the closing price as well as the minimum and maximum quotations registered for that day. A record is made daily, forming a pattern that may cover several weeks, months or even years. Some chartists insist that a new bar chart should be started as soon as a new futures position is opened.

However, it is common to continue the original chart with the new position following the position that has just expired. As the new position may have discounts or premiums in relation to the old position, the chart should be clearly marked to indicate where the new position starts and where the old position ends.

Continuous plotting can be done in various ways. One way is to show the first position until it expires and then to continue with the new first position. Another way is to show only one position until it expires and then to continue with the same month of the following year. The drawback of the second method is that once a position expires, e.g. in December 2004, and the next position taken is December 2005, prices may have changed significantly and the chart may therefore show either a large increase or decrease.

Trend lines on charts reveal significant trend changes but obscure subtle changes in supply and demand factors. The trend line is best suited for recording long-term changes in indices or other financial and economic data. The market registers three types of trends: a bullish trend when prices are rising, a bearish trend when prices are falling, and a steady or lateral trend when prices are neither rising nor falling. A steady trend sustained for a comparatively long period is known as a 'congestion area'. The larger this area, the greater the possibility that the market will begin a definite trend, either bullish or bearish.

The simplest patterns to recognize are those formed by the three types of trend lines. These are: the support line, which is drawn to connect the bottom points of a price move; the resistance line, which is drawn across the peaks of a trend; and the channel, which is the area between the support and resistance lines that contains a sustained price move.

Point and figure charts differ from the bar charts in two important respects. First, they ignore the passage of time. Unlike a bar chart, where lines are equidistant to mark distinct time periods, each column of the point and figure chart can represent any length of time. Second, the volume of trade is unimportant as it is thought merely to reflect price action and to contain no predictive importance. The measurement of change in price direction alone determines the pattern of the chart. The assumptions underlying the point and figure chart primarily concern the price of a commodity. It is assumed that the price, at any given time, is the commodity's correct valuation up to the instant the contract is closed. This price is the consensus of all buyers and sellers in the world and is the result of all the forces governing the laws of supply and demand.

Moreover, no other information needs to be included in this chart because the price is assumed to reflect all the essential information on the commodity.

Real time and delayed charts can be obtained from various sources, e.g. *www.theice.com*, *www.tradingcharts.com* and *www.coffeenetwork.com* – just to mention a few.

Daily and monthly coffee price futures charts are offered free of charge by *www.futures.tradingcharts.com* and are easy to access. See examples on the following page.

Figure 9.1   Example of a daily coffee futures price chart (December 2011); Coffee – ICE, 4 November 2011

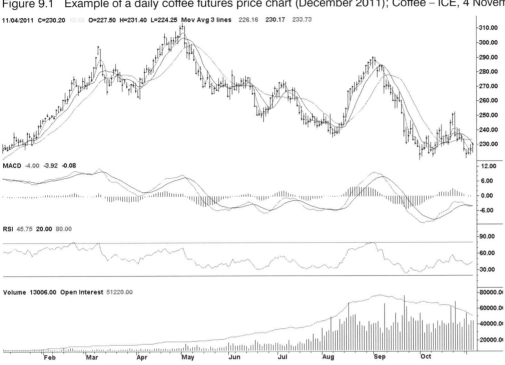

Chart courtesy of TradingCharts.com, Inc., *www.futures.tradingcharts.com.*
MACD: Moving average convergence/divergence.
RSI: Relative strength index.

Figure 9.2   Example of a monthly coffee futures price chart; Coffee – ICE, 31 October 2011

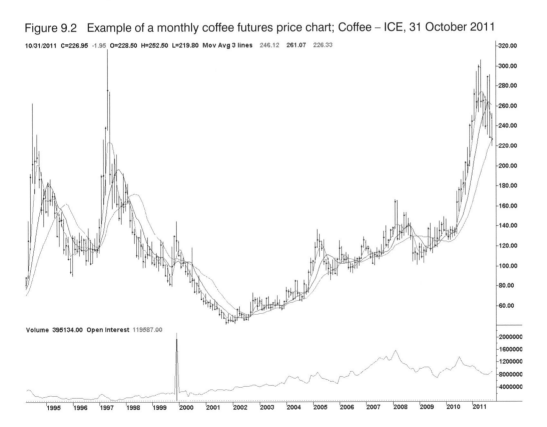

Chart courtesy of TradingCharts.com, Inc., *www.futures.tradingcharts.com*

RISK AND THE RELATION TO TRADE CREDIT

CHAPTER 10

RISK AND THE RELATION TO TRADE CREDIT

TYPES OF RISK

Risk in the coffee and general commodity trade can be divided into five main categories:

- **Physical and security risk.** Physical loss or damage as well as theft and fraud, will be covered by insurance against payment of a premium. See also chapter 5, Logistics and insurance.

- **Quality risk.** The goods are not what they are supposed to be – at worst they are not fit to be sold.

- **Price risk or market risk.** The price of goods may rise or fall to the detriment of the owner, depending on the type of transaction they have engaged in. The value of unsold stocks falls when demand declines or there is over supply. Conversely the cost of covering (buying in against) a short or forward sale increases when demand rises or there is a supply shortage.

- **Macroeconomic risk.** As recently as at the turn of the century the value of coffee generally was basically translated into price per United States dollar. Today, with wealth moving from older developed countries to newer, more powerful economies, the local value of coffee can and does easily move differently from its United States dollar price. A farmer in Brazil can see his price decline while at the same time a buyer in euros is experiencing a price increase. Macroeconomic moves in wealth create changes in currencies on a daily basis, resulting in a situation where for many exporters currency fluctuations now have a much greater impact on domestic coffee prices than ever before.

- **Performance risk.** One of the parties to a transaction does not fulfil its obligations, for example because of short supply or unexpected price movements, resulting in loss for the other party. A seller does not deliver, delivers late, or delivers the wrong quality. A buyer does not take up the documents, becomes insolvent or simply refuses to pay. In some countries this particular type of non-performance risk is also known as *del credere* risk.

IMPORTANT TRADE ASPECTS AND TERMINOLOGY

Long and short positions. 'Long' means unsold stocks, or bought positions against which there is no matching sale. The total unmatched quantity is the 'long position'. Short is the opposite, that is, sales exceed stocks and one has outstanding sales without matching purchases – the 'short position'. When large holders sell off their 'longs' the market speaks of 'liquidating'. Conversely, when traders buy in against 'shorts' then the reports speak of 'short covering'.

Physical and paper trade. There are two very different types of coffee trade. Exporters, importers and roasters handle green coffee: they trade 'physicals'. Other players trade purely on the futures markets and are known as 'paper' traders or technical traders because they do not habitually deliver or receive physical coffee. Paper traders include brokers acting on behalf of physical traders wishing to offset risk (hedging), market makers, individual speculators (day traders) and institutional speculators (funds).

Physical traders perform a supply function. Trading physicals requires in-depth product knowledge and regular access to producing countries. Futures traders, on the other hand, trade the risks players in the physical market wish to safeguard against. Most futures contracts are offset by matching counter transactions through the clearing houses that manage the contract settlements of the futures markets and debit or credit traders with losses or profits. Very rarely therefore do futures traders handle physical coffee. Instead, they specialize in market analysis and trendspotting. Coupled with considerable financial strength, this enables them to take on the risks the physical trade wishes to offset by providing market liquidity.

Exporters combine analytical ability with product knowledge. Like their clients they can put a value on physical coffee (quality), and they know which quality suits what buyer. Many paper or technical traders are not very conversant with 'quality', and do not need to be.

When physical traders wish to guard against future price falls on unsold stocks they sell futures, and the paper trade buys those futures contracts. When the delivery time draws near, the physical trade will want to buy those contracts back and the paper trade will then sell them.

Because the clearing house is always between buyer and seller (and deals only with approved parties) the identity of either is irrelevant. The system works because a futures contract represents a standard quantity of standard quality coffee, deliverable during a specified month (the trading position) and so matching trading positions long and short automatically cancel each other out, leaving just the price settlement.

First and second hand. Coffee sold directly from origin (from producing countries) is first hand – there were no intermediate holders. If the foreign buyer then re-offers that same coffee for sale, the market will know it as second hand. But international traders also offer certain coffees for sale independently from origin: in so doing they are going 'short' in the expectation of buying in later at a profit. To achieve such sales they may actually compete with origin by quoting lower prices. Market reports then refer to second hand offers or simply the second hand. Traders can buy and sell matching contracts many times, causing a single shipment to pass through a number of hands before reaching the end-user: a roaster. Such interlinked contracts are known as string contracts.

Volume of physicals versus futures and second hand. The volume of physicals is limited by how much coffee is available, but there is no such constraint on the trade in futures or second hand coffee. The huge volume of trade on the futures markets contributes strongly to the volatility of physicals. Futures can cause prices for physicals to move abruptly, sometimes for no immediately obvious reasons. In addition, the volume of trade in some individual coffees regularly exceeds actual production because many second hand or string contracts are either offset (washed out), or are executed through the repeated receiving and passing on of a single set of shipping documents. Producing countries are but a single factor in the daily trade and price movements.

The differential. This is the difference, plus or minus, between the price for a given trading position on the futures markets of New York (ICE, trading arabicas) or London (LIFFE, trading robustas), and a particular physical (green) coffee.

Briefly, the differential takes into account (i) differences between that coffee and the standard quality on which the futures market is based, (ii) the physical availability of that coffee (plentiful or tight), and (iii) the terms and conditions on which it is offered for sale. By combining the ex dock New York or London futures price and the differential, one usually obtains the FOB (free on board) price for the green coffee in question. This enables the market to simply quote, for example, 'Quality X from Origin Y for October shipment at New York December plus 5' (cts/lb). Traders and importers know the cost of shipping coffee from each origin to Europe, the United States, Japan or wherever, and so can easily recalculate 'plus 5' into a price landed final destination.

Price to be fixed – PTBF. Parties may agree to sell physical coffee at a differential (plus or minus) to the price, at an as yet undetermined point in the future, of a specific delivery month on the futures market, for example, 'New York December plus 5' (cts/lb) or 'LIFFE July minus 25' (US$/ton). The contract will state when and by whom the final price will be 'fixed': if by the seller then it is 'seller's call', if by the buyer then it is 'buyer's call'. See chapter 9, Hedging and other operations.

IN-HOUSE DISCIPLINE

AVOID OVER-TRADING

People often associate risk management with price protection, but there are many different types of risk and risk management. Exporters and traders can buy protection against many forms of risk, obviously at a cost. But there are other risks inherent to the trade in coffee that only they can 'manage'.

The serious exporter's long-term strategic objective is to trade steadily and profitably, and to seek regularity of business; not to chase potential windfall situations involving speculative moves with the potential to put the day-to-day business at risk. Solid seller-client relationships are founded on confidence and regularity of trade. Regular purchases maintain producer links; regular offers and sales help to convince clients to place at least part of their business 'with our company'.

Purely speculative trading has no place in such a strategy, but many an exporter has unwittingly fallen foul of speculative markets. When prices are low, the potential risk of a sudden rise is often high. Conversely, when prices are very high then the potential risk of a sudden fall increases accordingly. This conventional wisdom is reinforced by an old but accurate saying in the coffee trade: 'When prices are down coffee is never cheap enough, yet when prices are on the up then coffee is never too expensive.' In other words, when high prices fall the 'herd' does not buy, yet when low prices rise people buy all the way up and beyond. This often causes price movements to be exaggerated.

A speculative long position or stock of physicals, held in expectation of a price rise, needs to be financed. If one allows such speculation to take up most available working capital and the market turns – it falls – the competition will be able to buy and offer at the lower levels. The choice is then sell at a loss, or lose business and perhaps lose buyers as well by letting the competition in. The only consolation, perhaps, is that in theory the loss potential of long position holders is limited to their investment. Those with short positions potentially face an open-ended risk as no one knows how high a market may go.

Selling physicals short in anticipation of price falls usually does not require any direct investment (as opposed to selling on the futures markets where margin payments have to be put up), but the risk is entirely open ended. Should an unusual event occur, the market may rise beyond all reasonable expectation. In extreme cases it may become impossible to cover the shorts at any price. In a situation where uncovered sales are showing a serious loss one becomes reluctant to make further sales, even though buyers are now prepared to pay more. This again opens the door to the competition to grab both business and clients. Worse, with higher sales prices more can be bid in the local market, thus squeezing the short seller from both sides.

Quick turnaround? A trader who decides early enough that the market is definitely turning against them can quickly cover their shorts and go long. Or, in the reverse instance, sell stocks and in addition go short. But only if they can finance all these transactions. If they cannot, if they have overextended themselves by over-trading, then the party is over, at least for that season.

Price protection, hedging, options and other risk management tools may be available in theory. But such instruments will not necessarily save those who overextend themselves and do not manage their physical or position risk.

LONG AND SHORT AT THE SAME TIME

Strictly speaking, long or short represents the net difference between purchases and sales. But this assumes trading is in one type or quality of coffee only. What happens if stocks consist of one quality and sales are of another? For example, an exporter might believe that having at least some coffee in stock will act as a hedge against the shorts and limit exposure to price risk, even if stocks and shorts are of different qualities.

Or the expectation might be that the 'spread' (price difference) between the two types of coffee will change in the exporter's favour. In both cases the simple statement 'we are X tons long or short' hides the fact that there are not one but two positions. The qualities are not substitutional: the trader is long in quality A and short in quality B. If the market for B rises then the shorts must be covered. If funds must be liberated to do this then the longs must be sold.

But if others are short of B as well then covering may produce substantial losses and at the same time A may have to be sold at a loss simply to release the funds necessary to pay for the purchases of B. Incidentally, this does not change if the short sales were made on the basis of PTBF. Shortage or surplus in a particular type of physical coffee immediately forces the differential for that coffee up or down, often independently of the market as a whole.

Spread trading is the forecasting or anticipating of changes in price differences between two qualities or markets, for example between New York arabicas and London robustas. Arbitrage, on the other hand, is making use of (small) differences or distortions between different markets or positions, for the same commodity.

VOLUME LIMIT

Exporters deal with physical coffee. Unless they have easy access to a suitable futures market, they will always be directly exposed to physical or position risk. And that risk has to be managed by limiting or mitigating it. Any operation, large or small, should establish its exact position at least at the close of business every day.

The daily position report will show total stocks, forward purchases, and sales awaiting execution, concluding with an overall long or short position. At first glance it seems safe to assume that by imposing a volume limit, a maximum permitted volume or tonnage long or short, one avoids traders going 'overboard' and possibly putting the firm at risk.

In reality this is not the case. As mentioned above, long or short is the net difference between stocks and sales, but only if both are of the same quality. Therefore, a number of different position reports are required for the full picture to be seen:

- Tonnage and cost of stocks (including forward purchases) that cannot be offset against existing sales;
- Tonnage and estimated cost/value of uncovered (open) sales, i.e. sales for which coffee still has to be purchased;
- Tonnage and cost of stocks (including forward purchases) awaiting allocation against existing contracts, cost of shipments under execution, and total outstanding invoices (receivables).

FINANCIAL LIMIT

A volume limit is meant to avoid excessive risk. However, at a price of US$ 2,000/ton a 500-ton limit long or short represents US$ 1 million, but at US$ 4,000/ton the same 500 tons represents US$ 2 million. So, at US$ 2,000/ton, US$ 1 million is needed to pay for covering a short position of 500 tons; double that amount if the price goes to US$ 4,000/ton. Conversely, at US$ 2,000/ton a long position of 500 tons costs US$ 1 million to finance but US$ 2 million at US$ 4,000/ton. Clearly, because exporters deal in physical coffee that must be financed, the volume limit by itself is not enough.

A financial limit is needed as well to ensure the operation, the book, can be financed. However, the volume limit is equally important. A price change of US$ 200/ton against the exporter means a loss of US$ 100,000 for 500 tons; double that if lower prices had caused their financial limit to permit a position of 1,000 tons. To take a real-life example, in December 1999 the ICO 'other milds' indicator stood at 124 cts/lb ex dock: by the end of December 2001 the same indicator had fallen below 60 cts/lb and by the end of February 2011 it stood at no less than 296 cts/lb.

Both types of limit are needed therefore to protect against drastic price changes. The financial limit kicks in when prices rise, and the tonnage limit kicks in when prices fall. The objective is to avoid exceeding one's financing capacity or incurring unsustainable trading losses.

By adding the third position category (pending shipments and outstanding invoices) the daily position report will show both the funds applied by category, and the firm's total trading exposure. Unfulfilled contracts, shipments in progress and outstanding invoices should be subdivided to show the total exposure per individual client.

The combination of financial and volume limits is also important for those trading on the futures markets where financial leverage or gearing may enable traders to turn, for example, a margin investment of US$ 100,000 into a US$ 500,000 coffee position (if they are permitted to trade at the ratio of 5 to 1). In this situation a 1% position profit means a 5% profit on the actual investment; conversely, a 1% position loss means dropping 5% on the investment. (In futures the volume limit would be expressed as a number of contracts.)

MARGIN CALLS – A POTENTIAL HEDGE LIQUIDITY TRAP

Producers, traders and exporters are increasingly seeking ways and means to hedge price risks. When such hedging is done on a futures exchange, directly or through brokers, then deposits and margin calls are part of the deal. Usually producers and exporters sell futures short to hedge unsold crops and stocks. If futures prices then rise, additional and often substantial margin calls can pose real liquidity problems. There may be insufficient liquid funds available to cover the margin calls, even though the underlying trading position is sound and profitable. If there are heavily geared or leveraged speculative positions in the market, then margin calls by themselves can move the price of futures.

Hedge positions, and their associated potential margin demands, should also be included in the daily position report, as should any gearing or leverage involved in the futures transaction. The difficulty is that margin calls can be neither predicted nor quantified in advance, and in extreme cases a company's liquidity may not be adequate to finance them. Commodity banks understand this and their credit packages will make provision for margin calls to avoid otherwise sound operations being derailed.

Smaller banks in producing countries cannot always offer similar facilities, unless they act as agents for such commodity banks or other providers of risk management solutions.

CURRENCY RISK

The vast bulk of the world trade in coffee is expressed in United States dollars and coffee is known as a 'dollar commodity'. In many producing countries the local currency is not linked to the United States dollar. Exporters therefore face the risk that the dollar exchange rate will move adversely in relation to their own local currency, affecting both export revenues and internal coffee prices.

Usually, the currency risk can be limited by borrowing in the currency of sale, provided local regulations permit such foreign currency advances to be offset against the export proceeds. If advances are immediately converted into local currency that in turn is immediately used to pay for spot goods whose shipment will be invoiced in United States dollars, then the cost of goods is expressed in dollars and not local currency. If the cost of goods represents 80% of the sales value then one could say that exposure to currency risk is limited. But in many countries local banks are not always able to make substantial advances in United States dollars.

Historically, in many coffee producing countries the local currency was more likely to depreciate (exporters ought to profit on stocks bought in local currency) than appreciate (exporters are likely to lose because they will receive less local currency on export). But there have also been numerous examples, especially since the monetary crisis of 2008 and in subsequent years, where local currency movements in coffee producing countries have gone against exporters with their local currency appreciating against the United States dollar. Today, macro shifts in the wealth of nations are changing old currency and interest rate trends and international flows of capital are affecting relative currency rates and therefore the price of coffee. As a result, the supply and demand value of coffee does not always translate into the actual price that is paid.

Individual companies and bankers approach currency risk in different ways, but the guiding principle should always be that commodity export and currency speculation do not go together.

Exposure to potential currency risk needs to be reported and monitored in exactly the same way as purely coffee trade related risk. In many coffee producing countries currency risk can be hedged, but the complexity of currency markets and trading is beyond the scope of this guide.

RISK AND CREDIT

Risk is often assumed to concern only sellers and buyers, but there are other parties to a transaction. Usually finance for the deal is directly or indirectly provided by banks or other financial institutions whose risk is that after they have advanced funds to enable a transaction things somehow fall apart and part or all of the funds cannot be recovered. There are three principals to almost all transactions: sellers, buyers and financiers, each of whom have different but interlinked risk concerns. In other words, credit and risk mitigation are irrevocably linked. (Insurers or underwriters are obviously also party to risk but as service providers, not as principals.)

Few producers, traders, processors, exporters, importers, trade houses or roasters are able to finance turnover from 'own funds'. If they were able to do so then the financiers' preoccupations with risk would not concern them, except to say that in a well run business many of those concerns are taken into account as a matter of course. But if one aspires to borrow working capital then all the lender's preoccupations have to be addressed satisfactorily. Otherwise there is little chance of obtaining any finance.

Simply put, there are two perspectives to risk and risk management:

- The commercial or trade perspective is mainly preoccupied with managing physical and price risks, although performance risk also plays a role.
- The financial or lending perspective on the other hand is mainly concerned with performance risk.

All the other risks associated with commerce also feature, but a lender can insist on many types of risk 'insurance' against these, ranging from insurance against loss or theft to the hedging of unsold stocks or open positions. But what of the risk that a borrower does not perform – that is, someone becomes unable to refund a loan, misrepresents the company's financial or trading position, misstates the quality of goods financed, or engages in pure speculation without the knowledge of their financial backers?

What if the suppliers or buyers a borrower depends on default against that borrower? For example, unfavourable price movements cause a supplier to renege on sales contracts, thereby rendering the borrower unable to fulfil their own contractual obligations, through no fault of their own.

Each type of trade has its peculiarities and coffee is no exception. An added factor is that a coffee's value depends not only on supply and demand, but also on quality. No-one without at least some ability to assess and value quality would be expected to make a success of the physical or green coffee business as a trader, processor, exporter, importer or roaster. But assessing that quality, and therefore a coffee's commercial value, is not an exact science. Market analysis is not exact either, with many price movements difficult to anticipate or explain. These uncertainties complicate the business of raising loan finance because banks dislike uncertainty in any shape or form.

The risks that attach to monies lent for investment in visible physical assets (i.e. land and buildings) are very different from the risks on monies lent to finance trade in coffee. Commodity trade finance is a highly specialized activity, usually undertaken not by the average retail bank but rather by corporate lending or commodity trade finance banks.

The term *'trade finance'* is self-explanatory: these banks finance trade, not speculation. Prospective borrowers should understand this from the very beginning. Therefore, before any credit limit or credit line can be agreed, the types of transactions that are to be financed have to be agreed, to avoid each and every deal having to be individually approved. Usually, but not always, the borrower can then trade freely within the limits that have been agreed and needs to apply for additional approval only if, for example, they wish to increase their credit line.

Different risks are attached to financing the trade in coffee. Some of these could be termed trend risks, in that changing trends in the coffee world can have negative effects on those who borrow trade finance. Other more transaction specific risks attach to the type of coffee trade engaged in.

This discussion is limited to the financing of coffee that has been harvested, i.e. 'off the tree'. 'On tree' or production financing criteria would also be based on many of the considerations described below, but on many others as well. To discuss those is beyond the scope of this guide.

TREND RISKS

Market risk. World demand for coffee is relatively stable with limited growth potential only. Increasing price transparency means there is not that much scope for expansion of trade profitability other than through competition, consolidation, or expansion or diversification of activities. Diversification usually means getting involved with different or with a larger number of commercial counterparts, which can increase performance risk.

Margin (profitability) risk. The concentration of roaster buying power coupled with the large roasters' need for increased transparency in green coffee pricing puts pressure on margins, again potentially affecting trade profitability. Meanwhile costs rise because of changing buying patterns and a greater need for risk management (hedging). Having fewer and larger partners also means having larger performance risks. Margins are also likely to be affected as price transparency increases, certainly for the more standardized qualities of coffee.

Volatility risk. For many it is becoming more and more difficult to trade back-to-back (make matching purchases and sales simultaneously), and more and more position taking is required. While the general price risk can be hedged (the market as a whole rises or falls), it is impossible to hedge the differential risk or basis risk (the value of the coffee bought or sold rises or falls compared to the underlying futures market). Modern communications provide instant price news worldwide, bringing increased price volatility.

Country risk. This is a risk rating applied to all international lending, based on the lender's assessment of the political, social and economic climate in the individual country where the funds are to be employed. Country risk often weighs quite heavily in the total risk assessment attaching to the financing of trade with coffee producing countries. The more unstable a country or its economy, the poorer the country risk rating will be. Such ratings will also include an assessment of the probability that a country may suddenly introduce or reintroduce exchange controls or other limitations on financial transactions. Poor country ratings increase the cost of borrowing and may result in banks demanding loan guarantees from sources independent of the country concerned. If banks feel the country risk is unacceptably high they will buy country or credit insurance, the cost of which adds to the lending rate to be charged.

What is not always appreciated is that country risk also applies to the buyer's country of residence. If an exporter trades with bank-supplied finance then the bank will usually reserve the right to pre-approve the exporter's buyers and sometimes even the individual transactions. If a sale is to be made to an unusual destination, country risk will play a role in that approval process. It is easier for an international bank than for an individual exporter to make such judgement calls.

RISK IS NOT STATIC

General change or evolution has an effect on the positioning and exposure of exporters and traders or trade houses. Examples are the ever-increasing concentration of buying power in the hands of a small number of very large roasters, also now in the specialty trade, and the ongoing switch to the just-in-time supply chain. Large roasters concentrate more and more on their core business: the roasting and marketing of coffee. Procurement at origin, delivery and financing the supply chain is therefore increasingly entrusted to specialized trade houses and in-house trading firms, usually in the form of long-term supply contracts for a range of coffees. Such contracts may even stipulate delivery dates at roasting plants.

Another example of change or evolution in the marketplace is growing transparency in the coffee pricing chain. This limits trading margins, certainly for the more standardized qualities that very large end-users require. At the same time, near instantaneous global access to information means 'the market' as a whole learns more or less at the same time of important developments, which undoubtedly serves to increase price volatility.

All this evolutionary change impacts on the way the coffee trade does business and, by implication, changes the risks it incurs as well. Having fewer but very large business partners, for example, also means having fewer but larger performance risks, whereas the trader or trade house may be more or less forced to dance to their partner's tune.

The concentration of buying power is not limited to roasters. The same development is evident in the coffee trade, where today a small number of really large trade houses dominate.

The just-in-time supply system can be said to increase trade risks. But it also enables trade houses, especially larger ones, to add value because their turnover and their total range of activities both increase, often when they establish operations in producing countries in competition with local operators. The large trade houses' relatively easy access to cheaper international credit than is available to local operators has obviously facilitated their entry as direct players into origin markets.

CHANGING RISK AND SMALLER OPERATORS

Smaller exporters, traders and importers are having to become more professional and specialized if they are to maintain or add to their traditional functions. If they cannot satisfy the demands of the larger roasters then they must concentrate on niche markets and smaller counterparts, for example in the specialty market.

Their functions and margins may also be under threat from e-commerce or Internet trading at the retail end. This may not necessarily compete with them, but may limit their ability to maintain adequate margins. If trading margins are inadequate then turnover has to rise or other activities have to be added – again factors that can have an impact on risk.

If this involves them in more position taking, then their hedging requirements will increase accordingly, accompanied by exposure to margin calls. Smaller operators mostly lack the margin cushion that large houses with direct or indirect exchange membership enjoy. Large operators with direct access to the exchanges usually pay margin calls only over their net open futures position (long minus short). But for many in the industry, margin calls can present particularly unwelcome and difficult swings in liquidity. Perhaps this is one more reason why so much trading has been on a PTBF (price to be fixed) basis in recent years. Until such contracts have to be 'fixed', hedging is not necessarily required because the price remains open. See chapter 9 for more on trading PTBF.

Unless a transaction is back-to-back, banks usually require outright purchases at fixed prices to be hedged immediately, but of course such open hedges (sales or purchases) on the futures exchanges bring exposure to margin calls that need to be financed.

Importers dealing with the strongly growing specialty market need to 'carry' their customers: they must hold green coffee in stock for them, they must stock a range of different green coffees, and more often than not they must provide their clients with credit terms ranging from 30 to perhaps as much as 120 days after the actual delivery takes place. Risk attaches to all of these activities. See below for more on this.

Exporters wishing to sell to the specialty market often also have to guarantee a certain minimum availability over a certain period of time. This automatically translates into price risk on the unsold stock holdings that need to be maintained as a result.

Exporters wishing to secure a permanent foothold in the specialty market may have to make crop finance advances to certain producers in order to safeguard supplies from future crops, i.e. more risk again. Admittedly long-established and well-known exporters may be able to offset such transactions against forward sales to importers or roasters who also want to secure longer term supplies of that particular coffee, but not always.

Clearly, long-term industry trends require careful monitoring. Most change has an effect one way or another on a risk situation somewhere, sometime.

To these points one must add the risks attaching to the actual type of trade to be financed. These are the operational risks associated with the coffee operations that are to be conducted, and the transaction risks that attach to each and every individual transaction.

CREDIT INSURANCE AS A (CREDIT) RISK MANAGEMENT TOOL

Credit insurance is provided by specialized companies that assess the credit risk posed by an importer's (or roaster's) individual clients, particularly those requiring extended payment terms. Especially, smaller companies cannot afford the risk that a client fails to pay for goods delivered whereas their own banking (overdraft) facilities may also be dependent on having adequate credit insurance in place. Credit insurers in turn place limits on the amount of credit that can be insured for each individual buyer, but particularly in times of economic uncertainty, such limits can suddenly be sharply reduced or even withdrawn altogether. In such a situation, smaller importers/wholesalers, which rely on the security of the insurance, may have to either stop supplying certain clients altogether or demand cash up front.

NB: It is important not to confuse credit insurance with credit lines. The first refers to insuring the risk a buyer does not pay for goods received; the second refers to the amount of credit (or overdraft facility) a commercial bank is prepared to provide to an importer or trader.

Usually, credit insurers require importers to take out cover for all their clients – in other words, all or none. Whether to insure or not will depend on the type of business that is conducted and the premium required. If the great majority of clients are top roasting companies then the cost may not be warranted, or may simply be too high. Cost would appear to be one reason why the use of credit insurance is not widespread in the United States coffee market, although it is used in the specialty segment. In Europe it is fairly widely used, but mostly amongst smaller companies which do not normally sell (regularly) to the majors. Usually, the cost is relatively modest whereas for many importers/traders the willingness of a credit insurer to cover a (potential) client is a good indication of that client's financial standing. This is particularly important given that many smaller roasters demand extended credit terms. For a review of commonly used payment terms in the coffee trade see chapter 4.

WHY IS THE AVAILABILITY (OR ABSENCE) OF CREDIT INSURANCE IMPORTANT?

Here one has to differentiate between the two value chains. Coffee is mostly retailed through two separate market segments: supermarket chains and individual outlets as coffee shops, etc. Furthermore, especially for smaller operators, bank finance and credit risk are irrevocably linked with most bank funding conditional on having adequate credit risk insurance in place.

Supermarket chains are mostly serviced by the major roasting companies who in turn rely largely on trade houses for their green coffee supplies. Over time the tendency on the part of supermarket chains to demand ever more credit from suppliers has notably intensified. This in turn means similar demands from major roasters. For example, instead of buying on the basis of 'cash against documents on first presentation', some of the majors buy green coffee on the basis of 'payment on arrival', thus shifting a substantial financing burden on to their suppliers. Whilst accepting that major roasters present little or no credit risk, this shift still obliges potential suppliers to find the additional funding this necessitates. Major operators will find this easier than will their smaller counterparts, some of who may be unable to compete because they cannot raise the extended finance.

Smaller roasters and coffee shops (particularly specialty) are largely serviced by importers/traders and wholesalers. The provision of credit has always been an accepted way of doing business in this segment. This is particularly so in the specialty business where most small roasters expect to receive 30 or more days of credit from the date of delivery. However, when the economic climate worsens, as in 2008, so does the availability of finance. Even medium sized roasters started looking to their suppliers for additional credit by way of later payment, also because their own clients were seeking extended credit terms. Again, larger trade houses may deal with this more easily with this kind of situation, for example by channeling their specialty and smaller client business through separate companies that can afford to take out cover for all their clients.

For smaller operators, selling on (extended) credit is not really advisable without credit insurance, whereby the insurance company insures the risk that a buyer will not pay for goods received. This is central to the functioning of almost every retail supply chain, including coffee. Without access to adequate credit insurance many smaller importers/wholesalers may be unable to trade freely. If credit insurers experience underwriting losses then the likely reaction is to reduce exposure – at times by cancelling individual buyer coverage altogether. If that happens an importer may have to retreat from certain types of business and/or clients, irrespective of the availability of bank finance. It is important to note here that credit insurers do not reduce or cancel individual client limits without reason. General reductions may be linked to a deteriorating economic climate in the sector concerned whereas individual reductions may be because of information received or obtained, for example from annual accounts lodged by privately held companies with chambers of commerce or similar institutions.

FACTORING

Providing extended credit of course constrains one's liquidity, i.e. funds that are tied up in credit to buyers cannot be used for new trading. It is important to note here that credit insurance does not improve one's liquidity – the insurance only comes into play if a buyer defaults.

Factoring is one way around the liquidity problems associated with extending credit. It is the selling at a discount of a company's receivables (outstanding invoices) to a third party, the factor, who advances most (but not all) of the expected proceeds immediately, and pays the balance once the buyer in question has settled the amount due. This is at a cost, but the availability of the released funds for new business, i.e. the improved liquidity that is generated, probably offsets most if not all.

TRANSACTION SPECIFIC RISKS

OPERATIONAL RISKS

Different categories of traders have different strengths and weaknesses. Weaknesses can be equated with potential risks. See table 10.1.

There are also the in-house buying or trading companies of the very large roasters and some retail chains (which have coffee roasted for them by third parties), whose strength lies in buying power and strong financial resources that permit them to negotiate favourable terms of trade, either with trade houses or directly with origin. The fact that such in-house buying companies have a guaranteed outlet for their purchases obviously appeals to the banking system. In partnership with collateral management providers (discussed later in this chapter), this combination of interested bank and strong buyer is able to get closer to origin through all-encompassing credit packages that extend backwards from the roaster-buyer to the exporter and indirectly enable the exporter to purchase the necessary coffee at the farm gate.

Last but not least, there are speculative operations, technical or paper traders, and investment or commodity funds. The latter in particular have access to huge capital resources. They can invest in top-flight personnel and can afford to buy the best (and certainly the most expensive) analytical services available. But as they have no real trading function, they tend not to have much 'feel' for the physical market. Their risk exposure is therefore substantial. See table 10.2.

TRANSACTION RISKS

It is not always appreciated that lenders and borrowers have the same interest: that the transactions for which the funds are used come to a fruitful and profitable conclusion. Many of the average lender's preconditions are no more onerous than those any sensible owner or manager of an operation would apply in-house.

CONDITIONALITIES FOR CREDITS

GENERAL CONDITIONALITIES FOR CREDITS

When banks and other institutions finance trade in coffee they indirectly but automatically share in all these risks. Clearly

their assessment of the degree of risk presented by each borrower or type of operation plays a role in determining the credit line (the amount of finance to be provided), and what conditions and costs will apply.

As well as setting a limit on the amount of finance to be provided, banks will also stipulate under what circumstances and for which purposes funds may be drawn. For example, funds meant for trading coffee may not be used to finance other operations.

As a rule, international banks will only finance the trade in coffee in foreign currency (in most cases in United States dollars), and under an agreed set of pre-conditions, including limits on a borrower's total exposure to open and other risks, and a predetermined programme of actual transactions. The exact credit structure will depend to a large extent on an individual borrower's solvency, balance sheet and general standing. As a general rule smaller operators are likely to be subject to more stringent controls than substantial and well-known companies. Banks will also clearly distinguish between, and assess separately, the price (value) risks and the physical (goods) risks inherent in each lending operation.

Trade or commodity banks provide short-term credit to finance transactions from the purchase of stocks through to the collection of export or sales proceeds. Usually this means the credit is self-liquidating – funds lent for the purchase of a particular tonnage of coffee must be reimbursed when the proceeds are collected.

Put differently, credit buys stocks that turn into receivables (invoices on buyers, usually accompanied by documents of title such as shipping documents) that generate incoming funds, which automatically offset the original credit.

SECURITY STRUCTURE

To safeguard its funds and the underlying transaction flow the lender will establish a security structure. The elements can be summarized as follows.

Exporter. Assignment of accounts, mortgages on fixed assets, pledges of goods. Assignment of contracts, receivables, insurances. Business experience, track record. Fixed price contracts, risk management or hedging. Monitoring of trading 'book', independent audit of accounts.

Price risk during and after transaction. Agreed transaction structure, hedging tools, in-built margin call financing.

Contract reliability. Pre-approved buyers only; agreed transaction structure; fixed price or agreed hedging arrangement. (Who decides when and how price fixing takes place? For example, is it the trader or someone else? Are there specific time limits? For example, fix no later than so many days after date of contract, or so many days ahead of shipment.)

Table 10.1 Operational risks

Category	Strengths	Weaknesses
International multi-country traders or trade houses	Long-term supply contracts provide buying power and opportunities to add value by offering services. Global sourcing means being able to hedge some or much risk in-house while country risk is mitigated. Usually strong management and financial strength/backing	Global trade requires complex organization. Multi-location risk centres. Just-in-time commitments may translate into need to carry high stocks. Dependency on large roasters. Must be 'in the market' at all times.
Exporters	Local expertise. Can invest 'upstream' in processing and even production. Can add value by tailoring quality for niche markets.	Country risk if stability becomes problematic. Supply risk if crops are poor or fail. Often higher financing costs and competition from international trade houses. New exporter faces all these and also lacks track record and client base.
Importers	Local expertise. Can add value by adding services and servicing niche markets. Specialized products can mean higher margins.	Can face reducing client base because of concentrations of buying power. Services often include holding stocks and providing credit. Supply, quality and price risks on specialized products higher.

Table 10.2 Transaction risks

Category of risk	Transaction risks	Potential remedies
Speculative risk and volatility	The deal is not fully hedged or not hedged at all. Prices for physicals affected by speculation on futures markets. Differentials move 'against us'. Increasing visibility of prices brings more volatility.	Strict hedging rules and controls over 'open' positions. Strong management. Knowledgeable staff/brokers/agents. Pre-approved credit line for margin calls.
Performance risk (technical)	Supplier or buyer reneges on contract, for example because prices have moved sharply up or down. Inferior quality or weight is supplied. Coffee is rejected. Non-adherence to contract terms.	Deal only with well-established reputable parties on approved list. Possibly provide pre-finance. Establish independent quality and weight controls. Strong monitoring and administrative skills.
Performance risk (documentary)	Exporter presents inaccurate or invalid shipping documents. Documents are delayed or lost.	Standardize documentation and documentary processes. Facilitate access to electronic documentation systems.
Performance risk (financial)	One of the parties is declared insolvent.	Limit total exposure to any one client or supplier. Monitor changes in behaviour that may point to difficulties ahead, for example gradual slowing down of payments.
Currency risk	Currencies of purchase and sale are different. Currency rates move 'against us'.	Match currency of purchase, borrowing and sale. Strictly control 'open' positions. Use pre-finance expressed in United States dollars. Use forward cover.

Physical stocks. Stored in eligible (approved) warehouses. Properly marked, stored separately and identifiably. Commingling with other goods not permitted.

Stocks as security. Pledge agreement with title to the goods, i.e. warehouse warrants. (Note that depending on local law, warehouse receipts are not always documents of title in the legal sense and may need a court order to enforce rights.) Take ownership of the goods. Note that this does not protect the lender where export licenses are required, or where local law may require attached collateral to be auctioned locally – sometimes within just 14 days after the default is confirmed. How to ensure no other lender, creditor or authority may have prior assignment over the goods? For example, if the national revenue authority's claims take precedence the goods may remain blocked for long periods.

Stock values. Daily verification of market value versus credit outstanding, based on futures exchange values where goods are quoted, or valuation basis to be agreed. Top-up clause in lending agreement in case collateral value becomes inadequate. Monitoring of processing cycles and turnover speed.

Collateral management agreement (CMA). External legal opinion on the CMA itself, the fiduciary transfer of goods and the power of attorney to sell the goods. Due diligence on transport, shipping, warehousing, inspection and collateral management companies. (Due diligence is the thorough analysis of operations, standing, strengths and weaknesses, profitability and credit worthiness.) Performance insurance including cover against negligence and fraud by collateral manager. What pre-emptive rights, if any, do warehousemen and collateral managers have over goods under their control? Do their storage and management charges take precedence?

Export. Goods must comply with industry, government and contract specifications. In case of default, does a bank require any special licence to trade or export the goods? What will be the cost of export taxes, shipment and insurance? When does risk move from performance risk to payment risk? (Meaning at what stage does the lender get possession of actual negotiable shipping documents?) Are funds freely transferable in and out of the country? It is no good collecting local currency against an outstanding amount in foreign currency if that local currency is not convertible or transferable.

Buyer. Exposure to price risk and volatility (affects both exporter and importer). Due diligence; pre-approved buyers only. Limit total exposure to any one buyer. Buyer must accept that lender may execute contract in case of exporter default.

SPECIFIC CONDITIONALITIES

All or some of the following preconditions, the conditions precedent, must be met before any lending agreement will be considered.

- The borrower has obtained all necessary authorizations to export.

- All levies, fees and taxes are paid up to date.
- Legal opinion confirms the rights of the lender and the right to execute these without needing a court order.
- The borrower's entitlement to enter into the lending agreement is evidenced by, for example, a directors' or shareholders' resolution.
- Statements are available showing there are no outstanding or pending claims from tax or other authorities or institutions that could impinge upon the free and unconditional execution by the lender of its rights, or the free and unencumbered movement of the goods.
- Grading, bagging, inspection and quality certificates are available.
- The goods are and will be stored separately under the full control and responsibility of an approved collateral manager.
- Suitable commercial all risks insurance cover is in place, covering storage, in-country transit and loading onboard ship.
- Suitable political risk insurance cover is in place, covering seizure, confiscation, appropriation, exporter default due to export restrictions, riots, looting, war, contract frustration, and so on.
- Cash deposit or collateral deposit of X%.

Usually, the lending agreement will take effect only if:

- The goods are covered by fixed sales contract(s), pledged to the lender.
- All rights under the sales contract(s) are assigned to the lender with the acknowledgement of the buyer, authorizing the lender to execute the contract in case of default by the borrower.
- The export proceeds (receivables) under the contract(s) are pledged to the lender.
- The borrower's export account (escrow account) and other assets with the bank are also pledged to the lender. (An escrow account is an account under a third party's custody or control.)
- All insurance policies are assigned to the lender with acknowledgement that the lender is the loss payee or beneficiary.
- A collateral management agreement with an eligible and approved collateral manager is in place.
- The coffee (stock in trade) is pledged to the lender. Weekly stock statements are issued by eligible (approved) warehousing companies under collateral management agreements, or countersigned by an independent collateral manager confirming that the quantity and quality are equivalent to or higher than required for tender against the pledged sales contract(s).
- All relevant forwarding and shipping documents, issued by eligible (approved) transport, warehousing and shipping companies, are assigned to the lender.
- The transaction structure and control over the goods is such that there are no obvious 'gaps' in the transfer of title documents.

THE BORROWER'S BALANCE SHEET

The borrower's balance sheet is important – if it is not sound then not much else is likely to be sound either. But in any case international trade finance for coffee producers and exporters is nearly always, if not exclusively, based on realizable collateral security. Only very large 'blue chip' companies can obtain substantial credit lines on the strength of their balance sheets. At the other end of the borrowing scale are those who can obtain only fully collateralized credit (sometimes only against offsetting sales) because there is less balance sheet security.

Less substantial and smaller firms will usually be subject to detailed day-to-day scrutiny by both banks and collateral managers – more substantial or highly secured borrowers will fall somewhere in-between.

AVAILABILITY AND COST OF CREDIT

The availability of credit depends on a bank's overall exposure to a given country (each bank applies a 'country limit') or commodity, and the net collateral value (assets, stocks) an individual borrower may be able to provide (pledge). The ratio to pledgeable assets at which banks provide overdraft facilities varies, but will never be 100%.

Non-pledgeable assets are not considered, and banks always cap (set a limit to) their exposure to each individual borrower. Borrowers must appreciate that while gaining market share and making margins is important to banks, these are not the primary considerations when evaluating credit applications.

The cost of credit to a borrower is built up from the regular lending rate to include all the considerations discussed under trend and trade specific risks. Each consideration adds to the base lending rate until one arrives at an interest rate at which both the risk factors and the bank's profitability are adequately covered. This is why lending rates differ from country to country, and from borrower to borrower.

MONITORING

Monitoring of a borrower's entire operation is vital to avoid the chance that certain transactions are kept hidden – an 'audit trail' needs to be established. Even so, it can still be difficult for a bank to determine whether a client is entirely truthful with them, for example when it comes to forward transactions. Other than the exchange of contracts, a forward PTBF sale or purchase for completion six months ahead need not immediately generate visible action or disclosure, and could therefore be kept secret. Differential volatility has also proved to be a risk factor in itself. Unless a deal is back-to-back (the differential on both the purchase and the sale has been fixed), the company's position contains an unknown price risk. This is another reason why banks dislike financing unsold stocks.

Similarly, it is not always easy for banks to determine whether someone is speculating. The world has seen spectacular collapses of loss-making speculative operations in a number of commodities and markets, usually because at least some of 'the book' was hidden from both top management and the banks. Loss-making deals were kept secret and were rolled over until the loss became too high to manage. But there have also been instances where rogue traders declared insolvency while keeping profitable transactions hidden. Most banks will therefore regularly audit the borrower's procedures and administration, including retrospectively checking adherence to position limits and contract disclosure. This may be done as often as once a month.

Banks also watch for gradual changes in client behaviour. They will also control as much as possible the use of loan finance, for example by making payment direct to authorized suppliers and by using collateral managers. See later in this chapter for a review of collateral management.

In some producing countries local commercial banks have had bad experiences with lending to agriculture and commodity trading. Admittedly this has sometimes been due to government interference. Nevertheless, it has caused some local banks to cease such lending altogether, and others are now extra careful because soft commodity financing is dangerous and requires intimate knowledge of the trade.

The degree to which a bank follows the borrower's operation will vary from case to case. It is not unusual for a bank to price or 'quantify' its risk on a particular borrower on a daily basis. It is important to understand that unsold stocks will be valued at the purchase price or at market value, whichever is the lower. Stocks held against forward contracts that are to be shipped at some later stage, may also be valued on the same basis because they do not constitute receivables. This is because if shipment is subsequently frustrated then it is likely that neither the exporter nor the bank will be able to realize the sales value of the original contract and the goods may have to be disposed of at the then-ruling market price.

Cumbersome as all this may seem, the bank is a direct partner in the risk the business entails and as such is entitled to all relevant information. As with buyers, so too with banks: the early and frank disclosure of unexpected events usually leads to solutions being found. Good relationships and optimal support in banking are based on openness. For example, if a bank rules out a particular buyer perhaps the exporter should be grateful rather than annoyed, as the real message being conveyed is 'watch out.'

RISK MANAGEMENT AND CREDIT

RISK MANAGEMENT AS A CREDIT COMPONENT

Banks increasingly insist on risk management as a credit component but, as every trader or exporter knows, depending on just the futures markets for this can be quite restrictive (specifications, timing and financial requirements). Using futures does not always fit the bill for traders or their banks, or simply might not be possible. As a result, more and more 'off market' risk solutions are being created by the banks themselves, tailored to the individual client's requirements. Such individual packages can include facilities for the automatic financing of margin calls, for example, when an exporter sells PTBF 'buyer's call' to an importer or roaster on the bank's 'approved list' and wants to hedge (sell futures) to protect their base price.

For larger deals and more important clients the main commodity banks often create risk solution packages in-house. They do not necessarily offset these against the futures markets, but rather do so independently 'over the counter', sometimes even in-house. This may also be done at the request of the importer or roaster rather than the exporter. This can be important for exporters who otherwise may be unable to trade directly with large roasters who insist on buying PTBF 'buyer's call'. The golden rule is that the more the bank is involved in a transaction, for example if it is financing both the exporter and the receiver, the easier it will be to have access to tailored credit or risk management packages. But banks will never provide such facilities for transactions with unapproved buyers. Should there be a default the bank's loss could be double.

Obviously all of this comes at a cost, but at the same time it enables exporters at origin to compete on a more equal footing with the international trade. Once they can hedge their price risk, they will also be able to sell directly to roasters who habitually purchase 'buyer's call'.

The audit trail must always be clear and dependable. Much depends therefore on the quality of the control systems that are in place, their ability to prevent fraud and whether or not the fraud risk is insurable.

AVAILABILITY OF CREDIT IS NOT STATIC

In recent decades the international banking system has witnessed a number of serious disruptions and defaults, the net result of which have been much more stringent risk assessments for lending, and new rules on the ratio 'own capital to lending' banks must maintain. The higher the risk factor, the higher the ratio of own capital to such lending will have to be. Such rules 'block' capital, reduce the amount of available credit and increase costs. Despite globalization and talk of the world as a single marketplace, banks have in general become more selective as to how much, for what purpose and to whom they will lend in which countries.

Liberalization and deregulation in the 1980s and 1990s brought huge change in the export marketing of coffee worldwide: new rules, open markets and different players. But not all of the new players were creditworthy from an international banking perspective, whereas price volatility has become huge. As a result, from a banker's perspective

the financing of coffee trading became more risky and less attractive, i.e. less 'bankable'.

Add to this some fairly spectacular defaults caused by sudden price changes, over-trading, over-pricing and quality problems, and it is no surprise that many banks consider such business to be long on risks and short on margins. As a result the number of banks willing to lend to commodity producers and traders has been decreasing rather than increasing. But those that remain are more commodity-focused, they see new opportunities and have the expertise to gather the necessary information. Therefore, they have better insight into the actual business. Often such banks finance the entire chain, from roaster or importer back to the exporter, especially where the buyer actively supports the borrower's application.

Other initiatives aim to make risk management tools available to individual growers and smallholder groups as an integral part of producer credit. Electronic warehouse receipts will likely play a significant role in all this eventually. In general, though, modern coffee trade financing solutions are increasingly coming from specialized foreign banks rather than from banks in coffee producing countries.

RISK REMAINS RISK

Specialized commodity trade banks place trade credits where risk is manageable; that is, where collateral can be realized and genuine debts can relatively easily be recovered through a reasonably modern and properly functioning judicial system, and the funds so obtained can be remitted out of the country.

International trade houses co-exist well enough with all this, but local exporters may be faced with weak internal banking systems that are unable or unwilling to become substantially involved. They have to pay higher rates of interest, and they cannot easily or not at all directly access international finance. But the large commodity banks cannot easily or not at all work 'in the field' in producing countries either, so in-country financing requires local solutions. Sometimes this is achieved by a foreign bank taking a shareholding in a local bank. Even then, local banks remain first and foremost commercial institutions with specific limits and regulations. They cannot always accommodate modern risk management solutions, no matter which shareholder or international development agency backs them or provides the funding for specific packages.

It has to be recognized that risk remains risk for the seller and their bank until such time as the bank obtains receivables (invoices, with shipping documents) on a pre-approved foreign buyer. Even if the foreign bank is only involved 'at distance', perhaps by providing credit through a local bank and not directly to the borrower, it will nevertheless evaluate both the credit risk and the value in the entire transaction. That is also the case if the deal is 'fully collateralized', for example by warehouse receipts or warrants.

WAREHOUSE RECEIPTS AS COLLATERAL

In most countries a warehouse warrant automatically provides title to the goods, but with warehouse receipts this is not necessarily the case. National legislation may be unclear or silent on the enforceability (execution) of rights over the underlying goods. Although warehouse receipts have been in existence for centuries, not all country legislation recognizes them as negotiable documents of title. Even if the common law framework and trade legislation provide sufficient basis for using warehouse receipts as negotiable documents of title, banks and other creditors may still encounter unexpected obstacles when trying to execute a warehouse receipt and take title to the goods. In some countries there will be 'reasons' why a creditor may have title, but cannot enforce the rights this supposedly confers.

Where rights under a title are obtained, the execution still needs to be supported by legislation that will permit the creditor to trade or export the underlying goods. Does the creditor need a trade license? An export license? Can the sales proceeds be transferred out of the country? What are the chances of the execution process being interfered with or delayed? In some countries the execution of debt presents banks with huge problems. No credit risk assessment can therefore avoid examining the legal and sometimes physical difficulties surrounding the execution of the lender's rights.

The usefulness of warehouse receipts in general is well established, for example as a source of credit for producers of seasonal crops who may thus avoid having to sell during seasonal periods of oversupply and therefore low prices. But for the coffee export industry, warehouse receipts may represent only part of the answer to the banks' concerns about debt security and debt or collateral execution.

Freely negotiable warehouse receipts present a different potential for fraud, in that the documents themselves may be stolen or falsely endorsed. Some international collateral managers therefore prefer to issue their own, non-negotiable receipts as part of 'guaranteed total performance' packages, which they back with liability and indemnity insurance. It could be argued that the real value of such insurance will emerge only when a real claim (a really huge claim) arises, because insurance cover is only as good as what is stated in the policy document. One view is that only what is included is covered; the more attractive alternative view is that anything that is not specifically excluded is therefore covered by implication.

WAREHOUSE RECEIPTS – SUMMARY OF PRE-CONDITIONS

To recapitulate, in the context of coffee export trade finance, warehouse receipts may generally be considered as valid collateral if:

- The receipt is issued by an approved entity (public warehouseman, collateral manager).
- The goods are identifiable, records are maintained, and no commingling is permitted.
- No superior rights (liens) are held over the goods by the issuer (the warehouseman).
- The receipt can be transferred by endorsement or assignment (it is negotiable), or it is issued in favour of the lender.
- The receipt can be used to pledge or sell the underlying goods.
- Insurance cover against loss or unauthorized release of the underlying goods is adequate.
- No third party can have superior rights over the underlying goods.
- Local legislation enables the beneficial holder to enforce their rights over the underlying goods, that is, the debt the goods represent can be executed ahead of any claims that others (for example revenue authorities or warehousemen) may have.

TRADE CREDITS IN PRODUCING COUNTRIES

TRADE CREDIT TERMINOLOGY AND DEFINITIONS

- Physical coffee – green coffee.
- First hand – coffee sold from/by origin.
- Second hand – coffee subsequently sold on by overseas traders.
- Long – coffee bought in expectation of later sale.
- Short – coffee sold against expected future purchases or arrivals.
- Spot – immediately available coffee.
- Forward sales – coffee sold for later shipment, sometimes months ahead.
- Futures market – trades standard qualities and quantities of coffee for future delivery at pre-determined ports during specific months or trading positions.
- Paper trade or paper coffee – trade in futures and other contracts that are offset against each other, i.e. do not result in physical delivery of coffee.
- Differential – premium or discount of 'our coffee' with respect to the futures market.
- Outright sale or fixed price sale – the full selling price is set at the time of sale.
- PTBF – price to be fixed: selling now at a known differential against the futures market with the futures price being determined later.

- Fixing – the action to determine the futures price that, combined with the differential, will become the contract price for the physical coffee.
- PTBF seller's call – futures price to be called or fixed by the seller.
- PTBF buyer's call – futures price to be called or fixed by the buyer.
- Price risk or market risk – the risk that the coffee price generally moves against us.
- Basis risk or differential risk – the risk that the differential moves against us.
- Collateral – underlying security for advances, for example stocks.

TYPES OF COFFEE TRADE FINANCE

The most common types of coffee trade finance are the pre-financing of coffee to be purchased, advances against actual stock holdings and the financing of the goods during processing for export and shipment.

Pre-financing

Processors and exporters engage in pre-financing to secure future supplies of particular coffees. Bank support for such deals depends very much on the track record of the parties concerned, and whether the buyer has a guaranteed sale for that coffee. It is difficult enough to obtain finance for unsold stocks, let alone for 'promised' stocks.

This is one of the strengths of the trade houses that engage in long-term supply contracts with large roasters. They usually have a guaranteed outlet for their coffee with little performance risk and they are able to raise funds internationally, often at lower rates than those available in the producing country itself. But the individual exporter who deals with importers and smaller roasters will usually find that this type of buyer is not interested in providing any kind of finance; they may even be looking for credit themselves.

Collection credits and stock advances

The main issues with collection credits and stock advances are what proportion of the value can be borrowed, what type and quality of coffee will be collected or bought, at what prices, and how will the coffee be physically handled. It is often assumed that borrowing against stocks, or against coffees for which there is already a sales contract, is relatively risk free. But although the lender will have a formal lien over the goods, what if the weight or the quality is misstated? What if warehouse receipts are issued for non-existent goods? All exporters should ask themselves and their staff these same questions.

Pre-shipment finance

Pre-shipment finance is usually obtained when the ready goods are lodged for shipment (as pre-shipment finance) or when shipment has been made and the documents become available (as negotiation of documents). The term 'negotiation of documents' is often misunderstood – the bank merely makes an advance of all or part of the invoice value against receipt of the shipping documents, which it then presents to the buyer for payment. If the buyer does not pay, the bank has automatic recourse to the exporter because although it 'negotiated' the documents, it did not take over the non-performance risk, that is, the risk that the buyer would not pay. Letters of credit (see later in this chapter) are an option, but not all buyers are willing to establish them.

TRADE CREDIT AND ASSOCIATED RISKS

All the risks mentioned in other parts of this chapter are present. How do we know that the goods are what they are said to be? When a bill of lading simply reads 'received one container said to contain (STC) 20 tons of green coffee, shipper's stow and count', where does that leave everyone?

All forms of credit expose the lender to five types of risk:

- Physical risk: the goods are simply not there, or are somehow lost.
- Price risk or market risk: the market price falls and the loss cannot be recovered, or the quality is not up to standard and so the value of the goods is less than expected, also called value risk.
- Differential risk or basis risk: The domestic price of coffee does not move in tandem with international prices
- Currency risk: Fluctuating domestic currency rates may cause losses, for example when the domestic currency strengthens against the currency of sale.
- Performance risk: the foreign buyer does not buy the goods, reneges on the contract or is declared insolvent.

PHYSICAL RISK

When funds are advanced against stock in trade, the goods so financed are usually pledged to the lender as guarantee of repayment: they become the security or collateral. Banks do this by taking out a general lien over stocks and collectables (outstanding invoices) through which beneficial ownership rests with the bank until all outstanding advances have been refunded in full.

In long-established relationships banks may be satisfied with this. They may leave the management and physical control of the goods to the borrower, especially if general international guarantees are in place, for example from a trade house's parent company.

But for smaller operators, and certainly those in new or relatively recent relationships, the banks will want to be satisfied that checks and balances are in place. These checks could include having the goods stored by public warehousing companies that issue warrants or warehouse receipts in the bank's name or hand warrants to the bank 'endorsed in blank' which permits the bank to freely transfer or assume title. The bank's lien will extend to the proceeds of any insurance claim that may arise, since all the goods must be insured with an agreed insurer, on conditions acceptable to the bank. Even so, banks may still demand additional security guarantees

PRICE RISK OR MARKET RISK

In this context, price risk is the risk that the market as a whole (the price risk), or the differential (the differential or basis risk), will change to the borrower's disadvantage. Remember that banks do not normally encourage or finance speculation. Whether a bank will permit a client to hold stocks without hedging them depends on the relationship and the guarantees that the borrower may have provided.

Unless the goods have been bought to fulfil a fixed price contract, it is likely that the bank will insist on the regular hedging of the price risk on all stocks. In a general sense, smaller exporters especially should understand that banks are risk averse and do not like to finance speculative transactions. That is, they do not really approve of 'open' positions. Only the price risk can be hedged. The differential risk cannot be hedged.

DIFFERENTIAL RISK OR BASIS RISK

Banks are well aware that the differential risk can be substantial, especially for those trading single origin coffee, but also that it is difficult for banks to have insight into the way differentials move is and that as yet there is no immediately obvious solution for this. They therefore mostly depend on the borrower's track record and judgement, especially when coffee is bought against offsetting fixed price sales.

But where purchases are made against an open price sales contract (a PTBF contract that specifies only a selling differential) then the buying differential will only be determined when the physical coffee is bought and 'fixed'. If the market differential for that type of coffee has substantially changed since the sale was made, then the difference between the hedge price and the buying price of the physicals may be substantially different as well, which could cause the transaction to be unprofitable.

NB: Usually (but not always) differentials tend to be lower when futures prices are high, and higher when futures are low.

A differential of 'plus 10' on arabica when the 'C' contract is at 100 cts/lb may change to 'even money' in the producing country when the 'C' for example goes to 150 cts/lb. This is favourable for exporters who need to buy physicals against a PTBF sale because when they fix the purchase the physicals will only cost 'even money'.

A differential of 'minus 30' on robusta when LIFFE is at US$ 1,700/ton may perhaps change to 'even money' in the producing country when London goes to US$ 1,500/ton. This is unfavourable for exporters who need to buy physicals against a PTBF sale because when they fix the purchase the physicals will cost 'even money' against an open sale of 'minus 30'. Differentials in producing countries may also buck the general market trend, for example because of drought or other production problems.

CURRENCY RISK

When advances in United States dollars are immediately turned into coffee stocks that will later also be sold in United States dollars, then the currency risk can be considered limited and to be mostly of local concern. However, in the past decade changing international capital flows have led to increased volatility between currencies. Coffee is still a 'dollar commodity', but nowadays coffee prices worldwide are determined not only by supply and demand, but also by the relative value of the United Sates dollar to other world currencies. Major movements in exchange rates, especially for the Brazilian real or the Colombian peso, but also in other coffee producing countries, will affect the price of coffee. In some instances such price or currency changes could put original United States dollar advances at risk.

PERFORMANCE RISK

The first line of defence against performance risk is a correctly structured transaction. Further safeguards can then be put in place through the use of collateral management, beginning at the point of purchase and ending with the handing over of shipping documents. On the selling side this is more difficult, as it is impossible to know the financial status and health of all potential importers or roasters.

This is why banks will insist that trade is only with 'authorized buyers' – companies that are known and in which they have confidence. In addition the bank may require that a sales contract is in place before any monies are advanced to buy stocks. In that case selling PTBF facilitates matters. The contractual obligation to supply and accept the goods can be established without the buyer being committed to an actual price long in advance of the actual shipment: only the differential has to be agreed. (Many, if not most, roasters insist on buying 'PTBF buyer's call'.)

This resolves the performance issue, but still leaves open the questions of price and differential risk. As a general rule, most banks dislike advancing the entire cost of a purchase, often preferring to stick to a percentage of the value, say 80%. This provides reasonable cover against a worst case scenario. The percentage will vary according to the risk rating of the country where the borrower conducts their business, and the bank's assessment of the borrower.

COMMON ERRORS AND MISCONCEPTIONS

- Borrowers are not frank enough. If the bank feels it is not receiving all information, it will wonder why. In any case, banks do not want uncertainty – they want control. Shared knowledge is also beneficial to both parties and enables the bank to be proactive.
- Applications that are not based on adequate 'homework', result in a poor first impression or outright rejection.
- Borrowers do not realize how important it is to have quality independently audited financial statements ('financials'), delivered by reputable auditors.

- The internal control and reporting systems are inadequate.
- Transactions work when everyone wishes it – sudden change (weather, prices, buyer turns 'nasty' and politics) can alter this and result in 'blameless' default.
- It does not really help a bank to become the owner of the borrower's stocks. If these have to be sold off at a loss (10%–20% is not unusual) it may take years of new lending to recoup the money lost.
- The local legal system may make the realization of collateral or debt recovery difficult. If so, local collateral in whatever form, including warehouse receipts, may be (almost) without value.

LETTERS OF CREDIT

Letters of credit can serve a dual purpose:

- A guarantee of payment once shipment has been made, to reduce the exporter's credit risk;
- A means of advancing credit to an exporter, enabling goods to be bought and shipped.

In the first instance the exporter is paid against submission of the complete and correct set of shipping documents as stipulated in the letter of credit (L/C): the documentary

Table 10.3 What a borrower must show

Advances at each stage	Borrower must show	Ratio and cost of advance	Conditions	Financing of margin calls
1. Document negotiation	Real function, i.e. adds value. Track record. (Defaults are most likely to occur in the first three to five years of new operations.) Quality management. Understanding of the coffee business. Deals are correctly structured.	Ratio or percentage of advance: highest. Interest rate: lowest.	Sold to approved buyer. Documents and/or payment via bank.	Exposure has been hedged, or PTBF sale has been 'fixed'.
2. Pre-shipment	Appropriate business plan and reporting systems. In-house financial and volume limits. Clear document flows, proper stock rotation.	Ratio: lower. Cost: higher.	Pre-sold to approved buyer or hedged. Collateral manager.	Depending on package and borrower's 'book'.
3. Export processing	Own capital. Visible, permanent and pledgeable assets.	Ratio: lower again. Cost: higher again.	Pre-sold to approved buyer or hedged. Collateral manager.	Depending on package and borrower's 'book'.
4. Interior buying	Adequate warehousing and insurance. Access to collateral management.	Ratio: lowest or even nil. Cost: highest.	Pre-sold to approved buyer or hedged. Collateral manager.	Depending on package and borrower's 'book'.

credit. This is a guarantee of payment once shipment has been made. It is not a specifically designed instrument to enable one to raise credit, although occasionally banks may accept documentary credits as a form of collateral.

Documentary credits include:

- Sight letter of credit: payable on first sight (presentation) of the documents to the bank.
- Usance or time letter of credit: payable after a certain period has elapsed.
- In addition there is the performance credit or bid letter of credit, whose value is forfeited if the party concerned fails to perform (i.e. does not deliver, or does not establish the requisite documentary letter of credit). These are sometimes used for large, long-term supply contracts or in conjunction with tenders (a form of bid bond). For more on using documentary letters of credit see also chapter 4, Contracts.

ADVANCE CREDIT – THREE TYPES

Here the letter of credit becomes a means of raising credit. The buyer or (more likely) a bank agrees to release funds whenever an agreed set of circumstances arises and certain pre-conditions are met. In this category there are three main types of letters of credit.

Red clause letter of credit

This type of L/C is a combination of documentary and open credit in that it provides unsecured credit to an exporter against an agreed transaction. The issuing bank agrees to advance part of the estimated sales proceeds of the coffee to be shipped, without tender of the shipping documents. The balance is then paid once the shipping documents are presented. If a 'green clause' (see below) is included as well then the exporter can obtain additional advances upon submission of warehouse receipts as collateral. The issuing bank will issue strict directions to the correspondent bank in the exporter's country as to how, when, by whom and under what circumstances funds may be drawn. (The correspondent bank is a bank with which the issuing bank has an established relationship.)

A red clause letter of credit allows an exporter to obtain pre-shipment finance, although the amount of available credit is usually only part of the estimated value or even the sales value. This is one way for buyers to expand their sources of supply. Most buyers are reluctant to become involved in financing goods that have not yet been shipped, but exporter and buyer may be linked together through a normal contract with the trade bank establishing the red clause L/C against a registered contract with an approved buyer.

Advance letter of credit

This is similar to the red clause L/C, but it limits the amount that can be drawn without presentation of documents to a percentage of the invoice value and requires the exporter to present an original set of bills of lading before a specific date. Again, inclusion of a 'green clause' can extend the availability of credit through presentation of warehouse receipts as collateral.

Both red clause and advance letters of credit are used when local financing is not available or is available only at excessively high rates of interest. From the point of view of the trade bank or the buyer, the credit provided is unsecured.

Green clause letter of credit

This is a normal documentary letter of credit, which provides a secured form of credit in that exporters can draw an agreed percentage of the value of the goods to be shipped against presentation of warehouse receipts as collateral. Such receipts will be issued by an authorized party (public warehousing company, bonded warehouse, collateral manager), and issued or endorsed in favour of the bank in question. Proof of adequate insurance cover, with the bank as beneficiary, may also have to be submitted.

This type of credit can provide an exporter with working capital during the buying season and while export processing takes place. The credit will be revolving, in the sense that it must be self-liquidating with export proceeds offsetting the relevant outstanding advances in the order these were incurred. At the end of the season or other agreed period all outstanding advances are liquidated when the last shipment takes place. The advantage is that the lender (bank or buyer) has some control over the goods. Depending on their assessment of the exporter's reliability, the lender may decide to appoint someone to supervise the stocks on their behalf. This supervision is usually called collateral management. This is discussed in detail under 'Warehouse receipts as collateral' earlier in this chapter, and below.

UNIFORM CUSTOM AND PRACTICE FOR DOCUMENTARY CREDITS – UCP 600

Terms and conditions governing the issuance and execution by banks of letters of credit are laid down in what is known as the Uniform Custom and Practice for Documentary Credits, issued by the International Chamber of Commerce. Matters of particular interest to the commodity trade include the basic responsibilities of banks when examining documents tendered for payment under letters of credit governed by the Uniform Customs and Practice – UCP 600, and the requirements pertaining to different types of documents that may be tendered under letters of credit. However, UCP 600 only applies when the text of the credit expressly indicates that it is subject to these rules.

For a buyer to be under an obligation to open a letter of credit governed by the UCP 600, the sales contract needs to include an express condition imposing such an obligation on the buyer. Only with such a condition in place can the seller object if the buyer were to open a letter of credit that is not governed by the UCP, e.g. 'Payment by irrevocable letter of credit, incorporating UCP 600'. However, buyers may still stipulate in the credit that certain aspects of the UCP rules are excluded, provided this was laid down in the sales contract.

The major advantage of incorporating UCP 600 in the sales contract for a seller is that where the UCP 600 rules are incorporated, he or she will know in advance the criteria against which the banks will examine the shipping documents in deciding whether or not to pay under the credit. The major advantage for a buyer is that he or she will know in advance the criteria against which the price for the goods will be paid against tender of documents.

For a more detailed overview of UCP 600, see chapter 4, Contracts.

ALL-IN COLLATERAL MANAGEMENT

FUNCTIONS OF THE COLLATERAL MANAGER

The collateral manager (CM) is an independent operator who 'manages' the collateral (the stocks) for a fee on the bank's behalf. The action that triggers the release of bank funds usually determines the stage at which the collateral manager enters the process. Depending on circumstances this may entail CM personnel supervising or managing the borrower's premises, or the storage of goods at public warehouses owned and managed by the CM. Usually the CM is engaged by the borrower and the bank jointly, with the fees paid by the borrower.

To have true value for the banks the CM's obligations have to be guaranteed as well. This is usually done through appropriate liability and indemnity insurance, acceptable to the bank.

Today's collateral managers offer a host of services, described below:

Verification of funding:

- The funds are applied to the agreed purpose.
- The timing and level of advances applied for is as agreed or is realistic.
- The purchase price is as agreed or is realistic.

Verification of borrower's and warehouseman's insurance arrangements:

- Quality and scope of cover are acceptable.

- Lending bank is named as loss payee (beneficiary).
- Premiums are paid up to date.
- Premises and goods are adequately described.

Verification of premises:

- The premises are secure, safe and fit for storage.

Tally-in and weighing:

- Bags received are counted.
- Bags are weighed and stacked.

Verification of quality:

- The goods are what they are supposed to be.
- Goods can be monitored from farm gate to ship's hold.

Issue or certification of warehouse receipts:

- Certifying receipt of the goods.
- Providing proof of existence, which is collateral for funding.

Stock administration and control:

- Goods are properly accounted for.
- Goods cannot be dispatched independently.
- Goods are stored separately, they can be readily identified and no commingling is permitted at any time.

Export process:

- Supervision of export processing; quality control; goods match the sales contract.
- Goods are handed over against approved waybills, receipts or bills of lading.
- Waybills, receipts and bills of lading stipulate the bank as beneficial owner and are handled and dispatched correctly.

The stage at which the CM leaves the process depends on the bank. The bank's back office will have monitored the entire process and the CM's role often ends when the goods are handed over for shipment with the bank assuming title through the issue of bills of lading in the bank's name rather than the exporter's.

MODERN COLLATERAL MANAGEMENT FACILITATES CREDIT

Collateral management in coffee producing countries is a logical extension of the traditional 'supervision' business of independent verifiers and sworn weighers. Where previously such companies certified that goods loaded on ships were of the prescribed quality and weight, they now begin the verification process at the very first point in the collection marketing chain. Modern collateral management increasingly means that a single company coordinates all the logistics, guarantees the integrity of the physical circuit, and provides security over the export documentation process, thus eliminating all unsecured gaps. In other words, they are in the business of 'moving collateral'. As such they can play an essential role in the financing of coffee traders and processors or exporters, especially where the same bank is financing both the end-user and the exporter.

Some international CMs provide complete packages, linking customers with lending institutions on the strength of the CM's performance guarantee, based on standard packages and procedures which they apply worldwide. Should the coffee trade in future move into paperless trade with electronic documents of title and so on, then the role of the CM will take on more importance.

GUARANTEES

Banks need the guarantee that warehouse receipts will become receivables, that is, commercial invoices backed by negotiable bills of lading or other relevant documents of title to the goods. All the gaps and risks in the process from the first purchase to this point need to be quantified and covered. For CMs the risk is enormous. Cases of quality fraud, physical theft and document falsification do occur.

Therefore, if their guarantees are to be truly solid then they need to be backed by fidelity (indemnity) and liability insurance of a quality and level that is acceptable to banks. To be readily enforceable, the insurance policy, and if possible the underlying collateral management contract, must be based on an acceptable jurisdiction, for example English law.

If a CM's overseas parent company provides the guarantees, then it could be said that the collateral manager takes at least part of the country risk on board. This makes it easier for banks to approve certain lending operations, especially when the total credit and risk management package encompasses both the end-user and the producer or exporter.

Coupled with the 'total' credit and risk management packages offered by commodity banks, modern 'all in' collateral management has become an essential component of credit. The increased collateral and transaction security it offers facilitates access to credit, and can help to bring smaller producers and exporters closer to buyers and end-users in consuming countries.

TRADE CREDIT AND RISK – SMALLHOLDERS

CREDIT CHANNELS IN THE SMALLHOLDER SECTOR

Commercial credit for smallholders is linked to risk in much the same way as it is for commercial growers and exporters.

The risk principles are the same, although the detail may be different.

- Performance: Will the crop be delivered as agreed?
- Price: Will the value cover the outstanding credit?
- Value: Will the quality be acceptable and fit for sale?
- Collateral: Can any collateral be provided, and if it is, can it be realized?

Obviously it is difficult, if not entirely impossible, for the average commercial bank to evaluate performance risk, let alone potential quality and value, on an individual basis for thousands of smallholders.

PROVIDING COLLATERAL CAN PROVE DIFFICULT FOR SMALLHOLDERS

Land is nearly always unsuitable as collateral. Even though for most smallholders it may be their only form of visible asset, in many countries such land is often held through traditional ownership structures that make the realization (the sale in debt execution) of the collateral impossible. Even where rural agricultural land is held under title deed, communal and political pressure may make its sale impossible, so smallholder-owned land is often if not mostly unsuitable as collateral.

Crops on the tree are also not meaningful as collateral until they become goods entered into store against warehouse receipts. That is, credit will be advanced only once the harvest is stored. This is a most suitable arrangement for crops that might otherwise have to be sold quickly to raise cash during seasonal periods of oversupply and consequent low prices, but it is not necessarily right for coffee.

Even so, coffee is usually best marketed when it is still fresh (new crop). Prolonged storage, (beyond the usual marketing season), or retention for speculative purposes is not recommended.

The most likely credit channels for smallholders are therefore well run cooperatives or other forms of grower organizations, such as farmer groups that have the required critical mass and are in a position to guarantee and discipline their members. Credit to such organizations will then largely be based on the same principles discussed earlier in this section.

However, the search for alternative credit options has produced some interesting initiatives of which two are mentioned here by way of example. Both place a strong emphasis on development and sustainability issues.

Financial Alliance for Sustainable Trade

The Financial Alliance for Sustainable Trade, FAST, *www.fastinternational.org* is a member-driven, not-for-profit international organization. Its membership represents small and medium-sized enterprise (SME) producer organizations, commercial and socially oriented lenders, development focused NGOs, and other sustainable trade players. FAST's members are committed to promoting sustainable production and trade within their respective capacities.

FAST's mission is to facilitate a global collaborative effort among its members to ensure continued growth of the sustainable trade sector. This is done through increasing the number of producers in developing countries who can successfully access affordable trade finance and longer-term loans for infrastructure, tailored to their business needs as they enter sustainable markets and grow their businesses. SME's often face the problem that they are too small to benefit from infrastructural finance programmes and at the same time they are too big to qualify for micro-financing. This is where FAST comes in. See *www.fastinternational.org/en/node/733* where a substantial number of resources is available.

FAST also requires detailed information from potential borrowers such as: overview of the SME, amount required, certification, credit history, production and sales; business plan, organizational chart and financial statements (balance sheet and income statement for three years – cash flow projection for one year). See *www.fastinternational.org/en/node/681*

Sustainable Agriculture Guarantee Fund

This revolving fund – often just called Agri Fund – offers partial credit guarantees by way of stand-by letters of credit as risk mitigating instruments to financial intermediaries in South America, Africa and Asia. Agri Fund was initiated by Rabobank International in response to a call from the Dutch Government for ideas for public-private partnerships (PPP) that would contribute to improved access to financial services and commodity export markets for growers in developing countries.

The Agri Fund aims to enhance access to local financial services by agricultural cooperatives (or companies buying from small producers). This enables them to purchase, process and trade agricultural commodities in the international market on commercial and sustainable terms. Additionally, Agri Fund is committed to contributing towards achieving sustainable changes in the approach of local banks in emerging economies towards such cooperatives or companies through offering such banks adequate financial instruments.

The initiative has some unique characteristics, the most important of which is that finance is provided for production and export against sales contracts with pre-approved international buyers. Contracts can be basis Fixed Price or Price To Be Fixed (see chapter 9, Hedging), and usually are for execution within the same coffee campaign, i.e. from two to four months ahead of shipment. Other lenders often ask for additional security in the form of fixed assets, which then makes it impossible for borrowers to use these fixed assets as security for their long-term financial needs.

Agri Fund obtains security by using sales contracts with pre-approved buyers as collateral, leaving the borrower's fixed assets free to be used as collateral for other financing requirements. Agri Fund will issue (partial) credit guarantees and provide other financial products as a risk-mitigating instrument in favour of local financial intermediaries. This in turn allows these intermediaries to offer commercial finance for the production and export of agricultural produce at better pricing and conditions than would be possible without such risk mitigating instruments. Fundamental is that the risk mitigating instrument will be decreased on a step-by-step basis, phasing out during a period of three to four years. This means that the financial intermediary is expected to increase its share in the risk (phasing in), but in such a way that the conditions for the borrower will not deteriorate.

Go to *www.rabobank.com/guaranteefund* for more information and download the SAGF brochure from there or directly at *www.rabobank.com/content/images/G5334%20RI_MVO_fund-LR_tcm43-50951.pdf*.

RISK MANAGEMENT AND SMALLHOLDERS

Access to risk management solutions for small growers would not only facilitate access to credit, but would also reduce their exposure to price volatility. This in turn would also help them to plan ahead.

Of all coffee producing countries only Brazil has been able to establish a successful internal futures market for coffee, the Brazilian Mercantile and Futures Exchange. Growers in all other producing countries must look abroad, directly or indirectly, if they wish to make use of futures markets. See chapter 8, Futures markets, for details.

In many countries small growers and smallholders are mostly locked out of risk management markets anyway, for reasons that include a lack of knowledge, high costs and inappropriate contract sizes.

As for gaining access to credit, potential solutions include the aggregation of production and financial capacity through the establishment of cooperatives or other forms of producer groupings. Such groups can then decide how they approach price risk management: simply as an insurance that they purchase, or as part of the marketing process. Unfortunately it cannot be ignored that in a number of countries the performance record of cooperatives has not always been impressive.

But even so, the most likely credit channels for smallholders remain well-run cooperatives or other forms of grower organizations that have the required critical mass, and that are in a position to guarantee and discipline their members. But without some limitation of the price risk, without some form of management of the price risk, access to affordable credit will still remain a distant objective.

PRICE RISK MANAGEMENT AS PURE INSURANCE

Price risk management as pure insurance means there is no direct link between the insurance of the price risk and the marketing of the coffee.

Straight hedging by selling futures exposes the seller to margin calls, bringing with it the risk of potential hedge liquidity traps. Whether any lending institution or risk solution provider will finance such an operation without firm guarantees and collateral is doubtful. Indeed, the notion will be a non-starter for most, small growers and solution providers alike.

Buying put options, the right to sell futures at a stated price at some point in the future, is much simpler than hedging. The cost that needs to be financed is known up front, and no margin calls need to be faced. The premium will depend on circumstances, but can at times be very substantial. Even so, it may be easier to raise finance for this than for straight hedging. As always, the provider will still need to be reassured about how the cost of the option will eventually be recouped.

Tailored solutions. Risk solution providers tailor risk instruments to clients' requirements. For example, options can be graduated to extend over the usual marketing season by spreading equal portions over two or three futures trading positions, if so wished, at different strike prices. Each individual portion can then be exercised individually.

Alternatively the solution provider may simply guarantee a minimum price. Against payment of a premium, they undertake to make good any shortfall between the insured price (the minimum price the growers wish to secure) and the price ruling for the stated trading positions in New York or London, either at a given date or based on the average price over a number of trading days. The producer has bought a 'floor' – the guaranteed price less the cost of the premium. (Consumers would buy a 'cap' to protect themselves against future price rises.)

Swap agreements. Producers can also 'swap' price risk by giving up the benefits from future price rises in exchange for a guaranteed minimum price. Swap agreements could also cover more than one crop year, with tonnages and settlement dates set for each quarter.

The concept is nothing new, and has been extensively used to limit exposure to currency and interest rate fluctuations. Innumerable variables are possible, making it impossible to provide a standard model.

Note: Solution providers and commodity trade banks can put together different risk mitigation instruments, but only for parties with the required critical mass, who are organized and who can find and afford the finance necessary to buy the price insurance they require.

Note also that the World Bank offers price risk management training courses, both on CD-ROM and in workshop settings. Visit *www.agrisktraining.org* for more on this.

PRICE RISK MANAGEMENT AS PART OF MARKETING

Forward sales of physical coffee at a fixed price are the most straightforward form of price risk management as part of marketing. The size of the expected crop is reasonably well known, prices are satisfactory, and buyers have enough confidence in the seller to commit to them on a forward basis. This is perhaps the ideal situation, but it is seldom encountered nowadays. And when prices are very low, fixed price forward contracts look attractive only to the buyer.

Selling physicals forward 'PTBF buyer's call' means growers lose all control over the fixation level, and therefore the price, unless they simultaneously also sell a corresponding amount of futures. But this would expose them to margin calls and potential liquidity problems, assuming they could even find the funds to finance the initial deposits. For more on options, see chapter 9, Hedging.

Selling physicals forward 'PTBF seller's call' might appear to be the answer but this is not necessarily so either. Unless the seller fixes immediately, all such deals establish is a contractual obligation to deliver and accept physical coffee.

The PTBF sale sets the differential the buyer will pay in relation to the underlying futures position(s), but the general price risk and the decision when to fix remain entirely open. In other words, the PTBF sale does not mean the seller has made a price decision – that will only be the case once they fix. Many sellers are unable to bring themselves to fix at unattractive levels, and in falling markets a good number even roll fixations from one futures position to the next, preferring to pay the cost (usually the difference in price between the two positions) to gain more time in the hope that prices will eventually rise. This does not happen only when prices are generally low. In a falling market it is sometimes very difficult for sellers to accept that today they must fix at less than they could have done yesterday or the day before. To avoid such fixation traps one should set internal 'stops' so that fixing takes place automatically when a certain price (up or down) is reached. Such orders to fix can be given to whoever is responsible for the actual execution, basis GTC or 'good till cancelled'.

Note: When fixed price sales are not feasible the simple alternative is to sell PTBF and to fix immediately, thereby fixing both the base price and the differential which, together, make up the final sales price. If there are concerns about 'fixing too early' or 'what if the market goes up', then one also buys a call option accepting that the cost comes out of the sales price for the physicals.

MICROFINANCE

Microfinance is of particular importance to many smallholders in the coffee industry. Most of the world's coffee is produced by smallholders, but they often lack access to reasonably priced credit, particularly women coffee growers. (NB: the definition of smallholder varies from country to country.)

Many institutions today provide micro financing such as commercial banks, micro deposit taking institutions, NGO's and 'NGO-like microfinance institutions'. However, these are generally slanted towards the more urban areas and the financing of commercial activities. Cooperatives and 'village banks' as well as self-help groups usually have a greater rural outreach, but often their means and institutional capacities to finance the coffee sector are quite limited, not least also because of the remoteness of the areas many operate in.

A detailed review of microfinance is beyond the scope of this guide, but the following websites provide a good overview of on-line information sources, including downloadable training materials and links (not inclusive) to some of the better-known microfinance institutions.

General industry information, also providing links to individual websites

The Consultative Group to Assist the Poor (CGAP), *www.cgap.org* is a policy and research centre dedicated to advancing financial access to the world's poor. It is housed at the World Bank and supported by over 30 development agencies and private foundations.

The Microfinance Information Exchange (MIX), *www.mixmarket.org*, founded by CGAP, is the leading business information provider dedicated to strengthening the microfinance sector.

The Microfinance Gateway, *www.microfinancegateway.org*, also a product of CGAP, features research and publications, organization and consultant profiles and lists a very large number of microfinance institutions and their contact details.

MicroCapital publishes The MicroCapital Monitor, *www.microcapital.org,* and offers specialized news and information on international microfinance.

The Social Performance Task Force (SPTF), *www.sptf.info*, provides links and overviews of social performance tools, including tools specific to MFIs.

Planet Rating, *www.planetrating.com*, is a specialized microfinance ratings agency. It gives a comprehensive performance and risk analysis profile of microfinance institutions (MFIs) and also evaluates funds that invest in microfinance (microfinance investment vehicles or MIVs).

MicroRate, *www.microrate.com*, was the first agency to specialize in the evaluation of microfinance institutions that allows lenders and investors to measure the risk and the return on investment in microfinance.

MFTransparency, *www.mftransparency.org*, presents information on credit products and their prices for a number of MFIs and publishes country reports.

Training guides and best-practice resources

The Rural Finance Learning Center, *www.ruralfinance.org*, managed by the Food and Agricultural Organization, offers downloadable training materials for capacity building in the field of rural finance.

The Rural Finance Network, *www.ruralfinancenetwork.org*, hosts a virtual library of studies and training material in rural finance specific to eastern and southern Africa.

Women's World Banking (WWB), *www.swwb.org*, a network of 40 microfinance institutions and banks in 28 countries worldwide, hosts a virtual library of publications and case studies.

CERISE, *www.cerise-microfinance.org*, a network on best practices in microfinance, offers downloadable guides on rural microfinance for value chain development.

The Small Enterprise Education and Promotion (SEEP) Network, *www.seepnetwork.org*, offers downloadable microenterprise training materials also specifically for microfinance.

MicroLINKS (Microenterprise Learning Information and Knowledge Sharing), *www.microlinks.org*, a service of the USAID microenterprise development programme, offers downloadable training materials for the development of financial services, including value-chain finance.

The Microfinance Management Institute (MFMI), *www.themfmi.org*, a US-based NGO, offers downloadable training material for MFIs capacity building.

The Global Development Research Center (GDRC), *www.gdrc.org*, hosts a virtual library on microfinance news and case studies.

CHAPTER 11

COFFEE QUALITY

COFFEE QUALITY

TWO SPECIES AND TWO PROCESSING METHODS

Coffee (Coffea) is the major genus of the Rubiaceae family, which includes well over 500 genera and over 6,000 species. The genus Coffea itself comprises numerous species. Only two of them are currently of real economic importance:

- Coffea arabica, referred to in the trade as arabica and accounting for 60%-70% of world productio;
- Coffea canephora (or coffea robusta) called robusta in the trade and making up 30%-40% of world production.

Two other species are traded to a very limited extent: Coffea liberica (liberica), and coffea excelsa (excelsa).

The share of arabica fell from about 80% of world production in the 1960s to around 60% by the turn of the century. Initially this was because of strong growth of robusta production in Brazil and parts of Africa, but more recently because of the emergence of Asia as the world's leading robusta producing region.

The original arabica strains generally produce good liquors with acidity and flavour, but they are susceptible to pests and diseases. This has led to the development of a number of different varieties that show better tolerance. Some quality purists consider that some of these varieties lack the quality characteristics that created coffee's popularity. Others argue that the bottom line for many producers simply does not permit them to concentrate on just the traditional or original varieties.

There are two main primary processing methods: the unwashed or dry process, which produces naturals, and the washed or wet process, which produces washed coffees. In the dry process the ripe cherries are dried in their entirety after which they are mechanically decorticated to produce the green bean. In the washed or wet process the ripe cherries are pulped and fermented to remove the sticky sugary coating called mucilage that adheres to the beans (this can also be done mechanically), and the beans are then washed and dried.

There is a third process in which the ripe cherry is pulped and dried 'as is' with the mucilage still adhering to the parchment skin. Originally called semi-washed in Africa, this process is gaining considerable importance in Brazil where it occupies a place in-between the dry and wet processes and is simply called 'pulped natural'. In other countries, for example in the Great Lakes region of Central Africa, semi-washed coffee has been laboriously produced for many decades using small hand pulpers.

In all procedures the parchment skin is later removed mechanically after drying.

THE DEFINITION OF QUALITY

There are many differing views as to what constitutes 'quality'. But it can be said that the quality of a parcel of coffee comes from a combination of the botanical variety, topographical conditions, weather conditions, and the care taken during growing, harvesting, storage, export preparation and transport.

Botanical variety and topographical conditions are constants and therefore dominate the basic or inherent character of a coffee. Weather conditions are variable and cannot be influenced, resulting in fluctuating quality from one season to another.

Growing, harvesting, storage, export preparation and transport are variables that can be influenced. They involve intervention by human beings, whose motivation is a key factor in the determination of the end quality of a parcel of green coffee. Depending on their marketing priorities people's efforts will fluctuate between the highest possible level, regardless of the cost, and the bare minimum, in order to reduce costs and optimize revenues and margins. Efforts to promote quality are prejudiced by world market prices and the degree to which buyers are willing to reward attention to the safeguarding and improvement of quality with adequate premiums for better than average quality.

NB: The following sections are targeted mainly at assisting smaller operators, growers and exporters alike, to make headway in the development of coffee quality (and marketability). It therefore deals mostly with arabica quality as it relates to the quality expectations in the exemplary and medium quality segments of the market. Mainstream type coffees and robustas are dealt with separately, although the discussion on 'quality' is relevant to all those producing and exporting coffee. Quality requirements for exemplary type or fine robustas, and for those used in espresso, are largely comparable to those for arabica and just as stringent.

QUALITY AND AVAILABILITY DETERMINE THE TARGET MARKET

The trouble with the pursuit of quality is not just that the term itself is a somewhat nebulous concept. First of all, the vast bulk of world coffee exports consists of medium to average quality coffee: mainstream coffee. Secondly, the extra effort to produce top quality may not always be adequately rewarded and, thirdly, there is also a lively and substantial world trade in coffee of poor and inferior quality.

PROCESSING: SCHEMATIC OVERVIEW

Figure 11.1 Processing of coffee cherries and green coffee beans

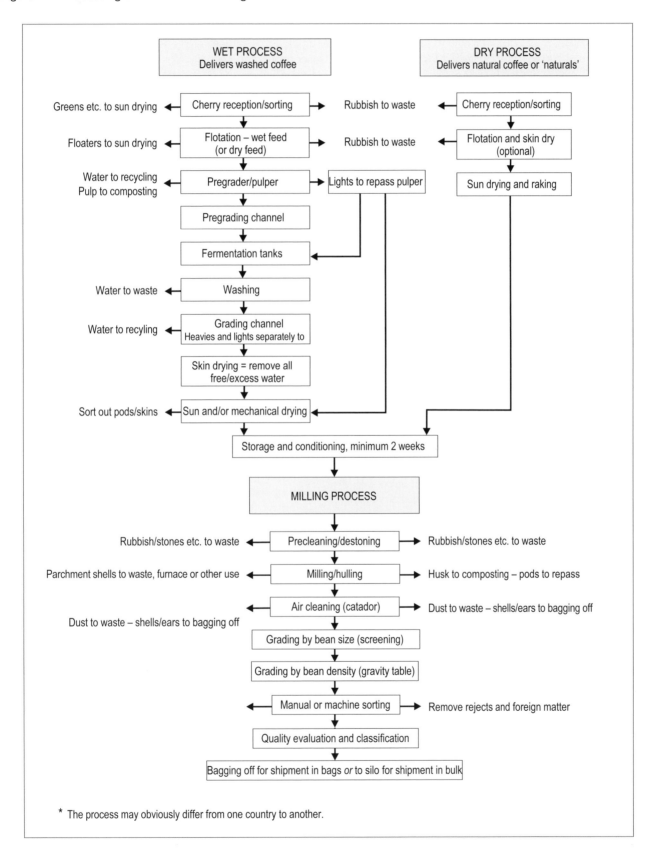

* The process may obviously differ from one country to another.

Quality discussions are further complicated when one separates coffee by species or by type of processing. There are arabicas and robustas, both wet and dry processed, and each with different quality aspects. Then there is also the question of whether the coffee will be sold as whole bean, as roast and ground, or as soluble. Appearances can also cause some confusion. It would be a mistake to think that quality means only exceptionally good looking (visually perfect), bold beans. Small bean coffees can also show excellent quality. Conversely, visually perfect, bold beans could in fact hide very unpleasant cup characteristics. The pursuit of quality is therefore not restricted to top or exemplary coffee.

This is probably just as well, because not everyone is capable of producing exemplary quality. In reality there is a market for almost everything, from expensive top quality to qualities at the other end of the spectrum. There is room in the marketplace for just about anyone who honours their contractual obligations and who adequately satisfies the market's quality expectations for the type of coffee they produce.

Different markets have different preferences. Producers and exporters should therefore know where their coffee is likely to receive the best response and, as far as possible, tailor the quality to the requirements of the buyer.

QUALITY SEGMENTATION – FOUR CATEGORIES

EXEMPLARY QUALITY

Exemplary quality coffees have a high intrinsic value with a fine or unique cup, and are usually of quite limited availability. They are mostly retailed under straight estate or origin names. These are usually very well presented washed coffees, including some superior washed robustas, but also include some naturals (Ethiopian Harars, Yemeni Mochas, some Indonesian arabicas) and top organic coffees. They are true niche coffees.

HIGH QUALITY

High-quality coffees are good cupping coffees, well presented, but not necessarily visually perfect. They are retailed both as straight origins and as blends. This category includes good quality, well-prepared organic coffees, and washed as well as superior quality natural robustas. The market for this quality band is much broader and includes a good percentage of today's specialty coffee.

MAINSTREAM QUALITY

Mainstream quality coffee is fair average quality, reasonably well presented, but certainly not visually perfect. It will offer a decent, clean but not necessarily impressive cup. Many robustas are included in this category. It is estimated that mainstream qualities account for 85%-90% of world coffee consumption, while the share of exemplary and high quality coffee is less than 15% of the world market.

Mainstream qualities are often traded on description. Descriptions can be fairly loosely written in the contracts, but usually there is some degree of quality understanding. That means seller and buyer have jointly established the quality parameters which the seller is expected to respect, for shipment after shipment. It is to be hoped that buyers will take this into consideration when talking price. The advantage to the buyer is that they are virtually certain that the coffee will do for them what they expect from it, and the seller knows the buyer will come back time and again for more of the same, irrespective of whether the market is up or down. This is one of the main factors that work towards creating market security. Although given how easily interchangeable they are, for most of the more mundane coffees, price will always play the major role. Note that no roaster will accept a coffee without tasting it first, regardless of how it was described, which means that no exporter should ship any coffee without having done the same.

Quality descriptions without an accompanying understanding between buyer and seller as to quality can lead to problems. For example, 'fair average quality (FAQ)', or simply specifying the screen size and defect count together with 'guaranteed clean cup' or 'sound merchantable quality', all leave much to the imagination. Such descriptions say the absolute minimum about a coffee's quality and therefore the quality often fluctuates within a fairly wide range. Deliveries can be good, mediocre or really disappointing. Although the buyer has a quality requirement, they are likely to be modest in their expectations of coffees bought on a relatively vague description. Usually, this is reflected in the price that is offered.

UNDERGRADES OR LOWGRADES

Finally, there are the undergrades or lowgrades, which are basically everything that does not fit into any of the earlier descriptions. There has traditionally been an active trade in undergrade coffees because there was a definite demand for them. Not everyone always knows 'the price' for such coffees, which can make trading them very opportunistic.

For the United States market, undergrade coffee is any type of coffee that grades below GCA type 6 (120 defects per 370 grams). In mid-2002, United States Customs regulations prohibited the importation of coffee below GCA type 8 (610 defects per 370 grams) with suggestions from some quarters that this should be raised to type 7 (240 defects per 370 grams). Other importing markets do not normally specify that particular grades of coffee should not be imported, relying instead on general food and hygiene regulations.

The ICO has introduced a set of worldwide minimum export standards in an attempt to remove the lowest coffees from the market altogether. The higher risk of mould and therefore OTA, a mycotoxin occurring in lowgrades is also likely to reduce the demand for such coffee. See also chapter 12.

As a result, it may be that over time lowgrades and rejects will lose some or most of their commercial value, thereby becoming part of the producer's or exporter's cost calculation rather than representing an exportable coffee.

QUALITY AND PRODUCTION

Much, but not all, quality evaluation is subjective, and many people buy certain coffees because they get what they want from them. All exporters should know the market for the type of coffee they produce; it is pointless to offer the wrong coffee to the wrong market. Once the 'right' quality is established, it then needs to be produced in the most efficient and consistent manner.

Production and processing systems influence quality. Exporters can never be certain of all the components and inputs that make up consistent quality, but they should know the basic norms in climate, soil and other agricultural factors in the growing areas. Once this is known exporters can adjust their processing techniques to get the best result for the given agricultural environment. Even annual variations in climate can often be at least partly offset by processing adjustments.

The best quality is obtained from selective picking in which only red, ripe cherries are gathered by hand in successive picking rounds until most of the crop has been harvested. When coffee prices are low, this time and labour consuming method is expensive whereas stripping allows individual pickers to harvest between three and four times more per day, thereby reducing the number of picking rounds quite considerably.

Mechanical harvesting is carried out using hand-held machines or by large wheeled mechanical harvesters, often self-propelled. This reduces the number of picking rounds still further. However, bulk mechanical harvesting is not feasible in areas where coffee trees may carry ripe cherries and flowers or pinheads at the same time, i.e. where the year's harvest is split between early crop and main crop for example.

It is true that modern technology allows for fairly effective separation of ripe, unripe and overripe cherries that can then be processed separately. But even so, it is difficult to produce exemplary quality coffee when the cherries are simply stripped all at once, regardless of the degree of maturity.

VARIETY, SOILS AND ALTITUDE

The vast number of different coffees traded in the market represent an almost immeasurable number of combinations of variety, soil and altitude. The better combinations can obviously aspire to better prices but growers, especially smallholders, cannot easily change their location, that is, change their soil type or altitude. Commercial growers however can relatively easily change the variety they grow: depending on their cropping cycle, modern commercial farms automatically replant 10%-15% of their tree park annually. But the choice of variety can be difficult. It is in the best interest of growers to stay informed of the types of coffee available for planting, and to match the best variety to the soils and the altitude conditions of their farms. For smallholders uprooting and replanting are especially costly undertakings, requiring careful consideration and realistic advice concerning all the potential consequences. This applies equally to any genetically modified (GM) coffee that may appear in future. As yet there is no commercially available GM coffee, but work in this area has been underway during past decades.

RAIN FED OR IRRIGATED

Stressed trees cannot produce decent, well-formed cherries. Coffee is drought resistant, but not drought proof. It has remarkable recuperative power from dry spells, but like all living things it needs water to produce.

Only very few coffees from marginal rainfall areas have made it to the ranks of truly notable coffees. These notable coffees have specific, inherent quality aspects (linked to their variety) which command premiums high enough to compensate for very low yields. Non-irrigated coffee in marginal rainfall areas usually shows the greatest seasonal quality variation.

WET OR DRY PROCESSED

Washed arabica not only needs adequate rainfall or irrigation for growth, but also requires water for wet processing. In many areas it has not been uncommon to see multiple washing stations (or wet beneficios) using common sources of water, either small rivers or streams. Below-average rainfall can then result in insufficient or poor quality water for washing, thereby affecting directly the quality that is produced. Fortunately, in many areas the introduction of small eco-friendly pulping units that require relatively little water to function is helping to minimize water usage.

The preparation of natural or dry processed coffee does not use water, but the trees still require adequate water for growth. Harvesting and drying need dry conditions and the best natural coffees are obtained from areas that have little rain in the harvesting season. Examples are Yemeni Mochas and some Ethiopian Harars, but the largest group of natural arabicas comes from Brazil, with the best originating from areas where the cherry matures and dries quickly.

COST AND YIELD VERSUS QUALITY

If their coffee lacks the inherent quality to make it a best-seller capable of commanding premium prices, then most growers, and specifically estates, cannot tolerate low yields unless their input costs are low as well. Estates, especially when using irrigation, can optimize yields much more easily than can most smallholders. This can be done by planting high yielding and/or disease-free varieties, by increasing planting densities, or by applying larger amounts of inputs, especially fertilizer (although excessive use of fertilizer can result in thin, almost bitter liquors).

There is an element of truth in the often heard lament that such actions at times reduce quality, especially when taken to excess, for example very dense plant populations necessitating very high fertilizer applications. But the bottom line return from higher yields of medium to sometimes mediocre quality is at times better than that from lower yields of superior quality, even when higher prices are obtained.

Estate managers can usually take these considerations into account and so make relatively well-informed decisions. But when smallholders replant it is sometimes perhaps more a case of being recommended to do so, rather than a well-informed choice on their part. Yet for many smallholders it is not an easy matter to maintain the level of inputs required by higher yielding hybrids. In times of trouble, such as when prices fall, they run into difficulty and may finally end up with neither yield nor quality. Respect for the old adage that 'low inputs equal low yields, but also low and therefore sustainable cost' has in the past kept many smallholders, especially those without access to irrigation, going but, as some would argue, perhaps it has also kept them poor.

ESTATE OR SMALLHOLDER GROWN

It is not true that smallholders can never match the quality standards of estates. For years and years many smallholders in Kenya have consistently outperformed large and well-managed estates while growing the same varieties. But much depends on the personal circumstances of each individual smallholder and it is fair to say that many smallholders in the world face daunting circumstances.

There are no accurate data on the proportions of estate and smallholder coffee in the total world production, partly because there is no definitive measure of what constitutes a smallholder. But it is believed that over half the world's coffee crop is grown on farms of less than five hectares.

In Africa only about 5%-6% of the annual output of about 15 million bags is grown on estates. The remaining 95% or so is grown by people whose holdings range from perhaps 1 or 2

to 10 hectares, to just a few hundred trees in all, sometimes even less than that.

The world's main resource of original coffees, and their future, probably lies within the smallholder sector. Ironically, because of the heterogeneity of most of these coffees (a single shipment is made up from many small growers), they often fail to get into the exemplary segment of the specialty market because they lack visual perfection, or they are 'unknown' and it is easier to market well-known coffees. On the other hand, their availability is also not always adequate or regular enough to match expectation, which limits their scope in the marketplace.

HIGH QUALITY ARABICA

PREPARING HIGH QUALITY ARABICA – THE BASICS

Before targeting a market one should understand one's own product, and know how it might fit into one or the other of the many niches that make up the world coffee market. Even where individual producers grow the same varieties, there are differences in tree age, tree care, fertilization, processing, general maintenance and sometimes irrigation that cause coffee quality to vary from farm to farm, within the same geographical area, on the same mountain slope, and so on. When these differences are not too obvious it is possible to mix or blend such coffees into a stable, reasonably even quality. When the differences are too great, any blend becomes as good (or as bad) as its lowest components. One cannot hide poor quality by mixing it with better coffee.

The degree of quality variation will depend on the size of the production area or region, the variables in that area (altitude, soil, water), the number of individual growers, whether the coffee faces north or south, and so on. Although not always appreciated as such, the same applies to individual estates, though to a lesser extent. Estates may also have excellent, good and mediocre blocks. By mixing all the coffee as it comes off the trees an estate may produce an acceptable product, and if the variability is not too great it can even be a good product. Mixing is often the only way to obtain commercially viable quantities and there is no problem with this as long as it is done on an informed basis.

Perhaps the most important message here is that the uninformed mixing of different qualities or production batches is nearly always bad for business and for profits. Knowledgeable buyers will always recognize mixing, and in the end the grower or exporter may have to start all over again. In the meantime the reputation of the coffee or even an entire region may have been affected.

The meaning of the word 'quality' is often misinterpreted. Unfortunately many producers and exporters appear to believe that all one needs to do to make quality coffee is to clean up the appearance of their usual standard coffee by some regrading and additional sorting. Expertise is sometimes lacking, not only at the producing end but also at the consuming end. Large quantities of so-called quality coffee are traded which show no quality at all.

This is regrettable because, in the end, indifferent quality causes consumers to lose interest, as happened for example in the United States after the World War II, with devastating consequences for consumption there. Fortunately, in recent years the market share of the United States specialty or gourmet segment has been growing strongly, which has helped to reverse that trend.

Accepting that not every grower, region or even country can produce absolute top quality, or visually perfect coffee, then the alternative must be to present the best possible coffee for those markets that show appreciation for that quality by rewarding the effort that goes into producing it. Without reward, growers cannot afford to invest the time and energy required to produce quality. The words 'present the best possible coffee' are used here because it is not the intention of this guide to praise or condemn any one cultivar or variety. Preferences in different markets vary, and so do the prospects of different varieties, types and qualities of coffee.

Other than the wild, extremely bitter tasting Mascarocoffea (found wild in the forest on Madagascar), inherently bad tasting coffee does not exist. Even the poor Mascaro has a selling point – it is entirely free of caffeine – but apparently it is also sterile when crossed.

True, certain new cultivars may not deliver the quality characteristics of the original lines and this disappoints many coffee enthusiasts. But there is no inherently bad coffee, at least not when it is still on the tree. What happens to degrade the quality from then onwards is nearly always caused by human intervention.

When discussing quality from the production perspective it is well to remember that someone, somewhere, is expected to drink the coffee. When recommending planting or replanting with disease-resistant or high-yielding hybrid varieties, one should ensure that the growers are exposed to all relevant information. So also, what is the expected quality and marketability of the coffee? What are the experiences with that coffee in the potential growers' own environment? The decision to change the variety one plants has to be an informed decision, one that includes an assessment of the quality and marketing potential.

DEFINING QUALITY

Who defines quality? Behind every successful importer and roaster stands a satisfied body of consumers. But the final judge for growers is, simply put, the importer (or roaster) who pays a satisfactory price for a coffee and who does so on a sustained basis. Once you know what this person takes into account when judging your coffee, you can relate this to your entire production process and see where you need to take corrective or supportive action.

The first impression can make or break a coffee's prospects. The first impression a potential buyer gets of any coffee is when a sample of the green coffee is put in front of them. If the green immediately creates a negative impression then the least that will happen is that the coffee will be subject to bias from then onwards. The worst scenario is that the sample is not even tasted and is simply thrown away.

Many exporters complain of getting no response to samples they send out, but green coffee buyers are usually very busy people. Getting them to take time out to taste a new coffee is not always easy, especially if their first impression is not very positive. Hence, the need to target one's markets. It is not just costly, but almost pointless to send samples to all and sundry in the hope of achieving the odd hit.

HIGH QUALITY ARABICA (GREEN)

The aspect (or style) and the colour should be 'even'

The green beans should be of compatible shape or style, colour and size. They, and the roasted beans or the roast must give an impression of being reasonably even. This is most important for coffee that is to be retailed as roasted whole beans. Buyers know the green bean aspects that affect the liquor negatively and they consider these when evaluating any sample, irrespective of how they might use the coffee. Buyers dislike uneven greens because they can pose problems during roasting. The resulting uneven roasts do not appeal to consumers and in any case tend to produce lower liquor quality than do even roasts. Usually, uneven colour indicates the mixed harvesting of immature and ripe cherry, which also reflects negatively in the cup.

The bean shape or style can vary with the cultivar. Usually coffee from the same cultivar will not show great variation in terms of shape and style, whereas uniformity of size is determined by the degree of size grading which takes place. But mixing different cultivars within a single consignment can produce uneven looking coffees, even if all the beans conform to the same screen size. This is especially so if coffee from different cultivars that produce solid and softish beans respectively are mixed into the same batch. Softish beans usually have quite a different shape and style from solid beans; this will be especially evident in the roast.

If different cultivars have been interplanted, as could be the case on a smallholding where there might be no room to separate them, then there is little to be done at the harvest stage. An estate with blocks of different cultivars on the other hand could harvest and process them on different days, and hold them separately for example by colour coding each batch.

If coffee is collected commercially from different geographical production areas, care should be taken to verify its compatibility before mixing it, if necessary by making small trial blends by hand in proportion to the quantities to be mixed (bulked).

Colour is very important

The colour should be even and bright, especially so for mild, washed arabicas, which should never be dull, mottled or faded (going whitish).

Buyers dislike greens of uneven, faded, blotchy or dull colour because this hints at poor processing, incorrect moisture content and/or premature ageing of the coffee. All of these translate into reduced liquor quality, progressively becoming dull (bland) and common (ordinary). Remember that the buyer knows the actual shipment will still take time to reach them, so if the advance sample sent by air already shows such signs, the coffee itself may look still worse on arrival.

Drying affects the colour

Like wet processing, drying is also of extreme importance. At this stage a coffee's quality can literally be destroyed. Correct harvesting, processing and drying require maximum management input: having spent an entire year tending to and investing in the crop, do not then entrust its harvest and handling to poorly trained, unsupervised labour. Many potential candidate coffees fail to make it to the specialty market, and certainly to the exemplary segment, because their green appearance shows shortcomings during drying and storage.

The green appearance of naturals (dried in the cherry) habitually shows a brownish tinge and beans with brown silver-skins (often called foxy beans). In naturals this is quite acceptable, but for wet-processed (washed) coffees these are negative aspects because they can translate into fruitiness, sourness and even an over-fermented taste. The knowledgeable liquorer will usually downgrade such a washed coffee even before it is liquored. But even if the liquor is satisfactory, the coffee may still be rejected because the green appearance suggests it could hide something – the coffee looks unreliable.

Causes of poor colour

Dullish and sometimes brownish greens often result from (too rapid) mechanical drying, which also tends to flatten the liquor quality. Uneven colour is usually a consequence of poor drying techniques.

Uneven, mottled greens, often with mottled, blotchy, whitish or soapy beans, suggest the coffee was spread too thickly when drying, that it was not turned often enough, or that it was dried too rapidly. Such beans subsequently show up as mottled beans (also called quakers by some) in the roast.

Mechanical drying is often used if the climate or the tonnage to be handled do not allow one to depend entirely on sun drying, that is, if the weather is too unreliable during the harvest season, or the quantities of cherry to be handled are simply too big. For washed robusta it is also a means of avoiding (secondary) fermentation. Collectors (those who buy parchment or dried coffee in cherry from small farmers) often use mechanical drying to bring the moisture content down to acceptable levels. Subsequent storage or conditioning in bulk bins with airflow capability then evens out the moisture content throughout the entire parcel or stack.

Brownish tinges in arabica greens can result from the harvesting of overripe cherries, or from allowing too many skins to enter the fermentation tanks. The use of dirty water, under-fermentation, insufficient washing after natural fermentation, or the mechanical removal of mucilage are other contributing causes. In washed arabicas foxy beans (where the silver-skin has turned reddish-brown) are usually due to the harvesting of overripe cherry, or keeping cherries overnight before pulping.

Fading is an indication of problems. A generally bleached or fading colour suggests that the coffee is ageing, or that it was over-dried, especially so in arabica. When the fading is more pronounced around the edges of the beans (which turn whitish) then this suggests the coffee was taken off the drying racks or grounds too early, or it was stored in moist, humid conditions, without adequate air circulation. If some of the beans are also generally softish and whitish then the experienced buyer knows such a coffee will never make it to the specialty market, let alone the roasted whole bean segment. Such a sample may find its way directly to the waste bin because such coffee has already lost its fresh taste and will definitely show a dull (bland) and common (ordinary) liquor.

Prolonged storage can be another cause of loss of colour (and quality). In this respect the Mesoamerican Development Institute first carried out experiments in 2005 in Costa Rica, storing green coffee in airtight cocoons and comparing quality against coffee from the same batch stored in the conventional manner. The two-piece hermetic storage cocoon consisted of a top cover and bottom floor that are joined with a PVC tongue and groove zipper, similar to those used to close environmental safety suits. Coffee stored in this manner was found to have retained colour, flavour and quality much better, also over prolonged periods and without risk of infestation by insects or fungi. Later experiments have confirmed this and advanced hermetic storage technology is now gaining considerable ground in both the storage and transportation of green coffee. Details of the original research and subsequent applications are available on *www.mesoamerican.org* and *www.grainpro.com*.

How to improve or maintain colour

When drying mechanically, experiment with the temperature. Some older types of dryers expose coffee to very high temperatures. Be careful coffee is not dried too rapidly or over-dried. Some modern (and quite simple) dryers use ambient air circulation, which minimizes such problems. Their suitability also depends on the prevailing climatic conditions.

For arabica coffee, try combining mechanical and sun drying, with the initial drying done mechanically followed by a finishing-off period of exposure to sunlight. This improves the colour generally and appears to reduce the effect on colour of the mechanical drying. Some flat bed dryers and pan dryers incorporate a sliding roof which permits managed exposure to sunlight.

When sun drying, do not spread drying coffee, cherry and parchment, thicker than one hand's width. Use an even drying surface and spread the coffee evenly, with no hills and valleys. Stir or turn the coffee regularly to ensure even drying. Cover parchment coffee during the hottest time of the day to avoid it cracking open and creating mottled beans. Cover all coffee during rain and at night. For smallholders, drying trays are an excellent drying method: easily taken out and returned to store. If they are used under plastic roofing, then one simultaneously achieves good air circulation, heat retention and cover against rain.

Moisture content and drying

There is no exact standard for ideal moisture content. Not all coffee is the same, and circumstances differ from country to country. In general, 11% is probably a good target for most coffee, but in any case larger roasters are increasingly prescribing what they consider an appropriate moisture content. Coffee above 12.5% moisture should never be shipped – the only exception could be some specialty coffees that traditionally have high moisture content, such as Indian monsooned coffees.

If past experience suggests buyers are generally satisfied then stick to good established practice and monitor the moisture content regularly. Remember that when coffee is dried on flat surfaces (such as tarpaulins or concrete) it will heat up and thus dry out more rapidly than when it is spread on raised tables or trays that allow air to circulate around it. When getting close to the moisture target, monitor every hour. Always use properly calibrated moisture meters and test them regularly, before each season. If in doubt about the exact percentage, take the coffee off a little earlier rather than letting it become noticeably over-dried. This is especially recommended if decent storage sheds or, better still, ventilated bins or silos are available for conditioning.

Apart from later loss of cup quality, under-drying may also cause mould. In severe cases, under-dried coffees may develop fungi and moulds. These have always been undesirable, but increasing consumer attention to mycotoxins in agricultural produce, specifically ochratoxin A (OTA), is a real cause for concern for some coffee producers. Clean, proper and efficient drying and storage of coffee is probably the best defence against mould growth

and its potential consequences. This and other food safety issues are reviewed in detail in chapter 12.

To repeat once more: many receivers stipulate a maximum permissible moisture content on both shipment and arrival. Producers and exporters need to develop appropriate moisture content management techniques if they are to cope with this.

Over-drying costs money. This makes it as serious as under-drying: not only is weight, and therefore money, lost unnecessarily, but the accompanying loss of colour also translates directly into lower liquor quality. When moisture drops below 10%, aroma, acidity and freshness begin to fade away and at 8% or below they have completely disappeared. For this reason the ICO wants to see shipments of coffee below 8% moisture content prohibited.

Like under-dried coffee, over-dried coffee should not be mixed with correctly dried coffee. The two are not compatible. Remember also that climatic conditions in many storage sheds are not ideal: they may be keeping the coffee dry but they are certainly not keeping it cool and the coffee may therefore continue drying out. Quality loss due to over-drying cannot be reversed, and is unacceptable. Over-dried coffee also breaks up more easily during milling. This increases the percentage of ears, shells and broken beans, which further reduces both the quality and the value.

Finally, do everything possible to avoid letting coffee sit around endlessly after it has been containerized for export. This can be especially problematic for landlocked countries from where coffee must travel long distances to the port of shipment. If containers are kept in the open, exposed to open sun in holding grounds, on railway flatcars or trucks it could lead to overheating and condensation. See also chapter 5.

Over-drying also affects the way a coffee roasts. Coffees with a moisture content as low as 8% may certainly take the average specialty roaster by surprise. This is because such coffees tend to roast to completion much faster than these roasters expect. Smaller specialty roasters do not always have moisture meters, and they can and do get into trouble with such coffees. Quite apart from the reduction in acidity and flavour that over-drying causes, the end-user may also be embarrassed – all good reasons never to buy that coffee again.

Appearance – avoid obvious defects

Coffees containing black beans, obvious stinkers, water-damaged beans and foreign matter stand no chance, not only in the quality market, but also not for the great majority of roasters. This should be obvious to anyone in the coffee business, so what follows is limited to the perhaps not so well recognized appearance (green) defects that put off quality buyers and cause them to reject one coffee in favour of another. This explains why seemingly good samples are rejected or why some buyers simply do not respond to them at all.

'Coated.' Silver-skin has adhered to more than half a bean's surface. The immediate consequence is that the green appearance suffers because the silver-skin obscures the bean's surface and true colour. Too much coatedness does not look good. The roaster also knows that the silver-skin tends to burn off during roasting and the resultant chaff can pose problems.

Coated beans are caused by drought and by trees over-bearing. Both of these tend to affect the cherry in similar ways, and the coffee's style and general aspect are usually not impressive. General coatedness can also result from under-fermentation. Beans that are entirely coated may originate from unripe cherry. Coffees with pronounced coatedness often produce common, ordinary liquors. The experienced coffee buyer will tend to instinctively discriminate against such coffees, also because the roast will usually contain ragged, soft and sometimes pale beans.

If possible one should not mix coffee from drought-affected trees with that of others. However, many coated beans will lose their silver-skin during hulling (or polishing, where this is installed). Very coated beans are usually also ragged and smaller or lighter than the norm and may be removed during grading and sorting.

Before rushing into polishing to remove the silver-skin, first establish whether the coatedness of your coffee is a problem and, if so, what the cause might be. Dry polishing as such adds nothing to coffee quality, but does improve the colour and overall appearance (unless the polisher has excessively heated the beans, which has the opposite effect). Correct (i.e. cool) polishing may make a coffee more easily saleable. Some robustas are (wet) polished as a matter of course, but for arabica it is advisable to first verify whether polishing makes commercial sense.

'Ragged or uneven.' Ragged refers to drought-affected and misshapen beans that give the green an uneven aspect. Too many ragged beans in a coffee suggest less than optimal quality in that neither green nor roast are pleasing to the eye and such coffee is not usually suitable for sale as whole roasted bean. Ragged coffees often produce mediocre liquors, but one cannot generalize because some sought-after original coffees show beans with naturally meandering centre cuts as a matter of course. Great care must be taken therefore to distinguish between the visual or cosmetic aspects of different coffees and the quality.

An uneven green can also be the result of mixing different coffees, for example a roundish bean (Bourbon) with a flattish bean (Typica), or a boat-shaped (Ethiopian) variety. Where possible it is probably best to leave decisions on the mixing of different cultivars and types to the buyer.

The fundamental causes of raggedness can be addressed only in the field. All processing can do is: separate light and heavy cherry before pulping (by grading or flotation: smallholders can even do this using a simple bucket or basin); systematic washing and grading after pulping; and intensive size and especially density separation during dry (export) processing. The most useful tool in this respect is without any doubt the gravity table (table densimétrique in French). Properly set and supervised, this machine will eliminate many, if not most, ragged beans.

'Pulper-nipped beans' are the result of incorrectly set pulpers. They are very difficult to remove during export grading and sorting. If those beans are discoloured as well they can also cause fermented, foul or unclean cups as described in the next paragraph. Experienced buyers will notice pulper-nipped beans and the risk message they convey.

Insect and pest damage

Controlling insects and other pests can be a problem, especially in countries where coffee is grown in small patches, sometimes of a few hundred trees only and often widely dispersed and scattered over substantial areas. Such conditions make effective treatment difficult. Insect damage in the beans suggests less than optimal care of the trees. It detracts from the coffee's visual attraction, and buyers know that insect damaged beans cause common, ordinary and sometimes tainted liquors.

Most insect damage may be quite obvious to the eye, but insects can also be the cause of invisible stinkers with dirty water penetrating an insect-stung (or pulper-nipped) bean during fermentation and causing an internal chemical reaction. Such beans may look sound on the outside, but can throw unclean or even fermented cups that degrade an entire consignment.

Insect and pest damage can be controlled only in the field. Eliminating damaged beans after harvesting costs more and does not address the root cause of the problem. However, the flotation (grading by density) of cherry before pulping is of great importance, as is the subsequent separation of parchment into lights and heavies in the washing and grading channel. These are important principles of wet processing. Smallholders who use hand pulpers should try floating the lights off in a bucket or basin filled with water before pulping – usually this makes a major difference to the end product.

Failing this, the coffee miller's best friend, the gravity table, presents the best and cheapest option for eliminating damaged and light beans. But of course the table works well only if it is properly set and operated; the attendants must know why they are doing what they are doing. Catadors (pneumatic separation using blast air) do the same job, but less efficiently, and work best if the coffee has first been size graded.

This is not the place to argue for or against the wet processing or washing of coffee. There is no doubt, however, that

---

Box 11.1   Screen sizes

Coffee is graded by size using rotating or shaking screens, replaceable metal sheets that have round holes in them that retain beans over a certain size and allow smaller beans to pass. Screen sizes are expressed as numbers (e.g. robusta grade one screen 16), or by letters (e.g. arabica grade AA – indicating a bold bean), or by descriptions (e.g. bold, medium or small bean). It all depends on the trade custom in any given country. Intermediate screen sizes (e.g. 16.5), are important in some producing countries but disregarded in others. However, nearly all coffee for export is graded to exclude the largest and smallest beans, as well as broken beans and other particles.

It is not always easy or possible to achieve a 100% accurate screen (e.g. nil passing through screen 16). Where a 100% accurate screen is required then marginally increasing the size of the holes to give a small tolerance in the screen may provide the required result.

Slotted screens with oblong slits (usually 4 mm or 4.50 mm wide) are used in some countries to remove peaberries (single oblong beans in a cherry, the result of a genetic aberration because normally there are two beans in a cherry), which are sought after in some consuming countries

Standard coffee round screen dimensions

Screen number	10	12	13	14	15	16	17	18	19	20
ISO dimensions (mm)	4.00	4.75	5.00	5.60	6.00	6.30	6.70	7.10	7.50	8.00

---

correctly operated washing stations are an important quality control tool, at the very start of the processing chain.

Bean size

'Below-size' and 'light beans' in a consignment are a direct consequence of inadequate size and density separation, partly during primary processing but mostly during dry or export processing. Not only do too many smalls and lights spoil the coffee's green appearance, but large and small, or heavy and light beans, also do not roast well together. This is because smalls and lights will over-roast during the time it takes for the roasting of the larger, heavier beans to be completed. There are strict limits to the proportion of smalls and lights roasters may tolerate in whole bean coffee; if a coffee exceeds their in-house tolerance for smalls and lights, then out it goes.

Not all size grading is accurate. Opinions differ on the accuracy of different size grading techniques (vibratory or flatbed versus rotary or cylinder graders for example). But, often, when operated at full design capacity, graders do not necessarily produce accurate separation, so the throughput must be regulated. This can be especially troublesome if a grader is directly auto-fed by a preceding processing unit, or if the product quality is quite variable. It is always advisable therefore to have a manufacturer commission any new milling, grading and sorting equipment, using the actual product that is to be handled. Regulating the intake flow by placing a buffer silo or feed hopper ahead of the grader can improve grading accuracy quite considerably, but constant supervision will always be necessary. The grading accuracy should be verified regularly, using hand or sample screens that should be kept handy, near the grader.

When grading whole bean type coffee, bear in mind that some very large beans may not be particularly attractive as they are often soft or misshapen. Such beans become especially noticeable in the roast appearance. They can be easily removed by the insertion of a large size screen (number 20 screen for example) ahead of the regular screens. This is also helpful when elephant beans are present (beans which have become inter-twined in the cherry and which nearly always break up, if not during milling then during roasting).

One easy way to quickly verify whether a shipment corresponds to the selling sample is to check the coffee's size and density composition. Pass 100 g or 200 g of the original sample and the shipment sample over the appropriate size screens and compare the percentages. Do the same with the lights by counting them. Many shipments appear visually to be a match, but turn out not to be when this simple test is applied. Buyers know this, and so should the exporter.

Bean density

'Lights,' 'shells' or 'ears,' and 'brokens' are all beans or parts of beans that are notably lighter in weight (i.e. less dense) than the average bean in a particular size grade. Note this distinction: although a small but solid bean will weigh less than a large one, it does not automatically follow that it is a light bean. Lights usually have natural causes such as drought, stress, or picking of immature cherry. All of these result in misshapen, shrivelled and soft beans. The breaking up of beans during hulling and other processing actions (including over-drying) results in shells, ears, brokens, chips and so on. Such beans and bits and pieces detract from the green appearance. They cause similar roasting problems to smalls in large bean grades, and they very definitely depress the cup quality.

Not only do light and broken beans reduce the flavour, acidity and body of a coffee, but they often also introduce a flattish, common or ordinary taste. They can turn a potentially fine cup into a mediocre one. Proper density separation is therefore of extreme importance, especially when the coffee beans to be dealt with are also somewhat heterogeneous (uneven) by nature.

Lights and brokens are removed pneumatically using strong airflows (catador), or by a fluidization process (gravity table). Both separate coffee by density but catadors are usually less accurate than gravity tables.

Catadors are most useful for the initial clean-up of a coffee, directly after hulling (and polishing if installed). The strong air current removes most chips and small lights that would otherwise complicate or slow the subsequent processing. However, gravity tables are at their most efficient when the coffee has already been size graded. This is because the size grader will have removed most of the remaining smalls, and the product to be separated is therefore already of reasonably uniform density.

Catador and gravity table settings must be based on the type and quality of the coffee under process and on the desired result. Constant, well-informed supervision is essential, especially if the product is not homogeneous, for example if there has been no prior size grading. Again, an intermediate buffer silo or feed hopper permitting variable feed can ensure that the intake flow is correctly set. This is essential if optimal results are to be achieved.

This applies to all grades of coffee, not only whole bean grades, because the value of the small bean coffees that are an inevitable by-product of the larger, whole bean, grades must also be maximized. Small lights, ears and chips in a grade of whole but small beans (C grade, pea-berry, screen 15 and even screen 14) cause exactly the same problems: they make the coffee awkward to roast and degrade the liquor quality. There are good markets for decent grinders (used for roast and ground only) if the coffee is homogeneous and properly graded.

Sorting

Bleached, mottled, whitish, blotchy, soapy and discoloured beans generally cannot be removed by size or density grading but there is no place for them in quality coffee (although there is probably some tolerance for them in the lower priced segment of the general market). Nearly all such beans are caused by moisture and drying problems, but discolouring can also be due to oxidization, contact with soil, metal, dirty water and so on. The gravity table can help, but in the end the only effective way to remove these beans is through manual or electronic sorting.

Not only do such beans effectively ruin the coffee's green appearance but they also show up in the roast as softs or quakers, pales, mottled beans and so on, and they definitely

affect the cup quality. The buyer of quality coffees will not tolerate such beans.

Modern sorting equipment is capable of many and extremely varied tasks. The most recent developments use laser technology. Such equipment can be quite costly though whereas in some countries sorting by hand is an important source of otherwise scarce employment. Deciding whether to hand or machine sort depends on individual circumstances, the tonnages to be sorted, and the cost of labour. Smaller producers of specialty coffee usually give their coffee at least a quick going over by hand, especially if labour is relatively cheap. Some expend much time and care on sorting, depending on their target market.

Individual countries and operators have different ideas, systems and methods when it comes to sorting green coffee and there is no point in discussing these here because different circumstances pose their own particular requirements and problems. But there are two general principles which are important.

- Know your sorting capabilities. When preparing advance samples for dispatch abroad, ensure that your expectations of your sorting capacity do not exceed reality. It is only human to remove more rather than fewer defects from an advance sample 'as the coffee will be properly sorted in any case'. It is exceedingly annoying for the buyer to find later that the coffee is 'almost' but not quite as well sorted as the advance sample.

- A good working environment and decent lighting is necessary for people to sort coffee efficiently and correctly. Many manual sorting processes still consist of people sitting on the floor in dark and dingy warehouses, each facing a heap of coffee. The sorters closest to the door can see the best – the remainder have to make do. This will never do for the preparation of quality coffee, whether arabica or robusta, because the sorting will be neither optimal nor even. This kind of operation is best kept hidden from visiting buyers altogether.

If sorting belts are too expensive, then at least invest in sorting tables and benches. These are easily made up by any competent carpenter. Such tables speed up the sorting process, which then is also more easily supervised. Sorting belts are moving conveyor belts, usually with auto-feed and auto-advance, providing room for 12 or 24 sorters to sit on either side. Sorting tables are tables with a fluorescent light over them, seating six or eight people. The tabletop is divided into squares with raised edges. A small hole in each square allows sorted coffee to fall into a bag attached underneath; rejects go into receptacles fixed to the table's edge.

Sampling

The golden rule of quality coffee is to do the best possible within one's capabilities. This means demonstrating first of all through the green appearance that a certain amount of care has gone into the coffee's preparation. Such care will automatically come through in the roast and in the liquor. If potential buyers do not see such signs of care in a green coffee sample they may discard it without even tasting it.

The liquor will always show a coffee's real character, however exciting or dull that may be, but at least the liquor should never show any of the obvious defects mentioned earlier. If it does, do not send the sample to someone who you know buys only quality. Apart from the rejection that will follow, you may inadvertently ruin any chance of future business with that buyer because you have demonstrated an obvious lack of expertise.

Samples must be representative. When you send a sample be sure that it is fully representative of the actual coffee or, if you do not have the coffee in stock, be sure that you can match the quality. It is useful to note the following sampling definitions:

- Stocklot samples are samples of the actual coffee that will be shipped if a contract is concluded.

- Approval samples are sent for coffees sold 'subject approval of sample'. Such samples must be drawn from the actual parcel intend for shipment. Remember, a sale subject to approval is not really a sale until the buyer approves the sample.

- Type samples represent a quality agreed with the buyer, expected to be matched in all respects. If you cannot match the sample quality in some respect, tell your buyer sooner rather than later.

- Indication samples are an indication of what you expect to be able to ship, usually followed later by an approval sample which shows what you actually propose to ship.

- Shipment or outturn samples are fully representative samples of the coffee that has actually been shipped.

HIGH QUALITY ARABICA (ROAST)

Type or quality

As with the green, first impressions are very important. A roast that is dull, uneven, open and/or soft (with ears or shells) immediately raises suspicion. Conversely, a bright or brilliant, even and solid roast is not just pleasing to the eye, but also suggests good cupping potential. For the average consumer of whole bean roasted coffee the most obvious eye-catching aspect is probably the evenness. An even roast is therefore a prerequisite for almost any coffee to make it to the end consumer in whole bean form. There are some exceptions: a few very well established naturals with less than optimal roast appearance are sold as whole bean, but these are coffees with an established reputation. The consumer is convinced they are good even if they do not 'look so good'. But 'new' coffees whose appearance does not match the general perception of what quality coffee should look like do not stand much chance in the whole bean market segment.

The potential causes and remedies for many individual roast defects have been identified earlier. The following therefore deals with more general roast defects that are under the control of producers and exporters.

An even roast is all-important. In an even roast almost all the beans have roasted to about the same colour and brightness, with a white or whitish centre-cut that is not too irregular. There should be few obvious defects, preferably none.

Wet-processed coffees usually produce the best roasts, especially when the parchment has been properly sun-dried. Brilliant roasts with white centre-cuts are a hallmark of well-prepared and well-dried coffee. Under-drying, on the other hand, produces dull roasts. The centre-cuts in particular are indicative of the care taken during the processing and drying of washed and semi-washed coffee. Naturals (dried in the cherry) usually show dullish roasts with brownish centre-cuts and this makes it difficult to present most of them as whole bean. Unless well managed, mechanical drying using hot air may also dull the roast appearance.

A brilliant or bright roast almost shines up at the viewer. It has a well defined, white to brilliantly white centre-cut and the beans are usually fairly hard or solid. When considering mixing or blending, one should always consider the roast of each individual component: mixing bright, solid roasts with dull and usually softer roasts may well result in an unattractive overall view that renders the coffee less suitable for presentation as whole bean.

Dull and dullish roasts lack lustre and brightness. This is usually caused by under-drying, or sometimes by mechanical drying. Over-fermentation and the picking of overripe cherry can also cause dull roasts and will especially affect the colour of the centre-cut.

In washed coffee, brownish centre-cuts or no centre-cuts are suggestive of overripes, over-fermentation, use of dirty water or the presence of too many skins in the fermentation tanks. But naturals usually tend towards duller roasts, and brownish or almost no centre-cuts as a matter of course.

Uneven roasts

There are many potential causes of uneven roasts. They include: the picking of immature or droughted cherry; uneven fermentation, including the mixing of different batches of washed or semi-washed coffee, which have not necessarily been fermented or washed to the same degree; too rapid or uneven drying; and insufficient separation of light coffee during primary and/or export processing. Incomplete fermentation causes dull roasts, and when mixed with brighter roasting coffee, gives an aspect of general unevenness.

Immature cherry usually translates into pales or semi-pales in the roast (beans which are yellowish to yellow in colour). But bleached or colourless green beans, including yellow beans or ambers, also cause pales in the roast. Not only do (bright) pales ruin the roast appearance and cause clearly visible yellow particles in ground coffee, they also introduce commonness into the liquor.

Mottled and blotchy beans are caused by uneven drying. The end consumer may not necessarily notice them as a defect, but their appearance in the roast suggests to examiners that the quality of the coffee is likely to deteriorate rather quickly. This may cause them to reject it altogether.

Softs, brokens and raggedness

'Softs' often go together with pales, but a roast can also present a general aspect of softness. In this case the beans are generally open, and the centre-cuts are not well defined and may be brownish in colour. Some cultivars have a tendency towards soft roasts, especially when grown at low altitudes, but in the main softs are caused by poor drying and immature (very coated) coffee.

Bleached, soapy, mottled, discoloured and blighted beans usually show up in the roast as softs or quakers, and also as pales. Careful sorting of the green beans helps to eliminate them, but it is difficult to achieve 100% accuracy.

Broken beans in a roast reflect inadequate separation during processing (both wet and dry), over-drying, incorrectly set equipment, and the presence of misshapen and deformed beans that have broken up during the roasting: all problems related to processing, although some cultivars do produce larger proportions of deformed beans (elephant beans). In some cases, drought or nutrition stress seems to result in larger numbers of small elephant beans (these are of considerable concern to the grower as they mostly break up during processing and roasting).

Ragged roasts also suggest the wrong coffees have been mixed together. For example, droughted coffee has been mixed with good coffee, or incompatible cultivars have been mixed such as larger flat-shaped beans with smaller, rounder or boat-shaped beans.

Measuring roast colour

Measuring roast colour is important. The type of roast – light, medium or dark – has a definite bearing on quality.

- The darker a roast, the less pronounced the acidity and different flavour aspects (as well as defects) of the liquor, but the heavier the body.
- The lighter a roast, the more pronounced the acidity and flavour (and defects), but the lighter the body.

Different markets roast coffee differently. Exporters should understand the type of roast their buyers need. But 'light, medium and dark' mean different things to different people: they are subjective terms. See also chapter 12, Quality control.

The Specialty Coffee Association of America (SCAA) has developed a points system to classify the degree – the colour – of different roast types. The system consists of eight numbered colour disks against which one matches a sample of finely ground, roasted coffee, usually pressed into a laboratory petri dish. In this way one assigns the roast an approximate number on what is commonly called the Agtron Gourmet Scale, ranging from #95 (lightest roast) at intervals of 10 down to #25 (the darkest common roast).

This helpful tool enables producers and roasters to speak the same language when discussing 'the roast' of a coffee. It is available from the SCAA's resource centre in Long Beach, California – see *www.scaa.org*.

HIGH QUALITY ARABICA (TASTE)

The importance of liquoring

First impressions are vitally important. If the green does not make it to the roasting room then the coffee will never be tasted. It is pointless therefore to send samples which do not demonstrate at least a minimal effort at creating a presentable product – the amount of effort one puts in depends on the market segment that is to be targeted or, perhaps, the premium one is trying to attract.

Remember that, in principle, there is no inherently bad coffee. If a coffee presents really poor quality, the cause can usually be traced to poor harvesting and post harvest processing, drying, storage and handling.

It is absolutely essential to maintain stringent standards of cleanliness at all stages, especially in wet processing. If this is done, almost any coffee has the potential to show a presentable green with at least a passable cup or liquor. How your potential buyer judges that liquor will depend on the type of coffee, and on how it matches their specific preferences and objectives. A buyer will not buy a coffee that does not fit their requirements, even though they may have appreciated it for what it was. Aspiring sellers therefore need to understand the requirements of the market segment they are thinking of targeting.

Without the ability to taste or liquor coffee one cannot be a successful exporter. All coffee is sold to be drunk, and someone, somewhere will taste a coffee before it is roasted. Sending out samples of obviously unsuitable or even unpleasant coffee is a recipe for disaster. It conveys the impression that the seller does not know his own product, or does not care. Such samples also suggest that the seller might ship unclean-tasting coffee and many buyers, especially smaller ones, will avoid them. Inexperienced suppliers represent potential danger. If on arrival the cup or liquor is no good, then the coffee cannot be used. This causes a shortfall in supply, which has to be made up from elsewhere, and the buyer has to find a way to dispose of the offending coffee, which meanwhile may be taking up finance and storage space.

Liquoring is also important for other reasons. A seller who cannot properly evaluate the quality of their own coffee also cannot value it against the price at which the competition or other origins are selling. Without liquoring it is nearly impossible to judge whether one's asking price, for example, is too high or too low.

Liquoring – the basics

At the very minimum the liquor has to be clean. There should be no off-flavours or taints in the cup. The liquor must be reliable and constant: the coffee should liquor the same every time it is tasted. When making up a shipment it is no good tasting a single cup and thinking that the coffee is fine, when many buyers as a matter of course will taste five or ten cups over two or more individual roasts.

When roasting your own coffee, remember the type of roast your buyer prefers and match it in your own preparation. But also remember that sometimes a lighter roast may accentuate defective liquor aspects that darker roasts tend to hide. Specialty roasters in particular usually roast small batches and taste every batch. This means a coffee will be tasted many times over. If it is unreliable (meaning different or even unclean cups simply 'appear' from time to time) this will be spotted. Bulk users of commercial grade coffee also sample very accurately and will easily spot an unreliable parcel. See also chapter 5.

What constitutes 'quality' is a subjective judgement. Quality is open to many interpretations, but experienced tasters will seldom disagree on whether a coffee is clean in the cup or not. What they may argue about is whether the type and degree of uncleanliness, or off-flavour, is such as to render the coffee unacceptable. Clearly one will be more tolerant of quality defects in a bargain-priced grinder to be used in the general mass market, than one would be of taste defects in a top-priced, supposedly exemplary coffee.

Experienced buyers have a fair idea what to expect from certain origins and types of coffee. They know what those coffees can be used for. And so a sun-dried natural may present flavours that buyers know, accept and even appreciate in that type of coffee, but that they will absolutely not accept in a washed coffee. For example, the full body and often somewhat heavy, fruity taste of many good naturals does not appeal to buyers looking for acidic coffees. The experienced liquorer will know what coffee suits which buyer or market. Anyone wishing to get into the business of selling quality will have to find this out if they want to make their mark.

Understand your buyer. Once a quality has been accepted it is most important to understand exactly why the buyer likes and continues to buy that particular coffee in preference to others. There can be many reasons, but the most important to mention here are continuity and mutual trust.

Continuity suggests not that this coffee is just an isolated happening, never to be seen again, but rather that the seller

knows where the coffee came from, how it was brought to the quality the buyer approved, and that within reason the seller can repeat the exercise in future. Of course, like wine, no coffee is exactly the same from season to season. There are good years, and then there are less good to sometimes even bad years. Experienced buyers know this and will never hold such variations against a seller.

Buyers hate exporters who knowingly ship coffee whose quality is not up to standard. If unforeseen circumstances mean one has difficulty in fulfilling a contract then the best and, really, the only option is always to inform your buyer as soon as you become aware of the problem. The buyer may be able to assist you by granting an extension to the shipping period, or may agree to take a slightly different quality (perhaps against a reduction in price), or may agree to release you from the contract. But the buyer will rightly be furious if the exporter simply ships a slightly different coffee hoping to get away with it. This can cause real and serious trouble, as shipping the wrong coffee disrupts the buyer's supply pipeline.

Roasters buy coffee for a specific objective. If on arrival it does not suit, it becomes virtually useless to them. It is no good then to offer a price allowance or discount to try and settle the matter. After all, if the roaster could have used a lower quality he or she would presumably have bought that in the first place.

Continuity and mutual trust mean both parties understand what is important in the coffee, that within reason they will continue to offer and buy that coffee, and that they can rely on each other to respect their obligations in every respect. Not all obligations are specified in the contract. For example, keeping buyers informed about the status of pending contracts is an unwritten obligation, whether the news to be passed on is good or not so good.

Serious liquor problems

There is a whole range of flavours, good and bad, whose impact on quality varies in importance depending on the type of coffee and on the type of buyer. But some flavours are unacceptable in any coffee to virtually all buyers, certainly in the quality business.

'Fermented' or 'foul' is a very objectionable taste, not unlike the odour of rotting coffee pulp. In its worst general form this is due to over-fermentation, cherry left to rot in heaps, the use of polluted water or stung beans with pollutants entering them. Foul-tasting cups can also be produced by single beans left behind in fermentation tanks or washing channels, or by beans that have been partly dried and then re-wetted again under unsanitary conditions.

If a few such stinker beans are irregularly spread throughout a shipment then this is a typical example of an unreliable coffee that occasionally produces an unclean or foul cup. Note that there is no such thing as only a little 'ferment', just as there is no such thing as being *almost honest*.

Most buyers would also consider 'sour' and 'onion' liquors as totally unacceptable, arguing that both are just a step away from ferment. This is a persuasive argument because sour and oniony liquors are caused by late pulping of cherry, and poor processing or drying techniques. Coffee does not naturally come off the tree with such taints. Remember that fermentation starts as soon as the cherry is picked. But there are clever blenders who know how to use such coffees in combination with other specific taste characteristics, and in so doing arrive at an acceptable final result. The real issue may therefore be whether such a coffee is over the top or not. In any case, as far as the quality market is concerned one is best advised to stay well clear of such coffees.

'Musty' or 'mouldy' is a very unpleasant coarse harsh flavour caused by the storage of under-dried coffee, or the re-wetting of coffee after it has already been dried. This flavour also suggests potential mould problems (see also chapter 12). 'Earthy' is a close relative. Contact with bare earth or dust are the main causes, which also imply poor drying arrangements, and the possibility of mustiness and mouldiness.

Very strong taints will also render a coffee virtually unusable: contact with petrol for example. Unclean can refer to any offensive off-flavour or taint. It can also be taken to indicate that an unspecified off-flavour is present.

Most of these taste defects tend to intensify with ageing. The common thread linking them all is that they are not to be tolerated in reasonably decent coffee.

NB: The information on mycotoxins (see also chapter 12, Quality control) in this guide has been drawn from industry experts, from the findings of the ICO/FAO project 'The enhancement of coffee quality by prevention of mould growth', and from the book *Coffee Futures: A Source Book of Some Critical Issues Confronting the Coffee Industry,* published by CABI Commodities (2001 – ISBN 958-332356-X) *www.cabi.org.*

Less serious liquor problems

Less serious liquor problems are difficult territory: very subjective and personal. What constitutes an acceptable or unacceptable liquor depends on the individual buyer's judgment, so it is vital to understand your buyer. Appreciate why the buyer takes certain coffees and not others – visit them and taste different coffees together, including your own.

'Fruity' or 'winey' are a good example of less serious liquor problems because, within reason, such flavours can add something interesting to a coffee. But the next step down is 'fruity-sour' and then 'sour', which is undesirable. Winey can move through 'oniony' to 'onion', which is a relative of ferment. Within reason, these are not always necessarily reasons to reject a coffee. However, in coffee to be used for espresso fruity or winey are not wanted under any circumstances because the espresso process often transforms them into rather different, intense and sometimes outright unpleasant tastes. So these tastes can be viewed as positive or negative – it all depends on the intensity and on the buyer's judgement. See also chapter 12.

'Ordinary', 'common' or 'coarse' tastes are strictly speaking not off-flavours. Just as there is a market for *vin ordinaire,* so there is one for *café ordinaire.* These flavour characteristics are usually caused by problems such as drought, serious stress or insect damage, or by processing or drying errors. Such liquors are therefore unlikely to find much favour in the quality market. But there are also disease resistant or high-yielding cultivars that present rather common liquors even though the coffee may be of attractive appearance and style. Sometimes such coffees may be upgraded through blending, perhaps by adding another coffee with an oniony, fruity or winey flavour. The result may not be a candidate for the exemplary market, but perhaps not a candidate for outright rejection either.

A 'woody' or 'aged' taste is not unsimilar and is the direct result of the ageing of a coffee, usually accompanied by loss of colour. It is not at all uncommon to find woody tasting coffee at the retail end of the specialty business because it sometimes takes months before coffees are roasted. Poorly dried coffees age more quickly than do well prepared ones, and lose colour more rapidly as well. The coffee 'fades' quickly. For 99 out of 100 offer samples from origin, a woody taste or fading appearance suggests a risk of premature ageing during shipment and the time spent awaiting final sale.

'Grassy' is a greenish taste that tends to obscure the liquor's finer aspects such as flavour or aroma. This taste is reminiscent of hay and is mostly found in early season coffee. Under-drying tends to accentuate grassiness. 'Bricky' is a close relative in that it also reduces flavour and acidity. Usually this commonish taste is associated with (slight) under-fermentation.

MAINSTREAM QUALITY

Mainstream is the main business

Mainstream quality makes up the bulk of the global trade in coffee. Standard type coffees are used by large and medium-sized roasters alike. These roasters have a supply obligation to keep the shelves in supermarkets and other retail stores filled with their product; a product that is always available and that is always the same in terms of appearance and taste. The largest roasters use many millions of bags of such coffee each year. For reasons of blend composition, logistics and simple supply security they cannot depend on just a single origin. Their main requirement therefore is that the supply be reliable, which means such coffees must be relatively easily substitutable and be available from a number of countries.

To satisfy their long-term delivery commitments for roasted coffee, roasters also enter into long-term purchase contracts, usually on the basis 'price to be fixed – buyer's call' (see also chapter 9, Hedging). Such long-term commitments almost inevitably mean the coffee trade sells such coffees short and expects to cover their sales later. Selling short is risky by itself but, as discussed in chapter 9, most of the risk can be hedged.

But selling a single origin short (in quantity and over an extended period) is exceedingly risky in case of later supply difficulties in that origin, so the trade instead sells a 'basket' of acceptable coffees from a number of different origins. For example, Guatemala, Prime Washed, and/or El Salvador, Central Standard, and/or Costa Rica, Hard Bean, against the appropriate delivery months of the New York arabica contract, the C. Or, Uganda, Standard Grade, and/or Côte d'Ivoire, Grade 2, against the LIFFE robusta contract.

The 'baskets' represent coffees that are acceptable for the same purpose in many blends of roasted coffee. Suppliers can fulfil their delivery commitments by providing one of the specified types. Each individual shipment is still subject to the roaster's final approval of quality on arrival. By coupling the use of these baskets with just-in-time delivery and the often imposed requirement that any coffee not approved on arrival be substituted immediately, one could say that the large roasters have taken most surprises out of the procurement process.

All except price; but even here their main objective is not to pay more than their competitors, rather than to look for bargains or play the market. Exporters must understand that there is no place for emotion in these buying processes. All that counts is price and performance.

Consequences of standardization

Interestingly, this standardization of mainstream quality not only means that below par coffees are not acceptable. It also means that coffees of better quality or better bean size are not wanted – and no premiums will be paid. The primary requirements are that the coffee must do for the blend what the roaster expects, and that every shipment is the same. There can be no question of accepting differences in quality, or of settling such differences through payment of allowances or through arbitration. If the coffee is not right then it will be rejected. Not only must the quality of each delivery be comparable to the previous one, it must also be uniform throughout the entire parcel, from bag to bag and from container to container. Consistency is the key.

All that has been said previously concerning respect for quality applies equally to mainstream or standard grades as well. Clearly, the quality of such coffees is not as exciting; it would be fair to say that as a rule standard type coffees are not particularly inspiring and offer easily matched cup quality. For standard quality, price is a much more important business factor than it is for exemplary or specialty coffee, where quality holds the key. Prices for standard quality are

generally also well known so the only way for an exporter to beat the competition is to be more efficient, more reliable, more consistent and more flexible.

Some accuse the large-scale roasting sector of gradually lowering the quality of retail coffee through technical innovation and product changes such as high-speed, high-yield roasting, steaming of robustas, the introduction of liquid coffee, etc.

Germany is sometimes quoted as an example of shifting quality preferences. In 1990, Colombian mild arabicas and Other mild arabicas accounted for 73% of green bean imports, with Colombia as top supplier. By 2010 Colombian mild arabicas and Other mild arabicas were only 26%. Indeed, Viet Nam alone provided almost 18% or 3.4 million bags against just 0.3 million bags or less than 2% from Colombia.

Others would argue that there simply is not enough quality coffee in the world to permit today's mega-roasters to raise the quality of standard blends without creating serious price distortions, although other agro-industrial products such as wine appear to cope easily enough with a widely segmented price structure.

Also, the demand pattern in some countries is shifting, as in Germany where acidic coffees are now in less demand.

Wherever the truth may lie, smaller origins and exporters cannot easily compete for what has become pure bulk commodity business. They have no competitive advantages and lack the economies of scale of larger players. It is impossible for them to add value because only large quantities of standard products are wanted. Mega-roasters have neither the time nor the inclination to deal with small quantities of exemplary coffees. Some do participate indirectly in the specialty business, but through separate business units. Despite the excitement of the specialty market, never overlook the fact that the mainstream business represents 85% or more of world coffee imports and should not be ignored.

ROBUSTA

Robusta – the species

Coffea canephora, popularly known as robusta because of the hardy nature of the plant, was first discovered in the former Belgian Congo in the 1800s. It is also known to be indigenous to the tropical forests around the Lake Victoria crescent in Uganda. It was introduced into Southeast Asia in 1900, after coffee rust disease wiped out all arabica cultivation in Ceylon in 1869 and destroyed most low altitude plantations in Java in 1876. Currently, it represents between 30% and 40% of world production. It is grown in West and Central Africa, throughout Southeast Asia, and in parts of South America including Brazil, where it is known as *Conillon*.

The robusta plant grows as a shrub or as a small tree up to 10 m in height. Generally, it is planted at lower densities than arabica because of the larger plant size. Robusta exists in many different forms and varieties in the wild. The cross-bred strains of this variety of coffee are often hard to identify, but two main types are generally recognized: *Erecta*, or upright forms, and *Nganda*, or spreading forms.

Robusta is a diploid species. It is a larger bush than the arabica plant, and with robust growth. The root system of robusta, though large, is rather shallow compared to arabica, with the mass of feeder roots being confined to the upper layers of the soil. The leaves are broad, large and pale green in colour. Flowers are white and fragrant, and are borne in larger clusters than in arabica. The flowers open on the seventh or eighth day after receiving rain. Unlike arabica, robusta is self-sterile, that is, its ovule cannot be fertilized with its own pollen and hence cross-pollination is necessary. The cherries are small, but larger in number per node than arabica, varying from 40 to 60 or more. They mature in about 10 to 11 months and are generally ready for harvest two months later than arabica.

Robusta beans are smaller than arabica beans. Depending on the plant strain, the bean shape is round, oval or elliptical with pointed tips. The colour of the beans depends on the method of processing – grey when washed and golden brown when prepared by the dry cherry or natural method of preparation. The caffeine content of robusta beans is nearly twice as high as that of arabica beans (2% to 2.5% versus 1.1% to 1.5%).

Under normal conditions robusta coffee possesses several useful characteristics such as high tolerance to leaf rust pathogen, white stem borer and nematode invasion, and the potential to give consistent yields. For these reasons, the cost of robusta cultivation is relatively low compared to the arabica variety. Inability to endure long drought conditions, late cropping, late stabilization of yields and somewhat less attractive quality compared to arabica, are some of the negative attributes of robusta coffee.

In general, robusta is harder than arabica and grows well at low altitudes, in open humid conditions, with the cost of production being lower than the arabica variety. In some countries (Uganda and India, for example) robusta is also cultivated at fairly high altitudes (above 1,200 m) and under shade. These features have helped in the production of dense beans, with better cupping characteristics than those normally expected in the robusta cup, which could aid in the preparation of specialty and possibly exemplary coffees.

Wet processing of robusta

The wet process helps to mute and mellow the striking notes of fruit and bitterness that are often at the core of the robusta cup. Wet processing helps in developing 'soft buttery notes'

in the cup, unlike the thick 'robust' notes that are observed in the average robusta cup. In a number of import markets, quality washed robusta has replaced a percentage of washed arabica in coffee blends. Such robustas have not only provided the froth and bubbles for the much sought after espresso, but have also helped in reducing the price of such blends. Robusta beans with robust but clean notes of strength and fruitiness (but not fermented, i.e. with a neutral liquor) also find ready acceptance in the preparation of soluble coffee.

Note, however, that the wet processing of robusta is riskier and more difficult because the mucilage in robusta coffee is thicker and stickier than it is in arabica. In some cases fermentation may not be complete even after 72 hours and, considering the high temperatures at the low altitude at which most robusta is grown, the process requires extremely careful monitoring to avoid over-fermentation. Such lengthy fermentation periods also require much more tank space than the average processing facility can economically operate, whereas large-scale friction (aqua) pulpers to strip mucilage are costly in terms of water and power use.

However, the development of small and sometimes mobile motorized processing units that combine depulping and frictional mucilage removal with minimal water use is creating new opportunities for smaller growers and smallholders to benefit from the growing demand for wet processed robustas. Some are combined with mechanical drying units to ensure rapid and uniform drying, thus avoiding the risk of secondary fermentation or off flavours. For information on such types of machines, also called eco-pulpers, visit for example *www.penagos.com* and *www.pinhalense.com.br*.

Defectives and off-tastes found in robusta, and their causes, do not differ markedly from those covered in the preceding section. All the concerns and limitations concerning quality and moisture content already stated are equally valid for robusta coffee, both dry and wet processed. Nevertheless it is appropriate to review some of them in the context of robusta production.

Defects in robusta coffees

Improper processing techniques, including use of incorrect equipment and improper handling, contribute to defects in quality. In washed robusta the major off-tastes caused by improper processing techniques are 'raw/green', 'fruity', 'overripe', 'fermented', 'medicinal', 'chemical', 'stinkers', 'stale', 'earthy', 'baggy/oily', 'spicy' and to an extent 'metallic'.

Unwashed or natural robusta coffee is less susceptible to quality deterioration. Off-tastes such as raw/green, fruity/fermented, overripe, medicinal, chemical and stale occur mainly because of negligence during processing.

Impact of immatures/greens, brown beans, fruity/overripe, fermented and medicinal off-tastes. Selective picking of cherries is essential for the production of high grade robusta. The quality of the bags or baskets used for collection during harvesting should also be carefully checked. Cherries collected in fertilizer bags or in bags previously used for chemicals could absorb an off-taste, especially when such bags are tightly tied and left unattended for a length of time or directly exposed to strong sunshine.

The raw/green off-taste in robusta coffee has been attributed to incorrect harvesting techniques. For economic reasons, selective picking may not be practised. This results in unripe cherries being pulped or dried along with ripe cherries. The green or immature beans present among the unripe cherries give a raw or green off-taste to the cup.

On the other hand, the presence of brown beans and an off-taste of overripe could occur when the cherries have been picked in an overripe or even already dried condition. Where feasible, growers are advised to sort the cherry after picking, to ensure that the coffee to be pulped (or dried in the cherry for natural preparation) does not contain unripe or overripe cherries that lower the cup quality.

Fermented and so-called medicinal off-tastes have been observed in natural (dry processed) robusta. The cause for these could be delays in spreading the cherries for drying or the deterioration of overripe cherry. (Late harvesting means general over-ripeness, resulting in poor cups.)

Causes of 'pulper-nipped' 'beans/cuts', 'stinkers', 'putrid/rotting off-taste'. Invariably, not all coffee cherries will be the same size. If they are not sorted on size, with the help of mechanical cherry sorters, hand sieves or flotation, it is very likely that the beans will be cut during pulping. This can also happen if the pulper has not been suitably adjusted or fitted with flexible chops. Micro-organisms can enter pulper-nipped beans through the injury and cause the formation of stinkers or black beans, adversely affecting quality.

Causes of earthy, fruity and fermented off-tastes. The water used for washing, as for all the stages of processing, should be clean to ensure the quality of the end product. Unclean water or water contaminated with fine silt, and recirculated water with a high solid content, could cause earthy, fruity or fermented and other off-tastes.

Causes of mouldy and faded beans and impact of improper drying and storage: During the preparation of natural robusta, spreading the cherries in thick layers with no or inadequate stirring and raking could result in mould formation. This can adversely affect the visual appearance and the cup quality of the cherry beans. Lack of protection from rain and night dew during drying can also cause mould growth. For more on this go to chapter 12, Quality control issues.

The fading (of the colour) of coffee and the cup being described as stale could be the result of inadequate drying facilities, storage of beans with a high moisture content, or the storage of well dried coffee in improperly ventilated warehouses. Stale cups can also be caused by improper storage on the farm, at the curing factory or at warehouses awaiting sale. Storage of coffee on the drying yards, inadequate covering of coffee

stacks, poorly ventilated warehouses, or stacking coffee in a haphazard manner up to the ceiling of the warehouse can all cause a stale off-taste to develop in the cup.

Spicy and chemical off-tastes could be due to packaging in poor quality bags or bags in which spices or fertilizers have been packed earlier. Storing coffee with spices, chemicals, fertilizers or fungicides could also cause these off-tastes. Remember that coffee beans readily absorb taints and odours that could lower their aromatic quality and, therefore, value.

Inspection and classification

Each coffee producing country has its own export presentation system. See examples under Grading and classification in chapter 1.

Whatever form this may take, it is essential to ensure that the coffee offered for sale does not contain excessive amounts of defective beans or foreign matter, and that it is clean in the cup. Some origins and exporters only assess robusta quality visually and do not liquor the coffee.

This is to be discouraged. Coffee is meant for human consumption and its taste is of paramount importance. The roaster liquors it before using it, so the shipper should liquor it before dispatching it.

Based on *visual* quality, robusta beans could be categorized into three grades: above FAQ (fair average quality), FAQ (average) and below FAQ. Note that for natural robusta wet-polishing helps to improve the appearance and, to some extent, also the quality.

Above average coffees would have good colour (grey with a hint of blue when washed and golden brown for naturals), possess uniformity in size and shape and conform to the prescribed grade specifications, emit a normal smell (cereal-like when washed and fruity when unwashed), and would contain hardly any defectives. The beans would be free of extraneous or foreign matter, mould or toxins, and have a moisture content definitely less than 12.5%.

Average coffees would be of a colour that is not faded, conform to the grade description, have no mould or fungal growth and contain a limited proportion of defects that do not adversely affect the cup quality.

Below average coffees could be of varying qualities, ranging from beans which have high moisture content and are defective such as broken beans, blacks, browns or extraneous matter, to very poor, bleached and mouldy beans. Remember that coffees with more than 12.5% moisture content should not be shipped, and that many receivers stipulate their own moisture content limits, both at the time of shipment and upon arrival.

Based on *liquor* quality, robusta beans could be classified as follows:

- Fine and special, where the liquor quality is soft, smooth and buttery, with good body, hardly any bitterness, and clean. This quality can be seen in robusta coffees which are washed and processed with care, in robusta beans grown at high altitudes and under shade, and in plant strains with the inherent characteristics of lower caffeine content, softness and mellow flavour notes.

- Good, where the liquor quality could be described as good body, neutral, light bitterness and clean, with a hint of chocolate notes.

- Average, with a cup quality of fair body, fair neutrality, average bitterness and clean.

- Below average, where the liquor, though of fair body, has harsh notes of the robusta fruit, is bitter though clean, and is flat with no flavour notes.

- Poor, a cup which is unclean, having medicinal, phenolic or rioy off-notes, or strong harsh robusta notes, with or without body, bitter and unpleasant to the taste.

What has been said above is not a universal methodology followed by all robusta producing origins. It is only a means to explain the quality attributes that could be encountered in a robusta cup and the manner in which these attributes could be classified. Individual buyers have their own classification and evaluation methods, but usually the attributes and ratings will be comparable to those above. See also chapter 1, World coffee trade.

Specific aspects affecting quality and price

High moisture content reduces coffee's shelf life. Beans that are at equilibrium and are inactive would have a moisture content of well below 12.5%. Beans with a high moisture content could be very actively respiring, giving up moisture and undergoing changes both physically and intrinsically. Physically, there would be a fading in colour and, depending on the moisture content, the temperature and the humidity of the surrounding area, the fading could intensify, resulting in bleaching and finally mould growth. Intrinsically, the cup quality could fade from a clean, strong and neutral cup to a 'woody', 'aged' and 'musty' cup.

Colour. Poor visual colour, such as a brownish or whitish appearance in washed robusta, or a green shrivelled appearance in natural robusta, could result in a low value. The brown appearance of the beans in washed robusta coffee is a direct indication of incorrect processing techniques. In the cup this could result in a fruity or fermented off-taste. The whitish appearance of a consignment would result in heavy discounts for the coffee, as again it reveals both incorrect processing techniques and improper storage conditions.

Greenish shrivelled beans in natural robusta reflect improper harvesting techniques; the farmer has stripped the coffee plant of berries that were at different stages of ripening. This visual defect detracts from the cleanliness and quality of a good cup of coffee.

Bean size could, to an extent, influence the price that is paid for a consignment of coffee. Large sized beans roast well and could have a better cup profile, provided the processing has been carried out carefully and correctly. Broken beans, on the other hand, could result not only in a high roasting loss, but also in charring of the beans and a poor cup quality. Many robusta producing origins sell their coffee based on the size of the beans and a permissible tolerance to defects, with a classification of AA or grade/type I and so on, each grade denoting the size of the beans and a measured tolerance of certain imperfections.

The defect count is the measured presence or absence of defects such as blacks, browns, greens, faded and bleached beans, insect damaged beans, pulper cuts, stinkers, sour beans and extraneous matter such as twigs, sticks or stones. The presence of defects could lower the value of coffee; their absence could result in a premium.

Cupping or cup quality would be the final determining factor for purchase or rejection of a consignment and for determining the price. The presence of defects could result in an unclean cup and thus lower the cup quality and price.

Steam cleaning

The steam treatment of coffee was developed by Professor Karl Lendrich, and was patented in Germany in 1933.

Briefly, the process was developed with the objective to make coffee more 'acceptable' to certain consumers who were reporting varying degrees of stomach discomfort when drinking regular coffee. The discussion as to exactly which chemical components of the coffee bean were/are responsible for this is ongoing, but 'mild' or 'stomach-friendly' coffees have been a regular feature of the German market ever since. Germany is the typical and possibly only significant market for this kind of product.

The original procedure consists of a relatively gentle steam-treatment lasting between 30 and 60 minutes during which the beans undergo chemical and physical changes. It is mostly, if not only, used on arabica where it reduces certain acids and also causes certain taste changes.

In recent years, steam treatment has increasingly been used to treat robusta because it was found that steam-treated robusta coffees were milder and could even develop some acidity. This first became of interest during periods of high coffee prices when the price difference between arabica and robusta made it attractive to include a certain percentage of steam treated robusta in a blend. However, this type of steam treatment is more severe in that higher temperatures are applied for longer periods. The end result of the harsher treatment results in a different taste experience and it is unlikely such coffees will be used to any great extent in high quality blends.

It is difficult to estimate the extent to which steam treated coffees are being used except to say that the never ending quest to reduce costs will certainly keep this process under the spotlight, especially when coffee prices are high. There are no statistics available as to actual usage, but trade sources suggest it is growing.

It is worth noting as well that further research has shown that certain phenolic compounds (causing off-flavours or taints) can also be reduced or eliminated through steam-treatment or steam cleaning. This then makes it possible to 'clean' coffees that otherwise would not have been useable, to a 'useable standard'. Therefore, if for example the price difference between arabica and robusta was to narrow substantially, then the steam cleaning of certain arabicas could also become a regular feature.

Robusta in espresso and other coffee beverages

Until very recently, the Western hemisphere and many South and Central American countries have been the producers and exporters of specialty coffees. While 75% to 80% of specialty coffee exports originate in Central or South America, the Caribbean and Hawaii, and over half the remaining 20% to 25% are produced in Africa, Asia's contribution barely exceeds 10%.

Historically, Colombia, Ethiopia, Jamaica and Kenya, which are considered as producers of gourmet coffees, produce only arabica. The North American consumer market, where the specialty phenomenon was born, has so far mostly bought robusta for use only as a filler or for soluble coffee preparation.

However, robusta coffees are strong in body and can be neutral and buttery in the cup. There are robusta varieties in Africa, India and Indonesia whose cup quality, when washed, is supremely soft and buttery. This taste profile, with the added attributes of high altitude and fairly low caffeine content, could help in creating designer and premium robusta coffees. (Liquor requirements and the liquoring of coffees for use in espresso blends are different from those used for traditional preparation, see also chapter 12, Quality control.)

Using only arabicas limits the diversity of coffees available for consumption. Robusta origins, and the special acceptable tastes inherent to robusta beans, could provide a solution. Price could be an additional reason for creating exemplary and specialty robustas. Robustas are traditionally cheaper than arabicas, so there is an opportunity to develop premium robustas that are less expensive than premium arabicas, thus catering to a new group of consumers.

A point worth mentioning is that on the consumer side there has been no rejection of quality robusta. Even before the birth of the gourmet and specialty coffee phenomenon, select food stores all over the world were offering roasted coffees by origin: monsooned robustas from India, washed robustas from Papua New Guinea, and from Indonesia the famous well washed robusta [originally called in Dutch *West Indische*

bereiding or WIB (West Indian preparation, or pulped)], have been very popular. Some have earned the status of being described as exemplary coffees. Increasing consumer awareness of the attractions of top quality robustas will in itself also help to promote such coffees.

Quality robusta can be used in the preparation of today's coffee beverages. Clean and fresh, strong bodied, neutral, with hardly any acidity and with an undercurrent of chocolate and malt notes, unwashed robustas can be used in the making of espresso, canned or liquid coffee, and regular or filter coffees.

Well washed, soft robustas provide the aromatic *crema* for strong espresso, provided they do not show fresh or fruity tastes that can be unpleasantly accentuated by the espresso extraction process. High-quality washed robusta coffees are excellent for fortification of milk-based drinks such as cappuccino and café latte, and as a component of high caffeine blends.

However, there are different tasting requirements when using arabica or robusta in espresso. The concentrated espresso cup exaggerates certain sensory aspects, not always positively. Only well-matured and absolutely clean cupping coffees can be considered, and their suitability can only definitively be established by submitting the sample to actual espresso extraction. See also chapter 12.

Robusta, espresso and specialty

Global consumption of espresso today is such that it has become a separate, stand-alone market alongside the market for whole bean coffee, and that for roast and ground coffee (R&G coffee). But, also in the espresso market one finds blends that consist of commonplace, if not ordinary coffees alongside really good quality. Basically, an entire range of qualities that are all sold as espresso. So, espresso can be both mainstream and specialty. The vast majority of espresso brands are blends.

Views on this tend to differ between the United States and Europe. The United States view is that, mostly, it ranks as specialty. This is probably due to the fact that for many in this market espresso is a relatively new consumer product and, one that is 'different'. Europe has known espresso for many, many decades and consumers there definitely look at it as a separate lifestyle product, but one whose quality can range from ordinary to truly exceptional – as is the case with traditional coffee.

What is beyond dispute is that the strong growth in the espresso segment has resulted in increased and new interest in robusta coffee. It is widely accepted that specialty (or gourmet) robustas exist and that there is also a market for them. As such, starting with the 2008 World Championship for Cup Tasters, held by the Specialty Coffee Association of Europe (*www.scae.com*), the tasting line-up for this event now includes premium robustas.

Additionally the Coffee Quality Institute (CQI – *www. coffeeinstitute.org*) has since early 2010 been working on the profiling of specialty robusta coffee (or fine robustas), thus providing further proof of the renewed interest in premium robusta coffees. To date, the project's main conclusion has been that selectively harvested and correctly processed robustas, both washed and natural, offer taste profiles that can be differentiated by their country and area of origin. Provided such coffees are correctly roasted (the robusta bean is harder than arabica, making the roasting process more difficult to manage) the cupping characteristics can yield scores of 80+ points on a 100-point scale.

The main taste difference between premium and commercial grade robustas is that premium robustas have a high sweet aspect (versus a low bitter aspect), whereas commercial grade robusta usually shows the exact opposite. The main obstacle to improved robusta quality, and therefore pricing, is the presence of defects that so often debase the cup quality to the minimum acceptable, which is the commercial grade product. Quality standards and quality controls for premium robustas therefore have to be of the same level as required for premium arabicas. See also chapter 12.

Bringing about fundamental change in the way the market perceives premium robustas requires both a radically different approach to robusta 'quality' by producers, and high-level promotion of fine robusta to the market at large. This has been done since 1999 for specialty arabicas through the Cup of Excellence initiative. Details at *www.cupofexcellence.org*.

CHAPTER 12

QUALITY CONTROL

QUALITY CONTROL

QUALITY CONTROL ISSUES

Quality control is essential, not only because of pricing considerations (better quality equals better price), but also to ensure that exports conform to food safety legislation in major import markets. It also helps to reduce waste and loss during the harvesting, processing and drying of coffee, and plays a role in the general move towards more sustainability in the coffee industry.

Quality control at the primary (farm gate) level can assume different forms:

- Government or coffee authorities attempt to 'police' harvesting, on-farm processing and drying. This is costly in terms of qualified staff and does not have a good track record.
- Penalties are imposed for lower than average quality. This is passive quality control: it does nothing to encourage better than minimal or average quality.
- Premiums are offered for better than average quality. This is active quality control: it rewards and encourages the production of better quality. It can be combined with a refusal to purchase lower quality but this does leave open the question of what then happens to such coffees.

Different producing countries have differing quality control systems and attach differing values to certain aspects of quality. General information on coffee quality standards can be found at *www.iso.org* (for instance, ISO 10470, a draft defect chart, but there are also many other ISO standards of interest to coffee exporters, including one detailing correct sampling procedures – look under ICS 67.140.20 Coffee and coffee substitutes). Information is also available from coffee authorities in producing countries.

When setting quality limits one should recognize that without active quality control, such as paying premiums for better quality, the maximum permissible limit (on defects, for instance) quickly becomes the new standard. And when setting export taxes, care should be taken not to penalize producers of better quality who manage to obtain premium prices as a result of their effort.

ICO MINIMUM EXPORT STANDARDS

Internationally, the very low coffee prices that resulted from surplus production in the late 1990s and early 2000s brought calls for the lowest qualities to be eliminated from the market altogether, and the ICO Council passed a resolution to this effect. Resolution 407 introduced mandatory minimum standards for coffee exports in February 2002, but this proved to be unenforceable so it was subsequently amended by Resolution 420 (May 2004), which recommends voluntary targets for the minimum quality export standards for both arabica and robusta. The objective remains to halt the export of substandard beans, thereby tightening supply lines in the expectation this will help lift prices. The ICO's Coffee Quality-Improvement Programme calls on producing members to endeavour to restrict the export of arabica coffee with more than 86 defects per 300 g sample or robusta coffee with more than 150 defects per 300 g.

The programme also asks members to endeavour not to allow arabica or robusta of any grade to be exported whose moisture content is below 8% or above 12.5%, with the proviso that this should not affect established, good and accepted commercial practice. Thus, where moisture percentages below 12.5% are currently being achieved, exporters should endeavour to maintain or decrease these.

It is accepted that specialty coffees that traditionally have a high moisture content, such as Indian monsooned coffees, are exempt, but Resolution 420 of 21 May 2004 (see *www.ico.org*) requires all producers to clearly identify on the Certificate of Origin any coffee which does not come up to the recommended standard. For the first six months of 2011 the ICO reported that 23 exporting members, accounting for nearly 40 million bags or over 72% of all exports during that period, provided information on the quality of the coffee they exported. Of these exports nearly 36 million bags (90%) were classified as being within the resolution's defects and moisture targets. The split was 92% arabica and 8% robusta.

ISO QUALITY SYSTEMS

ISO 9001 is a process-based quality management system that organizations can use to demonstrate the consistent quality of their products to customers and concerned regulatory institutions. Customer satisfaction is then further enhanced through continual improvement of their system. As an example, in a factory producing pencils it would be hopeless to inspect every single pencil manufactured – instead one monitors the process used to make them. Similarly one can describe in documented procedures, such as production manuals, the process of converting the fruit of the coffee tree into exportable green bean.

When an organization's quality management system complies with ISO 9001 and when the coffee is processed in accordance with these procedures, then the quality management system (not the product) can be ISO 9001 certified. During cultivation too many variables (weather, diseases, pests) are beyond the control of the producer. This is why in the case of green coffee the process in the ISO system starts when the cherry is picked, and ends when the container is delivered to the ship's side. This can work for estate coffee that is exported under its own name, but is less easy to apply to smallholder coffee because numerous small deliveries to collection points or washing stations automatically lose their identity. And blended coffee shipped in bulk gains an identity only upon loading.

Nevertheless, good harvesting and processing standards are essential to maintain quality, and ISO 9001 provides those who process their own coffee for export with identification and traceability for all the coffee produced. The batch number can lead back to the day of picking, where on the farm, what the weather was then, how long it took to dry the coffee, how well it was dried, and a number of other variables – all useful information in determining the cause of any quality problems that may subsequently arise. Perhaps none of this provides any immediate or direct economic advantage, but estate growers using the system say they have become better processors and are better able to provide the sort of quality guarantees that the larger commercial roasters demand. For current details go to *www.iso.org* and look for ISO 9001.

However, by themselves these ICO and ISO objectives do not provide answers to the ever more stringent food safety legislation being introduced at the consumer end, and the potential impact of this on coffee exporters. But ISO 22000 incorporates the requirements of the hazard analysis critical control points (HACCP) system developed by the Codex Alimentarius Commission. HACCP has increasingly become a mandatory requirement in the markets of various countries since the 1990s, most notably for non-farm food businesses in the EU since January 2006. As ISO 22000 is an auditable standard, certified companies can demonstrate their compliance to HACCP. Certification to ISO 22000 could facilitate acceptance by global food retailers, as it also covers the requirements of key standards developed by various global food retailer systems.

Tools on ISO 22000 and ISO 9001 have been developed by the International Trade Centre and are available on the Internet: see *www.intracen.org/eqm* and go to 'quality management'.

HB 17 ISO 22000 Food Safety Management Systems – An easy-to-use checklist for small business – Are you ready? is a software-based self-diagnostic tool on ISO 22000 (published in 2007). The tool helps small businesses operating in the food chain to understand the regulatory requirements for food safety and to make an assessment of their readiness to implement ISO 22000 and obtain some preliminary guidance on applying the standard.

HAZARD ANALYSIS CRITICAL CONTROL POINTS – WHAT IS IT?

The scope of quality control in developed countries has expanded enormously in recent years. Today, it encompasses not just the traditional commercial concerns with quality, but also all food health and hygiene concerns associated with modern consumerism. Coffee is part of the modern food chain and health concerns are increasingly shaping quality controls at the receiving end.

Gone are the days of settling claims on mould or contamination damage internally through the payment of a simple allowance. Not only may customs and health authorities in consuming countries order the destruction of 'hazardous' parcels, but they will also trace responsibility back to the source: the country, the shipper and even the individual grower. Relatively light-hearted sounding phrases such as tracking and tracing food products from 'farm to fork, stable to table or plough to plate' are, in fact, the political outcome of consumer pressure. People want to know their food is safe and if one particular sector of the food industry is found to pose a problem, then all other sectors are affected as well.

Food health and hygiene concerns are relatively easily addressed in developed countries. The difficulty for developing nations is that the resultant procedures and regulations are then applied equally to the food crops they export to developed countries. The import trade is increasingly passing such consumer-imposed food chain management issues on to exporting countries that, in most instances, have to find the answers or lose the business.

A particular food safety issue for coffee is concern over the presence in foods and beverages of ochratoxin A (OTA), a mycotoxin that is believed to cause kidney damage. OTA is a probable human renal carcinogen (cancer producing substance – IARC evaluation Class 2B). Although the toxicological status of OTA has not yet been settled, importing countries are increasingly paying attention to its occurrence in coffee and other products and are requiring the adoption of preventative measures.

HACCP is a management system in which food safety is addressed through the analysis and control of biological, chemical and physical hazards from raw food material production to manufacturing and consumption.

HACCP involves seven principles:

1. Analyse *hazards*, for instance microbiological (e.g. bacteria, viruses, moulds, toxins), chemical (e.g. pesticide residues), or physical (stones, wood, glass, etc.).

2. Identify *critical control points*. These are points in the food's production (from raw to processed to consumption) at which a potential hazard can be controlled or eliminated.

3. Establish *preventative measures* with critical limits (values) for each control point, such as a minimum drying time to ensure mould growth cannot progress.

4. Establish procedures to *monitor* the critical control points (e.g. how to ensure that adequate drying occurs).

5. Establish *corrective actions* to be taken when monitoring shows that a critical limit has not been met, such as disposing of potentially contaminated cherry.

6. Establish procedures to *verify* that the system is working properly. For example, test drying facilities for leaks or contamination.

7. Establish effective *record keeping* for documenting the HACCP system, such as records of hazards and control methods, the monitoring of safety requirements and actions taken to correct potential problems.

HACCP: HOW TO MANAGE?

Most enterprises in the coffee chain, including coffee producers and exporters, will at some point need to apply controls to guarantee product safety. These are usually represented in a concise process flow diagram with underlined points where hazards may occur. This must be documented in a HACCP plan. Any discrepancies found, and the countermeasures taken to correct them, must be registered.

In 2002, European Union food business operators were already being obliged to implement HACCP systems on the basis of existing legislation (Council Directive 93/43/EEC on the hygiene of foodstuffs). Many food processors and their suppliers have always had stringent quality controls that, in practice, were close to a HACCP system. The difference now is that a HACCP system requires a detailed description that can be subject to verification by food safety authorities. For example, supplying an inferior grade of green coffee that is otherwise sound is a quality issue and does not necessarily represent a food hazard. But a mouldy coffee does.

Control points can be divided into two groups: (i) The main group includes all those points where certain controls have to be applied and where loss of control may result in a low probability of a health risk. These are known as control points, or CP. (ii) The other group includes a very few points where loss of control may result in a high probability of illness. These are known as critical control points, or CCP. For example, quickly passing a critical stage in the coffee drying process seems like a vital critical point in the HACCP system.

Both HACCP and GAP (or Good Agricultural Practice – there is also GMP or Good Manufacturing Practice) are quality assurance systems, but they have different approaches. HACCP concentrates on a few critical points, whereas GAP tries to make all-round improvements. GAP is easier to set up but does not necessarily zero in on the most important steps that influence the occurrence or avoidance of toxins in coffee. See *www.fda.gov* and search under Food – H – HACCP for a good introduction to the subject. See also under Resources at *www.coffee-ota.org* for presentations on HACCP in the coffee chain with particular reference to the prevention of OTA.

The two processes are complimentary in that GAP will improve coffee quality, whereas HACCP will provide the type of disciplined monitoring and control that supermarket chains and food manufacturers increasingly demand. More importantly, it is only through the HACCP process that one can establish where OTA enters the system and where the fungi causing OTA first appear. This is essential if one is to meet EU and presumably in due course also United States requirements for the reduction and prevention of OTA contamination.

The World Trade Organization (WTO) offers a searchable database of member governments' measures related to the Sanitary and Phytosanitary (SPS) Agreement, thus making it easier to find out about other countries' food safety requirements and alerts.

The SPS Information Management System (SPS IMS) allows users to search and obtain information on measures that member governments have submitted to the WTO. These include notifications concerning new export and food safety requirements, specific trade concerns that governments have raised, documents of the WTO's sanitary and phytosanitary measures committee, details of the authorities who handle notifications and, particularly useful for those seeking information, member governments' national enquiry contacts.

The SPS Information Management System is available at *http://spsims.wto.org*. The site also offers a gateway into the SPS portal itself.

The International Portal on Food Safety, Animal and Plant Health – IPFSAPH is an alternative source. With over 35,000 records, the data sets incorporated into *www.ipfsaph. org* include WTO's SPS Information Management System (containing all WTO trade notifications and concerns) and IAEA's Clearance of Irradiated Foods Database.

HACCP AND THE UNITED STATES: FOOD SAFETY AND BIOTERRORISM

Imports of coffee into the United States are all subject to inspection by the U.S. Food and Drug Administration (FDA) under the provisions of the Federal Food, Drug and Cosmetic Act. To pass for importation coffee must be free of unapproved pesticide residues, have had no or only limited exposure to insect infestation in the field, and be free of all chemical and other contamination including mould and live insects. Insect damage by itself, pinholes for example, exceeding 10% may also lead to rejection. The Green Coffee Association (GCA) contracts routinely contain the clause 'no pass – no sale', which puts the responsibility for passing the FDA inspection firmly on the exporter.

Different events have in recent years catapulted both domestic and imported food security into top priority in the United States, with consequent strengthening of FDA surveillance of imported foods. This is visibly demonstrated by much stricter FDA and customs inspection of coffee containers and even coffee samples, and the distribution of an FDA Food Security Preventative Measures Guidance circular to food importing operations. These measures also include a large 'track and trace' element. For more information on all this and FDA coffee regulations go to – *www.fda.gov* and look for the New FDA Food Safety Modernization Act (FSMA) that was signed into law on 4 January 2011. Also, ask for the information booklet, Health, Safety and Security in the Importation of Green Coffee into the United States from the National Coffee Association of USA, Inc. – *www. ncausa.org*.

The Public Health Security and Bioterrorism Preparedness and Response Act requires all facilities engaged in the 'manufacturing, processing, packing or holding food for consumption in the United States' to be registered with the FDA. This includes all exporters of coffee or for that matter any other primary commodity exporting to the United States and some processing plants. This information needs to be updated each time there is a change. The regulations and much related information can be found on *www.fda.gov/ Food/FoodDefense/Bioterrorism*. The main point at issue here is that food shipments from unregistered suppliers are subject to refusal of admission into the United States. This includes coffee!

A fact sheet is available at *www.ncausa.org* whereas related information (on shipping security) is also available in chapter 5.

POTENTIAL HAZARDS

MYCOTOXINS, RESIDUES, CONTAMINATION

Mycotoxins are caused by contamination by some naturally occurring moulds. Not every type of mould produces mycotoxins. Mycotoxins are 'selective' in the sense that a given type of mycotoxin occurs in specific foodstuffs: aflatoxins in peanuts, grains and milk; patulin in apple juice; OTA in grains, grapes and derived products, beans and pulses, cocoa, coffee and others. OTA is the most relevant mycotoxin for coffee, but in the framework of an HACCP system it is recommended to envisage measures for mycotoxins in general.

Information on mycotoxins has been drawn from industry experts, from the findings of the ICO-FAO project 'The enhancement of coffee quality by prevention of mould growth', and the 2001 book *Coffee Futures* published by CABI Commodities, ISBN 958-332356-X.

The initial contamination of coffee with OTA takes place through spores in the air and in the ground. These spores may produce a mould, but only if the right circumstances (humidity and temperature) prevail. The importance of proper moisture management throughout the entire processing and supply chain cannot be overemphasized. Farmers, middlemen and exporters should also be aware that in a shipment of coffee OTA contamination (mould) may be very localized, making sampling extremely complex. Careful inspection of visual appearance and any mouldy or earthy smells can be a useful tool for checking.

Pesticide residues in coffee have only very rarely exceeded the limit values so far, but this does not mean that their monitoring is not a vital aspect of an HACCP system. It is absolutely essential that coffee growers maintain chemical registers that detail, in chronological order, the type and quantities of all chemicals used and the timing of their application. Only chemicals that have been approved for use on coffee may be used and then only within the withholding limits specified by the manufacturers. Exporters and shipping lines must ensure only clean containers are used, thus avoiding cross-contamination by previous cargoes. Go to *www.fao.org* and search for the Draft Code of Hygienic Practice for the Transport of Foodstuffs in Bulk and Semi-Packed Foodstuffs of the Codex Alimentarius Commission.

Hydrocarbon contamination is usually caused by jute coffee bags because of the 'batching oil' used to soften the jute fibres before spinning. There have been instances of contaminated oil being used (old engine oil for example).

The International Jute Organization has established specifications (IJO Standard 98/01) for the manufacture of jute bags to be used in the food industry – see *www.jute.org*.

- Analytical criteria. Ingredients used as batching oils must be non-toxic and approved for use in packaging materials that will come into contact with food. Batching oils must not contain compounds that could produce off-flavours or off-tastes in food packed in jute or sisal bags.

- Chemical criteria. The amount of unsaponifiable compounds (which cannot be converted into soap by boiling with alkali) shall be less than 1,250 mg/kg. The method described in British Standard 3845:1990 is recommended for the determination of the added oil content of jute yarn, rove and fabric. Method 2.401 of the International Union of Pure and Applied Chemistry (IUPAC) is recommended for determining unsaponifiable matter.

- Organoleptic criteria. Jute bags shall be analysed for their olfactory qualities. No undesirable odours, or odour untypical of jute, shall be present. No unacceptable odours shall develop after artificial ageing of the sacks. The ageing procedure to be followed shall be the one described in European Standard EN 766 for use on sacks for the transport of food.

To read the EU Packaging and Packaging Waste Directive (PPWD) go to *www.eur-lex.europa.eu* and search for Directive 62 of 1994 (94/62/EC). Subsequent changes and a consolidated version dated 20 April 2009 are found under the Bibliographic Notice.

Organizations and private companies in India and Bangladesh have developed a hydrocarbon-free lubricant, based on vegetable oil, to soften the jute fibre. It is a non-toxic, biodegradable oil, and bags made with it can be classified as food grade bags. However, the fact that vegetable oil is used for batching is in itself not sufficient. The oil used must be stable and may not turn rancid.

PESTICIDES: MAXIMUM RESIDUE LEVELS IN THE EU

The importance of the previous topic is emphasized by the fact that on 2 September 2008 European Union Regulation (EC) No. 396/2005 came into force for a large number of commodities, including green coffee beans. The Regulation harmonizes what was previously a highly fragmented number of national standards, applied by individual countries. This development is to be welcomed as it simplifies the trade in green coffee by ensuring that all stakeholders depart from the same assertions. Go to *www.eur-lex.europa.eu* and search for Regulation 396 of 2005. Subsequent changes and a consolidated version dated 1 January 2011 are found under the Bibliographic Notice.

It is important to note that the EU works on the basis that maximum residue level (MRLs) for active substances are set at very low default levels (currently 0.01 mg/kg) unless users provide justification to set them higher. The coffee trade has provided as much information as was obtained from producing countries to ensure that MRLs relevant to coffee were set at realistic levels. It is, however, not known whether all active substances used by different producing countries have in fact been so identified and assessed as not all countries provided such information.

However, the general consensus is that the current legislation does not adversely affect the trade in green coffee, although the cost and frequency of future inspections by EU authorities of arrivals in EU ports remains to be established. It should also be noted that from a contractual point of view green coffee refused entry for exceeding the MRLs requirements can be considered as not merchantable and therefore not in compliance with contractual obligations.

An MRL database is provided on *www.ec.europa.eu/food/plant/protection/pesticides/database_pesticide_en.htm*

– look for product reference 0620000 for the list of MRLs currently applicable to coffee beans. The website also provides the latest updates to the MRL database.

Other information sites are: *www.ec.europa.eu/food/plant/protection/pesticides/index_en.htm* and *www.ec.europa.eu/food/plant/protection/pesticides/legislation_en.htm*. See also the site of the European Food Safety Authority at *www.efsa.europa.eu*.

EU regulations quote permissible MRLs per kilogram whereas other countries/systems may express such limits in terms of, for example, parts per million or per billion. The comparison below is provided for ease of reference.

A mass concentration of	2 mg/kg = 2 ppm
A mass concentration of	2 µg/kg = 2 ppb

mg = milligram; µg = microgram; ppb = parts per billion; ppm = parts per million.

OBSOLETE PESTICIDES

When developed countries prohibit the use of dangerous chemicals a logical question arises: what to do about existing stocks in developing countries?

Over time stocks have accumulated worldwide of banned chemicals and pesticides, some of which are Persistent Organic Pollutants or POPs. Banning apart, these substances also become obsolete through ageing, rendering them less effective (past sell-by date) but no less unsafe. They may be left over from pest control campaigns or simply stay around because they are not wanted anymore.

Box 12.1   Persistent Organic Pollutants

Of the 21 POPs currently (2011) listed by the 2001 Stockholm Convention on Persistent Organic Pollutants, 14 are pesticides: aldrin, alpha hexachlorocyclohexane, beta hexachlorocyclohexane, chlordane, chlordocone, DDT, dieldrin, endrin, henxachlorenebenzene, heptachlor, lindane, mirex, pentachlorobenzene and toxaphene (campheclor).

DDT is, however, exempted for restricted use by some countries in anti-malaria campaigns.

The condition of obsolete pesticide stocks and waste can vary from well-stored products that could still be used, to products leaking from corroded drums and other containers into the soil. Disposal is sometimes attempted by dumping in pits or burning and covering with soil. Over time severe environmental harm in the form of soil and water pollution – often permanent – may occur. Storage sites are often unsupervised and pose severe health risks, particularly to children. Previous WHO estimates have suggested as many as 3 million people are poisoned by pesticides annually, most of them in developing countries.

There is also the risk that without formal cleanup and prevention measures, obsolete pesticides may be repackaged and reappear in the market under different names. Many are very persistent which, health and environmental hazards aside, also makes them effective as pesticides for long periods and renders them attractive for illegal resale.

Safe disposal requires sophisticated technology that, mostly, is not available in poorer developing countries. The quantities to be disposed of may however not warrant the establishment of such facilities in individual countries. In many cases this then leaves export to approved disposal facilities elsewhere as the best option. Not only are the costs of this extremely high, ranging from US$ 3,000/ton to US$ 5,000/ton, but the material to be disposed of is not homogeneous. There is therefore no blanket solution for the disposal of obsolete pesticides. It is clear though that unless the issue is properly addressed, future generations in affected countries will continue to suffer the consequences of illegal disposal of these substances, many of which are used in agriculture.

Coffee producing countries worldwide are not immune from this. Different products may have been used in the past that are now prohibited and whose safe disposal presents not only safety and logistical problems, but is also very expensive. Illegal repackaging and resale could cause enormous problems whereas contamination into export crops is a real possibility. Condemnation of a country's green coffee exports for containing residues of such substances would have very serious, long-term economic consequences.

In Africa alone it is estimated that there could be as much as 50,000 tons of obsolete pesticides. In response to requests for assistance from many African countries, the Africa Stockpiles Programme (ASP) was therefore created to help address issues around the identification, safeguarding, removal and safe disposal of obsolete pesticides, and to prevent future accumulation. Initially targeted at seven priority countries (as of early 2009) with more countries to be added in due course.

Some of the international organizations partnering with developing country governments in ASP include the Food and Agricultural Organization of the UN, the World Bank, The World Wide Fund for Nature, the Global Environment Facility, the African Development Bank, the Pesticides Action Network (PAN UK), and CropLife International. To note that some trade pesticide products do not necessarily indicate the active ingredients by name, making it difficult to identify them correctly. However, a useful comparison table of Pesticides Prohibited and Restricted in Coffee Standards was prepared by PAN UK in 2011 and is available on request from the 4C Coffee Association – *www.4c-coffeeassociation. org*. The table lists a number of products by their active ingredient.

See also *www.africastockpiles.net* and *www.fao.org/ agriculture/crops/obsolete_pesticides/en/*.

MOULD PREVENTION – OTA

Mould is undesirable in any product, and coffee is no exception. In recent years mould in coffee has increasingly become associated with concerns over the presence in food and beverages of OTA. The toxicological status of OTA has not yet been settled but most major importing countries are nevertheless paying increasing attention to its occurrence in coffee and other agricultural products, and are requiring preventative measures.

In the European Union the following maximum limits apply to finished coffee products, effective 1 March 2007: roasted coffee – 5 ppb (parts per billion); soluble coffee – 10 ppb. No limit has been set for green coffee but green coffee remains under review; and there is provision for annual reporting of the occurrence of OTA and prevention measures.

In the meantime, a number of individual European countries (Czech Republic, Finland, Greece, Hungary, Italy, Portugal, Spain and Switzerland) have their own legislation or customs regulations in place that also set (varying) maximum limits on green coffee. Italy has limits on finished coffee products while in some countries (e.g. the Netherlands) internal instructions for food safety inspectors are in place. Germany, Europe's largest importer, applies the EU limits.

The danger for producers is that once a producing country is identified publicly (for instance through the EU 'rapid alert' system used by customs authorities to distribute information on shipments with a food safety risk) as a potential source of OTA contamination, the reputation and marketability of its coffee are likely to suffer. Italy has already established a system to identify 'high-risk' origins. Identification of a shipment with an excessive OTA level automatically results in the producing country being placed on a 'high risk' list, and it will be removed again only once a number of 'clean' shipments have been received.

A further issue is how green coffee would be sampled for OTA. As yet there is no universally agreed OTA related sampling and testing method for green coffee and the danger is that individual countries will establish their own individual procedures. It is in everyone's interest that sampling and testing procedures are standardized worldwide, including producing countries, and that adequate preventative measures are taken in producing countries because it is there that the problem can be addressed at source. More information on testing green coffee for OTA at *www.europroxima.com/uk/food-safety/mycotoxins/* and *www. vicam.com*.

The importance of mould prevention cannot be stressed enough. Returning a shipment that is rejected at the external border of the EU is now subject to Article 21 of Regulation 882/2004 of 29 April 2004 on official controls. The relevant part of this article, applicable to green coffee and imported finished coffee products, reads as follows.

Re-dispatch of consignments shall be allowed by competent authority only if:

- The destination has been agreed with the feed or food business operator responsible for the consignment;

- The feed or food business operator has first informed the competent authority of the third country of origin or third country of destination, if different, of the reasons and circumstances preventing the placing on the market of the feed or food concerned within the Community;

- When the third country of destination is not the country of origin, the competent authority of the third country of destination has notified the competent authority of its preparedness to accept the consignment.

Logically then, failure or inability to re-export will result in destruction of a rejected consignment. Hence it is entirely possible that in time the well-known United States contract condition 'no pass no sale' could also be introduced for coffees shipped to Europe and elsewhere.

To note also that it is prohibited to mix foodstuffs complying with the maximum levels with foodstuffs exceeding these maximum limits. This does not affect green coffee for which there are no maximum limits, but would mean that it would not be permissible to mix equal volumes of, for example, roasted coffee containing 7 ppb of OTA with roasted coffee containing 2 ppb to achieve an average of 4.5 ppb.

Visit www.ecf-coffee.org and look under publications for extensive, practical information on OTA as an issue in the production and trading of green coffee, including details of relevant legislation on OTA in the European Union. Visit www.coffee-ota.org for more extensive coverage and click on Training Tool for presentations on HACCP and the prevention of OTA along the coffee chain, including a CD-ROM version.

For an overview of European Food Law generally go to www.ec.europa.eu/food/food/foodlaw/index_en.htm.

In the United States the presence of OTA in agricultural products is one of a number of food safety aspects that receive routine attention at the FDA. Although the FDA monitors for contaminants, including mould, based on a risk assessment analysis no specific guidelines exist concerning OTA levels in coffee products.

OTA – IN COFFEE

In coffee OTA is produced by fungi of the Aspergillus genus (A. ochraceus, A. carbonarius, A. niger). It is mostly concentrated in the husk, which suggests that naturals (coffees dried in the cherry) are most at risk of contamination. Identified factors affecting mycotoxin levels in the coffee chain include:

- Environmental factors: temperature, moisture, mechanical injury (insect or bird damage, micro-organisms);

- Harvesting factors: crop maturity, temperature, moisture;

- Primary processing: drying, removal of defects;

- Storage: temperature, moisture;

- Distribution and processing: condensation.

Studies have shown that the most important sources of OTA contamination in green coffee are (i) inadequate sun drying of cherries leading to OTA formation in the pods and parchment husks, and (ii) defectives (including black beans), pods and husks (and dust). The drying stage is the most favourable time for the development of OTA. Adequate drying to uniformly low moisture levels and avoiding local wet spots, caused for example by uneven drying, rewetting or condensation, is crucial in prevention. Simple and cheap devices for solar drying of coffee can be of great help in improving drying practices, including prevention of rewetting by rain or dew.

Tests have also shown that the presence of an earthy/mouldy smell in green coffee is an early indicator of the presence of mould damage. Not every mould is OTA-forming, but an earthy smell (or cup) should trigger further investigation. Similarly, visually clean coffees that show no visible damage (rewetted bags/beans, broken beans, insect-damaged beans) are very much less likely to be significantly contaminated. The use of green coffee with a higher contamination level than 15 ppb is not recommended. Given a reduction of OTA contamination through processing of 2/3rd (this is a conservative figure, used to be on the safe side as the actual reduction may be higher), green coffee with a contamination level of less than 15 ppb can reasonably be expected not to present any problem in the finished coffee.

The preventative steps listed in this section apply as much to wet processed coffees as they do to dry processed (natural) arabica and robusta. Good housekeeping is essential.

Prevention is currently the only available effective way at farm level to combat OTA, although it should be noted that the removal of mouldy cherry, or the reprocessing of mouldy coffee, does not guarantee that the clean bean will be free from micro particles or spores.

Visit www.coffee-ota.org for an overview of research work done and in progress. Visit also www.ecf-coffee.org and look under Publications for extensive, practical information on OTA as an issue in the production and trading of green coffee.

OTA – PREVENTION DURING PRODUCTION, HARVESTING AND PROCESSING

Production

Work being done by the Food and Agricultural Organization of the United Nations (FAO) indicates that under certain conditions some coffee may become contaminated with OTA, while still on the tree. Guidelines are therefore being developed that aim at minimizing any spore load from OTA-producing fungi in the plantation itself. Once these guidelines have been finalized, further information will be made available at www.coffee-ota.org.

Harvesting and processing

- Cover the soil below the trees with clean plastic during picking to prevent cherries coming into contact with dirt or soil, or getting mixed with old, mouldy cherries left behind from previous picking rounds or the previous season.

- Do not use cherries that have been in contact with bare earth – they are susceptible to developing mould growth.

- Process fresh cherry as soon as possible. Either pulp them or commence drying on the day they are picked. Do not store fresh cherry, especially if fully ripe or overripe, as such storage promotes mould growth; do not hold cherry in bags.

- Never dry on bare earth, because mould spores remain in the soil and can contaminate cherry. Use mats, trays or tarpaulins. Raised drying tables, allowing air circulation, remain one of the most effective drying systems though.

- During the first two to three days of drying ensure the layer of drying cherry is as thin as possible to speed the process. After this, the layer should not be more than 4 cm (1½ inch) thick. Drying cherry should constantly be raked and turned, and should be covered at night and during rainfall.

Never allow partly or wholly dried cherry to get wet again; protect it at all times against rain, morning dew and accidental wetting.

OTA – PREVENTION DURING PROCESSING

Prevention during wet processing

- Dispose of pulp from wet processing away from drying or clean coffee. Compost it before using as mulch in the field.

- Pulp on day of picking. Separate floaters and control water quality. Monitor the quality of fresh cherry. What proportion of unpulped cherry and, conversely, nipped/naked beans do you accept? Are skins effectively separated? Ensure these factors are monitored.

- Remove pulp and skins from parchment. Sanitize equipment daily.

- Skin dry wet parchment to remove water quickly. If necessary remove excess water with forced drying. Then dry the parchment slowly to avoid cracking. Turn regularly; do not spread more than 4 cm (1½ inch) thick.

- Remove any pods and skins from the parchment by hand.

- Use drying mats or drying tables where possible. Never dry on bare earth, because mould spores remain in the soil and can cause contamination. Use mats, trays or tarpaulins. Again, raised drying tables, allowing air circulation, remain one of the most effective drying systems.

Prevention during dry processing

- Site the dry processing or hulling plant in a dry area, away from swamps.

- Do not buy or process wet coffee. If you must, then keep it separate and dry it immediately and correctly.

- Keep equipment and buildings clean. Do not allow dust and husk to accumulate and so contaminate clean (green) coffee.

- Ensure clean coffee contains no husk; more than 90% of mould originates from the husk of sun-dried cherry. Remove also dust, mouldy beans, unhulled cherries (pods) and so forth.

- Avoid adding husk or pods on purpose (in order to reach a maximum permitted defect level in the specification).

- Use only clean, dry bags for storage. Always keep cleaned coffee in a separate area, well closed off from the hulling area and the waste husk disposal site.

- Ideally moisture content should be even throughout. Use correctly calibrated moisture meters and ensure all meters are recalibrated at the start of each season, preferably more often. See also chapter 11.

- The risk of fungi growth is at its strongest when coffee is stored with a moisture content of over 12.5% (ISO 6673) and at high temperatures (over 25° C).

- Cover bags during transport to avoid any chance of rewetting. Load and offload only during dry weather or under cover. Store in well-ventilated, leak-proof warehouses. Always store away from walls and on pallets to allow ventilation and avoid storm water damage.

Obvious indicators of potential OTA presence in green coffee include wet or mouldy bags or beans, the presence of husks and pods, an earthy or mouldy smell, and earthy notes in the cup itself. But, OTA has also been found in completely clean coffee.

The ICO agreed method of moisture content analysis is ISO standard 6673; heating at 105° C during 16 hours, or moisture measuring equipment calibrated to the same standard. The sampling method referred to in ISO 6673 is ISO 4072. For details go to *www.iso.org* or *www.ecf-coffee. org* – publications.

Websites where information on moisture meters can be obtained include *www.sinar.co.uk, www.farmcomp.fi/index. php?id=56, www.enercorp.com, www.agric.gov.ab.ca/ index.html* (search for moisture meters), *www.decagon. com/aqualab/* and *www.aqua-boy.co.uk*.

www.coffee-ota.org has extensive coverage on all aspects of the OTA issue.

OTA – PREVENTION DURING SHIPMENT

Condensation occurs because moisture is always present in the air and hygroscopic (water-attracting) materials such as coffee normally contain a certain amount of moisture as well. Coffee with a moisture content in excess of 12.5% (ISO 6673) should never be shipped, whether in containers or bagged, as beyond this point the risk of condensation and therefore fungi growth occurring becomes unacceptably high. Under ICO minimum export standards, the only exceptions could be specialty coffees that traditionally have a high moisture content, such as Indian monsooned coffees.

This is not to suggest that a moisture content of 12.5% is commercially acceptable for all coffee – for certain coffees, certain origins and certain buyers it is definitely not. The figure of 12.5% simply represents a known technical point at which the risk of damage from condensation and growth of mould during storage and transport becomes unacceptably high. Shippers who normally ship their coffee at *moisture percentages below 12.5%* should definitely continue to do so.

An increasing number of buyers now include a maximum permissible moisture content in purchasing contracts. Increasing preoccupations with food health and hygiene in consuming countries suggest strongly that exporters will be well advised to acquaint themselves with their buyers' requirements in this regard.

OTA – bagged coffee in containers

Condensation cannot always be avoided, but it is possible to avoid or reduce damage by observing these basic precautions.

- Containers must be technically impeccable: watertight; free of holes and free of corrosion on the roof or sides; and intact door locks, rubber and sealing devices. They must always be swept clean and must be dry and odourless.

- When stuffing takes place at the shipper's premises the shipper must inspect the containers. An inspector should go inside the container and close the doors. If any daylight is visible the container must be rejected immediately. Also check that all rubber door seals are whole and tight.

- The actual stuffing of the container should take place under cover, just in case a rain shower occurs. Bags should be sound: no leaking, slack or torn bags; no wet bags; and no stained bags. Containers should never be filled to absolute capacity – always leave sufficient room above the stow.

- Best practice is to line the container with cardboard (ideal) or two layers of kraft paper, preferably corrugated, with the corrugation facing the steel structure, so bags do not come in contact with unexposed metal from the container. When stuffing is complete, fit a double layer of kraft paper on top of the bags all the way to the floor in the doorway. This will ensure that the paper will, at least partly, absorb any condensation from the roof. Note that although desiccants or dry bags are meant to absorb moisture during the voyage they should only be used with the express prior permission of the receiver. Many receivers do not permit their use under any circumstances.

- When making a booking with the carrier always give the instruction 'stow away from heat, cool stow and sun/weather protected'. The term 'stow under deck' is no longer appropriate for modern container vessels.

Experience shows that most of the condensation problems encountered during maritime transport are caused at origin (containers are stuffed too early ahead of actual shipment, or not properly lined), or immediately after offloading (particularly for containers arriving in winter). It is therefore of utmost importance to limit both transit times and the dwell or intermediate storage periods and land legs of the transit as much as possible.

OTA – bulk coffee in containers

Recent years have seen a substantial increase in the movement of coffee in bulk, using normal dry containers fitted with a liner. One advantage is the savings for shippers on the cost of bags (and no need to dispose of them at the receiving end), minus the cost of the liner. Another advantage is the higher carrying capacity. But there are other, not always immediately apparent advantages.

Coffee shipped in bulk, using normal dry containers fitted with a liner, always arrives in a better condition than coffee in bags when shipped under similar conditions. Shipping in bulk avoids most of the problems associated with bagged cargo: no baggy smells, no weight losses due to handling, and generally better preservation of quality.

Air caught inside the closed liner is called interstitial air. Interstitial air in a bulk load hardly moves as the individual beans are obstructing the free flow of air, and so the hot air cannot easily move to the edge. As a result, there is less transport of moisture to the roof and walls and the risk of condensation is thereby reduced.

Provided correct liners and procedures are used, and the coffee is shipped at the correct moisture content, then the incidence of claims on bulk cargo is vastly reduced compared to bagged cargo – according to some by as much as two-thirds.

The general principles for choosing a container are the same as when shipping bagged coffee.

COFFEE TASTING (LIQUORING)

Before entering into this subject it is appropriate to look at some aspects of quality that aspiring tasters or 'cuppers' should understand.

BLENDING

Most roasted coffee sold is blended. Usually only specialty coffee roasters offer straight coffees, i.e. exclusively from individual origins and mostly at very high prices. However, the authors do not share the belief held by some that blended coffees are necessarily always inferior to straight origin coffees; it all depends on what the blend consists of, and at which market segment it is aimed. There are blended coffees that easily outclass some of the 'straight origin coffees' one finds on the average retail shelf.

To clarify the practice of blending it is important to note again that the global market for coffee consists of three broad quality segments:

- **Exemplary quality:** Coffees with a high intrinsic value because of their fine or unique cup quality (taste). Usually of quite limited availability and mostly retailed under straight origin or estate names. Because by their nature exemplary coffees are of limited availability their adherents usually know this and accept that their favourite coffee may not always be available, and may not taste exactly the same from year to year. Limited availability translates into high prices, i.e. a marketing advantage.

- **High quality or premium brands:** Good tasting coffees well presented but not necessarily visually perfect. Retailed both as straight origins and as blends. This quality band is much broader and includes a good number of today's specialty coffees. It is also produced by leading multinational coffee companies and marketed through supermarkets. High-quality or premium brands are expected to be available always, and to taste the same, also always. Therefore, for such a coffee to be marketed as a straight origin, the supply must be large enough to be offered throughout the year. If not, then the only option is to create the required quality from the mixing, the blending of a number of compatible coffees that, between them, can offer year-round availability.

- **Mainstream quality:** Coffees of average quality, reasonably well presented, but certainly not imperfect. It offers an average taste experience and probably accounts for over 90% of the world market. Mainstream coffees are produced, traded and roasted in large quantities. Most are blends for two main reasons: large roasters cannot rely on just one or two origins for security of supply, and more often than not, consumer tastes in different markets cannot be satisfied by just a single origin in any case.

To summarize:

- Blending a number of compatible coffees creates a taste or flavour profile that can be maintained, also when individual origin availability changes. If subsequently a particular coffee is not available then it is replaced by another (or others), always maintaining an unchanged taste profile.

- Blending broadens the roaster's choice of raw material and so enhances supply security; availability does not depend on a single origin only. Also, coffee is available when needed.

- Blending aims to maintain the preferred taste or flavour profile at the lowest possible cost. This means that coffees are interchanged, not only on the basis of quality but also on the basis of their cost. The more flexible the blend the greater the money saving possibilities, a fact that unfortunately at times clashes with the quality requirements, especially in the lower end of the market.

The relationship between blending and taste or flavour profiles

Flavour profiles are a description of the taste sensation the average coffee drinker will encounter from a particular coffee. The art of blending is the means by which a roaster strives to maintain the same taste, throughout the year or throughout the life of a particular brand. Recording a specification of the required end result, i.e. the taste or flavour profile, helps achieve this. Basic profiles standardize certain objectives. For example:

- For a fresh, clean cup with some acidity use washed or mild arabicas;

- For a more full-bodied cup add natural arabicas;

- For higher cup yield and lower prices: add robustas.

The blending action combines any or all of these three basic taste groups in different proportions to achieve a certain taste sensation. But, within each base group there are many potential supply options. For mainstream blends the number of potential supply options usually is quite large, whereas for higher quality and specialty blends the number of potential candidate coffees shrinks fairly rapidly. For top quality blends the number will be quite small. Water quality in the target market may also play a role, sometimes necessitating the production of slightly different versions of the same brand for different markets.

The blend master will profile the taste of each component of the blend by recording acidity, body, flavour, aftertaste etc. He will record the proportion of each component used in the final blend and will record the flavour profile of that final blend. The objective are:

- Stability: maintain the blend taste profile vis-à-vis the end-user, batch after batch.

- Security: select different coffees when availability changes or when the delivered quality of a purchase disappoints, by matching other coffees against the required profile.

- Profit: produce each batch at the lowest possible price by juggling components.

The blend master has the choice to blend the green coffee components first and then roast the mixture. Or, the blender can roast the individual components separately and blend them afterwards. This choice will depend on personal preference and appreciation of the blend components that are to be used.

Profiling also enables the blend master not to bother with coffees or origins for which he knows the flavour profile to be unsuitable. This is why so many samples that exporters send are never acknowledged or reported upon – the buyer knows they are unlikely to fit the required profile.

Finally, some specialty coffee flavour profiles have become incredibly complex, to the point where the average coffee consumer probably becomes completely lost and simply accepts that what is claimed is true. At the other end of the scale we find the erosion of blend quality, for example when quality is sacrificed because of higher prices or lack of availability.

Whatever the market, for an exporter the most important point to bear in mind is that having established a profile that a particular buyer accepts and uses, each and every subsequent delivery should be a full match. If at some stage this proves to be impossible then advise the buyer of the problem, openly and honestly. Never simply ship such a coffee and hope to get away with it.

THE ROAST

Coffee quality is assessed in terms of the green appearance, the roast appearance and by taste (cup or liquor).

The green appearance is discussed extensively in chapter 11.

Coffee quality is greatly influenced by the roasting process. Dark roasts tend to obscure the finer aspects but enhance the body. Light roasts emphasize acidity but result in a weaker brew. See chapter 11 for the Agtron system of roast colour measurements. The degree of roasting depends therefore on one's marketing objectives. From the professional taster's point of view, it is easier to detect quality and any off-flavours when coffee is roasted lighter rather than darker. A light roast also makes it easier to spot immature and green beans, which tend to show up as yellowish pale in colour rather than brown when roasted. All pales affect the cup quality, but extreme cases of pales (bright yellow beans) spoil the cup by giving it a 'quakery' or 'peanut' taste.

The roast of naturals (sun-dried coffees) tends to lack the bright whitish centre cuts of wet-processed arabicas. In general, dull roasts also suggest imperfectly processed or aged coffees, whereas bright roasts indicate freshness and good processing. The following descriptions are commonly used:

- **Fine roast**. Bright, brilliant, uniform and even, no pales.
- **Good to fine**. Bright, uniform, even, no pales.
- **Good roast**. Bright to dullish, reasonably even, occasional pale, no other defects such as ears or brokens.
- **Good to fair**. Dullish, slightly uneven, mottled, a few pales and other defects, can be soft and open.
- **Fair to poor**. Dull and uneven, a number of pales and other defects, generally soft and open, often containing many brokens.
- **Poor**. Anything below fair to poor.

Uneven bean size produces uneven roasts because small, broken and light beans roast faster than whole and solid beans. Very small pieces or chips may even burn up altogether. Some roasters prefer to roast coffees from

different origins separately and then to combine them afterwards. Strong growth in the specialty and whole bean segments of the consumer market has rekindled the emphasis on a coffee's roast appearance, and at the retail end the roast is perhaps the first thing the consumer really looks at.

THE CUP OR LIQUOR

The cup remains the most important determinant of a coffee's usefulness and value. All exporters grade coffee visually, by size and defect count, but not all cup test. Only the cup can reveal a coffee's true value, however, and exporters who cannot taste cannot bargain as equals with importers and roasters who always taste.

Taste is a highly subjective matter and different tasters or liquorers will have different opinions on the quality, appeal and value of a particular cup or liquor. There are no international cupping standards and nor is the terminology standardized. This adds to the subjectivity. Coffee tasting and wine tasting are comparable: both are done to determine quality, usefulness and price.

As a rule of thumb, cup characteristics can be loosely characterized in the following ways:

- **Robustas**. Mostly supplied as unwashed, sun-dried or naturals. Taste varies from neutral to coarse with strong robusta flavour. Neutral coffees are preferred for blending whereas those with strong robusta flavour are particularly suitable for soluble coffee. Well-prepared pulped and washed robustas are appreciated for their good body and neutral taste and the absence of off-flavours whereas there is growing interest in differentiating high quality or fine robustas by origin and cup characteristics.
- **Washed arabicas.** The most appreciated are those with a well-balanced (rounded) cup where good acidity and body, together with some flavour or aroma, complement each other. Marks for acidity range from pronounced through good, fair and slight to lacking; for body from heavy through good, medium and light to lacking; and for flavour from excellent through good, some and slight to lacking.
- **Unwashed arabicas or naturals.** This group (mainly Brazils, Ecuadors and sun-dried Ethiopians) tends to have less well-balanced body and acidity. Ecuadors are often fruity and occasionally sourish. Brazils frequently have a harsh or 'Rio' taste especially coffees grown in certain zones of the states of Espirito Santo, São Paulo and Rio de Janeiro. Unwashed Brazils that are free from 'Rio' or 'Rio taint' are known as soft or strictly soft and command a premium over hard or Rioish and Rio-type coffees.
- **Pulped Brazils.** This is a relatively new form of coffee from Brazil in which the cherry is pulped immediately after harvesting and is then sun-dried, so without fermentation or washing as in the normal wet process. Such coffees

tend to combine good body with a sweeter cup than is found in traditional Brazils that are dried in the cherry. These coffees are making inroads into the traditional market for secondary mild arabicas.

THE COFFEE LIQUORER (THE CUPPER)

Most people can acquire the liquoring technique, but it takes years of on-the-job training in the liquoring rooms of exporters, importers and roasters. Exporters must understand the preoccupations of the roasters, and a top liquorer will have experience of both sides of the 'divide'. Trading quality coffee is impossible without liquoring expertise. It remains surprising that not all producing countries offer formal training courses and official recognition to coffee professionals.

The liquorer's first objective is to determine if a coffee is acceptable in terms of type and standard. The less sophisticated the standard the easier it is to approve a coffee. But when it comes to better coffees then it is not only acceptability but also marketability that count. The liquorer must be able to assess not only a coffee's marketability and potential usage, but also its price range.

Marketability. Who can use this? Who wants this? Know your markets and know your buyers. Travel and cup test with them.

Price. What will they pay for this? Know the quality your competitors supply. Know what other origins offer. Again, travel, attend tradeshows and visit roasters. It is only by cupping your coffee against that of others that you can assess which has the advantage.

Tasting – traditional versus espresso

Following the introduction of soluble coffee in the 1950s, the next major change at the consumer level was the introduction of the home coffee-maker, the drip machine. This tended to split the market into roast and ground for those preferring convenience, and whole bean roasted for those who prefer to grind their own coffee at home. Further differentiation has come through the introduction of home coffee making machines that use pods, for example Nespresso and Senseo. But the next largest major change has probably been the huge inroads made by espresso in importing countries during the 1990s. Most coffee bars and cafés in the United States, Europe and Asia today have extended their product menu to include different types of espresso coffee.

Traditionally, coffee tasting has been done on the premise that the coffee would be used as soluble, roast and ground or whole bean. This permitted more or less the same methodology and terminology to be used to evaluate the quality. But there are significant differences between the brewing processes of traditional coffee and espresso, so much so that traditional liquoring alone cannot provide a correct evaluation of a coffee's suitability for use as espresso.

The steps before tasting the liquid coffee are always the same (examining the green and the roast, smelling the ground coffee and so on). For traditional tasting, about 10 g of ground coffee is brewed in cups containing about 230 g of boiling water. This is not a scientific process: the water temperature may vary, the weight is not always exactly 10 g and the water measure may not always be exactly right. The temperature of the water changes as the cups are poured and so on. But experienced cup testers know all this and so will taste more than a single cup per sample. They may also taste the sample various times. In the end it is the cup tester's personal assessment of all the different factors and sensations that determines what they will do with the sample in question. In real life consumers do not use a scientific process to prepare or evaluate their coffee either. They like it or they do not, and it is the cup tester's job to make sure they do.

But this method does not work for espresso. The espresso cup is a concentrated beverage, which can be said to exaggerate all the aromas, and fragrances found in the coffee bean.

Unlike the traditional coffee served in many bars and hotels, espresso must always be fresh. It can only be made on demand. The customer has to wait for the coffee, not the other way around. It was the desire to supply many cups of fresh coffee quickly and efficiently that led to a major innovation for traditional brewing systems. Italian inventors introduced the use of water pressure to speed up the extraction process.

Today, making espresso is a mixture of art and science. Italy is home to a large and fast-growing manufacturing and export business not only of espresso machines and all the accompanying accessories, but also of espresso coffee roasted and packed in Italy. Names such as Illy and Lavazza are but two of many found all over the world; they are even found in producing countries. The introduction of the espresso pod (pre-packed dosages of coffee ready for use 'as is' in the espresso machine), the growth of specialty coffee chains such as Starbucks, and increasingly efficient mini espresso machines for home use have all contributed to Italy's spectacular growth as a coffee processing and exporting centre.

Tasting – traditional versus espresso: differences to watch

Espresso is a brew obtained by percolation of hot, not boiling, water under pressure through a cake of roasted ground coffee. The energy of the water pressure is spent within the cake, according to *Espresso Coffee* by Andrea Illy and Rinantonio Viani, Academic Press, London 1995. The pressure accentuates taste aspects that are not immediately obvious in cups prepared in the traditional way. Sharp acidity turns into bitterness, freshness or slight fruitiness turns into sourness and fruity turns into fermented because all the flavour components are extracted. And this is not all; espresso is nearly always sugared, and the interaction of sugar and these intense flavours can again alter the final taste palette the taster encounters. Some flavours benefit, others are 'turned' and become negative.

For example, a pleasant tasting coffee that is slightly winey may be eminently suitable for sale as an exemplary quality in a niche market. But it will probably never make the grade for espresso, because once concentrated, the same winey flavour may turn into something quite unpleasant.

The other aspect to bear in mind is the foam or *crema* that is always present in every well made cup of espresso. Briefly, the machine pressure is allowed to drop, which permits the cup to be filled. The drop in pressure releases dissolved gases into the cup and this is what produces the foam. The foam must survive at least a few minutes before breaking up and starting to show the dark surface of the liquid itself. A perfect espresso looks as good as it tastes.

Some coffees produce excellent foam; others do not. Most espresso coffee is therefore a blend of different coffees that together produce the desired combination of both taste and cup appearance.

Green coffee exporters wanting to supply the important espresso market on a sustained basis must familiarize themselves with the differences between their traditional cupping and the basics of espresso liquoring. Better still, they should practice espresso liquoring alongside their traditional cupping by acquiring the necessary equipment.

The Q Coffee System of quality control

The Q Coffee System, developed by the Coffee Quality Institute, is an ongoing initiative to introduce internationally accepted standards for quality, both cup and grade, for the specialty coffee trade. The underlying assumption is that while anyone can state they have quality, companies that have their coffees graded through the Q Coffee System will have the ability to provide their customers a guarantee from a credible and independent third-party. The Q Coffee System is presented as an effective way to source coffees, allowing companies to develop specifications unique to them, and more effectively differentiate themselves against the competition.

Using technical standards developed by the Specialty Coffee Association of America (SCAA – *www.scaa.org*), the Q Coffee System institutes a common language for quality that makes quality less subjective, levelling the playing field for producers. In the Q Coffee System, three licensed Q graders, professionally accredited cuppers, evaluate the coffees. The scores are then averaged to produce a Q Certificate that includes a point rating and a cup profile of the coffee. The Q Certificate provides the necessary

information to communicate quality to customers and consumers, fostering their interest in the coffee you offer.

On the basis that sustainability begins with economic viability, the promoters of the Q Coffee System argue that it takes a market-based approach to economic viability, and therefore sustainability, by giving producers a tool to improve their incomes. The Q Coffee System also places roasters in a proactive position regarding responsible sourcing as opposed to a defensive one. Thus, the Q is a valuable component of corporate social responsibility programmes and an ideal complement to social and environmental certifications. Only with quality and cooperation can sustainability truly become a reality.

The Q Coffee System is presented visually below, reproduced courtesy of the Coffee Quality Institute from whom more information can be obtained – see *www.coffeeinstitute.org*.

The Q Coffee System – overview

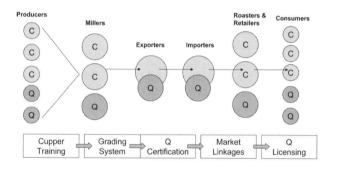

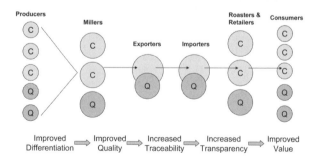

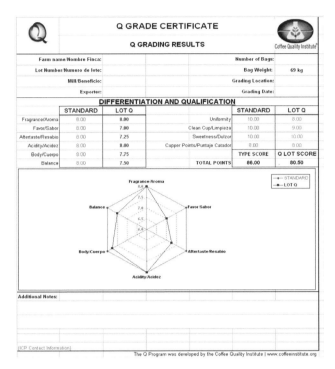

How the Q Coffee System works:

- Quality is defined, measured and standardized through internationally recognized protocols.
- Highly-skilled coffee cuppers (licenced Q graders) are utilized throughout origin and consuming countries.
- In-country partners are established at origin to manage and oversee coffee grading.
- Coffees are graded by three licenced Q graders, scores are averaged and provided in the form of a Q Certificate or technical report.

Building on the experience gained with creating the Q Coffee System in arabica, the Coffee Quality Institute has also developed a protocol and cupping form for fine robusta and commenced the training and licensing of R graders. For more information contact the CQI at *www.coffeeinstitute.org.*

CLASSIFICATION TERMS

GLOSSARY – GREEN OR RAW COFFEE

Ambers: Smooth yellowish beans caused by soil conditions.

Antestia-damaged: Beans damaged by the Antestia bug, resulting in black depressions on the bean, which is often completely shrivelled.

Black beans: Caused by harvesting immature beans or gathering them after they have dropped to the ground. Blacks are often taken as the yardstick for rating a defect count.

Blackish beans: Pulper-nipped beans which have partly oxidized.

Bleached beans: Colourless beans, often caused by drying too rapidly or over-drying. Also known as soapy and faded beans, usually associated with mechanical drying.

Blotchy beans: The result of uneven drying.

Broca-damaged beans: Beans partially eaten away by an insect (Stephanoderes hampei) which bores galleries through the bean.

Brown beans: Brown in colour. May be caused by faulty fermentation, improper washing or over drying – see also 'foxy'.

Coated beans: Beans to which the silverskin adheres. Caused by drought, over-bearing or harvesting of unripe cherries (see also chapter 11).

Crushed beans: Pulper-damaged beans, which often split and fade. Also caused by manual pounding of dry cherry to separate beans from husk (pilonnage in French).

Discoloured beans: Often pulper-damaged. Other causes are contact with earth, metal and foul water as well as damage after drying and beans left over in fermenting tanks (see also 'stinkers').

Drought-affected beans: Either coated or misshapen, pale and light in weight.

Dull, unnatural coloured beans: Due to faulty drying, often associated with metal contamination.

Ears: Part of a broken elephant bean.

Earthy beans: Smell of earth, caused by collecting beans fallen on bare ground.

Elephant beans: A generic aberration resulting in two beans being joined together – usually deformed and likely to break up during processing/roasting (see also 'ears', above).

Faded beans: Beans from old crop or dried too rapidly.

Flaky beans: Usually very thin, light and ragged (see also 'drought-affected', 'lights' and 'ragged').

Floats or floaters/lights: Under-developed, hollow beans – the fruit will float in water and is 'floated off' during wet processing. In washed coffee a sign of inadequate grading during wet processing.

Foxy beans: Rust or reddish coloured, a result either of harvesting overripe, sometimes yellow, cherries, delays in pulping, improper fermentation or faulty washing.

Green, water-damaged: Self-explanatory – usually brought about by dry parchment or hulled coffee becoming wet.

Hail-damaged beans: Show blackish circular marks on the oval side of the bean.

Light bean: Bean the specific weight of which is below normal – caused by drought or die-back.

Mottled beans: Are blotched, spotty or stained. Usually due to uneven drying.

Musty (mouldy) beans: Partial or wholly discoloured, whitish fur-like colour and texture (see also chapter 11). Show mould growth visible by the naked eye or evidence of mould attack.

Overripe: Brownish-yellow appearance; also known as foxy.

Peaberry: A single oblong or ovaloid roundish bean – a result of only one bean developing in a cherry instead of the usual two.

Pulper-nipped: Bean damaged by incorrect setting of the pulping knives – can become discoloured through oxidation during fermentation and may produce off-flavours.

Quakers: Blighted and undeveloped beans – show up as roast defects.

Ragged: This description often refers to drought-affected beans – harvesting a mixture of mature and immature cherries results in beans having a ragged appearance.

Stinkers: Beans which are over-fermented owing to improper cleaning of pulpers, fermenting tanks and washing channels.

Three-cornered beans: Semi-peaberry in character.

Withered: Light and shrivelled beans caused by drought or poor husbandry.

NB: The exporters/traders/roasters' technical vocabulary contains many more terms such as sticks, stones, pods (cherry), parchment, under-dried, under-fermented, etc. These are, however, all self-explanatory.

GLOSSARY – LIQUOR OR CUP

Acidy: A desirable flavour that is sharp and pleasing, but not biting. The term 'acid' as used by the coffee trade refers to coffee that is smooth and rich, and has verve, snap and life as against heavy, old and mellow taste notes.

Acrid: A burnt flavour that is sharp, bitter and perhaps irritating.

Astringent: A taste that causes puckering and a bitter impression.

Aftertaste: A taste that remains in the mouth longer than usual after eating or drinking.

Aroma: Usually, pleasant-smelling substances with the characteristic odour of coffee. Chemically, they are aldehydes, ketones, esters, volatile acids, phenols, etc.

Baggy: An undesirable taint, resembling the smell of a bag made from jute. Often observed in coffees that have been stored for long periods under unsuitable conditions.

Baked: Generally unpleasant characteristic. Sign of coffee having been over-roasted or roasted too slowly.

Balanced or round: Acidity and body are both present to the right extent.

Bitter: When strong, an unpleasant, sharp taste; biting like quinine. Similar to acidity, but lacking smoothness.

Bland or neutral: Tasting smooth and flavourless, lacking coffee flavour and characteristics. However, this is not necessarily always a negative comment.

Body: A taste sensation or mouth feeling of more viscosity, used to describe the mouth feel of a drink corresponding to a certain consistency or an apparent viscosity, but not an increase in true viscosity. Sought after in most if not all coffees.

Carbolic, chemical: Self-explanatory. Workers who have had wounds on legs treated with disinfectant and have then worked in tanks can cause this type of flavour. Certain emulsions in the manufacture of sacks are also a problem.

Carmelized: Burnt-like flavour; carmelized sugar flavour. Usually associated with spray-dried instant coffee, but sometimes found in roasted coffee.

Common, commonish: Poor liquor, lacking acidity but with full body. Usually associated with coated raw beans and softs and pales in roast.

Earthy: Self-explanatory. Not to be confused with grassy.

Fermented: Chemical flavour caused by enzymes on the green coffee sugars. Very unpleasant odour and taste. In its strongest form sometimes referred to as 'hidey' referring to smell of untreated animal hides.

Foul: Objectionable liquor often similar to rotten coffee pulp. Sometimes the most advanced stage of fruity and sour coffees. Causes are mostly bad factory preparation or the use of polluted water. It must be noted that one badly discoloured bean is sufficient to give a foul cup to an otherwise good liquor.

Fruity: First stage of sourness. Caused by overripe and yellow cherry or by fermentation with too many skins.

Grassy: A very pronounced green flavour can be most unpleasant.

Green, greenish: Flavour suggestive of hay. More common in early pickings. In some coffees this flavour is lost a few weeks after curing. Seldom found in coffees which have been thoroughly dried.

Harsh: A harshness of body. Coffee of immature raw appearance (but not necessarily from green cherry) frequently has a harsh taste. Drought-stricken or over-bearing trees producing mottled cherry frequently give this flavour.

Musty or mouldy: Self-explanatory. Caused by piling or bagging very wet parchment or by dry parchment getting wet. (See 'musty', under Green or raw coffee, above.)

Natural: Natural characteristic is the full body, slight bitterness indicative of natural processed coffee. It is a negative characteristic of a fully washed coffee.

Neutral: No predominant characteristics – can make a good base for blending.

Onion flavour: Often bordering on foul. Associated with the use of badly polluted and stagnant water.

Pungent: A taste sensation of overall bitterness of brew. A prickly, stinging, or piercing sensation not necessarily unpleasant.

Quakery: A peanutty taste, usually associated with pales in the roast.

Rioy or Phenolic: A taste with medicinal odour and off notes, slightly iodized phenolic or carbolic. Cannot be hidden by blending – always returns.

Rubbery: Odour and taste of rubber. Usually present in fresh robustas.

Sour, sourish: Unpleasant flavour, suggestive of rotting coffee pulp. Caused by faulty factory work, improper fermentation resulting in a continuation of the fermentation process during early stages of drying, overripe and yellow cherry, or delayed drying causing a heating of the coffee, excess fermentation with many skins. Discoloured pulper-nipped beans are a frequent cause (see also chapter 11).

Strong: Unbalanced liquor where body predominates to the point of being tainted.

Taint: A term used to denote the presence of flavours that are foreign to good clean liquor, but which cannot be clearly defined or placed in any category. It is often described as an offtaste or peculiar flavour for lack of a clear definition. Where the foreign flavour can be defined it is, of course, named accordingly.

Thin: Lacking body.

Twisty: A liquor which, although not directly unclean, is suspect and may become unclean.

Unclean: Self-explanatory. A coffee which has an undefined unclean taste.

Winey: A fruity taste similar to fresh wine. Not necessarily unpleasant when the taste is in the background.

Woody: A coarse common flavour peculiar to old crop coffee. Coffee stored at low altitudes with high temperatures and humidity (as in many ports of shipment) tends to become woody rather quickly. Storage at higher altitudes where feasible or in temperate climates is therefore recommended for long-term warehousing. All coffees, however, become woody if stored for too long.

PHENOLIC TASTE, RIO FLAVOUR AND FERMENTED

It is worthwhile to review these phenomena in some detail as they are often confused.

Phenolic taste

Synonyms for phenol include carbolic acid and hydroxybenzene. As far as is known the occurrence of phenolic taste, like a number of other off-tastes, is linked to the chemical composition of the bean. Such beans cannot be detected by visual inspection, nor is there any recognized method for combating their occurrence. Different sources offer differing causes, but it should be understood that not everyone understands the same by phenolic taste. For example, some cuppers wrongly identify certain types of over-fermentation as phenolic taste. Others believe it can be caused by poor sanitation or mould infestation during wet processing or drying but, although these may be variations on the same taste theme, the causes are not necessarily the same. See also chapter 11.

True phenolic beans, according to some, are more likely to be produced by drought and heat-affected trees. That is to say, the bean's chemical composition changes as a result of extreme growing conditions and so does the taste. If so, then the chemical change might in fact represent some kind of natural reaction, in response to the unfavourable environment. This appears to be entirely logical because healthy, vigorous trees always produce better quality than stressed trees. The most likely remedy would therefore appear to be the application of at least a minimal level of irrigation, assuming of course this resource is available.

Other beans that cause equally unpleasant off-tastes include what is known as invisible stinkers; beans that have been affected by chemical substances as carbolic acid for example; or beans that have suffered bacterial infection during the growing stage. These off-tastes may in some cases be mistaken for phenolic taste but it is important to recognize that the cause is different.

Invisible stinkers are beans that have been over-fermented during wet processing, but not to the point where actual decomposition sets in, i.e. they maintain a bluish-green appearance and are hard to spot. Or, the beans have suffered insect stings or minute cracks that allow fermentation water to enter and so continue the process. Beans that have been affected by unsanitary conditions or mould infestation during processing and drying are also invisible stinkers.

Bacterial infections can occur when coffee cherries are stung by insects while on the tree, with the sting damage allowing bacterial infection to take place, for example producing potato flavour or peasiness. This is fairly prevalent in certain countries.

These three groups of off-beans share one common trait: their chemical composition is different from that of sound beans. In most instances, they can only be recognized and removed through ultraviolet sorting.

The question of why beans of good green appearance nevertheless sometimes produce off-tastes has always been of interest because such beans can cause unexpected problems for roasters. This is particularly so for gourmet/specialty roasters who normally roast smallish batches that offer little chance of the offending bean being dispersed over a large quantity.

Already in June 1975, at the 7th International Scientific Colloquium on Coffee in Hamburg, the East African Industrial Research Organization in Nairobi presented a paper dealing with the identification of over-fermented beans (stinkers) through exposure to ultraviolet light that made such beans fluoresce because their chemical composition was different from that of sound beans. Yet, such beans were often unrecognizable with the naked eye, which is an important finding.

Note though that as coffee ages, its chemical composition changes as well. The resultant woody or old taste is in fact the result of chemical change. This means that as the beans age, so most or all of them begin to fluoresce. This makes it impossible to select the offending beans that were the original target. Therefore, as we understand it, for the ultraviolet sorting process to work well it should only be used for fresh coffee, promptly after milling. Also, the coffee should not be overly coated, i.e. not too much silver skin remains attached to the beans. Within these limitations we estimate that for certain producers ultraviolet sorting (or UV sorting) equipment may be of interest. For further information we suggest to visit www.Satake-USA.com. Some success has also been achieved using near infrared sorting to detect those infected beans not picked by ultra violet but this method remains experimental and only worthwhile in specific instances.

For more scientific questions and discussion we suggest visiting www.asic-cafe.org to make contact with the Association scientifique internationale du café (ASIC).

The difference between Rio flavour, phenolic taste and fermented

These taste phenomena have different causes such as climatic conditions, bacterial infection, contamination, poor sanitation, poor quality control, mismanagement, or a combination of some of these. Within each off-taste description one encounters varying degrees of intensity and, indeed, different 'tastes'. All unpleasant, but some are worse than others. This variability can and does lead to confusion amongst cuppers with some simply labeling an offending coffee as 'unclean' and discarding it. But for serious quality analysis, especially with a view to finding the cause of a particular off-taste, more in-depth evaluation is absolutely necessary. The authors' understanding is as follows:

> Rio flavour (or Rioy flavour) is typically associated with certain Brazilian coffees (but is also encountered elsewhere). A taste with medicinal odour and off notes, slightly iodised phenolic or carbolic. To note though that certain markets have an actual preference for 'astringent' or 'hardish' coffees. In Coffee – ISBN 0-582-46359-9 – Gordon Wrigley refers to Rio as a very characteristic harsh, even acid or acrid, flavour which is sometimes described as being medicinal or having an iodine flavour. Espresso Coffee: The Chemistry of Quality – ISBN 0-12-370670-X, edited by Andrea Illy and Rinantonio Viani – reports on Rioy beans as smelling 'dusty, musty, earthy,

woody, corky, cereal, iodine-like, phenolic; and tasting of bitterness, burned, rubbery, rioy, phenolic, acrid, pungent, earthy, corky, musty, stale and medicinal'.

In some countries Rio flavour is considered equivalent to phenolic, but there is an important difference. Phenolic taste is close in that when cupping phenolic beans separately one encounters a medicinal taste that is similar to Rio. However, true phenolic beans (the result of climatic conditions) can occur sporadically in a parcel (hence the earlier reference to UV sorting). However, Rio is usually encountered much more generally, making sorting more or less impossible.

The two, Rio (or Rioy) and phenolic, have in common that the taste cannot be hidden through blending, i.e. cannot be diluted through mixing with other coffees. The difference is that Rio flavour usually occurs as a general taste aspect, whereas true phenolic beans occur only sporadically and, under certain circumstances, can be identified through ultraviolet or UV sorting.

Fermented or over-fermented is quite different. Ferment covers a range of objectionable off-tastes, best described as being associated with decay. In its early stages 'ferment' can present itself as a sweetish, overripe, fruity/oniony taste that for some (not many) can still be acceptable. In its worst stage one can encounter a totally putrid, foul taste that is most off-putting. In between these extremes is found a quite a range of varying taste sensations. Note that for most roasters there is no such thing as 'just a little ferment'. See also chapter 11.

As a broad generalization one could perhaps briefly classify the causes of these different off-tastes as follows:

- Rio flavour: very high humidity during the growing season.
- Phenolic flavour: very hot and dry conditions during the growing season.
- Natural fermentation: overripe cherry left for some time on the tree.
- Fermentation/contamination: overripe cherry left for some time on the ground.
- Over-fermentation: poor management control during wet processing.

CHAPTER 13

CLIMATE CHANGE AND THE COFFEE INDUSTRY

CLIMATE CHANGE AND THE COFFEE INDUSTRY

RISING TEMPERATURES – CONSEQUENCES AND CHALLENGES

While climate change is just one of numerous factors affecting global coffee production, the International Coffee Organization considers it is likely to be one of the most important ones. Smallholders (who produce the majority of the world's coffee) are the most vulnerable group – and the least equipped to cope with the changes. Moreover, it is important to note that current initiatives to reduce the extent of global warming are mostly aimed at limiting further warming, not to rapidly reverse it.

Complexity and uncertainty make it hard to be precise, but it is generally accepted that climate change affects both arabica and robusta producers. Rising temperatures are expected to render certain producing areas less suitable or even completely unsuitable for coffee growing, meaning production may have to shift and alternative crops will have to be identified. Incidences of pests and diseases will increase and coffee quality is likely to suffer; both factors could limit the viability of current high quality producers. More coffee may need to be grown under irrigation, thereby increasing pressure on scarce water resources.

All the foregoing will increase the cost of production, whereas in the future fewer parts of the world may be suitable for coffee production. If so, then the already evident growth in concentration could become even more pronounced, bringing with it an increased risk of high volatility. For example, if an extreme event should severely curtail the output of one of the major producers.

SOME CONSIDERATIONS

New scientific evidence suggests that climate change is accelerating at a much faster pace than previously thought and that important tipping points, leading to irreversible changes in major Earth systems and ecosystems, may already have been reached or even overtaken. (Text taken from the foreword by Mr. Ban Ki-moon, UN Secretary-General, to the *Climate Change Science Compendium 2009,* published by the United Nations Environment Programme.)

Human beings depend for their livelihood on agriculture more than on any other economic activity. This is particularly true for small farmers in developing countries whose economic well-being and food security hinges primarily on farming. Because of this and its high dependence on climate, agriculture has received a great deal of attention promoting studies and debates over how developing countries might adapt to the impact of climate change. The subject is exceedingly complex, not only from the agricultural perspective, but also because of its implications for the global agricultural and trade policies that impact agricultural production and food security.

While climate change is just one of numerous factors that may affect global coffee production, it is nonetheless likely to be one of the most important ones. It is true that a great degree of uncertainty still exists with regard to how individual producing regions will be affected, and how climate change will affect overall coffee production. However, experts expect some changes to occur and these could be significant in some regions. To complicate matters further, the potential impact will not only vary between countries, but also within producing areas in individual countries, for example due to different altitudes.

Box 13.1   The Kyoto Protocol

The first formal global reaction to the need to isolate greenhouse gases (GHG) from the atmosphere and to limit their emission was materialized in a document called the Kyoto Protocol. See details in *www.unfccc.int/2860.php*.

The protocol arose from the need for defining **mechanisms for isolating GHG from the atmosphere** and **goals for limited GHG emissions.** The global response was materialized in a document called the Kyoto Protocol. The most publicized source of global warning are fossil fuels (electricity generation, manufacturing, transport, etc.). But deforestation in non-industrialized countries also contributes quite considerably as it reduces the available tree park. Trees are efficient absorbers of CO_2, whereas burning them releases carbon dioxide into the atmosphere.

Industries and others that produce GHG can calculate their emissions and offset these against certificates of emission reduction or CER. For example by investing in planting new trees or sources of renewable energy, either directly or (mostly) through the purchase of offset or renewable energy certificates generated by others who engage in these activities. The international market for such certificates is developing rapidly and is generally referred to as the emissions offset market. Much background information is available at *www.v-c-s.org*.

CLIMATE CHANGE AND COFFEE PRODUCTION

Climatic variability has always been the main factor responsible for the fluctuation of coffee yields in the world. Climate change, as a result of global warming, is expected to result in actual shifts on where and how coffee may be produced in future. This will affect millions of producers as well as all other participants in the value chain, right up to the end-consumer and presents a major challenge to the coffee industry. How to mitigate the impact?

The current change in global climate is – to an extent that is disputed, also among scientists – due to the burning of fossil energy (coal, oil, natural gas) and to the mineralization of organic matter as a result of land use. These processes are caused by humankind's exploitation of fossil resources, clearing of natural vegetation (forests for example) and use of these soils for agriculture. The result is a measurable increase in the carbon dioxide (CO_2) content of the atmosphere, an increase that results in global warming. This is so because CO_2 hinders the reflection of sunlight back into space, thereby trapping more of it in the Earth's atmosphere. Other contributing GHG are methane (CH_4), nitrous oxide (N_2O), hydro fluorocarbons (HFCs), per fluorocarbons (PFCs) and sulphur hexafluoride (SF_6).

It is important to note that different forms of agriculture, including coffee production, also contribute to GHG emissions, and hence to climate change. But so do all other links in the chain: processing, trading, transport, roasting, packaging, retailing, brewing, serving, etc. Thus, there is a need for all participants to collaborate on limiting coffee's contribution to the GHG problem. However, coffee growers are by far the most numerous group that is directly affected and the most vulnerable to the impact of global warming.

POSSIBLE EFFECTS OF CLIMATE CHANGE ON COFFEE PRODUCTION

(Text in this section is based on 'Global warming: the impact on global coffee' by Dr. Peter Baker and Dr. Jeremy Haggar.)

Quality: As temperature rises, coffee ripens more quickly leading to a fall in inherent quality. This statement is supported by the fact that low-grown arabica from tropical areas with higher temperatures mostly shows less quality in the cup compared to the same coffee grown at higher altitudes. The beans are softer and may well be larger but, lack that quality. In this regard it is estimated that if by the end of this century temperatures rise by 3° C (some experts believe an increase of up to 5° C is possible), then the lower altitude limit for growing good quality arabica may rise by some 15 ft (5 m) per annum, meaning that over time areas that are currently too cold for coffee could become suitable. But it is uncertain whether land at higher altitudes would in fact become available (or be rendered suitable) for coffee production.

Yield: If climatic events such as overly high temperatures occur during sensitive periods of the life of the crop, for example during flowering or fruit setting, then yields will be adversely affected, particularly if accompanied by reduced rainfall.

Pests and diseases: Higher temperatures will not only favour the proliferation of certain pests and diseases, but will also result in these spreading to regions where they were not normally present. Research suggest that the incidence of pests and diseases such as coffee berry borer, leaf miner, nematodes, coffee rust and others will increase as future temperatures rise. The consequent need for more control will make coffee production both more complicated and expensive.

Irrigation: Areas currently not requiring this may do so in the future due to increased evaporation that reduces the soil's moisture content. Other areas may experience increases in both rainfall and the variability thereof.

Erratic rains: Unseasonal rain during flowering affects fruit set, whereas rain during the harvest season will complicate the sun drying of coffee and affect quality.

As already mentioned, complexity and uncertainty make it hard to be precise. Nevertheless, there is a real possibility that fewer parts of the world will be suitable for growing coffee. If so, then the already evident growth in the concentration of production could become even more pronounced. This in turn could make global production more prone to high fluctuations, as any severe disruption in output from one of the major producers would drastically curtail global output. The cost of production will increase more than would have been the case without global warming and thirdly, competition from other crops for available arable land may increase. In the context of this brief review perhaps the most important point to note is that to date initiatives to reduce the extent of global warming are mostly aimed at limiting further warming, not to reverse it rapidly. This means everyone in the coffee value chain needs to adapt by taking actions to minimize and cope with the seemingly inevitable effects.

Events of recent years have shown the veracity of the foregoing paragraphs. Both floods and droughts are on the increase in a number of coffee producing countries, whereas there are widespread reports of pests and diseases moving into areas where previously they did not exist. Individual farmers in different countries complain of unseasonal rainfall affecting flowering and fruit set, with others cite drying and quality problems due to rain during the harvest season.

CLIMATE CHANGE AND SOIL DEGRADATION

According to the Intergovernmental Panel on Climate Change (IPCC) land management practices will be the most influential factor on the organic matter content of the soil during the next decades. Climate change is likely to increase the frequency and distribution of stronger winds and increased rainfall, both major determinants of erosion, likely leading to reduced soil capacity to hold water. This is of particular importance to crop production in semi-arid and arid areas, particularly if coupled with rising temperatures.

Water availability: In a warmer world, the hydrological cycle is expected to become more intense, likely to result in 'very wet' and 'very dry' areas compared to past measurements. Globally, the number of people exposed to extreme droughts at any one time is also expected to increase as a result of climate change.

Extreme events: These can influence agriculture quite heavily, but projecting their impact is hard. Probably the best known such event is the El Niño phenomenon that happens irregularly but dramatically affects the weather in many parts of the world. The term El Niño refers to the large-scale warming of surface waters of the Pacific Ocean every three to six years, which usually lasts for 9–12 months, but may continue for up to 18 months and dramatically affect the weather worldwide. Predicting the occurrence of El Niño events (but not their impact on agriculture) has only been possible since the 1980s when computing power became large enough to do so.

The impact of El Niño on coffee production has been closely studied in Colombia. During its occurrence in the Andean region of Colombia, rainfall decreases while sun intensity and temperatures increase. This causes production to fall in some regions, particularly in low-lying areas where rainfall is less than 1,500 mm/year and there is low retention of moisture and high exposure of the crop to sunlight. Lack of water during the critical stages of fruit development also brings about a high risk of black beans, small beans and other defects, as well as increased incidence of pests such as coffee berry borer.

POSSIBLE INTERVENTIONS AND SUPPORT MEASURES

This guide is part of ITC's mission to contribute to sustainable development through technical assistance in export promotion and international business development. As such the guide's main emphasis is on international green coffee trade matters, rather than on issues related to production. However, in recent years concern about the potential impact of climate change, coupled with the quest to achieve sustainability throughout the coffee value chain, is increasingly interlinking many producer and trade issues.

The information here highlights climate change and sustainability issues of particular relevance to the coffee industry, bearing in mind that it is not possible to offer a comprehensive insight into this enormous subject. Therefore, wherever possible sources of more extensive information are indicated.

Areas of possible intervention include:

- Changing agricultural practices;
- Creating social organization;
- Participating in new market strategies.

Strategic support areas include:

- Improving access to information;
- Establishing financial mechanisms;
- Investing in social capital.

ADAPTATION AND MITIGATION

Coffee production contributes to the emission of greenhouse gases (GHG) (as do other links in the chain). The industry therefore must not only focus on adaptation (help producers cope with climate change), but also on mitigation (reduce its own contribution to GHG emissions). It is important to differentiate between these two aspects, even though they are closely intertwined. Finally, the industry also needs to gear up to exploit the benefits that will spring from generating marketable carbon offset credits.

Short-term adaptation strategies include better farming practices and more efficient on-farm processing. Most progressive farmers apply these as a matter of course, but smallholders do not always have the necessary resources and/or knowledge to do so. Longer-term strategies include capacity building, mapping of climate data, improving soil fertility, examining different production models, developing/planting drought and disease resistant varieties. And some, in the extreme, diversify out of coffee and/or shift production to more suitable areas.

Short-term mitigation strategies include calculating and reducing the on-farm carbon footprint, and determining the feasibility of creating carbon sinks. A longer-term strategy would be to link producers, especially smallholders, with the carbon markets to exploit carbon footprint opportunities.

Smallholders produce the bulk of the world's coffee and the industry cannot afford steeply falling output in this sector. Yet, the ability of smallholders to cope with climate change is limited.

Not all views on how to go forward concur but these priority areas for smallholders are indicated:

Adaptation: Short-term technical solutions for adapting coffee production and processing to current climate variability, aimed at producers.

Long-term strategies to improve framework conditions for adaptation to future climate risks, and to build the necessary capacities including financing mechanisms.

Mitigation: Measures to reduce GHG and so contribute to climate protection and carbon credit generation, aimed at all participants in the value chain.

This is confirmed by previous surveys in the Mesoamerican region (the joint name for the Central American region and Mexico) that ranked five potential areas of intervention as follows:

- More important: (i) changes in agricultural practices and (ii) social organization.
- Important: (iii) participation in new marketing strategies.
- Less important: (iv) new economic activities, and (v) new cash crops.

Box 13.2   Carbon footprints and sinks

Carbon footprint opportunities arise from the wish by industry in developed countries to reduce or offset their carbon footprint, i.e. the total amount of GHG emissions caused directly or indirectly by an organization or a product.

Carbon sinks are natural or constructed reservoirs that can absorb or 'sequester' carbon dioxide from the atmosphere and include forests, soils, peat, permafrost, ocean water and carbonate deposits in the deep ocean. The most commonly referenced form of carbon sink is that of forests. Plants and trees absorb carbon dioxide from the atmosphere via photosynthesis, retain the carbon component as the building block of plant fibre and release oxygen back into the atmosphere. Therefore, long-lived, high biomass plants, such as trees and forests represent effective carbon sinks as long as they are maintained.

Carbon sequestration is the process of increasing the carbon content of a carbon reservoir other than the atmosphere. Biological approaches to sequestration include direct removal of carbon dioxide from the atmosphere through land-use change, afforestation, reforestation, and practices that enhance soil carbon in agriculture. Physical approaches include separation and disposal of carbon dioxide from flue gases or from processing fossil fuels to produce hydrogen- and carbon dioxide-rich fractions and long-term storage underground in depleted oil and gas reservoirs, coal seams and saline aquifers. Basically any process, activity or mechanism that removes a greenhouse gas, an aerosol, or a precursor of a greenhouse gas or aerosol from the atmosphere can be considered a carbon sink.

Strategic recommendations include, in addition to recognizing the value of human capital, i.e. the collective farming knowledge that already exists in the smallholder sector:

- Improving access to information, including market information, farming technology, etc., and developing the ability to interpret such information;
- Establishing financial mechanisms, including climate insurance, access to micro-credit to facilitate adaptation, i.e. organic, substitute crops, new varieties, shading, etc.;
- Investing in social capital, i.e. building structures that enable smallholders to access the resources necessary to adapt to climate change, access new markets and

exploit the social and environmental value of their farming activities.

Although considerable preparatory progress has been made in the development of both methodologies and tools, it is obvious that the industry as a whole is still in the preliminary stages of trying to transform strategy into widespread action.

CARBON CREDITS

Agricultural carbon credits, i.e. credits generated through agricultural practices like coffee production, are not eligible under the mandatory carbon market, including the Clean Development Mechanism (CDM). Therefore, marketable carbon credits do not yet feature in coffee production and by mid-2011 only one CDM project (the Coopeagri Forestry Project in Costa Rica) listed coffee growers among its indirect beneficiaries. For more information on all categories of CDM projects, visit *www.cdm.unfccc.int/Projects/index. html*.

There is more scope for land-use based projects under the smaller voluntary carbon offset market – this is discussed later in this chapter. Given the complexities surrounding CDM the general consensus among researchers appears to be that the voluntary carbon markets system presents the better option for coffee growers. Examples include the CarbonFix Standard AdapCC initiated Sierra Piura reforestation project in Peru, run by the CEPICAFE cooperative – *www.carbonfix. info/RSP*, and the Scolel Té project in Mexico – *www. planvivo.org/projects/registeredprojects/scolel-te-mexico*. Nevertheless, by late 2011 there were no obvious signs yet of any full-scale application in the coffee sector.

Meanwhile the retail end of the industry is increasingly looking across the supply chain to reduce the carbon footprint of products, including coffee, but so far measuring coffee's Product Carbon Footprint (PCF) has been costly and complex, whereas the calculating and reporting of PCFs is not always consistent. Nevertheless, for coffee an encouraging start has been made through a study sponsored by the major German roaster Tchibo, covering coffee produced in the United Republic of Tanzania and consumed in Germany – also mentioned later in this chapter. For more on soil carbon methodology see also *www.v-c-s. org/methodologies/adoption-sustainable-agricultural-land-management-salm*.

Developing carbon projects is both complicated and time consuming, whereas credible carbon monitoring methodologies for coffee farms have only recently come to the fore. But, a number of tools are now available and different initiatives are conducting or planning pilot projects that in due course should facilitate extending carbon projects to the majority of coffee producing countries. See for example the Cool Farm Tool, *www.sustainablefood.org/projects/ climate* and the Sustainable Agriculture Initiative, *www. saiplatform.org/activities/alias/climate-change*. Provided the necessary capacity building and legislative support in those countries is forthcoming, it may be assumed that progress will accelerate from 2011 onwards.

TERMINOLOGY

The debate over climate change has generated a host of terminology that is not always clear to the average reader.The United Nations Framework Convention on Climate Change (UNFCC) has therefore published a detailed Glossary of climate change acronyms that can be accessed at *www. unfccc.int/essential_background/glossary/items/3666.php.* The United Nation's Food and Agricultural Organization offers a similar but possibly somewhat more agriculture related glossary. Visit *www.fao.org/climatechange/en* and in particular *www.fao.org/climatechange/65923/en.*

MEASURING AND FORECASTING CLIMATE CHANGE

Global climate change models make projections about future climates based on current understanding of what drives climate change. These are then related to the potential impacts on crops, particularly cereal crops, given the importance of global food security.

Field experiments grow crops in controlled environments where variables can be varied, for example the concentration of different gases in the atmosphere; the availability of water; and temperature levels. This is crucial in understanding how climate change affects individual crops. However, incorporating the results into large-scale climate change models remains wrought with uncertainty.

Integrated climate-crop models attempt to address some of these problems, including the fact that individual crops react differently to outside drivers. But other factors, like changes in land use for example, may independently affect local climates, making it difficult for such models to be all-encompassing.

Statistical analysis of past climates is used to determine the impact on past crop production and to estimate how such crops may respond in future. But this assumes that adequate historical data is available, which is not always the case. Nor is it certain that past reactions will be repeated.

Climate change scenarios have been developed by the Intergovernmental Panel on Climate Change (IPCC – *www. ipcc.ch*), based on four different storylines of different future worlds. These differ in terms of projections in population growth, world gross domestic product changes, differences in per capita income between developed and developing countries, and the energy level of the economy (related to emission levels).

COMPLEXITY MIXED WITH UNCERTAINTY

Thus, models have to simplify certain parameters, some of which may have large implications on their outcome. Generally, uncertainties become larger the further into the future projections are made. Furthermore, there is a substantial scale-gap between large-scale global climate models (which generally have a resolution of over 100 km) and the small-scale of most farming systems (generally less than 10 km). Current climate modelling studies also have significant regional biases due to a lack of data in many developing countries, for example on precipitation patterns. Also, different crops are believed to react differently to CO_2 concentrations in the atmosphere. And finally there are events such as floods and droughts that are expected to become more frequent and more severe as a result of climate change. But predicting their impact is currently very difficult.

Most modelling studies related to agricultural crops include projections of:

- Changes in yields due to changes in seasonal climates;
- Changes in production potential in relation to factors such as yield, land availability and longer/shorter growing seasons;
- Crop response to changes in atmospheric conditions;
- Changes in prices and trade patterns due to climatic change;
- Changes in food security, i.e. the number of people at risk of hunger;
- Water run-off and related water stress.

However, there are other relevant aspects and potential impacts that are hard to include in current models.

COFFEE SPECIES AND CLIMATE CHANGE

Temperature and rainfall conditions are the main drivers when it comes to yield, i.e. production. In this respect the two main species, arabica and robusta that together account for about 99% of world production, have different requirements.

Arabica coffee evolved in the cool, shady environment of the Ethiopian highland forests where there is a single dry season coinciding with the winter months. The optimum temperature range is somewhere between 15° and 24° C. Much higher temperatures tend to impact negatively on both yield and quality. Rainfall requirements are between 1,500 mm and 2,000 mm per annum, although the use of irrigation today allows arabica to be grown also in areas with otherwise insufficient rainfall.

Robusta coffee evolved across lowland Equatorial Africa, particularly in the forests of the Congo River Basin and around the Lake Victoria Crescent in Uganda. It grows best in areas with abundant rainfall of around 2,000 mm per annum, at altitudes ranging from sea level to about 800 m.

Rainfall must be well distributed throughout most of the year because the robusta tree has a relatively shallow root system. The optimum temperature ranges from 22° to 26° C and the species is less tolerant of very high as well as very low temperatures than arabica.

HELPING PRODUCERS PREPARE

Potential strategies to make coffee producers better prepared include the following:

- **Detailed monitoring of changes in climate and production.** This would allow the mapping of areas prone to the spread of specific pests according to the likely impact of climate change. This would assist in determining which crops are best produced where and could help ensure that government guidance and assistance are correctly targeted.

- **Mapping of likely climate change within each coffee region.** The United Nations Framework Convention on Climate Change (UNFCC) assists least developed countries to identify their immediate priorities for adaptation options. Over 40 countries have received assistance to prepare their National Adaptation Programmes of Action and many have already submitted their action plans. See a list of proposed project details and plans at *www.unfccc. int/national_reports/napa/items/2719.php*.

- **Migration of production – latitudinal and altitudinal.** Latitudinal migration could be northwards or southwards in search of more appropriate climatic conditions. However, widespread latitudinal changes will be difficult given the susceptibility of both arabica and robusta to changes in the intensity and availability of sunlight that impact on the photosynthesis process. Effects range from a noticeable decrease of the growth phase to an inhibition of flower development. Altitudinal migration would move production to areas of higher altitude where the climate will become more suitable. After all, coffee does grow in areas outside the 'normal' tropical distribution range of coffee cultivation (Nepal and China's Yunnan province). Nevertheless, both movements in geographical location and in altitude may be restricted, for example by the potential impact on quality.

- **Estimating the potential impact of climate change on coffee quality.** Higher temperatures mean coffee will ripen more quickly, leading to a fall in quality. This means areas currently favourable for coffee production may no longer be so in 20 years, and others currently too cold may become suitable. But this dislocation of existing areas to new ones is highly problematic, given the increasing competition for fertile land across all regions.

- **Devising strategies to diversify out of coffee where necessary.** To date diversification has proven particularly challenging, mainly because of the lack of adequate substitute crops. However, with increasing pressure on food crops land currently used for coffee may become subject to competition from (more) profitable crops.

- **Evaluating available adaptation techniques, such as shade management systems.** Although originally a shade tree, coffee also prospers without shade in zones with adequate climate and soils. However, shade management is highly advisable when coffee is grown in less desirable areas, or in areas that will become affected by climate change. The main effects are decreasing air temperatures (as much as 3°–4° C), decreasing wind speeds and increasing air humidity. Shading also helps avoid large reductions in night temperatures at high elevations, or in high latitudes such as Parana State in Brazil.

- **High-density planting, vegetated soils and irrigation.** All these aim at maintaining and/or increasing organic matter and soil water retention capacity, thereby enhancing the viability of cultivation under adverse climatic conditions.

- **Genetic breeding.** The main objectives under this concept are the development of higher yields, better quality and strength, and longevity. However, it is equally important that genetic improvement based on selective breeding contributes to the long-term sustainability of coffee cultivation in lands potentially affected by climate change. Research on varieties that are less water demanding is equally important. Some research has focused on developing varieties that could cope with higher temperatures and remain highly productive at the same time.

WEBSITES ON CLIMATE CHANGE

www.unfccc.int/2860.php – United Nations Framework Convention on Climate Change (UNFCC). Home of the Kyoto Protocol – supports all institutions involved in the climate change process. Offers overviews of the Kyoto Protocol, the Clean Development Mechanism, data on greenhouse gases, national reports, science and CDM projects.

www.ccdcommission.org – The International Commission on Climate Change and Development offers a comprehensive overview of climate change and disaster risk reduction and offers recommendations to strengthen the resilience of vulnerable countries and communities in a comprehensive report entitled 'Closing the gap.'

www.unfccc.int/essential_background/glossary/items/3666. php offers an extensive glossary of climate change related acronyms and terminology.

www.gefweb.org – Global Environment Facility (GEF). Inter-governmental organization offering project funding for a large range of climate change and environment related issues to developing countries and countries with economies in transition.

www.unep.org/climatechange – United Nations Environment Programme (UNEP). Offers a wide range of insights and information on climate change related news and activities, including financing of climate change mitigation and adaptation.

www.undp.org/climatechange/adapt – United Nations Development Programme (UNDP). Provides resources in respect of the programming of climate change adaptation projects and their integration into mainstream development. Also offers an Adaptation Learning Mechanism (ALM). A global knowledge sharing platform, mapping good practices and information on climate adaptation.

www.fao.org/climatechange/en/ – Food and Agricultural Organization of the United Nations (FAO). Information and resources related to climate change with particular emphasis on food security and agriculture. Extensive glossary of climate change terminology.

www.odi.org.uk/themes/climate-change-environment/default. asp – Overseas Development Institute (ODI). Independent think tank on development issues, active in research on climate change issues in developing countries.

www.solutions-site.org The Horizon Solutions Site is a collaborative program with UNDP, UNEP, UNFPA, UNICEF, the IDRC, Yale and Horizon's colleagues at Harvard that presents answers to problems in environment, health, population and development, in case-studies (peer-reviewed), articles and exhibits.

www.sustainablecommodities.org – The Sustainable Commodity Initiative (a joint venture by IISD and UNCTAD) aims to promote sustainable practices in commodity production and trade. Site links into FAST (Finance Alliance for Sustainable Trade), SCAN (Sustainable Commodity Assistance Network), SSI (Reporting: State of Sustainability Initiatives) and COSA (Committee on Sustainability Analysis).

www.un.org/wcm/content/site/climatechange/gateway. This United Nations site offers a gateway to the work of over 30 UN organizations in the field of climate change, including a link to the World Meteorological Organization's Global Climate Observing System (*www.wmo.ch/pages/prog/gcos/index.php?name=about*).

www.climatehotmap.org/index.html is an initiative by a number of concerned NGO's, including the World Wildlife Fund, and offers an inter-active 'Early Warning Signs' map, detailing a number of potential global warming effects by region.

www.sdwebx.worldbank.org/climateportal/home. cfm?page=globlemap – The World Bank's Climate Change Data Portal. Provides information on climate change and a number of tools.

www.adaptationlearning.net – The United Nation's Development Programme's Adaptation Learning Mechanism is a knowledge-sharing platform on climate change.

www.isealalliance.org – The International Social and Environmental Accreditation and Labelling Alliance (ISEAL) is the global association for social and environmental standards systems. Site includes the complete output and documents

of the Social Accountability in Sustainable Agriculture project (SASA) and is of interest to coffee growers generally.

www.cgiar.org – The Consultative Group on International Agricultural Research (CGIAR) is a strategic partnership whose 64 members support 15 international research centres for which links and contact details are provided.

www.iwmi.cgiar.org – The International Water Management Institute (IWMI) is one of the 15 CGIAR-linked research centres. Its mission is to improve the management of land and water resources for food, livelihoods and nature. Look for its Water Policy Brief at *www.iwmi.cgiar.org/Publications/ Water_Policy_Briefs/PDF/WPB31.pdf*.

www.ifpri.org – The International Food Policy Research Institute (IFPRI) is another of the CGIAR-linked research centres and concentrates on food security issues. Their report entitled *'Climate change: Impact on agriculture and costs of adaptation'* presents research results that quantify climate-change impacts, assesses the consequences for food security, and estimates the investments that would offset the negative consequences for human well-being. Although not directly coffee-related, this analysis brings together, for the first time, detailed modelling of crop growth under climate change with insights from an extremely detailed global agriculture model, using two climate scenarios to simulate future climate.

http://www.wbcsd.org – The World Business Council for Sustainable Development (WBCSD) is a global business initiative. Although not directly relevant to coffee the site nevertheless offers interesting information, for example on water and forest products.

http://climatechange.worldbank.org – The World Bank offers the entire text of its report *Development and Climate Change – 2010*.

FROM STRATEGY TO ACTUAL RESPONSES

WHAT ARE THE PRIORITIES?

Smallholders are amongst the most vulnerable groups when it comes to the potential impact of climate change. Smallholders also produce the majority of the world's coffee, but for many their ability to adapt to climate change is limited by insufficient or no access to the resources and technical assistance that this requires. This is not to suggest that all such resources have been identified, far from it, but what is clear is that the coffee industry cannot afford severely reducing smallholder production, neither in terms of quantity nor in terms of quality and quality diversity. This therefore confirms the need for concerted industry-wide initiatives. But how?

NB. This brief discussion is limited to the coffee sector and as such no reference will be made to the debate on climate change between industrialized and developing countries.

Not all views on how to go forward concur, but it would seem reasonable to argue that there are three main areas for action to be undertaken as suggested in *Adaptation for Smallholders to Climate Change* by Mario Donga and Kathleen Jährmann – *www.adapcc.org/en/downloads.htm* – a joint project of Cafédirect and German International Cooperation (GIZ). Action areas include:

- Short-term technical solutions for adapting coffee production and processing to current climate variability, aimed at producers;

- Measures to reduce GHG and so contribute to climate protection and carbon credit generation, aimed at all participants in the value chain;

- Long-term strategies to improve framework conditions for adaptation to future climate risks and to build the necessary capacities – aimed at all in the value chain, but mostly producers.

Short-term technical solutions will vary from country to country and between areas in a single coffee producing country. Farmers are already experiencing climate change, they know their circumstances better than anyone and many have innovative ideas on how to combat at least some of the effects. In other words, external assistance is needed, but to be successful it should combine with local stakeholders to jointly develop adaptation and mitigation processes.

Measures to reduce GHG are equally important, but it is proving difficult for farmers to gain carbon offset credits, mostly because projects to reduce GHG emissions must demonstrate their additionality. That is to say, they must show an additional/added value effect in the GHG scenario. Under this concept coffee farms have to prove that they create GHG savings that are additional to anything that might happen anyway. Ironically, it is technically probably easier for other partners in the value chain to generate carbon offsets than it is for the grower. This is demonstrated by the fact that to date agri-based offsets are not widespread.

Long-term strategies at the production level are essential and require major industry support and supporting legislation. Many of these are identified and discussed in the ICO's paper on 'Climate Change and Coffee' – referred to earlier in this chapter. Suffice it here to add that the March 2009 Coffee Issues Management Forum (organized by the National Coffee Association of USA) identified producer sustainability as the prime priority issue with adaptation to climate change listed as the most important sub-issue under this heading. In the meantime, however, coffee producers require mostly short-term solutions to try and help them cope as things move along in the world of climate.

To a limited extent, progress towards mitigating the effects of climate change is assisted by adhering to Good Agricultural Practices or GAP, further aligned to coffee production through observance of one or more of the different certification or verification standards that are active. But, it is obvious that climate change itself cannot be adequately addressed at the individual farm level.

The reduction and trapping of GHG by coffee growers will very likely, if not automatically, also help towards mitigating at least some of the effects of climate change they are already experiencing.

While it is not possible to 'sell coffee or shade trees', it is possible to work towards producing carbon credits that can be traded, either through the mandatory CDM process, or through voluntary arrangements. For individual smallholders CDM type coffee carbon credits may be very difficult to achieve. For them the better route is probably through 'umbrella projects' that encompass larger areas and take a holistic approach to the issue as described later in this chapter.

REALISTICALLY, WHAT CAN BE DONE?

It is important to differentiate between mitigation and adaptation, i.e. actions that would help to reduce climate change, and actions that could help coffee growers to adapt to the impact of climate change.

- Coffee production itself contributes to GHG emissions. How can those emissions be reduced? And, how could carbon sinks be increased?

- In practical terms, what – if anything – can coffee growers do to adapt to the effects of climate change?

However, it is equally important to appreciate that, collectively, smallholders possess a vast amount of practical farming knowledge and history, meaning they understand what has changed or is changing in their area. The value of this human capital should not be ignored. A survey and policy brief in this regard, published by the Centro Agronómico Tropical de Investigación y Enseñanza (CATIE) in Costa Rica – *www.catie.ac.cr*, identifies three main responses by Mesoamerican coffee growers to past crises and ongoing change in the coffee sector. (September 2009 *'Building resilience to global change for coffee farmers in Mesoamerica'* by Hallie Eakin, Edwin Castellanos and Jeremy Haggar):

- Changes in agricultural practices, directed at reducing costs, improving soil fertility, or meeting sustainability criteria for new markets;

- Social organization, necessary for small producers to access new markets, technologies or support programs, and to help farmers recover or respond to global changes;

- Participation in new marketing strategies, to help them identify and develop the social and environmental value of their products.

Other responses have included diversification to non-agricultural activities, adopting more profitable crops, decreasing the area dedicated to coffee, lessening labour and input use, and even migration to urban centres or more developed countries.

Surveys that were conducted ranked five potential areas of intervention as follows:

- More important: (i) changes in agricultural practices and (ii) social organization;
- Important: (iii) participation in new marketing strategies;
- Less important: (iv) new economic activities, and (v) new cash crops.

In addition to recognizing the value of human capital, i.e. the collective farming knowledge that already exists in the smallholder sector, strategic recommendations include:

- Improving access to information, including market information, farming technology etc., and developing the ability to interpret such information.
- Establishing financial mechanisms, including climate insurance, access to micro-credit to facilitate adaptation, i.e. organic, substitute crops, new varieties, shading, etc.
- Investing in social capital, i.e. build structures that enable smallholders to access the resources necessary to adapt to climate change, access new markets and exploit the social and environmental value of their farming activities.

A number of projects elsewhere in the world have conducted or are conducting similar surveys. The indications are that the results may not be all that different.

ADAPTING TO CLIMATE CHANGE IN PRACTICE

Good farming practices automatically help conserve soil and water and in so doing also make it easier to adapt to global warming, while at the same time lessening its impact. But the necessary resources are not always available, especially not in the smallholder sector.

Hands-on options include the following:

- **In the field**
  - Mulching to reduce evaporation, avoid erosion and improve soil fertility;
  - Terracing/contouring, drainage and trapping/storing run-off rain water;
  - Planting hedges, planting contours to mitigate wind and water damage;
  - More effective irrigation and water resources management;
  - Shading to mitigate increased solar brilliance, reduce temperature variations and help retain moisture.
- **Processing**
  - Reduce water usage with eco-friendly pulpers;
  - Improve wastewater management and disposal;
  - Make effective use of all compostable materials;
  - Use solar energy, i.e. sun drying where feasible;
  - Use renewable energy sources for mechanical drying;

- Make better use of dry milling by-products (fuel, charcoal briquettes, board).
- **Longer-term options**
  - Strengthening institutions;
  - Improving access to climate data;
  - Mapping potential climate change impact on coffee areas;
  - Improving soil fertility;
  - Examining different production models, for example high density planting;
  - Developing/planting disease and drought resistant varieties;
  - Shifting production to more suitable areas where feasible;
  - Developing finance mechanisms to facilitate all or some of these.

Examples of climate mapping can be found at *www.ciat. cgiar.org*, Centro Internacional de Agricultura Tropical or International Center for Tropical Agriculture in Colombia, and at *www.iac.sp.gov.br*, Instituto Agronômico de Campinas (IAC) in Brazil.

- **Carbon sequestration and sinks**
  - Calculating and reducing the on-farm carbon footprint;
  - Determine the feasibility of creating marketable carbon sinks;
  - Linking smallholders to carbon markets to exploit carbon footprint opportunities.

The list above is obviously not exhaustive. Many – if not all – of the options are of course also promoted by the different certification and verification standards as Organic, Rainforest Alliance, Utz Certified, 4C Association and corporate standards as the Nespresso's AAA program, the Starbucks Coffee Company initiated C.A.F.E. (Coffee and Farmer Equity) Practices, and others.

The 4C Climate Code is an example of the work being done by a number of organizations to bring climate change adaptation and mitigation closer to the coffee producer. The (voluntary) add-on module identifies 15 principles and provides accompanying step by step indicators to measure progress from red (unacceptable) to green (compliant) in four main areas: Enabling Environment; Natural Resource Management; Soil and Crop Management; and GHG Emissions and Stocks.

Although the module is subject to further refinement, it nevertheless represents a practical roadmap for growers wishing to implement climate change adaptation and mitigation measures. The module is largely based on work done by a three-year public-private partnership in Kenya by Sangana Commodities Ltd and German International Cooperation. Further partners were the 4C Association, Tchibo GmbH and the World Bank's Bio-Carbon Fund.

The module, training manuals and further information, also on climate change generally, are available at *www.4c-coffeeassociation.org/en/work-on-climate-change-php*.

CARBON CREDITS

ORIGIN AND LIMITATIONS

A frequently encountered assumption is that coffee growers can (easily) benefit from what is called the carbon offset or carbon credit market. This because supermarket chains, other retailers and consumer organizations are, sometimes publicly so, asking the coffee distribution chain (importers, roasters, others) to move to what is called a carbon neutral product footprint. This is a situation wherein the carbon emissions (carbon-dioxide or CO_2) that the coffee chain produces are offset by carbon reducing activities. And yes, in principle coffee growing offers potential for this but it must be stressed that agri-based offsets are not widespread as yet – for reasons that are explained below.

It is important to have in mind that different ecosystems each have a distinct potential to trap carbon atoms. A tropical forest will isolate more carbon than a temperate forest, grasslands or an agricultural ecosystem. In the same way, different agricultural coffee systems have distinct potential to trap carbon atoms: forest coffee, smallholder plots, commercial plantations, coffee with or without shade, with or without intercropping, etc. But, whereas coffee production is often assumed not to contribute to GHG emissions, the fact is that auditing of an entire farming operation will reveal GHG leakages, the most obvious of which are the use of tractors, vehicles, electric motors, burning of firewood and the like that contribute to GHG emissions.

The Kyoto Protocol referred to at the beginning of this chapter created what is known as the Clean Development Mechanism (CDM). This allows developed countries to invest in projects in developing countries to reduce GHG emissions, and to promote sustainable development through structured projects that can result in the selling of Certified Emission Reductions (CER). CDM projects must demonstrate their additionality, i.e. they have an additional/added value effect in the GHG scenario. Under the additionality concept, coffee farms would have to prove that they create GHG savings that are additional to anything that might happen anyway. The additionality margin is always confronted against a baseline that is traced comparing the farms with and without the CDM Project.

WHAT DOES THIS MEAN?

- Established stands of both coffee and shade trees are not taken into account as they are part of an already existing situation. However, the conservation of existing forest cover and improvement of general agricultural practices, resulting in more eco-friendly coffee stands, are other

avenues towards earning carbon credits, provided net GHG gains can be shown.

- New activities such as the introduction of intercropping with suitable GHG absorbing plants, the planting of additional shade trees and the rehabilitation of degraded lands and hillsides can count. This could include the planting of additional coffee and shade trees, but only if it can be proven that the land in question had previously been in a prolonged state of degradation.

- The calculations to determine the net result of different activities are complex and the final result may only justify the effort if larger areas are covered. This makes it difficult if not impossible for individual smallholders to participate directly in carbon offsets.

The advantage of the CDM process is that it results in 'certified' carbon credits that offer the traceability and credibility as set out in the Kyoto Protocol procedures. These credits can be traded on established, formal markets with transparent pricing procedures. In practical terms, however, the CDM approach may not be the best suited for smallholder coffee because of the difficulty to measure the different coffee production processes accurately in terms of GHG impact.

CARBON CREDITS DEFINED

Carbon credits are a key component of national and international attempts to mitigate the growth in concentrations of GHG. One carbon credit is equal to one ton of carbon dioxide equivalents. It is the unit of measurement for the carbon market – much like a barrel of oil or liter of milk. Since there is more than one GHG and because each of them has different global warming potential, the carbon dioxide equivalent is the term used to standardize the unit of measurement. Carbon trading is an application of an emission trading approach, and to have a basis for comparison all GHG are calculated in CO_2 equivalents.

Greenhouse gas emissions are capped and then markets are used to allocate the emissions among the group of regulated sources. The idea is to allow market mechanisms to drive industrial and commercial processes in the direction of low emissions or 'less carbon intensive' approaches than they would use when there is no cost to emitting carbon dioxide and other GHG into the atmosphere. Because GHG mitigation projects generate credits, this approach can be used to finance carbon reduction projects between trading partners and around the world.

There are also companies that sell carbon credits to commercial and individual customers interested in lowering their carbon footprint on a voluntary basis. These offset traders purchase the credits from an investment fund or a carbon development company that has aggregated the credits from individual projects. The quality of the credits is based in part on the validation process and sophistication of the fund or development company that acted as the sponsor to the carbon project. This is reflected in their price. Non-CDM or voluntary units typically have less value than the units obtained through the Clean Development Mechanism. Their prices are risk-driven; more risk for the seller means higher price whereas more risk for the buyer means lower price. Voluntary market standards try to define quality by setting criteria; the stricter these are the better the quality of the certificate and, therefore, the higher the potential price.

There are two distinct types of carbon credits:

- Carbon Offset Credits (COCs): generated by clean forms of energy production, wind, solar, hydro and bio fuels.

- Carbon Reduction Credits (CRCs): generated by the collection and storage of carbon from the atmosphere through bio-sequestration (reforestation, forestation), ocean and soil collection and storage efforts.

Both approaches are recognized as effective ways to reduce the global carbon emissions crisis.

PRODUCT CARBON FOOTPRINTS

Industry in developed countries, including the coffee industry, is increasingly looking for ways to reduce their carbon footprint but, if the footprint cannot be reliably measured, how can it be managed?

Product carbon footprint (PCF) describes the sum of greenhouse gases accumulated during the full life cycle of a product (good or service) in a specified application.

This definition was developed by participants in the PCF Pilot Project Germany, an initiative that aims to draw up recommendations for the methodical development and international coordination for implementing a transparent and scientifically substantiated method for measuring PCF. An added objective is to adapt this within the coffee community to a common standard (or at least a benchmark) that will facilitate PCF measuring by coffee growers and others.

A pilot study *Privat Kaffee Rarity Machare* has been carried out on coffee from the United Republic of Tanzania. The results, together with other reports, are available at *www.pcf-projekt. de/main/results/case-studies.*

The major German roaster Tchibo GmbH partnered in this study, which identifies a number of stages in the coffee chain as contributors to emissions to the air, to the water and to the soil. The study offers schematic overviews of what takes place where, and what generates what in terms of GHG. Of interest here is the contribution to GHG emissions of the different processes within the producing country (on-farm cultivation, processing, transport, milling and packaging), and the consuming countries (overseas transportation, roasting, packaging, distribution, grinding/purchasing, consumption and waste disposal).

The authors conclude that in this particular case study the on-farm processes (production/processing and upstream processes, including the production of agro-chemicals) and the actual consumer phase (shopping and preparation) are the main CO_2 emission drivers. They point out however that the production methods on the two farms studied are

of a very high standard and more conventional production systems may produce different results.

The authors also comment that in many instances it is difficult to trace individual coffees back to their original production site given that so much coffee is mixed at origin and is shipped overseas in bulk. They recommend the coffee industry should develop harmonized standards for compensation methods within the coffee chain and stress the importance of ensuring both transparency and credibility when it comes to making public statements regarding PCF. Without consistency in the methods for calculation and reporting of PCF it can be difficult to compare published footprints. See *www.carbontrust.co.uk* for more.

To note here that the *Carbon Disclosure Project* at *www. cdproject.net* collects information on the carbon footprint of some 2,500 large companies worldwide, including the world's leading multinational roasting companies. Participants measure and disclose their greenhouse gas emissions and climate change strategies through the project in order that they can set reduction targets and make performance improvements. To access these reports one has to register with the project.

Of course there are many initiatives that deal with PCF reduction in industry generally, not limited to coffee. Slower vessel speeds, more efficient use of transport, using recycled packaging material, cleaner fuels and reduced energy use, but these are not within the scope of this discussion.

CLEAN DEVELOPMENT MECHANISM PROJECTS

The World Bank's Carbon Finance Unit website at *www. go.worldbank.org/9IGUMTMED0* provides useful information and tools in respect of the development and financing of CDM projects. It offers assistance with both capacity building and project preparation and it lists registered service providers. Project assistance includes preparation of the carbon documentation necessary to create a 'carbon asset' that will deliver marketable VERs (Verified Emission Reductions) or CERs (Certified Emission Reductions).

Also available are a CDM Methodology Overview, a CDM Methodology Database and a CDM Methodology Paper (reports on methodological issues, workshops, etc.). These provide easily accessible information that helps to understand the CDM rules of procedures and basic concepts of approved methodologies for CDM projects. However, the information provided in this section does not eliminate the need always to consult the approved methodologies and the guidance provided by the CDM Executive Board, which is recorded on the official CDM website and can be accessed at *www. cdm.unfccc.int.* Work is also ongoing on the development of a *Validation and Verification Manual.*

CDM projects are also listed at *www.carboncatalog.org/ projects,* whereas project documentation is available at *www. wbcarbonfinance.org.*

Also of interest to coffee producers is the Forest Carbon Partnership Facility (FCPF) at *www.forestcarbonpartnership. org/fcp*. It has information on ways to reduce emissions from deforestation and forest degradation (called REDD) by providing value to standing forests.

The majority of CDM projects appear to go to Asia and Latin America, in particular China, India and Brazil. As a result, the Carbon Finance Assist facility was created to promote a more widespread flow of CDM projects by offering assistance with the identification and creation of CDM projects. Visit *www. go.worldbank.org/T93VFJSRL0*. But for many coffee growers the CDM route is unfortunately still too cumbersome and may be out of reach.

THE VOLUNTARY MARKETS FOR CARBON OFFSETS

Voluntary markets do not require as much documentation and financial investment as do the mandatory (CDM) markets. However, prices are highly variable because the project developers have the freedom to adopt standards or not, to create new methodologies, and to have or not have third party verifications. To note also that as of late 2011 there were no indications yet of any full-scale application in the coffee sector.

Furthermore, this freedom of negotiation affects the prices of the credits as these are directly related to the quality and credibility of the methodology that was used, and the degree of verification by third part audits or other assurance mechanisms. Critics refer to a lack of regulated methodologies for setting up the credits and the impossibility of tracing back the volume of GHG alleged to have been sequestrated. Lack of regulations could possibly result in double counting of credits, intentionally or unintentionally, and having to trust that already purchased credits will be accounted for in the future. After all, projects can fail, whereas the standards or verification systems used could turn out to be inadequate.

The voluntary route is more appropriate for small or medium sized initiatives (projects) that may lack the capacity and knowledge to develop fully fledged CDM type coffee carbon credits. Widening the sphere of activities and extending the target areas might also result in more people or communities being able to participate. Additionally, investing in social or producer organization would facilitate smallholder access to the potential benefits offered by the carbon markets.

Standards leading to verified carbon credits that could potentially be adopted by coffee growers include the following:

- The Voluntary Carbon Standard, *www.v-c-s.org,* which has a useful section on agricultural land management (coffee trees, vegetation, soil and waste water).

- Plan Vivo, *www.planvivi.org,* whose Scolel Té project in Mexico includes a section dealing with shade trees in coffee plantations.

- CarbonFix, *www.carbonfix.info,* whose CarbonFix Standard was developed for climate forestation projects.

- The Chicago Climate Exchange, *www.theice.com/ccx. jhtml,* maintains an Offsets Registry Program to register verified emission reductions based on a comprehensive set of established protocols, including Forestry Carbon Sequestration.

See also *Making Sense of the Voluntary Carbon Market: A Comparison of Carbon Offset Standards* at *www. co2offsetresearch.org*.

The Climate, Community and Biodiversity Alliance Standards, *www.climate-standards.org,* include three kinds of credits: Approved, Silver and Gold depending on the findings of the audit process. However, if verified carbon credits are to be issued they must be verified by one of the other voluntary standards.

VOLUNTARY MARKET PROJECTS

Coffee farms generally and smallholdings especially do not contribute greatly to GHG emissions, but this is not to say that growers should not engage in mitigation measures, i.e. reduce their carbon footprint. However, coffee farms in many if not most countries often offer potential to increase their tree cover, either through the planting of (more) shade trees or by extending the total forest cover on a farm or in a demarcated area. Provided this is an additional activity, i.e. it would not happen without the incentive of earning carbon credits, such plantings can generate marketable carbon credits through the carbon sequestration process that the additional trees generate. An interesting aspect of forestry projects is that plantings can be monitored through satellite imagery, e.g. through Google Maps, *www.maps.google.com*.

It needs to be stressed again that credible reporting and verification of carbon credits requires that one carbon credit unit is always the same, regardless of where or how it was produced. To be credible a project therefore needs to be based on accepted standards and procedures, including transparent accreditation, validation and verification. It needs to be properly structured and adequate records must be kept. See also *www.adapcc.org/download/LPedroni-Carbon-Credits.pdf*.

ENVIRONMENTAL SERVICES

A particularly interesting discussion, potentially of great importance for the coffee sector, is whether maintaining shaded coffee farms, i.e. conserve existing shade trees and their carbon stocks, should count towards earning carbon credits. After all, coffee farms under shade conserve more carbon than coffee grown in direct sunlight, but at the cost of lower yields. There is therefore potentially an opportunity cost to adopting such conservation measures over sun grown coffee. Although in some cases this can be compensated for if linked to premium prices like for organic, the lack of incentives for farmers to provide environmental services in this way is evident. Furthermore, should farmers not be rewarded for conserving existing shade grown coffee as is proposed for forests under REDD (Reduce Emissions from Deforestation and Forest Degradation in Developing Countries)?

The current requirement is that farmers growing shade coffee plant additional trees before they may qualify for any carbon credits. In effect that means that the environmental services they already provide are being ignored.

WHERE TO GO, WHERE TO LOOK?

Many developing countries find it difficult to participate in the CDM. This is why the World Bank's BioCarbon Fund provides carbon finance for projects that sequester or conserve GHG in forests, agro- and other ecosystems. Visit *www.go.worldbank.org/IVUUKC9210*. By late 2011 the fund supported around 25 reforestation projects, three REDD projects Emissions from Deforestation and Forest Degradation in Colombia, Honduras and Madagascar (see the website), and is embarking on so-called soil carbon pilot projects. The BioCarbon fund is also working with Kenya's Green Belt Movement (GBM) on the reforestation of degraded land. This pilot project will pay local communities and provide them with the technology and knowledge to reforest these lands and manage the new forest. Carbon payments will allow GBM to expand this technique and its benefits to additional areas.

NB. Registering with the BioCarbon Fund website gives access to a number of documents, including reports on the state of the carbon markets (both CDM and voluntary).

Helpful information is also available from the Rainforest Alliance that has produced a manual entitled *Guidance on Coffee Carbon Development using the simplified Agroforestry Methodology*. This comprehensive manual deals with the entire project sequence – from identification to marketing carbon credits. It can be read in English and in Spanish at *www.rainforest-alliance.org/climate/documents/ coffee_carbon_guidance.pdf.*

Three interesting initiatives:

- CATIE, the Centro Agronómico Tropical de Investigación y Enseñanza in Costa Rica, *www.catie.ac.cr,* in 2004–2006 developed a technical manual on how to estimate carbon – *Carbon Capture and Development of Environmental Markets for Indigenous Cocoa Farms and Other Agroforestry Systems.*
- CATIE is also working with the Costa Rican Fondo Nacional de Financiamiento Forestal (FONAFIFO) on a *Payment for Environmental Services Scheme* to establish criteria for environmental payments to shaded coffee farms.
- The Rainforest Alliance, *www.rainforest-alliance.org,* with funding from the International Finance Corporation, completed a two-year project (2008/2009) entitled

Creating and testing a credible carbon monitoring methodology for Coffee Farms with the objective to combat climate change while promoting reforestation; enable farmers to sell the carbon these incremental trees take out of the atmosphere; avoid the high transaction costs usually associated with carbon offset projects; and develop methodology that can be used in other regions and sectors. A project outline is available at *www. rainforest-alliance.org/climate.cfm?id=carbon_coffee* with an update at *www.eco-index.org/search/results. cfm?ProjectID=1476.*

NB. See also The Global Forest and Trade Network at *www. gftn.panda.org.* GFTN is a WWF Global initiative and offers information, contacts and tools in respect of sustainable forest management and forest certification.

ADDITIONAL RELEVANT WEBSITES

These selected websites offer information on GHG emission issues, standards, offsets, product carbon footprints, project preparation and financing.

www.ipcc.ch – The Intergovernmental Panel on Climate Change (IPCC) is the leading scientific body for the assessment of climate change. It reviews and assesses the most recent scientific, technical and socio-economic information produced worldwide relevant to the understanding of climate change. Very informative technical insights in the origin, potential effects and mitigation of GHG emissions are available.

www.cdm.unfccc.int/index.html – The Clean Development Mechanism allows emission-reduction (or emission removal) projects in developing countries to earn Certified Emission Reduction (CER) credits, each equivalent to one ton of CO_2. CER can be traded and sold and used by industrialized countries to meet a part of their emission reduction targets under the Kyoto Protocol.

www.usaid.gov/our_work/environment/climate – The United States Agency for International Development (USAID) supports climate change initiatives in a number of countries. Visit this website for an overview.

www.pcf-projekt.de – The Product Carbon Footprint Pilot Project Germany aims at the methodical development and international coordination for implementing transparent and scientifically substantiated methods for measuring PCF. Site offers explanations of how PCF are measured and a number of downloadable studies, including one on coffee from the United Republic of Tanzania.

www.v-c-s.org – Verified Carbon Standard Association (VCS) aims to standardize and provide transparency and credibility to the voluntary offset market, thereby enhancing consumer and government confidence in voluntary offsets, by creating a trusted and tradable voluntary offset credit, the Verified Carbon Unit (VCU). VCS provides much information on standards for the reduction of GHG, project regulations and certification, and the marketing of Certificates of Emission Reduction or CER.

www.climatestandards.org – The Climate, Community and Biodiversity Alliance (CCB) is a private sector-civil society partnership. It aims at setting standards to be used for the identification of projects that simultaneously address climate change, support local communities and conserve biodiversity.

www.co2offsetresearch.org – The Carbon Offset Research and Education Initiative (CORE) is a project of the Stockholm Environment Institute and provides an analysis and synthesis of the most influential offset programmes and activities.

www.carbontrust.co.uk/Pages/Default.aspx – The Carbon Trust is a United Kingdom Government initiative to accelerate the move towards a low carbon economy. It offers advice on reducing carbon footprints and helps develop low carbon methodologies and products. In particular look for the report entitled *The Carbon Trust three stage approach to developing a robust offsetting strategy.*

www.cdmgoldstandard.org – The Gold Standard Foundation is a civil society initiative that operates a certification service for premium carbon credits. Apart from the Gold Standard the site also lists accredited service providers in different fields, including project development financing.

www.carbonneutral.com – The Carbon Neutral Company is a private sector carbon offset and management business.

www.carbonfootprint.com – Carbon Footprint Ltd is a carbon management and offset consultancy. Site includes calculator and management tools.

www.ieta.org – The International Emissions Trading Association aims to develop a functional international framework for trading in GHG emission reductions. The site offers a number of publications and explanations.

www.chicagoclimatex.com and *www.ecx.eu* are formal exchanges for the pricing and trading of carbon offsets. They offer information on how and by who this can be done.

www.ecosystemmarketplace.com – The Ecosystem Marketplace, a private initiative of Forest Trends, is a leading source of news, data, and analytics on markets, prices and payments for ecosystem services such as water quality, carbon sequestration and biodiversity. The site offers wide-ranging information on environmental markets, ecosystem markets and carbon markets and a comprehensive glossary. It also offers a number of tools.

Finally, a very useful listing of a large number of annotated and thematically sorted links to websites focusing on climate protection and development is available from the German International Cooperation (GIZ, previously GTZ) website. Go to *www.gtz.de* and in particular *www.gtz.de/en/themen/umwelt-infrastruktur/umweltpolitik/4859.htm.* Note: With the change from GTZ to GIZ existing GTZ website links are likely to change.

Acknowledgement: Several parts of this chapter are based on the report *Climate Change and Coffee* published by the International Coffee Organization (ICO) in September 2009. The full report, including a list of selected organizations that are funding mitigation and adaptation to climate change initiatives, is available on the ICO website. See *www.dev.ico.org/documents/icc-103-6-r1e-climate-change.pdf.* The ICO's permission to make use of this report is gratefully acknowledged.

CHAPTER 14

QUESTIONS & ANSWERS AT *WWW.THECOFFEEGUIDE.ORG*

QUESTIONS & ANSWERS AT *WWW.THECOFFEEGUIDE.ORG*

In 2005, ITC opened the Coffee Guide website *www. thecoffeeguide.org* – a continuously updated version of this guide. Over the years, the website's Questions & Answers service has posted more than 240 detailed answers to questions from users – with priority given to questions from producing countries.

Here are just a few of the many questions raised over the years with two examples of answers posted in the website's Q&A Archive – in English, French and Spanish.

QA 004 Should desiccants (or dry-sacs) be used in containers or not?

QA 010 Are the ECC Contract (Europe) and the GCA Contract (New York) valid for sales to markets outside Europe and North America, particularly Japan?

QA 018 What are the credit risks involved in direct sales?

QA 032 How to approach potential buyers?

QA 051 What role do investment funds play in the coffee trade?

QA 054 In market analysis, what is the difference between 'fundamentals' and 'technicals'?

QA 061 When damage occurs en route to an FCL shipment, who is responsible?

QA 064 In percentage terms, how much soluble coffee can be extracted from roasted coffee beans?

QA 079 What prevents growers from marketing finished products direct to (wholesale) consumers?

QA 088 Is there a standard form for cup tasting, i.e. to record coffee quality?

QA 100 In a Code of Conduct or coffee standard, what is the difference between certification and verification?

QA 103 Affordable credit for small growers versus price risk: what are the options?

QA 104 In coffee tasting: when, if at all, does 'fruity' pass from acceptable to unacceptable?

QA 116 How should one approach the Japanese market?

QA 126 Can growers use put options to manage price risk?

QA 126 Is delayed payment sufficient cause to cancel a contract?

QA 128 What is the exact difference between a Trademark and a Geographical Indication?

QA 131 How to differentiate between the mainstream and the specialty industry?

QA 134 What duties are payable and what documentation do US Customs require to clear green coffee imports?

QA 142 What is the function of 'middlemen' in the coffee chain? Are they necessary?

QA 144 Are consumer tastes in Germany changing?

QA 145 Who is liable for missing bags when container seals show no sign of tampering?

QA 150 For robusta, is there any difference in yield between dry and wet processing?

QA 163 Why vacuum-pack coffee?

QA 168 How to export very small lots, say 50 bags or less?

QA 172 What is the meaning of 'squeeze' in London robusta futures?

QA 175 Does polishing add value to quality coffee?

QA 178 What are the differences between pulped natural, semi-washed and washed coffee?

QA 180 On what grounds, if any, could a buyer reject a shipment and what would the consequences be?

QA 181 How do destoners and catadors work?

QA 199 What can a buyer do when his shipper defaults?

QA 208 If quality deteriorates during (delayed) transit, who is responsible?

QA 209 Who is liable for fumigation costs on arrival of infested shipments?

QA 212 Can brokers usually link coffee producers and importers on a commission basis?

QA 215 Damage during loading – who should initiate insurance action?

QA 218 Who is responsible when bags go missing from an LCL/FCL shipment?

QA 227 Why and how deliver coffee from origin to the London LIFFE futures market?

QA 237 Why do some producing countries use altitude in their descriptions and others bean size?

QA 238 Under ECC, who is liable when arrival weights show a loss of over 0.5%?

QA 242 What are the terms of trade and premium for 4C-compliant coffee?

ANSWER TO QUESTION 032

Question: *How to approach potential buyers?*

Asked by: Cooperative – Central Africa

Background: Until now we have always sold our coffee to local exporters but our members are pressing us to establish an alternative sales channel by entering the export market. We have never approached any roasters or importers and we wonder what the best approach would be, i.e. how do we convince potential buyers to take us seriously? After all, no one knows us and we, basically, know no one either.

Answer: Importers and roasters receive many approaches, some serious but many not. Many aspiring sellers approach potential buyers on a hit or miss basis, hoping one or two of their missives may bring a result. But most of these approaches are recognized for what they are and end up in the wastepaper basket.

Our first recommendation is to peruse ITC's Coffee Guide in some considerable detail, including the advice given under 'I want to sell coffee' on our homepage.

This apart, we do not think there is an 'ideal way' in which to approach potential buyers, but we can point out some of the more common factors that play a role in determining whether a buyer may see you as a potential supplier.

Know your coffee. Is it exemplary quality? Specialty quality? Mainstream quality? How have your prices compared with those of others around you? Answers to these questions will suggest which market segment to target.

Know yourself. What quantities can you realistically supply over what period of time? Can you afford to reserve some of your production to back your export drive? Trying to raise interest without having the coffee to back it is pointless. Is your interest in exporting purely price driven, or are you looking for diversification? Trying for top dollar from day one is equally self-defeating.

Have a story and state your credentials. Know your area, know what makes you different. Explain how you grow and process your coffee, how you will export it, what you are able to do to support your buyer, what you expect in return. How long have you been in the coffee business? How has your business progressed? Provide names and addresses of those you have done business with, both in your own country and abroad; which associations you are a member of. State your long-term vision, but be brief. At this stage no one has the time to read more than three pages.

Send a fact sheet. Give information on variety, altitude, soils, annual rainfall, location, annual production by grade and or type, harvesting/marketing season, labour practices, processing system, anti-pollution measures, warehousing, dry processing, distance to port, shipping opportunities to the target market, etc. Be transparent.

Send a sample. A sample (500 g) is better than a thousand words (just like a picture). A sample suggests you understand the importance of quality, that you know your quality and that you have confidence in it. But be sure you send the right sample. It should be fully representative of what you can supply and drawn from a parcel of coffee that itself is fully homogeneous. Understand that the buyer takes a risk when making a first purchase – if the coffee that arrives is no good, what can he do? Propose that shipments can be checked by a third party, both as regards quality and weight. Ask for comments on the quality and suitability of your coffee. What is the buyer's preferred method of doing business? If you can, propose setting up appointments to visit buyers. This demonstrates your seriousness and will go a long way to establishing interest. Get samples to them before you arrive so that you can cup your samples (and others that may compete against you) together.

Do not make generalized statements about what you can do. Instead be precise and factual. Show that you understand the importance of correct contract execution, the absolute need to ship precisely the quality that was sold, the need for documentation to be in order, etc. Buyers need convincing that you understand these issues and that you are capable of satisfying their requirements.

Do not make promises you cannot keep. If necessary explain you are a novice but that you are keen to learn.

Do not make claims you know not to be true. Not only will a buyer quickly pick this up but bear in mind that buyers also talk to each other.

Remember that many roasters, for example in the United States, are not keen to deal direct and prefer to buy through exporters/importers. Therefore, do not concentrate on one sector only, but investigate what will be your best options in each individual market. Recognize the importance of intermediaries. Futures markets, language barriers, different time zones, the risk of default on both sides, etc., all support the need for exporters, importers, local agents, traders and brokers.

Match your client to yourself. If you are producing 80 tons annually, do not go to one of the majors like Kraft, Sara Lee or Nestlé. But also do not spend a fortune wooing a roaster who only needs 40 bags a year.

Posted 19 July 2005

Related chapter(s): 03 – Niche markets, environment and social aspects; 02 – The markets for coffee

Related Q&A: QA 029

ANSWER TO QUESTION 142

Question: *What is the function of 'middlemen' in the coffee chain? Are they necessary?*

Asked by: Grower – West Africa

Background: Why are there are so many middlemen in the coffee chain between grower and roaster? They must charge a lot for their services because grower prices are very low compared to retail prices for roasted coffee. Are these people really necessary and why should we not be able to sell direct?

Answer: Many people who compare grower prices with retail prices for roasted coffee, particularly specialty coffee, wonder who benefits from the mark up.

The discussion over 'middlemen' often fails to recognize the many stages coffee (and similar commodities) pass through between grower and consumer: Collection, primary processing, export processing, marketing, financing, transport to port, export clearing and shipping, import discharge and clearing, inland transportation to roaster, roasting, packaging, marketing, promotion, distribution/wholesale and retail to final consumer. All these are necessary stages that involve third parties, i.e. middlemen, because someone has to perform these functions, obviously at a cost that of course includes a profit margin. Therefore, removing the 'middle*man*' does not remove the 'middle *function*'.

Put differently, everyone who handles coffee between the grower and the end-consumer, including the roaster and the retailer, is a middleman. But at the same time, we would all agree that roasting and retailing are not functions a grower or a grower organization could easily undertake, if at all, and so people do not see roasters and retailers as middlemen. Yet, different value chain data indicate that over 80% of the mark up (costs and margins) on specialty coffee in fact goes to these last two sectors.

Internal marketing systems in individual producing countries have different intermediate marketing stages and layers so we will not comment on these. Similarly, it is relatively pointless to delve into roasting and retailing activities because these are functions most individual growers cannot undertake. This then leaves us with the functions performed in the transition between exporter and roaster.

Exporters and importers carry out specific service functions but, more importantly, they also assume a number of risks. Thus, whereas both growers (or roasters) wishing to deal direct can probably purchase the transitional services they need (shipping, clearing, insurance etc.), they will also have to assume the additional risks this entails.

For a grower exporting direct some of these risks include:

- Credit risk (the roaster does not pay – please see Q&A 018 and 035 that deal with precisely this);
- Quality risk (the goods are rejected on arrival, either by customs or by the roaster).

For the roaster importing direct some of the major risks will be:

- Performance risk (the goods are not shipped), and again;
- Quality risk (the goods are rejected by customs, or the quality is not what had been agreed).

These are typical examples of the risk-taking function exporters and importers assume as a matter of course.

Other examples include:

- Currency risk (coffee bought in one currency, sold in another);
- Shipping risk (goods are delayed or damaged en route);
- Provision of extended credit and so on.

In our view there are basically no unnecessary functions in the value chain. But of course there are additional margins that could accrue to growers if they are prepared to extend the number of functions they carry out themselves, for example, by exporting themselves. However, contrary to popular belief, the major costs and margins are not incurred by exporters and importers as evidenced by the example on the next page of a value chain for Kenya specialty coffee to the United States.

Although the calculations in the example were made when coffee prices were quite low, the findings are corroborated by a further study (ERR-38 – March 2007) released by the Economic Research Service of the United States Department of Agriculture. This study found that, on average, a 10-cent increase in the cost of a pound of green coffee beans in a given quarter results in a 2-cent increase in manufacturer and retail prices in the current quarter. If a cost change persists for several quarters, it will be incorporated into manufacturer prices approximately cent-for-cent with the commodity cost change. Given the substantial fixed costs and markups involved in coffee manufacturing, this translates into about a 3% change in retail prices for a 10% change in commodity prices. The study also noted that cross-sectional price differences were substantially larger at the retail level than at the wholesale level.

In our example some 87% of the retail cost of roasted coffee is incurred at the roaster and retailer level whereas the grower price represents around 7% of the retail value. However, this assumes a straightforward transaction, but many smaller roasters regularly require importers to hold stocks on their behalf. Delivery then has to be spread over a number of months, at fixed prices and at extended credit terms, thereby of course increasing the 'middleman's' costs.

	US$/kg green coffee	US$/kg R&G	Percentage split
Retail price per kg roasted coffee		24.36	100%
Retail costs and margin		8.05	33.1%
Wholesale price		16.31	
Roaster profit (gross)		1.74	7.1%
Roaster overheads		1.22	5.0%
Roaster marketing/ advertising		4.09	16.9%
Roasting/packaging/ distribution		6.04	24.9%
In-plant cost to roaster per kg roasted		3.23	
In-plant cost to roaster per kg green	2.72		
Transport to roaster	0.02		
Insurance/financing (incl. hedging)	0.11		
Warehousing	0.04		1.0%
Traders' margin	0.04		
Port charges	0.02		
CIF landed cost per kg roasted		2.97	
CIF landed cost per kg green	2.50		
Freight and shipping costs	0.12		0.5%
FOB price per kg roasted		2.83	
FOB price per kg green	2.38		
Exporter costs and margin	0.21		0.9%
Levies	0.09		0.3%
Marketing agent and milling*	0.17		0.7%
Cooperative primary processing	0.43		1.8%
Grower price per kg roasted		1.75	7.2%
Grower price per kg green	1.47		

Source: Various reports and ITC's own estimates.

* Current legislation in Kenya requires growers wishing to sell direct (i.e. bypassing the auction system) to employ a marketing agent. The need for this link between grower and exporter is not entirely clear.

Note: Percentages do not add up due to rounding; Conversion green/ roasted – ratio of 1.19 as per ICO rules.

Exporting smaller quantities (less than a container load) is also quite difficult. This is one of the reasons why roasters taking part in Cup of Excellence auctions (*www. cupofexcellence.org*) rely on exporters and importers to ship/import their purchases. Further proof that for many growers the number of 'middleman' functions they can assume is, in fact, quite limited.

A similar calculation for mainstream coffee to Germany concluded that 84% of the roast and ground retail value accrued to the roasting and retail segments. About 6% went to processing cum export costs and intermediaries, leaving about 10% of the R&G retail value for the grower.

Posted 23 March 2007

Related chapter(s): 01 – World coffee trade; 03 – Niche markets, environment and social aspects; 02 – The markets for coffee

Related Q&A: Q&A 018, 032, 035, 046, 065, 079, 083, 090, 094